Betty Crocker's

ANNUAL RECIPES

2·O·O2

Bac-Os, BETTY CROCKER, Bisquick, Chicken Helper, Cinnamon Toast Crunch, Country Corn Flakes, Gold Medal, Potato Buds, Suddenly Salad, and SuperMoist are registered trademarks of General Mills, Inc.
Better for Bread is a trademark of General Mills, Inc.
This edition published by arrangement with Hungry Minds, Inc.

GENERAL MILLS, INC.

Betty Crocker Kitchens

Manager, Publishing: Lois Tlusty
Recipe Development: Betty Crocker Kitchens Home Economists
Food Stylists: Betty Crocker Kitchens Food Stylists
Photography: Photographic Services Department

Cover and Interior Designer: Joanna Williams

ISBN   1–57954–527–0   hardcover

10 9 8 7 6 5 4 3 2 1   hardcover

Cover: Brownie Torte with Raspberry Sauce (page 262)

For more great ideas visit www.bettycrocker.com.

C O N T E N T S

Sour Cream and Chive Rolls, page 235

Introduction

Welcome to the very first edition of *Betty Crocker's Annual Recipes*!

We've collected more than 240 of your favorites from the past year of *Betty Crocker* magazine in one convenient volume of easy, great-tasting recipes. Combined with best-ever cooking tips and creative serving suggestions, these special selections are sure to please your hungry family!

Enjoy breakfasts like Spicy Pumpkin Pancakes and Bacon and Swiss Waffles. Try quick lunches or light dinners like Grilled Portabella Mushroom Sandwiches or Chicken Quesadillas. Make super salads like Spring Vegetable Pasta Salad or Caribbean Chicken Salad.

Looking for clever ideas to help you in the kitchen? Lots of helpful tips are included with the recipes to make your life easier—and tastier!

Pasta makes a big splash in entrées like Shanghai Chicken and Noodles and Linguine with Grilled Shrimp and Vegetables. Heat up the barbecue for Jamaican Jerk Pork Chops with Mango Salsa and Grilled Antipasto Pizza. Or, impress company with dinners like Spinach-Stuffed Chicken Breasts or Salmon with Cranberry Pistachio Sauce. And serve up luscious desserts like Brownie Butterscotch Squares, Lemon Berry Tart or White Chocolate Cheesecake.

Looking for a quick meal? Recipes with a "Quick" label can be on the table in 30 minutes or less. And if you want to cut the fat in your diet, look for the recipes marked "Low Fat." Main dishes with this label have 6 grams of fat or less per serving, while side dishes and desserts have 3 grams or less.

Cook your way through the year using our "Calendar of Delicious Dishes"—a seasonal list of all the recipes in the book to help you plan meals no matter what the time of year. Or, if you're planning a holiday meal or a special get-together with friends, use our "Celebrate!" menus to decide what to serve, right down to snacks and beverages.

Plus, you can work up your appetite just by looking at the beautiful photographs of finished dishes.

We hope you'll join us as we begin our annual celebration of a year of delicious recipes!

Betty Crocker

A Calendar of Delicious Dishes

You can always count on Betty Crocker for mouthwatering, family-pleasing recipes. The list below will help you decide what to make no matter what the time of year. Recipes from this book are categorized by season based on the availability of ingredients (you'll find pumpkin recipes listed under "Fall"), the cooking method (many of the grilling recipes are listed under "Summer"), or the overall "feel" of the dish (you'll find hearty, rib-sticking Beef Pot Pie with Potato Crust under "Winter"). Look under "Any Time of Year" for those dishes that aren't associated with one particular season. Of course, you can always use your creative impulses to mix and match recipes from various seasons depending on your own personal tastes and cravings!

Spring

Summer

Savory Corn on a Stick, page 218

Fall

California Pizza, page 48

Winter

Caribbean Jerk Pork and Rice Casserole, page 197

Beef, Bacon and Noodle Bake, page 188

Any Time of Year

Brownie Torte with Raspberry Sauce, page 262

Pasta with Bacon, Caramelized Onions and Cheddar Cheese, page 98

Rise and Shine

Breakfasts and Brunches Worth Waking Up For

Orange Almond Mini-Muffins

Prep: 15 min   Bake: 15 min

¾ cup milk
⅓ cup vegetable oil
¼ cup frozen (thawed) orange juice concentrate
2 teaspoons grated orange peel
½ teaspoon almond extract
1 egg, slightly beaten
2¼ cups Gold Medal® all-purpose flour
½ cup granulated sugar
3 teaspoons baking powder
¼ teaspoon salt
⅓ cup finely chopped blanched almonds
2 tablespoons coarse sugar crystals (decorating sugar), if desired
2 tablespoons finely chopped blanched almonds, if desired

1. Heat oven to 400°. Grease bottom only of 24 small muffin cups, 1¾ × 1 inch, or line with paper baking cups.

2. Beat milk, oil, juice concentrate, orange peel, almond extract and egg in large bowl with spoon until blended. Stir in flour, granulated sugar, baking powder and salt all at once just until flour is moistened (batter will be lumpy). Stir in ⅓ cup almonds. Divide batter evenly among cups. Sprinkle with sugar crystals and 2 tablespoons almonds.

3. Bake 10 to 15 minutes or until light golden brown. Immediately remove from pan to wire rack.

24 muffins.

1 Muffin: Calories 110 (Calories from Fat 45); Fat 5g (Saturated 1g); Cholesterol 10mg; Sodium 95mg; Carbohydrate 15g (Dietary Fiber 1g); Protein 2g
% Daily Value: Vitamin A 0%; Vitamin C 2%; Calcium 4%; Iron 4%
Diet Exchanges: 1 Starch

BETTY'S TIPS

✿ Variation
To make 12 regular-size muffins, grease just the bottoms of 12 muffin cups, 2½ × 1¼ inches. Bake 20 to 25 minutes.

Cranberry Poppy Seed Muffins

Prep: 5 min   Bake: 20 min   Stand: 5 min

1¾ cups Original Bisquick®
½ cup sugar
¼ cup plain yogurt
½ cup milk
1 tablespoon poppy seed
1 teaspoon grated lemon peel
1 egg
½ cup fresh or frozen (thawed) cranberries

1. Heat oven to 400°. Grease bottom only of 12 medium muffin cups, 2½ × 1¼ inches, or line with paper baking cups.

2. Stir all ingredients except cranberries just until moistened. Stir in cranberries. Fill muffin cups about ¾ full.

3. Bake 18 to 20 minutes or until golden brown. Let stand 5 minutes; remove from pan.

12 muffins.

1 Muffin: Calories 120 (Calories from Fat 25); Fat 3g (Saturated 1g); Cholesterol 20mg; Sodium 260mg; Carbohydrate 21g (Dietary Fiber 0g); Protein 2g
% Daily Value: Vitamin A 0%; Vitamin C 0%; Calcium 6%; Iron 4%
Diet Exchanges: 1 Starch, ½ Fruit, ½ Fat

BETTY'S TIPS

✿ Success Hint
Overmixing can make muffins tough, heavy or rubbery. Muffin batter should not be beaten as much as cake batter. Mix only until the dry ingredients are moistened. It will still be slightly lumpy, which is typical of muffin batter.

✿ Special Touch
Drizzle these warm muffins with a glaze made by mixing ½ cup powdered sugar and 1 to 2 tablespoons milk or whipping (heavy) cream until smooth and thin enough to drizzle.

Cranberry Poppy Seed Muffins

Banana Toffee Drop Scones

Prep: 10 min   Bake: 13 min per sheet

2½   cups Original Bisquick
½   cup English toffee bits
¼   cup sugar
¼   cup whipping (heavy) cream
½   teaspoon vanilla
1   egg
2   medium bananas, mashed (¾ cup)
Milk
Additional sugar

1. Heat oven to 425°. Grease 2 cookie sheets.

2. Stir Bisquick, toffee bits, ¼ cup sugar, whipping cream, vanilla, egg and bananas until soft dough forms. Drop by 10 heaping tablespoonfuls onto cookie sheets (5 per cookie sheet). Brush tops with milk; sprinkle with additional sugar. Refrigerate second cookie sheet while first cookie sheet bakes.

3. Bake 11 to 13 minutes or until golden brown. Serve warm.

10 scones.

1 Scone: Calories 185 (Calories from Fat 65); Fat 7g (Saturated 3g); Cholesterol 30mg; Sodium 440mg; Carbohydrate 29g (Dietary Fiber 1g); Protein 3g
% Daily Value: Vitamin A 2%; Vitamin C 0%; Calcium 6%; Iron 6%
Diet Exchanges: 1 Starch, 1 Fruit, 1 Fat

BETTY'S TIPS

✿ Substitution
You can use ½ cup miniature semi-sweet chocolate chips instead of the English toffee bits.

✿ Special Touch
Use white coarse sugar crystals (decorating sugar) on top instead of the granulated sugar for an extra-special look.

Banana Blueberry Bread

Prep: 15 min   Bake: 1 hr 10 min   Cool: 1 hr 10 min

1   cup butter or margarine, softened
1⅔   cups sugar
4   eggs
5   medium ripe bananas, mashed
1   cup reduced-fat sour cream
2   teaspoons vanilla
3   cups Gold Medal all-purpose flour
2   teaspoons baking soda
1   teaspoon salt
1   cup dried blueberries

1. Move oven rack to low position so that tops of pans will be in center of oven. Heat oven to 350°. Grease bottoms only of 2 loaf pans, 8½ × 4½ × 2½ or 9 × 5 × 3 inches.

2. Beat butter and sugar in large bowl with electric mixer on medium speed until blended. Stir in eggs until well blended. Add bananas, sour cream and vanilla. Beat until smooth. Stir in flour, baking soda and salt just until moistened. Stir in blueberries. Pour into pans.

3. Bake 1 hour to 1 hour 10 minutes or until toothpick inserted in center comes out clean. Cool 10 minutes. Loosen sides of loaves from pans; remove from pans. Cool completely on wire rack, about 1 hour. Wrap tightly and store in refrigerator up to 1 week.

2 loaves (24 slices each.)

1 Slice: Calories 125 (Calories from Fat 45); Fat 5g (Saturated 3g); Cholesterol 30mg; Sodium 140mg; Carbohydrate 19g (Dietary Fiber 1g); Protein 2g
% Daily Value: Vitamin A 4%; Vitamin C 2%; Calcium 0%; Iron 2%
Diet Exchanges: ½ Starch, ½ Fruit, 1 Fat

BETTY'S TIPS

✿ Substitution
You can use nuts instead of the blueberries.

✿ Success Hint
Grease only the bottoms of loaf pans for nut breads. The ungreased sides allow the batter to cling while rising during baking, which helps form a gently rounded top. If sides are greased, the edges of the loaf may have ridges.

Cranberry Whole Wheat Bread

Prep: 10 min   Bake: 4 hr

1-Pound Recipe (8 slices)

¾	cup water
2	tablespoons honey
1	tablespoon butter or margarine, softened
1¼	cups Gold Medal Better for Bread™ flour
¾	cup Gold Medal whole wheat flour
1	teaspoon salt
¼	teaspoon ground mace
1¼	teaspoons bread machine or active dry yeast
⅓	cup dried cranberries

1½-Pound Recipe (12 slices)

1	cup plus 2 tablespoons water
¼	cup honey
2	tablespoons butter or margarine, softened
2	cups Gold Medal Better for Bread flour
1¼	cups Gold Medal whole wheat flour
1½	teaspoon salt
¾	teaspoon ground mace
2	teaspoons bread machine or active dry yeast
½	cup dried cranberries

1. Make 1-Pound Recipe with bread machines that use 2 cups flour, or make 1½-Pound Recipe with bread machines that use 3 cups flour.

2. Measure carefully, placing all ingredients except cranberries in bread machine pan in the order recommended by the manufacturer. Add cranberries at the Raisin/Nut signal.

3. Select Whole Wheat or Basic/White cycle. Use Medium or Light crust color. Do not use delay cycle. Remove baked bread from pan, and cool on wire rack.

1 loaf.

1 Slice: Calories 155 (Calories from Fat 20); Fat 2g (Saturated 0g); Cholesterol 0mg; Sodium 300mg; Carbohydrate 34g (Dietary Fiber 4g); Protein 4g
% Daily Value: Vitamin A 0%; Vitamin C 8%; Calcium 0%; Iron 8%
Diet Exchanges: 2 Starch

BETTY'S TIPS

✪ Success Hint
If your bread machine doesn't have a Raisin/Nut signal, add the cranberries 5 to 10 minutes before the last kneading cycle ends. Check your bread machine's use-and-care book to find out how long the last cycle runs.

✪ Substitution
You can use raisins if you don't have dried cranberries handy. Actually, any dried berry will do—you also may want to try dried cherries or blueberries. For a triple-berry treat, mix cranberries, cherries and blueberries together, and use the same amount as if you were using just the cranberries.

Cherry Swirl Coffee Cake

Cherry Swirl Coffee Cake

Prep: 20 min   Bake: 25 min

    4   cups Original Bisquick
    ½   cup sugar
    ¼   cup margarine or butter, melted
    ½   cup milk
    1   teaspoon vanilla
    1   teaspoon almond extract
    3   eggs
    1   can (21 ounces) cherry pie filling
        Glaze (below)

1. Heat oven to 350°. Grease jelly roll pan, 15½ × 10½ × 1 inch, or 2 square pans, 9 × 9 × 2 inches. Mix all ingredients except pie filling and Glaze; beat vigorously 30 seconds.

2. Spread two-thirds of the batter (about 2½ cups) in jelly roll pan or one-third of the batter (about 1¼ cups) in each square pan. Spread pie filling over batter (filling may not cover batter completely). Drop remaining batter by tablespoonfuls onto pie filling.

3. Bake 20 to 25 minutes or until light brown. While warm, drizzle with Glaze. Serve warm or cool.

18 servings.

Glaze

    1   cup powdered sugar
 1 to 2 tablespoons milk

Stir ingredients until smooth and thin enough to drizzle.

1 Serving: Calories 220 (Calories from Fat 65); Fat 7g (Saturated 2g); Cholesterol 35mg; Sodium 430mg; Carbohydrate 37g (Dietary Fiber 1g); Protein 3g
% Daily Value: Vitamin A 4%; Vitamin C 0%; Calcium 6%; Iron 4%
Diet Exchanges: 1 Starch, 1½ Fruit; 1 Fat

BETTY'S TIPS

❂ **Substitution**
You could also use 1 can of apricot, peach or blueberry pie filling for an easy flavor variation of this recipe.

❂ **Variation**
This recipe is easy to cut in half. Use one 9-inch square pan. Use 2 eggs, and substitute a 10-ounce jar of fruit preserves for the pie filling. Divide remaining ingredient amounts in half.

Betty ... MAKES IT EASY

Sweet Potato Caramel Twist Coffee Cake

Prep: 25 min   Bake: 30 min

Fold dough into thirds; press edges together to seal. Cut crosswise into twelve 1-inch strips.

⅓ cup margarine or butter
½ cup packed brown sugar
¼ cup corn syrup
½ cup chopped pecans
2 ½ cups Original Bisquick
⅔ cup mashed canned vacuum-pack sweet potatoes
⅓ cup milk
2 tablespoons margarine or butter, softened
3 tablespoons packed brown sugar

1. Heat oven to 400°. Melt ⅓ cup margarine in ungreased square pan, 9 × 9 × 2 inches, in oven. Stir in ½ cup brown sugar and the corn syrup. Sprinkle with pecans.

2. Mix Bisquick, sweet potatoes and milk until dough forms a ball. Place dough on surface dusted with Bisquick. Knead lightly 10 times. Roll or pat into 12-inch square. Spread 2 tablespoons margarine over dough. Sprinkle 3 tablespoons brown sugar over margarine. Fold dough into thirds; press edges together to seal. Cut crosswise into twelve 1-inch strips. Twist ends of each strip in opposite directions. Arrange twists on pecans in pan.

Twist ends of each strip in opposite directions.

3. Bake 25 to 30 minutes or until golden brown. Immediately place heatproof serving plate upside down onto pan; turn plate and pan over. Leave pan over coffee cake 1 minute. Serve warm.

12 servings.

1 Serving: Calories 280 (Calories from Fat 125); Fat 14g (Saturated 2g); Cholesterol 0mg; Sodium 470mg; Carbohydrate 37g (Dietary Fiber 1g); Protein 3g
% Daily Value: Vitamin A 20%; Vitamin C 2%; Calcium 6%; Iron 6%
Diet Exchanges: 1 Starch, 1 Vegetable, 1 Fruit, 2½ Fat

Italian Pancake Dunkers

Quick & Low-Fat

Italian Pancake Dunkers

Prep: 10 min   Cook: 13 min

1   cup pizza or spaghetti sauce
2   cups Original Bisquick
1   cup milk
2   eggs
½   cup shredded mozzarella cheese (2 ounces)
½   cup finely chopped pepperoni
¼   cup finely chopped green bell pepper
2   teaspoons Italian seasoning
1   small tomato, finely chopped (½ cup)

1. Heat pizza sauce until warm; keep warm. Stir Bisquick, milk and eggs until blended. Stir in remaining ingredients.

2. Spoon batter by tablespoonfuls onto hot griddle (grease griddle if necessary); spread slightly.

3. Cook until edges are dry. Turn; cook until golden. To serve, dunk pancakes into sauce.

40 pancakes.

1 Pancake: Calories 45 (Calories from Fat 20); Fat 2g (Saturated 1g); Cholesterol 15mg; Sodium 150mg; Carbohydrate 5g (Dietary Fiber 0g); Protein 2g
% Daily Value: Vitamin A 2%; Vitamin C 2%; Calcium 2%; Iron 2%
Diet Exchanges: ½ Starch

BETTY'S TIPS

☺ Success Hint
Don't flip 'em more than once! Repeated cooking on both sides toughens rather than browns the pancakes.

☺ Serve-With
These wonderful pancakes are just the fun, new breakfast or brunch idea you've been looking for. Serve them with kabobs of fresh fruit skewered alternately with cubes of cheese.

Chocolate Swirl Coffee Cake

Prep: 15 min   Bake: 25 min

⅓   cup flaked coconut
¼   cup chopped nuts
¼   cup sugar
3   tablespoons butter or margarine, melted
2   cups Original Bisquick
¼   cup sugar
⅔   cup water or milk
1   egg
⅓   cup semisweet chocolate chips, melted

1. Heat oven to 400°. Grease square pan, 8 × 8 × 2 inches. Mix coconut, nuts, ¼ cup sugar and 1 tablespoon of the butter; set aside.

2. Mix Bisquick, ¼ cup sugar, the water, egg and remaining 2 tablespoons butter; beat vigorously 30 seconds. Spread batter in pan. Spoon chocolate over batter; lightly swirl batter several times for marbled design. Sprinkle coconut mixture evenly over top.

3. Bake 20 to 25 minutes or until top is light golden brown and cake feels firm when touched in center. Serve warm.

12 servings.

1 Serving: Calories 200 (Calories from Fat 90); Fat 10g (Saturated 4g); Cholesterol 25mg; Sodium 310mg; Carbohydrate 25g (Dietary Fiber 1g); Protein 3g
% Daily Value: Vitamin A 2%; Vitamin C 0%; Calcium 4%; Iron 4%
Diet Exchanges: 1 Starch, ½ Fruit, 2 Fat

BETTY'S TIPS

☺ Time-Saver
Melt the chocolate chips in the microwave. Place in a small microwavable bowl or glass measuring cup, and microwave uncovered on Medium (50%) 1 minute 30 seconds to 2 minutes. The chips won't change shape, so stir until smooth.

☺ Do-Ahead
This coffee cake is best served warm, but you can microwave a piece for 10 to 15 seconds on High to bring back that fresh-from-the-oven taste.

Spicy Pumpkin Pancakes

Prep: 10 min   Bake: 10 min

Maple-Pecan Syrup (below)

2⅓ cups Original Bisquick
⅓ cup canned pumpkin (not pumpkin pie mix)
1¼ cups milk
¼ cup vegetable oil
2 tablespoons sugar
¼ teaspoon ground cinnamon
¼ teaspoon ground nutmeg
¼ teaspoon ground ginger
2 eggs

1. Make Maple-Pecan Syrup; keep warm. Stir remaining ingredients until blended.

2. Pour batter by slightly less than ¼ cupfuls onto hot griddle (grease griddle if necessary).

3. Cook until edges are dry. Turn; cook until golden brown. Serve with syrup.

18 pancakes.

Maple-Pecan Syrup

1 cup maple-flavored syrup
1 tablespoon butter or margarine
¼ cup chopped pecans

Heat syrup and margarine until margarine is melted; remove from heat. Stir in pecans.

1 Pancake: Calories 180 (Calories from Fat 70); Fat 8g (Saturated 2g); Cholesterol 25mg; Sodium 270mg; Carbohydrate 26g (Dietary Fiber 1g); Protein 2g
% Daily Value: Vitamin A 12%; Vitamin C 0%; Calcium 4%; Iron 4%
Diet Exchanges: 1 Starch, 1 Fruit, 1 Fat

Spicy Pumpkin Pancakes

Bacon and Swiss Waffles

Prep: 10 min   Bake: 15 min

      2 cups Original or Reduced Fat Bisquick
  1½ cups milk
      2 eggs
      1 cup shredded Swiss cheese (4 ounces)
      8 slices bacon, crisply cooked and crumbled
           (½ cup)

1. Heat waffle iron; grease if necessary. Stir Bisquick, milk and eggs in large bowl until blended. Stir in cheese and bacon.

2. Pour batter by slightly less than 1 cupfuls onto center of hot waffle iron.

3. Bake until steaming stops and waffle is golden brown. Carefully remove waffle.

Twelve 4-inch waffles.

1 Waffle: Calories 165 (Calories from Fat 80); Fat 9g (Saturated 4g); Cholesterol 50mg; Sodium 400mg; Carbohydrate 14g (Dietary Fiber 0g); Protein 7g
% Daily Value: Vitamin A 4%; Vitamin C 0%; Calcium 16%; Iron 4%
Diet Exchanges: 1 Starch, ½ High-Fat Meat, 1 Fat

Smoked Salmon and Egg Wraps

Prep: 10 min   Cook: 10 min   Bake: 10 min

12   eggs
2   tablespoons milk or water
½   teaspoon seasoned salt
¼   cup chopped fresh or 1 tablespoon dried dill weed
12   flour tortillas (8 inches in diameter)
1   package (4½ ounces) smoked salmon, broken into pieces
½   cup finely chopped red onion
1½   cups shredded Havarti cheese (6 ounces)
Dill weed sprigs, if desired

1. Heat oven to 350°. Line jelly roll pan, 15½ × 10½ × 1 inch, with aluminum foil. Beat eggs, milk and seasoned salt thoroughly with fork or wire whisk until a uniform yellow.

2. Spray 12-inch nonstick skillet with cooking spray. Pour egg mixture into skillet. As mixture begins to set at bottom and side, gently lift cooked portions with spatula so that thin, uncooked portion can flow to bottom. Avoid constant stirring. Cook 8 to 10 minutes or until eggs are thickened throughout but still moist. Stir in chopped dill weed.

3. Spoon about ⅓ cup eggs down center of each tortilla. Top with salmon, onion and cheese. Fold opposite sides of each tortilla over filling (sides will not meet in center). Roll up tortilla, beginning at one of the open ends. Place wraps, seam sides down, in pan. Cover with foil. Bake about 10 minutes or until cheese is melted. Garnish with dill weed sprigs.

12 servings.

1 Serving: Calories 280 (Calories from Fat 125); Fat 14g (Saturated 5g); Cholesterol 220mg; Sodium 500mg; Carbohydrate 25g (Dietary Fiber 2g); Protein 16g
% Daily Value: Vitamin A 10%; Vitamin C 0%; Calcium 16%; Iron 12%
Diet Exchanges: 1½ Starch, 2 Medium-Fat Meat

BETTY'S TIPS

☺ **Variation**
Use flavored tortillas to add extra color and flavor to these wraps.

☺ **Do-Ahead**
Refrigerate wraps up to 2 hours before serving, and bake 13 to 15 minutes.

☺ **Special Touch**
Wrap a pretty napkin or piece of brightly colored food-safe paper around each egg wrap. Choose colors to coordiante with your centerpiece for a special, festive look.

Smoked Salmon and Egg Wraps

Green Chili Egg and Potato Bake

Prep: 15 min   Bake: 1 hr   Stand: 10 min

3 cups frozen diced hash brown potatoes, thawed

½ cup frozen whole kernel corn, thawed

¼ cup chopped drained roasted red bell peppers (from 7-ounce jar)

1 can (4 ounces) chopped green chilies, drained

1½ cups shredded Colby–Monterey Jack cheese (6 ounces)

10 eggs

½ cup small curd creamed cottage cheese

½ teaspoon dried oregano leaves

¼ teaspoon garlic powder

4 medium green onions, chopped (¼ cup)

1. Heat oven to 350°. Spray rectangular baking dish, 11 × 7 × 1½ inches, with cooking spray. Layer potatoes, corn, bell peppers, chilies and 1 cup of the cheese in baking dish.

2. Beat eggs, cottage cheese, oregano and garlic powder with electic mixer on medium speed until smooth. Slowly pour over potato mixture in dish. Sprinkle with onions and remaining ½ cup cheese.

3. Cover and bake 30 minutes. Uncover and bake about 30 minutes longer or until knife inserted in center comes out clean. Let stand 5 to 10 minutes before cutting.

8 servings.

1 Serving: Calories 270 (Calories from Fat 125); Fat 14g (Saturated 7g); Cholesterol 290mg; Sodium 510mg; Carbohydrate 21g (Dietary Fiber 2g); Protein 17g
% Daily Value: Vitamin A 18%; Vitamin C 22%; Calcium 18%; Iron 8%
Diet Exchanges: 1 Starch, 2 Medium-Fat Meat, 1 Vegetable, ½ Fat

BETTY'S TIPS

☻ **Substitution**
An 11-ounce can of whole kernel corn with red and green bell peppers, drained, can be substituted for the frozen corn and roasted red bell peppers.

☻ **Serve-With**
Serve this southwestern-style dish with mild or medium chunky-style salsa.

☻ **Do-Ahead**
Get a head start on this crowd-pleasing brunch dish by assembling it up to 24 hours ahead of time. Cover and refrigerate, then bake as directed.

Green Chili Egg and Potato Bake

Hearty Breakfast Bake

Prep: 20 min   Bake: 40 min   Cool: 5 min

1   package (12 ounces) bulk pork sausage

4   medium green onions, thinly sliced

1   medium red bell pepper, chopped

1   package (8 ounces) sliced mushrooms (3 cups)

½   bag (20-ounce size) refrigerated loose-pack hash brown potatoes (2½ cups)

2   cups shredded Swiss cheese (8 ounces)

1   cup Original Bisquick

2   cups milk

⅛   teaspoon pepper

5   eggs

1. Heat oven to 400°. Grease rectangular baking dish, 13 × 9 × 2 inches.

2. Cook sausage in 10-inch skillet over medium-high heat, stirring frequently, until no longer pink; drain. Layer sausage, onions, bell pepper, mushrooms, potatoes and cheese in baking dish. Mix remaining ingredients. Pour over ingredients in baking dish.

3. Bake uncovered 35 to 40 minutes or until knife inserted in center comes out clean. Cool 5 minutes.

12 servings.

1 Serving: Calories 240 (Calories from Fat 125); Fat 14g (Saturated 6g); Cholesterol 120mg; Sodium 470mg; Carbohydrate 17g (Dietary Fiber 1g); Protein 13g
% Daily Value: Vitamin A 14%; Vitamin C 18%; Calcium 26%; Iron 6%
Diet Exchanges: 1 Starch, 1 High-Fat Meat, 1 Vegetable, 1 Fat

BETTY'S TIPS

✪ Health Twist

For 7 grams of fat and 200 calories per serving, spray baking dish with cooking spray. Use turkey sausage instead of the pork sausage, reduced-fat Swiss cheese, fat-free (skim) milk, 1¼ cups fat-free cholesterol-free egg product instead of the 5 eggs and Reduced Fat Bisquick instead of the Original Bisquick. Stir in ½ teaspoon salt with the egg mixture.

✪ Do-Ahead

To make this the night before, assemble recipe in baking dish and refrigerate overnight. Bake at 400° about 1 hour or until knife inserted in center comes out clean.

Vegetable Strata

Prep: 15 min   Chill: 2 hr   Bake: 1 hr 15 min   Stand: 10 min

- 8 slices whole wheat bread
- 1 bag (1 pound) frozen broccoli, green beans, pearl onions and red peppers (or other combination), thawed and drained
- 2 cups shredded sharp Cheddar cheese (8 ounces)
- 8 eggs, slightly beaten
- 4 cups milk
- ½ teaspoon salt
- ½ teaspoon ground mustard
- ¼ teaspoon pepper
- ⅛ teaspoon ground red pepper (cayenne)

1. Cut each bread slice diagonally into 4 triangles. Arrange half of the bread in ungreased rectangular pan, 13 × 9 × 2 inches. Top with vegetables. Sprinkle with cheese. Top with remaining bread.

2. Beat remaining ingredients until blended; pour over bread. Cover and refrigerate at least 2 hours but no longer than 24 hours.

3. Heat oven to 325°. Cover and bake 30 minutes. Uncover and bake about 45 minutes longer or until knife inserted in center comes out clean. Let stand 10 minutes before cutting.

8 servings.

1 Serving: Calories 325 (Calories from Fat 160); Fat 18g (Saturated 9g); Cholesterol 250mg; Sodium 600mg; Carbohydrate 23g (Dietary Fiber 3g); Protein 21g
% Daily Value: Vitamin A 26%; Vitamin C 24%; Calcium 36%; Iron 10%
Diet Exchanges: 1 Starch, 1 High-Fat Meat, 1 Skim Milk, 1 Fat

BETTY'S TIPS

✪ Substitution
White or rye bread can be used instead of the whole wheat.

✪ Success Hint
Don't throw away that day-old bread! Slightly dried-out bread slices are perfect for soaking up all the wonderful flavors in this dish.

Mexican Brunch Wedges

Prep: 20 min   Bake: 35 min   Cool: 5 min

- 1½ cups Original Bisquick
- ⅓ cup very hot water
- 6 ounces chorizo sausage, casing removed and sausage crumbled
- 3 eggs, beaten
- 1 cup sour cream
- 1 cup shredded mozzarella cheese (4 ounces)
- 4 medium green onions, sliced (¼ cup)
- ⅓ cup coarsely chopped red bell pepper

1. Heat oven to 425°. Grease 12-inch pizza pan. Mix Bisquick and hot water until soft dough forms. Press dough on bottom and up side of pan, using hands dipped in Bisquick. Bake 10 minutes.

2. While crust is baking, cook sausage in 10-inch skillet, stirring frequently, until brown; drain.

3. Mix eggs, sour cream, cheese and onions; pour over crust. Sprinkle sausage and bell pepper over egg mixture. Bake about 25 minutes or until set. Cool 5 minutes.

6 to 8 servings.

1 Serving: Calories 410 (Calories from Fat 250); Fat 28g (Saturated 13g); Cholesterol 165mg; Sodium 920mg; Carbohydrate 22g (Dietary Fiber 1g); Protein 18g
% Daily Value: Vitamin A 12%; Vitamin C 8%; Calcium 24%; Iron 10%
Diet Exchanges: 1½ Starch, 2 High-Fat Meat, 2 Fat

BETTY'S TIPS

✪ Substitution
For a milder version of this recipe, use bulk pork sausage instead of the chorizo sausage.

✪ Variation
Ham and Cheddar Wedges are easy to make using 1 cup of finely chopped fully cooked ham instead of the sausage and Cheddar instead of mozzarella cheese.

✪ Did You Know?
Chorizo is a highly seasoned, coarsely ground pork sausage flavored with garlic, chili powder and other spices. It is widely used in both Mexican and Spanish cooking.

Mexican Brunch Wedges

Key West Fruit Salad

Prep: 20 min   Cook: 5 min   Chill: 2 hr

¾ cup sugar

¼ cup water

¼ cup fresh or bottled Key lime juice

2 to 3 tablespoons tequila

1 teaspoon grated Key lime or regular lime peel

14 cups cut-up fresh fruit (pineapple, strawberries, kiwifruit, grapes)

1. Heat sugar and water to boiling in 1½-quart saucepan; reduce heat. Simmer uncovered about 2 minutes, stirring constantly, until sugar is dissolved; remove from heat. Stir in lime juice and tequila.

2. Let lime dressing stand until room temperature. Cover and refrigerate about 2 hours or until cool.

3. Stir lime peel into dressing. Carefully toss fruit and dressing. Serve immediately.

28 servings.

1 Serving: Calories 65 (Calories from Fat 0); Fat 0g (Saturated 0g); Cholesterol 0mg; Sodium 0mg; Carbohydrate 17g (Dietary Fiber 2g); Protein 1g
% Daily Value: Vitamin A 0%; Vitamin C 56%; Calcium 0%; Iron 2%
Diet Exchanges: 1 Fruit

BETTY'S TIPS

☺ **Substitution**
If you don't have tequila on hand, use 2 tablespoons of lime juice instead.
You can also use regular lime juice instead of the Key lime juice.

☺ **Success Hint**
If you are serving a smaller group, pour desired amount of dressing over fruit. Cover and refrigerate remaining dressing up to 1 week.

☺ **Do-Ahead**
Make the dressing up to a day ahead of time and store covered in the refrigerator.

Rio Grande Melon Salad

Prep: 25 min

Honey Lime Dressing (below)

4 cups watermelon balls

2 mangoes or papayas, peeled, seeded and sliced

½ honeydew melon, peeled, seeded and thinly sliced

1 cup seedless red grape halves

Lettuce leaves

1. Make Honey Lime Dressing; refrigerate until serving.

2. Arrange watermelon, mangoes, melon and grapes on lettuce leaves. Drizzle with dressing.

8 servings.

Honey Lime Dressing

½ cup vegetable oil

½ teaspoon grated lime peel

¼ cup lime juice

2 tablespoons honey

Shake all ingredients in tightly covered container.

1 Serving: Calories 240 (Calories from Fat 125); Fat 14g (Saturated 2g); Cholesterol 0mg; Sodium 15mg; Carbohydrate 30g (Dietary Fiber 2g); Protein 1g
% Daily Value: Vitamin A 22%; Vitamin C 76%; Calcium 2%; Iron 2%
Diet Exchanges: 2 Fruit, 3 Fat

BETTY'S TIPS

☺ **Success Hint**
Need help cutting a mango? Score the skin lengthwise into fourths with a knife, and peel like a banana. Cut the peeled mango lengthwise close to both sides of the seed, then slice.

☺ **Special Touch**
Many pretty salad greens, such as red leaf, curly endive and Bibb, are available. Line each salad plate with a combination of greens for an assortment of colors and textures. For a dramatic presentation, line a deep platter with salad greens and arrange the fruit on top. Or arrange fruit in glass dishes.

Watermelon Wedges with Mango Berry Salsa

Prep: 20 min

3 medium mangoes, cut lengthwise in half, pitted and coarsely chopped (3 cups)

1 pint (2 cups) strawberries, coarsely chopped

2 to 3 small jalapeño chilies, seeded and finely chopped (1 tablespoon)

¼ cup chopped fresh mint leaves

2 tablespoons lime juice

2 tablespoons honey

12 wedges watermelon, 1½ inches thick

1. Mix all ingredients except watermelon.

2. To serve, spoon mango salsa over watermelon wedges.

12 servings.

1 Serving: Calories 155 (Calories from Fat 20); Fat 2g (Saturated 0g); Cholesterol 0mg; Sodium 10mg; Carbohydrate 35g (Dietary Fiber 3g); Protein 2g
% Daily Value: Vitamin A 76%; Vitamin C 100%; Calcium 4%; Iron 4%
Diet Exchanges: 2 Fruit, ½ Fat

BETTY'S TIPS

❂ **Success Hint**

To make quick work of cutting watermelon wedges, cut a whole melon lengthwise in half. Cut each half crosswise into 1½-inch-thick slices. Then cut each slice in half.

To easily cut up a mango, score the skin lengthwise into fourths with a knife, and peel off the skin as you would a banana. Cut mango lengthwise close to both sides of the seed. Then chop, slice or dice the mango as needed.

❂ **Do-Ahead**

This fruity salsa can be made ahead and refrigerated for an impromptu snack or refreshing dessert. Chilling the salsa ahead helps blend the flavors.

Watermelon Wedges with Mango Berry Salsa

Lime Mint Melon Salad

Prep: 20 min   Chill: 2 hr

1½   cups ½-inch cubes honeydew melon
      (½ medium)
1½   cups ½-inch cubes cantaloupe (½ medium)
  1   teaspoon grated lime peel
  3   tablespoons lime juice
  2   tablespoons chopped fresh or 1 tablespoon
      dried mint leaves
  1   teaspoon honey
  ¼   teaspoon salt

1. Toss all ingredients in medium glass or plastic bowl.

2. Cover and refrigerate about 2 hours or until chilled.

6 servings.

1 Serving: Calories 40 (Calories from Fat 0); Fat 0g (Saturated 0g); Cholesterol 0mg; Sodium 110mg; Carbohydrate 9g (Dietary Fiber 1g); Protein 1g
% Daily Value: Vitamin A 22%; Vitamin C 48%; Calcium 0%; Iron 0%
Diet Exchanges: ½ Fruit

BETTY'S TIPS

⊛ **Success Hint**
Select a cantaloupe by smelling the soft stem end. Sweetness means ripeness.

⊛ **Variation**
Instead of cubing the melons, cut into balls with a melon baller.

Lime Mint Melon Salad

Easy Street

Super-Simple Lunches and Light Meals

French Onion Burgers

Prep: 10 min   Grill: 15 min

2 pounds ground beef
1 envelope (about 1½ ounces) onion soup mix
8 ounces French onion dip (1 cup)
½ cup dry bread crumbs
⅛ teaspoon pepper
   Lettuce leaves
8 slices tomato
8 kaiser rolls, split and toasted
   Ketchup, if desired
   Pickle planks, if desired

1. Heat coals or gas grill. Mix beef, soup mix (dry), onion dip, bread crumbs and pepper. Shape mixture into 8 patties, about ¼ inch thick.

2. Grill patties uncovered 4 to 6 inches from medium heat 10 to 15 minutes, turning once, until no longer pink in center and juice is clear. Place lettuce leaves and tomato slices on bottom halves of rolls; top with burgers, ketchup and pickles. Top with remaining roll halves.

8 servings.

1 Serving: Calories 465 (Calories from Fat 215); Fat 24g (Saturated 9g); Cholesterol 75mg; Sodium 900mg; Carbohydrate 36g (Dietary Fiber 2g); Protein 28g
% Daily Value: Vitamin A 2%; Vitamin C 4%; Calcium 10%; Iron 22%
Diet Exchanges: 2 Starch, 3 Medium-Fat Meat, 1 Vegetable, 1 Fat

BETTY'S TIPS

☺ Time-Saver
If this recipe makes too many burgers for your family, freeze half of the grilled burgers and you'll have the makings of an emergency meal.

☺ Special Touch
To toast kaiser rolls, hamburger buns or hot dog buns, grill cut sides down about 4 minutes or until golden brown.

Italian Turkey Burgers

Prep: 10 min   Grill: 16 min

1 pound ground turkey breast
⅓ cup tomato pasta sauce
3 tablespoons finely chopped red onion
4 slices (1 ounce each) provolone cheese, cut in half
1 baguette (16 inches), cut into 4-inch pieces
4 lettuce leaves
4 slices red onion
   Additional tomato pasta sauce, if desired

1. Brush grill rack with vegetable oil. Heat coals or gas grill. Mix turkey, ⅓ cup pasta sauce and chopped onion. Shape mixture into 4 patties, each about ¾ inch thick and the approximate shape of the baguette pieces.

2. Cover and grill patties 4 to 6 inches from medium heat 12 to 15 minutes, turning once, until no longer pink in center and juice is clear. Top patties with cheese. Cover and grill about 1 minute longer or until cheese is melted.

3. Slice baguette pieces horizontally in half. Place lettuce leaves on bottom halves; top with burgers and onion slices. Top with remaining baguette halves. Serve with additional pasta sauce.

4 servings.

1 Serving: Calories 365 (Calories from Fat 90); Fat 10g (Saturated 5g); Cholesterol 95mg; Sodium 680mg; Carbohydrate 34g (Dietary Fiber 2g); Protein 37g
% Daily Value: Vitamin A 10%; Vitamin C 6%; Calcium 22%; Iron 18%
Diet Exchanges: 2 Starch, 4 Very Lean Meat, 1 Vegetable, 1 Fat

BETTY'S TIPS

☺ Success Hint
Because of their lower fat content, turkey patties may stick to the grill unless it is oiled first. For safety reasons, always brush the grill rack with oil before lighting the coals or turning the gas on.

☺ Variation
For more Italian flavor, mix 1 teaspoon Italian seasoning in with the turkey, pasta sauce and chopped onion.

Italian Turkey Burgers

Grilled Portabella Mushroom Sandwiches

Prep: 10 min   Grill: 10 min

Lemon Herb Basting Sauce (at right)
4   fresh large portabella mushroom caps
1   medium red onion, cut into ¼-inch slices
4   whole wheat hamburger buns, split
4   lettuce leaves
4   tomato slices

1. Heat coals or gas grill for direct heat. Make Lemon Herb Basting Sauce.

2. Brush mushrooms and onion slices with basting sauce. Cover and grill mushrooms 5 to 6 inches from medium heat 5 minutes. Add onions. Cover and grill about 5 minutes, turning and brushing mushrooms and onions with sauce occasionally, until vegetables are tender.

3. Brush cut sides of buns with remaining sauce. Fill each bun with lettuce, mushroom, tomato and onion.

4 servings.

Lemon Herb Basting Sauce
½   cup olive or vegetable oil
1   tablespoon chopped fresh or 1 teaspoon dried thyme leaves
2   tablespoons Dijon mustard
2   tablespoons lemon juice
1   teaspoon grated lemon peel

Shake all ingredients in tightly covered container.

1 Serving: Calories 305 (Calories from Fat 190); Fat 21g (Saturated 3g); Cholesterol 0mg; Sodium 370mg; Carbohydrate 27g (Dietary Fiber 4g); Protein 6g
% Daily Value: Vitamin A 10%; Vitamin C 10%; Calcium 4%; Iron 14%
Diet Exchanges: 1 Starch, 3 Vegetable, 3 Fat

BETTY'S TIPS

⊙ **Substitution**
Focaccia bread, about 8 inches in diameter, can be used instead of the buns. Cut the bread horizontally in half, and spread cut sides with the basting sauce.

Quick

Grilled Barbecue Subs

Prep: 15 min   Grill: 15 min

- 2 loaves (1 pound each) French bread
- 1 pound sliced fully cooked ham
- 1 pound sliced salami
- 8 ounces sliced Swiss cheese
- 8 ounces sliced Cheddar cheese
- ½ cup barbecue sauce

1. Heat coals or gas grill for direct heat. Cut bread loaves horizontally in half. Arrange half of ham, salami and cheeses on each bottom loaf half. Spread barbecue sauce over sandwich fillings. Add tops of loaves; secure with toothpicks.

2. Wrap each loaf in heavy-duty aluminum foil. Cover and grill 3 to 4 inches from medium heat about 15 minutes or until cheese is melted and sandwiches are hot.

12 servings.

1 Serving: Calories 505 (Calories from Fat 215); Fat 24g (Saturated 12g); Cholesterol 80mg; Sodium 1580mg; Carbohydrate 44g (Dietary Fiber 2g); Protein 30g
% Daily Value: Vitamin A 8%; Vitamin C 0%; Calcium 34%; Iron 18%
Diet Exchanges: 3 Starch, 3 Medium-Fat Meat, 1 Fat

BETTY'S TIPS

⚙ **Pack 'n Go**
Make these hearty subs either ahead of time or at your picnic site. If you plan to take the ingredients, start the grill when you begin assembling the sandwiches.

⚙ **Variation**
Go beyond regular barbecue sauces and experiment with hot and spicy, honey-mustard or hickory-smoked barbecue sauce for a different sub every time!

Quick

Salmon Patties

Prep: 15 min   Cook: 12 min

- 1 cup soft bread crumbs
- 8 medium green onions, chopped (½ cup)
- ½ cup Original or Reduced Fat Bisquick
- 1 tablespoon Dijon mustard
- ¼ teaspoon pepper
- 2 eggs, slightly beaten
- 1 can (14¾ ounces) red salmon, drained and flaked
- 2 tablespoons margarine or butter
- ½ cup dill dip

1. Stir together all ingredients except margarine and dill dip. Shape mixture into 4 patties, using heaping ½ cupful for each patty.

2. Melt margarine in 10-inch nonstick skillet over medium heat. Cook patties in margarine over medium-high heat 10 to 12 minutes, turning once, until brown and cooked through. Serve with dill dip.

4 servings.

1 Serving: Calories 420 (Calories from Fat 190); Fat 21g (Saturated 7g); Cholesterol 165mg; Sodium 1310mg; Carbohydrate 32g (Dietary Fiber 1g); Protein 27g
% Daily Value: Vitamin A 12%; Vitamin C 2%; Calcium 34%; Iron 18%
Diet Exchanges: 2 Starch, 3 Lean Meat, 2 Fat

BETTY'S TIPS

⚙ **Substitution**
Do you prefer **Tuna Patties?** Two cans (6 ounces each) tuna, drained, can be used instead of the salmon.

⚙ **Variation**
These tasty **Salmon Patties** make a hearty sandwich meal. Place 1 patty, lettuce, thick slices of tomato, dill dip or additional mustard if desired between slices of rye bread.

⚙ **Do-Ahead**
Cook Salmon Patties up to 24 hours before serving; cover and refrigerate. To serve, heat on cookie sheet in 400° oven 10 minutes.

Greek-Style Tuna Salad Sandwiches

Prep: 10 min

- 1 can (12 ounces) tuna, drained and flaked
- ½ cup chopped drained roasted red bell peppers (from 7-ounce jar)
- ½ cup crumbled feta cheese or shredded mozzarella cheese
- 1 medium stalk celery, chopped (½ cup)
- 1 loaf (1 pound) French bread
- ¼ cup Italian dressing

1. Mix tuna, bell peppers, cheese and celery.

2. Cut bread into four 4-inch pieces; cut each piece horizontally in half. For each sandwich, remove some of the bread from center of slices; discard bread or save for another use.

3. Drizzle dressing on cut sides of bread; spread over bread. Fill each sandwich with ½ cup tuna mixture. Serve immediately, or wrap securely with plastic wrap and refrigerate up to 24 hours.

4 servings.

1 Serving: Calories 360 (Calories from Fat 110); Fat 12g (Saturated 6g); Cholesterol 50mg; Sodium 1310mg; Carbohydrate 44g (Dietary Fiber 2g); Protein 21g
% Daily Value: Vitamin A 6%; Vitamin C 0%; Calcium 8%; Iron 20%
Diet Exchanges: 3 Starch, 2 Lean Meat

BETTY'S TIPS

☼ Substitution
Canned sliced pimientos, drained, can be used instead of the roasted bell peppers.

☼ Special Touch
Add ½ cup chopped drained pepperoncini peppers (bottled Italian peppers) instead of the roasted bell peppers. Pepperoncini peppers have a slightly sweet and spicy-hot flavor.

Italian Vegetable Focaccia Sandwich

Prep: 5 min

- 1 round focaccia bread (10 to 12 inches in diameter)
- 2 cups shredded mozzarella cheese (8 ounces)
- 2 cups deli marinated Italian vegetable salad, drained and coarsely chopped

1. Cut focaccia vertically in half, then horizontally in half. Sprinkle bottom halves of focaccia with 1 cup of the cheese. Spread vegetables over cheese. Sprinkle with remaining cheese.

2. Top with tops of bread. Cut each half into 3 wedges.

6 servings.

1 Serving: Calories 340 (Calories from Fat 145); Fat 16g (Saturated 6g); Cholesterol 55mg; Sodium 960mg; Carbohydrate 33g (Dietary Fiber 2g); Protein 18g
% Daily Value: Vitamin A 20%; Vitamin C 2%; Calcium 32%; Iron 14%
Diet Exchanges: 2 Starch, 1½ High-Fat Meat, 1 Vegetable

BETTY'S TIPS

☼ Variation
This easy sandwich filling works great in crusty Italian or French rolls as well—and makes the sandwiches more portable. Slice off the top of each roll, and remove half of the soft bread from inside. Layer the cheese and vegetable salad inside the rolls.

☼ Did You Know?
Focaccia is an Italian bread shaped into a large, flat round, then often drizzled with olive oil and topped with Parmesan cheese. It can be found in the bakery, deli or frozen-foods section of the grocery store.

Quick

Curried Egg Salad Sandwiches

Prep: 10 min

6 hard-cooked eggs, chopped
¼ cup mayonnaise or salad dressing
2 tablespoons chutney
¼ teaspoon curry powder
8 slices hearty whole-grain or rye bread
½ medium cucumber, thinly sliced

1. Mix all ingredients except bread and cucumber.

2. Spread egg salad on 4 slices bread. Top with cucumber and remaining bread.

4 servings.

1 Serving: Calories 355 (Calories from Fat 190); Fat 21g (Saturated 5g); Cholesterol 325mg; Sodium 470mg; Carbohydrate 31g (Dietary Fiber 4g); Protein 15g
% Daily Value: Vitamin A 10%; Vitamin C 4%; Calcium 8%; Iron 16%
Diet Exchanges: 2 Starch, 1½ High-Fat Meat, 1 Fat

BETTY'S TIPS

○ **Time-Saver**
Save time by purchasing hard-cooked eggs, available in your supermarket deli or dairy case.

○ **Health Twist**
If you're trying to reduce the fat in your diet, use fat-free mayonnaise.

○ **Variation**
Serve this zesty egg salad on marbled rye bread available in the bakery of your supermarket.

Curried Egg Salad Sandwiches

Mexican Layered Sandwich

Mexican Layered Sandwich

Prep: 15 min

4 flour tortillas (8 inches in diameter)
2 large lettuce leaves, shredded (½ cup)
½ pound thinly sliced cooked turkey
½ cup purchased spicy guacamole
½ cup shredded Cheddar cheese
1 can (2¼ ounces) sliced ripe olives, drained
⅓ cup chopped red bell pepper
3 medium green onions, sliced
2 tablespoons chopped fresh cilantro or parsley
¼ cup sour cream
Salsa, if desired

1. Place 1 tortilla on serving platter. Top with lettuce, half of the turkey and another tortilla.

2. Reserve 1 tablespoon guacamole; spread remaining guacamole evenly over second tortilla. Sprinkle with half each of the cheese, olives, bell pepper and green onions.

3. Top with third tortilla and remaining turkey; sprinkle with cilantro. Top with remaining tortilla. Spread sour cream evenly over sandwich. Sprinkle with remaining cheese, olives, bell pepper and green onions. Top with reserved guacamole.

4. Serve immediately, or cover and refrigerate up to 3 hours. To serve, cut into 6 wedges. Serve with salsa.

6 servings.

1 Serving: Calories 230 (Calories from Fat 110); Fat 12g (Saturated 4g); Cholesterol 35mg; Sodium 840mg; Carbohydrate 21g (Dietary Fiber 3g); Protein 13g
% Daily Value: Vitamin A 12%; Vitamin C 42%; Calcium 12%; Iron 10%
Diet Exchanges: 1 Starch, 1 Lean Meat, 1 Vegetable, 1½ Fat

BETTY'S TIPS

✪ **Variation**

For more spice, use the new jalapeño- or cilantro-flavored tortillas available in the supermarket.

Honey Mustard Chicken Sandwiches

Prep: 10 min   Grill: 20 min

- ¼ cup Dijon mustard
- 2 tablespoons honey
- 1 teaspoon dried oregano leaves
- ⅛ to ¼ teaspoon ground red pepper (cayenne)
- 4 boneless skinless chicken breast halves (about 1¼ pounds)
- 4 whole-grain sandwich buns, split
- 4 slices tomato
- Leaf lettuce

1. Heat coals or gas grill. Mix mustard, honey, oregano and red pepper. Brush on chicken.

2. Cover and grill chicken 4 to 6 inches from medium heat 15 to 20 minutes, brushing frequently with mustard mixture and turning occasionally, until juice is no longer pink when centers of thickest pieces are cut. Discard any remaining mustard mixture. Serve chicken on buns with tomato and lettuce.

4 servings.

1 Serving: Calories 240 (Calories from Fat 45); Fat 5g (Saturated 1g); Cholesterol 60mg; Sodium 400mg; Carbohydrate 25g (Dietary Fiber 3g); Protein 27g
% Daily Value: Vitamin A 4%; Vitamin C 12%; Calcium 6%; Iron 14%
Diet Exchanges: 1½ Starch, 3 Very Lean Meat, ½ Fat

BETTY'S TIPS

☺ **Variation**
On rainy days, broil the chicken instead. Place it on a rack in the broiler pan, and brush with the mustard mixture. Broil with tops 4 to 6 inches from heat 15 to 20 minutes, turning once and brushing with additional mustard mixture.

☺ **Special Touch**
Prepare some ice-cold kabobs to serve with these sandwiches. Spear any combination of cut-up fresh fruits with toothpicks or skewers. These would be great to keep in the fridge for a pick-me-up as the temperature rises. Dipping the fruit in lemon juice will keep it from turning brown while refrigerated.

Adobe Chicken Wraps

Prep: 10 min

- 1½ cups chopped cooked chicken
- ½ cup salsa
- 1 can (15 ounces) black beans, rinsed and drained
- 1 can (7 ounces) whole kernel corn, drained
- 6 spinach or regular flour tortillas (8 to 10 inches in diameter)
- ⅓ cup sour cream
- Additional salsa, if desired

1. Mix chicken, ½ cup salsa, the beans and corn. Divide chicken mixture among tortillas, spreading to within 2 inches of bottom of each tortilla. Top each with sour cream.

2. Fold one end of the tortilla up about 1 inch over filling; fold right and left sides over folded end, overlapping. Fold remaining end down. Serve with additional salsa.

6 servings.

1 Serving: Calories 340 (Calories from Fat 80); Fat 9g (Saturated 3g); Cholesterol 40mg; Sodium 680mg; Carbohydrate 51g (Dietary Fiber 7g); Protein 21g
% Daily Value: Vitamin A 4%; Vitamin C 10%; Calcium 12%; Iron 22%
Diet Exchanges: 3 Starch, 1½ Lean Meat, 1 Vegetable

BETTY'S TIPS

☺ **Substitution**
If you don't have leftover chicken on hand, pick up roast chicken at your supermarket deli or use canned chunk chicken.

☺ **Variation**
Zest it up! Toss sprigs of fresh cilantro on top of the filling, then roll 'em up.

Honduran Chicken Salad Wraps

Prep: 10 min

4 cups chopped cooked chicken (1¼ pounds)
2 cups coarsely shredded cabbage (½ pound)
1 large tomato, diced (1 cup)
¾ cup salad dressing or mayonnaise
1 to 2 teaspoons red pepper sauce
1 teaspoon salt
6 flour tortillas (10 inches in diameter)

1. In a large bowl, mix chicken, cabbage, tomato, salad dressing, red pepper sauce and salt.

2. Divide chicken mixture among tortillas; roll up.

6 servings.

1 Serving: Calories 484 (Calories from Fat 278); Fat 31g (Saturated 5g); Cholesterol 100mg; Sodium 604mg; Carbohydrate 21g (Dietary Fiber 2g); Protein 31g
% Daily Value: Vitamin A 7%; Vitamin C 30%; Calcium 10%; Iron 18%
Diet Exchanges: 1 Starch, 4 Meat, ½ Vegetable, 5 Fat

BETTY'S TIPS

✿ Success Hint

The red pepper sauce adds a lot of zip. You may want to start with 1 teaspoon or less, then add more to your own tastes. Sliced green onions or chopped fresh cilantro would be nice additions to this recipe.

Honduran Chicken Salad Wraps

Super Summer Subs

Prep 20 min

Club-Style Filling, Mediterranean Filling or Western Barbecue Filling (below)

3 cups shredded roasted chicken (from a deli rotisserie chicken)

6 soft hoagie or crusty submarine sandwich rolls (about 6 inches), split

Choose one or more of the fillings and layer with chicken on rolls.

6 servings.

Club-Style Filling

Spread 1/2 cup honey mustard on cut sides of rolls. Layer with 4 ounces thinly sliced cooked roast beef or fully cooked ham. Top with chicken. Add 6 tablespoons sliced ripe or pimiento-stuffed olives, 2 medium tomatoes, sliced, and, if desired, spinach leaves.

Mediterranean Filling

Spread 1/2 cup hummus on cut sides of rolls. Layer with 1 small red onion, thinly sliced, 2 ounces feta cheese, crumbled (1/2 cup), 24 spinach leaves and the chicken.

Western Barbecue Filling

Spread 1/2 cup guacamole on cut sides of rolls. Layer with chicken. Drizzle with 1/4 cup barbecue sauce. Add 1 small green bell pepper, thinly sliced.

1 Serving: Calories 425 (Calories from Fat 100); Fat 11g (Saturated 3g); Cholesterol 70mg; Sodium 1370mg; Carbohydrate 52g (Dietary Fiber 4g); Protein 33g
% Daily Value: Vitamin A 6%; Vitamin C 12%; Calcium 10%; Iron 24%
Diet Exchanges: 3 Starch, 3 Lean Meat, 1 Vegetable

BETTY'S TIPS

✿ Pack 'n Go

Roll individual subs in plastic wrap, waxed paper or aluminum foil. Use a permanent marker to label different flavors of sandwiches.

✿ Crowd Pleaser

You can easily double or triple these subs for the whole gang. Use one filling or a variety of fillings, depending on crowd preferences.

✿ Substitution

Many flavors of hummus and feta cheese are available. Pick up a flavored kind (sun-dried tomato, roasted garlic) to give the Mediterranean sub a flavor twist.

Super Summer Subs

Cheesy Roast Beef Wraps

Cheesy Roast Beef Wraps

Prep: 10 min   Cook: 5 min

Cheesy Dipping Sauce (below)

¼ cup yellow mustard

6 garden vegetable-flavored flour tortillas (8 inches in diameter)

¾ pound thinly sliced cooked roast beef

1 cup lightly packed spinach leaves

1 medium bell pepper, cut into strips

1. Make Cheesy Dipping Sauce.

2. Spread 2 teaspoons mustard over each tortilla. Top with roast beef, spinach and bell pepper. Roll up tortillas. Serve with sauce.

6 servings.

Cheesy Dipping Sauce

1 jar (16 ounces) process cheese sauce or spread

2 tablespoons milk

4 medium green onions, sliced (¼ cup)

Heat cheese sauce and milk in 1½-quart saucepan over medium heat, stirring constantly, until smooth. Stir in green onions. Serve warm.

1 Serving: Calories 520 (Calories from Fat 260); Fat 29g (Saturated 15g); Cholesterol 90mg; Sodium 1600mg; Carbohydrate 33g (Dietary Fiber 2g); Protein 34g
% Daily Value: Vitamin A 20%; Vitamin C 34%; Calcium 52%; Iron 22%
Diet Exchanges: 2 Starch, 4 Lean Meat, 1 Vegetable, 3 Fat

BETTY'S TIPS

⊙ **Substitution**

Use thinly sliced cooked turkey or chicken instead of the roast beef.

⊙ **Time-Saver**

No time for the cheese sauce? Serve these wraps with additional mustard or with creamy Italian dressing, honey mustard dressing or salsa for dipping.

Beef and Provolone Pinwheels

Prep: 10 min

¼ cup mayonnaise or salad dressing
2 cloves garlic, finely chopped
2 flour tortillas (8 to 10 inches in diameter)
1 cup fresh spinach
¼ pound thinly sliced cooked roast beef
6 slices (¾ ounce each) provolone cheese
1 medium tomato, thinly sliced

1. Mix mayonnaise and garlic in small bowl. Spread mixture evenly over tortillas.

2. Top tortillas with layers of spinach, beef, cheese and tomato; roll up tightly. Cut each tortilla into 12 pieces; secure with toothpicks. Serve immediately or refrigerate until serving.

8 servings.

1 Serving: Calories 111 (Calories from Fat 69); Fat 8g (Saturated 2g); Cholesterol 16mg; Sodium 75mg; Carbohydrate 6g (Dietary Fiber 0g); Protein 5g
% Daily Value: Vitamin A 9%; Vitamin C 9%; Calcium 5%; Iron 6%
Diet Exchanges: ½ Meat, 1 Fat

BETTY'S TIPS

⊘ **Substitution**
In place of the regular roast beef, try Cajun- or Italian-seasoned roast beef from the deli. Or if you prefer, use sliced cooked turkey.

⊘ **Time-Saver**
Ready-to-use chopped garlic, available in jars in the produce section of the grocery store, is very convenient. Use 1 teaspoon of this already chopped garlic instead of chopping the 2 cloves of garlic.

⊘ **Do-Ahead**
Wrap tortilla rolls (unsliced) individually in plastic wrap and refrigerate for up to 24 hours.

Beef and Provolone Pinwheels

Burrito BLT Wraps

Prep: 10 min

2 cups bite-size pieces lettuce

1½ cups shredded Cheddar cheese (6 ounces)

⅓ cup mayonnaise or salad dressing

8 slices bacon, crisply cooked and crumbled

1 large tomato, chopped (1 cup)

6 flour tortillas (8 to 10 inches in diameter)

1. Toss all ingredients except tortillas.

2. Place lettuce mixture on tortillas. Fold up bottom third of each tortilla; roll up to form a cone shape with folded end at bottom.

6 servings.

1 Serving: Calories 380 (Calories from Fat 235); Fat 26g (Saturated 9g); Cholesterol 45mg; Sodium 590mg; Carbohydrate 26g (Dietary Fiber 2g); Protein 14g
% Daily Value: Vitamin A 8%; Vitamin C 10%; Iron 10%
Diet Exchanges: 1 Starch, 1 High-Fat Meat, 2 Vegetable, 3 Fat

BETTY'S TIPS

⊙ **Serve-With**
Cinnamon fried ice cream without the frying? Coarsely crush Cinnamon Toast Crunch® cereal over scoops of vanilla or chocolate ice cream—easy! Top with a drizzle of chocolate sauce or honey if you like.

⊙ **Variation**
Spread each tortilla with 2 tablespoons guacamole before adding the lettuce mixture.

Stromboli Hero

Prep: 15 min

1 round focaccia bread (8 or 9 inches in diameter)

¼ cup Italian dressing

4 or 5 leaves leaf lettuce

¼ pound sliced provolone cheese

¼ pound sliced fully cooked ham

¼ pound sliced salami

8 pepperoncini peppers (bottled Italian peppers), cut lengthwise in half

1. Cut bread horizontally in half. Drizzle dressing evenly over cut sides of bread.

2. Layer lettuce, cheese, ham, salami and peppers on bottom half of bread. Top with top half. Secure loaf with toothpicks or small skewers. Cut into 6 wedges.

6 servings.

1 Serving: Calories 355 (Calories from Fat 180); Fat 20g (Saturated 7g); Cholesterol 40mg; Sodium 1200mg; Carbohydrate 30g (Dietary Fiber 2g); Protein 16g
% Daily Value: Vitamin A 34%; Vitamin C 96%; Calcium 16%; Iron 14%
Diet Exchanges: 2 Starch, 1½ Medium-Fat Meat, 2 Fat

BETTY'S TIPS

⊙ **Substitution**
You can use an unsliced 8- or 10-inch round loaf of Italian or sourdough bread instead of the focaccia. If you don't have pepperoncini peppers, use sliced tomatoes, sliced red onion or bell pepper rings.

⊙ **Time-Saver**
Before cutting the sandwich into wedges, wrap it securely with plastic wrap and refrigerate up to 6 hours.

Montana Panini

Montana Panini

Prep: 10 min   Cook: 5 min

Avocado Ranch Dressing (below)
12 slices sourdough bread, ½ inch thick
 3 tablespoons butter or margarine, softened
 ¾ pound thinly sliced cooked deli turkey
12 slices turkey bacon, crisply cooked and broken in half
 1 large tomato, sliced
 6 slices (1 ounce each) Colby–Monterey Jack cheese

1. Make Avocado Ranch Dressing. Spread one side of each bread slice with butter. Turn 6 bread slices butter sides down; top with turkey, bacon, tomato, cheese and dressing. Top with remaining bread slices, butter sides up.

2. Cover and cook sandwiches in 12-inch skillet over medium heat 4 to 5 minutes, turning once, until bread is crisp and cheese is melted.

6 servings.

Avocado Ranch Dressing
 ¼ cup ranch dressing
 1 small avocado, pitted, peeled and mashed

Mix ingredients.

1 Serving: Calories 540 (Calories from Fat 325); Fat 36g (Saturated 13g); Cholesterol 95mg; Sodium 1760mg; Carbohydrate 31g (Dietary Fiber 3g); Protein 27g
% Daily Value: Vitamin A 16%; Vitamin C 6%; Calcium 22%; Iron 14%
Diet Exchanges: 2 Starch, 3 High-Fat Meat, 2 Fat

BETTY'S TIPS

⚙ **Did You Know?**
Turkey bacon has the same smoky flavor as pork bacon, but it has much less fat. One slice of regular bacon weighs in at about 6 grams of fat per slice. And turkey bacon? A slice has about 0.5 gram of fat.

Ham Bagels with Honey Mustard Cream Cheese

Prep: 5 min

 ½ cup whipped cream cheese spread
 2 tablespoons Dijon mustard
 1 tablespoon honey
 4 bagels, cut horizontally in half
 8 ounces deli-style sliced fully cooked ham

1. Mix cream cheese, mustard and honey.

2. Spread cream cheese mixture over cut sides of bagels. Top with ham and remaining bagel halves.

4 servings.

1 Serving: Calories 360 (Calories from Fat 110); Fat 12g (Saturated 6g); Cholesterol 50mg; Sodium 1310mg; Carbohydrate 44g (Dietary Fiber 2g); Protein 21g
% Daily Value: Vitamin A 6%; Vitamin C 0%; Calcium 8%; Iron 20%
Diet Exchanges: 3 Starch, 2 Lean Meat

BETTY'S TIPS

⚙ **Substitution**
Use your favorite flavor of bagel—honey wheat, onion, pumpernickel and white are tasty with ham.

You can use sliced smoked turkey instead of ham.

⚙ **Time-Saver**
Spread the bagels with the cream cheese and then spread with 3 tablespoons honey mustard instead of mixing the Dijon mustard and honey.

Chicken Quesadillas

Prep: 10 min   Cook: 15 min

2	cups shredded cooked chicken
1/4	cup chopped fresh cilantro
8	flour tortillas (8 inches in diameter)
1	cup shredded Monterey Jack cheese (4 ounces)
1	can (4 ounces) chopped green chilies, drained
	Salsa, if desired

1. Heat coals or gas grill for direct heat. Mix chicken and cilantro.

2. Place 1 tortilla on 30 × 18-inch piece of heavy-duty aluminum foil. Top with one-fourth of the chicken mixture, 1/4 cup of the cheese and one-fourth of the chilies. Top with another tortilla. Wrap foil securely around tortillas; pierce top of foil packet once or twice with fork to vent steam.

3. Repeat with remaining tortillas, chicken mixture, cheese and chilies. Cover and grill foil packets, seam sides up, 4 to 6 inches from medium heat about 15 minutes or until cheese is melted.

4. Cut quesadillas into wedges. Serve with salsa.

4 servings.

1 Serving: Calories 505 (Calories from Fat 180); Fat 20g (Saturated 8g); Cholesterol 85mg; Sodium 760mg; Carbohydrate 50g (Dietary Fiber 3g); Protein 34g
% Daily Value: Vitamin A 14%; Vitamin C 32%; Calcium 32%; Iron 22%
Diet Exchanges: 3 Starch, 3 Medium-Fat Meat, 1 Vegetable, 1 Fat

BETTY'S TIPS

⊕ **Success Hint**
Use deli roasted chicken if you don't have leftover cooked chicken on hand.

⊕ **Serve-With**
For a super-quick side dish, combine hot cooked rice with salsa or with melted process cheese spread. Top with sliced ripe olives and chopped green onions for a festive look.

⊕ **Variation**
If you don't want to heat up the grill, cook the filled tortillas in a 10-inch skillet over medium-high heat 4 to 6 minutes, turning after 2 minutes, until light golden brown.

Chicken Quesadillas

Betty . . .

MAKES IT EASY

Quick & Low-Fat

Chicken and Fruit in Foil

Prep: 12 min   Grill: 15 min

- 1 pound cut-up boneless chicken breast for stir-fry
- 2 large firm ripe pears, sliced
- 1 large cooking apple, sliced
- ½ cup malt vinegar
- 2 tablespoons chopped fresh or 1 teaspoon dried sage leaves
- ½ teaspoon salt

1. Heat coals or gas grill. Place chicken, pears and apple on one side of four 18 × 12-inch sheets of heavy-duty aluminum foil. Top with malt vinegar, sage and salt.

2. Fold foil over chicken and fruit so edges meet. Seal edges, making tight ½-inch fold; fold again. Allow space on sides for circulation and expansion.

3. Cover and grill packets 4 to 5 inches from medium heat 10 to 15 minutes or until chicken is no longer pink in center. Place packets on plates. Cut large X across top of packet; fold back foil.

4 servings.

1 Serving: Calories 225 (Calories from Fat 35); Fat 4g (Saturated 1g); Cholesterol 70mg; Sodium 360mg; Carbohydrate 26g (Dietary Fiber 4g); Protein 25g
% Daily Value: Vitamin A 0%; Vitamin C 6%; Calcium 2%; Iron 8%
Diet Exchanges: 3 Very Lean Meat, 2 Fruit

Fold foil over chicken and fruit so edges meet.

Seal edges, making tight ½-inch fold; fold again.

Cut large X across top of packet; fold back foil.

Vegetable Kabobs with Mexican Cheese Sauce

Vegetable Kabobs with Mexican Cheese Sauce

Prep: 10 min   Microwave: 5 min   Grill: 15 min

12 small red potatoes
2 tablespoons water
2 medium zucchini, cut into 1-inch pieces
12 whole mushrooms
12 cherry tomatoes
2 tablespoons vegetable oil
1 jar (8 ounces) mild salsa-flavor process cheese sauce or spread

1. Heat coals or gas grill. Place potatoes and water in 2-quart microwavable casserole. Cover and microwave on High 3 to 5 minutes or until partially cooked; drain.

2. Thread potatoes, zucchini, mushrooms and tomatoes alternately on each of six 15-inch metal skewers, leaving space between each piece. Brush vegetables with oil.

3. Cover and grill kabobs 4 to 6 inches from medium heat about 15 minutes, brushing once with oil, until zucchini is crisp-tender.

4. While kabobs are grilling, heat cheese sauce as directed on jar. Serve with kabobs.

6 servings.

1 Serving: Calories 225 (Calories from Fat 100); Fat 11g (Saturated 4g); Cholesterol 20mg; Sodium 190mg; Carbohydrate 27g (Dietary Fiber 3g); Protein 7g
% Daily Value: Vitamin A 16%; Vitamin C 20%; Calcium 6%; Iron 12%
Diet Exchanges: 1 Starch, 2 Vegetable, 2 Fat

BETTY'S TIPS

☺ Success Hint
Using square metal skewers (instead of round) helps keep the food from spinning when you turn the skewers.

☺ Variation
Jumbo pitted ripe olives would be fun to use with the mushrooms and cherry tomatoes.

Spanish Chicken Supper

Prep: 10 min Grill: 20 min

3 medium unpeeled baking potatoes, cut into ½-inch cubes
2 medium green or red bell peppers, chopped
1 large onion, coarsely chopped
12 large pimiento-stuffed olives, chopped
1 can (14½ ounces) diced tomatoes with roasted garlic, undrained
1 tablespoon Gold Medal all-purpose flour
3 teaspoons chili powder
1 teaspoon salt
1½ pounds chicken breast tenders (not breaded)

1. Heat coals or gas grill for direct heat. Mix potatoes, bell peppers, onion, olives and tomatoes in large bowl. Stir in flour, 2 teaspoons of the chili powder and ½ teaspoon of the salt. Spoon mixture into large heavy-duty aluminum foil bag.

2. Sprinkle remaining 1 teaspoon chili powder and ½ teaspoon salt over chicken. Arrange chicken on top of vegetables. Double-fold open end of bag. Slide foil bag onto cookie sheet to carry to grill.

3. Slide foil bag onto grill. Grill 4 to 5 inches from medium-high heat about 20 minutes or until potatoes are tender and chicken is no longer pink in center.

6 servings.

1 Serving: Calories 240 (Calories from Fat 45); Fat 5g (Saturated 1g); Cholesterol 70mg; Sodium 800mg; Carbohydrate 25g (Dietary Fiber 4g); Protein 28g
% Daily Value: Vitamin A 22%; Vitamin C 46%; Calcium 6%; Iron 14%
Diet Exchanges: 1 Starch, 3 Very Lean Meat, 2 Vegetable

BETTY'S TIPS

☺ Pack 'n Go
This packet is a great take-along meal. Add vegetable mixture and chicken to the foil bag, and carefully pack in a cooler until grilling time.

☺ Did You Know?
You can make your own foil packet with two 18 × 15-inch sheets of heavy-duty aluminum foil. Place vegetable mixture on one sheet of foil; top with chicken. Cover with the other sheet of foil, and tightly seal the edges.

Spicy Sausage Pizza Pie

Prep: 15 min   Bake: 25 min

- 1 pound Italian or bulk pork sausage
- 1 can (8 ounces) pizza sauce
- ½ teaspoon dried oregano leaves
- 2 cups Original Bisquick
- ¼ cup process cheese spread (room temperature)
- ¼ cup hot water
- Green and red bell pepper rings, if desired
- 1 cup shredded mozzarella cheese (4 ounces)

1. Heat oven to 375°. Grease large cookie sheet. Cook sausage in 10-inch skillet over medium-high heat, stirring occasionally, until no longer pink; drain. Stir in pizza sauce and oregano; set aside.

2. Stir Bisquick, cheese spread and hot water until soft dough forms. Place on surface dusted with Bisquick; roll in Bisquick to coat. Shape into ball; knead 5 times. Roll dough into 14-inch circle; fold circle in half. Place on cookie sheet; unfold. Spread sausage mixture over crust to within 2 inches of edge. Fold edge over mixture. Top with bell pepper rings. Sprinkle with cheese.

3. Bake 23 to 25 minutes or until crust is light golden brown and cheese is melted.

8 servings.

1 Serving: Calories 280 (Calories from Fat 155); Fat 17g (Saturated 6g); Cholesterol 35mg; Sodium 990mg; Carbohydrate 21g (Dietary Fiber 1g); Protein 12g
% Daily Value: Vitamin A 4%; Vitamin C 6%; Calcium 18%; Iron 8%
Diet Exchanges: 1 Starch, 1 High-Fat Meat, 1 Vegetable, 2 Fat

California Pizza

Prep: 20 min   Bake: 25 min

- 1 can (8 ounces) tomato sauce
- 1 teaspoon dried oregano leaves
- ½ teaspoon dried basil leaves
- ½ teaspoon salt
- ¼ teaspoon garlic powder or onion powder
- ⅛ teaspoon pepper
- 2 cups Original Bisquick
- ½ cup cold water
- 1½ cups shredded Monterey Jack cheese (6 ounces)
- 2 cups cut-up cooked chicken
- ½ cup sliced ripe olives
- 1 medium avocado, sliced

1. Heat oven to 425°. Grease 12-inch pizza pan. Stir together tomato sauce, oregano, basil, salt, garlic powder and pepper; set aside.

2. Stir Bisquick and cold water until soft dough forms. Press dough in pizza pan, using hands dipped in Bisquick; pinch edge to form ½-inch rim. Sprinkle ½ cup of the cheese over dough. Spread tomato sauce over top. Top with chicken and olives. Sprinkle with remaining 1 cup cheese.

3. Bake 20 to 25 minutes or until crust is golden brown and cheese is bubbly. Garnish with avocado slices.

8 servings.

1 Serving: Calories 310 (Calories from Fat 155); Fat 17g (Saturated 6g); Cholesterol 50mg; Sodium 980mg; Carbohydrate 23g (Dietary Fiber 2g); Protein 18g
% Daily Value: Vitamin A 12%; Vitamin C 4%; Calcium 22%; Iron 12%
Diet Exchanges: 1 Starch, 2 Medium-Fat Meat, 1 Vegetable, 1 Fat

BETTY'S TIPS

⊛ **Substitution**
One cup of pizza sauce can be used instead of the tomato sauce, oregano, basil, salt, garlic powder and pepper.

⊛ **Success Hint**
To prevent the avocado from turning brown, brush the cut surfaces with lemon juice.

⊛ **Did You Know?**
If you don't have a pizza pan, press the dough into a 13-inch circle on a greased cookie sheet, using hands dipped in Bisquick. Pinch the edge to form a ½-inch rim.

California Pizza

Hot Sub Deep-Dish Pizza

Prep: 15 min   Bake: 20 min

3	cups Original Bisquick
²⁄₃	cup very hot water
2	tablespoons vegetable oil
1¼	cups pizza or spaghetti sauce
8 to 10	slices assorted thinly sliced deli or luncheon meats
1	large green bell pepper, thinly sliced into rings
2	tablespoons Italian dressing
6	slices (1 ounce each) Cheddar cheese, cut diagonally in half

1. Move oven rack to lowest position. Heat oven to 425°. Grease jelly roll pan, 15½ × 10½ × 1 inch, or cookie sheet.

2. Stir Bisquick, very hot water and oil until dough forms; beat vigorously 20 strokes. Press dough in bottom and up sides of pan, using hands dipped in Bisquick. Or pat into rectangle, 13 × 10 inches, on cookie sheet; pinch edges to form ¾-inch rim. Spread pizza sauce over crust. Top with meats and bell pepper rings. Drizzle with dressing. Add cheese.

3. Bake 15 to 20 minutes or until crust is brown and cheese is melted.

8 servings.

1 Serving: Calories 360 (Calories from Fat 190); Fat 21g (Saturated 7g); Cholesterol 30mg; Sodium 1000mg; Carbohydrate 32g (Dietary Fiber 1g); Protein 12g
% Daily Value: Vitamin A 8%; Vitamin C 22%; Calcium 20%; Iron 12%
Diet Exchanges: 2 Starch, 1 High-Fat Meat, 2 Fat

BETTY'S TIPS

✿ Health Twist
To reduce the fat to 11 grams and the calories to 280 per serving, use Reduced Fat Bisquick, fat-free Italian dressing and reduced-fat Cheddar cheese.

✿ Variation
Have it your way! Any combination of ham, turkey, large slices of pepperoni, summer sausage, bologna or other cold cuts will work in this recipe. The possibilities are endless!

Hot Sub Deep-Dish Pizza

Barbecue Cheeseburger Pizza

Prep: 15 min   Bake: 15 min

1	pound ground beef
1½	cups barbecue sauce
1½	cups Original Bisquick
¼	cup very hot water
1	tablespoon vegetable oil
	Dill pickle slices, if desired
5	slices process American cheese, cut diagonally in half

1. Move oven rack to lowest position. Heat oven to 450°. Grease 12-inch pizza pan. Cook beef in 10-inch skillet over medium heat, stirring occasionally, until brown; drain. Stir in ½ cup of the barbecue sauce; set aside.

2. Stir Bisquick, very hot water and oil until dough forms; beat vigorously 20 strokes. Press dough in pizza pan, using hands dipped in Bisquick; pinch edge to form ½-inch rim. Spread remaining 1 cup barbecue sauce over crust. Top with beef mixture and pickle slices. Top with cheese.

3. Bake 12 to 15 minutes or until crust is brown and cheese is melted.

8 servings.

1 Serving: Calories 300 (Calories from Fat 160); Fat 18g (Saturated 7g); Cholesterol 45mg; Sodium 920mg; Carbohydrate 20g (Dietary Fiber 1g); Protein 16g
% Daily Value: Vitamin A 8%; Vitamin C 2%; Calcium 12%; Iron 12%
Diet Exchanges: 1 Starch, 2 High-Fat Meat

BETTY'S TIPS

❂ **Substitution**
One pound of bulk pork sausage would make a tasty variation for this recipe.

❂ **Serve-With**
Quickly finish off this meal by making a salad of bagged coleslaw mix with your favorite purchased coleslaw dressing and serving halved ripe, juicy pears.

❂ **Did You Know?**
After you grease the pizza pan or cookie sheet, sprinkle the pan with cornmeal for added crust crispness.

Fajita Pizza

Prep: 20 min   Bake: 15 min

- 2 tablespoons vegetable oil
- ½ pound boneless skinless chicken breasts, cut into ⅛- to ¼-inch strips
- ½ medium bell pepper, cut into thin strips
- 1 small onion, sliced
- ½ cup salsa or picante sauce
- 1½ cups Original Bisquick
- ⅓ cup very hot water
- 1½ cups shredded mozzarella cheese

1. Move oven rack to lowest position. Heat oven to 450°. Grease 12-inch pizza pan. Heat 10-inch skillet over medium-high heat. Add oil; rotate skillet to coat bottom and side. Cook chicken in oil 3 minutes, stirring frequently. Stir in bell pepper and onion. Cook 3 to 4 minutes, stirring frequently, until vegetables are crisp-tender and chicken is no longer pink in center. Stir in salsa; set aside.

2. Stir Bisquick and very hot water until soft dough forms; beat vigorously 20 strokes. Press dough in pizza pan, using hands dipped in Bisquick; pinch edge to form ½-inch rim. Sprinkle ¾ cup of the cheese over crust. Top with chicken mixture. Sprinkle with remaining ¾ cup cheese.

3. Bake 12 to 15 minutes or until crust is brown and cheese is melted.

8 servings.

1 Serving: Calories 215 (Calories from Fat 100); Fat 11g (Saturated 4g); Cholesterol 30mg; Sodium 490mg; Carbohydrate 16g (Dietary Fiber 1g); Protein 14g
% Daily Value: Vitamin A 4%; Vitamin C 8%; Calcium 20%; Iron 6%
Diet Exchanges: 1 Starch, 2 Lean Meat, 1 Fat

BETTY'S TIPS

✪ Success Tip
Sprinkling part of the cheese onto the unbaked pizza crust helps to prevent the crust from becoming soggy. The cheese will separate the crust from the moist toppings.

✪ Time-Saver
Get the whole family involved! Young children can set the table, wash vegetables and load the dishwasher. Older children can shred cheese, cut up vegetables and help assemble recipes. What child wouldn't be proud of helping to make this pizza!

Fajita Pizza

Sun-Dried Tomato and Prosciutto Pizza

Prep: 5 min   Bake: 8 min

1 package (10 ounces) ready-to-serve thin pizza crust
¼ cup sun-dried tomato spread
3 ounces thinly sliced prosciutto, cut into thin strips
2 tablespoons shredded fresh basil leaves
1 cup finely shredded mozzarella cheese (4 ounces)

1. Heat oven to 450°. Place pizza crust on ungreased cookie sheet. Spread with tomato spread. Top with prosciutto, basil and cheese.

2. Bake about 8 minutes or until cheese is melted. Cut into small squares or wedges.

8 servings.

1 Serving: Calories 150 (Calories from Fat 40); Fat 4g (Saturated 2g); Cholesterol 10mg; Sodium 500mg; Carbohydrate 20g (Dietary Fiber 2g); Protein 10g
% Daily Value: Vitamin A 2%; Vitamin C 0%; Calcium 6%; Iron 4%
Diet Exchanges: 1 Starch, 1 Medium-Fat Meat

BETTY'S TIPS

✿ Success Hint
Prosciutto is a dry-cured Italian ham usually sliced thin. Look for it in the deli section as well as in the prepackaged sliced meat section of your supermarket.

✿ Serve-With
This zesty pizza would be great served with a frosty mug of beer or any mixed drink of your choice.

Cranberry Orange Turkey Flatbread

Prep: 15 min   Bake: 10 min

2¼ cups original Bisquick
⅔ cup milk
2 teaspoons vegetable oil
⅔ cup cranberry-orange crushed fruit (from 12-ounce tub)
1 cup ½-inch pieces cooked turkey
1 cup shredded mozzarella or provolone cheese (4 ounces)
   Orange peel strips, if desired

1. Heat oven to 450°. Stir Bisquick and milk until soft dough forms; beat 30 seconds. If dough is too sticky, gradually mix in enough Bisquick (up to ¼ cup) to make dough easy to handle.

2. Place dough on surface generously dusted with Bisquick; gently roll in Bisquick to coat. Shape into ball; knead 10 times. Pat or roll on ungreased cookie sheet into 12-inch circle. Brush with oil. Spread with crushed fruit. Sprinkle with turkey and cheese.

3. Bake about 10 minutes or until golden brown. Garnish with orange peel strips. Cut into wedges.

8 servings.

1 Serving: Calories 260 (Calories from Fat 90); Fat 10g (Saturated 3g); Cholesterol 25mg; Sodium 590mg; Carbohydrate 32g (Dietary Fiber 1g); Protein 12g
% Daily Value: Vitamin A 2%; Vitamin C 2%; Calcium 18%; Iron 6%
Diet Exchanges: 1 Starch, 1 Medium-Fat Meat, 1 Fruit, 1 Fat

BETTY'S TIPS

✿ Substitution
Either 1 cup of chopped fully cooked ham or chicken would work well in this flavorful flatbread.

✿ Variation
Make this into 24 individual 2-inch appetizers by cutting the rolled dough with 2-inch cutter dipped in Bisquick; top as directed.

Toss It Together

Sensational, Satisfying Salads

Chopped Asian Salad

Prep: 25 min

Lime Dressing (at right)
2 cups chopped escarole
1 cup chopped cooked chicken
1 small jicama, peeled and chopped (1 cup)
1 large papaya, peeled, seeded and chopped (1 cup)
1 large yellow or red bell pepper, chopped (1 cup)
½ cup dry-roasted peanuts
¼ cup chopped fresh cilantro

1. Make Lime Dressing.

2. Place remaining ingredients except peanuts and cilantro in large bowl. Pour dressing over salad; toss to coat.

3. Top with peanuts and cilantro.

4 servings.

Lime Dressing

⅓ cup frozen (thawed) limeade concentrate
¼ cup vegetable oil
1 tablespoon rice or white vinegar
1 teaspoon grated gingerroot
¼ teaspoon salt

Shake all ingredients in tightly covered container.

1 Serving: Calories 385 (Calories from Fat 215); Fat 24g (Saturated 4g); Cholesterol 30mg; Sodium 260mg; Carbohydrate 31g (Dietary Fiber 6g); Protein 17g
% Daily Value: Vitamin A 8%; Vitamin C 100%; Calcium 6%; Iron 8%
Diet Exchanges: 1½ Lean Meat, 3 Vegetable, 1 Fruit, 4 Fat

BETTY'S TIPS

✪ Substitution

In-season peaches and nectarines are wonderfully juicy and luscious. Either can be used instead of the papaya if you prefer.

✪ Variation

It's easy to make this a seafood salad. Just use 1 cup cooked small shrimp or crabmeat instead of the chicken.

Chopped Asian Salad

Tijuana Caesar Salad

Tijuana Caesar Salad

Prep: 30 min   Bake: 9 min per sheet

   Cooking spray
6 flour tortillas (6 to 8 inches in diameter)
1 teaspoon garlic salt
1 teaspoon ground cumin or chili powder
⅔ cup Caesar dressing
4 teaspoons grated lemon peel
2 tablespoons lemon juice
12 cups bite-size pieces romaine (12 ounces)
8 ounces jicama, peeled and cut into cubes
   (2 cups)
2 medium red bell peppers, cut into thin strips
   (2 cups)
½ cup shredded Parmesan cheese

1. Heat oven to 375°. Spray 2 cookie sheets with cooking spray. Spray tortillas lightly with cooking spray. Sprinkle with garlic salt and cumin. Cut each tortilla in half, then crosswise into ½-inch strips. Place tortilla strips on cookie sheets. Bake each cookie sheet 7 to 9 minutes or until crisp.

2. Mix dressing, lemon peel and lemon juice. Toss romaine, jicama, bell peppers, cheese, tortilla strips and dressing mixture in large bowl. Sprinkle with additional shredded Parmesan cheese if desired. Serve immediately.

8 servings.

1 Serving: Calories 225 (Calories from Fat 100); Fat 12g (Saturated 3g); Cholesterol 5mg; Sodium 620mg; Carbohydrate 27g (Dietary Fiber 4g); Protein 6g
% Daily Value: Vitamin A 28%; Vitamin C 100%; Calcium 14%; Iron 12%
Diet Exchanges: 1 Starch, 2 Vegetable, 2 Fat

BETTY'S TIPS

☺ Variation
Add 1 pound cooked small shrimp or grilled boneless, skinless chicken breasts to make a hearty main-dish salad for another occasion.

☺ Did You Know?
Jicama is sometimes called Mexican potato. It is a sweet, crunchy vegetable with a thin brown skin that should be peeled.

Italian Layered Salad

Prep: 20 min   Chill: 2 hr

6 cups bite-size pieces iceberg lettuce
   (1 pound)
1 bag (16 ounces) broccoli slaw (6 cups)
1 can (15 to 16 ounces) garbanzo beans, rinsed
   and drained
½ cup chopped red onion
1 medium red bell pepper, chopped (1 cup)
1 cup mayonnaise or salad dressing
½ cup creamy Italian dressing
¼ cup shredded Asiago cheese (1 ounce)
2 tablespoons chopped fresh parsley

1. Layer lettuce, broccoli slaw, beans, onion and bell pepper in deep 3-quart serving dish.

2. Mix mayonnaise and Italian dressing until well blended. Spread over vegetables. Sprinkle with cheese. Cover and refrigerate at least 2 hours until chilled or overnight. Sprinkle with parsley just before serving.

16 servings.

1 Serving: Calories 185 (Calories from Fat 135); Fat 15g (Saturated 3g); Cholesterol 10mg; Sodium 210mg; Carbohydrate 12g (Dietary Fiber 3g); Protein 4g
% Daily Value: Vitamin A 10%; Vitamin C 76%; Calcium 4%; Iron 6%
Diet Exchanges: 2 Vegetable, 3 Fat

BETTY'S TIPS

☺ Substitution
Shredded Parmesan cheese or the shredded three-cheese blend of Parmesan, Romano and Asiago can be substituted for the Asiago cheese.

☺ Success Hint
Iceberg lettuce will keep up to one week in the refrigerator. If you plan to use the lettuce within a day or two, remove the core by striking the core against a flat surface, then twisting the core and lifting it out. Hold the lettuce head, cored end up, under running cold water to separate and clean leaves, then turn it over and drain thoroughly. Refrigerate in a sealed plastic bag or a bowl with an airtight lid.

Spring Greens Fruit Salad

Prep: 15 min

½ cup champagne vinegar or white wine vinegar

¼ cup olive or vegetable oil

2 tablespoons honey

1 tablespoon chopped fresh or ½ teaspoon dried marjoram leaves

Pinch of salt

6 cups mixed baby greens

2 cups sliced strawberries

2 peaches, pitted and thinly sliced

1 cup diced Gouda cheese (4 ounces)

½ cup hazelnuts, toasted and coarsely chopped

1. Mix vinegar, oil, honey, marjoram and salt.

2. Mix baby greens, strawberries, peaches and cheese in large serving bowl. Add vinegar mixture; toss to coat. Sprinkle with hazelnuts.

12 servings.

1 Serving: Calories 145 (Calories from Fat 100); Fat 11g (Saturated 3g); Cholesterol 10mg; Sodium 110mg; Carbohydrate 9g (Dietary Fiber 2g); Protein 4g
% Daily Value: Vitamin A 6%; Vitamin C 32%; Calcium 10%; Iron 2%
Diet Exchanges: ½ High-Fat Meat, ½ Fruit, 1½ Fat

BETTY'S TIPS

⊙ **Substitution**

Cheddar, Jarlsberg or Gruyère cheese can be used instead of the Gouda cheese.

⊙ **Success Hint**

Toast hazelnuts in an ungreased heavy skillet over medium-low heat 5 to 7 minutes, stirring frequently until browning begins, then stirring constantly until golden brown.

Use strawberries as soon as possible after buying them. If storing them for a day or two, place in a single layer in a jelly roll pan lined with paper towels. Cover the berries with paper towels and refrigerate.

Spring Greens Fruit Salad

Layered Gazpacho Salad

Prep: 15 min   Chill: 1 hr

Lemon-Garlic Vinaigrette (below)
1   bag (8 ounces) Mediterranean lettuce blend
2   medium tomatoes, diced (2 cups)
2   medium cucumbers, diced (2 cups)
1   medium green bell pepper, chopped (1 cup)
½   cup finely chopped red onion
2   hard-cooked eggs, chopped
1   cup seasoned croutons

1. Make Lemon-Garlic Vinaigrette. Place lettuce in large glass bowl. Layer tomatoes, cucumbers, bell pepper and onion on lettuce. Pour vinaigrette over onion. Cover and refrigerate 1 to 2 hours to blend flavors.

2. Sprinkle eggs and croutons over salad. Toss before serving.

8 to 10 servings.

Lemon-Garlic Vinaigrette
½   cup olive or vegetable oil
¼   cup red wine vinegar
2   tablespoons lemon juice
1   teaspoon salt
¼   teaspoon pepper
1   clove garlic, finely chopped

Shake all ingredients in tightly covered container.

1 Serving: Calories 190 (Calories from Fat 145); Fat 16g (Saturated 3g); Cholesterol 55mg; Sodium 380mg; Carbohydrate 10g (Dietary Fiber 3g); Protein 3g
% Daily Value: Vitamin A 28%; Vitamin C 48%; Calcium 4%; Iron 6%
Diet Exchanges: 2 Vegetable, 3 Fat

BETTY'S TIPS

✪ Substitution
Bags of salad greens are convenient to use, but they do cost a bit more money. If you prefer, you can use 8 cups bite-size pieces salad greens.

✪ Time-Saver
You can use about ¾ cup purchased Italian dressing instead of the Lemon-Garlic Vinaigrette.

Betty . . .

A Garden of Greens

Salad greens don't mean just lettuces anymore! Today's selection of greens ranges from slightly sweet to peppery and pungent, from smooth and slender to crinkled and curved, from pale green to deep hunter green. Deliciously different from iceberg lettuce, these new greens are a great way to create an unforgettable salad.

MILD GREENS

Lollo Rosso is a crinkly leaf lettuce. Although restaurants use it as a garnish, the green leaves with crimson or burgundy edges add texture, color and a mild flavor to salads.

Mâche, also know as corn salad or lamb's lettuce, has a mild nutty flavor. Its delicate, dark green leaves have a soft velvety appearance and resemble a spoon shape.

Oakleaf is a loose leaf green with small thin leaves and a characteristic oak-leaf shape. Different varieties of oakleaf offer different colors (yellow-green, red, bronze), but they all have a buttery texture and mild sweet flavor.

SPRING SALAD MIX

Mesclun, often called Spring Salad Mix, is not one green but actually a mix of young greens that are bitter, sweet and tart. Although somewhat pricey, this combination of flavors is a convenient way to enjoy a variety of greens.

SPICY GREENS

Dandelion Greens are bright green with jagged-edged leaves that have a tangy flavor with astringent overtones. The distinctive flavor and pretty shape make these greens a nice addition to salads.

Arugula, once an upscale restaurant offering, is now more mainstream and is excellent in most any salad. Also called rocket, arugula's slightly bitter, peppery, dark green leaves add all-around zest to any salad.

Mustard Greens have a distinct zesty bite. Younger, smaller leaves will be milder but still quite assertive. Depending on the type of green, leaves may range from green to purple and be flat or curly. Use in combination with milder greens, such as any leaf lettuce or romaine.

Mizuna, also spelled mizuma, is a Japanese green with slender white stalks and dark feathery leaves. It's actually a member of the Brassica family, which includes broccoli, cauliflower and Brussels sprouts. Good in mixed-green salads, the slender, crunchy leaves have a slightly nutty, peppery flavor.

Mâche

Oakleaf

Dandelion Greens

DRESSING OF THE GREENS

Mix greens for optimum flavor, texture and eye appeal. Mix mild-flavored greens with more assertive ones. While some of these greens may not be available in supermarkets, look for them at local farmers' markets.

▓ Dressing greens, meaning to toss with a salad dressing, is done carefully so the greens are not overwhelmed. Start by tossing with a small amount of dressing. Toss just before serving so the greens won't become wilted and limp.

▓ Loose leaf lettuces pair well with lighter dressings, such as vinaigrettes. More intense greens, such as arugula, are good with stronger-flavored dressings. Spicy greens are assertive and need to be combined with milder greens. Use these and other mixes, such as mesclun, with a variety of dressings.

▓ Dress greens that have a heartier taste and bite more generously than you would milder greens.

Arugula

Lollo Rosso

Mustard Greens

Mesclun

Mizuna

Asian Coleslaw

Prep: 10 min

- 1 bag (16 ounces) coleslaw mix
- 1 can (11 ounces) mandarin orange segments, drained
- 1 small jicama (about 1 pound) peeled and cut into ½-inch cubes (2 cups)
   Peanut Dressing (below)
- ½ cup peanuts

1. Toss coleslaw mix, orange segments and jicama in large bowl.

2. Make Peanut Dressing. Toss with coleslaw mixture. Sprinkle with peanuts.

12 to 15 servings.

Peanut Dressing

- ½ cup Italian dressing
- 2 tablespoons peanut butter
- 1 tablespoon soy sauce

Mix all ingredients with wire whisk until smooth.

1 Serving: Calories 120 (Calories from Fat 80); Fat 9g (Saturated 1g); Cholesterol 0mg; Sodium 210mg; Carbohydrate 10g (Dietary Fiber 3g); Protein 3g
% Daily Value: Vitamin A 2%; Vitamin C 42%; Calcium 4%; Iron 4%
Diet Exchanges: 2 Vegetable, 1½ Fat

BETTY'S TIPS

⚙ **Substitution**
   You can also use 4 cups of shredded cabbage instead of the bag of coleslaw mix.

Asian Coleslaw

Mediterranean Grilled Potato Salad

Prep: 10 min   Cook: 20 min   Grill: 10 min

1½   pounds small red potatoes
½   teaspoon salt
2   tablespoons olive or vegetable oil
     Basil Vinaigrette (below)
1   small red bell pepper, chopped (½ cup)
½   cup pitted ripe olives

1. Place potatoes in 2-quart saucepan; add enough water just to cover potatoes. Add salt. Cover and heat to boiling; reduce heat to low. Cook covered about 15 minutes or until potatoes are just tender; drain. Cool slightly; cut potatoes in half. Toss with oil.

2. Heat coals or gas grill for direct heat. Cover and grill potatoes 5 to 6 inches from medium heat 5 to 10 minutes, turning occasionally, until golden brown and tender.

3. Make Basil Vinaigrette. Toss potatoes, bell pepper, olives and vinaigrette.

6 to 8 servings.

Basil Vinaigrette

⅓   cup olive or vegetable oil
3   tablespoons white wine vinegar
2   tablespoons chopped fresh basil leaves
1   teaspoon Dijon mustard
1   teaspoon salt

Shake all ingredients in tightly covered container.

1 Serving: Calories 260 (Calories from Fat 160); Fat 18g (Saturated 2g); Cholesterol 0mg; Sodium 520mg; Carbohydrate 25g (Dietary Fiber 3g); Protein 2g
% Daily Value: Vitamin A 4%; Vitamin C 18%; Calcium 2%; Iron 10%
Diet Exchanges: 1½ Starch, 1 Vegetable, 2½ Fat

BETTY'S TIPS

⊛ **Substitution**
Chopped fresh oregano can be used instead of the basil.

⊛ **Variation**
Cut ½ medium red onion into wedges, and grill with the potatoes about 10 minutes.

If you have a grill basket, go ahead and cook the potatoes in the basket on the grill.

Creamy Potato Salad

Prep: 15 min   Cook: 35 min   Chill: 4 hr

6   medium round red or white potatoes
     (2 pounds), peeled
1½   cups mayonnaise or salad dressing
1   tablespoon white or cider vinegar
1   tablespoon yellow mustard
1   teaspoon salt
¼   teaspoon pepper
2   medium stalks celery, chopped (1 cup)
8   medium green onions, chopped (½ cup)
4   hard-cooked eggs, chopped
     Paprika, if desired

10 servings.

1 Serving: Calories 330 (Calories from Fat 250); Fat 28g (Saturated 5g); Cholesterol 105mg; Sodium 480mg; Carbohydrate 17g (Dietary Fiber 2g); Protein 4g
% Daily Value: Vitamin A 4%; Vitamin C 4%; Calcium 2%; Iron 4%
Diet Exchanges: 1 Starch, 5 ½ Fat

BETTY'S TIPS

⊕ **Health Twist**
For 1 gram of fat and 90 calories per serving, substitute ½ cup fat-free mayonnaise and 1 cup plain fat-free yogurt for the 1½ cups mayonnaise. Use 2 eggs.

⊕ **Did You Know?**
What's the difference between mayonnaise and salad dressing? Although very similar in flavor and appearance, salad dressing is usually a bit sweeter than mayonnaise.

1. Place potatoes in 3-quart saucepan; add enough water just to cover potatoes. Cover and heat to boiling; reduce heat to low. Cook covered 30 to 35 minutes or until potatoes are tender, drain. Cool slightly; cut potatoes into cubes.

2. Mix mayonnaise, vinegar, mustard, salt and pepper in large glass or plastic bowl. Add potatoes, celery and onion; toss. Stir in eggs. Sprinkle with paprika. Cover and refrigerate at least 4 hours to blend flavors but no longer than 24 hours.

Creamy Potato Salad

Spring Vegetable Pasta Salad

Prep: 35 min   Chill: 2 hr

Lemon Mayonnaise (below)

2 packages (16 ounces each) medium pasta shells

3 pounds asparagus, blanched and cut into 4-inch pieces

2 pounds snap pea pods, blanched

16 medium green onions, sliced (1 cup)

2 medium yellow bell peppers, coarsely chopped (2 cups)

1. Make Lemon Mayonnaise.

2. Cook and drain pasta as directed on package. Rinse with cold water; drain.

3. Mix pasta and remaining ingredients in large bowl. Stir in Lemon Mayonnaise until well mixed. Cover and refrigerate 1 to 2 hours or until chilled.

24 servings.

Lemon Mayonnaise

2 cups mayonnaise or salad dressing

1 cup plain fat-free yogurt

½ cup lemon juice

¼ cup chopped fresh or 1 tablespoon dried tarragon leaves

1 teaspoon salt

Mix all ingredients until well blended.

1 Serving: Calories 310 (Calories from Fat 145); Fat 16g (Saturated 2g); Cholesterol 10mg; Sodium 220mg; Carbohydrate 36g (Dietary Fiber 3g); Protein 8g
% Daily Value: Vitamin A 4%; Vitamin C 74%; Calcium 6%; Iron 14%
Diet Exchanges: 2 Starch, 1 Vegetable, 3 Fat

BETTY'S TIPS

⚙ **Success Hint**

To blanch the asparagus and pea pods, plunge them into boiling water for 10 to 15 seconds or until they turn bright green. Remove from boiling water, then plunge into pan of ice and water to stop the cooking; drain.

⚙ **Variation**

If you're lucky enough to have leftover pasta salad, toss in some cooked chicken for a delicious main-dish salad.

⚙ **Special Touch**

If you think some of your guests would prefer a more traditional salad, cut this recipe in half and serve potato salad as a second salad.

Dijon Ham and Pasta Salad

Prep: 5 min   Cook: 12 min

- 1 package Berry Crocker Suddenly Salad® classic pasta salad mix
- 3 tablespoons cold water
- 2 tablespoons vegetable oil
- 2 tablespoons Dijon mustard
- 1 cup cubed fully cooked ham

1. Cook and drain pasta mix as directed on package. Rinse with cold water until chilled; drain.

2. Stir together seasoning mix (from salad mix), water, oil and mustard in large bowl. Stir in pasta and ham. Toss with topping (from salad mix). Serve immediately, or cover and refrigerate up to 2 hours before serving.

4 servings.

1 Serving: Calories 325 (Calories from Fat 110); Fat 12g (Saturated 2g); Cholesterol 30mg; Sodium 740mg; Carbohydrate 39g (Dietary Fiber 2g); Protein 17g
% Daily Value: Vitamin A 0%; Vitamin C 0%; Calcium 4%; Iron 12%
Diet Exchanges: 2 1/2 Starch, 1 1/2 Lean Meat, 1 Fat

BETTY'S TIPS

✿ Variation
If you're an artichoke lover, stir in a 14-ounce can of artichoke hearts (drained and cut into fourths) with the ham.

Italian Ham and Pasta Salad

Prep: 20 min   Chill: 1 hr

- 5 cups cooked penne pasta
- 2 cups broccoli flowerets (5 ounces)
- 1/2 cup coarsely chopped bell pepper
- 2 tablespoons finely chopped onion
- 1 pound fully cooked ham, cut into julienne strips
- 1/2 cup Italian dressing

1. Mix all ingredients except Italian dressing in large bowl. Pour dressing over mixture; toss.

2. Cover and refrigerate at least 1 hour to blend flavors.

6 servings.

1 Serving: Calories 380 (Calories from Fat 145); Fat 16g (Saturated 4g); Cholesterol 45mg; Sodium 1300mg; Carbohydrate 38g (Dietary Fiber 3g); Protein 24g
% Daily Value: Vitamin A 4%; Vitamin C 64%; Calcium 2%; Iron 16%
Diet Exchanges: 2 Starch, 2 Medium-Fat Meat, 2 Vegetable, 1/2 Fat

BETTY'S TIPS

✿ Substitution
Cubes of cooked chicken breast or turkey ham could easily be used in place of the ham in this pasta salad.

✿ Variation
There are several forms of Italian dressing on the market—choose your favorite. Try a zesty Italian or a creamy Italian in this recipe.

Italian Ham and Pasta Salad

Asian Noodle Salad

Asian Noodle Salad

Prep: 20 min   Cook: 20 min

Sesame Dressing (below)

1 package (8 to 10 ounces) Chinese curly noodles

½ pound snap pea pods, cut in half

1 pound pork tenderloin, cut into ¼-inch slices

1 teaspoon finely chopped gingerroot

1 medium bell pepper, cut into strips

1½ medium carrots, shredded (1 cup)

8 medium green onions, sliced (½ cup)

1 tablespoon sesame seed, toasted

1. Make Sesame Dressing. Cook noodles as directed on package, adding pea pods for last 1 to 2 minutes; drain. Rinse with cold water; drain.

2. Spray 10-inch skillet with cooking spray. Cook pork and gingerroot in skillet 4 to 6 minutes, stirring occasionally, until pork is slightly pink in center.

3. Toss noodles, bell pepper, carrots, onions and pork with half of the dressing. Sprinkle with sesame seed. Serve with remaining dressing.

4 servings.

Sesame Dressing

½ cup rice vinegar

¼ cup honey

2 tablespoons vegetable oil

2 tablespoons sesame oil

1 tablespoon soy sauce

Shake all ingredients in tightly covered container.

1 Serving: Calories 670 (Calories from Fat 190); Fat 21g (Saturated 4g); Cholesterol 70mg; Sodium 300mg; Carbohydrate 87g (Dietary Fiber 6g); Protein 39g
% Daily Value: Vitamin A 100%; Vitamin C 100%; Calcium 8%; Iron 36%
Diet Exchanges: 5 Starch, 3 Lean Meat, 2 Vegetable, 1 Fat

BETTY'S TIPS

◎ **Substitution**
Sesame oil adds a wonderful, nutty flavor to this Asian-inspired salad. If you don't have any on hand, you can use vegetable oil instead.

◎ **Success Hint**
To toast sesame seed, cook in ungreased heavy skillet over medium heat about 2 minutes, stirring frequently until browning begins, then stirring constantly until golden brown.

Asparagus and Tomato Pasta Salad

Prep: 15 min   Chill: 30 min

3 cups uncooked rotini pasta (9 ounces)
1 pound asparagus, cut into 2-inch pieces (2 cups)
   Dijon Vinaigrette (below)
¾ cup chopped yellow bell pepper
2 large tomatoes, cut into 2-inch pieces (2 cups)
   Freshly cracked pepper, if desired

1. Cook pasta as directed on package, adding asparagus for last 2 minutes; drain. Rinse with cold water; drain.

2. Make Dijon Vinaigrette. Toss pasta, asparagus, bell pepper, tomatoes and vinaigrette in large bowl. Cover and refrigerate at least 30 minutes to blend flavors but no longer than 24 hours.

3. Serve salad with pepper.

4 servings.

Dijon Vinaigrette
¼ cup garlic-flavored vegetable oil
2 tablespoons balsamic vinegar
1 tablespoon Dijon mustard
½ teaspoon salt

Shake all ingredients in tightly covered container.

1 Serving: Calories 490 (Calories from Fat 145); Fat 16g (Saturated 2g); Cholesterol 0mg; Sodium 400mg; Carbohydrate 78g (Dietary Fiber 5g); Protein 14g
% Daily Value: Vitamin A 26%; Vitamin C 68%; Calcium 4%; Iron 24%
Diet Exchanges: 4 Starch, 3 Vegetable, 2 Fat

BETTY'S TIPS

✪ Substitution
Look for a variety of new flavored oils, including garlic-flavored oil, in your supermarket. If they're not available in your area, use olive or vegetable oil instead.

✪ Success Hint
If using pasta for a salad, rinse it under cold running water to remove the excess starch and to keep the pasta from sticking together.

Pasta Salad Niçoise

Prep: 15 min   Cook: 10 min

1¼ cups uncooked gemelli pasta
    Zesty Italian Dressing (at right)
1   can (12 ounces) albacore tuna, drained and flaked
3   hard-cooked eggs, cut into fourths
1   medium tomato, coarsely chopped
1   ripe avocado, pitted, peeled and coarsely chopped
2   tablespoons sliced ripe olives
    Lettuce leaves

1. Cook and drain pasta as directed on package. Rinse with cold water; drain. Meanwhile, make Zesty Italian Dressing.

2. Toss pasta, dressing, tuna, eggs, tomato, avocado and olives in large bowl. Serve immediately, or cover and refrigerate about 2 hours but no longer than 24 hours. Serve on lettuce.

4 servings.

Zesty Italian Dressing
¼ cup Italian dressing
¼ cup chopped fresh basil leaves
¼ teaspoon crushed red pepper, crumbled
2 cloves garlic, finely chopped

Shake all ingredients in tightly covered container.

1 Serving: Calories 436 (Calories from Fat 191); Fat 21g (Saturated 4g); Cholesterol 190mg; Sodium 473mg; Carbohydrate 32g (Dietary Fiber 3g); Protein 29g
% Daily Value: Vitamin A 23%; Vitamin C 18%; Calcium 6%; Iron 21%
Diet Exchanges: 2 Starch, 3 Meat, ½ Vegetable, 4 Fat

Pasta Salad Niçoise

Grilled Asparagus and Fennel Pasta Salad

Grilled Asparagus and Fennel Pasta Salad

Prep: 15 min   Cook: 20 min   Grill: 15 min

½ pound asparagus, cut into 2-inch pieces

2 medium fennel bulbs, cut into thin wedges

1 medium red onion, cut into thin wedges

1 tablespoon olive or vegetable oil

½ teaspoon salt

3 cups uncooked rainbow rotini pasta (9 ounces)

Vinaigrette (at right)

1 navel orange, peeled and coarsely chopped

1. Heat coals or gas grill for direct heat. Toss asparagus, fennel, onion, oil and salt until vegetables are coated. Place in grill basket. Grill 5 to 6 inches from medium heat 10 to 15 minutes, stirring vegetables or shaking grill basket frequently, until vegetables are crisp-tender. Cool slightly.

2. While vegetables are grilling, cook and drain pasta as directed on package. Rinse with cold water; drain. Make Vinaigrette.

3. Toss vegetables, pasta, orange and Vinaigrette. Serve immediately, or cover and refrigerate up to 2 hours before serving.

4 servings.

Vinaigrette

⅓ cup white balsamic vinegar

¼ cup olive or vegetable oil

½ teaspoon sugar

¼ teaspoon salt

Shake all ingredients in tightly covered container.

1 Serving: Calories 540 (Calories from Fat 170); Fat 19g (Saturated 3g); Cholesterol 0mg; Sodium 510mg; Carbohydrate 86g (Dietary Fiber 8g); Protein 14g
% Daily Value: Vitamin A 8%; Vitamin C 32%; Calcium 10%; Iron 26%
Diet Exchanges: 5 Starch, 2 Vegetable, 2 Fat

BETTY'S TIPS

✪ Substitution
Grill any of your favorite vegetables. Try 1-inch pieces of bell peppers and sliced zucchini, yellow summer squash and mushrooms.

White wine vinegar can be used in place of the white balsamic vinegar.

✪ Success Hint
Use extra-virgin olive oil for the very best flavor.

Chicken Parmesan Pasta Salad

Prep: 10 min   Cook: 12 min

1 package Betty Crocker Suddenly Salad roasted garlic Parmesan pasta salad mix
¼ cup mayonnaise or salad dressing
¼ cup milk
2 cups cubed cooked chicken or turkey
1 medium cucumber, coarsely chopped (1 cup)
1 medium tomato, seeded and coarsely chopped (¾ cup)

1. Cook and drain pasta mix as directed on package. Rinse with cold water until chilled; drain.

2. Stir together seasoning mix (from salad mix), mayonnaise and milk in large bowl. Stir in pasta and remaining ingredients. Toss with topping (from salad mix). Serve immediately, or cover and refrigerate up to 2 hours before serving.

6 to 8 servings.

1 Serving: Calories 320 (Calories from Fat 110); Fat 12g (Saturated 3g); Cholesterol 45mg; Sodium 800mg; Carbohydrate 35g (Dietary Fiber 1g); Protein 19g
% Daily Value: Vitamin A 12%; Vitamin C 10%; Calcium 6%; Iron 12%
Diet Exchanges: 2 Starch, 1½ Medium-Fat Meat, 1 Vegetable, 1 Fat

BETTY'S TIPS

⚙ **Variation**
Cut-up cooked ham or roast beef can be substituted for the chicken.

Cheese-Filled Tortellini Salad

Prep: 15 min   Chill: 2 hr

1 package (9 ounces) refrigerated or dried cheese-filled tortellini

1 package (9 ounces) refrigerated or dried cheese-filled spinach tortellini

Basil Caper Dressing (at right)

2 medium carrots, sliced (1 cup)

2 medium green onions, thinly sliced (2 tablespoons)

2 tablespoons chopped fresh basil leaves or parsley

1 tablespoon freshly grated or shredded Parmesan cheese

1/8 teaspoon pepper

1. Cook and drain plain and spinach tortellini as directed on packages. Rinse with cold water; drain.

2. Make Basil Caper Dressing. Place tortellini and remaining ingredients in large glass or plastic bowl. Add dressing; toss until evenly coated. Cover and refrigerate at least 2 hours to blend flavors but no longer than 24 hours. Toss before serving.

6 servings.

Basil Caper Dressing

1/3 cup extra-virgin olive oil

2 tablespoons fresh lemon juice

2 tablespoons chopped fresh or 2 teaspoons dried basil leaves

2 tablespoons capers

Shake all ingredients in tightly covered container.

1 Serving: Calories 250 (Calories from Fat 155); Fat 17g (Saturated 4g); Cholesterol 70mg; Sodium 140mg; Carbohydrate 18g (Dietary Fiber 1g); Protein 7g
% Daily Value: Vitamin A 36%; Vitamin C 8%; Calcium 8%; Iron 8%
Diet Exchanges: 1 Starch, 1 Vegetable, 3 Fat

BETTY'S TIPS

✪ Substitution

Although refrigerated pasta cooks in just minutes, you can also use the dried tortellini. It will take just a bit longer to cook.

We prefer extra-virgin olive oil for the very best flavor. But you can also use regular olive oil or vegetable oil.

Tortellini Broccoli Salad

Prep: 20 min   Chill: 1 hr

1 package (7 ounces) cheese-filled tortellini
   Garlic Vinaigrette (below)
1 medium carrot, sliced (½ cup)
2 cups broccoli flowerets
2 medium green onions, sliced (2 tablespoons)

1. Cook and drain tortellini as directed on package. Rinse with cold water; drain. Make Garlic Vinaigrette.

2. Mix carrot, broccoli, onions and vinaigrette in large glass or plastic bowl. Add tortellini; toss until evenly coated. Cover and refrigerate at least 1 hour to blend flavors but no longer than 24 hours.

4 servings.

Garlic Vinaigrette
   ¼ cup cider or balsamic vinegar
   2 tablespoons olive or vegetable oil
   1 tablespoon chopped fresh or 1 teaspoon dried basil leaves
   ¼ teaspoon paprika
   ⅛ teaspoon salt
   1 clove garlic, finely chopped

Shake all ingredients in tightly covered container.

1 Serving: Calories 170 (Calories from Fat 100); Fat 11g (Saturated 3g); Cholesterol 40mg; Sodium 125mg; Carbohydrate 14g (Dietary Fiber 2g); Protein 5g
% Daily Value: Vitamin A 72%; Vitamin C 74%; Calcium 6%; Iron 8%
Diet Exchanges: ½ Starch, 2 Vegetable, 2 Fat

BETTY'S TIPS

❂ **Substitution**
If you have leftover ham, chop it and add it to make a main-meal salad!

❂ **Time-Saver**
Supermarket salad bars can be a real time-saver. Rather than chopping the vegetables yourself, why not buy the already sliced carrots, broccoli and onions from the salad bar?

To save more time, use ⅓ cup purchased balsamic vinaigrette dressing or another vinaigrette dressing of your choice.

❂ **Special Touch**
For brightly colored vegetables, blanch them by immersing in boiling water for a few seconds and then plunging into ice water to stop the cooking process.

Shrimp Paella Salad

Prep: 15 min   Cook: 5 min

4 slices bacon, cut up
1 clove garlic, finely chopped
2 cups cooked rice
1 cup frozen green peas, thawed
⅓ cup chopped drained roasted red bell peppers (from 7-ounce jar)
2 tablespoons lemon juice
¼ teaspoon paprika
4 to 6 drops red pepper sauce
1 package (12 ounces) frozen cooked peeled and deveined shrimp, thawed and drained
Lettuce leaves

1. Cook bacon in 12-inch skillet over medium heat, stirring occasionally, until crisp. Drain fat, reserving 1 tablespoon in skillet. Drain bacon on paper towel.

2. Cook garlic in bacon fat in skillet over medium heat about 1 minute, stirring occasionally, until softened. Stir in bacon and remaining ingredients except lettuce.

3. Serve shrimp mixture on lettuce. Sprinkle with additional paprika if desired.

4 servings.

1 Serving: Calories 215 (Calories from Fat 35); Fat 4g (Saturated 1g); Cholesterol 125mg; Sodium 270mg; Carbohydrate 28g (Dietary Fiber 2g); Protein 19g
% Daily Value: Vitamin A 20%; Vitamin C 42%; Calcium 4%; Iron 20%
Diet Exchanges: 2 Starch, 2 Very Lean Meat

BETTY'S TIPS

✪ Success Hint
Depending on the saltiness of the bacon, you may need to add ¼ teaspoon salt to the salad.

✪ Do-Ahead
Prepare the salad up to a day ahead of time, and store covered in the refrigerator.

Caesar Tuna Salad in Pasta Shells

Prep: 15 min   Cook: 18 min

16 uncooked jumbo pasta shells
2 cans (6 ounces each) albacore tuna in water, drained
1 cup cherry tomatoes, cut into fourths
1 package (10 ounces) frozen cut green beans, cooked and drained
⅓ cup sliced ripe olives
¼ cup mayonnaise or salad dressing
¼ cup creamy Caesar dressing
Pinch of pepper
Leaf lettuce leaves
2 hard-cooked eggs, chopped

1. Cook and drain pasta shells as directed on package. Rinse with cold water; drain.

2. Mix tuna, tomatoes, green beans and olives in medium bowl. Mix mayonnaise, Caesar dressing and pepper; toss with tuna mixture.

3. Spoon about ¼ cup tuna mixture into each pasta shell. Arrange shells on lettuce leaves. Sprinkle with eggs.

4 servings.

1 Serving: Calories 670 (Calories from Fat 385); Fat 43g (Saturated 7g); Cholesterol 160mg; Sodium 1150mg; Carbohydrate 43g (Dietary Fiber 4g); Protein 32g
% Daily Value: Vitamin A 16%; Vitamin C 20%; Calcium 8%; Iron 24%
Diet Exchanges: 2 Starch, 3 Lean Meat, 2 Vegetable, 6½ Fat

BETTY'S TIPS

✪ Health Twist
Transform this salad into a low-fat favorite by using fat-free mayonnaise and reduced-fat Caesar dressing. You'll reduce the fat to 16 grams and the calories to 435 for each serving.

✪ Serve-With
Complete the meal with soft breadsticks or crusty sourdough bread.

✪ Special Touch
For a special presentation, serve the pasta shells on a platter lined with burgundy-colored radicchio and bright green leaf lettuce leaves.

Quick

Seafood Caesar Salad

Prep: 10 min

1 bag (7½ ounces) complete Caesar salad mix
1 package (8 ounces) frozen flake-style imitation crabmeat, thawed
4 medium green onions, sliced (¼ cup)
1 ripe avocado, pitted, peeled and cubed

1. Divide lettuce from salad mix among 4 plates.

2. Mix crabmeat, onions, avocado and salad dressing from salad mix. Spoon over lettuce. Sprinkle with Parmesan cheese and croutons from salad mix.

4 servings.

1 Serving: Calories 250 (Calories from Fat 155); Fat 17g (Saturated 4g); Cholesterol 27mg; Sodium 870mg; Carbohydrate 14g (Dietary Fiber 4g); Protein 14g
% Daily Value: Vitamin A 28%; Vitamin C 32%; Calcium 14%; Iron 8%
Diet Exchanges: 1 Lean Meat, 3 Vegetable, 3 Fat

BETTY'S TIPS

✪ Substitution
You can use 8 ounces of cooked medium shrimp instead of the imitation crabmeat.

If you prefer, you can use 4 cups torn romaine, ⅓ cup Caesar dressing, ¼ cup Parmesan cheese and ½ cup seasoned croutons instead of the Caesar salad mix.

✪ Special Touch
Sprinkle with additional shredded Parmesan cheese.

Shrimp Rice Salad

Prep: 10 min   Chill: 30 min

3 cups cold cooked rice
⅓ cup pitted ripe olives, cut in half
⅓ cup zesty Italian dressing
¼ teaspoon pepper
4 medium green onions, sliced (¼ cup)
2 medium tomatoes, chopped (1½ cups)
¾ pound cooked peeled deveined medium shrimp, thawed if frozen
   Lettuce leaves

1. Toss all ingredients except lettuce.

2. Cover and refrigerate 30 minutes to blend flavors. Serve on lettuce.

4 servings.

1 Serving: Calories 345 (Calories from Fat 100); Fat 11g (Saturated 2g); Cholesterol 170mg; Sodium 450mg; Carbohydrate 41g (Dietary Fiber 2g); Protein 22g
% Daily Value: Vitamin A 10%; Vitamin C 28%; Calcium 6%; Iron 28%
Diet Exchanges: 2 Starch, 2 Very Lean Meat, 2 Vegetable, 1½ Fat

BETTY'S TIPS

✪ Success Hint
Don't store tomatoes in the refrigerator. Cold temperatures ruin the flavor and make the flesh pulpy.

✪ Variation
Experiment a little bit with this salad by using 3 cups of cooked couscous instead of rice.

✪ Did You Know?
Rice can be placed in an airtight container or resealable plastic food-storage bag and refrigerated up to 5 days or frozen up to 6 months.

Shrimp Rice Salad

Honey Mustard Grilled Salmon and Pasta Salad

Honey Mustard Grilled Salmon and Pasta Salad

Prep: 20 min   Grill: 15 min

Honey Mustard Dressing (at right)
1- pound salmon fillet, ½ inch thick (about
   1 pound), cut into 4 pieces
2 medium bell peppers, cut into ¾-inch pieces
1 medium zucchini, cut into ¾-inch pieces
2 cups uncooked fusilli (corkscrew) pasta
   (6 ounces)
2 cups fresh baby salad greens
1 tablespoon chopped fresh or ½ teaspoon
   dried dill weed

1. Heat coals or gas grill for direct heat. Make Honey
   Mustard Dressing.

2. Brush salmon with about 2 tablespoons of the
   dressing. Toss bell peppers, zucchini and 1 tablespoon of the dressing. Place vegetables in grill
   basket. Place salmon, skin side down, on grill. Cover
   and grill salmon and vegetables 4 to 6 inches from
   medium heat 10 to 15 minutes, shaking grill basket to
   turn vegetables occasionally, until salmon flakes
   easily with fork and vegetables are crisp-tender.

3. Cook and drain pasta as directed on package. Rinse
   with cold water; drain. Mix pasta, vegetables and
   about ¼ cup of the dressing.

4. Arrange salad greens on 4 plates. Top with pasta mixture. Place salmon on pasta and vegetables. Drizzle
   each serving with 2 to 3 tablespoons of the dressing.
   Sprinkle with dill weed. Serve with remaining
   dressing.

4 servings.

Honey Mustard Dressing

½ cup white balsamic vinegar or white wine
   vinegar
¼ cup olive or vegetable oil
¼ cup honey
¼ cup Dijon mustard
2 teaspoons lemon juice
¼ teaspoon salt
¼ teaspoon ground mustard

Shake all ingredients in tightly covered container.

1 Serving: Calories 550 (Calories from Fat 200); Fat 22 (Saturated 4g);
Cholesterol 75mg; Sodium 760mg; Carbohydrate 60g (Dietary Fiber 4g);
Protein 32g
% Daily Value: Vitamin A 30%; Vitamin C 54%; Calcium 6%; Iron 20%
Diet Exchanges: 3 Starch, 2 Lean Meat, 3 Vegetable, 3 Fat

BETTY'S TIPS

✺ Did You Know?

White balsamic vinegar is lighter and sweeter in flavor than
its darker partner, making it perfect for dressing crisp and delicate salad greens. Although new to supermarket shelves, this
vinegar is sure to become a popular staple in many kitchen
cupboards.

Grilled Seafood Salad

Prep: 20 min   Marinate: 30 min   Grill: 10 min

	Shallot Thyme Vinaigrette (below)
12	uncooked large shrimp, peeled and deveined
1	pound swordfish, marlin or tuna steaks, ¾ to 1 inch thick
1	medium bulb fennel, cut into wedges
10	cups bite-size pieces mixed salad greens
½	small red onion, thinly sliced
12	cherry tomatoes, cut in half
12	pitted Kalamata or ripe olives

1. Make Shallot Thyme Vinaigrette. Place shrimp and fish in shallow glass or plastic dish or heavy-duty resealable plastic food-storage bag. Add ¼ cup of the vinaigrette; turn shrimp and fish to coat. Cover dish or seal bag and refrigerate 30 minutes. Reserve remaining vinaigrette.

2. Heat coals or gas grill for direct heat. Remove shrimp and fish from marinade; reserve marinade. Cover and grill fish and fennel 5 to 6 inches from medium heat 5 minutes; brush with marinade. Add shrimp. Cover and grill 5 minutes, turning and brushing fish, fennel and shrimp with marinade 2 or 3 times, until shrimp are pink and firm, fish flakes easily with fork and fennel is tender. Discard any remaining marinade.

3. Arrange salad greens on serving platter. Cut fish into bite-size pieces. Arrange fish, fennel, shrimp and remaining ingredients on greens. Serve with reserved vinaigrette.

6 servings.

Shallot Thyme Vinaigrette

⅓	cup olive or vegetable oil
¼	cup balsamic vinegar
2	tablespoons white wine vinegar
1	tablespoon finely chopped shallot
1	tablespoon chopped fresh or 1 teaspoon dried thyme leaves
1	tablespoon Dijon mustard
¼	teaspoon salt

Shake all ingredients in tightly covered container.

1 Serving: Calories 235 (Calories from Fat 125); Fat 14g (Saturated 2g); Cholesterol 60mg; Sodium 480mg; Carbohydrate 16g (Dietary Fiber 8g); Protein 19g
% Daily Value: Vitamin A 68%; Vitamin C 58%; Calcium 12%; Iron 20%
Diet Exchanges: 2 Lean Meat, 3 Vegetable, 1 Fat

Cut root end and leaves off fennel.

Cut fennel into wedges.

Italian Chicken Salad

Prep: 10 min   Marinate: 15 min   Grill: 20 min

⅓ cup raspberry vinegar

2 tablespoons balsamic vinegar

¼ cup water

1 envelope (0.7 ounce) Italian dressing mix

1 tablespoon olive or vegetable oil

4 boneless skinless chicken breast halves (about 1¼ pounds)

6 cups bite-size pieces mixed salad greens

2 roma (plum) tomatoes, chopped (⅔ cup)

1. Mix vinegars and water in medium bowl. Stir in dressing mix. Stir in oil. Divide dressing mixture in half.

2. Place chicken in shallow glass or plastic dish or heavy-duty resealable plastic food-storage bag. Pour half of the dressing mixture over chicken; turn chicken to coat. Cover dish or seal bag and refrigerate 15 minutes. Cover and refrigerate remaining dressing mixture.

3. Heat coals or gas grill for direct heat. Remove chicken from marinade; reserve marinade. Cover and grill chicken 4 to 6 inches from medium heat 15 to 20 minutes, turning and brushing with marinade occasionally, until juice of chicken is no longer pink when centers of thickest piece are cut. Discard any remaining marinade.

4. Cut chicken into slices. Serve chicken on salad greens with remaining dressing mixture. Top with tomatoes.

4 servings.

1 Serving: Calories 205 (Calories from Fat 80); Fat 9g (Saturated 2g); Cholesterol 75mg; Sodium 135mg; Carbohydrate 5g (Dietary Fiber 2g); Protein 28g
% Daily Value: Vitamin A 54%; Vitamin C 32%; Calcium 6%; Iron 12%
Diet Exchanges: 4 Very Lean Meat, 1 Vegetable, 1 Fat

Thai Chicken Salad

Prep: 20 min

Peanut Sauce (at right)
- 3- pound deli roasted chicken
- 4 cups shredded lettuce
- ½ cup chopped fresh Italian parsley
- 8 medium green onions, thinly sliced (½ cup)
- 1 package (6 ounces) wide chow mein noodles
- ½ cup dry-roasted peanuts

1. Make Peanut Sauce; set aside.

2. Remove chicken from bones; cut into bite-size pieces (about 3 cups).

3. Toss lettuce, chicken, parsley and onions in large bowl. Place lettuce mixture in center of large serving plate. Arrange noodles around edge of plate. Sprinkle peanuts over lettuce mixture. Drizzle sauce over salad.

6 to 8 servings.

Peanut Sauce
- ¼ cup reduced-sodium soy sauce
- ¼ cup creamy peanut better
- 2 tablespoons packed brown sugar
- 2 tablespoons sesame oil
- 2 tablespoons rice vinegar
- 1 tablespoon grated gingerroot
  Dash of ground red pepper (cayenne)
- 1 clove garlic, finely chopped.

Mix all ingredients with wire whisk until smooth

1 Serving: Calories 525 (Calories from Fat 335); Fat 37g (Saturated 8g); Cholesterol 100mg; Sodium 450mg; Carbohydrate 13g (Dietary Fiber 2g); Protein 37g
% Daily Value: Vitamin A 12%; Vitamin C 12%; Calcium 6%; Iron 16%
Diet Exchanges: 1 Starch, 5 Medium-Fat Meat, 2 Fat

BETTY'S TIPS

✪ Substitution
If you aren't concerned about sodium, you can use regular soy sauce.

Betty... ON WHAT'S NEW

Vinegars: Flavor Power

Vinegar may not get much respect. Its name, after all, comes from the French *vin aigre*, or "sour wine," which is exactly what vinegar is. How a vinegar tastes depends on the starting liquid (wine, beer, cider), storage conditions, acid level and whether the vinegar is infused with fruits or herbs.

1. **Balsamic vinegar,** originally from Modena, Italy, is fast becoming an all-time favorite vinegar. It is dark brown with a mild, sweet flavor. Made from the juice of sweet white grapes, balsamic vinegar must be aged in wooden casks at least 10 years, making it a more expensive vinegar. *White balsamic vinegar* is made from white wine vinegar and the musts (freshly pressed juice) of white grapes. It is a clear vinegar with a subtle tang. If you can't find balsamic vinegar, a good substitute is red wine vinegar plus a small amount of sugar. White wine vinegar can be substituted for white balsamic vinegar.

2. **Cider vinegar,** made from the juice of apples, is the most widely used vinegar. It's golden brown with a sharp bite and subtle apple flavor. Try raspberry, rice, champagne or wine vinegar as substitutes.

3. **Fruit vinegars** are vinegars infused with fruits, such as raspberries or strawberries. **Herb vinegars** are infused with garlic, basil or other herbs. If you don't have fruit vinegar, try cider vinegar. White wine vinegar can be substituted for herb vinegars.

4. **Malt vinegar** is made from beer or malted barley. It is dark brown with an assertive flavor and is the perfect serve-with for English-style fish and chips. Use lemon juice if you don't have malt vinegar.

5. **Rice vinegar** is popular in Chinese and Japanese cuisines. This pale gold vinegar is made from rice wine or sake, giving it slightly sweet overtones and a mild tang. To substitute, try cider or white wine vinegar or three parts white vinegar with one part water.

6. **Sherry and champagne vinegars** start with their respective beverages. Sherry vinegar has a deep color and rich flavor. Champagne vinegar has a pale color and delicate flavor. Substitute balsamic vinegar for sherry vinegar and white wine, rice or raspberry vinegar for champagne vinegar.

7. **White (or distilled) vinegar** is made from grain alcohol. It's clear with a strong, sharp flavor and is most often used for pickling, processing and even as a household cleaner. You can substitute malt or cider vinegar, but the color may be affected.

8. **Wine vinegars** are made from white, red and rosé wines. The color and flavor of the vinegar depend on the type of wine used. Red wine vinegar is heartier with more body. You can substitute balsamic vinegar for red wine vinegar and rice or cider vinegar for white wine vinegar.

MAKING THE PERFECT MATCH

When dressing greens, the general rule is to pair milder greens with light dressings such as vinaigrettes. More-intense greens, such as arugula and spinach, are good with stronger-flavored dressings.

- For assertive, bitter greens such as arugula and mustard greens, use balsamic or sherry vinegar.

- For milk greens such as Bibb or Boston lettuce, use cider vinegar or a fruit vinegar.

- For a mixture of greens such as mesclun, try wine, champagne or rice vinegar.

- A well-balanced vinaigrette blends one part vinegar (or acid) with three parts oil.

- For creamy dressings, use white wine, rice, champagne or another pale-colored vinegar to prevent discoloring.

Caribbean Chicken Salad

Prep: 15 min   Cook: 12 min

1   pound boneless skinless chicken breast halves, cut into ½-inch strips

2   tablespoons blackened seasoning blend

1   tablespoon vegetable oil

4   cups bite-size pieces mixed salad greens

1   medium papaya, peeled, seeded and diced (1½ cups)

½   medium red onion, sliced (¾ cup)

1   small red bell pepper, chopped (½ cup)

⅔   cup fruit-flavored vinaigrette

1. Place chicken in heavy-duty resealable plastic food-storage bag. Sprinkle seasoning blend over chicken; seal bag and shake until chicken is evenly coated.

2. Heat oil in 10-inch nonstick skillet over medium-high heat. Cook chicken in oil 10 to 12 minutes, stirring frequently, until no longer pink in center. Remove chicken from skillet; drain on paper towels.

3. Toss salad greens, papaya, onion and bell pepper in large bowl; divide evenly among 4 plates. Top with chicken. Drizzle with vinaigrette.

4 servings.

1 Serving: Calories 220 (Calories from Fat 55); Fat 6g (Saturated 1g); Cholesterol 70mg; Sodium 840mg; Carbohydrate 18g (Dietary Fiber 2g); Protein 26g
% Daily Value: Vitamin A 52%; Vitamin C 94%; Calcium 4%; Iron 8%
Diet Exchanges: 3 Very Lean Meat, 2 Vegetable, ½ Fruit, 1 Fat

BETTY'S TIPS

✪ Success Hint
Need help cutting a papaya? Use a sharp knife to peel the papaya, then cut it in half and use a spoon to scoop out the seeds. Cut into ½-inch pieces.

✪ Health Twist
For 3 grams of fat and 170 calories per serving, use ¾ pound boneless skinless chicken breast halves, cook the chicken in cooking spray instead of oil and use a fat-free fruit-flavored vinaigrette.

✪ Variation
For a sizzling grilled salad, sprinkle 4 boneless skinless chicken breast halves with the seasoning blend and grill as directed for Italian Chicken Salad (page 86).

Caribbean Chicken Salad

Beef and Blue Cheese Salad

Prep: 10 min

Zesty Italian Dressing (below)

6 cups bite-size pieces mixed salad greens

8 ounces cooked roast beef, cubed

1 cup cherry tomatoes, cut in half

½ cup crumbled blue cheese

4 medium green onions, sliced (¼ cup)

1. Make Zesty Italian Dressing.

2. Divide salad greens among 4 plates. Top with remaining ingredients. Serve with dressing.

4 servings.

Zesty Italian Dressing

⅓ cup Italian dressing

1 teaspoon Worcestershire sauce

Shake all ingredients in tightly covered container.

1 Serving: Calories 260 (Calories from Fat 145); Fat 16g (Saturated 5g); Cholesterol 65mg; Sodium 490mg; Carbohydrate 8g (Dietary Fiber 3g); Protein 24g
% Daily Value: Vitamin A 62%; Vitamin C 42%; Calcium 16%; Iron 18%
Diet Exchanges: 3 Lean Meat, 2 Vegetable, 2 Fat

BETTY'S TIPS

⊙ **Substitution**
If you'd rather have turkey than roast beef, use cubed cooked turkey or smoked turkey from the deli.

⊙ **Time-Saver**
Purchase cooked roast beef at the deli to streamline preparation of this salad. Or use leftover grilled steak or beef.

Using Your Noodle

Perfect Pasta in All Shapes and Sizes

Grilled Italian Sausages
with Pasta and Vegetables

Prep: 15 min   Grill: 20 min

1¼ pounds Italian sausage links (4 or 5 links)

2 large bell peppers, cut lengthwise into fourths

¾ cup Italian dressing

2 cups uncooked penne pasta (6 ounces)

4 roma (plum) tomatoes, chopped

2 tablespoons chopped fresh or ½ teaspoon dried basil leaves

1. Heat coals or gas grill for direct heat. Grill sausages 4 to 6 inches from medium heat 15 to 20 minutes, turning frequently, until no longer pink in center.

2. Brush bell pepper pieces with about 2 tablespoons of the dressing. Add to grill for last 10 minutes of cooking time, turning frequently, until crisp-tender.

3. Meanwhile, cook and drain pasta as directed on package.

4. Cut sausages into ½-inch slices; cut bell peppers into 1½-inch pieces. Toss pasta, sausages, bell peppers, tomatoes and remaining dressing. Sprinkle with basil.

5 servings.

1 Serving: Calories 565 (Calories from Fat 335); Fat 37g (Saturated 9g); Cholesterol 70mg; Sodium 1090mg; Carbohydrate 38g (Dietary Fiber 3g); Protein 30g
% Daily Value: Vitamin A 12%; Vitamin C 56%; Calcium 8%; Iron 16%
Diet Exchanges: 2 Starch, 2 High-Fat Meat, 2 Vegetable, 3½ Fat

BETTY'S TIPS

✪ Success Hint
Use plenty of water and make sure you heat it to a vigorous boil before adding the pasta.

You can use either hot or mild Italian sausages.

✪ Special Touch
For a pretty presentation, use one green and one yellow bell pepper.

Grilled Italian Sausages with Pasta and Vegetables

Easy Bacon Cheeseburger Lasagna

Prep: 30 min   Chill: 2 hr   Bake: 1 hr 15 min   Stand: 10 min

1½ pounds ground beef

2 medium onions, chopped (1 cup)

¼ teaspoon salt

⅛ teaspoon pepper

2 cans (15 ounces each) chunky tomato sauce

1 cup water

1 egg

1 container (15 ounces) ricotta cheese

1 cup shredded Swiss cheese (4 ounces)

¼ cup chopped fresh parsley

8 slices bacon, crisply cooked and crumbled (½ cup)

12 uncooked lasagna noodles

2 cups shredded Cheddar cheese (8 ounces)

1. Grease rectangular baking dish, 12 × 9 × 2 inches. Cook beef, onions, salt and pepper in 12-inch skillet over medium-high heat, stirring occasionally, until beef is brown; drain. Stir in tomato sauce and water. Heat to boiling; reduce heat to medium-low. Simmer uncovered 10 minutes.

2. Beat egg in medium bowl. Stir in ricotta cheese, Swiss cheese, parsley and ¼ cup of the bacon.

3. Spread about 1 cup of the beef mixture in baking dish. Top with 4 uncooked noodles. Spread half of the ricotta mixture, 2 cups beef mixture and ¾ cup of the Cheddar cheese over noodles. Repeat layers, starting with 4 noodles. Top with remaining noodles, beef mixture, Cheddar cheese and bacon. Spray 15-inch length of aluminum foil with cooking spray. Cover lasagna with foil, sprayed side down. Refrigerate at least 2 hours but no longer than 24 hours.

4. Heat oven to 350°. Bake covered 45 minutes. Uncover and bake about 30 minutes longer or until bubbly and golden brown. Cover and let stand 10 minutes before cutting.

8 servings.

1 Serving: Calories 605 (Calories from Fat 305); Fat 34g (Saturated 17g); Cholesterol 140mg; Sodium 1140mg; Carbohydrate 37g (Dietary Fiber 3g); Protein 41g
% Daily Value: Vitamin A 36%; Vitamin C 14%; Calcium 46%; Iron 22%
Diet Exchanges: 2 Starch, 5 Medium-Fat Meat, 1 Vegetable, 1 Fat

BETTY'S TIPS

☺ Success Hint

The great thing about this recipe is you don't have to cook the noodles first. But if you like, you can also make it with cooked lasagna noodles—just omit the 1 cup water and proceed as directed.

☺ Serve-With

So you like your cheeseburgers with all the fixin's? If so, top off this variation with chopped tomatoes and shredded lettuce.

Quick

Ravioli with Peppers and Sun-Dried Tomatoes

Prep: 5 min   Cook: 15 min

2   packages (9 ounces each) refrigerated Italian sausage-filled ravioli (any variety)

½   cup julienne sun-dried tomatoes packed in oil and herbs, drained and 2 tablespoons oil reserved.

1   bag (1 pound) frozen stir-fry bell peppers and onions, thawed and drained

1   cup shredded provolone or Havarti cheese (8 ounces)

1. Cook and drain ravioli as directed on package.

2. Heat oil from tomatoes in 12-inch skillet over medium heat. Cook bell pepper mixture in oil 2 minutes, stirring occasionally. Stir in tomatoes and ravioli. Cook, stirring occasionally, until hot.

3. Sprinkle with cheese. Cover and cook 1 to 2 minutes or until cheese is melted.

6 servings.

1 Serving: Calories 385 (Calories from Fat 215); Fat 24g (Saturated 11g); Cholesterol 135mg; Sodium 870mg; Carbohydrate 26g (Dietary Fiber 3g); Protein 19g
% Daily Value: Vitamin A 40%; Vitamin C 40%; Calcium 28%; Iron 14%
Diet Exchanges: 1 Starch, 2 Medium-Fat Meat, 2 Vegetable, 2½ Fat

BETTY'S TIPS

❂ **Substitution**
Use shredded mozzarella cheese if you don't have provolone or Havarti.

❂ **Did You Know?**
Havarti cheese is typically mild and is named for the town in Denmark where it first originated.

Ravioli with Peppers and Sun-Dried Tomatoes

Pasta with Bacon, Caramelized Onions and Cheddar Cheese

Prep: 10 min   Cook: 40 min

6 medium onions, thinly sliced (4 cups)
2 tablespoons olive or vegetable oil
2 tablespoons butter or margarine
1 package (16 ounces) uncooked fettuccine
½ pound sliced bacon
1½ cups whipping (heavy) cream
2 cups shredded Cheddar cheese (8 ounces)

1. Place onions, oil and butter in 3-quart micro-wavable casserole. Microwave uncovered on Medium-High (70%) 20 to 30 minutes, stirring occasionally, until onions are golden brown. Drain onions.

2. Meanwhile, cook and drain fettuccine as directed on package. Cook bacon in 10-inch skillet over low heat, turning occasionally, until crisp; drain on paper towels. Chop bacon into small pieces.

3. Heat whipping cream to boiling in 2-quart saucepan. Mix in 1 cup of the cheese and the onions. Pour over fettuccine; toss to coat. Top with remaining 1 cup cheese; sprinkle with bacon.

8 servings.

1 Serving: Calories 717 (Calories from Fat 446); Fat 50g (Saturated 25g); Cholesterol 117mg; Sodium 419mg; Carbohydrate 51g (Dietary Fiber 2g); Protein 19g
% Daily Value: Vitamin A 39%; Vitamin C 9%; Calcium 33%; Iron 18%
Diet Exchanges: 3 Starch, 1½ Meat, 1 Vegetable, 9 Fat

Pasta with Bacon, Caramelized Onions and Cheddar Cheese

Baked Chicken Dijon

Prep: 30 min   Bake: 30 min

- 3 cups uncooked farfalle (bow-tie) pasta (6 ounces)
- 2 cups cubed cooked chicken
- 1/3 cup diced roasted red bell peppers (from 7-ounce jar)
- 2 cups frozen broccoli cuts (from 1-pound bag)
- 1 can (10¾ ounces) condensed cream of chicken or cream of mushroom soup
- 1/3 cup chicken broth
- 3 tablespoons Dijon mustard
- 1 tablespoon finely chopped onion
- 1/2 cup shredded Parmesan cheese

1. Heat oven to 375°. Grease 2½-quart casserole. Cook and drain pasta as directed on package.

2. Mix pasta, chicken, bell peppers and broccoli in casserole. Mix soup, broth, mustard and onion; stir into pasta mixture. Sprinkle with cheese.

3. Cover and bake about 30 minutes or until hot and cheese is melted.

6 servings.

1 Serving: Calories 315 (Calories from Fat 80); Fat 9g (Saturated 3g); Cholesterol 45mg; Sodium 690mg; Carbohydrate 37g (Dietary Fiber 2g); Protein 24g
% Daily Value: Vitamin A 10%; Vitamin C 20%; Calcium 12%; Iron 16%
Diet Exchanges: 2 Starch, 2½ Lean Meat, 1 Vegetable

BETTY'S TIPS

☺ Substitution
You can use fresh broccoli instead of frozen. Just add it to the boiling pasta for the last 2 to 3 minutes of cooking.

☺ Special Touch
Add a splash of wine! For a special occasion, use 1/3 cup dry white wine instead of the chicken broth.

Quick

Shanghai Chicken and Noodles

Prep: 15 min   Cook: 10 min

- 1¼ pounds boneless, skinless chicken breast halves
- 12 ounces uncooked fettuccine
- 1 bag (1 pound) fresh (refrigerated) stir-fry or chop suey vegetables (about 5 cups)
- 1 cup sliced mushrooms (3 ounces)
- 1/4 cup hoisin sauce

1. Cut chicken into 1/4-inch slices. Cook and drain fettuccine as directed on package.

2. While fettuccine is cooking, spray nonstick wok or 12-inch skillet with cooking spray; heat over medium-high heat. Add chicken; stir-fry 3 to 4 minutes or until brown. Add vegetables and mushrooms; stir-fry about 3 minutes or until vegetables are crisp-tender and chicken is no longer pink in center.

3. Stir hoisin sauce into chicken mixture. Heat to boiling, stirring constantly. Boil and stir 1 minute. Add fettuccine; toss until well coated and heated through.

6 servings.

1 Serving: Calories 385 (Calories from Fat 65); Fat 7g (Saturated 2g); Cholesterol 115mg; Sodium 270mg; Carbohydrate 51g (Dietary Fiber 5g); Protein 35g
% Daily Value: Vitamin A 66%; Vitamin C 2%; Calcium 6%; Iron 22%
Diet Exchanges: 3 Starch, 3 Very Lean Meat, 1 Vegetable

BETTY'S TIPS

☺ Variation
Try 1¼ pounds pork tenderloin, cut into 1/4-inch slices, in place of the chicken.

☺ Did You Know?
Hoisin sauce is a thick, reddish brown sauce also referred to as Peking sauce. Made from a mixture of soybeans, garlic, chili peppers and various spices, the sauce has many applications in Asian cooking. Look for it in the ethnic-foods section or with the bottled condiments in your supermarket.

Roasted Vegetable and Chicken Manicotti

Prep: 25 min   Bake: 1 hr

 1 pound asparagus, cut into 2-inch pieces (3 cups)
 1 medium red bell pepper, cut into 12 pieces
 1 medium onion, cut into thin wedges
 1 cup halved mushrooms
 1 tablespoon olive or vegetable oil
 ½ teaspoon lemon pepper
 ¼ teaspoon salt
 12 uncooked manicotti shells
 1 envelope (1.8 ounces) white sauce mix
 2¼ cups milk
 ¼ teaspoon dried marjoram leaves
 1½ cups shredded Havarti cheese (6 ounces)
 2 cups diced cooked chicken

1. Heat oven to 450°. Toss asparagus, bell pepper, onion, mushrooms, oil, lemon pepper and salt until vegetables are coated. Spread in ungreased jelly roll pan, 15½ × 10½ × 1 inch. Bake about 20 minutes or until vegetables are crisp-tender. Cool slightly. Coarsely chop vegetables.

2. While vegetables are baking, cook and drain manicotti as directed on package. Mix sauce mix and milk in 1½-quart saucepan. Heat to boiling, stirring constantly. Stir in marjoram; remove from heat.

3. Reserve 1 cup vegetables for topping. Mix remaining vegetables, 1 cup of the cheese, the chicken and ½ cup of the sauce. Spread about ¼ cup sauce in bottom of ungreased rectangular baking dish, 13 × 9 × 2 inches. Spoon chicken mixture into manicotti shells; arrange in dish. Spoon remaining sauce over manicotti. Sprinkle with remaining 1 cup vegetables and ½ cup cheese.

4. Cover and bake 30 minutes. Uncover and bake about 10 minutes or until bubbly.

6 servings.

1 Serving: Calories 485 (Calories from Fat 225); Fat 25g (Saturated 10g); Cholesterol 75mg; Sodium 670mg; Carbohydrate 39g (Dietary Fiber 3g); Protein 29g
% Daily Value: Vitamin A 46%; Vitamin C 20%; Calcium 28%; Iron 16%
Diet Exchanges: 2 Starch, 3 Lean Meat, 2 Vegetable, 2½ Fat

BETTY'S TIPS

❂ Substitution
Havarti is a mild, smooth Danish cheese. Mozzarella cheese is a good substitute.

❂ Do-Ahead
Roast and chop the vegetables up to a day ahead of time, and cover and refrigerate. Prepare the manicotti as directed.

Roasted Vegetable and Chicken Manicotti

Linguine Pasta with Spicy Chicken Sauce

Linguine Pasta with Spicy Chicken Sauce

Prep: 10 min   Cook: 20 min

8 ounces uncooked linguine

2 tablespoons olive or vegetable oil

2 cloves garlic, finely chopped

2 teaspoons anchovy paste

1 red jalapeño chili, seeded and finely chopped

2 tablespoons chopped sun-dried tomatoes packed in oil

1 tablespoon chopped fresh or 1 teaspoon dried oregano leaves

½ pound boneless, skinless chicken breasts, cut into 1-inch pieces

2 medium red or yellow bell peppers, cut into 1 × ¼-inch strips

½ cup dry red wine or chicken broth

½ cup freshly grated or shredded Parmesan cheese

1. Cook and drain linguine as directed on package.

2. While linguine is cooking, heat oil in 12-inch skillet over medium-high heat. Cook garlic, anchovy paste, chili and tomatoes in oil about 5 minutes, stirring frequently, until garlic just begins to turn golden.

3. Stir in oregano, chicken, bell peppers and wine. Cover and cook about 10 minutes, stirring occasionally, until chicken is no longer pink in center.

4. Add linguine and ¼ cup of the cheese to mixture in skillet; toss until linguine is evenly coated. Sprinkle with remaining ¼ cup cheese.

4 servings.

1 Serving: Calories 420 (Calories from Fat 125); Fat 14g (Saturated 4g); Cholesterol 35mg; Sodium 490mg; Carbohydrate 52g (Dietary Fiber 3g); Protein 24g
% Daily Value: Vitamin A 30%; Vitamin C 100%; Calcium 20%; Iron 18%
Diet Exchanges: 3 Starch, 2 Lean Meat, 1 Vegetable, 1 Fat

Asiago Chicken and Cavatappi

Prep: 10 min Cook: 20 min

1½ cups uncooked cavatappi pasta (5 ounces)

¾ cup boiling water

½ cup julienne strips sun-dried tomatoes (not oil-packed)

1 pound boneless, skinless chicken breasts, cut into ½-inch pieces

¼ teaspoon garlic pepper

¼ teaspoon salt

2 cups frozen baby bean and carrot blend (from 1-pound bag)

¼ cup chopped fresh parsley

¼ cup shredded Asiago cheese (1 ounce)

1. Cook and drain pasta as directed on package. While pasta is cooking, pour boiling water over tomatoes; let stand 10 minutes.

2. Meanwhile, spray 12-inch nonstick skillet with cooking spray; heat over medium heat. Cook chicken, garlic pepper and salt in skillet 2 to 3 minutes, stirring constantly, until chicken is brown. Stir in tomato mixture and vegetables. Cover and cook about 5 minutes, stirring occasionally, until chicken is no longer pink in center and vegetables are crisp-tender.

3. Stir in pasta; cook and stir until thoroughly heated. Stir in parsley. Sprinkle with cheese.

4 servings.

1 Serving: Calories 250 (Calories from Fat 55); Fat 6g (Saturated 2g); Cholesterol 70mg; Sodium 620mg; Carbohydrate 22g (Dietary Fiber 4g); Protein 31g
% Daily Value: Vitamin A 100%; Vitamin C 8%; Calcium 12%; Iron 16%
Diet Exchanges: 1 Starch, 4 Very Lean Meat, 1 Vegetable

BETTY'S TIPS

❂ **Substitution**
Parmesan cheese is a good substitute if Asiago isn't available.

❂ **Success Hint**
Place parsley in a glass measuring cup and use kitchen scissors to quickly chop it.

Betty...
ON BASICS

Basil Pesto

Prep: 10 min

- 1 cup chopped fresh basil leaves
- ½ cup freshly grated Parmesan cheese
- ½ cup pine nuts
- ½ cup chopped fresh parsley
- ½ cup olive or vegetable oil
- 1 teaspoon salt
- ¼ teaspoon pepper
- 3 cloves garlic

1. Place all ingredients in food processor or blender. Cover and process until smooth.

2. Use pesto immediately, or cover and refrigerate up to 5 days or freeze up to 1 month.

About 1½ cups pesto.

¼ Cup: Calories 280 (Calories from Fat 250); Fat 28g (Saturated 5g); Cholesterol 5mg; Sodium 560mg; Carbohydrate 4g (Dietary Fiber 2g); Protein 5g
% Daily Value: Vitamin A 6%; Vitamin C 6%; Calcium 14%; Iron 6%
Diet Exchanges: 1 Vegetable, 5½ Fat

Cover and process all ingredients in food processor or blender until smooth.

Pesto Ravioli with Chicken

Prep: 15 min   Cook: 15 min

2 teaspoons olive or vegetable oil

1 pound chicken breast tenders (not breaded)

¾ cup chicken broth

1 package (9 ounces) refrigerated cheese-filled ravioli

3 small zucchini, cut into ¼-inch slices

1 large red bell pepper, thinly sliced

¼ cup Basil Pesto (at left)

Freshly grated Parmesan cheese, if desired

1. Heat oil in 12-inch skillet over medium-high heat. Cook chicken in oil about 4 minutes, turning occasionally, until brown. Remove chicken from skillet.

2. Add broth and ravioli to skillet. Heat to boiling; reduce heat. Cover and simmer about 4 minutes or until ravioli are tender.

3. Stir zucchini, bell pepper and chicken into ravioli. Cook over medium-high heat about 3 minutes, stirring occasionally, until vegetables are crisp-tender and chicken is no longer pink in center. Toss with pesto. Sprinkle with cheese.

4 servings.

1 Serving: Calories 355 (Calories from Fat 160); Fat 18g (Saturated 5g); Cholesterol 130mg; Sodium 890mg; Carbohydrate 17g (Dietary Fiber 3g); Protein 34g
% Daily Value: Vitamin A 32%; Vitamin C 72%; Calcium 18%; Iron 14%
Diet Exchanges: 1 Starch, 4 Lean Meat, 1 Fat

BETTY'S TIPS

⚙ **Success Hint**
Be sure to use a 12-inch skillet, or you'll have a difficult time tossing all the ingredients. You can also use a Dutch oven if you don't have a large skillet.

Pesto Ravioli with Chicken

Linguine with Grilled Shrimp and Vegetables

Prep: 15 min   Cook: 20 min   Grill: 11 min

2 tablespoons olive or vegetable oil

1 tablespoon lemon juice

½ teaspoon garlic salt

¼ teaspoon pepper

1½ pounds asparagus, cut into 2-inch pieces

1½ cups baby-cut carrots, cut lengthwise in half

1½ pounds uncooked fresh or frozen large shrimp, peeled and deveined

12 ounces uncooked linguine

Lemon Mustard Dressing (at right)

1. Heat coals or gas grill for direct heat. Mix oil, lemon juice, garlic salt and pepper in large glass bowl. Add asparagus and carrots; toss until coated. Place vegetables in grill basket; reserve remaining oil mixture. Grill 5 to 6 inches from medium heat 5 minutes, stirring vegetables frequently.

2. While vegetables are grilling, add shrimp to oil mixture; toss until coated. Add shrimp to vegetables. Grill 4 to 6 minutes, stirring or shaking grill basket frequently, until shrimp are pink and firm.

3. Meanwhile, cook and drain linguine as directed on package. Make Lemon Mustard Dressing. Toss linguine, shrimp, vegetables and dressing until coated.

6 servings.

Lemon Mustard Dressing

¼ cup olive or vegetable oil

2 teaspoons grated lemon peel

¼ cup lemon juice

1 tablespoon Dijon mustard

1 teaspoon chopped fresh or ¼ teaspoon dried rosemary leaves, crumbled

2 teaspoons honey

¼ teaspoon garlic salt

Shake all ingredients in tightly covered container.

1 Serving: Calories 420 (Calories from Fat 135); Fat 15g (Saturated 2g); Cholesterol 105mg; Sodium 260mg; Carbohydrate 54g (Dietary Fiber 4g); Protein 21g
% Daily Value: Vitamin A 100%; Vitamin C 34%; Calcium 6%; Iron 24%
Diet Exchanges: 3 Starch, 1 Very Lean Meat, 2 Vegetable, 2 Fat

BETTY'S TIPS

☺ Success Hint

Check veggies frequently, and remove them from the grill basket as soon as they are done.

For the very best flavor, grate just the yellow part of the lemon peel. the white pith underneath the zest tastes bitter and should be avoided.

Lemons will yield more juice if you bring them to room temperature and roll them gently between your palms before squeezing.

☺ Special Touch

Garnish with lemon wedges and fresh rosemary sprigs.

Marinara Shrimp and Vegetable Bowls

Prep: 10 min   Cook: 20 min

1   package (7 ounces) uncooked vermicelli
1   tablespoon olive or vegetable oil
2   cloves garlic, finely chopped
1   small red onion, cut into wedges
1   medium zucchini, cut into 2 × ¼-inch strips
1   medium yellow summer squash, cut into
    2 × ¼-inch strips
¼   teaspoon salt
1   pound uncooked fresh or frozen medium or
    large shrimp, peeled and deveined
1   cup marinara sauce
2   tablespoons chopped fresh or ½ teaspoon
    dried basil leaves

4 servings.

1 Serving: Calories 350 (Calories from Fat 65); Fat 7g (Saturated 1g); Cholesterol 105mg; Sodium 580mg; Carbohydrate 56g (Dietary Fiber 4g); Protein 20g
% Daily Value: Vitamin A 20%; Vitamin C 18%; Calcium 6%; Iron 26%
Diet Exchanges: 3 Starch, 1 Very Lean Meat, 2 Vegetable, 1 Fat

BETTY'S TIPS

⊗ **Substitution**
You can also use either two zucchini or two summer squash instead of one each.

Use your favorite flavor of spaghetti or marinara sauce.

1. Cook and drain vermicelli as directed on package.

2. While vermicelli is cooking, heat oil in 10-inch skillet over medium heat. Cook garlic and onion in oil 2 to 3 minutes, stirring frequently, until onion is crisp-tender. Stir in zucchini, yellow squash and salt. Cook 2 to 3 minutes, stirring frequently, just until squash is tender; remove from skillet.

3. Add shrimp to skillet. Cook and stir 1 to 2 minutes or until shrimp are pink and firm.

4. Heat marinara sauce in 1-quart saucepan over medium heat until hot. Divide vermicelli among 4 bowls; toss each serving with about 2 tablespoons marinara sauce. Top with vegetables and shrimp. Drizzle with remaining marinara sauce. Sprinkle with basil.

Marinara Shrimp and Vegetable Bowls

Crab and Spinach Casserole

Prep: 20 min   Bake: 20 min

2 cups uncooked gemelli (twist) pasta (8 ounces)

1 package (1.8 ounces) leek soup mix

2 cups milk

1 package (8 ounces) refrigerated imitation crabmeat chunks

2 cups baby spinach leaves, stems removed

1/4 cup freshly shredded Parmesan cheese

1. Heat oven to 350°. Spray 1 1/2-quart casserole or square baking dish, 8 × 8 × 2 inches, with cooking spray. Cook and drain pasta as directed on package.

2. While pasta is cooking, mix soup mix and milk in 1-quart saucepan. Heat to boiling, stirring constantly.

3. Cut up larger pieces of crabmeat if desired. Mix pasta, crabmeat and spinach in baking dish. Pour soup mixture over pasta mixture; stir gently to mix. Spread evenly. Sprinkle with cheese.

4. Bake uncovered about 20 minutes or until bubbly and light golden brown.

4 servings.

1 Serving: Calories 345 (Calories from Fat 55); Fat 6g (Saturated 2g); Cholesterol 25mg; Sodium 960mg; Carbohydrate 55g (Dietary Fiber 4g); Protein 22g
% Daily Value: Vitamin A 66%; Vitamin C 14%; Calcium 18%; Iron 18%
Diet Exchanges: 3 Starch, 1 Very Lean Meat, 1 Vegetable, 1/2 Skim Milk

BETTY'S TIPS

✪ Substitution
One cup of leftover cooked chicken can be used in place of the crabmeat in this casserole.

✪ Time-Saver
Pick up a bag of prewashed spinach for this recipe. (Tear the larger leaves into 1 1/2-inch pieces). It saves time and eliminates the extra water that would cling to the leaves if you rinsed them yourself.

Poached Salmon in Orzo Broth

Prep: 30 min   Cook: 15 min

2 cups hot water

12 dried shiitake mushrooms (1 ounce)

4 cups chicken broth

3 cloves garlic, finely chopped

⅓ cup uncooked orzo or rosamarina pasta

1- pound salmon fillet, skinned and cut into
4 pieces

½ cup sliced drained roasted red bell peppers

2 cups thinly sliced spinach leaves (2 ounces)

⅓ cup thinly sliced fresh basil leaves (¼ ounce)

4 medium green onions, sliced diagonally
(¼ cup)

Shredded Parmesan cheese, if desired

1. Pour hot water over mushrooms in medium bowl.
Let stand about 20 minutes or until soft. Drain mushrooms, reserving liquid. Rinse with warm water; drain.
Squeeze out excess moisture from mushrooms. Remove and discard stems; cut caps into ½-inch strips.

2. Strain mushroom liquid through a fine wire mesh
sieve or coffee filter into 4-quart Dutch oven. Stir in
broth and garlic. Heat to boiling over medium-high
heat. Stir in orzo; reduce heat. Add salmon. Simmer
uncovered about 10 minutes or until salmon flakes
easily with fork. Carefully remove salmon with
slotted spatula; keep warm.

3. Stir mushrooms, bell peppers, spinach, basil and
onions into broth mixture. Cook about 2 minutes or
until spinach is wilted and orzo is tender.

4. Place a piece of salmon in each individual bowl;
spoon vegetable-orzo broth over top. Sprinkle with
cheese.

4 servings.

1 Serving: Calories 265 (Calories from Fat 70); Fat 8g (Saturated 2g);
Cholesterol 75mg; Sodium 1110mg; Carbohydrate 18g (Dietary Fiber
2g); Protein 32g
% Daily Value: Vitamin A 44%; Vitamin C 32%; Calcium 6%; Iron 16%
Diet Exchanges: 1 Starch, 4 Very Lean Meat, 1 Vegetable, ½ Fat

BETTY'S TIPS

✿ Success Hint
Use a long, thin boning or filleting knife to carefully remove the skin from the salmon fillet. That way, you'll be sure
not to serve up any fish scales with the soup!

✿ Serve-With
Serve each bowl with a spoonful of Basil Pesto (page 104)
or refrigerated pesto atop a toasted small baguette slice.

Italian Pasta Pie

Italian Pasta Pie

Prep: 15 min   Bake: 30 min   Stand: 5 min

4	ounces uncooked capellini (angel hair) pasta
18 to 25	slices baguette or French bread, about ¼ inch thick
2	tablespoons margarine or butter, melted
¾	cup shredded Swiss cheese (3 ounces)
2	tablespoons chopped fresh or 2 teaspoons dried basil leaves
1	container (10 ounces) refrigerated Alfredo pasta sauce
3	medium roma (plum) tomatoes, chopped
2	medium green onions, sliced (2 tablespoons)
1	tablespoon grated Romano or Parmesan cheese

1. Heat oven to 400°. Cook and drain pasta as directed on package.

2. While pasta is cooking, brush bread with margarine. Line bottom and side of pie plate, 9 × 1½ inches, with bread, margarine sides up and slightly overlapping slices. Bake about 10 minutes or until light brown.

3. Reduce oven temperature to 350°. Stir Swiss cheese and 1 tablespoon of the basil into Alfredo sauce. Toss sauce and pasta. Spoon into baked crust. Sprinkle with tomatoes, onions and Romano cheese.

4. Bake 15 to 20 minutes or until hot. Let stand 5 minutes before cutting. Sprinkle with remaining 1 tablespoon basil.

6 servings.

1 Serving: Calories 430 (Calories from Fat 225); Fat 25g (Saturated 13g); Cholesterol 60mg; Sodium 540mg; Carbohydrate 39g (Dietary Fiber 2g); Protein 14g
% Daily Value: Vitamin A 22%; Vitamin C 4%; Calcium 30%; Iron 12%
Diet Exchanges: 2½ Starch, 1 High-Fat Meat, 3 Fat

BETTY'S TIPS

❂ **Serve-With**

What a delicious way to use up any leftover French bread you have. It makes a toasted crust for this creamy pasta pie. Just add a vegetable or salad, and your meal is complete.

Quick & Low-Fat

Mexican Macaroni and Cheese

Prep: 5 min   Cook: 15 min

2	cups uncooked small macaroni shells (7 ounces)
½	cup fat-free half-and-half
¼	cup sliced ripe olives
½	teaspoon salt
1	small red bell pepper, chopped (½ cup)
1	can (4 ounces) chopped green chilies, drained
4	slices fat-free American cheese (2 ounces)

1. Cook and drain macaroni as directed on package.

2. Stir in remaining ingredients. Cook over low heat about 5 minutes, stirring occasionally, until cheese is melted and sauce is hot.

4 servings.

1 Serving: Calories 285 (Calories from Fat 20); Fat 2g (Saturated 0g); Cholesterol 0mg; Sodium 980mg; Carbohydrate 56g (Dietary Fiber 3g); Protein 14g
% Daily Value: Vitamin A 10%; Vitamin C 28%; Calcium 6%; Iron 16%
Diet Exchanges: 3 Starch, 1 Vegetable, ½ Skim Milk

BETTY'S TIPS

❂ **Substitution**

Wagon wheel pasta can be used instead of the macaroni shells.

We like the rich flavor of the half-and-half, but you can also use skim milk.

Four-Cheese Fettuccine

Prep: 10 min   Cook: 15 min

1 package (16 ounces) uncooked fettuccine

2 tablespoons olive or vegetable oil

2 tablespoons butter or margarine

4 medium green onions, chopped (¼ cup)

1 tablespoon chopped fresh parsley

½ cup ricotta cheese

½ cup crumbled feta cheese (2 ounces)

¾ cup shredded Asiago cheese (3 ounces)

¾ cup freshly grated or shredded Parmesan cheese

½ teaspoon pepper

Chopped fresh parsley, if desired

1. Cook and drain fettuccine as directed on package.

2. While fettuccine is cooking, heat oil and butter in 12-inch skillet over medium heat. Cook onions and 1 tablespoon parsley in oil mixture about 4 minutes, stirring occasionally, until onions are tender.

3. Stir in ricotta and feta cheeses; reduce heat to low. Cook about 2 minutes, stirring frequently, until cheeses are melted.

4. Add fettuccine, Asiago and Parmesan cheeses and pepper to mixture in skillet. Cook about 4 minutes, tossing gently, until cheeses are melted and fettuccine is evenly coated. Sprinkle with parsley.

6 servings.

1 Serving: Calories 500 (Calories from Fat 205); Fat 23g (Saturated 10g); Cholesterol 115mg; Sodium 470mg; Carbohydrate 52g (Dietary Fiber 2g); Protein 23g
% Daily Value: Vitamin A 12%; Vitamin C 2%; Calcium 44%; Iron 20%
Diet Exchanges: 3½ Starch, 1½ High-Fat Meat, 2 Fat

BETTY'S TIPS

❂ **Success Hint**

Amazingly simple to prepare, this dish has a sophisticated taste because of the four cheeses. It is important not to overcook the cheeses in the skillet, however, because they could stick and burn.

You may want to use Italian flat-leaf parsley instead of curly-leaf parsley for this dish. The slightly strong flavor of the flat-leaf complements the cheeses.

Four-Cheese Fettuccine

Lasagna Primavera

Prep: 25 min   Bake: 1 hr   Stand: 15 min

12 uncooked lasagna noodles

3 cups frozen broccoli flowerets, thawed and well drained

3 large carrots, coarsely shredded (2 cups)

1 can (14½ ounces) diced tomatoes, well drained

2 medium bell peppers, cut into ½-inch pieces

1 container (15 ounces) ricotta cheese

½ cup grated Parmesan cheese

1 egg

2 containers (10 ounces each) refrigerated Alfredo pasta sauce

1 package (16 ounces) shredded mozzarella cheese (4 cups)

1. Heat oven to 350°. Cook and drain noodles as directed on package.

2. Cut broccoli flowerets into bite-size pieces if necessary. Mix broccoli, carrots, tomatoes and bell peppers in large bowl. Mix ricotta cheese, Parmesan cheese and egg in small bowl.

3. Spread ⅔ cup Alfredo sauce in ungreased rectangular pan, 13 × 9 × 2 inches. Top with 4 noodles. Spread half of the cheese mixture and 2½ cups of the vegetables over noodles. Spoon ⅔ cup sauce in dollops over vegetables. Sprinkle with 1 cup of the mozzarella cheese.

4. Top with 4 noodles; spread with remaining cheese mixture and 2½ cups of vegetables. Spoon ⅔ cup sauce in dollops over vegetables. Sprinkle with 1 cup mozzarella cheese. Top with remaining 4 noodles and vegetables. Spoon remaining sauce in dollops over vegetables. Sprinkle with remaining 2 cups mozzarella cheese.

5. Bake uncovered 45 minutes to 1 hour or until bubbly and hot in center. Let stand 15 minutes before cutting.

8 servings.

1 Serving: Calories 665 (Calories from Fat 370); Fat 41g (Saturated 25g); Cholesterol 150mg; Sodium 880mg; Carbohydrate 42g (Dietary Fiber 4g); Protein 37g
% Daily Value: Vitamin A 100%; Vitamin C 42%; Calcium 36%; Iron 14%
Diet Exchanges: 2 Starch, 4 High-Fat Meat, 2 Vegetable, 1 Fat

BETTY'S TIPS

✿ Success Hint

Slightly undercook the pasta when making lasagna because it cooks again in the oven.

Make sure you thoroughly drain the broccoli and tomatoes so the lasagna won't be watery. Use a paper towel to remove any excess moisture from the broccoli.

Fettuccine Primavera

Prep: 12 min   Cook: 10 min

8   ounces uncooked fettuccine

1   tablespoon olive or vegetable oil

1   cup broccoli flowerets

1   cup cauliflowerets

1   cup frozen green peas, rinsed to separate

2   medium carrots, thinly sliced (1 cup)

1   small onion, chopped (¼ cup)

1   container (10 ounces) refrigerated Alfredo pasta sauce

1   tablespoon grated Parmesan cheese

1. Cook and drain fettuccine as directed on package.

2. While fettuccine is cooking, heat oil in 12-inch skillet over medium-high heat. Cook broccoli, cauliflowerets, peas, carrots and onion in oil 6 to 8 minutes, stirring frequently, until vegetables are crisp-tender.

3. Stir Alfredo sauce into vegetable mixture; cook until hot. Stir in fettuccine; heat through. Sprinkle with cheese.

4 servings.

1 Serving: Calories 525 (Calories from Fat 270); Fat 30g (Saturated 16g); Cholesterol 125mg; Sodium 400mg; Carbohydrate 53g (Dietary Fiber 6g); Protein 17g
% Daily Value: Vitamin A 100%; Vitamin C 28%; Calcium 26%; Iron 18%
Diet Exchanges: 3 Starch, 2 Vegetable, 5 Fat

BETTY'S TIPS

⊛ **Substitution**

Look for refrigerated Alfredo sauce next to the fresh pasta in the supermarket. If you're counting calories and fat, purchase the light variety.

If you like, use linguine or spaghetti instead of the fettuccine.

Roasted Vegetable and Pasta Casserole

Prep: 20 min   Cook: 25 min   Bake: 1 hr 5 min

3 cups uncooked penne pasta (9 ounces)
2 medium red, green or yellow bell peppers, each cut into 12 pieces
1 cup mushrooms, cut in half
1 medium zucchini, cut into 1½ inch pieces (2 cups)
1 tablespoon olive or vegetable oil
½ teaspoon Italian seasoning
¼ teaspoon salt
1 envelope (1.8 ounces) white sauce mix
2 cups milk
1 cup shredded Havarti cheese (4 ounces)
1 cup shredded Cheddar cheese (4 ounces)

1. Heat oven to 450°. Spray square baking dish, 8 × 8 × 2 inches, with cooking spray. Cook and drain pasta as directed on package.

2. While pasta is cooking, toss bell peppers, mushrooms, zucchini, oil, Italian seasoning and salt to coat. Spoon into ungreased jelly roll pan, 14½ × 10½ × 1 inch. Bake uncovered about 20 minutes or until crisp-tender. Cool slightly. Coarsely chop vegetables.

3. Reduce oven temperature to 350°. Mix sauce mix (dry) and milk in 4-quart saucepan. Heat to boiling over medium heat, stirring constantly; remove from heat. Stir in cheeses until melted. Stir in pasta until well coated.

4. Spoon half of pasta mixture into baking dish. Reserve about ½ cup of the vegetables. Spoon remaining vegetables evenly over pasta. Top with remaining pasta. Sprinkle with reserved vegetables.

5. Cover and bake 30 minutes. Uncover and bake 10 to 15 minutes longer or until bubbly.

6 servings.

1 Serving: Calories 525 (Calories from Fat 225); Fat 25g (Saturated 11g); Cholesterol 45mg; Sodium 690mg; Carbohydrate 57g (Dietary Fiber 3g); Protein 21g
% Daily Value: Vitamin A 26%; Vitamin C 32%; Calcium 32%; Iron 18%
Diet Exchanges: 3 Starch, 1 High-Fat Meat, 2 Vegetable, 3 Fat

BETTY'S TIPS

⊕ **Serve-With**
Serve with a packaged ready-to-eat Caesar salad from the produce section.

⊕ **Do-Ahead**
This meatless casserole can be prepared and refrigerated up to 24 hours ahead of time. Bake as directed.

Gorgonzola Rigatoni with Vegetables

Prep: 10 min   Cook: 15 min

3 cups uncooked rigatoni pasta (9 ounces)
2 cups broccoli flowerets
1 can (12 ounces) evaporated fat-free milk
1 tablespoon cornstarch
½ cup crumbled Gorgonzola cheese (2 ounces)
1 small tomato, chopped (½ cup)
1 jar (6 ounces) sliced mushrooms, drained
10 pitted ripe olives, cut in half
½ teaspoon salt
¼ teaspoon pepper
Oregano sprigs, if desired

1. Cook and drain pasta as directed on package.

2. While pasta is cooking, place steamer basket in ½ inch water in saucepan or skillet (water should not touch bottom of basket). Place broccoli in basket. Cover tightly and heat to boiling; reduce heat to medium-low. Steam about 3 minutes or until crisp-tender.

3. Mix milk and cornstarch in 3-quart saucepan using wire whisk. Heat to boiling over medium heat, stirring constantly; reduce heat to low. Stir in cheese; continue stirring 2 to 3 minutes or until cheese is melted.

4. Stir broccoli, tomato, mushrooms, olives, salt and pepper into cheese sauce; heat through. Serve over pasta. Garnish with oregano.

4 servings.

1 Serving: Calories 435 (Calories from Fat 65); Fat 7g (Saturated 3g); Cholesterol 10mg; Sodium 830mg; Carbohydrate 79g (Dietary Fiber 6g); Protein 20g
% Daily Value: Vitamin A 16%; Vitamin C 38%; Calcium 26%; Iron 24%
Diet Exchanges: 4 Starch, 4 Vegetable, ½ Fat

BETTY'S TIPS

⊙ **Substitution**
Gorgonzola cheese proves the old adage that a little goes a long way! Its strong and tangy flavor packs a tasty punch without adding a lot of fat and calories. You can also try blue cheese or feta cheese in this recipe.

Chipotle Peanut Noodle Bowls

Prep: 15 min   Cook: 15 min

½ cup creamy peanut butter
½ cup apple juice
2 tablespoons soy sauce
2 chipotle chilies in adobo sauce (from 7-ounce can), seeded and chopped
1 teaspoon adobo sauce (from can of chilies)
¼ cup chopped fresh cilantro
4 cups water
2 medium carrots, cut into julienne strips (½ cups)
1 medium red bell pepper, cut into julienne strips
1 package (8 to 10 ounces) Chinese curly noodles
2 tablespoons chopped peanuts

1. Mix peanut butter, apple juice, soy sauce, chilies and adobo sauce until smooth. Stir in the cilantro.

2. Heat water to boiling in 2-quart saucepan. Add carrots and bell pepper; cook 1 minute. Remove from water with slotted spoon. Add noodles to water; cook and drain as directed on package.

3. Toss noodles with peanut butter mixture; divide noodles among 4 bowls. Top with carrots and bell pepper. Sprinkle with peanuts.

4 servings.

1 Serving: Calories 530 (Calories from Fat 180); Fat 20g (Saturated 4g); Cholesterol 0mg; Sodium 730mg; Carbohydrate 74g (Dietary Fiber 7g); Protein 20g
% Daily Value: Vitamin A 100%; Vitamin C 28%; Calcium 4%; Iron 24%
Diet Exchanges: 4 Starch, 2 Vegetable, 3 Fat

BETTY'S TIPS

⊙ **Success Hint**
If you like a bit more kick in the sauce, don't remove the seeds from the chilies.

⊙ **Serve-With**
Enjoy this fabulous restaurant-style supper with crusty bread, fresh melon slices and iced tea.

Chipotle Peanut Noodle Bowls

Penne with Tomato and Smoked Cheese

Prep: 20 min   Bake: 30 min

- 3 cups uncooked penne pasta (9 ounces)
- 1 can (14½ ounces) diced tomatoes, undrained
- 2 cups Alfredo pasta sauce
- 1 cup shredded smoked mozzarella cheese (4 ounces)

1. Heat oven to 350°. Grease 1½-quart casserole. Cook and drain pasta as directed on package.

2. While pasta is cooking, heat tomatoes to boiling in 2-quart saucepan; reduce heat to medium. Cook uncovered 6 to 8 minutes, stirring occasionally, until liquid has evaporated.

3. Heat Alfredo sauce in 2-quart saucepan over medium-low heat until warm. Stir in cheese until melted.

4. Mix sauce, pasta and tomatoes. Pour into casserole. Bake uncovered about 30 minutes or until hot in center.

6 servings.

1 Serving: Calories 580 (Calories from Fat 270); Fat 30g (Saturated 18g); Cholesterol 90mg; Sodium 540mg; Carbohydrate 59g (Dietary Fiber 3g); Protein 21g
% Daily Value: Vitamin A 28%; Vitamin C 8%; Calcium 38%; Iron 16%
Diet Exchanges: 4 Starch, 1½ High-Fat Meat, 3 Fat

BETTY'S TIPS

✿ **Special Touch**
Sprinkle crumbled cooked bacon over top of the baked casserole for an even smokier flavor.

✿ **Time-Saver**
When you need a meal that's quick and easy, assemble this dish the night before and refrigerate overnight. Bake as directed.

Quick

Lemon Pepper Pasta and Asparagus

Prep: 10 min   Cook: 15 min

- 2 cups uncooked farfalle (bow-tie) pasta (4 ounces)
- ¼ cup olive or vegetable oil
- 1 medium red bell pepper, chopped (1 cup)
- 1 pound asparagus, cut into 1-inch pieces
- 1 teaspoon grated lemon peel
- ½ teaspoon salt
- ½ teaspoon freshly ground pepper
- 3 tablespoons lemon juice
- 1 can (15 to 16 ounces) navy beans, rinsed and drained
  Freshly ground pepper, if desired

1. Cook and drain pasta as directed on package.

2. While pasta is cooking, heat oil in 12-inch skillet over medium-high heat. Cook bell pepper, asparagus, lemon peel, salt and ½ teaspoon pepper in oil, stirring occasionally, until vegetables are crisp-tender.

3. Stir lemon juice and beans into vegetable mixture. Cook until beans are hot. Add pasta; toss. Sprinkle with pepper.

4 servings.

1 Serving: Calories 380 (Calories from Fat 135); Fat 15g (Saturated 2g); Cholesterol 0mg; Sodium 710mg; Carbohydrate 55g (Dietary Fiber 9g); Protein 15g
% Daily Value: Vitamin A 42%; Vitamin C 30%; Calcium 10%; Iron 24%
Diet Exchanges: 3 Starch, 2 Vegetable, 2 Fat

BETTY'S TIPS

✿ **Substitution**
Fresh asparagus is now available year-round in most produce departments, so this light and refreshing recipe can be enjoyed more often. For a flavor twist, try fresh lime juice and peel instead of the lemon.

✿ **Variation**
For tasty **Lemon Pepper Pasta and Shrimp,** add ½ pound cooked peeled deveined shrimp with the beans in step **3.** Continue as directed.

Betty... ON WHAT'S COOKING

Perfect Pasta

Using your noodle to create perfect pasta is simply a matter of having the know-how! With the ever-increasing passion for pasta, you'll want to understand the basics of cooking it. **Here are 10 tips to perfect pasta:**

1. **Use a generous amount of water,** at least 1 quart of water for every 4 ounces of pasta. Be sure the **water is boiling vigorously** before adding the pasta.
2. **Do not add oil** to the cooking water; it isn't necessary, and sauces won't cling to oil-coated pasta.
3. **Salt,** which isn't necessary for proper cooking of pasta, does enhance the flavor. **Add ½ teaspoon for each 8 ounces of pasta** immediately after the water starts to boil. Or add dried herbs for a different flavor boost.
4. **Cook pasta uncovered at a fast, continuous boil.** This helps the pasta cook more evenly and prevents sticking.
5. **Gradually add pasta** to the boiling water, and then **stir to prevent sticking.** Stir the pasta occasionally during cooking, as well.
6. Always **follow package directions** for timings. Fresh pasta takes less cooking time than dried or frozen pasta. Size and shape will greatly alter cooking time, too.
7. If you're going to use cooked pasta in a casserole or any recipe with additional cooking time, **slightly undercook the pasta** so it won't become mushy with the additional cooking. Check pasta after 5 minutes of cooking to test doneness.
8. Correctly cooked pasta should be tender but firm to the bite (called al dente). **Check for doneness at the minimum cook time** by carefully removing a piece of pasta, letting it cool and then tasting.
9. **Thoroughly drain** the cooked pasta. Excess water will dilute the sauce.
10. Don't rinse cooked pasta unless directed to in a recipe. If using the pasta in a chilled salad, **immediately rinse with cold water** to stop the cooking process and reduce the temperature.

THE LONG AND SHORT OF PASTA YIELDS

As a rule, one ounce of dried pasta will yield about ½ cup of cooked pasta. If you are using fresh pasta, you will need slightly more. Yields will vary with the shape and size of the pasta. Plan on between ½ to ¾ cup of cooked pasta for a side-dish serving and 1 to 1½ cups for a main-dish serving.

7 ounces of uncooked macaroni (2 cups) will yield **4 cups** of cooked macaroni.

7 to 8 ounces of uncooked spaghetti will yield **4 cups** of cooked spaghetti.

8 ounces of uncooked noodles (4 to 5 cups) will yield **4 to 5 cups** of cooked noodles.

Mostaccioli with Roasted Tomato and Garlic

Prep: 15 min   Bake: 1 hr   Cook: 15 min

¼	cup olive or vegetable oil
8 to 10	medium roma (plum) tomatoes, cut in half
1	teaspoon sugar
¼	teaspoon salt
	Freshly ground pepper
1	unpeeled bulb garlic
2	cups uncooked mostaccioli pasta (6 ounces)
¼	cup chopped fresh or 1 tablespoon dried basil leaves
1	cup crumbled feta or cubed mozzarella cheese (4 ounces)

1. Heat oven to 300°. Line cookie sheet with aluminum foil; generously brush with 1 tablespoon of the oil. Arrange tomato halves, cut sides up, in single layer on cookie sheet; brush with 4 teaspoons of the oil. Sprinkle with sugar, salt and pepper.

2. Cut ½ inch off top of garlic bulb; drizzle 2 teaspoons of the oil over garlic bulb. Wrap in aluminum foil; place on cookie sheet with tomatoes. Bake 55 to 60 minutes or until garlic is soft when pierced with a knife and tomatoes have begun to shrivel; cool slightly.

3. Cook and drain pasta as directed on package. Squeeze garlic into remaining 1 tablespoon oil and mash until smooth; toss with pasta. Add tomato and basil; toss. Top with cheese. Serve immediately.

4 servings.

1 Serving: Calories 380 (Calories from Fat 125); Fat 14g (Saturated 5g); Cholesterol 25mg; Sodium 480mg; Carbohydrate 53g (Dietary Fiber 3g); Protein 13g
% Daily Value: Vitamin A 18%; Vitamin C 18%; Calcium 16%; Iron 16%
Diet Exchanges: 3 Starch, 2 Vegetable, 2 Fat

BETTY'S TIPS

⊙ **Substitution**

You can use 3 large tomatoes, sliced, in place of the roma tomatoes. The roasting time is the same, and the flavor will be just as sweet.

⊙ **Time-Saver**

You can roast the tomatoes and garlic and toss with the pasta, basil and cheese ahead of time. It's delicious served at room temperature with crusty Italian bread.

Mostaccioli with Roasted Tomato and Garlic

The Thrill
of the Grill

Fun Fixin's in the Great Outdoors

Lemon Shrimp Kabobs with Squash

Prep: 20 min   Marinate: 30 min   Grill: 12 min

¼ cup lemon juice

3 tablespoons honey

1 teaspoon chopped fresh or ½ teaspoon dried rosemary leaves, crumbled

1½ pounds uncooked fresh or frozen large shrimp in shells

3 medium zucchini, cut into 1-inch slices

2 medium yellow summer squash, cut into 1-inch slices

1 small bell pepper, cut into 1-inch wedges

1 small lemon, cut into wedges

1. Mix lemon juice, honey and rosemary in shallow glass or plastic dish. Add shrimp, stirring to coat. Cover and refrigerate 30 minutes, stirring occasionally.

2. Heat coals or gas grill. Remove shrimp from marinade; reserve marinade. Thread shrimp, zucchini, yellow squash and bell pepper alternately on each of six 15-inch metal skewers, leaving space between pieces.

3. Cover and grill kabobs 5 to 6 inches from medium heat about 12 minutes, turning and brushing 2 or 3 times with marinade, until shrimp are pink and firm. Discard any remaining marinade. To serve, peel shrimp. Serve with lemon wedges.

6 servings.

1 Serving: Calories 115 (Calories from Fat 10); Fat 1g (Saturated 0g); Cholesterol 105mg; Sodium 130mg; Carbohydrate 15g (Dietary Fiber 3g); Protein 14g
% Daily Value: Vitamin A 10%; Vitamin C 26%; Calcium 4%; Iron 14%
Diet Exchanges: 1 Very Lean Meat, 3 Vegetable

BETTY'S TIPS

✿ Substitution
Wooden skewers can be used instead of metal ones. To prevent them from burning, soak the skewers in water 30 minutes before using.

✿ Time-Saver
For no-mess marinating, place the shrimp and marinade in a heavy-duty resealable plastic bag.

Lemon Shrimp Kabobs with Squash

Skewered Shrimp with Apricot Curry Glaze

Prep: 15 min   Marinate: 30 min   Grill: 8 min

3 tablespoons vegetable oil

3 tablespoons apricot preserves

1½ tablespoons white wine vinegar

2¼ teaspoons Dijon mustard

2¼ teaspoons curry powder

1¼ teaspoons finely chopped garlic

1½ pounds uncooked large shrimp, peeled and deveined

Shredded lettuce

Lemon wedges

1. Mix oil, preserves, vinegar, mustard, curry powder and garlic in shallow glass or plastic dish. Add shrimp, turning to coat with glaze. Cover and refrigerate 15 to 30 minutes.

2. Heat coals or gas grill. Remove shrimp from glaze; reserve glaze. Thread shrimp on six 10- to 12-inch skewers, leaving space between. (If using bamboo skewers, soak them in water 30 minutes before using.)

3. Grill kabobs uncovered 4 to 6 inches from medium heat 6 to 8 minutes, brushing several times with glaze and turning once, until shrimp are pink and firm. Discard any remaining glaze.

4. Place shredded lettuce on platter, arrange skewers of shrimp on top. Garnish with lemon wedges.

6 servings.

1 Serving: Calories 212 (Calories from Fat 80); Fat 9g (Saturated 1g); Cholesterol 175mg; Sodium 221mg; Carbohydrate 8g (Dietary Fiber 0g); Protein 23g
% Daily Value: Vitamin A 0%; Vitamin C 0%; Calcium 8%; Iron 19%
Diet Exchanges: 3 Meat, 1½ Fat

Skewered Shrimp with Apricot Curry Glaze

Herbed Seafood

Prep: 20 min   Grill: 10 min

½   pound bay scallops

½   pound orange roughy fillets, cut into 1-inch pieces

½   pound uncooked fresh or frozen large shrimp, peeled and deveined

2   tablespoons chopped fresh or 2 teaspoons dried marjoram leaves

½   teaspoon grated lemon peel

⅛   teaspoon white pepper

3   tablespoons butter or margarine, melted

2   tablespoons lemon juice

4   cups hot cooked pasta or rice

1. Heat coals or gas grill for direct heat. Spray 18-inch square of heavy-duty aluminum foil with cooking spray.

2. Arrange scallops, fish and shrimp on foil, placing shrimp on top. Sprinkle with marjoram, lemon peel and white pepper. Drizzle with butter and lemon juice. Bring corners of foil up to center and seal loosely.

3. Cover and grill foil packet 4 inches from medium heat 8 to 10 minutes or until scallops are white, fish flakes easily with fork and shrimp are pink and firm. Serve seafood mixture over pasta.

4 servings.

1 Serving: Calories 355 (Calories from Fat 80); Fat 9g (Saturated 2g); Cholesterol 140mg; Sodium 270mg; Carbohydrate 41g (Dietary Fiber 2g); Protein 30g
% Daily Value: Vitamin A 12%; Vitamin C 0%; Calcium 6%; Iron 24%
Diet Exchanges: 3 Starch, 3 Very Lean Meat

BETTY'S TIPS

⚙ **Substitution**

Bay scallops are sweeter, more succulent and more expensive than the larger, more available (but less tender) sea scallops. If you use sea scallops, cut each in half.

Halibut with Lime and Cilantro

Prep: 10 min   Marinate: 15 min   Grill: 20 min

Lime Cilantro Marinade (below)

2   halibut or salmon steaks (about ¾ pound)
Freshly ground pepper to taste

½   cup salsa

1. Make Lime Cilantro Marinade in shallow glass or plastic dish or heavy-duty resealable plastic food-storage bag. Add fish, turning several times to coat with marinade. Cover and refrigerate 15 minutes, turning once.

2. Heat coals or gas grill for direct heat. Remove fish from marinade; discard marinade. Cover and grill fish 4 to 6 inches from medium heat 10 to 20 minutes, turning once, until fish flakes easily with fork. Sprinkle with pepper. Serve with salsa.

2 servings.

Lime Cilantro Marinade

2   tablespoons lime juice

1   tablespoon chopped fresh cilantro

1   teaspoon olive or vegetable oil

1   clove garlic, finely choppd

Mix all ingredients.

1 Serving: Calories 125 (Calories from Fat 25); Fat 3g (Saturated 1g); Cholesterol 75mg; Sodium 280mg; Carbohydrate 4g (Dietary Fiber 1g); Protein 27g
% Daily Value: Vitamin A 10%; Vitamin C 12%; Calcium 4%; Iron 4%
Diet Exchanges: 4 Very Lean Meat

BETTY'S TIPS

⚙ **Success Hint**

You may want to consider using a grill basket when grilling delicate fish because it can break apart easily. Be sure to spray the basket with cooking spray or lightly brush it with vegetable oil before adding the fish.

For best results, marinate fish only up to 2 hours. If the fish marinates longer, it will begin to toughen.

Grilled Tuna Steaks with Ginger Orange Marinade

Prep: 15 min   Marinate: 1 hr   Grill: 20 min

1½ pounds tuna steaks, ¾ to 1 inch thick
Ginger Orange Marinade (below)
Orange wedges, if desired

1. If fish steaks are large, cut into 6 serving pieces. Make Ginger Orange Marinade in shallow glass or plastic dish or heavy-duty resealable plastic food-storage bag. Add fish; turn to coat with marinade. Cover dish or seal bag and refrigerate, turning once, at least 1 hour but no longer than 2 hours.

2. Heat coals or gas grill for direct heat. Remove fish from marinade; reserve marinade. Cover and grill fish about 4 inches from medium heat 15 to 20 minutes, brushing 2 or 3 times with marinade and turning once, until fish flakes easily with fork. Discard any remaining marinade. Serve fish with orange wedges.

6 servings.

Ginger Orange Marinade

¼ cup orange juice
2 tablespoons olive or vegetable oil
1 teaspoon finely chopped gingerroot
¼ teaspoon salt
Pinch of ground red pepper (cayenne)
1 clove garlic, crushed

Mix all ingredients.

1 Serving: Calories 150 (Calories from Fat 70); Fat 8g (Saturated 2g); Cholesterol 60mg; Sodium 150mg; Carbohydrate 1g (Dietary Fiber 0g); Protein 19g
% Daily Value: Vitamin A 2%; Vitamin C 6%; Calcium 0%; Iron 4%
Diet Exchanges: 2½ Lean Meat

BETTY'S TIPS

⊘ **Substitution**
For variety, try this recipe using swordfish or halibut steaks instead of the tuna steaks.

⊘ **Success Hint**
Plan on about 40 minutes for the charcoal to be ready for cooking. It will take only 10 minutes for a gas grill to be at medium heat.

If the tuna sticks to the grill, try using a metal pancake turner to carefully loosen it.

⊘ **Did You Know?**
The sooner the grill is cleaned after using, the easier cleaning will be!

Grilled Salmon with Nectarine Salsa

Prep: 10 min   Grill: 20 min

2 pounds salmon fillets

½ cup lemon juice

4 medium nectarines, chopped

½ cup chopped fresh cilantro

2 teaspoons chopped jalapeño chili

1. Heat coals or gas grill for direct heat. Place salmon in ungreased rectangular baking dish, 11 × 7 × 1½ inches. Drizzle with ¼ cup of the lemon juice.

2. Remove salmon from baking dish. Place skin sides down on grill. Cover and grill 4 to 6 inches from medium heat 10 to 20 minutes until salmon flakes easily with fork.

3. Mix remaining ¼ cup lemon juice and remaining ingredients. Serve nectarine salsa over salmon.

4 servings.

1 Serving: Calories 340 (Calories from Fat 110); Fat 12g (Saturated 3g); Cholesterol 125mg; Sodium 150mg; Carbohydrate 18g (Dietary Fiber 2g); Protein 42g
% Daily Value: Vitamin A 16%; Vitamin C 34%; Calcium 4%; Iron 8%
Diet Exchanges: 6 Very Lean Meat, 1 Fruit, ½ Fat

BETTY'S TIPS

⊙ Substitution

Two medium mangoes, cut into ½-inch pieces, can be used instead of the nectarines.

⊙ Success Hint

Fish usually takes about 10 minutes to grill for each inch of thickness. Add more time if the fillet is thicker. If you have 2 thinner pieces, grill them for slightly less time.

To prevent fish from sticking to the grill, spray the cold grill rack with cooking spray or brush lightly with vegetable oil. To avoid fire flare-ups, don't spray over the hot coals.

Grilled Salmon with Nectarine Salsa

Spice-Rubbed Grilled Chicken

Prep: 10 min   Grill: 2 hr 15 min   Stand: 10

1 tablespoon packed brown sugar
1½ teaspoons chili powder
½ teaspoon seasoned salt
½ teaspoon ground ginger
¼ teaspoon garlic powder
¼ teaspoon ground allspice
¼ teaspoon coarsely ground pepper
4- to 4½- pound whole broiler-fryer chicken
Zesty Peach Sauce (at right)

1. If using charcoal grill, place drip pan directly under grilling area, and arrange coals around edge of firebox. Heat coals or gas grill for indirect heat.

2. Mix all ingredients except chicken and Zesty Peach Sauce. Fold wings of chicken across back with tips touching. Tie or skewer drumsticks to tail. Sprinkle spice mixture inside cavity and all over outside of chicken; rub with fingers. Insert barbecue meat thermometer so tip is in thickest part of inside thigh muscle and does not touch bone.

3. Cover and grill chicken, breast side up, over drip pan or over unheated side of gas grill and 4 to 6 inches from low heat 2 hours to 2 hours 15 minutes, turning every 20 minutes until thermometer reads 180° and juice is no longer pink when center of thigh is cut. Let stand 10 minutes. Serve with sauce.

6 servings.

Zesty Peach Sauce

½ cup peach preserves
⅓ cup chili sauce
1 tablespoon chopped fresh chives
1 teaspoon chili powder

Heat all ingredients to boiling in 1-quart saucepan; reduce heat. Simmer uncovered 5 minutes, stirring occasionally.

1 Serving: Calories 395 (Calories from Fat 160); Fat 18g (Saturated 5g); Cholesterol 115mg; Sodium 410mg; Carbohydrate 23g (Dietary Fiber 1g); Protein 36g
% Daily Value: Vitamin A 8%; Vitamin C 4%; Calcium 2%; Iron 10%
Diet Exchanges: 5 Lean Meat, 1½ Fruit, ½ Fat

BETTY'S TIPS

☺ Substitution
One tablespoon chopped green onion can be used instead of the chives.

☺ Success Hint
To grill with indirect heat, place a drip pan directly under the grilling area and arrange the coals around the edge of the firebox. For a dual-burner grill, heat only one side and place food over the burner that is not lit.

Spice-Rubbed Grilled Chicken

Grilled Asian Chicken Drumsticks

Prep: 10 min   Grill: 1 hr

2 tablespoons soy sauce
1 tablespoon olive or vegetable oil
1 teaspoon Dijon mustard
¼ teaspoon salt
⅛ teaspoon ground red pepper (cayenne)
2 cloves garlic, finely chopped
8 chicken drumsticks (about 1½ pounds)

1. Heat coals or gas grill for direct heat. Mix all ingredients except chicken; brush over chicken.

2. Cover and grill chicken, bone sides down, 4 to 6 inches from medium heat 15 to 20 minutes; turn. Cover and grill 20 to 40 minutes longer, turning 2 or 3 times, until juice of chicken is no longer pink when centers of thickest pieces are cut.

4 servings.

1 Serving: Calories 240 (Calories from Fat 120); Fat 14g (Saturated 4g); Cholesterol 85mg; Sodium 710mg; Carbohydrate 1g (Dietary Fiber 0g); Protein 29g
% Daily Value: Vitamin A 0%; Vitamin C 0%; Calcium 4%; Iron 14%
Diet Exchanges: 4 Lean Meat

BETTY'S TIPS

⚙ **Substitution**
If you have a family of chicken-thigh lovers, by all means substitute thighs for the drumsticks.

⚙ **Time-Saver**
When you're in a hurry, use 1 teaspoon of ready-to-use minced garlic that's available in jars in the produce department of your supermarket.

⚙ **Serve-With**
Cooked Chinese noodles make a terrific accompaniment.

Jerk Chicken Kabobs

Prep: 10 min   Marinate: 1 hr   Grill: 15 min

6 boneless skinless chicken thighs (about 1¼ pounds, cut into 1-inch cubes)
⅓ cup jerk seasoning sauce
1 cup canned or fresh pineapple chunks
2 medium red bell peppers, each cut into 12 wedges
½ medium onion, cut into 12 wedges and separated

1. Mix chicken and ¼ cup of the jerk sauce in shallow glass or plastic dish or resealable plastic food-storage bag. Cover dish or seal bag and refrigerate 1 hour, stirring occasionally.

2. Heat coals or gas grill for direct heat. Drain chicken; discard marinade. Thread chicken, pineapple, bell peppers and onion alternately on each of six 15-inch metal skewers, leaving space between pieces. Brush vegetables with remaining jerk sauce.

3. Cover and grill kabobs 4 to 6 inches from medium heat about 15 minutes or until chicken is no longer pink in center and vegetables are tender.

6 servings.

1 Serving: Calories 190 (Calories from Fat 70); Fat 8g (Saturated 2g); Cholesterol 55mg; Sodium 80mg; Carbohydrate 11g (Dietary Fiber 1g); Protein 20g
% Daily Value: Vitamin A 22%; Vitamin C 66%; Calcium 2%; Iron 10%
Diet Exchanges: 3 Lean Meat, 1 Vegetable, ½ Fruit

BETTY'S TIPS

⚙ **Success Hint**
Leave about ¼ inch space between the pieces on the skewers to allow for even cooking.

⚙ **Serve-With**
For an easy and delicious summer supper, serve grilled kabobs with hot buttered basmati rice.

Grilled Citrus Chicken

Prep: 12 min   Marinate: 2 hr   Grill: 20 min

Citrus Marinade (below)

6 boneless, skinless chicken breast halves (about 1¾ pounds)

1. Make Citrus Marinade in shallow glass or plastic dish or resealable plastic food-storage bag. Add chicken; turn to coat with marinade. Cover dish or seal bag and refrigerate, turning chicken occasionally, at least 2 hours but no longer than 24 hours.

2. Heat coals or gas grill for direct heat. Remove chicken from marinade; reserve marinade. Cover and grill chicken 4 to 6 inches from medium heat 15 to 20 minutes, turning and brushing with marinade occasionally, until juice of chicken is no longer pink when centers of thickest pieces are cut.

3. Heat remaining marinade to boiling; boil and stir 1 minute. Serve with chicken.

6 servings.

Citrus Marinade

½ cup frozen orange juice concentrate, thawed

¼ cup vegetable oil

¼ cup lemon juice

2 tablespoons grated orange peel

½ teaspoon salt

1 clove garlic, finely chopped

Mix all ingredients.

1 Serving: Calories 265 (Calories from Fat 115); Fat 13g (Saturated 2g); Cholesterol 75mg; Sodium 270mg; Carbohydrate 10g (Dietary Fiber 0g); Protein 27g
% Daily Value: Vitamin A 2%; Vitamin C 30%; Calcium 2%; Iron 6%
Diet Exchanges: 4 Lean Meat, ½ Fruit

BETTY'S TIPS

❂ **Success Hint**

For extra-moist grilled chicken, use a pair of tongs instead of a fork to turn the pieces. A fork will pierce the meat and let too many of the juices run out, drying out the chicken.

❂ **Serve-With**

Round out this terrific meal with Easy Grilled Vegetables (page 223).

Three-Herb Chicken

Three-Herb Chicken

Prep: 10 min   Marinate: 30 min   Grill: 55 min

Herb Marinade (below)
4   chicken thighs (about 1 pound)
4   chicken drumsticks (about 1 pound)

1. Make Herb Marinade in shallow glass or plastic dish or heavy-duty resealable plastic food-storage bag. Add chicken thighs and drumsticks; turn to coat with marinade. Cover dish or seal bag and refrigerate, turning chicken occasionally, at least 30 minutes but no longer than 24 hours.

2. Heat coals or gas grill for direct heat. Remove chicken from marinade; reserve marinade. Cover and grill chicken, skin sides down, 5 to 6 inches from medium heat 15 minutes. Turn chicken; brush with marinade. Cover and grill 20 to 40 minutes longer, brushing occasionally with marinade, until juice of chicken is no longer pink when centers of thickest pieces are cut. Discard any remaining marinade.

4 servings.

Herb Marinade

$\frac{1}{2}$ cup vegetable oil
$\frac{1}{2}$ cup lime juice
2   tablespoons chopped fresh or 2 teaspoons dried basil leaves
2   tablespoons chopped fresh or 2 teaspoons dried oregano leaves
2   tablespoons chopped fresh or 2 teaspooons dried thyme leaves
1   teaspoon onion powder
$\frac{1}{4}$ teaspoon lemon pepper

Mix all ingredients.

1 Serving: Calories 435 (Calories from Fat 305); Fat 34g (Saturated 7g); Cholesterol 105mg; Sodium 115mg; Carbohydrate 2g (Dietary Fiber 0g); Protein 30g
% Daily Value: Vitamin A 4%; Vitamin C 4%; Calcium 2%; Iron 10%
Diet Exchanges: 4 High-Fat Meat

BETTY'S TIPS

✿ **Time-Saver**
Microwave the chicken to partially cook it before grilling. Not only does this save time, but it can also help prevent overcooked, burned chicken. Place chicken in microwavable dish with thickest parts to the outside edge. Cover with plastic wrap, folding back one corner to allow steam to escape. Microwave on High 10 to 12 minutes, rotating dish $\frac{1}{2}$ turn after 5 minutes, until edges begin to cook; drain. Immediately put chicken on heated grill; grill 15 to 20 minutes until juice of chicken is no longer pink when centers of thickest pieces are cut.

✿ **Special Touch**
Garnish individual servings with lime slices or sprigs of fresh basil, oregano or thyme.

Spicy Thai Chicken Wings

Prep: 25 min   Marinate: 1 hr   Grill: 1 hr

20	chicken wings (about 4 pounds)
¼	cup dry sherry or chicken broth
¼	cup oyster sauce
¼	cup honey
3	tablespoons chopped fresh cilantro
2	tablespoons chili sauce
2	tablespoons grated lime peel
4	medium green onions, chopped (¼ cup)
3	cloves garlic, finely chopped

1. Cut each chicken wing at joints to make 3 pieces; discard tip. Cut off excess skin; discard.

2. Mix remaining ingredients in heavy-duty resealable plastic food-storage bag or large glass bowl. Add chicken; turn to coat with marinade. Seal bag or cover dish and refrigerate, turning once, at least 1 hour.

3. Heat coals or gas grill for direct heat. Remove chicken from marinade; reserve marinade. Cover and grill chicken 6 inches from medium heat 45 to 60 minutes, brushing frequently with marinade and turning once, until juice of chicken is no longer pink when centers of thickest pieces are cut. Discard any remaining marinade.

8 servings.

1 Serving: Calories 312 (Calories from Fat 163); Fat 18g (Saturated 5g); Cholesterol 65mg; Sodium 555mg; Carbohydrate 12g (Dietary Fiber 0g); Protein 22g
% Daily Value: Vitamin A 10%; Vitamin C 11%; Calcium 3%; Iron 11%
Diet Exchanges: 3 High-Fat Meat, ½ Vegetable, 2 Fat

BETTY'S TIPS

✿ Time-Saver
Purchase chicken drummettes (you'll need about 40) instead of chicken wings. Drummettes are cut up and ready for marinating.

✿ Do-Ahead
You can prepare and grill these zesty wings up to 24 hours ahead. Place in a rectangular pan, cover with foil and refrigerate. To reheat, place the covered pan in the oven at 350° for 20 to 25 minutes or until heated through.

Barbecued Chicken Nachos

Prep: 10 min   Grill: 10 min

8	cups corn tortilla chips
1½	cups cut-up cooked chicken
⅔	cup barbecue sauce
1	can (15 ounces) chili beans in sauce, undrained
1	can (2¼ ounces) sliced ripe olives, drained
2 to 3	medium roma (plum) tomatoes, chopped (1 cup)
3	cups shredded Colby–Monterey Jack Cheese (12 ounces)

1. Heat coals or gas grill for direct heat. Spray two 30 × 18-inch pieces of heavy-duty aluminum foil with cooking spray. Spread tortilla chips on centers of foil pieces. Mix chicken and barbecue sauce. Spoon chili beans, chicken mixture, olives, tomatoes and cheese on chips.

2. Wrap foil securely around tortilla chips. Cover and grill foil packets, seam sides up, 4 to 6 inches from medium heat 8 to 10 minutes or until cheese is melted.

8 servings.

1 Serving: Calories 410 (Calories from Fat 235); Fat 26g (Saturated 11g); Cholesterol 65mg; Sodium 1050mg; Carbohydrate 26g (Dietary Fiber 4g); Protein 22g
% Daily Value: Vitamin A 18%; Vitamin C 8%; Calcium 28%; Iron 14%
Diet Exchanges: 1½ Starch, 3 Lean Meat, 3 Fat

BETTY'S TIPS

✿ Substitution
You can chop one large tomato to use in place of the roma tomatoes.

✿ Time-Saver
When you're in a hurry, use a package of frozen diced cooked chicken, which you can thaw quickly in the microwave.

Pesto Chicken Packets

Prep: 15 min   Grill: 25 min

- 4 boneless skinless chicken breast halves (about 1¼ pounds)
- 8 roma (plum) tomatoes, cut into ½ inch slices
- 4 small zucchini, cut into ½-inch slices
- ½ cup basil pesto

1. Heat coals or gas grill. Place 1 chicken breast half, 2 sliced tomatoes and 1 sliced zucchini on one side of four 18 × 12-inch sheets of heavy-duty aluminum foil. Spoon 2 tablespoons pesto over chicken mixture on each sheet.

2. Fold foil over chicken and vegetables so edges meet. Seal edges, making right ½-inch fold; fold again. Allow space on sides for circulation and expansion.

3. Cover and grill packets 4 to 5 inches from medium heat 20 to 25 minutes or until juice of chicken is no longer pink when centers of thickest pieces are cut. Place packets on plates. Cut large X across top of packet; fold back foil.

4 servings.

1 Serving: Calories 330 (Calories from Fat 180); Fat 20g (Saturated 4g); Cholesterol 75mg; Sodium 330mg; Carbohydrate 10g (Dietary Fiber 3g); Protein 31g
% Daily Value: Vitamin A 12%; Vitamin C 26%; Calcium 14%; Iron 14%
Diet Exchanges: 4 Very Lean Meat, 2 Vegetable, 3 Fat

BETTY'S TIPS

⚙ **Time-Saver**
Instead of using foil packets, try using heavy-duty foil bags made especially for grilling.

⚙ **Did You Know?**
Pesto is a sauce made of fresh basil, garlic, oil, pine nuts and grated cheese. A variety of pesto flavors are now available, and you may want to experiment with one of them in this recipe. Or, make your own using the recipe on page 104.

Pesto Chicken Packets

Pan-Asian Turkey Packets

Prep: 20 min   Grill: 20 min

1¼ pounds turkey breast tenderloins (2 large)

¾ pound asparagus spears, cut into 1½-inch pieces

2 medium carrots, cut into julienne strips

1 cup picante sauce

¼ cup chunky peanut butter

2 tablespoons honey

2 tablespoons orange juice

1 tablespoon Gold Medal all-purpose flour

1 teaspoon soy sauce

½ teaspoon grated gingerroot

1. Heat coals or gas grill for direct heat. Cut each turkey tenderloin crosswise into ³/₄-inch slices. Place half the slices of each tenderloin on one side of each of 4 sheets of heavy-duty aluminum foil, 18 × 12 inches. Top each with equal amounts of asparagus and carrots.

2. Mix remaining ingredients until well blended. Carefully pour one-fourth of sauce over each portion of turkey and vegetables. Fold other half of foil over turkey and vegetables so edges meet. Seal edges, making a tight ¹/₂-inch fold; fold again. Allow space on sides for circulation and expansion. Repeat folding to seal each side. Place foil packets on cookie sheet to carry to grill.

3. Cover and grill packets 4 to 5 inches from medium-high heat 15 to 20 minutes or until turkey is no longer pink in center and vegetables are tender. Place foil packets on plates. To serve, cut a large X across top of packet; fold back foil.

4 servings.

1 Serving: Calories 335 (Calories from Fat 90); Fat 10g (Saturated 2g); Cholesterol 95mg; Sodium 410mg; Carbohydrate 25g (Dietary Fiber 4g); Protein 40g
% Daily Value: Vitamin A 100%; Vitamin C 26%; Calcium 6%; Iron 18%
Diet Exchanges: 4 Lean Meat, 5 Vegetable

BETTY'S TIPS

⊗ **Variation**

If you want to make this a one-packet meal, use a large heavy-duty aluminum foil bag instead of the individual packets. Be sure to add 5 to 10 minutes to the grilling time.

⊗ **Special Touch**

Garnish these packets with chopped roasted peanuts or sliced green onions. Both add flavor and a bit of crunch.

Summer Herb Steaks

Prep: 10 min   Grill: 11 min

¼ cup Dijon mustard

2 teaspoons chopped fresh or ½ teaspoon dried rosemary leaves, crumbled

1 teaspoon coarsely ground pepper

2 cloves garlic, finely chopped

4 beef boneless top loin steaks, about 1 inch thick (about 1 pound)

1. Heat coals or gas grill for direct heat. Mix mustard, rosemary, pepper and garlic; spread on both sides of beef.

2. Grill beef uncovered 4 to 5 inches from medium heat 1 minute on each side to seal in juices. Cover and grill 8 to 9 minutes longer for medium doneness, turning once.

4 servings.

1 Serving: Calories 125 (Calories from Fat 35); Fat 4g (Saturated 1g); Cholesterol 50mg; Sodium 230mg; Carbohydrate 2g (Dietary Fiber 1g); Protein 21g
% Daily Value: Vitamin A 0%; Vitamin C 0%; Calcium 2%; Iron 12%
Diet Exchanges: 3 Very Lean Meat

BETTY'S TIPS

⊙ **Serve-With**
Make a meal celebrating life's simple pleasures—steak, grilled corn on the cob and baked potatoes with sour cream and real butter.

⊙ **Did You Know?**
Top loin is one of the lower-fat cuts of meat. Other "skinny" cuts include eye round, top round, round tip, tenderloin and sirloin.

Grilled Tequila Lime Steak

Prep: 15 min   Marinate: 6 hr   Grill: 25 min

2- pound beef boneless top round steak about 1 inch thick
Tequila Marinade (below)

1 cup thick-and-chunky salsa

1. Pierce beef with fork several times on both sides. Make Tequila Marinade in shallow glass or plastic dish or heavy-duty resealable plastic food-storage bag. Add beef; turn to coat with marinade. Cover dish or seal bag and refrigerate, turning beef occasionally, at least 6 hours but no longer than 24 hours.

2. Heat coals or gas grill for direct heat. Remove beef from marinade; reserve marinade. Cover and grill beef 4 to 5 inches from medium heat 20 to 25 minutes for medium doneness, brushing occasionally with marinade and turning once. Discard any remaining marinade.

3. Cut beef across grain into thin slices. Serve with salsa.

8 servings.

Tequila Marinade

¼ cup lime juice

2 tablespoons vegetable oil

2 tablespoons tequila

½ teaspoon salt

½ teaspoon ground cumin

½ teaspoon ground red pepper (cayenne)

2 cloves garlic, finely chopped

Mix all ingredients.

1 Serving: Calories 155 (Calories from Fat 65); Fat 7g (Saturated 2g); Cholesterol 55mg; Sodium 250mg; Carbohydrate 3g (Dietary Fiber 1g); Protein 21g
% Daily Value: Vitamin A 2%; Vitamin C 10%; Calcium 0%; Iron 12%
Diet Exchanges: 3 Lean Meat

BETTY'S TIPS

⊙ **Substitution**
If you don't have any tequila on hand, you can use lime juice instead.

⊙ **Did You Know?**
Piercing the meat with the tines of a fork helps the marinade penetrate the meat.

Pesto-Stuffed Steaks

Pesto-Stuffed Steaks

Prep: 20 min   Grill: 14 min

- 2   beef rib eye steaks, 1½ inches thick (about 2 pounds)
- ¼   cup basil pesto
- 2   tablespoons finely shredded Parmesan cheese
- 1   tablespoon olive or vegetable oil

1. Heat coals or gas grill. Make horizontal cut in side of each steak, forming a pocket (do not cut through to opposite side).

2. Mix pesto and cheese; spread evenly on insides of pockets; press pockets closed. Drizzle oil over beef.

3. Cover and grill beef 4 to 5 inches from medium heat 12 to 14 minutes for medium doneness, turning once. To serve, cut beef into thick strips.

4 servings.

1 Serving: Calories 410 (Calories from Fat 235); Fat 26g (Saturated 8g); Cholesterol 110mg; Sodium 380mg; Carbohydrate 1g (Dietary Fiber 0g); Protein 43g
% Daily Value: Vitamin A 2%; Vitamin C 0%; Calcium 18%; Iron 20%
Diet Exchanges: 6 Lean Meat, 2 Fat

BETTY'S TIPS

☺ Substitution
New York strip or sirloin steak can be substituted for the rib eye.

☺ Success Hint
To retain beef juices, turn the steaks with tongs instead of piercing them with a fork.

☺ Serve-With
Serve with a side dish of tomatoes. Drizzle tomato halves with olive oil, and sprinkle with garlic pepper. Either serve fresh or add to the grill the last 3 to 4 minutes before beef is done.

Quick

Texas T-Bones

Prep: 10 min   Grill: 14 min

- 4   beef T-bone steaks, about ¾ inch thick (10 to 12 ounces each)
- 2   cloves garlic, cut in half
- 4   teaspoons black peppercorns, crushed
- ¼   cup butter or margarine, softened
- 1   tablespoon Dijon mustard
- ½   teaspoon Worcestershire sauce
- ¼   teaspoon lime juice
  Salt and pepper, if desired

1. Heat coals or gas grill for direct heat. Trim fat on beef steaks to ¼-inch thickness. Rub garlic on beef. Press peppercorns into beef.

2. Mix remaining ingredients except salt and pepper; set aside.

3. Cover and grill beef 4 to 5 inches from medium heat 10 to 14 minutes for medium doneness, turning once. Sprinkle with salt and pepper. Serve with butter mixture.

4 servings.

1 Serving: Calories 260 (Calories from Fat 190); Fat 21g (Saturated 6g); Cholesterol 50mg; Sodium 180mg; Carbohydrate 1g (Dietary Fiber 0g); Protein 17g
% Daily Value: Vitamin A 10%; Vitamin C 0%; Calcium 0%; Iron 8%
Diet Exchanges: 2½ High-Fat Meat

BETTY'S TIPS

☺ Success Hint
Place peppercorns in a heavy-duty resealable plastic food-storage bag and crush into small pieces with a rolling pin.

Let the beef stand for a few minutes after grilling. This allows the meat juices, which have been driven to the center of the meat by the searing heat, to return to the surface. The result is a juicier, tastier piece of meat.

Glazed Beef Tenderloin with Herbed New Potatoes

Prep: 15 min   Marinate: 1 hr   Grill: 13 min

⅓ cup steak sauce

1½ tablespoons packed brown sugar

4 beef tenderloin steaks, about 1 inch thick (about 1 pound)

8 small new potatoes (1 pound), cut lengthwise in half

2 tablespoons water

Cooking spray

1 teaspoon chopped fresh or ¼ teaspoon dried rosemary leaves, crumbled

1 teaspoon chopped fresh or ¼ teaspoon dried thyme leaves

¼ teaspoon paprika

½ teaspoon salt

¼ teaspoon pepper

1. Mix steak sauce and brown sugar in shallow glass or plastic dish; reserve 2 tablespoons sauce. Add beef to remaining sauce (about ¼ cup); turn to coat with sauce. Cover and refrigerate, turning beef 2 or 3 times, at least 1 hour but no longer than 24 hours.

2. Heat coals or gas grill for direct heat. Place potatoes and water in 2-quart microwavable casserole. Cover and microwave on High 3 to 5 minutes or until potatoes are just tender. Place potatoes on sheet of heavy-duty aluminum foil. Spray potatoes with cooking spray; sprinkle with rosemary, thyme and paprika. Wrap securely in foil.

3. Grill beef and packet of potatoes uncovered 4 to 6 inches from medium heat 7 minutes. Turn beef and potatoes; brush reserved sauce over beef. Grill about 6 minutes longer for medium beef doneness; remove from heat. Sprinkle salt and pepper over potatoes.

4 servings.

1 Serving: Calories 260 (Calories from Fat 65); Fat 7g (Saturated 3g); Cholesterol 55mg; Sodium 660mg; Carbohydrate 28g (Dietary Fiber 2g); Protein 23g
% Daily Value: Vitamin A 2%; Vitamin C 10%; Calcium 2%; Iron 18%
Diet Exchanges: 2 Starch, 2 Lean Meat

BETTY'S TIPS

✿ Success Hint

Make sure the grill is hot before adding the steaks. A hot grill quickly sears the outside of the steaks, sealing the outside of the meat so the inside stays juicy and tender.

When handling the steaks, use tongs or a spatula instead of a fork, so you won't pierce the meat during cooking and allow the juices to seep out.

Glazed Beef Tenderloin with Herbed New Potatoes

Beef Kabobs with Chilied Plum Sauce

Prep: 15 min   Cook: 30 min   Grill: 15 min

Chilied Plum Sauce (below)

2 pounds beef bone-in sirloin, cut into 1-inch pieces

24 whole medium mushrooms

3 medium yellow summer squash or zucchini, cut into 1-inch slices

2 medium bell peppers, cut into 1½-inch pieces

1 large onion, cut into 1-inch pieces

½ cup Italian dressing

1. Heat coals or gas grill for direct heat. Make Chilied Plum Sauce.

2. Thread 4 or 5 pieces of beef alternating with mushrooms, squash, bell peppers and onion on each of sixteen 10- to 12-inch metal skewers, leaving a space between pieces.

3. Cover and grill kabobs 4 to 5 inches from medium heat 10 to 15 minutes for medium beef doneness, turning and brushing 2 or 3 times with dressing. Serve kabobs with sauce for dipping.

8 servings.

Chilied Plum Sauce

1 can (16½ ounces) purple plums, drained and chopped

1 can (6 ounces) frozen lemonade concentrate, thawed

¼ cup butter or margarine

1 small onion, chopped (¼ cup)

¼ cup chili sauce

1 tablespoon Dijon mustard

1. Place plums and lemonade concentrate in blender. Cover and blend on medium speed until smooth; set aside.

2. Melt butter in 2-quart saucepan over medium heat. Cook onion in butter about 2 minutes, stirring occasionally, until tender. Stir in plum mixture, chili sauce and mustard. Heat to boiling over medium-high heat; reduce heat. Simmer uncovered 15 minutes, stirring occasionally.

1 Serving: Calories 340 (Calories from Fat 125); Fat 14g (Saturated 5g); Cholesterol 70mg; Sodium 310mg; Carbohydrate 34g (Dietary Fiber 3g); Protein 23g
% Daily Value: Vitamin A 18%; Vitamin C 38%; Calcium 2%; Iron 18%
Diet Exchanges: 2 Medium-Fat Meat, 4 Vegetable, 1 Fruit, 1 Fat

BETTY'S TIPS

☺ Do-Ahead
Make the Chilied Plum Sauce up to 48 hours ahead of time; cover and refrigerate. You can serve the sauce cold or reheat until hot.

☺ Special Touch
Line a large serving platter or tray with hot cooked rice or couscous, and serve the kabobs on top.

Italian Sausages with Peperonata

Prep: 20 min   Grill: 33 min

4   uncooked hot or mild Italian sausage links
    (about 1 pound)
    Peperonata (below)
1   can (4 ounces) sliced ripe olives, drained
4   hot dog buns, split

1. Heat coals or gas grill for direct heat. Cover and grill
   sausages 4 to 5 inches from medium heat about 25
   minutes, turning occasionally, until no longer pink in
   center.

2. While sausages are grilling, make Peperonata; place
   in grill basket. Cover and grill 5 to 8 minutes or until
   bell peppers and onion are crisp-tender. Stir in
   olives.

3. Serve sausages on buns with Peperonata.

4 servings.

Peperonata

2   medium yellow bell peppers, cut into
    $\frac{1}{2}$-inch strips
2   medium red bell peppers, cut into $\frac{1}{2}$-inch
    strips
1   large onion, sliced and separated into rings
2   cloves garlic, finely chopped
1   tablespoon chopped fresh or 1 teaspoon
    dried basil leaves
2   teaspoons chopped fresh or $\frac{1}{2}$ teaspoon
    dried oregano leaves
1   tablespoon olive or vegetable oil
2   teaspoons lemon juice
$\frac{1}{2}$ teaspoon salt
$\frac{1}{4}$ teaspoon pepper

Toss all ingredients.

1 Sandwich: Calories 545 (Calories from Fat 280); Fat 31g (Saturated
9g); Cholesterol 65mg; Sodium 1670mg; Carbohydrate 47g (Dietary Fiber
5g); Protein 24g
% Daily Value: Vitamin A 72%; Vitamin C 100%; Calcium 16%; Iron 6%
Diet Exchanges: 2 Starch, 2 High-Fat Meat, 3 Vegetable, 2$\frac{1}{2}$ Fat

BETTY'S TIPS

✿ Substitution
Use a variety of colored bell peppers—red, orange, yellow
or green.

If you don't like olives, just omit them from the Peperonata.

✿ Variation
If you have leftover Peperonata, serve it on grilled steak
sandwiches or fajitas.

Pork Ribs with Smoky Barbecue Sauce

Prep: 10 min   Grill: 1 hr 10 min   Cook: 20 min

4   pounds pork loin back ribs (not cut into serving pieces)

1   tablespoon vegetable oil

4   teaspoons chopped fresh or 1½ teaspoons dried thyme leaves

Smoky Barbecue Sauce (below)

1. If using charcoal grill, place drip pan directly under grilling area, and arrange coals around edge of firebox. Heat coals or gas grill for indirect heat. Brush meaty sides of pork with oil. Sprinkle with thyme.

2. Cover and grill pork, meaty sides up, over drip pan or over unheated side of gas grill and 4 to 5 inches from medium heat 1 hour 10 minutes or until no longer pink when cut near bone.

3. While pork is grilling, make Smoky Barbecue Sauce. Brush sauce over pork 2 or 3 times during last 15 minutes of grilling. Heat any remaining sauce to boiling; boil and stir 1 minute. Cut pork into serving pieces. Serve with sauce.

4 servings.

Smoky Barbecue Sauce

½   cup ketchup

¼   cup water

3   tablespoons packed brown sugar

2   tablespoons white vinegar

2   teaspoons celery seed

¼   teaspoon liquid smoke

¼   teaspoon red pepper sauce

Heat all ingredients to boiling in 1-quart saucepan; reduce heat. Simmer uncovered 15 minutes, stirring occasionally.

1 Serving: Calories 910 (Calories from Fat 605); Fat 67g (Saturated 24g); Cholesterol 265mg; Sodium 440mg; Carbohydrate 13g (Dietary Fiber 0g); Protein 64g
% Daily Value: Vitamin A 2%; Vitamin C 2%; Calcium 10%; Iron 24%
Diet Exchanges: 8½ High-Fat Meat, 1 Fruit

Pork Ribs with Smoky Barbecue Sauce

Grilled Southwestern Pork Chops

Prep: 5 min   Marinate: 1 hr   Grill: 12 min

8   pork loin or rib chops, about ½ inch thick
    (about 2 pounds)
    Chili Rub (below)

1. Remove excess fat from pork. Make Chili Rub; rub evenly on both sides of pork. Cover and refrigerate 1 hour to blend flavors.

2. Heat coals or gas grill for direct heat. Cover and grill pork 4 to 6 inches from medium heat 10 to 12 minutes, turning frequently, until slightly pink when cut near bone.

8 servings.

Chili Rub

1   tablespoon chili powder
1   teaspoon ground cumin
¼   teaspoon ground red pepper (cayenne)
¼   teaspoon salt
1   large clove garlic, finely chopped

Mix all ingredients.

1 Serving: Calories 170 (Calories from Fat 70); Fat 8g (Saturated 3g); Cholesterol 65mg; Sodium 120mg; Carbohydrate 1g (Dietary Fiber 0g); Protein 23g
% Daily Value: Vitamin A 6%; Vitamin C 0%; Calcium 0%; Iron 4%
Diet Exchanges: 3 Lean Meat

BETTY'S TIPS

✪ **Substitution**
The Chili Rub is also delicious on chicken breasts.

✪ **Serve-With**
Serve with rice and beans, corn on the cob and a salad of sliced oranges, sliced avocado and red onion rings.

Jamaican Jerk Pork Chops with Mango Salsa

Prep: 20 min   Marinate: 30 min   Grill: 15 min

Jamaican Jerk Seasoning (below)

4   pork loin or rib chops, about ¾ inch thick (about 2 pounds)

Mango Salsa (at right)

1. Prepare Jamaican Jerk Seasoning. Rub seasoning into pork. Cover and refrigerate at least 30 minutes but no longer than 1 hour.

2. Heat coals or gas grill for direct heat. Cover and grill pork chops 4 to 6 inches from medium heat about 15 minutes, turning once, until slightly pink when cut near bone. Serve pork with Mango Salsa.

4 servings.

Jamaican Jerk Seasoning

2   teaspoons dried thyme leaves

1   teaspoon ground allspice

1   teaspoon packed brown sugar

½   teaspoon salt

½   teaspoon cracked black pepper

¼ to ½   teaspoon ground red pepper (cayenne)

¼   teaspoon crushed dried sage leaves

4   cloves garlic, finely chopped

Mix all ingredients.

Mango Salsa

1   mango, peeled, pitted and chopped (1 cup)

½   small red onion, finely chopped

1   tablespoon finely chopped fresh or 1 teaspoon dried mint leaves

1   small jalapeño chili, finely chopped (2 to 3 teaspoons)

2   tablespoons lime juice

⅛   teaspoon salt

Mix all ingredients in nonmetal bowl. Cover and refrigerate until serving.

1 Serving: Calories 215 (Calories from Fat 70); Fat 8g (Saturated 3g); Cholesterol 65mg; Sodium 410mg; Carbohydrate 14g (Dietary Fiber 2g); Protein 24g
% Daily Value: Vitamin A 30%; Vitamin C 32%; Calcium 2%; Iron 10%
Diet Exchanges: 1 Starch, 3 Very Lean Meat, 1 Fat

BETTY'S TIPS

✿ Substitution
Mango adds a tropical flavor that particularly enhances pork and chicken. If mangoes are not available, canned mango, or fresh or frozen (thawed) peaches are a good substitute.

✿ Time-Saver
You can use two tablespoons of purchased Jamaican jerk blend seasoning, which is available in the supermarket with the spices, instead of making your own jerk seasoning.

Jamaican Jerk Pork Chops with Mango Salsa

Peach- and Mustard-Glazed Pork Tenderloin

Prep: 10 min   Marinate: 1 hr   Grill: 25 min   Cook: 2 min

Peach Mustard Marinade (below)
2   pork tenderloins (about ¾ pound each)

1. Make Peach Mustard Marinade in shallow glass or plastic dish or heavy-duty resealable plastic food-storage bag. Add pork; turn to coat with marinade. Cover dish or seal bag and refrigerate, turning pork occasionally, at least 1 hour but no longer than 8 hours.

2. Heat coals or gas grill for direct heat. Remove pork from marinade; reserve marinade. Cover and grill pork 4 to 5 inches from medium heat 20 to 25 minutes, brushing occasionally with marinade and turning once, until pork is slightly pink in center.

3. Heat remaining marinade to boiling; boil and stir 1 minute. Cut pork into slices. Serve with marinade.

6 servings.

Peach Mustard Marinade
½   cup peach preserves
2   tablespoons Dijon mustard
2   teaspoons vegetable oil
¼   teaspoon dried thyme leaves
¼   teaspoon salt

Mix all ingredients.

1 Serving: Calories 230 (Calories from Fat 55); Fat 6g (Saturated 2g); Cholesterol 65mg; Sodium 280mg; Carbohydrate 18g (Dietary Fiber 0g); Protein 24g
% Daily Value: Vitamin A 0%; Vitamin C 2%; Calcium 0%; Iron 8%
Diet Exchanges: 4 Very Lean Meat, 1 Fruit, 1 Fat

BETTY'S TIPS

❂ **Substitution**
Apricot preserves can be used instead of the peach preserves in this recipe.

❂ **Did You Know?**
Zippered plastic food-storage bags are great for mess-free marinating. Place meat in bag, fold over the top and squeeze out all the air, allowing marinade to completely coat the food. When it's time to grill, take the bag outside and transfer marinated meat to the grill.

Southwest Pork Packets

Prep: 15 min   Stand: 5 min   Grill: 20 min

2 cups uncooked instant rice
1 can (14½ ounces) chicken broth
1 tablespoon Mexican seasoning
1 can (15 ounces) whole kernel corn, drained
1 small bell pepper, chopped (½ cup)
4 medium green onions, sliced (¼ cup)
4 pork boneless rib or loin chops, ¾ to 1 inch thick (1¼ pounds)
2 teaspoons Mexican seasoning
   Salsa, if desired

1. Heat coals or gas grill. Spray half of one side of four 18 × 12-inch sheets of heavy-duty aluminum foil with cooking spray.

2. Mix rice, broth and 1 tablespoon Mexican seasoning in large bowl; let stand about 5 minutes or until broth is absorbed. Stir in corn, bell pepper and onion.

3. Sprinkle each pork chop with ½ teaspoon Mexican seasoning; place in center of sprayed foil. Spoon rice mixture over pork. Fold foil over pork and rice so edges meet. Seal edges, making tight ½-inch fold; fold again. Allow space on sides for circulation and expansion.

4. Grill packets 4 to 6 inches from medium heat 15 to 20 minutes or until pork is slightly pink when cut near bone. Place packets on plates. Cut large X across top of packets; fold back foil. Serve with salsa.

4 servings.

1 Serving: Calories 560 (Calories from Fat 125); Fat 14g (Saturated 4g); Cholesterol 90mg; Sodium 760mg; Carbohydrate 70g (Dietary Fiber 4g); Protein 42g
% Daily Value: Vitamin A 4%; Vitamin C 22%; Calcium 6%; Iron 28%
Diet Exchanges: 4 Starch, 4 Lean Meat, 2 Vegetable

Orange Barbecued Ham

Prep: 15 min   Marinate: 4 hr   Grill: 1 hr 45 min

1 cup orange juice

¼ cup honey

2 tablespoons chopped fresh chives

2 tablespoons vegetable oil

4- pound fully cooked boneless ham

1 cup barbecue sauce

¼ cup orange marmalade

1 teaspoon ground mustard

1. Mix orange juice, honey, chives and oil in medium bowl. Make cuts on top of ham about ½ inch apart and ¼ inch deep in diamond pattern. Place ham in large heavy-duty resealable plastic food-storage bag. Pour orange juice mixture over ham; turn to coat. Refrigerate at least 4 hours but no longer than 24 hours, turning occasionally.

2. Heat coals or grill for indirect heat. Remove ham from marinade; reserve marinade. Cover and grill ham over low heat 1 hour 15 minutes to 1 hour 30 minutes, brushing with marinade 2 or 3 times and turning once or twice, until heated through. Discard remaining marinade.

3. While ham is grilling, mix barbecue sauce, marmalade and mustard in 2-quart saucepan. Cook over low heat 5 to 10 minutes, stirring occasionally, until well blended. Brush sauce on ham. Grill 10 to 15 minutes longer or until glazed. Serve ham with remaining sauce.

16 servings.

1 Serving: Calories 215 (Calories from Fat 90); Fat 10g (Saturated 3g); Cholesterol 55mg; Sodium 1580mg; Carbohydrate 9g (Dietary Fiber 0g); Protein 22g
% Daily Value: Vitamin A 2%; Vitamin C 4%; Calcium 0%; Iron 8%
Diet Exchanges: 3 Lean Meat, ½ Fruit

BETTY'S TIPS

⊘ Substitution
Two tablespoons chopped green onions can be used instead of the chives.

⊘ Success Hint
To grill with indirect heat, place a drip pan directly under the grilling area and arrange the coals around the edge of the firebox. For a dual burner grill, heat only one side and place food over the burner that is not lit. For a single burner grill, place food in an aluminum-foil pan or on several layers of aluminum foil and use low heat.

Betty...
ON WHAT'S COOKING

Fire Up for Grilled Vegetables

▦ When grilling vegetables, think of them as being either soft or hard. Softer vegetables, such as zucchini, eggplant and bell peppers, will not need precooking. Harder vegetables, such as potatoes and carrots, should be cut into 1-inch pieces and precooked. To precook a vegetable, bring a small amount of water to boiling in a medium saucepan; add vegetable. Reduce heat, cover and simmer 5 to 10 minutes or until crisp-tender (potatoes should be almost tender); drain.

▦ **Grill over medium coals,** turning occasionally, until tender.

▦ **Arrange vegetables perpendicular** to the wires on the grill rack so they won't fall into the coals.

▦ Keep vegetables from sticking to a basket, skewers or grill surface by **marinating them or brushing them lightly with olive oil** or an oil-herb mixture.

▦ Use vegetable pieces of similar size for kabobs, and **precook hard vegetables.** If you're using bamboo or wooden skewers, soak them in water before threading so they won't burn.

GRILL HELPERS

▦ **Perforated aluminum foil sheets** can be placed directly on a heated grill to reduce the risk of stray veggies falling into the coals, help reduce flare-ups and keep mess to a minimum (they're disposable).

▦ **A grill basket** or a hinged grill basket is a great piece of equipment! With the hinged basket, instead of turning each vegetable on the grill, a twist of your wrist flips the basket and turns all the vegetables (or kabobs) over at once. The spaces are big enough to brush on marinade with ease.

▦ **Savu™ smoker bags** (savu means "smoke" in Finnish) are a great way to smoke vegetables (or any food) using a covered grill or a conventional oven. No need to soak wood chips or fight billowing clouds of smoke. Check local grocery stores.

GRILLING TIMES

Vegetables are grilled 4 to 5 inches over medium coals, and times are approximate. Check at the minimum time to test for doneness.

5–10 minutes
Carrot pieces or small whole carrots
Whole mushrooms
New potatoes or potato pieces*
Small whole onions or $\frac{1}{2}$-inch slices
Whole asparagus spears

10–15 minutes
Bell pepper strips (1 inch)
Eggplant slices ($\frac{1}{4}$ inch)
Pattypan squash (1 inch)
Zucchini or yellow squash slices ($\frac{3}{4}$ inch)
Whole green beans

20–30 minutes
Corn on the cob

Should be precooked (see guidelines above).

Grilled Antipasto Pizza

Grilled Antipasto Pizza

Prep: 10 min   Grill: 16 min

¼ pound small whole mushrooms (1½ cups)

1 medium yellow bell pepper, cut into 8 pieces

¼ cup Italian dressing

1 package (16 ounces) ready-to-serve original pizza crust (12 inches in diameter)

1 cup shredded mozzarella cheese (4 ounces)

2 roma (plum) tomatoes, thinly sliced

4 medium green onions, sliced (¼ cup)

¼ cup sliced ripe olives

1. Heat coals or gas grill for direct heat. Toss mushrooms, bell pepper and 2 tablespoons of the dressing. Place vegetables in grill basket.

2. Cover and grill vegetables 4 to 5 inches from medium heat 4 to 6 minutes, shaking grill basket to turn vegetables occasionally, until bell pepper is crisp-tender. Coarsely chop vegetables.

3. Brush pizza crust with remaining 2 tablespoons dressing. Sprinkle with ½ cup of the cheese. Arrange tomatoes on cheese. Top with grilled vegetables, onions, olives and remaining ½ cup cheese.

4. Place pizza directly on grill. Cover and grill 4 to 6 inches from medium heat 8 to 10 minutes or until crust is crisp and cheese is melted.

8 servings.

1 Serving: Calories 240 (Calories from Fat 90); Fat 10g (Saturated 3g); Cholesterol 10mg; Sodium 440mg; Carbohydrate 32g (Dietary Fiber 2g); Protein 8g
% Daily Value: Vitamin A 4%; Vitamin C 26%; Calcium 12%; Iron 12%
Diet Exchanges: 2 Starch, 2 Fat

BETTY'S TIPS

⊙ **Substitution**
If you don't have a grill basket, a sheet of heavy-duty foil that has a few holes poked in it also works.

⊙ **Serve-With**
Enjoy this easy grilled vegetable pizza as an appetizer (just cut into small pieces), or serve it as the main course with a fresh spinach salad and watermelon wedges.

Garden Vegetable Medley

Prep: 15 min   Grill: 30 min

 2   medium Yukon gold potatoes, cut into ⅛-inch slices
1½   cups baby-cut carrots
 ¼   pound whole green beans
 2   tablespoons butter or margarine, melted
 ½   teaspoon salt
 ¼   teaspoon dried oregano leaves
 ¼   teaspoon garlic pepper
 ¼   teaspoon ground cumin

1. Heat coals or gas grill for direct heat. Toss all ingredients. Spoon mixture onto 24 × 18-inch piece of heavy-duty aluminum foil. Wrap foil securely around vegetable mixture.

2. Cover and grill foil packet 4 to 6 inches from medium heat 25 to 30 minutes or until vegetables are tender.

4 servings.

1 Serving: Calories 135 (Calories from Fat 55); Fat 6g (Saturated 4g); Cholesterol 15mg; Sodium 360mg; Carbohydrate 22g (Dietary Fiber 4g); Protein 2g
% Daily Value: Vitamin A 100%; Vitamin C 10%; Calcium 2%; Iron 6%
Diet Exchanges: 1 Starch, 1 Vegetable, 1 Fat

Fold foil in half over vegetables.

Turn edges over twice on all 3 open sides to seal securely.

Grilled Double Cheese and Herb Bread

Prep: 10 min   Grill: 3 min

4 slices Italian bread, ½-inch thick

1 tablespoon chopped fresh or ½ teaspoon dried basil leaves

1 tablespoon chopped fresh or ½ teaspoon dried oregano leaves

¼ teaspoon garlic powder

½ cup shredded Colby or mild Cheddar cheese (2 ounces)

½ cup shredded Havarti cheese (2 ounces)

1. Heat coals or gas grill for direct heat. Spray both sides of each bread slice with cooking spray. Sprinkle one side with basil, oregano and garlic powder. Top with cheeses.

2. Cover and grill bread 4 to 6 inches from medium heat 2 to 3 minutes or until bread is toasted and cheese is melted.

4 servings.

1 Serving: Calories 185 (Calories from Fat 90); Fat 10g (Saturated 6g); Cholesterol 30mg; Sodium 350mg; Carbohydrate 15g (Dietary Fiber 1g); Protein 10g
% Daily Value: Vitamin A 6%; Vitamin C 0%; Calcium 16%; Iron 6%
Diet Exchanges: 1 Starch, 1 High-Fat Meat

BETTY'S TIPS

⊙ **Substitution**

Sourdough bread can be used instead of the Italian bread.

Use your favorite cheese combination in place of the Colby and Havarti.

Grilled Double Cheese and Herb Bread

One-Dish Wonders

Easy Entrées in a Single Pot

Picadillo Chicken Paella

Prep: 15 min   Bake: 1 hr 5 min

1   cup uncooked regular long-grain rice
½   pound smoked chorizo sausage, sliced
¼   cup raisins
1   can (14½ ounces) stewed tomatoes, undrained
1   can (14½ ounces) chicken broth
½   teaspoon ground turmeric
4   chicken legs, skin removed if desired
4   chicken thighs, skin removed if desired
¼   teaspoon seasoned salt
¼   teaspoon paprika
1   cup frozen green peas, thawed

1. Heat oven to 375°. Spray rectangular baking dish, 13 × 9 × 2 inches, with cooking spray.

2. Mix rice, sausage, raisins, tomatoes, broth and turmeric in baking dish. Arrange chicken on top; press into rice mixture. Sprinkle chicken with seasoned salt and paprika.

3. Cover and bake 30 minutes. Uncover and bake about 30 minutes longer or until liquid is absorbed and juice of chicken is no longer pink when centers of thickest pieces are cut. Stir in peas. Bake uncovered 5 minutes.

4 servings.

1 Serving: Calories 780 (Calories from Fat 340); Fat 38g (Saturated 13g); Cholesterol 150mg; Sodium 1660mg; Carbohydrate 61g (Dietary Fiber 4g); Protein 53g
% Daily Value: Vitamin A 10%; Vitamin C 12%; Calcium 8%; Iron 32%
Diet Exchanges: 4 Starch, 3 Medium-Fat Meat

BETTY'S TIPS

❂ Serve-With
This festive Spanish dish is a meal in itself. Complete the menu with crusty French bread and, for dessert, lemon sorbet.

Rosemary Lemon Roasted Turkey

Prep: 10 min   Bake: 4 hr   Stand: 15 min

6   sprigs rosemary
3   lemons, cut into quarters
12- to 14-   pound turkey
2   tablespoons vegetable oil
1   teaspoon garlic salt

1. Heat oven to 325°. Place rosemary and lemon quarters in cavity of turkey. Place turkey, breast side up, on rack in shallow roasting pan. Brush with oil. Sprinkle with garlic salt.

2. Bake uncovered 3 hours 30 minutes to 4 hours or until thermometer reads 180° and juice of turkey is no longer pink when center of thigh is cut. Let stand 15 minutes before serving.

12 to 15 servings.

1 Serving: Calories 385 (Calories from Fat 205); Fat 23g (Saturated 6g); Cholesterol 140mg; Sodium 170mg; Carbohydrate 0g (Dietary Fiber 0g); Protein 44g
% Daily Value: Vitamin A 14%; Vitamin C 0%; Calcium 4%; Iron 22%
Diet Exchanges: 6 Lean Meat, 1 Fat

BETTY'S TIPS

❂ Success Hint
To thaw the turkey, place turkey in original wrap in a baking pan (to collect liquid) in the refrigerator for 2 to 3 days.

❂ Special Touch
For a pretty presentation, garnish with fresh rosemary and sage leaves. Add lemon halves and lemon wedges, red grapes and whole cranberries to the platter.

Rosemary Lemon Roasted Turkey

Salsa Arroz con Pollo

Salsa Arroz con Pollo

Prep: 15 min   Bake: 1 hr 30 min

1   cup uncooked regular long-grain rice

1   cup frozen whole kernel corn

1   can (14½ ounces) chicken broth

1   can (14½ ounces) salsa-style diced tomatoes with green chilies, undrained

1   can (15 ounces) black beans, rinsed and drained

3   tablespoons Gold Medal all-purpose flour

1   teaspoon chili powder

½   teaspoon ground cumin

½   teaspoon salt

3- to 3½-   pound cut-up broiler-fryer chicken, skin removed if desired

1. Heat oven to 375°. Mix rice, corn, broth, tomatoes and beans in ungreased rectangular baking dish, 13 × 9 × 2 inches.

2. Mix flour, chili powder, cumin and salt in heavy-duty resealable plastic food-storage bag. Add chicken, 2 pieces at a time; seal bag and shake until chicken is evenly coated. Arrange chicken, meaty sides up, on rice mixture.

3. Cover and bake 1 hour 15 minutes. Uncover and bake 10 to 15 minutes longer or until liquid is absorbed and juice of chicken is no longer pink when centers of thickest pieces are cut.

6 servings.

1 Serving: Calories 490 (Calories from Fat 135); Fat 15g (Saturated 4g); Cholesterol 85mg; Sodium 970mg; Carbohydrate 57g (Dietary Fiber 7g); Protein 39g
% Daily Value: Vitamin A 10%; Vitamin C 12%; Calcium 10%; Iron 28%
Diet Exchanges: 3 Starch, 4 Lean Meat, 2 Vegetable

BETTY'S TIPS

✪ Success Hint

Using a resealable plastic bag for coating the chicken saves cleanup and makes evenly coating the chicken a breeze!

Quick

Szechuan Chicken and Pasta

Prep: 5 min   Cook: 25 min

1   pound boneless skinless chicken breasts, cut into ¾- to 1-inch pieces

1   small red onion, cut into thin wedges

2   cups water

1½   cups uncooked fusilli (corkscrew) pasta (5 ounces)

1   bag (1 pound 5 ounces) frozen Szechuan stir-fry mix with vegetables, Szechuan sauce and peanuts

1. Spray 12-inch nonstick skillet with cooking spray; heat over medium-high heat. Add chicken and onion; stir-fry 3 to 5 minutes or until chicken is light brown.

2. Stir in water; heat to boiling. Stir in pasta. Cook 8 to 10 minutes, stirring occasionally, until pasta is almost tender (do not drain).

3. Stir in packet of sauce mix from stir-fry mix until well blended. Stir in vegetables; reduce heat to medium. Cover and cook 8 to 9 minutes, stirring occasionally, until vegetables are crisp-tender. Sprinkle with peanuts from stir-fry mix.

4 servings.

1 Serving: Calories 380 (Calories from Fat 90); Fat 10g (Saturated 2g); Cholesterol 50mg; Sodium 620mg; Carbohydrate 49g (Dietary Fiber 7g); Protein 30g
% Daily Value: Vitamin A 18%; Vitamin C 38%; Calcium 8%; Iron 22%
Diet Exchanges: 3 Starch, 2 Lean Meat, 1 Vegetable

Savory Baked Chicken and Potato Dinner

Prep: 15 min   Bake: 40 min

4   boneless skinless chicken breast halves
(about 1¼ pounds)

¼   cup Dijon mustard

¾   cup Original or Reduced Fat Bisquick

1½   pounds small red potatoes, cut into fourths

1   medium bell pepper, cut into
½-inch pieces

1   medium onion, cut into 16 wedges

¼   cup grated Parmesan cheese

1   teaspoon paprika

1. Heat oven to 400°. Spray jelly roll pan,
15½ × 10½ × 1 inch, with cooking spray.

2. Brush chicken with 2 tablespoons of the mustard,
then coat with Bisquick. Place 1 chicken breast half in
each corner of pan. Place potatoes, bell pepper and
onion in center of pan; brush vegetables with remaining 2 tablespoons mustard. Spray chicken and
vegetables with cooking spray; sprinkle evenly with
cheese and paprika.

3. Bake uncovered 35 to 40 minutes, stirring vegetables
after 20 minutes, until potatoes are tender and juice
of chicken is no longer pink when centers of thickest
pieces are cut.

4 servings.

1 Serving: Calories 375 (Calories from Fat 55); Fat 6g (Saturated 2g);
Cholesterol 60mg; Sodium 510mg; Carbohydrate 54g (Dietary Fiber 5g);
Protein 31g
% Daily Value: Vitamin A 14%; Vitamin C 46%; Calcium 6%; Iron 24%
Diet Exchanges: 3 Starch, 2 Lean Meat, 2 Vegetable

BETTY'S TIPS

✿ Substitution

Regular yellow mustard can be used if you don't have Dijon
on hand. Or use a favorite flavored mustard of your choice.

✿ Serve-With

This oven meal is almost complete by itself. Add a bagged
salad mix, your family's favorite rolls and, for dessert, serve
warm Microwave Apple Crisp (page 281).

Savory Baked Chicken and Potato Dinner

Swiss Steak and Gravy

Prep: 10 min   Cook: 8 hr

- 6 beef cubed steaks (8 ounces each)
- ½ teaspoon salt
- ½ teaspoon pepper
- 1 small onion, chopped (¼ cup)
- 1 jar (6 ounces) sliced mushrooms, undrained
- 2 cans (10¾ ounces each) condensed golden mushroom soup

1. Sprinkle beef with salt and pepper. Place beef in 3½- to 4-quart slow cooker, sprinkling onion and mushrooms with liquid between layers of beef. Pour soup over beef.

2. Cover and cook on low heat setting 7 to 8 hours or until beef is tender.

6 servings.

1 Serving: Calories 330 (Calories from Fat 115); Fat 13g (Saturated 4g); Cholesterol 115mg; Sodium 1100mg; Carbohydrate 10g (Dietary Fiber 1g); Protein 44g
% Daily Value: Vitamin A 0%; Vitamin C 0%; Calcium 6%; Iron 24%
Diet Exchanges: ½ Starch, 6 Very Lean Meat, 2 Fat

BETTY'S TIPS

✪ Substitution
Two cups sliced fresh mushrooms can be used instead of the mushrooms in the jar. No additional liquid is needed.

✪ Variation
You can add 2 cups baby-cut carrots to this Swiss Steak. Place the carrots in the bottom of the slow cooker.

Easy Sloppy Joe Bake

Prep: 15 min   Bake: 30 min

- 1 pound ground beef
- 1 medium onion, chopped (½ cup)
- 1 can (15½ ounces) original sloppy joe sauce
- 1 cup shredded Cheddar cheese (4 ounces)
- 1 cup Original Bisquick
- ½ cup milk
- 1 egg

1. Heat oven to 400°. Cook beef and onion in oven-proof 10-inch skillet over medium heat, stirring occasionally, until beef is brown; drain. Stir in sloppy joe sauce. Sprinkle with cheese.

2. Stir remaining ingredients until blended. Pour over beef mixture.

3. Bake uncovered about 30 minutes or until golden brown.

6 servings.

1 Serving: Calories 375 (Calories from Fat 205); Fat 23g (Saturated 10g); Cholesterol 100mg; Sodium 920mg; Carbohydrate 20g (Dietary Fiber 1g); Protein 23g
% Daily Value: Vitamin A 10%; Vitamin C 8%; Calcium 18%; Iron 14%
Diet Exchanges: 1 Starch, 3 Medium-Fat Meat, 1½ Fat

BETTY'S TIPS

✪ Substitution
For a change of pace, use 1 pound of bulk pork sausage or ground chicken or turkey instead of the ground beef.

✪ Time-Saver
Use ½ cup frozen chopped onion or 2 tablespoons instant minced onion instead of the fresh onion.

✪ Special Touch
Serve this easy supper with slices of crisp, juicy apples.

Orange Teriyaki Beef with Noodles

Orange Teriyaki Beef with Noodles

Prep: 5 min   Cook: 15 min

1   pound beef boneless sirloin, cut into thin strips
1   can (14½ ounces) beef broth
¼   cup teriyaki stir-fry sauce
2   tablespoons orange marmalade
    Dash of ground red pepper (cayenne)
1½ cups snap pea pods
1½ cups uncooked fine egg noodles (3 ounces)

1. Spray 12-inch skillet with cooking spray; heat over medium-high heat. Cook beef in skillet 2 to 4 minutes, stirring occasionally, until brown. Remove beef from skillet; keep warm.

2. Add broth, stir-fry sauce, marmalade and red pepper to skillet. Heat to boiling. Stir in pea pods and noodles; reduce heat to medium. Cover and cook about 5 minutes or until noodles are tender.

3. Stir in beef. Cook uncovered 2 to 3 minutes or until sauce is slightly thickened.

4 servings.

1 Serving: Calories 230 (Calories from Fat 35); Fat 4g (Saturated 1g); Cholesterol 65mg; Sodium 1210mg; Carbohydrate 24g (Dietary Fiber 1g); Protein 25g
% Daily Value: Vitamin A 0%; Vitamin C 10%; Calcium 2%; Iron 18%
Diet Exchanges: 1 Starch, 3 Very Lean Meat, 2 Vegetable

BETTY'S TIPS

❂ **Serve-With**
Garnish this dish with orange slices and chopped fresh chives. For a great salad, pick up a bag of prewashed spinach and toss with mandarin orange segments. Top it off with a sweet-and-sour dressing and chopped green onions.

❂ **Did You Know?**
A variety of teriyaki sauces are available in the Asian-foods section of the grocery store. Some are thick and some are a bit thinner, so you may want to experiment to find the one you like best.

Curried Coconut Beef with Winter Vegetables

Prep: 25 min   Bake: 1 hr 30 min

1   tablespoon vegetable oil
2   pounds beef stew meat
1   large onion, chopped (1 cup)
2   cloves garlic, finely chopped
1   can (14 ounces) coconut milk (not cream of coconut)
2   tablespoons lemon juice
1½ tablespoons curry powder
1   tablespoon packed brown sugar
3   medium carrots, chopped (1½ cups)
2   medium parsnips, peeled and chopped (1 cup)
1   medium sweet potato, peeled and chopped (1½ cups)
1   teaspoon salt
¼   teaspoon pepper
    Chopped fresh cilantro, if desired

1. Heat oven to 350°. Heat oil in 4-quart ovenproof Dutch oven over medium-high heat. Cook beef in oil, stirring occasionally, until brown.

2. Stir in onion and garlic. Cook 2 to 3 minutes, stirring occasionally, until onion is crisp-tender. Stir in coconut milk, lemon juice, curry powder and brown sugar. Cover and place in oven; bake about 1 hour or until beef is tender.

3. Stir in remaining ingredients except cilantro. Cover and bake about 30 minutes or until vegetables are tender. Garnish with cilantro.

6 servings.

1 Serving: Calories 495 (Calories from Fat 260); Fat 29g (Saturated 16g); Cholesterol 80mg; Sodium 510mg; Carbohydrate 35g (Dietary Fiber 7g); Protein 30g
% Daily Value: Vitamin A 100%; Vitamin C 20%; Calcium 6%; Iron 24%
Diet Exchanges: 2 Starch, 3 High-Fat Meat, 1 Vegetable

BETTY'S TIPS

❂ **Serve-With**
For a cozy winter supper for family or friends, serve with a crisp green salad, warm dinner rolls and hot coffee, cider or tea.

Roasted Beef Tenderloin

Prep: 15 min   Bake: 50 min   Stand: 15 min

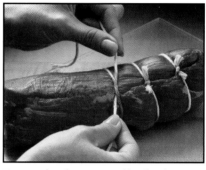

Tie turned-under portion of beef with string at about 1½-inch intervals.

1	beef tenderloin (about 2½ pounds)
1	tablespoon olive or vegetable oil
½	teaspoon coarsely ground pepper
½	teaspoon dried marjoram leaves
¼	teaspoon coarse kosher salt, coarse sea salt or regular salt

1. Heat oven to 425°.

2. Turn small end of beef under about 6 inches. Tie turned-under portion of beef with string at about 1½-inch intervals. Place beef on rack in shallow roasting pan. Brush with oil. Sprinkle with pepper, marjoram and salt. Insert meat thermometer so tip is in thickest part of beef.

3. Bake uncovered 40 to 50 minutes or until thermometer reads at least 140°. Cover beef with tent of aluminum foil and let stand about 15 minutes or until thermometer reads 145°. (Temperature will continue to rise about 5°, and beef will be easier to carve.) Remove string from beef before carving.

6 servings.

1 Serving: Calories 230 (Calories from Fat 110); Fat 12g (Saturated 4g); Cholesterol 80mg; Sodium 170mg; Carbohydrate 0g (Dietary Fiber 0g); Protein 30g
% Daily Value: Vitamin A 0%; Vitamin C 0%; Calcium 0%; Iron 14%
Diet Exchanges: 4 Lean Meat

Ham and Broccoli Cheese Pot Pie

Prep: 10 min   Bake: 35 min

1 bag (16 ounces) frozen broccoli cuts, thawed and drained
2 cups cut-up fully cooked ham
2 cans (11 ounces each) condensed Cheddar cheese soup
¼ cup milk
2 cups Original Bisquick
1 cup milk
2 tablespoons yellow mustard
2 eggs

1. Heat oven to 400°. Mix broccoli, ham, soup and ¼ cup milk in ungreased rectangular baking dish, 13 × 9 × 2 inches.

2. Stir remaining ingredients until blended. Pour over ham mixture.

3. Bake uncovered about 35 minutes or until crust is golden brown.

6 servings.

1 Serving: Calories 425 (Calories from Fat 190); Fat 21g (Saturated 8g); Cholesterol 115mg; Sodium 2280mg; Carbohydrate 39g (Dietary Fiber 3g); Protein 23g
% Daily Value: Vitamin A 42%; Vitamin C 32%; Calcium 26%; Iron 16%
Diet Exchanges: 2 Starch, 2 High-Fat Meat, 2 Vegetable

BETTY'S TIPS

✿ Substitution
Two cups of cut-up cooked chicken or turkey would also work well. Keep this recipe in mind for using up leftovers from the Thanksgiving turkey!

✿ Serve-With
Purchase cut-up deli fruits for a salad, and let everyone enjoy top-your-own-ice-cream sundaes for dessert.

Quick

Stove-Top Lasagna

Prep: 10 min   Cook: 18 min

1 pound bulk Italian sausage
1 medium onion, chopped (½ cup)
1 medium green bell pepper, chopped (1 cup)
3 cups uncooked mafalda (mini-lasagna noodle) pasta (6 ounces)
2½ cups water
½ teaspoon Italian seasoning
1 jar (26 to 30 ounces) tomato pasta sauce (any variety)
1 jar (4½ ounces) sliced mushrooms, drained

1. Cook sausage, onion and bell pepper in 4-quart Dutch oven over medium-high heat, stirring occasionally, until sausage is no longer pink; drain.

2. Stir in remaining ingredients. Heat to boiling, stirring occasionally; reduce heat. Simmer uncovered 10 to 12 minutes or until pasta is tender.

6 servings.

1 Serving: Calories 460 (Calories from Fat 180); Fat 20g (Saturated 6g); Cholesterol 45mg; Sodium 1370mg; Carbohydrate 56g (Dietary Fiber 4g); Protein 18g
% Daily Value: Vitamin A 26%; Vitamin C 18%; Calcium 6%; Iron 18%
Diet Exchanges: 3 Starch, 1 High-Fat Meat, 2 Vegetable, 2 Fat

BETTY'S TIPS

✿ Substitution
If you don't have mafalda pasta, you can use pieces of broken regular lasagna noodles instead.

✿ Variation
For a popular pizza variation, substitute 2 cans (15 ounces each) pizza sauce for the pasta sauce and add ½ cup diced pepperoni.

Lazy-Day Lasagna

Prep: 15 min   Bake: 1 hr   Stand: 15 min

1   container (15 ounces) ricotta cheese
½   cup grated Parmesan cheese
2   tablespoons chopped fresh parsley
1   tablespoon chopped fresh or 1½ teaspoons dried oregano leaves
2   jars (28 ounces each) tomato pasta sauce
12   uncooked lasagna noodles (12 ounces)
2   cups shredded mozzarella cheese (8 ounces)
¼   cup grated Parmesan cheese
    Additional shredded mozzarella cheese, if desired

1. Heat oven to 350°. Mix ricotta cheese, ½ cup Parmesan cheese, the parsley and oregano.

2. Spread 2 cups of the pasta sauce in ungreased rectangular pan, 13 × 9 × 2 inches. Top with 4 uncooked noodles; spread ricotta mixture over noodles. Spread with 2 cups pasta sauce; top with 4 noodles. Repeat with 2 cups pasta sauce and 4 noodles. Sprinkle with 2 cups mozzarella cheese. Spread with remaining pasta sauce. Sprinkle with ¼ cup Parmesan cheese.

3. Cover and bake 30 minutes. Uncover and bake about 30 minutes longer or until hot in center. Sprinkle with additional mozzarella cheese. Let stand 15 minutes before cutting.

8 servings.

1 Serving: Calories 500 (Calories from Fat 160); Fat 19g (Saturated 8g); Cholesterol 35mg; Sodium 1340mg; Carbohydrate 64g (Dietary Fiber 4g); Protein 24g
% Daily Value: Vitamin A 26%; Vitamin C 26%; Calcium 50%; Iron 16%
Diet Exchanges: 4 Starch, 1½ Medium-Fat Meat, 1 Vegetable, 1 Fat

BETTY'S TIPS

☺ **Time-Saver**
To prepare lasagna ahead of time, cover unbaked lasagna tightly with aluminum foil and refrigerate up to 24 hours. About 1½ hours before serving, heat oven to 350°. Bake covered 45 minutes. Uncover and bake 15 to 20 minutes longer or until hot and bubbly. Sprinkle with additional mozzarella cheese. Let stand 15 minutes before cutting.

Fish Florentine

Prep: 10 min   Bake: 30 min

¾   pound mild-flavored fish fillets, about ½ inch thick
1   cup milk
1   cup shredded Cheddar cheese (4 ounces)
¾   cup Original or Reduced Fat Bisquick
1   teaspoon lemon juice
⅛   teaspoon pepper
2   eggs
1   small onion, chopped (¼ cup)
1   package (10 ounces) frozen chopped spinach, thawed and squeezed to drain
    Lemon wedges, if desired

1. Heat oven to 400°. Grease rectangular baking dish, 11 × 7 × 1½ inches. Place fish in single layer in baking dish. Stir together remaining ingredients except lemon wedges; spread over fish to edge of baking dish.

2. Bake uncovered about 30 minutes or until light brown. Serve with lemon wedges.

6 servings.

1 Serving: Calories 245 (Calories from Fat 110); Fat 12g (Saturated 6g); Cholesterol 125mg; Sodium 440mg; Carbohydrate 14g (Dietary Fiber 1g); Protein 21g
% Daily Value: Vitamin A 32%; Vitamin C 4%; Calcium 24%; Iron 8%
Diet Exchanges: ½ Starch, 2½ Lean Meat, 1 Vegetable, 1 Fat

BETTY'S TIPS

☺ **Success Hint**
Good choices of mild-flavored fish fillets include cod, flounder, haddock, halibut, orange roughy and sole.

☺ **Serve-With**
For a quick cheese sauce, heat a can of condensed Cheddar cheese soup with 1 soup can of milk. Stir in sliced green onions for added color and flavor.

Slow Cooker Christmas Chili

Slow Cooker Christmas Chili

Prep: 15 min   Cook: 7 hr 15 min

1   pound beef boneless round steak, cut into ½-inch pieces
2   medium stalks celery, cut into ½-inch pieces (1 cup)
1   large onion, chopped (1 cup)
2   cans (14½ ounces each) diced tomatoes, undrained
1   can (15 ounces) tomato sauce
3   teaspoons chili powder
2   teaspoons ground cumin
¼   teaspoon dried oregano leaves
¼   teaspoon ground cinnamon
1   medium bell pepper, cut into 1-inch pieces (1 cup)
1   can (15 to 16 ounces) kidney beans, rinsed and drained

1. Mix all ingredients except bell pepper and beans in 3½- to 4-quart slow cooker.

2. Cover and cook on low heat setting 6 to 7 hours or until beef and vegetables are tender.

3. Stir in bell pepper and beans. Cook uncovered on high heat setting about 15 minutes or until slightly thickened.

8 servings.

1 Serving: Calories 170 (Calories from Fat 25); Fat 3g (Saturated 1g); Cholesterol 30mg; Sodium 640mg; Carbohydrate 24g (Dietary Fiber 6g); Protein 18g
% Daily Value: Vitamin A 16%; Vitamin C 30%; Calcium 6%; Iron 22%
Diet Exchanges: 1 Starch, 1 Lean Meat, 2 Vegetable

BETTY'S TIPS

✿ Substitution
You can use a 28-ounce can of whole tomatoes instead of the diced tomatoes. Use a spoon to break up the whole tomatoes in the slow cooker.

✿ Special Touch
Add some zip to your serving bowls by brushing the edges of the bowls with shortening or butter, then sprinkling with chili powder.

White Chicken Chili

Prep: 15 min   Cook: 5 hr 20 min

6   skinless chicken thighs (1½ pounds)
1   large onion, chopped (1 cup)
2   cloves garlic, finely chopped
1   can (14½ ounces) chicken broth
1   teaspoon ground cumin
1   teaspoon dried oregano leaves
½   teaspoon salt
¼   teaspoon red pepper sauce
2   cans (15 to 16 ounces each) great Northern beans, rinsed and drained
1   can (15 ounces) white shoepeg corn, drained
3   tablespoons lime juice
2   tablespoons chopped fresh cilantro

1. Remove excess fat from chicken. Mix onion, garlic, broth, cumin, oregano, salt and pepper sauce in 3½- to 6-quart slow cooker. Add chicken.

2. Cover and cook on low heat setting 4 to 5 hours or until chicken is tender.

3. Remove chicken from slow cooker. Use 2 forks to remove bones and shred chicken into pieces. Discard bones; return chicken to slow cooker. Stir in beans, corn, lime juice and cilantro. Cover and cook on low heat setting 15 to 20 minutes or until beans and corn are hot.

8 servings.

1 Serving: Calories 265 (Calories from Fat 45); Fat 5g (Saturated 2g); Cholesterol 30mg; Sodium 540mg; Carbohydrate 39g (Dietary Fiber 8g); Protein 24g
% Daily Value: Vitamin A 0%; Vitamin C 6%; Calcium 12%; Iron 30%
Diet Exchanges: 2½ Starch, 2 Very Lean Meat

BETTY'S TIPS

✿ Substitution
If you can't find white shoepeg corn, you can use regular whole kernel corn.

✿ Success Hint
If you like chili with a little kick, increase the red pepper sauce to ½ teaspoon.

Southwest Chicken Soup

Prep: 15 min   Cook: 8 hr 30 min

1   pound boneless skinless chicken thighs
2   medium sweet potatoes, peeled and cut into 1-inch pieces (2 cups)
1   large onion, chopped (1 cup)
2   cans (14½ ounces each) salsa-style diced tomatoes with green chilies, undrained
1   can (14½ ounces) chicken broth
1   teaspoon dried oregano leaves
½   teaspoon ground cumin
1   cup frozen whole kernel corn
½   cup chopped green bell pepper
2   tablespoons chopped fresh cilantro

1. Remove fat from chicken. Cut chicken into 1-inch pieces. Mix chicken, sweet potatoes, onion, tomatoes, broth, oregano and cumin in 3½- to 4-quart slow cooker.

2. Cover and cook on low heat setting 7 to 8 hours. Stir in corn and bell pepper. Cover and cook on high heat setting about 30 minutes or until chicken is no longer pink in center and vegetables are tender.

3. Spoon soup into individual bowls. Sprinkle with cilantro.

6 servings.

1 Serving: Calories 225 (Calories from Fat 65); Fat 7g (Saturated 2g); Cholesterol 45mg; Sodium 560mg; Carbohydrate 24g (Dietary Fiber 4g); Protein 20g
% Daily Value: Vitamin A 90%; Vitamin C 34%; Calcium 8%; Iron 14%
Diet Exchanges: 1½ Starch, 2 Lean Meat

BETTY'S TIPS

⚙ **Serve-With**
Serve this hearty soup with a mixed-greens salad and warm corn bread sticks.

Low Fat

Easy Multi-Bean Soup

Prep: 10 min   Cook: 10 hr 15 min

5   cans (14½ ounces each) chicken or vegetable broth
1   package (20 ounces) 15- or 16-dried bean soup mix, sorted and rinsed
4   medium carrots, chopped (2 cups)
3   medium stalks celery, chopped (1½ cups)
1   large onion, chopped (1 cup)
2   tablespoons tomato paste
1   teaspoon salt
1   teaspoon Italian seasoning
½   teaspoon pepper
1   can (14½ ounces) diced tomatoes, undrained

1. Mix all ingredients except tomatoes in 5- to 6-quart slow cooker.

2. Cover and cook on low heat setting 8 to 10 hours or until beans are tender.

3. Stir in tomatoes. Cover and cook on high heat setting about 15 minutes or until hot.

12 servings.

1 Serving: Calories 170 (Calories from Fat 10); Fat 1g (Saturated 0g); Cholesterol 0mg; Sodium 1040mg; Carbohydrate 37g (Dietary Fiber 9g); Protein 12g
% Daily Value: Vitamin A 46%; Vitamin C 8%; Calcium 14%; Iron 26%
Diet Exchanges: 2 Starch, 1 Vegetable

BETTY'S TIPS

⚙ **Substitution**
You can also use small amounts of various leftover dried beans you may have in your cupboard. Mix them together to make 2¼ cups of beans, and use them instead of purchasing a package of bean soup mix.

You can use either chicken or vegetable broth to prepare this great-tasting soup. If you are vegetarian, go ahead and use the vegetable broth. But if you're simply looking for a meatless soup, we prefer the richer flavor of chicken broth.

Mexican Minestrone

Prep: 10 min   Cook: 8 hr

2 cans (15 ounces each) black beans, rinsed and drained

2 cans (14½ ounces each) Mexican-style stewed tomatoes, undrained

1 can (14½ ounces) chicken broth

1 can (12 ounces) vacuum-packed whole kernel corn, undrained

1 or 2 medium red potatoes, cut into ½-inch pieces

1 cup salsa

1 cup cut-up green beans

Mix all ingredients in 3½- to 6-quart slow cooker. Cover and cook on low heat setting 6 to 8 hours or until vegetables are tender.

8 to 10 servings.

1 Serving: Calories 148 (Calories from Fat 9); Fat 1g (Saturated 0g); Cholesterol 0mg; Sodium 835mg; Carbohydrate 30g (Dietary Fiber 8g); Protein 8g
% Daily Value: Vitamin A 10%; Vitamin C 38%; Calcium 6%; Iron 13%
Diet Exchanges: 1 Starch, 1 Vegetable

BETTY'S TIPS

⊘ **Special Touch**
Surround individual servings with baked tortilla chips to add some contrasting crunch.

If you're serving a crowd of cheese lovers, try sprinkling a little shredded sharp Cheddar or Monterey Jack over each serving.

Mexican Minestrone

Cioppino

Prep: 20 min   Cook: 4 hr 45 min

- 2 large onions, chopped (2 cups)
- 2 medium stalks celery, finely chopped
- 5 cloves garlic, finely chopped
- 1 can (28 ounces) diced tomatoes, undrained
- 1 bottle (8 ounces) clam juice
- 1 can (6 ounces) tomato paste
- ½ cup dry white wine or water
- 1 tablespoon red wine vinegar
- 1 tablespoon olive or vegetable oil
- 2½ teaspoons Italian seasoning
- ¼ teaspoon sugar
- ¼ teaspoon crushed red pepper
- 1 dried bay leaf
- 1 pound firm-fleshed white fish, cut into 1-inch pieces
- 12 ounces uncooked medium shrimp, peeled and deveined
- 1 can (6½ ounces) chopped clams with juice, undrained
- 1 can (6 ounces) crabmeat, drained
- ¼ cup chopped fresh parsley

1. Mix all ingredients except fish, shrimp, clams, crabmeat and parsley in 5- to 6-quart slow cooker.

2. Cover and cook on high heat setting 3 to 4 hours or until vegetables are tender.

3. Stir in fish, shrimp, clams and crabmeat. Cover and cook on low heat setting 30 to 45 minutes or until fish flakes easily with fork. Remove bay leaf. Stir in parsley.

8 servings.

1 Serving: Calories 190 (Calories from Fat 35); Fat 4g (Saturated 1g); Cholesterol 100mg; Sodium 570mg; Carbohydrate 15g (Dietary Fiber 3g); Protein 26g
% Daily Value: Vitamin A 18%; Vitamin C 30%; Calcium 12%; Iron 50%
Diet Exchanges: 3 Very Lean Meat, 3 Vegetable

BETTY'S TIPS

✤ Serve-With
Be sure to serve plenty of crusty bread with this fish stew so everyone can sop up every last drop of the wonderful broth in the bottom of the bowl.

Cioppino

Low Fat

Split Pea and Yam Soup

Prep: 10 min   Cook: 9 hr

- 7   cups water
- ¾   teaspoon salt
- ½   teaspoon Italian seasoning
- ¼   teaspoon pepper
- 2   small yams (¾ pound), peeled and cut into ½-inch pieces
- 1   medium potato, peeled and cut into ½-inch pieces (1 cup)
- 1   medium onion, finely chopped (½ cup)
- 1   package (16 ounces) dried yellow split peas (2¼ cups)
- 1   package (6 ounces) sliced Canadian-style bacon, coarsely chopped

1. Mix all ingredients in 3½- to 4-quart slow cooker.

2. Cover and cook on low heat setting 8 to 9 hours or until split peas are tender. Stir well before serving.

8 servings.

1 Serving: Calories 260 (Calories from Fat 20); Fat 2g (Saturated 1g); Cholesterol 10mg; Sodium 490mg; Carbohydrate 38g (Dietary Fiber 13g); Protein 18g
% Daily Value: Vitamin A 32%; Vitamin C 6%; Calcium 2%; Iron 12%
Diet Exchanges: 2 Starch, 1 Lean Meat, 2 Vegetable

BETTY'S TIPS

❂ Substitution

For a tasty meatless soup, use vegetable or chicken broth instead of the water and omit the Canadian-style bacon.

Wild Rice Soup

Prep: 20 min   Cook: 20 min

- 2   tablespoons margarine or butter
- 2   medium stalks celery, sliced (1 cup)
- 1   medium carrot, coarsely shredded (1 cup)
- 1   medium onion, chopped (½ cup)
- 1   small green bell pepper, chopped (½ cup)
- ¼   cup Original or Reduced Fat Bisquick
- ½   teaspoon salt
- ¼   teaspoon pepper
- 1   cup water
- 1   can (10½ ounces) condensed chicken broth
- 1½ cups cooked wild rice
- 1   cup half-and-half
- ⅓   cup slivered almonds, toasted
- ¼   cup chopped fresh parsley

1. Melt margarine in 3-quart saucepan over medium-high heat. Cook celery, carrot, onion and bell pepper in margarine about 4 minutes, stirring occasionally, until tender.

2. Stir in Bisquick, salt and pepper. Stir in water, broth and wild rice. Heat to boiling, stirring frequently; reduce heat to low. Cover and simmer 15 minutes, stirring occasionally.

3. Stir in half-and-half, almonds and parsley. Heat just until hot (do not boil).

5 servings.

1 Serving: Calories 260 (Calories from Fat 145); Fat 16g (Saturated 5g); Cholesterol 20mg; Sodium 700mg; Carbohydrate 24g (Dietary Fiber 3g); Protein 8g
% Daily Value: Vitamin A 32%; Vitamin C 24%; Calcium 10%; Iron 8%
Diet Exchanges: 1 Starch, 2 Vegetable, 3 Fat

BETTY'S TIPS

❂ Success Hint

To toast almonds, cook in ungreased heavy skillet over medium-low heat 5 to 7 minutes, stirring frequently until browning begins, then stirring constantly until golden brown.

Celebrate!

Whether you're gearing up for a party, planning a holiday meal, or hosting a family get-together, turn to Betty's best menus to help you make every occasion special. All of the menus include ideas for side dishes, beverages, or snacks that you can easily purchase or make without a recipe.

New Year's Eve

Easy Holiday Paella (page 211)
Curried Coconut Beef with Winter Vegetables (page 165)
Seasoned popcorn
Brownie Torte with Raspberry Sauce (page 262)
White Chocolate Macadamia Nut Cookies (page 247)
Hot cocoa with marshmallows
Your favorite sparkling cider or champagne

Super Bowl Party

Stromboli Hero (page 39)
Fajita Pizza (page 52)
Baked tortilla chips with guacamole dip
Brownie Butterscotch Squares (page 241)
On-the-Trail Monster Cookies (page 248)
Soda and beer

Valentine's Day

Swiss Steak and Gravy (page 163)
Baked potatoes with sour cream and chives
Mixed greens tossed with your favorite vinaigrette
White Chocolate Cheesecake (page 261)
Your favorite sparkling cider or wine

Passover

Salmon with Cranberry Pistachio Sauce (page 212)
Warm Caramelized Vegetables (page 224)
Steamed asparagus
Double Chocolate Meringues (page 277)
Red wine and grape juice

Easter

Easy Glazed Baked Ham (page 198)
Spring Greens Fruit Salad (page 60)
Warm Caramelized Vegetables (page 224)
Bread Machine Dinner Rolls (page 236)
Key Lime Coconut Angel Cake (page 255)
Rainbow Egg Cookies (page 244)
Your favorite wine or cider

Mother's Day

Rio Grande Melon Salad (page 20)
Mostaccioli with Roasted Tomato
and Garlic (page 120)
Layered Gazpacho Salad (page 61)
Strawberry Rhubarb Trifle (page 283)
Freshly brewed iced tea
with lemon

Father's Day

Texas T-Bones (page 139)
Garden Vegetable Medley (page 154)
Baked beans
Grilled Double Cheese and Herb Bread (page 156)
Caramelized Peach and Raspberry Shortcakes
(page 258)
Your favorite fruit punch

Family Reunion

Spice-Rubbed Grilled Chicken (page 128)
Strip Steaks with Chipotle Peach Glaze (page 184)
Creamy Potato Salad (page 66)
Corn with Garlic Cilantro Butter (page 217)
Pesto-Stuffed Tomatoes (page 220)
S'Mores Mousse Dessert (page 274)
Triple Chocolate Torte (page 267)
Birch beer or lemonade

4th of July

Pork Ribs with Smoky Barbecue Sauce (page 144)
Mediterranean Grilled Potato Salad (page 65)
Easy Grilled Vegetables (page 223)
Savory Corn on a Stick (page 218)
Strawberry Margarita Cake (page 259)
Watermelon Wedges with Mango Berry Salsa (page 21)
Your favorite punch

Bridal Shower

Lime Mint Melon Salad (page 22)
Pesto Ravioli with Chicken (page 105)
Garden Couscous Salad (page 227)
Lemon Raspberry Cake (page 252)
Cranberry Herbal Tea Granita (page 286)
Mimosas or orange juice

End of Summer

Barbecued Chicken Nachos (page 134)

Grilled Southwestern Pork Chops (page 145)

Vegetable Kabobs with Mexican Cheese Sauce (page 47)

Angel Berry Summer Pudding (page 285)

Ice-cold lemonade

Back-to-School Lunch

Cheesy Roast Beef Wraps (page 37)

Mini pretzels

Baby carrots

Chocolate Chip Pecan Pie Bars (page 241)

Fruit juice box

Halloween

Easy Multi-Bean Soup (page 172)

Cranberry Whole Wheat Bread (page 5)

Grandma's Gingersnaps (page 247)

Praline Pumpkin Dessert (page 281)

Hot apple cider with cinnamon sticks

Thanksgiving

Rosemary Lemon Roasted Turkey (page 158)

Cranberry Stuffing (page 231)

Caesar Green Beans (page 217)

Sour Cream and Chive Rolls (page 235)

Cranberry Orange Biscotti (page 243)

Irish coffee or your favorite herbal tea

Christmas

Roasted Beef Tenderloin (page 166)

Whipped Maple Sweet Potatoes (page 231)

Italian Christmas Veggies (page 225)

Garlic Bread Wreath (page 236)

Caramel Creme Brownie Trifle (page 282)

Eggnog Cream Puffs (page 278)

Homemade or purchased eggnog

Hanukkah

Brisket with Cranberry Gravy (page 190)

Potato latkes with applesauce

Steamed green beans

Hot Fruit Compote (page 286)

Bowl of walnuts

Rugalach

Red wine or seltzer

Come for Dessert

Pumpkin Hazelnut Torte (page 268)

Chocolate Swirl Coffee Cake (page 11)

Pistachio Cranberry Fudge (page 250)

Your favorite gourmet coffee
with whipped cream

Birthday Party for Kids

Beef and Provolone Pinwheels (page 38)

Trail mix of mini pretzels, peanuts, raisins, and cereal squares

Lemonade Party Cake (page 255)

Bear Cookie Pops (page 242)

Vanilla milkshakes

Sunday Brunch

Key West Fruit Salad (page 20)

Smoked Salmon and Egg Wraps (page 14)

Sweet Potato Caramel Twist Coffee Cake (page 8)

Orange Almond Mini-Muffins (page 2)

Punch of half orange juice, half cranberry juice

Your favorite gourmet coffee

The Main Event

Savory Main Dishes That Aim to Impress

Strip Steaks with Chipotle Peach Glaze

Prep: 10 min   Grill: 10 min

½ cup peach preserves

¼ cup lime juice

1 chipotle chili in adobo sauce (from 7-ounce can), seeded and chopped

1 teaspoon adobo sauce (from can of chilies)

2 tablespoons chopped fresh cilantro

8 beef boneless strip steaks (about 6 ounces each)

1 teaspoon garlic pepper

½ teaspoon ground cumin

½ teaspoon salt

4 peaches, cut in half and pitted, if desired
Cilantro sprigs

1. Heat coals or gas grill for direct heat. Mix preserves, lime juice, chili and adobo sauce in 1-quart saucepan. Heat over low heat, stirring occasionally, until preserves are melted. Stir in chopped cilantro; set aside. Sprinkle each beef steak with garlic pepper, cumin and salt.

2. Cover and grill beef 4 to 6 inches from medium heat 8 to 10 minutes for medium doneness, turning once or twice and brushing with preserves mixture during last 2 minutes of grilling. Add peach halves to grill for last 2 to 3 minutes of grilling just until heated.

3. Heat any remaining preserves mixture to boiling; boil and stir 1 minute. Serve with steaks and peaches. Garnish with cilantro sprigs.

8 servings.

1 Serving: Calories 315 (Calories from Fat 110); Fat 12g (Saturated 5g); Cholesterol 95mg; Sodium 250mg; Carbohydrate 14g (Dietary Fiber 0g); Protein 37g
% Daily Value: Vitamin A 0%; Vitamin C 6%; Calcium 2%; Iron 8%
Diet Exchanges: 5 Lean Meat, 1 Fruit

BETTY'S TIPS

✪ **Substitution**
You can use ½ teaspoon garlic powder and ½ teaspoon coarsely ground black pepper instead of the 1 teaspoon garlic pepper.

✪ **Success Hint**
Brush the grill rack with vegetable oil or spray it with cooking spray before heating the grill. This prevents food from sticking and makes cleaning the grill easier (and spraying the cold grill is safer).

Strip Steaks with Chipotle Peach Glaze

Chili Diablo Steak and Pasta

Chili Diablo Steak and Pasta

Prep: 20 min   Cook: 20 min   Grill: 12 min

- 2 slices bacon, cut into ½-inch pieces
- 1 medium onion, chopped (½ cup)
- 1 small green bell pepper, chopped (½ cup)
- 1 chipotle chili in adobo sauce (from 7-ounce can), seeded and chopped
- 1 teaspoon adobo sauce (from can of chilies)
- ¾ cup chili sauce
- ¾ cup beef broth
- 1 can (15 ounces) black beans, rinsed and drained
- 6 cups uncooked mafalda (mini-lasagna noodle) pasta (12 ounces)
- 1½- pound beef boneless top sirloin steak, about 1 inch thick
- ½ teaspoon garlic pepper
- ½ teaspoon salt
- ¼ teaspoon chili powder
- 1 avocado, peeled, pitted and sliced
- 2 tablespoons fresh cilantro leaves, if desired

1. Cook bacon in 10-inch nonstick skillet over medium heat, stirring occasionally, until crisp. Stir in onion and bell pepper. Cook 2 to 3 minutes, stirring occasionally, until crisp-tender. Stir in chipotle chili and adobo sauce. Cook and stir 1 minute. Stir in chili sauce and broth. Heat to boiling; reduce heat. Simmer 5 minutes, stirring occasionally. Stir in beans; heat through.

2. Cook and drain pasta as directed on package.

3. While pasta is cooking, heat coals or gas grill for direct heat. Sprinkle beef with garlic pepper, salt and chili powder. Grill beef 4 to 6 inches from medium heat 8 to 12 minutes for medium doneness, turning once.

4. To serve, toss pasta with about 1 cup sauce. Cut beef across grain into thin slices; arrange over pasta mixture. Drizzle and serve with remaining sauce. Garnish with avocado and cilantro.

6 servings.

1 Serving: Calories 525 (Calories from Fat 100); Fat 11g (Saturated 3g); Cholesterol 60mg; Sodium 1100mg; Carbohydrate 77g (Dietary Fiber 9g); Protein 39g
% Daily Value: Vitamin A 12%; Vitamin C 18%; Calcium 8%; Iron 38%
Diet Exchanges: 5 Starch, 3 Lean Meat, 1 Vegetable

BETTY'S TIPS

✪ Substitution

Bow-tie pasta can be used in place of the mini-lasagna noodles.

Beef sirloin steak is a tender but less-expensive cut of meat, which makes it a good choice for entertaining a group. You could also use strip steak, which is more tender but also more expensive.

✪ Success Hint

Chipotle chilies are often sold canned in adobo sauce, which is a smoky, spicy tomato-based concoction. Look for the chilies in larger supermarkets or Mexican markets.

Beef, Bacon and Noodle Bake

Prep: 20 min   Bake: 1 hr 55 min

4	slices bacon, cut into ¾-inch pieces
1½	pounds beef stew meat
½	teaspoon peppered seasoned salt
1	medium onion, chopped (½ cup)
1½	cups baby-cut carrots
1	can (14½ ounces) diced tomatoes with basil, garlic and oregano, undrained
1	jar (12 ounces) beef gravy
1	cup water
2	cups uncooked wide egg noodles (4 ounces)
1½	cups frozen whole green beans

1. Heat oven to 325°. Spray rectangular baking dish, 13 × 9 × 2 inches, with cooking spray.

2. Cook bacon in 12-inch nonstick skillet over medium-high heat 3 minutes, stirring occasionally. Stir in beef, seasoned salt and onion. Cook, stirring occasionally, until beef is brown.

3. Spoon beef mixture into baking dish. Stir in carrots, tomatoes, gravy and water. Cover and bake 1 hour 30 minutes.

4. Stir in noodles and green beans. Cover and bake 20 to 25 minutes or until beef, noodles and beans are tender.

6 servings.

1 Serving: Calories 350 (Calories from Fat 155); Fat 17g (Saturated 6g); Cholesterol 85mg; Sodium 680mg; Carbohydrate 22g (Dietary Fiber 3g); Protein 30g
% Daily Value: Vitamin A 52%; Vitamin C 12%; Calcium 6%; Iron 24%
Diet Exchanges: 1 Starch, 3 Medium-Fat Meat, 2 Vegetable

BETTY'S TIPS

⊘ **Substitution**
Not a green bean lover? Substitute your favorite frozen vegetable or frozen vegetable medley.

⊘ **Serve-With**
Serve with thick slices of hearty bread to sop up all of the flavorful juices.

Beef Pot Pie with Potato Biscuit Crust

Prep: 15 min   Bake: 35 min

½-	pound piece deli roast beef, cubed (1½ cups)
2	cups frozen vegetables (from 16-ounce bag)
1	medium onion, chopped (½ cup)
1	jar (12 ounces) beef gravy
	Potato Biscuit Crust (below)

1. Heat oven to 375°. Heat beef, vegetables, onion and gravy to boiling in 3-quart saucepan, stirring frequently; boil and stir 1 minute. Keep warm.

2. Make Potato Biscuit Crust. Pour beef mixture into ungreased rectangular baking dish, 11 × 7 × 1½ inches. Carefully unfold crust onto beef mixture.

3. Bake uncovered 30 to 35 minutes or until crust is golden brown.

4 to 6 servings.

Potato Biscuit Crust

⅔	cup Betty Crocker Potato Buds® mashed potatoes (dry)
⅔	cup hot water
1½	cups Original Bisquick
2 to 3	tablespoons milk
1	tablespoon freeze-dried chives

Mix potatoes and water in medium bowl; let stand until water is absorbed. Stir in Bisquick, milk and chives until dough forms. Turn dough onto surface dusted with Bisquick; gently roll in Bisquick to coat. Shape into ball; knead 10 times. Pat into 11 × 7-inch rectangle. Fold crosswise into thirds.

1 Serving: Calories 350 (Calories from Fat 90); Fat 10g (Saturated 3g); Cholesterol 30mg; Sodium 1750mg; Carbohydrate 51g (Dietary Fiber 5g); Protein 19g
% Daily Value: Vitamin A 30%; Vitamin C 6%; Calcium 12%; Iron 20%
Diet Exchanges: 3 Starch, 1 Medium-Fat Meat, 1 Vegetable

BETTY'S TIPS

⊘ **Variation**
For a hearty chicken pot pie, use 1½ cups chopped cooked chicken and a jar of chicken gravy instead of the beef and beef gravy.

Fiesta Taco Casserole

Prep: 15 min   Bake: 30 min

1   pound ground beef
1   can (15 to 16 ounces) spicy chili beans in sauce, undrained
1   cup salsa
2   cups coarsely broken tortilla chips
4   medium green onions, sliced (¼ cup)
1   medium tomato, chopped (¾ cup)
1   cup shredded Cheddar or Monterey Jack cheese (4 ounces)
    Tortilla chips, if desired
    Shredded lettuce, if desired
    Additional salsa, if desired

1. Heat oven to 350°. Cook beef in 10-inch skillet over medium heat 8 to 10 minutes, stirring occasionally, until brown; drain. Stir in beans and 1 cup salsa. Heat to boiling, stirring occasionally.

2. Place broken tortilla chips in ungreased 2-quart casserole. Top with beef mixture. Sprinkle with onions, tomato and cheese.

3. Bake uncovered 20 to 30 minutes or until hot and bubbly. Arrange tortilla chips around edge of casserole. Serve with lettuce and additional salsa.

4 servings.

1 Serving: Calories 615 (Calories from Fat 315); Fat 35g (Saturated 14g); Cholesterol 95mg; Sodium 1490mg; Carbohydrate 47g (Dietary Fiber 9g); Protein 37g
% Daily Value: Vitamin A 18%; Vitamin C 26%; Calcium 22%; Iron 34%
Diet Exchanges: 3 Starch, 4 High-Fat Meat

BETTY'S TIPS

❂ **Health Twist**
For 17 grams of fat and 455 calories per serving, use ground turkey breast and reduced-fat Cheddar cheese.

❂ **Serve-With**
Enjoy this family-pleasin' casserole with a tossed salad with cut-up avocado and corn bread with honey and butter.

Fiesta Taco Casserole

Brisket with Cranberry Gravy

Prep: 5 min   Cook: 2 hr

2- to 2½- pound fresh beef brisket (not corned beef)
   ½ teaspoon salt
   1 can (16 ounces) whole berry cranberry sauce
   1 can (15 ounces) tomato sauce
   1 medium onion, chopped (½ cup)

1. Rub surface of beef with salt. Place beef in 10-inch skillet.

2. Mix cranberry sauce, tomato sauce and onion; pour over beef. Heat to boiling over medium-high heat. Stir; reduce heat to low. Cover and simmer 1½ to 2 hours or until beef is tender.

3. To serve immediately, cut beef across grain into thin slices. Serve with gravy.

6 to 8 servings.

1 Serving: Calories 401 (Calories from Fat 70); Fat 9g (Saturated 3g); Cholesterol 111mg; Sodium 784mg; Carbohydrate 36g (Dietary Fiber 2g); Protein 41g
% Daily Value: Vitamin A 9%; Vitamin C 17%; Calcium 3%; Iron 28%
Diet Exchanges: 1½ Vegetable, ½ Fruit, 6 Meat

Caramelized Onion Pot Roast

Prep: 25 min   Cook: 9 hr

2½- pound beef boneless chuck roast
   ½ teaspoon salt
   ¼ teaspoon pepper
   1 tablespoon olive or vegetable oil
   4 medium onions, sliced
   1 cup beef broth
   ½ cup beer or apple juice
   2 tablespoons Dijon mustard
   1 tablespoon packed brown sugar
   1 tablespoon cider vinegar
   Horseradish, if desired

1. Spray 12-inch skillet with cooking spray; heat over medium-high heat. Cook beef in skillet 5 minutes, turning once, until brown. Sprinkle with salt and pepper; remove from skillet.

2. Reduce heat to medium. Add oil to skillet. Cook onions in oil 12 to 14 minutes, stirring frequently, until brown. Stir in broth, beer, mustard, brown sugar, and vinegar. Spoon half of the onion mixture in 4- to 5-quart slow cooker. Place beef on onions. Spoon remaining onion mixture over beef.

3. Cover and cook on low heat setting 8 to 9 hours or until beef is tender.

4. Remove beef and onions from slow cooker and place on serving platter. Spoon some of the beef juices from slow cooker over beef. Serve with horseradish.

6 servings.

1 Serving: Calories 410 (Calories from Fat 215); Fat 24g (Saturated 9g); Cholesterol 115mg; Sodium 530mg; Carbohydrate 10g (Dietary Fiber 2g); Protein 40g
% Daily Value: Vitamin A 0%; Vitamin C 4%; Calcium 2%; Iron 26%
Diet Exchanges: ½ Starch, 5 Medium-Fat Meat

BETTY'S TIPS

۞ Special Touch
To make gravy, remove beef and onions from slow cooker. Skim off fat from beef juices, and pour juices into saucepan. Mix 1 tablespoon cornstarch with 2 tablespoons water, and stir into beef juices. Boil and stir 1 minute or until thickened.

Italian Sausage Lasagna

Prep: 25 min   Cook: 50 min

18 uncooked lasagna noodles

2 pounds ground beef or bulk Italian sausage

½ small onion, chopped (¼ cup)

Pepper to taste

1 can (28 ounces) tomato sauce

½ cup olive or vegetable oil

2 teaspoons dried oregano leaves

2 teaspoons dried basil leaves

1 package (16 ounces) process cheese spread loaf, cut into ¼-inch slices

2 cups shredded mozzarella cheese (8 ounces)

1. Heat oven to 350°. Spray rectangular baking dish, 13 × 9 × 2 inches, with olive oil–flavored cooking spray. Cook and drain noodles as directed on package.

2. Cook beef and onion in 10-inch skillet over medium-high heat, stirring occasionally and seasoning to taste with pepper, until beef is brown; drain. Stir in tomato sauce, oil, oregano and basil. Heat to boiling, stirring occasionally; reduce heat to low. Simmer uncovered 10 to 15 minutes.

3. Place layer of cooked noodles in baking dish. Spoon one-third of the sauce over noodles. Top with half of sliced cheese. Add another layer of noodles and sauce; sprinkle with half of the mozzarella cheese. Add remaining noodles, sauce and sliced cheese. Sprinkle with remaining mozzarella cheese.

4. Cover and bake 30 minutes. Uncover and bake 10 to 20 minutes longer or until hot in center.

8 servings.

1 Serving: Calories 863 (Calories from Fat 454); Fat 50g (Saturated 20g); Cholesterol 124mg; Sodium 1573mg; Carbohydrate 56g (Dietary Fiber 3g); Protein 46g
% Daily Value: Vitamin A 36%; Vitamin C 23%; Calcium 68%; Iron 39%
Diet Exchanges: 3 Starch, 6 Meat, 1½ Vegetable, 7 Fat

Italian Sausage Lasagna

Savory Italian Sausage and Biscuits

Prep: 15 min   Bake: 20 min

½ pound fully cooked mild Italian turkey sausages, cut into ¾-inch slices

1 bag (1 pound) frozen zucchini, cauliflower, Italian green beans, baby lima beans and sliced carrots, thawed and drained

1 jar (14 ounces) tomato pasta sauce (any variety)

1 can (8 ounces) Italian-style tomato sauce

1 cup Original Bisquick

⅓ cup milk

¾ teaspoon Italian seasoning

2 tablespoons grated Parmesan cheese

1. Heat oven to 400°. Grease 2-quart casserole.

2. Stir sausage slices, vegetables, pasta sauce and tomato sauce in 10-inch skillet; heat to boiling. Pour into baking dish.

3. Stir Bisquick, milk and Italian seasoning until soft dough forms. Drop dough by 6 spoonfuls onto vegetable mixture. Sprinkle with cheese.

4. Bake uncovered 18 to 20 minutes or until biscuits are golden brown.

6 servings.

1 Serving: Calories 265 (Calories from Fat 100); Fat 11g (Saturated 3g); Cholesterol 25mg; Sodium 1140mg; Carbohydrate 35g (Dietary Fiber 4g); Protein 12g
% Daily Value: Vitamin A 58%; Vitamin C 18%; Calcium 12%; Iron 12%
Diet Exchanges: 1 Starch, 4 Vegetable, 2 Fat

BETTY'S TIPS

⊘ **Substitution**
You can use any 1-pound blend of frozen vegetables that your family prefers.

⊘ **Serve-With**
Complete this meal with a bagged green salad, a cluster of grapes and Chocolate Chip Pecan Pie Bars (page 241) for dessert.

Swiss Pork Chop and Potato Casserole

Prep: 20 min   Bake: 1 hr 5 min

1   envelope (1.8 ounces) white sauce mix

2   cups milk

1   cup shredded Swiss cheese (4 ounces)

½   teaspoon dried rosemary leaves, crumbled

3   medium Yukon gold potatoes, peeled and sliced (4 cups)

1   medium sweet potato, peeled and sliced (1½ cups)

1   medium onion, thinly sliced (1½ cups)

4   bone-in pork loin chops, ½ inch thick

½   teaspoon peppered seasoned salt

1. Heat oven to 350°. Spray rectangular baking dish, 11 × 7 × 1½ inches, with cooking spray. Mix sauce mix and milk in 1½-quart saucepan. Heat to boiling over medium heat, stirring constantly. Stir in cheese and rosemary until cheese is melted.

2. Layer half of the Yukon gold potatoes, all of the sweet potato and half of the onion in baking dish. Spread about half of the sauce over top. Layer with remaining potatoes and onion; cover with remaining sauce. Cover and bake 30 minutes.

3. While potatoes are baking, spray 12-inch nonstick skillet with cooking spray; heat over medium-high heat. Sprinkle both sides of pork chops with seasoned salt. Cook pork in skillet 4 to 5 minutes, turning once, until brown.

4. Place pork on potatoes. Bake uncovered 30 to 35 minutes or until pork is slightly pink when cut near bone and potatoes are tender.

4 servings.

1 Serving: Calories 455 (Calories from Fat 160); Fat 18g (Saturated 9g); Cholesterol 100mg; Sodium 670mg; Carbohydrate 38g (Dietary Fiber 3g); Protein 38g
% Daily Value: Vitamin A 72%; Vitamin C 16%; Calcium 42%; Iron 10%
Diet Exchanges: 2 Starch, 4 Lean Meat, 1 Vegetable, 1 Fat

BETTY'S TIPS

☺ **Substitution**
Sprinkle the pork chops with salt and pepper if you don't have peppered seasoned salt.

☺ **Serve-With**
Complete the meal with a broccoli raisin salad from the deli.

Betty... MAKES IT EASY

Apricot Pistachio Rolled Pork

Prep: 30 min   Marinate: 2 hr 15 min   Bake: 2 hr 30 min   Stand: 20 min

- 4- pound pork boneless top loin roast (single uncut roast)
- ½ cup chopped dried apricots
- ½ cup chopped pistachio nuts
- 2 cloves garlic, finely chopped
- ¼ teaspoon salt
- ¼ teaspoon pepper
- ¼ cup apricot brandy or apricot nectar
- ¼ cup apricot preserves
- 3 tablespoons chopped pistachio nuts

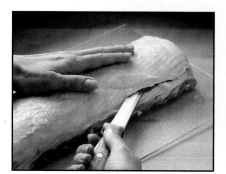

Cut horizontally down length of pork.

1. To cut pork roast, cut horizontally down length of pork about ½ inch from top of pork to within ½ inch of opposite side; open flat. Turn pork. Repeat with other side, cutting from the inside edge to the outer edge; open flat.

2. Sprinkle apricots, ½ cup nuts, the garlic, salt and pepper over pork to within 1 inch of edges. Beginning with edge of second cut side, tightly roll up pork. Secure with toothpicks, or tie with string. Place in glass baking dish. Pierce pork all over with metal skewer. Brush entire surface with brandy. Let stand 15 minutes. Brush again with brandy. Cover and refrigerate at least 2 hours but no longer than 24 hours.

3. Heat oven to 325°. Place pork, fat side up, on rack in shallow roasting pan. Insert meat thermometer so tip is in center of thickest part of pork roll. Bake uncovered 1 hour 30 minutes.

Turn pork. Repeat with other side of pork, cutting from the inside edge to the outer edge.

4. Brush preserves over pork. Sprinkle with 3 tablespoons nuts. Bake 30 to 60 minutes longer or until meat thermometer reads 155°. Cover pork with tent of aluminum foil and let stand 15 to 20 minutes or until thermometer reads 160°. (Temperature will continue to rise about 5°, and pork will be easier to carve.) Cut into slices.

12 servings.

1 Serving: Calories 240 (Calories from Fat 80); Fat 9g (Saturated 8g); Cholesterol 80mg; Sodium 150mg; Carbohydrate 11g (Dietary Fiber 1g); Protein 30g
% Daily Value: Vitamin A 6%; Vitamin C 0%; Calcium 2%; Iron 12%
Diet Exchanges: 4 Very Lean Meat, 1 Fruit, 1 Fat

Pork Crown Roast with Cranberry Stuffing

Prep: 20 min   Bake: 3 hr 20 min   Stand: 20 min

7½- to 8- pound pork crown roast (about 14 to 16 ribs)
2 teaspoons salt
1 teaspoon pepper
Cranberry Stuffing (page 231)

1. Heat oven to 325°. Sprinkle pork with salt and pepper. Place pork, bone ends up, on rack in shallow roasting pan. Wrap bone ends in aluminum foil to prevent excessive browning. Insert meat thermometer so tip is in thickest part of meat and does not touch bone or rest in fat. Place small heatproof bowl or crumpled aluminum foil in crown to hold shape of roast evenly.

2. Bake uncovered 2 hours 30 minutes to 3 hours 20 minutes or until thermometer reads 155°.

3. While pork is baking, make Cranberry Stuffing. One hour before pork is done, remove bowl and fill center of crown with stuffing. Cover only stuffing with aluminum foil for first 30 minutes.

4. Remove pork from oven, cover with tent of aluminum foil and let stand 15 to 20 minutes or until thermometer reads 160°. (Temperature will continue to rise about 5°, and pork will be easier to carve.)

5. Remove foil wrapping; place paper frills on bone ends if desired. To serve, spoon stuffing into bowl and cut pork between ribs.

12 servings.

1 Serving: Calories 575 (Calories from Fat 270); Fat 30g (Saturated 15g); Cholesterol 150mg; Sodium 1040mg; Carbohydrate 22g (Dietary Fiber 3g); Protein 42g
% Daily Value: Vitamin A 12%; Vitamin C 6%; Calcium 6%; Iron 14%
Diet Exchanges: 1 Starch, 6 Lean Meat, ½ Fruit, 2 Fat

BETTY'S TIPS

Success Hint

This special roast may be on hand at your supermarket during the holidays, but call the meat department ahead of time to make sure. The fancy paper frills usually come with the roast.

Caribbean Jerk Pork and Rice Casserole

Prep: 20 min   Bake: 1 hr

1 pound pork boneless loin, cut into ¾-inch pieces

1½ teaspoons jerk seasoning (dry)

1 teaspoon grated gingerroot

1 tablespoon vegetable oil

½ cup coarsely chopped red bell pepper

1 can (8 ounces) pineapple tidbits, drained and juice reserved

¼ cup lime juice

1 cup uncooked regular long-grain rice

2 tablespoons honey

4 medium green onions, cut into ¼-inch pieces

¼ cup salted cashew pieces

2 tablespoons chopped fresh cilantro

1. Heat oven to 350°. Spray rectangular baking dish, 11 × 7 × 1½ inches, with cooking spray.

2. Mix pork, 1 teaspoon of the jerk seasoning and the gingerroot. Heat oil in 10-inch skillet over medium-high heat. Cook pork mixture and bell pepper in oil 3 to 5 minutes, stirring occasionally, until pork is brown. Spoon into baking dish.

3. Mix reserved pineapple juice, lime juice and enough water to equal 2 cups. Pour over pork mixture. Stir in rice, honey and remaining ½ teaspoon jerk seasoning.

4. Cover and bake 45 minutes. Stir in pineapple and onions. Sprinkle with cashews. Bake uncovered about 15 minutes or until pork is no longer pink and liquid is absorbed. Sprinkle with cilantro.

4 servings.

1 Serving: Calories 510 (Calories from Fat 145); Fat 16g (Saturated 4g); Cholesterol 70mg; Sodium 400mg; Carbohydrate 63g (Dietary Fiber 2g); Protein 31g
% Daily Value: Vitamin A 12%; Vitamin C 40%; Calcium 4%; Iron 18%
Diet Exchanges: 3 Starch, 3 Lean Meat, 1 Fruit, ½ Fat

BETTY'S TIPS

⊛ **Success Hint**
Pop the pork in the freezer for about 30 minutes to make it easier to cut.

⊛ **Serve-With**
Treat your family to a culinary trip to the Caribbean with this Jamaican-inspired dish. Serve with warm baguettes and mango sorbet as a sure cure for the winter blues!

Caribbean Jerk Pork and Rice Casserole

Easy Glazed Baked Ham

Prep: 10 min   Bake: 1 hr 30 min   Stand: 15 min

6- pound fully cooked smoked bone-in ham
Brown Sugar Orange Glaze (below)

1. Heat oven to 325°. Place ham on rack in shallow roasting pan. Insert meat thermometer in thickest part of ham. Bake uncovered about 1 hour 30 minutes or until thermometer reads 135° to 140°.

2. While ham is baking, make Brown Sugar Orange Glaze. Brush over ham during last 45 minutes of baking.

3. Remove ham from oven, cover with tent of aluminum foil and let stand 10 to 15 minutes for easier carving.

20 servings.

Brown Sugar Orange Glaze

½ cup packed brown sugar
2 tablespoons orange or pineapple juice
½ teaspoon ground mustard

1 Serving: Calories 125 (Calories from Fat 35); Fat 4g (Saturated 1g); Cholesterol 40mg; Sodium 890mg; Carbohydrate 7g (Dietary Fiber 0g); Protein 15g
% Daily Value: Vitamin A 0%; Vitamin C 0%; Calcium 0%; Iron 6%
Diet Exchanges: 2 Lean Meat, ½ Fruit

BETTY'S TIPS

⊚ **Success Hint**
Adjust the oven rack to the lowest position.

⊚ **Variation**
For an unglazed baked ham, omit the Brown Sugar Orange Glaze and step **2.**

⊚ **Special Touch**
Garnish with halved blood oranges and kumquats, lemon leaves and orange slices.

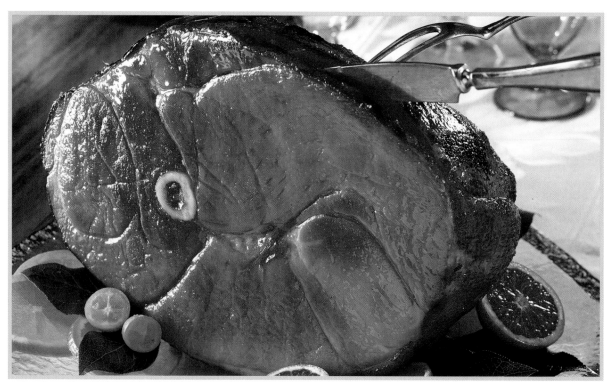

Easy Glazed Baked Ham

Black Sesame Chicken with Roasted Red Pepper Sauce

Prep: 25 min   Bake: 20 min

⅓ cup butter or margarine, melted

6 boneless skinless chicken breast halves (about 2 pounds)

1 package (6 ounces) chèvre (goat) cheese with herbs

⅓ cup black sesame seed

1 teaspoon olive or vegetable oil
   Roasted Red Pepper Sauce (below)

1. Heat oven to 425°. Spray rectangular pan, 13 × 9 × 2 inches, with cooking spray. Place melted butter in large shallow bowl.

2. Cut 2-inch horizontal slit in each chicken breast half. Stuff 1 tablespoon cheese in each pocket. Dip each chicken breast into butter; sprinkle with sesame seed.

3. Heat oil in 12-inch nonstick skillet over medium heat. Cook chicken in oil until brown on both sides. Place chicken in pan. Drizzle with any remaining butter.

4. Bake uncovered 15 to 20 minutes or until chicken is no longer pink in center. Meanwhile, prepare Roasted Red Pepper Sauce; keep warm. Serve chicken in pool of sauce, or drizzle sauce over chicken.

6 servings.

Roasted Red Pepper Sauce

1 jar (7 ounces) roasted red bell peppers, drained

1 clove garlic, finely chopped

1 teaspoon sugar

¼ teaspoon salt
   Pinch of ground red pepper (cayenne)

1 tablespoon sour cream

Place all ingredients except sour cream in mini food processor or blender. Cover and process until smooth. Heat mixture in 1-quart saucepan over medium heat, stirring occasionally, until hot; remove from heat. Strain if desired; stir in sour cream.

1 Serving: Calories 410 (Calories from Fat 250); Fat 28g (Saturated 12g); Cholesterol 120mg; Sodium 320mg; Carbohydrate 6g (Dietary Fiber 2g); Protein 35g
% Daily Value: Vitamin A 22%; Vitamin C 46%; Calcium 18%; Iron 14%
Diet Exchanges: 5 Medium-Fat Meat, 1 Vegetable

BETTY'S TIPS

⚙ **Do-Ahead**
You can make the sauce up to 24 hours ahead. Refrigerate and heat just before serving.

⚙ **Substitution**
Black sesame seed adds a dramatic look to this dish, but regular sesame seed, toasted, can also be used. If you aren't fond of chèvre cheese, use garlic-herb cream cheese spread.

⚙ **Serve-With**
If you're looking for something new to serve this holiday season, try this flavorful entrée. We suggest serving with cooked couscous and steamed broccoli rabe or green beans.

Chicken and Corn Bread Stuffing Casserole

Prep: 15 min   Bake: 15 min

1   can (10¾ ounces) condensed 98% fat-free cream of chicken or celery soup
¾   cup fat-free (skim) milk
1   package (10 ounces) frozen mixed vegetables, thawed and drained
1   medium onion, finely chopped (½ cup)
½   teaspoon ground sage or poultry seasoning
2   cups cut-up cooked chicken
1½   cups corn bread stuffing mix
⅛   teaspoon pepper
    Paprika, if desired

1. Heat oven to 400°. Spray 3-quart casserole with cooking spray.

2. Heat soup and milk to boiling in 3-quart saucepan over high heat, stirring frequently. Stir in mixed vegetables, onion and sage. Heat to boiling, stirring frequently; remove from heat.

3. Stir in chicken and stuffing mix. Spoon into casserole. Sprinkle with pepper and paprika. Bake uncovered about 15 minutes or until hot in center.

4 servings.

1 Serving: Calories 285 (Calories from Fat 55); Fat 6g (Saturated 2g); Cholesterol 60mg; Sodium 1060mg; Carbohydrate 34g (Dietary Fiber 4g); Protein 28g
% Daily Value: Vitamin A 28%; Vitamin C 22%; Calcium 14%; Iron 12%
Diet Exchanges: 2 Starch, 2½ Very Lean Meat, 1 Vegetable

BETTY'S TIPS

⊘ **Substitution**
You can substitute cut-up leftover turkey for the chicken.

⊘ **Serve-With**
This comfy casserole is a wonderful reminder of an old-fashioned turkey dinner, without all the work! Try serving with a side of cranberry sauce spiked with a little orange-flavored liqueur or orange juice and grated orange peel.

Creamy Layered Chicken Dinner

Prep: 10 min   Bake: 40 min

4   boneless skinless chicken breast halves (about 1¼ pounds)
4   slices process Swiss cheese
1   package Betty Crocker Chicken Helper® chicken and stuffing
1   can (4 ounces) mushroom pieces and stems, drained
1½   cups hot water
1   cup hot water
2   tablespoons margarine or butter, melted

1. Heat oven to 375°. Place chicken in ungreased rectangular baking dish, 13 × 9 × 2 inches; cover with cheese slices. Sprinkle with Stuffing and mushrooms.

2. Mix 1½ cups hot water and the Seasoning Mix; pour over stuffing. Stir 1 cup hot water and the Gravy Mix with wire whisk until smooth; pour over mixture in dish. Drizzle with margarine.

3. Cover and bake 20 minutes. Uncover and bake 15 to 20 minutes longer or until top is golden brown and juice of chicken is no longer pink when centers of thickest pieces are cut.

4 servings.

1 Serving: Calories 395 (Calories from Fat 145); Fat 16g (Saturated 6g); Cholesterol 90mg; Sodium 1120mg; Carbohydrate 29g (Dietary Fiber 2g); Protein 36g
% Daily Value: Vitamin A 12%; Vitamin C 0%; Calcium 22%; Iron 14%
Diet Exchanges: 2 Starch, 4 Lean Meat

BETTY'S TIPS

⊘ **Substitution**
Four ounces of sliced fresh mushrooms can be used instead of the canned mushrooms.

⊘ **Serve-With**
Add a crisp green salad and Bisquick biscuits to complete this kid-friendly meal.

Spinach-Stuffed Chicken Breasts

Prep: 30 min   Bake: 40 min

16 boneless skinless chicken breast halves (about 5 pounds)

4 cups spinach leaves, shredded (6 ounces)

8 slices bacon, crisply cooked and crumbled (½ cup)

2 cups shredded mozzarella cheese (8 ounces)

½ cup chopped drained roasted red bell peppers (from 7-ounce jar)

2 tablespoons chopped fresh or 2 teaspoons dried marjoram leaves

2 tablespoons Italian dressing

½ teaspoon seasoned salt

Paprika, if desired

1. Heat oven to 375°. Spray 2 rectangular baking dishes, 13 × 9 × 2 inches, with cooking spray. Cut 3- to 4-inch horizontal slit in thick side of each chicken breast half; set aside.

2. Mix spinach, bacon, cheese, bell peppers and half of the marjoram. Spoon 3 to 4 tablespoons into pocket in each chicken breast. Secure with toothpicks or small skewers. Place in baking dishes. Brush dressing over tops of chicken breasts. Sprinkle with seasoned salt, remaining marjoram, and paprika.

3. Bake uncovered 35 to 40 minutes or until juice of chicken is no longer pink when centers of thickest pieces are cut.

16 servings.

1 Serving: Calories 215 (Calories from Fat 80); Fat 9g (Saturated 3g); Cholesterol 85mg; Sodium 250mg; Carbohydrate 1g (Dietary Fiber 0g); Protein 32g
% Daily Value: Vitamin A 10%; Vitamin C 8%; Calcium 12%; Iron 6%
Diet Exchanges: 4½ Very Lean Meat, 1½ Fat

BETTY'S TIPS

☺ Time-Saver
Use ½ cup Bac-Os® bacon-flavored bits or chips instead of the cooked bacon.

☺ Do-Ahead
After arranging the stuffed chicken breasts in the pans, cover and refrigerate for up to 4 hours, then bake just before your family celebration. You may need to add about 5 minutes to the bake time.

Spinach-Stuffed Chicken Breasts

Do-Ahead Chicken Leek Strata

Prep: 20 min   Chill: 4 hr   Bake: 1 hr 5 min   Stand: 10 min

   2 tablespoons butter or margarine
   2 cups sliced leeks (about 2 pounds)
  24 slices French bread, each $\frac{1}{2}$ inch thick (from 1-pound loaf)
   2 cups chopped cooked chicken or turkey
   2 tablespoons chopped fresh or 2 teaspoons dried dill weed
   3 cups shredded mozzarella cheese (12 ounces)
   8 eggs, beaten
   4 cups milk
   1 teaspoon salt
  $\frac{1}{4}$ teaspoon pepper

1. Melt butter in 2-quart saucepan over medium heat. Cook leeks in butter about 3 minutes, stirring frequently, until softened; remove from heat.

2. Line bottom of ungreased rectangular baking dish, 13 × 9 × 2 inches, with half of the bread slices. Sprinkle with chicken and dill weed; layer with leeks. Sprinkle 2 cups of the cheese over leeks. Top with remaining bread slices; sprinkle with remaining 1 cup cheese.

3. Mix remaining ingredients; pour over bread mixture. Cover tightly and refrigerate at least 4 hours but no longer than 24 hours. About 1¼ hours before serving, heat oven to 325°. Uncover and bake 1 hour to 1 hour 5 minutes or until knife inserted in center comes out clean. Let stand 10 minutes before serving.

12 servings.

1 Serving: Calories 355 (Calories from Fat 135); Fat 15g (Saturated 7g); Cholesterol 185mg; Sodium 750mg; Carbohydrate 31g (Dietary Fiber 2g); Protein 26g
% Daily Value: Vitamin A 14%; Vitamin C 2%; Calcium 38%; Iron 14%
Diet Exchanges: 2 Starch, 3 Lean Meat, 1 Fat

BETTY'S TIPS

✪ Success Hint
Purchase leeks with brightly colored leaves and an unblemished white portion. The smaller the leek, the more tender it will be. Refrigerate in a plastic bag up to 5 days. Before using, trim the root and leaf ends. Slit the leeks from top to bottom and wash thoroughly to remove dirt trapped between leaf layers.

Chicken and Rice with Autumn Vegetables

Prep: 15 min   Bake: 30 min

   1 package (about 6 ounces) chicken-flavored rice mix or rice and vermicelli mix
   2 cups 1-inch pieces butternut squash
   1 medium zucchini, cut lengthwise in half, then crosswise into $\frac{3}{4}$-inch slices
   1 medium red bell pepper, cut into 1-inch pieces (1 cup)
   4 boneless skinless chicken breast halves (about 1¼ pounds)
   2 cups water
  $\frac{1}{2}$ cup garlic-and-herb spreadable cheese

1. Heat oven to 425°. Mix rice, contents of seasoning packet, squash, zucchini and bell pepper in ungreased rectangular pan, 13 × 9 × 2 inches.

2. Spray 10-inch skillet with cooking spray; heat over medium-high heat. Cook chicken in skillet 5 minutes, turning once, until brown. Remove chicken from skillet.

3. Add water to skillet; heat to boiling. Pour boiling water over rice mixture; stir to mix. Stir in cheese. Place chicken on rice mixture.

4. Cover and bake about 30 minutes or until liquid is absorbed and juice of chicken is no longer pink when centers of thickest pieces are cut.

4 servings.

1 Serving: Calories 340 (Calories from Fat 125); Fat 14g (Saturated 7g); Cholesterol 105mg; Sodium 320mg; Carbohydrate 23g (Dietary Fiber 2g); Protein 32g
% Daily Value: Vitamin A 76%; Vitamin C 58%; Calcium 8%; Iron 14%
Diet Exchanges: 1 Starch, 4 Lean Meat, 2 Vegetable

BETTY'S TIPS

✪ Substitution
Buttercup squash can be used if butternut is not available. Butternut squash is a long, tan-colored squash with a bulbous end; the buttercup variety is round with a flat bottom and dark green color. Buttercup has a drier texture, but both are sweet tasting.

Santa Fe Chicken Tortellini Casserole

Prep: 15 min   Bake: 35 min

1 package (9 ounces) refrigerated cheese-filled tortellini

3 tablespoons olive or vegetable oil

2 cups broccoli flowerets

1 medium onion, chopped (½ cup)

1 medium red bell pepper, chopped (1 cup)

3 tablespoons Gold Medal all-purpose flour

¾ cup milk

¾ cup chicken broth

1 teaspoon ground cumin

4 cups cut-up cooked chicken

¾ cup shredded Monterey Jack cheese (3 ounces)

½ cup shredded Colby cheese (2 ounces)

½ cup crushed tortilla chips, if desired

1. Heat oven to 325°. Grease 3-quart casserole. Cook and drain tortellini as directed on package.

2. Heat 1 tablespoon of the oil in 10-inch skillet over medium-high heat. Cook broccoli, onion and bell pepper in oil about 3 minutes, stirring frequently, until crisp-tender. Remove broccoli mixture from skillet.

3. Cook flour and remaining 2 tablespoons oil in same skillet over low heat, stirring constantly, until smooth. Stir in milk, broth and cumin. Heat to boiling over medium heat, stirring constantly; remove from heat. Stir in chicken, Monterey Jack cheese, tortellini and broccoli mixture. Spoon into casserole.

4. Bake uncovered 25 to 35 minutes or until hot in center. During last several minutes of baking, sprinkle with Colby cheese and tortilla chips; bake until cheese is melted.

6 servings.

1 Serving: Calories 480 (Calories from Fat 250); Fat 28g (Saturated 10g); Cholesterol 145mg; Sodium 490mg; Carbohydrate 20g (Dietary Fiber 2g); Protein 39g
% Daily Value: Vitamin A 30%; Vitamin C 58%; Calcium 26%; Iron 14%
Diet Exchanges: 1 Starch, 5 Medium-Fat Meat, 1 Vegetable

BETTY'S TIPS

☺ Success Hint

Broken chips at the bottom of the chip bag are perfect for topping off this casserole. You also can place whole chips in a resealable plastic bag and crush them with a rolling pin.

☺ Serve-With

For a true taste of the Southwest, pass around individual bowls of salsa, sour cream and sliced ripe olives.

Mou Shu Chicken

Mou Shu Chicken

Prep: 10 min   Cook: 20 min

1 tablespoon vegetable oil
1 bag (16 ounces) coleslaw mix
1 package (8 ounces) sliced mushrooms
1½ cups shredded cooked chicken
1 tablespoon grated gingerroot
3 tablespoons hoisin sauce
1¼ cups Original Bisquick
1¼ cups milk
1 egg
8 green onions, chopped (½ cup)

1. Heat oil in 4-quart Dutch oven over medium-high heat. Cook coleslaw mix, mushrooms, chicken and gingerroot in oil about 10 minutes, stirring frequently, until vegetables are tender. Stir in hoisin sauce. Reduce heat; keep warm.

2. Stir Bisquick, milk and egg in medium bowl until blended. Stir in onions.

3. Lightly grease 10-inch skillet; heat over medium-high heat. Pour slightly less than ¼ cup batter into skillet; rotate skillet to make a thin pancake, 5 to 6 inches in diameter. Cook until bubbles break on surface; turn. Cook other side until golden brown. Keep warm while making remaining pancakes.

4. Spoon about ½ cup chicken mixture onto each pancake; roll up.

12 servings.

1 Serving: Calories 125 (Calories from Fat 45); Fat 5g (Saturated 1g); Cholesterol 35mg; Sodium 280mg; Carbohydrate 14g (Dietary Fiber 2g); Protein 8g
% Daily Value: Vitamin A 4%; Vitamin C 12%; Calcium 8%; Iron 8%
Diet Exchanges: 1 Starch, 1 Lean Meat

BETTY'S TIPS

✿ Variation
Add an extra spark of color and flavor by stirring in ½ red bell pepper, thinly sliced, with the coleslaw, mushrooms and chicken. One clove garlic, finely chopped, could also be added with the other vegetables.

✿ Did You Know?
Mou Shu is traditionally made of shredded pork, dried lily buds, a special variety of mushroom called tree ears, scallions, soy sauce, and seasonings, all of which are stir-fried, mixed with strips of cooked eggs and rolled in thin pancakes.

Corn Bread–Topped Chicken Pot Pie

Prep: 25 min   Bake: 22 min   Stand: 5 min

1 pound boneless skinless chicken breasts, cut into ½-inch pieces

½ teaspoon peppered seasoned salt

1 large onion, chopped (1 cup)

1 jar (12 ounces) home-style chicken gravy

1 bag (1 pound) frozen broccoli, cauliflower and carrots

½ cup sour cream

1 pouch (6.5 ounces) Betty Crocker golden corn muffin and bread mix

⅓ cup milk

2 tablespoons margarine or butter, melted

1 egg

2 tablespoons shredded Parmesan cheese

1. Heat oven to 400°. Spray rectangular baking dish, 13 × 9 × 2 inches, and 12-inch nonstick skillet with cooking spray. Sprinkle chicken with seasoned salt. Cook chicken and onion in skillet over medium-high heat 4 to 6 minutes, stirring occasionally, until chicken is brown.

2. Stir in gravy. Heat to boiling; reduce heat to medium-low. Cover and cook about 5 minutes, stirring occasionally, until chicken is no longer pink in center. While chicken is cooking, place vegetables in colander. Rinse with hot water until thawed. Remove chicken mixture from heat. Stir in vegetables and sour cream; keep warm.

3. Stir corn bread mix, milk, margarine and egg just until moistened (batter will be lumpy). Spoon chicken mixture into baking dish. Drop batter by spoonfuls around edges of warm chicken mixture. Sprinkle cheese over batter.

4. Bake uncovered 20 to 22 minutes or until corn bread is deep golden brown. Let stand 5 minutes before serving.

4 servings.

1 Serving: Calories 680 (Calories from Fat 245); Fat 27g (Saturated 12g); Cholesterol 150mg; Sodium 1920mg; Carbohydrate 75g (Dietary Fiber 7g); Protein 41g
% Daily Value: Vitamin A 46%; Vitamin C 32%; Calcium 32%; Iron 28%
Diet Exchanges: 5 Starch, 4 Lean Meat, 1½ Fat

BETTY'S TIPS

✪ Substitution
This recipe will work with lots of other vegetable combinations. Let your family pick their favorite, or you can substitute leftover cooked vegetables for the frozen vegetables.

✪ Success Hint
Make sure that the chicken filling is still hot before dropping the corn bread batter on top to ensure that the corn bread will bake throughout.

✪ Serve-With
Enjoy grapes and apple wedges with this family-pleasin' meal.

Southern Turkey and Lentil Casserole

Prep: 15 min   Cook: 15 min   Bake: 1 hr 10 min

4   slices bacon, cut into ½-inch pieces

2   medium carrots, chopped (1 cup)

1   medium onion, chopped (½ cup)

1   cup dried lentils (8 ounces), sorted and rinsed

1   can (15 to 16 ounces) black-eyed peas, rinsed and drained

1   can (14½ ounces) stewed tomatoes with garlic, oregano and basil, undrained

1   can (14½ ounces) chicken broth

1½ cups ½-inch cubes cooked turkey or chicken

2   tablespoons chili sauce

   Chopped fresh parsley, if desired

1. Heat oven to 350°. Spray rectangular baking dish, 13 × 9 × 2 inches, with cooking spray.

2. Cook bacon, carrots and onion in 10-inch nonstick skillet over medium heat 3 to 5 minutes, stirring occasionally, until vegetables are crisp-tender. Stir in lentils. Cook 3 minutes, stirring occasionally.

3. Spoon mixture into baking dish. Stir in black-eyed peas, tomatoes, broth, turkey and chili sauce.

4. Cover and bake 1 hour to 1 hour 10 minutes or until liquid is absorbed. Sprinkle with parsley.

5 servings.

1 Serving: Calories 330 (Calories from Fat 65); Fat 7g (Saturated 2g); Cholesterol 40mg; Sodium 990mg; Carbohydrate 51g (Dietary Fiber 16g); Protein 32g
% Daily Value: Vitamin A 44%; Vitamin C 12%; Calcium 8%; Iron 38%
Diet Exchanges: 3 Starch, 2 Very Lean Meat, 1 Vegetable

BETTY'S TIPS

❂ **Substitution**
Ketchup can be used in place of the chili sauce for this delicious casserole.

❂ **Time-Saver**
Freeze leftover cooked turkey for use in recipes. Cool the turkey completely, then package it in small measured amounts. Label and date the packages.

❂ **Serve-With**
Serve this southern-inspired casserole with thick slices of whole-grain bread and lots of fresh fruit.

Southern Turkey and Lentil Casserole

Chipotle Grilled Turkey Breast

Prep: 10 min   Grill: 2 hr   Stand: 5 min

8 to 10   cloves garlic, peeled
2- to 2½- pound bone-in turkey breast half
          Chipotle Sweet 'n Spicy Marinade (below)

1. Heat coals or gas grill for indirect heat. Tuck garlic cloves under skin of turkey. Make Sweet 'n Spicy Marinade.

2. Place turkey on grill; brush with marinade. Cover and grill turkey over drip pan and 5 to 6 inches from medium heat 1 hour 30 minutes to 2 hours, turning occasionally and brushing with marinade, until meat thermometer reads 170° and juice is no longer pink when center is cut. Let stand 5 minutes before serving. Discard any remaining marinade.

6 servings.

Chipotle Sweet 'n Spicy Marinade

⅓ cup real maple syrup
2 tablespoons vegetable oil
1 or 2 chipotle chilies in adobo sauce (from 7-ounce can)
1 tablespoon soy sauce
1 or 2 cloves garlic, peeled

Place all ingredients in mini food processor or blender. Cover and process until smooth.

1 Serving: Calories 255 (Calories from Fat 100); Fat 11g (Saturated 3g); Cholesterol 80mg; Sodium 230mg; Carbohydrate 10g (Dietary Fiber 0g); Protein 29g
% Daily Value: Vitamin A 2%; Vitamin C 4%; Calcium 2%; Iron 6%
Diet Exchanges: 4 Lean Meat, ½ Fruit

BETTY'S TIPS

○ **Success Hint**
When using indirect heat, food is cooked away from the heat. When using coals, arrange them around the edge of the firebox, and place a drip pan under the grilling area. If using a dual-burner gas grill, heat only one side, and place the food under the burner that is not lit. For single-burner gas grills, place food in a foil tray or on several layers of aluminum foil and use low heat.

○ **Substitution**
Maple-flavored syrup or honey can be used instead of the real maple syrup in the marinade.

Herb Cornish Hens with Cranberry Orange Sauce

Prep: 15 min   Bake: 1 hr 15 min   Cook: 5 min

4   Rock Cornish hens (about 2 pounds each)
2   tablespoons roasted garlic-flavored vegetable oil or plain vegetable oil
1   teaspoon salt
1   teaspoon dried thyme leaves
½   teaspoon pepper
    Cranberry Orange Sauce (below)
    Thyme sprigs, if desired

1. Heat oven to 350°. Place hens, breast sides up, on rack in shallow roasting pan. Brush with oil. Sprinkle inside and out with salt, dried thyme and pepper. Insert meat thermometer so tip is in thickest part of inside thigh muscle and does not touch bone.

2. Bake uncovered 1 hour to 1 hour 15 minutes or until thermometer reads 180° and juice of hens is no longer pink when center of thigh is cut.

3. While hens are baking, make Cranberry Orange Sauce. To serve, cut each hen in half along backbone and breastbone from tail to neck, using kitchen scissors. Serve hens with sauce. Garnish with thyme sprigs.

8 servings.

Cranberry Orange Sauce

1   can (16 ounces) whole berry cranberry sauce
3   tablespoons sweet orange marmalade
2   teaspoons grated gingerroot
1   clementine tangerine, peeled and sectioned

Heat cranberry sauce in 1-quart saucepan over low heat, stirring constantly, until melted. Stir in marmalade, gingerroot and clementine sections. Cook 1 minute. Serve warm.

1 Serving: Calories 410 (Calories from Fat 205); Fat 23g (Saturated 6g); Cholesterol 150mg; Sodium 390mg; Carbohydrate 28g (Dietary Fiber 1g); Protein 24g
% Daily Value: Vitamin A 4%; Vitamin C 4%; Calcium 2%; Iron 6%
Diet Exchanges: 3½ Medium-Fat Meat, 2 Fruit, ½ Fat

BETTY'S TIPS

⊗ **Substitution**
One can of mandarin orange segments, drained, can be used instead of the clementine.

⊗ **Variation**
If you're not a fan of ginger, omit the gingerroot in the sauce.

⊗ **Serve-With**
Add steamed pea pods and cooked white and wild rice to complete this merry meal.

Easy Holiday Paella

Easy Holiday Paella

Prep: 30 min   Bake: 55 min

¾ pound uncooked large shrimp, peeled and deveined

¾ pound sea scallops, cut in half

2 tablespoons olive or vegetable oil

Generous pinch plus 1 teaspoon saffron threads

6 cloves garlic, finely chopped

5 medium onions, chopped (2½ cups)

2 cans (14½ ounces each) diced tomatoes with garlic and onion, undrained

1 can (14 ounces) artichoke hearts, drained and coarsely chopped

¾ pound smoked turkey sausage, cut into ¼-inch slices and slices cut in half

2 cups uncooked basmati rice

4 cups chicken broth

1 teaspoon paprika

Chopped fresh parsley, if desired

1. Heat oven to 375°. Spray 2 rectangular baking dishes, 11 × 7 × 1½ inches, with cooking spray. Toss shrimp and scallops with 1 tablespoon of the oil and generous pinch of the saffron threads in medium bowl; cover and refrigerate.

2. Heat remaining 1 tablespoon oil in 4-quart Dutch oven over medium heat. Cook garlic and onions in oil about 5 minutes, stirring frequently, until onions are crisp-tender. Stir in tomatoes, artichokes and sausage. Cook 2 minutes, stirring frequently. Stir in rice. Spread half of rice mixture evenly in each baking dish.

3. Heat broth, paprika and 1 teaspoon saffron threads to boiling in 2-quart saucepan. Pour 2 cups broth mixture evenly over rice mixture in each baking dish. Cover and bake 35 minutes.

4. Place shrimp and scallops on top of rice mixture. Cover and bake 15 to 20 minutes or until shrimp are pink and firm and scallops are white. Sprinkle with parsley.

8 to 10 servings.

1 Serving: Calories 400 (Calories from Fat 90); Fat 10g (Saturated 2g); Cholesterol 70mg; Sodium 1190mg; Carbohydrate 57g (Dietary Fiber 5g); Protein 26g
% Daily Value: Vitamin A 10%; Vitamin C 20%; Calcium 12%; Iron 28%
Diet Exchanges: 3 Starch, 2 Lean Meat, 2 Vegetable

BETTY'S TIPS

⚙ **Substitution**
You can replace the sea scallops with ¾ pound whole bay scallops.

We love the wonderful nutty flavor of basmati rice, but you also can use regular long-grain rice.

Salmon with Cranberry Pistachio Sauce

Prep: 10 min   Cook: 20 min   Broil: 10 min

Cranberry Pistachio Sauce (below)
2- pound salmon fillet
2 tablespoons fresh lime juice
2 tablespoons butter or margarine, melted
½ teaspoon salt
Chopped pistachio nuts, if desired

1. Make Cranberry Pistachio Sauce; keep warm. Set oven control to broil. Spray broiler pan rack with cooking spray. Place fish, skin side down, on rack in broiler pan. Mix lime juice, butter and salt; pour over fish.

2. Broil with top 4 inches from heat 8 to 10 minutes or until fish flakes easily with fork. Top fish with sauce. Sprinkle with nuts.

8 servings.

Cranberry Pistachio Sauce

1 pound fresh cranberries
1 cup sugar
1 jar (10 ounces) red currant jelly
1 cup orange juice
½ cup chopped pistachio nuts

Mix cranberries, sugar, jelly and orange juice in 2-quart saucepan. Heat to boiling; reduce heat. Simmer uncovered 20 minutes, skimming off any foam that collects on surface. Remove from heat. Stir in nuts.

1 Serving: Calories 450 (Calories from Fat 110); Fat 12g (Saturated 2g); Cholesterol 65mg; Sodium 320mg; Carbohydrate 68g (Dietary Fiber 4g); Protein 22g
% Daily Value: Vitamin A 6%; Vitamin C 20%; Calcium 2%; Iron 8%
Diet Exchanges: 3 Lean Meat, 4½ Fruit, ½ Fat

BETTY'S TIPS

❂ Success Hint
Leftover Cranberry Pistachio Sauce will keep for 1 week covered in the refrigerator. You can also fill a decorative jar with sauce to give as a hostess or holiday gift.

❂ Variation
For an easy and festive appetizer, top cream cheese with chilled Cranberry Pistachio Sauce. Sprinkle with chopped pistachio nuts, and serve with crackers.

Salmon with Cranberry Pistachio Sauce

Tuna Linguine Casserole

Prep: 20 min   Bake: 25 min

8   ounces uncooked linguine
1   cup frozen broccoli flowerets
1   package (1.8 ounces) leek soup mix
1½ cups milk
    Pinch of pepper
1   can (6 ounces) albacore tuna, drained
2   tablespoons chopped drained roasted red bell peppers (from 7-ounce jar)
1   tablespoon margarine or butter, melted
¼   cup plain dry bread crumbs

1. Heat oven to 350°. Spray square baking dish, 8 × 8 × 2 inches, with cooking spray. Cook and drain linguine as directed on package, adding broccoli for last 2 minutes of cook time.

2. While linguine is cooking, mix soup mix and milk in 1-quart saucepan. Heat to boiling over medium heat, stirring constantly. Stir in pepper.

3. Mix linguine, broccoli, tuna, bell peppers and soup mixture; spoon into baking dish. Mix margarine and bread crumbs; sprinkle over linguine mixture.

4. Bake uncovered 20 to 25 minutes or until top is golden brown.

4 servings.

1 Serving: Calories 410 (Calories from Fat 65); Fat 7g (Saturated 3g); Cholesterol 35mg; Sodium 580mg; Carbohydrate 55g (Dietary Fiber 4g); Protein 36g
% Daily Value: Vitamin A 26%; Vitamin C 22%; Calcium 10%; Iron 24%
Diet Exchanges: 3 Starch, 3 Very Lean Meat, 2 Vegetable, ½ Fat

BETTY'S TIPS

❂ **Substitution**

If you don't have any roasted red bell peppers on hand, use sliced pimientos, drained, instead.

This casserole is also delicious made with regular water-packed tuna instead of the slightly more expensive albacore tuna.

Quick & Low-Fat

Creamy Crab au Gratin

Prep: 15 min   Bake: 15 min

1½ cups sliced mushrooms (4 ounces)
2   medium stalks celery, sliced (1 cup)
1   can (14½ ounces) chicken broth
¾   cup fat-free half-and-half
3   tablespoons Gold Medal all-purpose flour
½   teaspoon red pepper sauce
2   packages (8 ounces each) refrigerated imitation crabmeat chunks or 2 cups chopped cooked crabmeat
1   cup soft bread crumbs (about 1½ slices bread)

1. Heat oven to 400°. Lightly spray rectangular baking dish, 11 × 7 × 1½ inches, with cooking spray.

2. Spray 3-quart saucepan with cooking spray; heat over medium heat. Cook mushrooms and celery in saucepan about 4 minutes, stirring constantly, until celery is tender. Stir in broth. Heat to boiling; reduce heat.

3. Beat half-and-half, flour and pepper sauce with wire whisk until smooth; stir into vegetable mixture. Heat to boiling, stirring constantly. Boil and stir 1 minute. Stir in crabmeat.

4. Spoon crabmeat mixture into baking dish. Top with bread crumbs. Bake uncovered about 15 minutes or until heated through.

4 servings.

1 Serving: Calories 200 (Calories from Fat 20); Fat 2g (Saturated 1g); Cholesterol 350mg; Sodium 1540mg; Carbohydrate 24g (Dietary Fiber 1g); Protein 23g
% Daily Value: Vitamin A 8%; Vitamin C 2%; Calcium 6%; Iron 8%
Diet Exchanges: ½ Starch, 2 Very Lean Meat, 2 Vegetable, ½ Skim Milk

BETTY'S TIPS

❂ **Serve-With**

Forget ordinary tuna casserole, and try this enticing Crab au Gratin. Not only will you be pleased by its extraordinary flavor, you'll also applaud that it's low in fat. Steam some fresh pea pods to serve alongside.

Veggie Casserole with Dill Drop Biscuits

Prep: 15 min   Bake: 22 min

1   medium onion, chopped (½ cup)
1   bag (1 pound) frozen carrots, green beans and cauliflower (or other combination)
1   package (9 ounces) frozen broccoli cuts
1   container (10 ounces) refrigerated Alfredo pasta sauce
2¼ cups Original Bisquick
⅔   cup milk
¾   teaspoon dried dill weed

1. Heat oven to 400°. Spray 10-inch nonstick skillet with cooking spray; heat over medium-high heat. Cook onion in skillet 2 to 3 minutes, stirring occasionally, until crisp-tender. Stir in carrot mixture, broccoli and Alfredo sauce; reduce heat to medium. Cover and cook 5 to 6 minutes, stirring occasionally, until hot. Spoon into ungreased square baking dish, 8 × 8 × 2 inches.

2. Mix Bisquick, milk and dill weed until soft dough forms. Drop dough by 9 spoonfuls onto hot vegetable mixture.

3. Bake 18 to 22 minutes or until biscuits are golden brown.

6 servings.

1 Serving: Calories 380 (Calories from Fat 200); Fat 22g (Saturated 10g); Cholesterol 35mg; Sodium 880mg; Carbohydrate 39g (Dietary Fiber 4g); Protein 10g
% Daily Value: Vitamin A 34%; Vitamin C 34%; Calcium 22%; Iron 12%
Diet Exchanges: 2 Starch, 2 Vegetable, 4 Fat

BETTY'S TIPS

✪ Health Twist
Use reduced-fat Alfredo sauce to reduce the fat to 12 grams per serving. Look for it in the refrigerated and pasta sauce sections of your grocery store.

Veggie Casserole with Dill Drop Biscuits

All Things Aside

Creative Accompaniments to Match Any Meal

Caesar Green Beans

Caesar Green Beans

Prep: 10 min   Cook: 10 min

> 2   cups water
> ¾   pound green beans (3 cups)
> ¼   cup Caesar dressing
> 2   tablespoons dried cranberries

1. Heat water to boiling in 2-quart saucepan. Add beans. Heat to boiling. Boil uncovered 5 minutes. Cover and boil 2 to 5 minutes longer or until crisp-tender; drain. Toss with dressing.

2. Place beans in serving bowl. Sprinkle with cranberries.

6 servings.

1 Serving: Calories 100 (Calories from Fat 80); Fat 9g (Saturated 1g); Cholesterol 5mg; Sodium 250mg; Carbohydrate 6g (Dietary Fiber 2g); Protein 1g
% Daily Value: Vitamin A 2%; Vitamin C 0%; Calcium 2%; Iron 2%
Diet Exchanges: 1 Vegetable, 1½ Fat

BETTY'S TIPS

❂ Variation
If you don't have dried cranberries on hand, sprinkle with freshly grated Parmesan cheese or sliced toasted almonds.

To toast almonds, bake uncovered in ungreased shallow pan in 350° oven about 10 minutes, stirring occasionally, until golden brown. Or cook in ungreased heavy skillet over medium-low heat 5 to 7 minutes, stirring frequently until browning begins, then stirring constantly until golden brown.

Corn with Garlic Cilantro Butter

Prep: 10 min   Stand: 2 hr   Grill: 30 min

> 6   ears corn in husks
>   Garlic Cilantro Butter (below)

1. Place corn (in husks) in large container; cover with cold water. Let stand 2 hours.

2. Make Garlic Cilantro Butter.

3. Heat coals or gas grill for direct heat. Cover and grill corn in husks 4 to 6 inches from medium heat 20 to 30 minutes or until corn is tender. Remove husks. Serve corn with Garlic Cilantro Butter.

6 servings.

Garlic Cilantro Butter

> ⅓   cup butter or margarine, softened
> 2   tablespoons chopped fresh cilantro
> ½   teaspoon grated lime peel
> ¼   teaspoon garlic salt
> ¼   teaspoon ground cumin
> ¼   teaspoon black and red pepper blend or black pepper

Mix all ingredients. Cover and refrigerate until serving.

1 Serving: Calories 210 (Calories from Fat 110); Fat 12g (Saturated 7g); Cholesterol 25mg; Sodium 180mg; Carbohydrate 25g (Dietary Fiber 3g); Protein 3g
% Daily Value: Vitamin A 12%; Vitamin C 4%; Calcium 0%; Iron 4%
Diet Exchanges: 1½ Starch, 2 Fat

BETTY'S TIPS

❂ Success Hint
Store fresh corn in a plastic bag in the refrigerator for up to a day. It's best eaten the day it's purchased.

❂ Did You Know?
Soaking the corn in cold water helps tenderize it and also helps prevent the husks from burning while grilling. If you're short on time, soak the corn for 15 minutes and grill the corn as directed.

Savory Corn on a Stick

Prep: 20 min   Microwave: 14 min   Stand: 5 min

4   ears corn
2   tablespoons zesty Italian dressing
2   tablespoons shredded fresh Parmesan
    cheese

1. Husk corn, remove silk and cut each ear in half. Use metal skewer or ice pick to make a hole through center of one end of each piece of corn. Insert 6-inch bamboo skewers through corn.

2. Brush corn with Italian dressing. Place corn in rectangular microwavable dish, 11 × 7 × 1½ inches. Cover with plastic wrap, folding back one corner to vent.

3. Microwave on High 9 to 14 minutes, rotating dish ¼ turn every 5 minutes, until tender. Let stand 5 minutes. Sprinkle with Parmesan cheese before serving.

4 servings.

1 Serving: Calories 155 (Calories from Fat 45); Fat 5g (Saturated 1g); Cholesterol 5mg; Sodium 120mg; Carbohydrate 26g (Dietary Fiber 3g); Protein 5g
% Daily Value: Vitamin A 2%; Vitamin C 4%; Calcium 4%; Iron 4%
Diet Exchanges: 1½ Starch, 1 Fat

BETTY'S TIPS

✪ Variation
Do you want traditional buttered corn? Try using spray butter for a quick and easy way to flavor cooked corn. You can omit the bamboo skewers and still enjoy this savory corn.

Savory Corn on a Stick

Portabellas with Corn Salsa

Prep: 15 min   Broil: 5 min   Cool: 5 min

3 tablespoons white balsamic vinegar

2 tablespoons olive or vegetable oil

½ teaspoon sugar

¼ teaspoon salt

2 packages (6 ounces each) fresh portabella mushrooms, stems removed

1 cup frozen whole kernel corn, cooked and drained

1 cup chopped roma (plum) tomatoes

½ cup sliced ripe olives

¼ cup chopped fresh parsley

1. Mix vinegar, oil, sugar and salt. Reserve ¼ cup for corn salsa.

2. Spray broiler pan with cooking spray. Place mushrooms, stem sides up, in pan. Brush lightly with vinegar mixture. Broil about 6 inches from heat 2 minutes. Turn mushrooms; brush with remaining vinegar mixture. Broil 2 to 3 minutes longer or until tender. Remove from pan; cool 5 minutes.

3. Mix corn, tomatoes, olives, parsley and reserved vinegar mixture. Cut mushrooms into ½ -inch slices. Serve with corn salsa.

8 servings.

1 Serving: Calories 70 (Calories from Fat 35); Fat 4g (Saturated 1g); Cholesterol 0mg; Sodium 150mg; Carbohydrate 8g (Dietary Fiber 2g); Protein 2g
% Daily Value: Vitamin A 2%; Vitamin C 6%; Calcium 0%; Iron 6%
Diet Exchanges: 1½ Vegetable, ½ Fat

BETTY'S TIPS

⊙ **Substitution**

Any chopped fresh tomatoes can be used instead of the roma tomatoes. Regular balsamic vinegar can be used instead of white balsamic vinegar.

⊙ **Special Touch**

Arrange portabellas the full length of a ceramic platter and spread the corn salsa lengthwise over the center of the mushrooms.

Pesto-Stuffed Tomatoes

Prep: 20 min   Microwave: 4 min   Stand: 2 min

4   medium tomatoes (1¼ to 1½ pounds total)

2   tablespoons shredded fresh Parmesan cheese

2   tablespoons pine nuts

2   tablespoons chopped fresh or 2 teaspoons dried basil leaves

1½ teaspoons olive or vegetable oil

½   teaspoon garlic salt

¼   teaspoon pepper

2   slices bread, torn into crumbs

1   tablespoon shredded fresh Parmesan cheese

1. Cut ¼-inch slice from stem end of each tomato; scoop out pulp. Discard seeds; chop pulp. Mix pulp, 2 tablespoons Parmesan cheese, the nuts, basil, oil, garlic salt and pepper. Gently stir in bread crumbs. Fill tomatoes with mixture.

2. Place tomatoes in 4 small microwaveable custard cups or arrange in circle in shallow round microwaveable dish. Cover loosely with waxed paper.

3. Microwave on High 3 to 4 minutes or until tender. Sprinkle with 1 tablespoon Parmesan cheese. Cover and let stand about 2 minutes or until cheese is melted.

4 servings.

1 Serving: Calories 120 (Calories from Fat 55); Fat 6g (Saturated 2g); Cholesterol 5mg; Sodium 290mg; Carbohydrate 13g (Dietary Fiber 2g); Protein 5g
% Daily Value: Vitamin A 8%; Vitamin C 20%; Calcium 8%; Iron 6%
Diet Exchanges: 3 Vegetable, 1 Fat

BETTY'S TIPS

✪ Substitution
One-fourth cup prepared basil pesto can be used in place of the cheese, nuts, basil, olive oil, garlic salt and pepper.

✪ Success Hint
If fresh tomatoes need to ripen, store them at room temperature in a brown paper bag or in a fruit-ripening bowl with other fruits. Don't let them stand in the sun to ripen or they will become mushy.

✪ Did You Know?
The tomato is not a vegetable but a fruit—a berry, to be exact.

Pesto-Stuffed Tomatoes

Easy Grilled Vegetables

Easy Grilled Vegetables

Prep: 10 min   Marinate: 1 hr   Grill: 15 min

12 pattypan squash, about 1 inch in diameter

2 medium red or green bell peppers, each cut into 6 pieces

1 large red onion, cut into ½-inch slices

⅓ cup Italian dressing

Freshly ground pepper, if desired

1. Place squash, bell peppers and onion in rectangular baking dish, 13 × 9 × 2 inches. Pour dressing over vegetables. Cover and let stand 1 hour to blend flavors.

2. Heat coals or gas grill for direct heat. Remove vegetables from marinade; reserve marinade. Place vegetables in grill basket or directly on grill rack.

3. Cover and grill vegetables 4 to 5 inches from medium heat 10 to 15 minutes, turning and brushing vegetables with marinade 2 or 3 times, until crisp-tender. Sprinkle with pepper.

6 servings.

1 Serving: Calories 70 (Calories from Fat 35); Fat 4g (Saturated 1g); Cholesterol 0mg; Sodium 85mg; Carbohydrate 9g (Dietary Fiber 3g); Protein 2g
% Daily Value: Vitamin A 26%; Vitamin C 72%; Calcium 2%; Iron 4%
Diet Exchanges: 2 Vegetable, ½ Fat

BETTY'S TIPS

☺ Substitution
One medium zucchini, cut into 1-inch pieces, can be used in place of the squash. If you like mushrooms, go ahead and add them for the last 10 minutes of grilling.

☺ Success Hint
If you don't have a grill basket, make sure the vegetable pieces are large enough so they don't fall through the grill rack. Cut the vegetables the same size so they'll cook in the same amount of time. Or remove vegetables from the grill as they are done.

Warm Caramelized Vegetables

Prep: 20 min   Cook: 18 min

4 pounds small red potatoes, cut into 1-inch pieces

1 teaspoon salt

2 pounds asparagus, cut into 2-inch pieces

⅔ cup butter or margarine

2 large onions, chopped (2 cups)

½ cup balsamic vinegar

½ cup packed brown sugar

½ teaspoon salt

Freshly ground pepper, if desired

1. Heat 1 inch water to boiling in 4-quart Dutch oven. Add potatoes and 1 teaspoon salt. Heat to boiling; reduce heat to medium. Cover and cook about 12 minutes or until tender; drain and set aside.

2. Heat 1 inch water to boiling in 3-quart saucepan. Add asparagus. Heat to boiling; reduce heat to medium. Cover and cook 5 to 6 minutes or until crisp-tender; drain and set aside with potatoes.

3. While vegetables are cooking, melt butter in 12-inch skillet over medium-high heat. Cook onions in butter about 10 minutes, stirring occasionally, until golden brown. Stir in vinegar, brown sugar and ½ teaspoon salt.

4. Pour onion mixture over potatoes and asparagus; stir until coated. Sprinkle with pepper.

12 servings.

1 Serving: Calories 275 (Calories from Fat 100; Fat 11g (Saturated 6g); Cholesterol 25mg; Sodium 380mg; Carbohydrate 44g (Dietary Fiber 4g); Protein 4g
% Daily Value: Vitamin A 10%; Vitamin C 22%; Calcium 4%; Iron 12%
Diet Exchanges: 3 Vegetable, 2 Fruit, 2 Fat

BETTY'S TIPS

✪ Substitution
Balsamic vinegar is dark brown and has a rich, mellow and slightly sweet flavor. It's a great flavor booster, but if you don't have any on hand, you can use cider or red wine vinegar with a little sugar.

✪ Do-Ahead
You may want to cook the potatoes ahead of time to lessen last-minute stove-top preparation. The caramelized onions could be prepared ahead, as well. It's best to cook the asparagus right before serving, though, then add to the skillet of reheated potatoes and onions.

Italian Christmas Veggies

Prep: 10 min   Cook: 7 min

⅓ cup fat-free Italian Parmesan dressing

2 medium zucchini, cut into ¼-inch slices (2 cups)

1 medium red bell pepper, cut into ½-inch slices

1 cup sliced mushrooms

1 cup sliced onion

2 tablespoons dry white wine

3 tablespoons shredded Parmesan cheese

1. Cook dressing, zucchini, bell pepper, mushrooms and onion in 10-inch skillet over medium-high heat about 5 minutes, stirring frequently, until dressing almost evaporates.

2. Stir in wine. Cover and cook about 2 minutes or until vegetables are crisp-tender. Sprinkle with cheese.

6 servings.

1 Serving: Calories 35 (Calories from Fat 10); Fat 1g (Saturated 1g); Cholesterol 0mg; Sodium 170mg; Carbohydrate 6g (Dietary Fiber 1g); Protein 2g
% Daily Value: Vitamin A 12%; Vitamin C 34%; Calcium 4%; Iron 2%
Diet Exchanges: 1 Vegetable

BETTY'S TIPS

☼ Substitution

For a little variety, use one yellow summer squash in place of one of the zucchini. You also can use chicken broth instead of the wine.

Roasted Autumn Vegetables

Prep: 20 min   Bake: 45 min

2 medium Yukon gold potatoes, cut into eighths

1 medium red onion, cut into 16 wedges and separated

1 small butternut squash, peeled, seeded and cut into 1-inch pieces

1 large red garnet sweet potato, peeled and cut into 1-inch pieces

1 pound baby-cut carrots

2 tablespoons olive or vegetables oil

1 tablespoon chopped fresh or 1 teaspoon dried sage leaves

1 tablespoon chopped fresh or 1 teaspoon dried rosemary leaves

½ teaspoon salt

1 clove garlic, finely chopped

1. Heat oven to 425°. Spray jelly roll pan, 15½ × 10½ × 1 inch, with cooking spray. Place vegetables in pan. Pour oil over vegetables. Sprinkle with remaining ingredients. Stir to coat.

2. Bake uncovered 35 to 45 minutes, stirring occasionally, until vegetables are crisp-tender.

8 servings.

1 Serving: Calories 125 (Calories from Fat 35); Fat 4g (Saturated 1g); Cholesterol 0mg; Sodium 170mg; Carbohydrate 24g (Dietary Fiber 4g); Protein 2g
% Daily Value: Vitamin A 100%; Vitamin C 16%; Calcium 4%; Iron 6%
Diet Exchanges: 1 Starch, 2 Vegetable

BETTY'S TIPS

☼ Success Hint

If the baby carrots are large, cut them in half.

Check veggies at the minimum cooking time, and remove them from the pan as soon as they are done.

☼ Health Twist

Omit the olive oil and instead spray the pan and vegetables with olive oil–flavored cooking spray to reduce the calories to 90 and the fat to 0 grams per serving.

Garden Couscous Salad

Garden Couscous Salad

Prep: 15 min   Chill: 1 hr

2   cups cooked couscous
1   cup sliced zucchini
1   cup garbanzo beans, rinsed and drained
¼   cup chopped red bell pepper
2   medium green onions, sliced (2 tablespoons)
    Yogurt Curry Dressing (below)
    Lettuce leaves

1. Mix all ingredients except Yogurt Curry Dressing and lettuce in large bowl.

2. Make Yogurt Curry Dressing. Stir into couscous mixture. Cover and refrigerate at least 1 hour to blend flavors but no longer than 6 hours.

3. Serve salad on lettuce.

4 to 6 servings.

Yogurt Curry Dressing
½   cup plain yogurt
2   tablespoons olive or vegetable oil
½   teaspoon salt
¼   teaspoon curry powder

Mix all ingredients.

1 Serving: Calories 250 (Calories from Fat 90); Fat 10g (Saturated 2g); Cholesterol 0mg; Sodium 600mg; Carbohydrate 36g (Dietary Fiber 5g); Protein 9g
% Daily Value: Vitamin A 18%; Vitamin C 36%; Calcium 8%; Iron 10%
Diet Exchanges: 2 Starch, 1 Vegetable, 1½ Fat

BETTY'S TIPS

⊙ **Substitution**
Cooked white or brown rice can be used instead of couscous.

Herbed Orzo Pilaf

Prep: 15 min   Cook: 25 min

1   package (16 ounces) rosamarina or orzo pasta
¼   cup pine nuts
2   tablespoons olive or vegetable oil
2   cloves garlic, finely chopped
1½ cups sliced mushrooms (4 ounces)
8   medium green onions, sliced (½ cup)
2   cups sliced roma (plum) tomatoes
¼   cup shredded fresh or 1 tablespoon dried basil leaves
½   teaspoon salt

1. Cook and drain pasta as directed on package.

2. While pasta is cooking, cook nuts in 12-inch skillet over medium heat 2 to 3 minutes, stirring constantly, until toasted. Remove from skillet.

3. Add 1 tablespoon of the oil and the garlic to skillet. Cook and stir over medium-high heat 1 minute. Stir in mushrooms and onions. Cook about 2 minutes, stirring occasionally, until crisp-tender.

4. Stir in tomatoes, pasta, basil, salt and remaining 1 tablespoon oil. Cook over medium heat, stirring occasionally, until heated through. Spoon into serving dish; sprinkle with nuts.

16 servings.

1 Serving: Calories 135 (Calories from Fat 25); Fat 3g (Saturated 1g); Cholesterol 0mg; Sodium 80mg; Carbohydrate 25g (Dietary Fiber 2g); Protein 4g
% Daily Value: Vitamin A 2%; Vitamin C 4%; Calcium 0%; Iron 8%
Diet Exchanges: 1 Starch, 2 Vegetable, ½ Fat

BETTY'S TIPS

⊙ Do-Ahead
Cook the pasta as directed on the package, but undercook it by a minute or two. Drain, then rinse with cold water and drain again. Toss with a teaspoon of olive or vegetable oil. Refrigerate in a tightly covered container or resealable plastic food storage bag up to 5 days. When making the pilaf, add pasta to the skillet after cooking mushrooms and green onions, and heat through. Then stir in the remaining ingredients and heat through.

Herbed Orzo Pilaf

Grilled Herbed New Potatoes

Prep: 10 min   Grill: 15 min

2 tablespoons olive or vegetable oil

1 tablespoon chopped fresh or ½ teaspoon dried rosemary leaves

1 tablespoon chopped fresh or ½ teaspoon parsley flakes

½ teaspoon lemon pepper

¼ teaspoon salt

8 small red potatoes, cut into fourths

Sour Cream Sauce (below)

1. Heat coals or gas grill for direct heat. Mix oil, rosemary, parsley, lemon pepper and salt. Add potatoes; toss to coat. Place potatoes in grill basket.

2. Cover and grill potatoes 4 to 6 inches from medium heat 10 to 15 minutes, shaking grill basket to turn potatoes occasionally, until tender.

3. Make Sour Cream Sauce. Serve with potatoes.

4 servings.

Sour Cream Sauce

⅓ cup sour cream

1 tablespoon chopped fresh or ½ teaspoon dried rosemary leaves

¼ teaspoon lemon pepper

⅛ teaspoon garlic powder

Mix all ingredients.

1 Serving: Calories 290 (Calories from Fat 100); Fat 11g (Saturated 3g); Cholesterol 10mg; Sodium 220mg; Carbohydrate 47g (Dietary Fiber 5g); Protein 5g
% Daily Value: Vitamin A 2%; Vitamin C 20%; Calcium 4%; Iron 14%
Diet Exchanges: 3 Starch, 1 Fat

BETTY'S TIPS

☉ Substitution

If you don't have lemon pepper, use pepper instead and add some freshly grated lemon peel.

☉ Serve-With

Serve this recipe as a terrific accompaniment to Grilled Salmon with Nectarine Salsa (page 127). Add a tossed salad and iced tea to complete the meal.

Smashed Red Potatoes with Gorgonzola Cheese

Prep: 10 min   Cook: 25 min

1½   pounds small red potatoes, cut in half
 3   tablespoons butter or margarine, softened
⅓   cup buttermilk
 1   package (4 ounces) crumbled Gorgonzola cheese
½   teaspoon salt
     Pinch of pepper

1. Place potatoes in 3-quart saucepan; add enough water (salted if desired) to cover. Cover and heat to boiling; reduce heat. Simmer about 20 minutes or until potatoes are tender; drain. Shake potatoes in saucepan over low heat to dry.

2. Add butter, buttermilk, cheese, salt and pepper to potatoes. Lightly mash with fork or back of spoon, keeping some larger pieces of potato.

6 servings.

1 Serving: Calories 215 (Calories from Fat 100); Fat 11g (Saturated 5g); Cholesterol 15mg; Sodium 560mg; Carbohydrate 24g (Dietary Fiber 2g); Protein 7g
% Daily Value: Vitamin A 12%; Vitamin C 8%; Calcium 12%; Iron 6%
Diet Exchanges: 1½ Starch, 2 Fat

BETTY'S TIPS

✿ **Success Hint**

If you make the potatoes ahead of time, keep them warm by setting the saucepan over a double boiler or larger pan of simmering water, or place the potatoes in a slow cooker on the low heat setting for 2 to 3 hours.

You can easily double this recipe to feed a larger group. Just be certain you have a large Dutch oven to allow for boiling 3 pounds of potatoes.

✿ **Special Touch**

Sprinkle chopped fresh chives or toasted chopped walnuts over smashed potatoes before serving. To toast walnuts, cook in an ungreased skillet over medium heat 5 to 7 minutes, stirring frequently until nuts begin to brown, then constantly until light brown.

Smashed Red Potatoes with Gorgonzola Cheese

Whipped Maple Sweet Potatoes

Prep: 15 min   Bake: 1 hr 15 min

- 3 pounds red garnet sweet potatoes or yams
- 2 tablespoons maple-flavored syrup
- 2 tablespoons butter or margarine, softened
- ½ teaspoon salt
  Ground nutmeg to taste
  Additional maple-flavored syrup, if desired

1. Heat oven to 350°. Pierce potatoes with fork. Place potatoes in square pan, 9 × 9 × 2 inches. Cover and bake about 1 hour 15 minutes or until potatoes can be easily pierced with a knife.

2. Slip off skins. Beat potatoes with electric mixer on medium speed until no lumps remain. Add 2 table-spoons syrup, the butter, salt and nutmeg. Continue beating until potatoes are light and fluffy. Drizzle with additional syrup.

6 servings.

1 Serving: Calories 180 (Calories from Fat 35); Fat 4g (Saturated 1g); Cholesterol 0mg; Sodium 260mg; Carbohydrate 38g (Dietary Fiber 4g); Protein 2g
% Daily Value: Vitamin A 100%; Vitamin C 28%; Calcium 4%; Iron 4%
Diet Exchanges: 1 Starch, 1½ Fruit, ½ Fat

BETTY'S TIPS

⊙ **Do-Ahead**
Cover and refrigerate whipped sweet potatoes up to 24 hours. Reheat in microwave oven or in slow cooker on low heat setting until warm.

⊙ **Special Touch**
Sprinkle chopped toasted pecans over sweet potatoes.

Cranberry Stuffing

Prep: 15 min   Bake: 45 min

- 1 cup butter or margarine
- 1½ cups chopped celery (stalks and leaves)
- 1 medium onion, finely chopped (¾ cup)
- 9 cups soft bread cubes (about 15 slices bread) or corn bread cubes
- ½ cup dried cranberries
- 2 tablespoons chopped fresh or 1½ teaspoons dried sage leaves
- 1 tablespoon chopped fresh or 1 teaspoon dried thyme leaves
- 1½ teaspoons salt
- ½ teaspoon pepper

1. Heat oven to 350°. Grease a 3-quart casserole or 13 × 9 × 2-inch rectangular baking dish. Melt butter in 10-inch skillet over medium heat. Cook celery and onion in butter, stirring frequently, until onion is tender. Stir in about one-third of the bread cubes.

2. Place celery mixture in large bowl. Add remaining bread cubes and ingredients; toss. Place in baking pan. Cover and bake 30 minutes. Uncover and bake 15 minutes longer.

12 servings.

1 Serving: Calories 160 (Calories from Fat 100); Fat 11g (Saturated 7g); Cholesterol 30mg; Sodium 370mg; Carbohydrate 15g (Dietary Fiber 2g); Protein 2g
% Daily Value: Vitamin A 8%; Vitamin C 4%; Calcium 2%; Iron 4%
Diet Exchanges: 1 Starch, 2 Fat

BETTY'S TIPS

⊙ **Substitution**
Use 2 teaspoons poultry seasoning instead of the sage and thyme.

⊙ **Variation**
This recipe makes 9 cups of stuffing, enough for a 12-pound turkey. If you like to cook your stuffing in the bird, stuff the turkey just before roasting.

⊙ **Did You Know?**
Look for dried cranberries in the dried fruits section or the produce department of your supermarket. If they are unavail-able, you can also use raisins or dried blueberries.

Slow Cooker Sourdough and Wild Rice Stuffing

Prep: 25 min   Bake: 15 min   Cook: 7 hr 30 min

8	cups cubed sourdough bread
3	cups chicken broth
½	cup uncooked wild rice
⅓	cup dried porcini mushroom pieces
3	medium stalks celery, chopped (1½ cups)
1	medium onion, chopped (½ cup)
¼	cup chopped fresh parsley
¼	cup butter or margarine, melted
1	teaspoon dried basil leaves
1	teaspoon dried thyme leaves
½	teaspoon ground sage
½	teaspoon salt
¼	teaspoon pepper
¾	cup chicken broth

1. Heat oven to 300°. Spread bread cubes in single layer in large roasting pan or baking pan. Bake 10 to 15 minutes or until lightly toasted; set aside.

2. Place 3 cups broth, the wild rice and mushrooms in 4- or 5-quart slow cooker. Cover and cook on high heat setting 3 hours.

3. Add remaining ingredients except ¾ cup broth to wild rice mixture. Add bread cubes. Pour ¾ cup broth over bread mixture; toss gently. Cover and cook on low heat setting 4 hours to 4 hours 30 minutes.

12 servings.

1 Serving: Calories 135 (Calories from Fat 45); Fat 5g (Saturated 1g); Cholesterol 0mg; Sodium 630mg; Carbohydrate 19g (Dietary Fiber 2g); Protein 5g
% Daily Value: Vitamin A 6%; Vitamin C 2%; Calcium 4%; Iron 6%
Diet Exchanges: 1 Starch, 1 Vegetable, 1 Fat

BETTY'S TIPS

⚙ **Substitution**
If you prefer to use regular white mushrooms instead of the dried porcini mushroom pieces, stir in 1 cup chopped mushrooms with the wild rice.

You can use plain white or whole wheat bread cubes instead of the sourdough.

Slow Cooker Sourdough and Wild Rice Stuffing

Sour Cream and Chive Rolls

Sour Cream and Chive Rolls

Prep: 30 min   Cool: 20 min   Rise: 1 hr   Bake: 20 min

¾ cup sour cream

2 tablespoons shortening

2¼ cups Gold Medal all-purpose flour

2 tablespoons sugar

1 teaspoon salt

1 package regular or quick active dry yeast

⅓ cup very warm water (120° to 130°)

1 egg

1½ tablespoons chopped fresh chives

1. Heat sour cream and shortening over medium heat, stirring frequently, until shortening is melted. Cool about 20 minutes or until lukewarm.

2. Mix 1¼ cups of the flour, the sugar, salt and yeast in large bowl. Add sour cream mixture, water and egg; beat with spoon until smooth. Stir in remaining 1 cup flour and the chives until smooth. Scrape batter from side of bowl. Cover and let rise in warm place about 30 minutes or until double.

3. Grease 12 medium muffin cups, 2½ × 1¼ inches. Stir down batter by beating about 25 strokes. Spoon into muffin cups. Let rise uncovered 20 to 30 minutes or until batter rounds over tops of cups.

4. Heat oven to 400°. Bake 15 to 20 minutes or until golden brown.

12 rolls.

1 roll: Calories 150 (Calories from Fat 55); Fat 6g (Saturated 2g); Cholesterol 25mg; Sodium 210mg; Carbohydrate 21g (Dietary Fiber 1g); Protein 4g
% Daily Value: Vitamin A 2%; Vitamin C 0%; Calcium 2%; Iron 6%
Diet Exchanges: 1½ Starch, 1 Fat

BETTY'S TIPS

✿ Variation
Make flavorful **Herb Rolls.** Omit sour cream and chives. Use 1 cup very warm water; do not melt shortening. Add 1 teaspoon caraway seed, ½ teaspoon dried sage leaves and ¼ teaspoon ground nutmeg to the flour mixture. Add shortening with the water and egg.

✿ Do-Ahead
Make 2 batches of these rolls for hearty appetites! Bake them earlier in the day, then warm the rolls in the microwave. Place 8 to 10 rolls on a microwavable plate or in a napkin-lined basket and microwave uncovered on Medium (50%) 1 minute. Continue to microwave, checking every 15 seconds, until warm.

Garlic Bread Wreath

Prep: 20 min   Rise: 3 hr   Bake: 30 min

¼ cup shredded Parmesan cheese
1 loaf (1 pound) frozen white bread dough (from 3-pound package), thawed
1 tablespoon olive or vegetable oil
1 small clove garlic, finely chopped

1. Grease cookie sheet. Spray outside of 6-ounce custard cup with cooking spray; place upside down on center of cookie sheet.

2. Sprinkle 2 tablespoons of the cheese over flat surface. Roll bread dough in cheese into 24-inch rope. Place rope on cookie sheet and form into circle around custard cup; pinch ends to seal.

3. Make cuts in dough at about 1½-inch intervals from the outer edge of the circle, cutting two-thirds of the way through, using kitchen scissors. Lift and turn every other section of dough toward center of the circle. Cover and let rise in warm place 2 to 3 hours or until double. (Dough is ready if indentation remains when touched.)

4. Heat oven to 350°. Mix oil and garlic; brush over dough. Sprinkle with remaining 2 tablespoons cheese. Bake 25 to 30 minutes or until golden brown. Remove custard cup.

8 servings.

1 Serving: Calories 170 (Calories from Fat 35); Fat 4g (Saturated 1g); Cholesterol 2mg; Sodium 350mg; Carbohydrate 28g (Dietary Fiber 1g); Protein 6g
% Daily Value: Vitamin A 0%; Vitamin C 0%; Calcium 10%; Iron 10%
Diet Exchanges: 2 Starch

BETTY'S TIPS

☺ Serve-With
Fill the center of the wreath with a dish of olive oil garnished with fresh rosemary sprigs or a dish of sun-dried tomato butter. To make the butter, beat ¼ cup softened butter with 2 tablespoons chopped, drained, oil-packed sun-dried tomatoes.

Low-Fat

Bread Machine Dinner Rolls

*Prep: 20 min   Dough Cycle: 1 hr 30 min
Rest: 10 min   Rise: 40 min   Bake: 15 min*

1 cup water
2 tablespoons butter or margarine, softened
1 egg
3¼ cups Gold Medal Better for Bread flour
¼ cup sugar
1 teaspoon salt
3 teaspoons bread machine or active dry yeast
Butter or margarine, melted, if desired

1. Measure carefully, placing all ingredients except melted butter in bread machine pan in the order recommended by the manufacturer. Select Dough/Manual cycle. Do not use delay cycle.

2. Remove dough from pan, using lightly floured hands. Cover and let rest 10 minutes on lightly floured surface.

3. Grease large cookie sheet. Divide dough into 15 equal pieces. Shape each piece into a ball. Place 2 inches apart on cookie sheet. Cover and let rise in warm place 30 to 40 minutes or until double. (Dough is ready if indentation remains when touched.)

4. Heat oven to 375°. Bake 12 to 15 minutes or until golden brown. Brush tops with melted butter. Serve warm, or cool on wire rack.

15 rolls.

1 Roll: Calories 135 (Calories from Fat 20); Fat 2g (Saturated 0g); Cholesterol 15mg; Sodium 170mg; Carbohydrate 26g (Dietary Fiber 1g); Protein 4g
% Daily Value: Vitamin A 2%; Vitamin C 0%; Calcium 0%; Iron 8%
Diet Exchanges: 1½ Starch, ½ Fat

BETTY'S TIPS

☺ Do-Ahead
After you have shaped the dough into rolls and placed them on the cookie sheet, cover with plastic wrap. You can refrigerate them from 4 hours up to 48 hours. Before baking, remove the rolls from the refrigerator and remove plastic wrap. Cover with kitchen towel and let rise in a warm place about 2 hours or until double. Bake the rolls as directed.

Bread Machine Dinner Rolls

Sweet Potato Cranberry Knots

Prep: 30 min   Rise: 2 hr 10 min   Bake : 20 min

2¼ to 2¾ cups Gold Medal Better for Bread flour
  ¼ cup sugar
  1 teaspoon salt
  ½ teaspoon ground cinnamon
  1 package quick active dry yeast
  ¼ cup butter or margarine, softened
  ¾ cup lukewarm water (95°)
  ¾ cup mashed drained sweet potatoes packed in syrup (from 23-ounce can)
  ½ cup dried cranberries
     Butter or margarine, melted

1. Mix 1 cup of the flour, the sugar, salt, cinnamon and yeast in large bowl. Add ¼ cup butter and the water. Beat with electric mixer on low speed 1 minute scraping bowl frequently. Add sweet potatoes. Beat on medium speed 1 minute, scraping bowl frequently. Stir in cranberries and enough remaining flour, ½ cup at a time, to make dough easy to handle.

2. Place dough on lightly floured surface. Knead about 5 minutes or until smooth and springy. Place dough in large bowl greased with shortening, turning dough to grease all sides. Cover and let rise in warm place 1 hour to 1 hour 30 minutes or until double. (Dough is ready if indentation remains when touched.)

3. Heat oven to 375°. Spray cookie sheet with cooking spray. Gently push fist into dough to deflate. Divide dough into 12 equal pieces. Roll each piece into 8-inch rope; tie into knot. Place on cookie sheet.

4. Brush knots with melted butter. Cover and let rise in warm place about 40 minutes or until double. Bake 14 to 20 minutes or until golden brown.

12 rolls.

1 Roll: Calories 185 (Calories from Fat 55); Fat 6g (Saturated 2g); Cholesterol 5mg; Sodium 270mg; Carbohydrate 33g (Dietary Fiber 3g); Protein 3g
% Daily Value: Vitamin A 18%; Vitamin C 6%; Calcium 0%; Iron 8%
Diet Exchanges: 1 Starch, 1 Fruit, 1 Fat

BETTY'S TIPS

❂ **Variation**
For a citrus twist, add 1 teaspoon freshly grated orange peel with the sweet potatoes.

❂ **Do-Ahead**
Rolls can be made up to a day ahead of time. Reheat in the microwave just before serving.

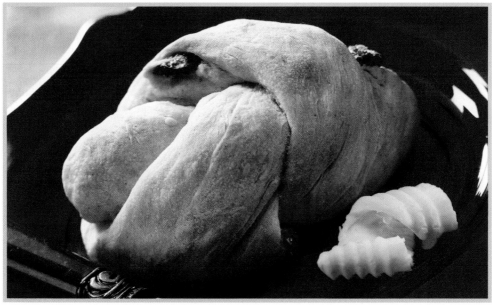

Sweet Potato Cranberry Knots

Sweet Treats

Cookies, Candies and Other Confections

Chocolate Chip Pecan Pie Bars

Chocolate Chip Pecan Pie Bars

Prep: 20 min   Bake: 45 min   Chill: 2 hr

1½	cups Original Bisquick
1	cup powdered sugar
¼	cup firm margarine or butter
4	eggs, beaten
1	cup dark corn syrup
¼	cup margarine or butter, melted and cooled
1	teaspoon vanilla
1	bag (6 ounces) semisweet chocolate chips (1 cup)
1½	cups chopped pecans (6 ounces)

1. Heat oven to 350°. Mix Bisquick and powdered sugar in medium bowl. Cut in margarine, using pastry blender or crisscrossing 2 knives, until crumbly. Press firmly in bottom of ungreased rectangular pan, 13 × 9 × 2 inches. Bake 15 minutes; cool.

2. Beat eggs, corn syrup, margarine and vanilla in large bowl with spoon until smooth. Stir in chocolate chips and pecans. Pour over crust.

3. Bake 25 to 30 minutes or until golden brown and set. Refrigerate at least 2 hours until chocolate is firm. For bars, cut into 6 rows by 6 rows.

36 bars.

1 Bar: Calories 145 (Calories from Fat 70); Fat 8g (Saturated 2g); Cholesterol 25mg; Sodium 125mg; Carbohydrate 8g (Dietary Fiber 1g); Protein 2g
% Daily Value: Vitamin A 4%; Vitamin C 0%; Calcium 2%; Iron 2%
Diet Exchanges: 1 Starch, 1½ Fat

BETTY'S TIPS

⊙ **Success Hint**
Use the size of pan specified in the recipe. Bars made in a larger pan will be dry and overbaked; those made in a smaller pan will be underbaked.

⊙ **Time-Saver**
Buy a bag of already-chopped pecans to save on prep time.

Brownie Butterscotch Squares

Prep: 10 min   Bake: 30 min   Cool: 3 hr

1	package Betty Crocker Supreme Original brownie mix (with chocolate syrup pouch)
¼	cup water
⅓	cup vegetable oil
2 or 3	eggs
⅔	cup sugar
⅔	cup light corn syrup
1	cup butterscotch-flavored chips
½	cup peanut butter
2	cups Country® Corn Flakes cereal

1. Heat oven to 350°. Bake brownie mix for either fudge-like or cakelike brownies, using water, oil and eggs, as directed on package for 13 × 9 × 2-inch pan. Cool completely, about 2 hours.

2. Mix sugar and corn syrup in 2-quart saucepan. Heat to boiling, stirring constantly; remove from heat. Stir in butterscotch chips and peanut butter until melted. Stir in cereal. Immediately spread over cooled brownies.

3. Cool brownies completely, about 1 hour. For squares, cut into 8 rows by 4 rows. Store tightly covered.

32 squares.

1 Square: Calories 210 (Calories from Fat 80); Fat 9g (Saturated 3g); Cholesterol 15mg; Sodium 110mg; Carbohydrate 30g (Dietary Fiber 0g); Protein 2g
% Daily Value: Vitamin A 0%; Vitamin C 0%; Calcium 2%; Iron 6%
Diet Exchanges: 1 Starch, 1 Fruit, 2 Fat

BETTY'S TIPS

⊙ **Pack 'n Go**
Expect oohs and aahs when serving these butterscotch- and peanut butter-topped brownies. Use a plastic knife (rather than a sharp knife) to easily cut brownies.

⊙ **Variation**
Nut lovers can stir ½ cup of chopped peanuts into the brownie batter.

Bear Cookie Pops

Prep: 15 min   Bake: 13 min per sheet   Cool: 32 min

- 1 pouch (1 pound 1.5 ounces) Betty Crocker peanut butter cookie mix
- ⅓ cup vegetable oil
- 1 egg
- 24 flat round candies (about ½ inch in diameter)
- 12 milk chocolate kisses, unwrapped
- 1 tube (0.68 ounce) Betty Crocker red decorating gel

1. Heat oven to 375°. Stir cookie mix, oil and egg in medium bowl until soft dough forms.

2. Shape dough into 12 balls, using 1½ tablespoons dough for each. Place balls about 4 inches apart on ungreased cookie sheet. Shape remaining dough into 24 balls, using 1 teaspoon dough for each.

3. Insert wooden stick with round ends into side of each large ball; place 2 small balls next to each large ball for ears. Press balls evenly until about ¼ inch thick.

4. Bake 11 to 13 minutes or until edges begin to brown. Cool 2 minutes; remove from cookie sheet to wire rack. Cool completely, about 30 minutes.

5. Add 2 small candies on each cookie for eyes and 1 chocolate kiss for nose, using gel to attach. Squeeze on gel for mouth.

12 cookie pops.

1 Cookie Pop: Calories 275 (Calories from Fat 115); Fat 13g (Saturated 3g); Cholesterol 25mg; Sodium 210mg; Carbohydrate 35g (Dietary Fiber 0g); Protein 4g
% Daily Value: Vitamin A 0%; Vitamin C 0%; Calcium 0%; Iron 2%
Diet Exchanges: 1½ Starch, 1 Fruit, 2 Fat

BETTY'S TIPS

☺ **Variation**

Make **Bear Paws!** Shape dough into 12 balls; place on cookie sheet. Insert stick into side of each ball; press dough until ¼ inch thick. Press 4 jelly beans into each cookie about ½ inch from edge for toe pads. Press 1 semisweet chocolate chip at end of each jelly bean for claws. Bake as directed; cool completely. Spread each cookie with 1 teaspoon chocolate ready-to-spread frosting for paw pad.

☺ **Special Touch**

If you are serving birthday cake at the party, wrap up a couple of cookies for each child as a party gift. It's a great way to send party fun home!

Bear Cookie Pops

Cranberry Orange Biscotti

Prep: 25 min   Bake: 45 min   Cool: 15 min

⅔ cup sugar
½ cup vegetable oil
1 tablespoon grated orange peel
1½ teaspoons vanilla
2 eggs
2½ cups Gold Medal all-purpose flour
¾ cup dried cranberries, coarsely chopped
1 teaspoon baking powder
¼ teaspoon baking soda
¼ teaspoon salt

1. Heat oven to 350°. Beat sugar, oil, orange peel, vanilla and eggs in large bowl. Stir in remaining ingredients.

2. Place dough on lightly floured surface. Knead until smooth. Shape half of dough at a time into 10 × 3-inch rectangle on ungreased cookie sheet.

3. Bake 25 to 30 minutes or until toothpick inserted in center comes out clean. Cool on cookie sheet 15 minutes.

4. Cut rectangles crosswise into ½-inch slices. Place slices, cut sides down, on cookie sheet.

5. Bake about 15 minutes, turning once, until crisp and light brown. Immediately remove from cookie sheet to wire rack; cool.

About 3 dozen cookies.

1 Cookie: Calories 80 (Calories from Fat 25); Fat 3g (Saturated 1g); Cholesterol 10mg; Sodium 40mg; Carbohydrate 13g (Dietary Fiber 1g); Protein 1g
% Daily Value: Vitamin A 0%; Vitamin C 2%; Calcium 0%; Iron 2%
Diet Exchanges: 1 Starch

BETTY'S TIPS

⊛ **Do-Ahead**
Store biscotti in an airtight container for up to 4 weeks. For longer storage, freeze biscotti in an airtight freezer container; label. Freeze no longer than 3 months. Let stand at room temperature to thaw.

⊛ **Special Touch**
Melt 3 ounces semisweet baking chocolate or white baking bar and ½ teaspoon shortening. Drizzle chocolate over biscotti or dip half of each biscotti into melted chocolate. Place on waxed paper until chocolate is set.

Betty... MAKES IT EASY

Rainbow Egg Cookies

Prep: 40 min   Bake: 9 min per sheet   Cool: 30 min

- 1 pouch Betty Crocker sugar cookie mix
- ½ cup margarine or butter, melted
- ¼ cup Gold Medal all-purpose flour
- 1 egg
- 3 food colors
  White coarse sugar crystals or granulated sugar, if desired
- ½ tub Betty Crocker Rich & Creamy vanilla ready-to-spread frosting

1. Heat oven to 375°. Stir cookie mix, margarine, flour and egg until soft dough forms. Divide dough evenly among 3 bowls; tint each dough by stirring in desired food color. (See chart below for a guide to mixing colors. For a variety of colors, make several batches of cookies.)

2. Shape ⅓ cup of each color of dough into a rope about 5 inches long and 1 inch in diameter. Place ropes side by side and a little more than ¼ inch apart on floured surface; roll until ¼ inch thick. Cut with 2- to 2½-inch egg-shaped cookie cutter so each cookie has 3 colors. Sprinkle with sugar. Place 2 inches apart on ungreased cookie sheet. Repeat with remaining dough. (When rerolling dough scraps, carefully lay matching colors together. For marbled cookies, mix colors of dough scraps but don't mix colors too much or they won't be distinct.)

3. Bake 7 to 9 minutes or until edges are light golden brown. Cool 1 minute; remove from cookie sheet to wire rack. Cool completely, about 30 minutes. Spread frosting on bottoms of half the cookies. Top with remaining cookies.

18 sandwich cookies.

1 Sandwich Cookie: Calories 245 (Calories from Fat 100); Fat 11g (Saturated 7g); Cholesterol 30mg; Sodium 105mg; Carbohydrate 36g (Dietary Fiber 0g); Protein 1g
% Daily Value: Vitamin A 4%; Vitamin C 0%; Calcium 0%; Iron 2%
Diet Exchanges: 1 Starch, 1 Fruit, 2 Fat

Place ropes side by side and a little more than ¼ inch apart on floured surface; roll until ¼ inch thick.

Cut with 2- to 2½-inch egg-shaped cookie cutter so each cookie has 3 colors.

To make the colors of Rainbow Egg Cookies as shown in the photograph, use the proportions of liquid food color in this chart as a guide.

Color	Number of Drops of Liquid Food Color
Orange	2 drops yellow and 2 drops red
Peach	4 drops yellow and 1 drop red
Lime green	3 drops yellow and 1 drop green
Turquoise blue	3 drops blue and 1 drop green
Purple	3 drops red and 2 drops blue
Rose	5 drops red and 1 drop blue

Grandma's Gingersnaps

Grandma's Gingersnaps

Prep: 20 min   Bake: 12 min per sheet   Cool: 2 min

1	cup shortening
¼	cup butter or margarine
⅓	cup molasses
1⅔	cups sugar
2	eggs
4	cups Gold Medal all-purpose flour
3	teaspoons baking soda
2	teaspoons ground cinnamon
1	teaspoon salt
1	teaspoon ground cloves
1	teaspoon ground ginger
	Additional sugar

1. Heat oven to 350°. Melt shortening and butter in 1-quart saucepan over low heat. Cool 15 minutes.

2. Mix shortening mixture, molasses, 1⅔ cups sugar and the eggs in large bowl until well blended. Stir in remaining ingredients except additional sugar.

3. Shape dough into 1-inch balls. Roll in sugar. Place about 2 inches apart on ungreased cookie sheet.

4. Bake 10 to 12 minutes or until set. Cool 1 to 2 minutes; remove from cookie sheet to wire rack.

About 6 dozen cookies.

1 Cookie: Calories 90 (Calories from Fat 35); Fat 4g (Saturated 1g); Cholesterol 5mg; Sodium 90mg; Carbohydrate 12g (Dietary Fiber 0g); Protein 1g
% Daily Value: Vitamin A 0%; Vitamin C 0%; Calcium 0%; Iron 2%
Diet Exchanges: ½ Starch, 1 Fat

BETTY'S TIPS

✪ **Variation**
For **Giant Gingersnaps,** shape dough by rounded measuring tablespoonfuls or using #24 cookie/ice-cream scoop into balls. Bake 12 to 15 minutes.

For a real ginger zing, add ¼ cup chopped crystallized ginger to the dough before shaping into balls.

✪ **Special Touch**
Melt 3 packages (6 ounces each) white baking bar, broken up, and 1 tablespoon shortening. Dip half of each cookie into melted mixture; sprinkle with chopped crystallized ginger. Place on waxed paper until coating is set.

White Chocolate Macadamia Nut Cookies

Prep: 20 min   Bake: 12 min per sheet

1	bag (10 ounces) white baking chips (1⅔ cups)
⅔	cup sugar
⅔	cup butter or margarine, softened
1	teaspoon vanilla
2	eggs
2½	cups Gold Medal all-purpose flour
1	teaspoon baking soda
1	teaspoon cream of tartar
1	cup coarsely chopped macadamia nuts

1. Heat oven to 325°. Place 1 cup of the baking chips in 2-cup microwavable measuring cup. Microwave uncovered on Medium (50%) 3 to 4 minutes or until chips are softened. Stir chips until smooth; cool.

2. Beat sugar, butter, vanilla and eggs in large bowl with electric mixer on medium speed until creamy. Beat in melted chips on low speed. Stir in flour, baking soda and cream of tartar. Stir in remaining ⅔ cup baking chips and the nuts.

3. Drop dough by rounded teaspoonfuls about 2 inches apart onto ungreased cookie sheet. Bake 10 to 12 minutes; remove from cookie sheet to wire rack.

About 4 dozen cookies.

1 Cookie: Calories 110 (Calories from Fat 55); Fat 6g (Saturated 3g); Cholesterol 15mg; Sodium 50mg; Carbohydrate 12g (Dietary Fiber 0g); Protein 2g
% Daily Value: Vitamin A 2%; Vitamin C 0%; Calcium 2%; Iron 2%
Diet Exchanges: 1 Starch, 1 Fat

BETTY'S TIPS

✪ **Variation**
Make these cookies extra-special for a graduation or shower by dipping into candy coating.

Melt 16 ounces of vanilla-flavored candy coating (almond bark) as the package directs. Stir in enough paste food color until coating is desired color (Liquid food color would stiffen the coating). If you like, divide the coating in half and tint each a different color.

Dip half of each cooled cookie into coating, and place on waxed paper until firm. If dipping cookies into 2 colors, let first color set before dipping again.

On-the-Trail Monster Cookies

Prep: 10 min   Bake: 15 min per sheet

1 cup granulated sugar
1 cup packed brown sugar
½ cup butter or margarine, softened
½ cup butter-flavor or regular shortening
1½ cups quick-cooking or old-fashioned oats
2 teaspoons vanilla
2 eggs
2 cups Gold Medal all-purpose flour
1 teaspoon baking powder
1 teaspoon baking soda
1 cup peanut butter
2 cups candy-coated chocolate candies
1 cup peanuts
¾ cup raisins

1. Heat oven to 375°. Beat sugars, butter and shortening in large bowl with electric mixer on medium speed, or mix with spoon. Stir in oats, vanilla and eggs. Stir in flour, baking powder and baking soda thoroughly. Stir in peanut butter. Stir in candies, peanuts and raisins.

2. Drop dough by scant ¼ cupfuls about 2 inches apart onto ungreased cookie sheet; flatten to ¾-inch thickness.

3. Bake 13 to 15 minutes or just until cookies are set and begin to brown. Cool 1 minute; remove from cookie sheet to wire rack.

About 3 dozen cookies.

1 Cookie: Calories 265 (Calories from Fat 125); Fat 15g (Saturated 5g); Cholesterol 20mg; Sodium 110mg; Carbohydrate 32g (Dietary Fiber 2g); Protein 5g
% Daily Value: Vitamin A 2%; Vitamin C 0%; Calcium 4%; Iron 6%
Diet Exchanges: 2 Starch, 2½ Fat

BETTY'S TIPS

⊙ **Time-Saver**
If you don't have time to make a batch of these irresistible cookies, **Striped S'mores** are a quick sweet treat. Thread a large marshmallow on a skewer. Heat over a campfire or grill, turning frequently, until golden brown. Place between bottoms of 2 fudge-striped shortbread cookies and press tightly.

⊙ **Variation**
For cookies with a less-monstrous size but the same big taste, drop dough by rounded tablespoonfuls and flatten slightly. Bake 9 to 10 minutes. You'll make about 60 cookies.

On-the-Trail Monster Cookies

Pistachio Cranberry Fudge

Prep: 15 min   Microwave: 5 min   Chill: 2 hr

- 1½ bags (12-ounce size) semisweet chocolate chips (3 cups)
- 2 cups miniature marshmallows or 16 large marshmallows, cut in half
- 1 can (14 ounces) sweetened condensed milk
- 1 teaspoon vanilla
- 1 cup pistachio nuts
- ½ cup dried cranberries or chopped candied cherries
- ¼ cup white baking chips, melted, if desired

1. Line square pan, 9 × 9 × 2 inches, with aluminum foil, leaving 1 inch of foil overhanging at 2 opposite sides of pan. Grease foil with butter.

2. Place chocolate chips, marshmallows and milk in 8-cup microwavable measuring cup. Microwave uncovered on High 3 to 5 minutes, stirring every minute, until marshmallows and chips are melted and can be stirred smooth.

3. Stir in vanilla, nuts and cherries. Immediately pour into pan. Drizzle with melted white baking chips. Refrigerate about 2 hours or until firm.

4. Remove fudge from pan, using foil edges to lift. Cut into 9 rows by 8 rows, or cut into diamond shapes.

6 dozen candies.

1 Candy: Calories 75 (Calories from Fat 35); Fat 3g (Saturated 2g); Cholesterol 5mg; Sodium 15mg; Carbohydrate 11g (Dietary Fiber 1g); Protein 1g
% Daily Value: Vitamin A 0%; Vitamin C 0%; Calcium 2%; Iron 2%
Diet Exchanges: 1 Fruit, 1 Fat

BETTY'S TIPS

✪ **Variation**
For a scrumptious new flavor twist, omit the cranberries, substitute hazelnuts for the pistachios and add 2 tablespoons hazelnut liqueur with the nuts.

If you like luscious, creamy chocolate fudge, just leave out the nuts and cranberries for a smooth, rich chocolate treat.

Hazelnut Coffee Caramels

Prep: 5 min   Cook: 20 min   Cool: 2 hr

- ½ cup chopped hazelnuts
- ¾ cup butter or margarine
- 2 cups packed brown sugar
- 1 cup corn syrup
- 2 tablespoons instant espresso coffee (dry)
- 1 tablespoon hazelnut syrup (coffee flavoring)
- 1 can (14 ounces) sweetened condensed milk
- Chocolate-covered coffee beans, if desired

1. Line square pan, 8 × 8 × 2 inches, with aluminum foil, leaving 1 inch of foil overhanging at 2 opposite sides of pan. Butter foil that lines bottom and sides of pan. Sprinkle hazelnuts in pan.

2. Heat butter, brown sugar, corn syrup, coffee, hazelnut syrup and milk to boiling in heavy 3-quart saucepan. Cook over medium heat, stirring frequently, to 245° on candy thermometer or until small amount of mixture dropped into cup of very cold water forms a firm ball. Pour into pan. Cool completely, about 2 hours.

3. Remove mixture from pan, using foil edges to lift. Cut into 8 rows by 6 rows, separating caramels as they are cut. Garnish with coffee beans. Wrap pieces individually in plastic wrap or waxed paper.

4 dozen candies.

1 Candy: Calories 135 (Calories from Fat 45); Fat 5g (Saturated 2g); Cholesterol 10mg; Sodium 45mg; Carbohydrate 21g (Dietary Fiber 0g); Protein 1g
% Daily Value: Vitamin A 2%; Vitamin C 0%; Calcium 4%; Iron 0%
Diet Exchanges: 1½ Fruit, 1 Fat

BETTY'S TIPS

✪ **Substitution**
Feeling nutty? Use your favorite nut in this recipe, and use vanilla for the hazelnut syrup.

✪ **Special Touch**
Oh, what a gift—wonderful to give and even better to receive! Package these treats in holiday cellophane (found in party stores), and place in a clear coffee mug with a small bag of hazelnut coffee. Tie gold ribbons on the mug, and it's ready for a great office gift.

Grand Finales

Cakes, Pies and Other Happy Endings

Lemon Raspberry Cake

Prep: 10 min   Bake: 20 min   Cool: 1 hr 10 min

1 package Betty Crocker SuperMoist® lemon cake mix
1¼ cups water
⅓ cup vegetable oil
3 eggs
6 tablespoons raspberry preserves
Lemon Buttercream Frosting (below)

1. Heat oven to 350°. Grease and flour 3 round pans, 9 × 1½ inches. Make cake mix as directed on package, using water, oil and eggs. Pour into pans.

2. Bake 18 to 20 minutes or until toothpick inserted in center comes out clean. Cool 10 minutes; remove from pans to wire rack. Cool completely, about 1 hour.

3. Fill layers with raspberry preserves. Frost side and top of cake with Lemon Buttercream Frosting. Store covered in refrigerator.

16 servings.

Lemon Buttercream Frosting

1¼ cups butter or margarine, softened
2 teaspoons grated lemon peel
3 tablespoons lemon juice
3 cups powdered sugar

Beat butter, lemon peel and lemon juice in medium bowl with electric mixer on medium speed 30 seconds. Gradually beat in powdered sugar. Beat 2 to 3 minutes longer or until light and fluffy.

1 Serving: Calories 420 (Calories from Fat 200); Fat 22g (Saturated 4g); Cholesterol 40mg; Sodium 410mg; Carbohydrate 54g (Dietary Fiber 0g); Protein 2g
% Daily Value: Vitamin A 20%; Vitamin C 2%; Calcium 6%; Iron 2%
Diet Exchanges: Not Recommended

BETTY'S TIPS

✪ Success Hint
You'll need one medium lemon for the frosting. A medium lemon yields 2 to 3 teaspoons of grated lemon peel and about 3 tablespoons of juice.

If you have only two round pans, refrigerate one-third of the batter while you bake two pans. Let a pan cool before washing it, then grease and flour before adding batter for the third layer.

✪ Special Touch
Garnish top of cake with fresh raspberries and strips of lemon peel.

Lemon Raspberry Cake

Key Lime Coconut Angel Cake

Quick

Key Lime Coconut Angel Cake

Prep: 25 min

1 round (10 inches in diameter) angel food cake
1 can (14 ounces) sweetened condensed milk
⅓ cup Key lime or regular lime juice
1 teaspoon grated lime peel
1 container (12 ounces) frozen whipped topping, thawed
1 cup flaked coconut
  Sliced kiwifruit and strawberries, if desired

1. Cut angel food cake horizontally into 3 layers. Place bottom layer, cut side up, on serving plate.

2. Beat milk, lime juice and lime peel in large bowl with wire whisk until smooth and thickened. Fold in whipped topping.

3. Spread 1 cup lime mixture evenly over top of first layer of cake. Place second layer of cake carefully on bottom layer; spread evenly with 1 cup lime mixture. Top with remaining layer of cake.

4. Frost top and side of cake with remaining lime mixture. Sprinkle with coconut. Garnish cake with kiwifruit and strawberries.

16 servings.

1 Serving: Calories 295 (Calories from Fat 80); Fat 9g (Saturated 4g); Cholesterol 10mg; Sodium 250mg; Carbohydrate 49g (Dietary Fiber 1g); Protein 6g
% Daily Value: Vitamin A 2%; Vitamin C 4%; Calcium 10%; Iron 2%
Diet Exchanges: 2 Starch, 1 Fruit, 2 Fat

BETTY'S TIPS

❂ **Substitution**
If you have time, bake a Betty Crocker angel food cake mix.

❂ **Success Hint**
Use a flexible metal or plastic spatula and a light touch when frosting the cake.

An electric knife works great for cutting the cake into layers.

Lemonade Party Cake

Prep: 20 min   Bake: 35 min   Cool: 15 min   Chill: 2 hr

1 package Betty Crocker SuperMoist lemon cake mix
1¼ cups water
⅓ cup vegetable oil
3 eggs
1 can (6 ounces) frozen lemonade concentrate, thawed
¾ cup powdered sugar
1 tub Betty Crocker Whipped fluffy white or lemon ready-to-spread frosting
  Colored sugar, if desired

1. Heat oven to 350°. Bake cake mix, using water, oil and eggs, as directed on package for 13 × 9 × 2-inch pan. Cool 15 minutes.

2. Mix lemonade concentrate and powdered sugar. Poke long-tined fork into top of warm cake every ½ inch, wiping fork occasionally to reduce sticking. Drizzle lemonade mixture evenly over top of cake.

3. Cover and refrigerate about 2 hours or until chilled. Spread frosting over top of cake. Sprinkle with colored sugar. Store loosely covered in the refrigerator.

12 servings.

1 Serving: Calories 280 (Calories from Fat 70); Fat 8g (Saturated 2g); Cholesterol 40mg; Sodium 450mg; Carbohydrate 50g (Dietary Fiber 0g); Protein 2g
% Daily Value: Vitamin A 0%; Vitamin C 4%; Calcium 6%; Iron 2%
Diet Exchanges: 2 Starch, 1 Fruit, 1½ Fat

BETTY'S TIPS

❂ **Substitution**
If you can't find a 6-ounce can of lemonade, buy a 12-ounce can and use ¾ cup.

❂ **Variation**
Try frozen pink lemonade or limeade concentrate instead of the regular lemonade.

Golden Pound Cake

Prep: 15 min   Bake: 1 hr 20 min   Cool: 1 hr 20 min

3 cups Gold Medal all-purpose flour

1 teaspoon baking powder

¼ teaspoon salt

2¾ cups sugar

1¼ cups butter or margarine, softened

1 teaspoon vanilla or almond extract

5 eggs

1 cup evaporated milk

1. Heat oven to 350°. Grease and flour 12-cup bundt cake pan or angel food cake pan (tube pan), 10 × 4 inches. Mix flour, baking powder and salt; set aside.

2. Beat sugar, butter, vanilla and eggs in large bowl with electric mixer on low speed 30 second, scraping bowl constantly. Beat on high speed 5 minutes, scraping bowl occasionally. Beat in flour mixture alternately with milk on low speed. Pour into pan.

3. Bake 1 hour 10 minutes to 1 hour 20 minutes until toothpick inserted in center comes out clean. Cool 20 minutes. Remove from pan to wire rack. Cool completely, about 1 hour.

16 servings.

1 Serving: Calories 390 (Calories from Fat 155); Fat 17g (Saturated 10g); Cholesterol 105mg; Sodium 200mg; Carbohydrate 54g (Dietary Fiber 1g); Protein 6g
% Daily Value: Vitamin A 14%; Vitamin C 0%; Calcium 8%; Iron 8%
Diet Exchanges: Not Recommended

BETTY'S TIPS

✪ **Variation**
For zesty **Triple Ginger Pound Cake,** add 1 tablespoon grated gingerroot, 2 teaspoons ground ginger and ½ cup finely chopped crystallized ginger with the flour mixture.

✪ **Special Touch**
For a festive look, cut cake into 3 horizontal layers, and layer cake with whipped cream and crushed hard peppermint candies.

Golden Pound Cake

Berry Phyllo Shortcakes

Prep: 10 min   Chill: 30 min   Bake: 12 min   Cool: 10 min

4 cups raspberries
2 cups blueberries
¼ cup sugar
2 teaspoons grated lemon peel
8 frozen (thawed) phyllo sheets
(16 × 12 inches)
2 tablespoons butter or margarine, melted
1 quart lemon sherbet

1. Mix raspberries, blueberries and 2 tablespoons of the sugar. Refrigerate 30 minutes.

2. Meanwhile, heat oven to 350°. Spray cookie sheet with cooking spray. Mix remaining 2 tablespoons sugar and the lemon peel; set aside.

3. Unroll phyllo; cover with waxed paper, then with damp cloth to keep from drying out. Place 1 phyllo sheet on work surface; brush with butter. Continue layering phyllo and brushing each sheet with butter. After brushing top sheet, sprinkle with lemon peel mixture; gently press into phyllo.

4. Cut layered phyllo into 6 rows by 4 rows. Place on cookie sheet. Bake 10 to 12 minutes or until golden brown. Remove from cookie sheet to wire rack. Cool 10 minutes.

5. Place phyllo piece on each serving plate; top with sherbet and berries. Add another phyllo piece; top with additional sherbet and berries.

12 servings.

1 Serving: Calories 190 (Calories from Fat 35); Fat 4g (Saturated 2g); Cholesterol 10mg; Sodium 95mg; Carbohydrate 39g (Dietary Fiber 3g); Protein 2g
% Daily Value: Vitamin A 2%; Vitamin C 18%; Calcium 4%; Iron 4%
Diet Exchanges: 1 Starch, 1½ Fruit, ½ Fat

BETTY'S TIPS

⊙ **Success Hint**
For best results, thaw phyllo completely and work quickly with each layer.

⊙ **Variation**
Use sliced strawberries instead of raspberries for this colorful dessert.

⊙ **Do-Ahead**
Save some preparation time on the day of your celebration by baking phyllo shortcake pieces up to 24 hours ahead of time. Store in an airtight container.

Caramelized Peach and Raspberry Shortcakes

Prep: 15 min   Cook: 10 min   Cool: 10 min

3   tablespoons butter or margarine

¼   cup packed brown sugar

2   tablespoons amaretto

2   medium peaches, peeled and cut up

1   cup raspberries
    Amaretto Whipped Cream (below)

6   sponge shortcake cups
    Sliced almonds, if desired

1 Serving: Calories 320 (Calories from Fat 170); Fat 19g (Saturated 12g); Cholesterol 100mg; Sodium 170mg; Carbohydrate 36g (Dietary Fiber 2g); Protein 3g
% Daily Value: Vitamin A 20%; Vitamin C 14%; Calcium 4%; Iron 4%
Diet Exchanges: Not Recommended

1. Melt butter in 10-inch skillet over medium-low heat. Stir in brown sugar. Cook 2 minutes, stirring constantly. Stir in amaretto and peaches. Cook 3 to 4 minutes, stirring occasionally, until peaches are coated with mixture. Cool 10 minutes. Gently stir in raspberries.

2. Make Amaretto Whipped Cream. Top each shortcake cup with peach-raspberry mixture and Amaretto Whipped Cream. Sprinkle with almonds.

6 servings.

Amaretto Whipped Cream

1   cup whipping (heavy) cream

2   tablespoons packed brown sugar

1   teaspoon cornstarch

1   teaspoon amaretto

Beat all ingredients in chilled medium bowl with electric mixer on high speed until stiff.

BETTY'S TIPS

⊙ **Pack 'n Go**
If you're taking these shortcakes to a picnic, omit the Amaretto Whipped Cream and take along a can of whipped cream topping instead.

⊙ **Substitution**
Amaretto is an almond-flavored liqueur. If you don't have any on hand, you can use 1 teaspoon almond extract in the fruit mixture and ¼ teaspoon almond extract in the whipped cream.

Strawberry Margarita Cake

Prep: 10 min   Bake: 33 min   Cool: 1 hr

¾ cup bottled strawberry-flavored nonalcoholic margarita drink mix

1 package Betty Crocker SuperMoist white cake mix

⅓ cup vegetable oil

3 egg whites

1 tablespoon grated lime peel

1 container (8 ounces) frozen whipped topping, thawed (3 cups)

Strawberries, if desired

1. Heat oven to 350°. Grease bottom only of rectangular pan, 13 × 9 × 2 inches. Add enough water to drink mix to measure 1¼ cups.

2. Beat cake mix (dry), drink mix, oil and egg whites in large bowl with electric mixer on low speed 2 minutes. Pour into pan.

3. Bake 28 to 33 minutes or until toothpick inserted in center comes out clean. Cool completely, about 1 hour.

4. Gently stir lime peel into whipped topping; spread over top of cake. Garnish with strawberries. Store covered in refrigerator.

12 servings.

1 Serving: Calories 255 (Calories from Fat 115); Fat 13g (Saturated 3g); Cholesterol 0mg; Sodium 310mg; Carbohydrate 31g (Dietary Fiber 0g); Protein 3g
% Daily Value: Vitamin A 0%; Vitamin C 0%; Calcium 4%; Iron 4%
Diet Exchanges: 1 Starch, 1 Fruit, 2½ Fat

BETTY'S TIPS

✿ Success Hint
You'll usually find the bottled margarita drink mix in the soft drink section of the grocery store.

Strawberry Margarita Cake

White Chocolate Cheesecake

White Chocolate Cheesecake

Prep: 40 min   Bake: 1 hr   Cool: 30 min   Chill: 8 hr

1 cup crushed chocolate wafer cookies

2 tablespoons butter or margarine, melted

3 packages (8 ounces each) cream cheese, softened

½ cup sugar

3 eggs

1 teaspoon vanilla

1 bag (12 ounces) white baking chips (2 cups), melted

½ cup half-and-half

Cran-Raspberry Sauce (below)

1. Heat oven to 325°. Mix crushed cookies and butter. Press evenly in bottom of springform pan, 9 × 10 × 3 inches. Refrigerate while making filling.

2. Beat cream cheese in large bowl with electric mixer on medium speed until smooth. Gradually add in sugar until smooth. Beat in eggs, one at a time. Beat in vanilla, melted chips and half-and-half until blended. Pour over crust; smooth top.

3. Bake 55 to 60 minutes or until center is set; cool 30 minutes. Cover and refrigerate at least 8 hours.

4. Run metal spatula along side of cheesecake to loosen; remove side of pan. Serve cheesecake with Cran-Raspberry Sauce. Store covered in refrigerator.

16 servings.

Cran-Raspberry Sauce

½ cup cranberry juice cocktail

2 tablespoons sugar

2 teaspoons cornstarch

1 package (12 ounces) frozen raspberries, thawed and juice reserved

Mix cranberry juice cocktail, sugar and cornstarch in 1-quart saucepan. Cook over medium heat, stirring constantly, until mixture thickens and boils. Remove from heat; cool 30 minutes. Stir in raspberries and reserved juice. Cool completely.

1 Serving: Calories 350 (Calories from Fat 190); Fat 21g (Saturated 13g); Cholesterol 85mg; Sodium 250mg; Carbohydrate 34g (Dietary Fiber 2g); Protein 8g
% Daily Value: Vitamin A 14%; Vitamin C 4%; Calcium 8%; Iron 6%
Diet Exchanges: Not Recommended

BETTY'S TIPS

❂ Do-Ahead

Cover cooled cheesecake with aluminum foil and refrigerate no longer than 3 days. Cover and refrigerate Cran-Raspberry Sauce no longer than 2 days.

❂ Special Touch

Garnish with sugared cranberries and mint leaves cut to resemble holly leaves. To sugar cranberries, roll frozen cranberries in granulated sugar.

Brownie Torte with Raspberry Sauce

Prep: 15 min   Bake: 20 min   Cool: 1 hr

½ cup sugar

½ cup butter, softened*

3 eggs

⅔ cup semisweet chocolate chips, melted and cooled

¼ cup Gold Medal all-purpose flour
Raspberry Sauce (below)

1. Heat oven to 400°. Grease and flour round pan, 8 × 1½ inches.

2. Beat sugar and butter in medium bowl with electric mixer on medium speed until smooth. Stir in eggs and melted chocolate until smooth and blended. Stir in flour. Pour into pan.

3. Bake 18 to 20 minutes or until toothpick inserted in center comes out clean. Cool 10 minutes; remove from pan. Cool completely, about 1 hour. Serve with Raspberry Sauce.

8 servings.

Raspberry Sauce

1 package (10 ounces) frozen raspberries in juice, thawed, drained and juice reserved

¼ cup sugar

2 tablespoons cornstarch

Add enough water to reserved juice to measure 1¼ cups. Mix sugar and cornstarch in 1½-quart saucepan.

Stir in juice mixture and raspberries. Heat to boiling over medium heat, stirring frequently. Boil and stir 1 minute; cool. Strain sauce through a strainer to remove seeds.

*Do not use margarine in this recipe.

1 Serving: Calories 335 (Calories from Fat 160); Fat 18g (Saturated 10g); Cholesterol 110mg; Sodium 100mg; Carbohydrate 42g (Dietary Fiber 3g); Protein 4g
% Daily Value: Vitamin A 12%; Vitamin C 4%; Calcium 2%; Iron 6%
Diet Exchanges: Not Recommended

BETTY'S TIPS

✿ **Variation**
Make the spectacular plate design shown here with **White Truffle Sauce.** Chop 6 ounces white chocolate baking bar and heat with 2 tablespoons butter in heavy 2-quart saucepan over low heat, stirring constantly, until melted (mixture will be thick and grainy.) Stir in ½ cup whipping (heavy) cream until smooth. Refrigerate about 2 hours or until chilled. (For detailed instructions, see page 265.)

Brownie Torte with Raspberry Sauce

Betty ... ON WHAT'S NEW

Irresistible Plate Appeal

Ordinary desserts become extraordinary when you begin by dressing up your plates. Simple-to-create, edible plate designs provide a splash of color and a ripple of flavor to all types of desserts. Express your creativity with new techniques, and experiment with your own designs.

DESIGN BASICS

- Choose plain plates that will show off your design. Color is important, too. A light-colored plate will accent darker sauces, such as chocolate; darker plates will highlight pale-colored sauces.

- Sauce consistency is important so your design holds its shape. A sauce should be thin enough so you can easily draw a knife or toothpick through it. To test, spoon sauce onto a plate; it should stand up and not spread.

- Use a plastic squeeze bottle for dispensing the sauce. It provides even control and flow.

- Use contrasting colors and flavors within the design to create interest.

- Be sure the design is prominent around the edge of the plate where it will be seen once the dessert is placed in the center.

STAMP IT

1. Choose a simple design—the simpler, the better.

2. Be sure to use clean foam stamps, not the hard block stamps. Stamps with some open areas, rather than solid stamps, work best. Small stamps, 3/4 inch to 1 1/4 inches, are good to start with. You'll find foam stamps at most craft stores.

3. Use purchased chocolate-flavored syrup. It has a good consistency that evenly coats the stamp. Pour the syrup onto a small plate and dip the stamp into it, or "paint" the syrup directly on the stamp with a small brush.

4. Try your first design on a piece of waxed paper or other smooth surface to see how it looks and to make sure you have the right amount of syrup.

5. Carefully place the stamp on the plate (flatter plates work best) and gently roll the stamp, making sure all areas touch the plate. Then lift the stamp straight up to remove it from the plate.

HERRINGBONE WAVE

1. Cover a dessert plate with sauce.

2. Using a contrasting sauce, make vertical lines at 1-inch intervals.

3. Using a knife tip or toothpick, draw through the lines in alternating directions.

ZIGZAG DESIGN

1. Using sauce, create zigzag pattern on plate.

2. Rotate the plate one-fourth turn, and repeat the zigzag pattern.

Triple Chocolate Torte

Triple Chocolate Torte

Prep: 15 min   Bake: 50 min   Freeze: 4 hr

1 package (1 pound 3.8 ounces) Betty Crocker fudge brownie mix

1¼ cups milk

1 package (4-serving size) white chocolate pudding and pie filling mix

1 container (8 ounces) frozen whipped topping, thawed (3½ cups)

⅓ cup miniature semisweet chocolate chips

1 pint (2 cups) raspberries or strawberries, if desired

1. Heat oven to 325°. Spray bottom only of springform pan, 9 × 3 inches, with cooking spray. Make brownie mix as directed on package, using water, oil and eggs. Spread in pan.

2. Bake 45 to 50 minutes or until toothpick inserted in center comes out clean. Cool completely. (Do not remove side of pan.)

3. Beat milk and pudding mix in large bowl with wire whisk about 2 minutes or until thickened. Fold in whipped topping and chocolate chips. Pour over brownie.

4. Cover and freeze at least 4 hours before serving. Remove side of pan. Serve with raspberries. Store covered in freezer.

16 servings.

1 Serving: Calories 205 (Calories from Fat 45); Fat 11g (Saturated 3g); Cholesterol 20mg; Sodium 210mg; Carbohydrate 25g (Dietary Fiber 1g); Protein 2g
% Daily Value: Vitamin A 0%; Vitamin C 0%; Calcium 2%; Iron 2%
Diet Exchanges: 1 Starch, 1 Fruit, 1½ Fat

BETTY'S TIPS

⊗ **Special Touch**
For a spectacular presentation, drizzle chocolate topping on the dessert plates before adding the torte. Or drizzle chocolate topping over the top of the torte, and garnish with chocolate-dipped strawberries or raspberries.

Pumpkin Hazelnut Torte

Prep: 25 min   Bake: 30 min   Cool: 1 hr 10 min   Chill: 1 hr

1 can (15 ounces) pumpkin (not pumpkin pie mix)
2½ cups Original Bisquick
1 cup sugar
¾ cup ground hazelnuts or walnuts
¼ cup shortening
1 cup milk
1 teaspoon pumpkin pie spice
1 teaspoon vanilla
2 eggs
Pumpkin Cream (right)

1. Heat oven to 350°. Grease and flour 2 round pans, 9 × 1½ inches. Reserve 1 cup pumpkin for Pumpkin Cream. Beat remaining pumpkin and remaining ingredients except Pumpkin Cream in large bowl with electric mixer on low speed 30 seconds, scraping bowl constantly. Beat on medium speed 4 minutes, scraping bowl occasionally. Divide batter evenly between pans.

2. Bake 25 to 30 minutes or until toothpick inserted in center comes out clean. Cool 10 minutes; remove from pans. Cool completely, about 1 hour.

3. Make Pumpkin Cream. Place cake layer, rounded side down, on serving plate; spread with half of cream. Top with second layer, rounded side up. Spread remaining cream on top. Refrigerate 1 hour before serving. Store covered in refrigerator.

12 servings.

Pumpkin Cream

¾ cup powdered sugar
1½ cups whipping (heavy) cream
½ teaspoon vanilla
¼ teaspoon pumpkin pie spice
Reserved 1 cup pumpkin

Beat all ingredients except pumpkin in chilled large bowl on high speed until stiff. Gently fold in pumpkin.

1 Serving: Calories 390 (Calories from Fat 190); Fat 21g (Saturated 9g); Cholesterol 70mg; Sodium 390mg; Carbohydrate 47g (Dietary Fiber 2g); Protein 5g
% Daily Value: Vitamin A 100%; Vitamin C 2%; Calcium 12%; Iron 10%
Diet Exchanges: Not Recommended

BETTY'S TIPS

✿ Success Hint
You will need a 3-ounce package of hazelnuts for ¾ cup ground hazelnuts.

✿ Special Touch
Garnish the top of the torte with finely chopped and whole hazelnuts.

Pumpkin Hazelnut Torte

Pumpkin Cream Cheese Pie

Pumpkin Cream Cheese Pie

Prep: 20 min   Bake: 52 min   Cool: 30 min   Chill: 4 hr

Pecan Shortbread Cookie Crust (right)

1   cup sugar

3   tablespoons Gold Medal all-purpose flour

1   package (8 ounces) plus 1 package (3 ounces) cream cheese, softened

1   teaspoon ground cinnamon

¼   teaspoon ground nutmeg

¼   teaspoon ground ginger

¼   teaspoon ground cloves

3   eggs

1   can (15 ounces) pumpkin (not pumpkin pie mix)

1   tablespoon milk

1. Heat oven to 375°. Bake Pecan Shortbread Cookie Crust; cool.

2. Beat sugar, flour and cream cheese in large bowl with electric mixer on low speed until smooth; reserve ½ cup. Add remaining ingredients except milk to cream cheese mixture. Beat on medium speed, scraping bowl constantly, until smooth. Pour into crust.

3. Stir milk into reserved cream cheese mixture. Spoon over pumpkin mixture. Cut through cream cheese and pumpkin mixtures with knife in S-shape curves in one continuous motion. Turn pie plate one-fourth turn and repeat.

4. Cover crust with 3-inch strip of aluminum foil to prevent excessive browning; remove foil for last 15 minutes of baking. Bake 35 to 40 minutes or until knife inserted in center comes out clean. Cool 30 minutes. Cover loosely and refrigerate at least 4 hours before serving. Store covered in refrigerator.

8 servings.

Pecan Shortbread Cookie Crust

1½   cups packed crushed shortbread cookies with pecans (about 16 cookies)

3   tablespoons butter or margarine, melted

3   tablespoons Gold Medal all-purpose flour

Mix all ingredients. Press firmly on bottom and up side of ungreased pie plate, 9 × 1¼ inches. Bake about 12 minutes or until light brown.

1 Serving: Calories 510 (Calories from Fat 270); Fat 30g (Saturated 13g); Cholesterol 130mg; Sodium 270mg; Carbohydrate 54g (Dietary Fiber 3g); Protein 9g
% Daily Value: Vitamin A 100%; Vitamin C 2%; Calcium 6%; Iron 14%
Diet Exchanges: Not Recommended

BETTY'S TIPS

❂ Do-Ahead
Bake the crust the day before. Pour in the filling when you are ready to bake the pie. Or you can use a refrigerated or frozen pie crust.

❂ Special Touch
Top with a dollop of whipped cream and miniature candy pumpkin, peanut brittle, crushed gingersnaps or chocolate-covered coffee beans.

Lemon Berry Tart

Prep: 30 min   Bake: 15 min   Cool: 45 min   Chill: 1 hr

Cookie Crust (below)
½ cup lemon curd (from 10-ounce jar)
1 package (8 ounces) cream cheese, softened
2 cups berries or sliced fruits

1. Bake and cool Cookie Crust.

2. Beat lemon curd and cream cheese with electric mixer on medium speed until smooth. Spread over crust. Refrigerate at least 1 hour until slightly firm. Just before serving, arrange berries on lemon mixture.

8 servings.

Cookie Crust

1¼ cups Gold Medal all-purpose flour
½ cup butter or margarine, softened
3 tablespoons packed brown sugar
1 egg

Heat oven to 400°. Mix all ingredients until dough forms. Press firmly and evenly against bottom and side of ungreased tart pan, 9 × 1 inch. Bake 13 to 15 minutes or until light golden brown. Cool completely, about 45 minutes.

1 Serving: Calories 275 (Calories from Fat 205); Fat 23g (Saturated 14g); Cholesterol 95mg; Sodium 180mg; Carbohydrate 38g (Dietary Fiber 2g); Protein 6g
% Daily Value: Vitamin A 18%; Vitamin C 26%; Calcium 4%; Iron 8%
Diet Exchanges: Not Recommended

BETTY'S TIPS

⊛ **Success Hint**
Showcase any combination of berries and sliced fruit on this tart. Try strawberries and blueberries with nectarine or papaya slices. Add a few blackberries for a dramatic color accent. You'll probably need to make two tarts to serve all of your guests!

⊛ **Did You Know?**
Lemon curd is a creamy mixture made by cooking lemon juice, sugar, butter and egg yolks until thickened. Look for lemon curd jars at the supermarket in the jam and jelly section or at gourmet shops.

Lemon Berry Tart

S'Mores Mousse Dessert

Prep: 20 min   Bake: 10 min   Cool: 20 min   Chill: 2 hr

2¼ cups cinnamon graham cracker crumbs (30 squares)

⅓ cup butter or margarine, melted

1 jar (7 ounces) marshmallow creme

2 cups chocolate fudge topping (not hot fudge topping)

2½ cups frozen (thawed) whipped topping

3 cups miniature marshmallows

1. Heat oven to 350°. Grease rectangular pan, 13 × 9 × 2 inches. Mix 2 cups of the cracker crumbs and the butter in medium bowl. Press on bottom of pan. Bake 10 minutes. Cool completely, about 20 minutes.

2. Mix marshmallow creme and 1 cup chocolate topping in large bowl until smooth. Fold in whipped topping and 2 cups of the marshmallows. Spoon filling evenly over cooled crust.

3. Sprinkle remaining ¼ cup cracker crumbs and 1 cup marshmallows over top of dessert. Drizzle remaining 1 cup chocolate topping over top of dessert.

4. Spray a piece of aluminum foil with cooking spray. Tightly cover dessert with foil, sprayed side down. Refrigerate at least 2 hours or freeze up to 3 days. Cut into squares.

12 servings.

1 Square: Calories 430 (Calories from Fat 145); Fat 16g (Saturated 7g); Cholesterol 20mg; Sodium 210mg; Carbohydrate 69g (Dietary Fiber 1g); Protein 4g
% Daily Value: Vitamin A 4%; Vitamin C 0%; Calcium 6%; Iron 6%
Diet Exchanges: Not Recommended

BETTY'S TIPS

✪ Pack 'n Go
For on-the-go outings, freeze this yummy dessert ahead of time. Pack in a cooler to transport. By the time you're ready for dessert, it will have thawed enough to give you a creamy dessert that's easy to cut.

✪ Success Hint
You can crush graham crackers a couple different ways. Place squares in a plastic food-storage bag, seal the bag and crush crackers with a rolling pin or the flat side of a meat mallet. Or use a mini- or standard-size food processor to quickly make the crumbs.

S'Mores Mousse Dessert

Double Chocolate Meringues

Double Chocolate Meringues

Prep: 20 min   Bake: 1 hr   Cool: 3 hr 30 min

3 egg whites
¼ teaspoon cream of tartar
¾ cup sugar
¼ cup finely chopped hazelnuts
  Bittersweet Chocolate Sauce (below)
1 quart chocolate ice cream

1. Heat oven to 275°. Cover cookie sheet with heavy brown paper or cooking parchment paper.

2. Beat egg whites and cream of tartar in medium bowl with electric mixer on high speed until foamy. Beat in sugar, 1 tablespoon at a time; continue beating until stiff and glossy. Do not underbeat. Fold in hazelnuts. Drop meringue by ⅓ cupfuls in 8 mounds onto paper. Shape into circles, building up sides.

3. Bake 1 hour. Turn off oven; leave meringues in oven with door closed 1 hour 30 minutes. Finish cooling at room temperature, about 2 hours. Make Bittersweet Chocolate Sauce. Fill each meringue with scoop of ice cream. Serve with sauce.

8 meringues.

Bittersweet Chocolate Sauce

¼ cup butter or margarine
1½ ounces unsweetened baking chocolate, cut into pieces
¾ cup sugar
¼ cup baking cocoa
¼ cup half-and-half
⅛ teaspoon salt
1 teaspoon vanilla

Melt butter and chocolate in 1-quart saucepan over low heat, stirring constantly. Stir in sugar, cocoa, half-and-half and salt. Heat slowly to boiling; do not stir. Remove from heat; stir in vanilla. Serve warm.

1 Meringue: Calories 420 (Calories from Fat 170); Fat 19g (Saturated 11g); Cholesterol 40mg; Sodium 150mg; Carbohydrate 60g (Dietary Fiber 3g); Protein 5g
% Daily Value: Vitamin A 10%; Vitamin C 0%; Calcium 8%; Iron 8%
Diet Exchanges: Not Recommended

BETTY'S TIPS

☺ Success Hint
Want to make sure the meringues are crisp? Bake them on a dry day because humid weather causes lower volume and less-crisp shells. If meringues soften, heat them in a 200° oven until crisp.

☺ Special Touch
To make the lovely swirl designs on your serving plates as shown, see page 264. Experiment with your favorite sweet dessert sauces!

Eggnog Cream Puffs

Prep: 20 min   Cook: 5 min   Bake: 40 min

1 cup water
½ cup butter or margarine
1 cup Gold Medal all-purpose flour
4 eggs
Eggnog Cream (below)
Powdered sugar

1. Heat oven to 400°. Heat water and butter to rolling boil in 2½-quart saucepan. Stir in flour. Stir vigorously over low heat about 1 minute or until mixture forms a ball; remove from heat. Beat in eggs at once; continue beating until smooth.

2. Drop dough by scant ¼ cupfuls about 3 inches apart onto ungreased cookie sheet. Bake 35 to 40 minutes or until puffed and golden. Cool away from draft.

3. Make Eggnog Cream. Cut off tops of puffs; pull out any soft dough. Fill puffs with Eggnog Cream; replace tops. Sprinkle with powdered sugar. Serve immediately. Store covered in refrigerator.

10 to 12 servings.

Eggnog Cream

1 package (4-serving size) vanilla instant pudding and pie filling mix
1 cup milk
1 teaspoon ground nutmeg
1 teaspoon rum extract
¼ teaspoon ground ginger
2 cups whipping (heavy) cream

Beat all ingredients except cream in large bowl with electric mixer on low speed 1 to 2 minutes or until smooth. Add cream. Beat on high speed 1 to 2 minutes or until soft peaks form.

1 Serving: Calories 360 (Calories from Fat 245); Fat 27g (Saturated 12g); Cholesterol 140mg; Sodium 320mg; Carbohydrate 23g (Dietary Fiber 0g); Protein 6g
% Daily Value: Vitamin A 28% Vitamin C 0%; Calcium 8%; Iron 4%
Diet Exchanges: Not Recommended

BETTY'S TIPS

⊙ **Do-Ahead**
Fill the cream puffs, and cover and refrigerate up to 3 hours. Sprinkle with powdered sugar just before serving.

⊙ **Special Touch**
Instead of sprinkling the cream puffs with powdered sugar, brush the tops with light corn syrup and sprinkle with colored sugar or nonpareils.

Eggnog Cream Puffs

Praline Pumpkin Dessert

Praline Pumpkin Dessert

Prep: 10 min   Bake: 1 hr

1   can (15 ounces) pumpkin (not pumpkin pie mix)
1   can (12 ounces) evaporated milk
3   eggs
1   cup sugar
4   teaspoons pumpkin pie spice
1   package Betty Crocker SuperMoist white cake mix
1½ cups chopped pecans or walnuts
¾   cup butter or margarine, melted

1. Heat oven to 350°. Grease rectangular pan, 13 × 9 × 2 inches. Mix pumpkin, milk, eggs, sugar and pumpkin pie spice until smooth. Pour into pan.

2. Sprinkle cake mix (dry) over pumpkin mixture. Sprinkle with pecans. Pour melted margarine over top.

3. Bake uncovered 50 to 60 minutes or until knife inserted in center of dessert comes out clean.

12 servings.

1 Serving: Calories 510 (Calories from Fat 250); Fat 28g (Saturated 5g); Cholesterol 60mg; Sodium 510mg; Carbohydrate 61g (Dietary Fiber 3g); Protein 7g
% Daily Value: Vitamin A 98%; Vitamin C 2%; Calcium 16%; Iron 0%
Diet Exchanges: Not Recommended

BETTY'S TIPS

☺ **Success Hint**
Be sure to use canned pumpkin, not pumpkin pie mix, for this yummy dessert. Pumpkin pie mix contains sugar and spices—not just pumpkin.

☺ **Serve-With**
This fabulous pumpkin dessert is delicious with a scoop of cinnamon ice cream or a dollop of whipped cream.

Quick

Microwave Apple Crisp

Prep: 15 min   Microwave: 10 min

4   medium tart cooking apples, peeled and sliced (4 cups)
⅔   cup packed brown sugar
⅔   cup quick-cooking or old-fashioned oats
½   cup Original or Reduced Fat Bisquick
3   tablespoons stick margarine or butter, softened
¾   teaspoon ground cinnamon
¾   teaspoon ground nutmeg

1. Arrange apples in ungreased 1-quart microwavable casserole or square microwavable dish, 8 × 8 × 2 inches. Stir remaining ingredients until crumbly. Sprinkle over apples.

2. Microwave uncovered on High 7 to 10 minutes, rotating dish ½ turn after 5 minutes, until apples are tender. Serve warm.

6 servings.

1 Serving: Calories 255 (Calories from Fat 70); Fat 8g (Saturated 4g); Cholesterol 15mg; Sodium 190mg; Carbohydrate 47g (Dietary Fiber 3g); Protein 2g
% Daily Value: Vitamin A 4%; Vitamin C 2%; Calcium 4%; Iron 6%
Diet Exchanges: 1 Starch, 2 Fruit, 1 Fat

BETTY'S TIPS

☺ **Success Hint**
Good choices of cooking apples include Rome Beauty, Golden Delicious and Greening.

☺ **Variation**
You can pop this simple dessert in the oven to bake. Grease square pan or baking dish, 8 × 8 × 2 inches. Decrease oats to ½ cup and increase margarine to ⅓ cup. Bake in 375° oven about 30 minutes or until topping is golden brown and apples are tender.

☺ **Special Touch**
Serve this warm, fragrant dessert topped with a dollop of whipped cream or a scoop of cinnamon ice cream.

Caramel Cream Brownie Trifle

Prep: 20 min   Bake: 30 min   Cool: 1 hr   Chill: 2 hr

1	package (1 pound 3.8 ounces) Betty Crocker fudge brownie mix
¼	cup water
½	cup vegetable oil
2	eggs
1	package (4-serving size) chocolate fudge instant pudding and pie filling mix
2	cups milk
¼	cup caramel topping
1	container (8 ounces) frozen whipped topping, thawed
1	cup chopped walnuts

1. Heat oven to 350°. Bake brownie mix as directed on package for fudgelike brownies, using water, oil and eggs, in rectangular pan, 13 × 9 × 2 inches. Cool completely, about 1 hour.

2. Make pudding mix as directed on package for pudding, using milk; refrigerate. Cut brownies into 1-inch pieces. Thoroughly stir caramel topping into whipped topping.

3. Layer half each of the brownies, pudding, walnuts and whipped topping mixture in 3-quart glass bowl; repeat.

4. Cover and refrigerate at least 2 hours before serving but no longer than 24 hours. Store covered in refrigerator.

20 servings.

1 Serving: Calories 215 (Calories from Fat 110); Fat 12g (Saturated 3g); Cholesterol 15mg; Sodium 120mg; Carbohydrate 25g (Dietary Fiber 1g); Protein 3g
% Daily Value: Vitamin A 2%; Vitamin C 0%; Calcium 4%; Iron 2%
Diet Exchanges: 1 Starch, ½ Fruit, 2 Fat

BETTY'S TIPS

✿ Special Touch
Garnish with chocolate shavings or chocolate curls. To make the curls, pull a vegetable peeler across a milk chocolate candy bar, using long, thin strokes. (The curls will be easier to make if the chocolate is slightly warm, so let the chocolate stand in a warm place for about 10 minutes.) Use a toothpick to lift the curls from the chocolate to the trifle.

Drizzle the whipped topping mixture with additional caramel topping and sprinkle with additional chopped walnuts.

Strawberry Rhubarb Trifle

Prep: 20 min   Cook: 25 min   Cool: 30 min   Chill: 4 hr

½   pound rhubarb, cut into ½-inch pieces (2 cups)

1   cup sugar

¼   cup orange juice

2   cups sliced strawberries

2   packages (4-serving size each) tapioca or vanilla pudding and pie filling mix (not instant)

2½   cups milk

2   cups frozen (thawed) whipped topping

1   package (16 ounces) frozen pound cake loaf

½   cup orange marmalade

1   cup medium-size whole strawberries, if desired

   Shredded orange peel, if desired

1. Mix rhubarb, sugar and orange juice in 2-quart saucepan. Heat to boiling over medium heat; reduce heat to low. Cook about 15 minutes, stirring occasionally, until rhubarb is tender and mixture starts to thicken slightly. Cool 30 minutes. Refrigerate about 2 hours or until chilled. Stir in sliced strawberries.

2. While rhubarb mixture is cooling, mix pudding mix and milk in 2-quart saucepan. Cook over medium heat 6 to 7 minutes, stirring constantly, until mixture boils. Cool 15 minutes. Refrigerate at least 2 hours until chilled. Fold in whipped topping.

3. Cut pound cake horizontally in half. Spread marmalade over bottom half. Top with top half. Cut into 18 slices. Place 9 slices in bottom of 2½- to 3-quart trifle or serving bowl.

4. Spoon half of the rhubarb mixture over cake; top with half of the pudding. Repeat layers with remaining cake, rhubarb mixture and pudding. Cover and refrigerate at least 2 hours until chilled.

5. Arrange whole strawberries on top of trifle. Garnish with orange peel. Store covered in refrigerator.

12 servings.

1 Serving: Calories 410 (Calories from Fat 125); Fat 14g (Saturated 6g); Cholesterol 45mg; Sodium 180mg; Carbohydrate 68g (Dietary Fiber 2g); Protein 5g
% Daily Value: Vitamin A 4%; Vitamin C 44%; Calcium 12%; Iron 6%
Diet Exchanges: Not Recommended

Angel Berry Summer Pudding

Angel Berry Summer Pudding

Prep: 25 min   Chill: 4 hr

2   packages (4-serving size each) vanilla instant pudding and pie filling mix

4   cups milk

¾   teaspoon rum extract

1   round angel food cake (10 inches in diameter), torn into bite-size pieces

4   cups sliced strawberries

2   cups raspberries
    Frozen (thawed) whipped topping, if desired

1. Make pudding mixes as directed on package for pudding, using 4 cups milk and adding rum extract.

2. Spoon one-third of the pudding into bottom of rectangular baking dish, 13 × 9 × 2 inches. Layer with half of the cake pieces and half of the berries. Repeat layers, ending with remaining pudding.

3. Cover and refrigerate at least 4 hours. Garnish each serving with a dollop of whipped topping.

12 servings.

1 Serving: Calories 260 (Calories from Fat 20); Fat 2g (Saturated 1g); Cholesterol 5mg; Sodium 560mg; Carbohydrate 57g (Dietary Fiber 3g); Protein 7g
% Daily Value: Vitamin A 4%; Vitamin C 62%; Calcium 12%; Iron 4%
Diet Exchanges: 2 Starch, 2 Fruit

BETTY'S TIPS

✪ Pack 'n Go
Sure to be a crowd pleaser, this fruit and pudding dessert should remain chilled. Tote in an insulated pack with ice packs. Return any leftover pudding to the cooler.

✪ Substitution
Seize the season by enjoying other combinations of summer berries in this simple trifle-like dessert. We suggest blueberries or blackberries.

White Chocolate Bread Pudding

Prep: 30 min   Bake: 1 hr 50 min

2   cups whipping (heavy) cream

2   cups half-and-half

8   ounces white baking bars (white chocolate cut into ¼- to ½-inch pieces)

1½   cups sugar

8   egg yolks

1   teaspoon vanilla

¼   teaspoon salt

1   baguette (about 25 inches), thinly sliced

1   package (12 ounces) frozen raspberries, thawed
    Fresh raspberries, if desired

1. Heat oven to 325°. Grease shallow 3-quart casserole. Heat whipping cream and half-and-half to boiling in 3-quart saucepan over medium-high heat, stirring constantly. Stir in baking bar pieces; remove from heat.

2. Beat sugar, egg yolks, vanilla and salt in large bowl with mixer on medium speed until creamy. Gradually add cream mixture, beating constantly, until smooth.

3. Line bottom and side of casserole with baguette slices. Pour 2 cups of the cream mixture over bread. Let stand a few minutes until bread absorbs mixture. Add remaining baguette slices. Pour remaining cream mixture, 2 cups at a time, over bread; let stand a few minutes until bread absorbs mixture. Place casserole in roasting pan; place in oven. Pour boiling water in pan until 1 inch deep.

4. Bake uncovered 45 minutes. Cover with aluminum foil and bake about 1 hour 5 minutes longer or until knife inserted 1 inch from edge comes out clean.

5. Place raspberries in blender. Cover and blend on high speed until smooth; strain seeds. Serve warm bread pudding with raspberry sauce and fresh raspberries.

10 servings.

1 Serving: Calories 575 (Calories from Fat 290); Fat 32g (Saturated 19g); Cholesterol 245mg; Sodium 240mg; Carbohydrate 66g (Dietary Fiber 2g); Protein 8g
% Daily Value: Vitamin A 22%; Vitamin C 4%; Calcium 16%; Iron 8%
Diet Exchanges: Not Recommended

Hot Fruit Compote

Prep: 15 min   Bake: 45 min

    1   can (28 ounces) pear halves in heavy syrup
    1   can (28 ounces) peach halves in heavy syrup
    1   can (20 ounces) pineapple chunks in juice
    ½   cup dried apricots
    ½   cup dried prunes
    ½   cup dried cherries or raisins
    2   tablespoons packed brown sugar
    ¼   cup brandy, if desired
    ½   teaspoon ground cinnamon
    ¼   teaspoon ground nutmeg
    ½   cup slivered almonds, if desired

1. Heat oven to 375°. Drain canned fruit, reserving syrup and juice; mix syrup and juice. Cut pears and peaches into bite-size pieces. Layer canned and dried fruit in 3-quart casserole or rectangular baking dish, 13 × 9 × 2 inches.

2. Mix brown sugar and brandy; pour over fruit. Pour reserved juice mixture over fruit just until fruit is covered; discard remaining juice mixture. Sprinkle cinnamon, nutmeg and almonds over fruit.

3. Bake uncovered about 45 minutes or until bubbly. Serve warm or cool.

10 servings.

1 Serving: Calories 248 (Calories from Fat 30); Fat 3g (Saturated 0g); Cholesterol 0mg; Sodium 11mg; Carbohydrate 53g (Dietary Fiber 3g); Protein 3g
% Daily Value: Vitamin A 13%; Vitamin C 14%; Calcium 5%; Iron 9%
Diet Exchanges: 3 Fruit, 1 Fat

BETTY'S TIPS

⊕ **Do-Ahead**
You can prepare this elegant dessert the day before and reheat it just before serving.

Low Fat

Cranberry Herbal Tea Granita

Prep: 15 min   Freeze: 5 hr   Stand: 20 min

    5   whole cloves
    1   slice orange
    2   cups water
    ½   cup sugar
    1   stick cinnamon
    3   tea bags red zesty herbal tea flavored with hibiscus, rose hips and lemongrass
    1½ cups cranberry juice cocktail
    1½ cups pineapple juice
        Fresh fruit, if desired

1. Insert cloves into peel of orange slice. Heat water, sugar, cinnamon and orange slice to boiling in 2-quart saucepan, stirring occasionally; remove from heat. Add tea bags; cover and let steep 5 minutes. Remove tea bags, cinnamon stick and orange slice.

2. Stir cranberry and pineapple juices into tea. Pour into 2-quart nonmetal bowl or square baking dish, 8 × 8 × 2 inches. Cover and freeze about 2 hours or until partially frozen. Stir with fork or wire whisk. Cover and freeze 3 hours longer, stirring every 30 minutes and breaking up any large chunks.

3. Remove from freezer 20 minutes before serving. Spoon into stemmed glasses. Garnish with fruit.

8 servings.

1 Serving: Calories 105 (Calories from Fat 0); Fat 0g (Saturated 0g); Cholesterol 0mg; Sodium 0mg; Carbohydrate 26g (Dietary Fiber 0g); Protein 0g
% Daily Value: Vitamin A 0%; Vitamin C 36%; Calcium 0%; Iron 0%
Diet Exchanges: 1½ Fruit

BETTY'S TIPS

⊕ **Time-Saver**
If you don't want the hassle of whisking every 30 minutes, stir granita after 2 hours, then cover and freeze 3 hours or overnight. To serve, scrape surface of granita with fork and spoon into glasses.

⊕ **Special Touch**
Garnish with festive kiwifruit stars. To easily make the stars, cut slices of kiwifruit with a small, deep star-shaped cookie cutter.

Cranberry Herbal Tea Granita

Index

Note: <u>Underscored</u> page references indicate Betty's Tips or boxed text. **Bold** page references indicate photographs.

helpful **nutrition** and **cooking** information

nutrition guidelines

We provide nutrition information for each recipe that includes calories, fat, cholesterol, sodium, carbohydrate, fiber and protein. Individual food choices can be based on this information.

Recommended intake for a daily diet of 2,000 calories as set by the Food and Drug Administration

Total Fat	Less than 65g
Saturated Fat	Less than 20g
Cholesterol	Less than 300mg
Sodium	Less than 2,400mg
Total Carbohydrate	300g
Dietary Fiber	25g

criteria used for calculating nutrition information

- The first ingredient was used wherever a choice is given (such as ⅓ cup sour cream or plain yogurt).
- The first ingredient amount was used wherever a range is given (such as 3- to 3½-pound cut-up broiler-fryer chicken).
- The first serving number was used wherever a range is given (such as 4 to 6 servings).
- "If desired" ingredients and recipe variations were not included (such as sprinkle with brown sugar, if desired).
- Only the amount of a marinade or frying oil that is estimated to be absorbed by the food during preparation or cooking was calculated.

ingredients used in recipe testing and nutrition calculations

- Ingredients used for testing represent those that the majority of consumers use in their homes: large eggs, 2% milk, 80%-lean ground beef, canned ready-to-use chicken broth and vegetable oil spread containing not less than 65 percent fat.
- Fat-free, low-fat or low-sodium products were not used, unless otherwise indicated.
- Solid vegetable shortening (not butter, margarine, nonstick cooking sprays or vegetable oil spread as they can cause sticking problems) was used to grease pans, unless otherwise indicated.

equipment used in recipe testing

We use equipment for testing that the majority of consumers use in their homes. If a specific piece of equipment (such as a wire whisk) is necessary for recipe success, it is listed in the recipe.

- Cookware and bakeware without nonstick coatings were used, unless otherwise indicated.
- No dark-colored, black or insulated bakeware was used.
- When a pan is specified in a recipe, a metal pan was used; a baking dish or pie plate means ovenproof glass was used.
- An electric hand mixer was used for mixing only when mixer speeds are specified in the recipe directions. When a mixer speed is not given, a spoon or fork was used.

cooking terms glossary

Beat: Mix ingredients vigorously with spoon, fork, wire whisk, hand beater or electric mixer until smooth and uniform.

Boil: Heat liquid until bubbles rise continuously and break on the surface and steam is given off. For rolling boil, the bubbles form rapidly.

Chop: Cut into coarse or fine irregular pieces with a knife, food chopper, blender or food processor.

Cube: Cut into squares ½ inch or larger.

Dice: Cut into squares smaller than ½ inch.

Grate: Cut into tiny particles using small rough holes of grater (citrus peel or chocolate).

Grease: Rub the inside surface of a pan with shortening, using pastry brush, piece of waxed paper or paper towel, to prevent food from sticking during baking (as for some casseroles).

Julienne: Cut into thin, matchlike strips, using knife or food processor (vegetables, fruits, meats).

Mix: Combine ingredients in any way that distributes them evenly.

Sauté: Cook foods in hot oil or margarine over medium-high heat with frequent tossing and turning motion.

Shred: Cut into long thin pieces by rubbing food across the holes of a shredder, as for cheese, or by using a knife to slice very thinly, as for cabbage.

Simmer: Cook in liquid just below the boiling point on top of the stove; usually after reducing heat from a boil. Bubbles will rise slowly and break just below the surface.

Stir: Mix ingredients until uniform consistency. Stir once in a while for stirring occasionally, often for stirring frequently and continuously for stirring constantly.

Toss: Tumble ingredients (such as green salad) lightly with a lifting motion, usually to coat evenly or mix with another food.

metric conversion chart

Volume

U.S. Units	Canadian Metric	Australian Metric
¼ teaspoon	1 mL	1 ml
½ teaspoon	2 mL	2 ml
1 teaspoon	5 mL	5 ml
1 tablespoon	15 mL	20 ml
¼ cup	50 mL	60 ml
⅓ cup	75 mL	80 ml
½ cup	125 mL	125 ml
⅔ cup	150 mL	170 ml
¾ cup	175 mL	190 ml
1 cup	250 mL	250 ml
1 quart	1 liter	1 liter
1½ quarts	1.5 liters	1.5 liters
2 quarts	2 liters	2 liters
2½ quarts	2.5 liters	2.5 liters
3 quarts	3 liters	3 liters
4 quarts	4 liters	4 liters

Weight

U.S. Units	Canadian Metric	Australian Metric
1 ounce	30 grams	30 grams
2 ounces	55 grams	60 grams
3 ounces	85 grams	90 grams
4 ounces (¼ pound)	115 grams	125 grams
8 ounces (½ pound)	225 grams	225 grams
16 ounces (1 pound)	455 grams	500 grams
1 pound	455 grams	½ kilogram

Measurements

Inches	Centimeters
1	2.5
2	5.0
3	7.5
4	10.0
5	12.5
6	15.0
7	17.5
8	20.5
9	23.0
10	25.5
11	28.0
12	30.5
13	33.0

Temperatures

Fahrenheit	Celsius
32°	0°
212°	100°
250°	120°
275°	140°
300°	150°
325°	160°
350°	180°
375°	190°
400°	200°
425°	220°
450°	230°
475°	240°
500°	260°

Note: The recipes in this cookbook have not been developed or tested using metric measures. When converting recipes to metric, some variations in quality may be noted.

THE BLACK POWER BROKERS

ARTHUR L. ELLIS

CENTURY TWENTY ONE PUBLISHING

PUBLISHED BY

CENTURY TWENTY ONE PUBLISHING
POST OFFICE BOX 8
SARATOGA, CALIFORNIA 95070

LIBRARY OF CONGRESS CARD CATALOG NUMBER

79-65252

I.S.B.N.

0-86548-009-5

TABLE OF CONTENTS

CHAPTER 1

INTRODUCTION

The crisis of leadership in Northern American black communities is fundamentally a function of the peculiar and historical context of race caste in the American social system.[1]

The profound consequences of this reality are not to be found alone, in the social trauma which blacks have suffered as a people, but as well, in the systematic distortion of knowledge about the internal dynamics which function within the black community as positive, effective forces of socialization, cohesion and self determination. Knowles and Prewitt note in their study, Institutional Racism in America, for example:

> From Myrdal to Moynihan, there has been a tendency to picture the black sub-culture as pathological. These commentators see the damage wrought by oppression without being able to recognize the strength born admist suffering. Such judgements rest upon the assumption that the dominant white society which excersises racism's controls, is the healthy organism into which the sick ghetto should dissolve. As they overemphasize the health of a racist society, they are compelled to see little but pathology in the life of its victims. Black culture and personality are depicted one-sidedly in terms of the scars of oppression. Furthermore, the black man and his milieu are defined purely in terms of reaction to the white world. It is as though the truth of the general proposition that "man makes his own history" is granted, but in this case its special form as "the white man makes the blackman's history". Thereby, the value, creativity, and potential of the black qua black is denied.[2]

I am concerned, in this study, with one particular aspect of this general problem; the pervasive ignorance about functional leadership within the black community. An additional, primary interest is the identification of specific social instrumentalities which serve as mechanisms for the identification, observation and training of such leadership.

Haryou-Act,[3] the community corporation of the Central Harlem community, serves as the social instrumentality for the analysis of functional leadership in the ghetto. We are primarily concerned, here, with civic leadership as defined in terms of functions performed "in the work of civic organizations and the activity involved in the raising and settling of community issues".[4]

The major objective is, thus, to illustrate the dynamic aspect of leadership function by analyzing actions of certain men and women, who determine by what they do, or do not do; by decisions they make or refrain from making, the development, character syntality and survival potential of certain forms of community organizations. Board of directors members and executive staff of Haryou-Act serve as the

1

population for the analysis, of this form of leadership.[5]

The logic of the approach is consistent with other leadership studies insofar as it introduces early one basic assumption: That the functions of leadership are best understood within a particular social context. Philip Selznick finds, for example, that, "The functions of leadership will be understood only as we develop a better understanding of the main types of groups and the recurrent problems they face".[6] Thus in his view, "a theory of leadership is dependent on a theory of social organization". Jenkin's adds, that

Leadership is specific to the particular situation under investigation; who becomes the leader in a given group engaging in a particular activity and what the leadership characteristics are in a given case are a function of the specific situation.......[7]

M. Elaine Burgess finds

In the study of race and power relations, the community is the research setting. It is only recently that social scientists have moved to the local level to observe these relationships. Yet such phenomena can fruitfully be observed at this level.[8]

And finally, Myrdal warns,

The study of leadership and followership should not start from an attempt to define on a priority grounds the two principle concepts involved. In this tangled and uncultivated field of study such an attempt would almost inevitably land the investigator in hollow and doctrinal squabbles on the meaning of words. We have only to settle that we are discussing the role and importance of individual persons in the sphere of social and political Power.[9]

The rationale for the utilization of Haryou-Act as the appropriate Social organizational instrumentality or mechanism for the analysis of functional leadership is consistent with the above. I am in fundamental agreement with those who view leadership as 'a process' which occurs within a 'particular social situation'.[10]

There is an additional crisis in leadership which makes this study relevant and of moment. Default of leadership at the highest level of national government in America, though not new with respect to the problems of black people,[11] is most recently reflected in a basic change in social philosophy as articulated in National policies and priorities established by President Richard M. Nixon's administration. I believe the New York Times analysis is correct in its assessment.

The philosophy that lay behind the President's budget was viewed in some quarters as a repudiation of four decades of social change - a reversion to the do nothing Federal Governments and every-man-for-himself ideology of the Hoover era.......[12]

Clearly the importance of 'mustering' the most qualitative and committed community leadership available is unquestionable, given such 'reversals' at the National level. For black people, in black communities, the crisis is the more profound.

An analysis of leadership in Central Harlem, her community institutionals, programs or organizations which proceeds without first establishing the dynamic and peculiar social history which is Harlem, is meaningless. Only in Harlem could a Haryou-Act have been conceived. Only the 'Capital' of Black America or the 'Apple' of its eye, evidenced the capacity and character to give birth to the 'creature of controversy'.[13] In this instance we will be defining leadership, somewhat the way in which Bogardus does; in terms of "conjuncture". That is as

> a concurrence of a social situation that involves conflict and crisis, capable persons to meet the social situation, and opportunity to exercise these capabilities.[14]

Thus, a brief historical sketch of Harlem is presented in the study, so as to enable understanding the types of functional leaders who emerge, in the Haryou-Act process. Certain questions[15] are explored and answered as the study proceeds. Fundamental, among them are: Who were the initial leaders in Haryou? Why did they become involved in the program? Has the Haryou leadership pattern changed? If so, how? Who are the 'new' Haryou leaders? In what way does Haryou represent a legitimate social instrumentality or mechanism for leadership identification, selection, training and change? What are the functions of Haryou leaders? In what ways is Haryou leadership dysfunctional to organizational values and goals? What are Haryou's organizational values and goals? What relationships do Haryou leaders have with other Harlem institutions or community systems? With institutions external to Harlem? What kinds of behavior are associated with Haryou leadership behavior? How is such behavior associated with the broader community or social context? Are specific group affiliations and individual factors significant for Haryou leadership functions? What emerges as the process of leadership change in the Haryou program? How are the results of leadership behavior evaluated? In answering these and other questions, we find it helpful to construct a new typology of leadership. One which deals with the kinds of peculiar 'tasks' and 'functions' relegated to those who would assume leadership in Harlem. Thus, some departure from the conventional models of black leadership, i.e., accommodation, protest, militant etc. is discernable: though reference to existing theories of leadership are often relied upon.[16]

Constant themes throughout the study relate to analysis' of processes of policy and 'critical decision'; the effects of leadership functions on Haryou 'character' or 'syntality'; the functional relationships between certain forms of leadership and organizational 'integrity'; and finally the functional and dysfunctional effects of leadership default respecting organizational values and goals.[17]

Theoretical and Literary Referents

> Evaluation (of leadership), takes on a special importance because of the strong pragmatic emphasis upon leadership in our culture. It is not enough to know what leadership is; the demand is for knowledge about good leadership in order to secure as much of it as possible, as soon as possible.[18]

In black culture, however, we find that leadership takes on a special 'dual' form. Thus I am interested in such questions as, "good leadership" defined by whom and for what purposes.[19]

An intensive review of current studies and conventional literature related to leadership is presented in this analysis. A major finding is that students of the problem have been so preoccupied with conceptualizing black communities as sub-communities; to be studied only as functional to the broader American power system, that few systematic efforts are directed at internal dynamics, related to leadership modes.[20] The point of departure in my study, however, is more akin to the insights of Ralph Ellison, who, in an unpublished review of Gunnar Myrdal's An American Dilemma wrote:

> But can a people live and develop for three hundred years simply by reacting? Are American Negroes simply the creation

of white men, or have they at least helped to create
themselves out of what they found around them? Men have
made a way of life in caves and upon cliffs, why cannot
negroes have made a life upon the horns of the white
man's dilemma?[21]
There is little question regarding the trauma which racist controls
have heaped upon the black ghetto. But the recognition that social
and cultural bonds with distinctive strengths, as well as weaknesses
have been forged received little commentary in the literature.[22] This
kind of perspective assisted me in weaving through the proliferate
theory and literature related to leadership as an area of inquiry.

To have settled with 'functionalism' as the broad theoretical framework, within which organizational theory and leadership theories are
specified, is consistent with the announced bias. The logic of the
approach is consistent with the findings of Seeman and Morris in their
studies of leadership. They, for example find that some 'mix' of
theoretical orientations for a substantive analysis of leadership
phenomena is essential.[23] In their study, A General Framework For The
Study of Leadership, they construct a Paradigm for the analysis of leadership which is of immeasureable assistance in the present study.[24]
Their call for an 'interdisciplinary' approach to problems associated
with studying leadership, has important insights for social policy generally, and social work specifically.[25]

The reader will, therefore, recognize throughout this study, concepts drawn from a variety theoretical orientations which cut across a
number of academic disciplines. The integration of concepts from
theories of power and social change, formal and informal organization,
functional analysis and leadership; crosscut disciplines of policital
science sociology, social psychology and social work.

My major concern in the study, utilizing this approach to theory,
is to effectively illuminate, through a qualitative analysis of Haryou
Leadership, the process by which their varied functions serve specific
organizational maintenance and change needs. An additional and major
approach to leadership theory, that made by Philip Selznick, is important to my analysis. His study Leadership In Administration, helped
develop much insight regarding Haryou leadership. Selznick's other
works, TVA and The Grass Roots, and The Organizational Weapon, are often
referred to.[26]

Particular note is made, however, to the process of development in
Leadership and Administration. Here, though Selznick develops an analytical model which deals with large formal organizations, I find a
wealth of relevant material useful in the present analysis, of a community organization. The conceptualization of functional 'types' of leaders
i.e., 'creative' and 'institutional' leaders; and the ascription of
functions dealing with the defense of institutional integrity and critical decision-making fit neatly into my conceptual model of leadership
typology and function. The manner by which institutionalization is
viewed as a 'process' and that 'happens' to an organization over time
is consistent with one subsidiary hypothesis here; that is, to the functional relevance of particular modes of leadership behavior at given
times, in an organizations development. Selznick finds in this regard:

It (institutionalization) is something that happens to an
organization over time, reflecting the organization's own
distinctive history, the people who have been in it, the
group it embodies and the vested interest they have created,
and the way it has adapted to its environment.[27]

Institutionalization, is finally, to Selznick, "a process of value infusion".[28] I find this a most provocative, relevant approach to

4

conceptualizing functional leadership in Haryou; and though not of
immediate relevance to the present study, to an analysis of Haryou and
its organizational functions within the Central Harlem community.

Additional contributions of Selznick's orientation, relate to the
finding that; "leadership is the kind of work done to meet the needs
of a social situation"; and further,

> however, it does not follow that the nature of leadership varies
> within each social situation. If that were so, there would be
> nothing determinate about it: its study would be a scientific
> blind alley. In fact, of course, we assume that significant
> leadership patterns are relatively few; and that these patterns
> are related to types of social situations.29

A final comment regarding Selznick's contributions relates to his
work in TVA and The Grass Roots. Here, the integration of the complex
theoretical concepts of power, organization and political leadership
are effectively bridged. The analysis of the policy and organizer
leadership functions as performed by certian power interests at the
community and regional levels discussed by Selznick are familiar to the
enlightened observer of the Haryou scene; particularly in the manner by
which organizational and community decisions are made. The familiarity
of concepts of 'maximum feasible participation' of local and indigenous
interests groups and individuals precipitate almost identical crisis in
organizational survival; reference Haryou and the 'Authority'. Finally,
identification of those processes and tactics utilized at policy making
levels, by Board of Directors members and their power cliques are
reminiscent of the experience being analyzed here.30

In The Organizational Weapon, concepts of organizational and
leadership 'strain' and 'adaption'; 'group alienation', 'crisis precipitation' are keys which are useful in the analysis of Haryou and its
leadership.31

Turning for the moment from the contributions made by Selznick, I
have found the contributions of Robert K. Merton and his theory of
Functional Analysis particularly enlightening.32 In addition to utilizing his 'Paradigm for Functional Analysis', which serves as a model at
varying points during my analysis, his major work in Social Theory and
Social Structure, served the purpose of a resource for reviewing many
of the theoretical and conceptual contributions of 'functionalists'
such as Talcott Parsons, Branislaw Malinowski, Emile Durkheim.33
Additional references to the literature re: reference group theory
found in the American Soldier, studies were made as a direct result of
Merton's writings.34 Functional analysis as a primary framework for the
present study of leadership will be commented upon somewhat further, in
the methodological section of the study. Other contributors to the
functionalist orientation used in the study are Harry Bredemeier and
Richard Stephenson, in their work The Analysis of Social Systems; Don
Martindale, editor in his monograph, Functionalism in the Social Sciences;
Martin F. Spencer, The Nature and Value of Functionalism in Anthropology
and Robert T. Holt, in A Proposed Structural-Functional Framework for
Political Science. 35

Turning, at this point to additional theoretical contributions to
the analysis of leadership, I have found the literature related to
social and political power and powerlessness of immense relevance. The
writings of Dr. Kenneth B. Clark, with particular respect to the designing and structure of Haryou have been and are invaluable to my dissertation. Such works include, the Haryou planning document, Youth in the
Ghetto: The Consequences of Powerlessness; Dark Ghetto; A Relevant War

<u>Against Poverty</u>; <u>The Present Dilemma and Challenges of Negro Elected Officials</u> (in The Black Man in American Politics); and <u>The Civil Rights Movements</u>; <u>Momentum and Organization</u>, (in Daedalus Vol. 2, The Negro American).[36]

Though the present study borrows much from the basic power and social change frameworks within which Dr. Clark conceptualizes the problems of the ghetto, and further, views his orientation as fundamental to an indepth analysis of social pathology within Harlem; I am fundamentally in disagreement with his approach to the problem of Leadership. Dr. Clark states in his book, <u>A Relevant War Against Poverty</u> that:

> The effective use of the potential power of Negro masses
> and the ability of Negro leaders to discipline and mobilize
> that power for constructive social change, may well be de-
> termined by the ability of a critical mass of Negroes to
> the capacity for genuine and sustained respect for those
> Negroes who are worthy of confidence and respect. The present
> unrealities and distortions of ghetto life make it difficult
> to differentiate between empty flamboyance and valid achievement;
> between hysterical, cynical, verbal manipulation and sound
> judgement. It is difficult for the uneducated, exploited, and
> despised Negro to know whom he can trust and whom he must con-
> tinue to suspect.[37]

I reject this analysis of the problem of leadership in the black community. For, in addition to its similarity to the kind of 'elitist' leadership concept once articulated by WEB Dubois (Re: The Talented Tenth),[38] Dr. Clark's suggestion is in conflict with the infact reality, of ghetto leadership styles and functions.[39] I explore this matter as the dissertation proceeds.

As my analysis proceeds, the reader finds a variety of referrants to power theory as it is articulated in political science literature. The contributions in this regard of Dr. Charles V. Hamilton and Stokely Carmichael, in the book, <u>Black Power</u>, and the continuous writings of Dr. Hamilton in The Harvard Law Review and The New York Times and most recently in the book <u>The Black Preacher</u>, are worth particular mention.[40] In addition, M. Elaine Burgess' well developed research, <u>The Study of Leadership In A Southern City</u>, though not a political science treatise, was illuminating.[41] Particular note here is made to Miss Burgess' organization and methodology in conducting her study. Floyd Hunter's work in <u>Community Power Structure</u>; <u>A Study of Decision Makers</u>; and Everett C. Ladd's book, <u>Negro Political Leadership in the South</u>, are added 'power' studies of relevance here.[42] The latter are relevant primarily as they share my concern for developing the concept of 'functional leadership' though they deal primarily with political leadership within a race relations framework. Secondarily, (though this certainly applies to Miss Burgess as well), these authors have facilitated new insight re: the development of leadership typologies. In this regard, Eugene Litwak in the treatment of his 'Balance' theories respecting bureaucratic and 'primary' groups, their leadership and 'linkages' make a major contribution.[43]

In some instances, these studies provide contrasts from the study of leadership in Haryou. Particularly in view of their settings in Southern American communities. For I am, in this study, about the analysis of a community system within a Northern urban ghetto, with its peculiar realities and subterfuge. In this regard, one political scientist, James Q. Wilson, utilizing a power theory orientation, has in his Chicago studies provided a somewhat more relevant leadership analysis.[44] Wilson's implications regarding the differences in community organizational and

6

leadership styles which exist between blacks in the North and South are, to some degree echoed in my analysis. His findings that South Side Chicago, as a ghetto does not represent as sophisiticated a constellation of leaders and organizations as Central Harlem serve as additional impetus for systematic investigation of the present topic.[45]

Finally, for the purpose of the present review of relevant concepts of power, are the contributions of Gunnar Myrdal, in his classic, An American Dilemma.[46] Myrdal's study, long ago, provided the basic seeds of inquiry about the true nature of leadership in the ghetto; and has served as impetus to me, for many years, to begin the task implicit in this study. The dated nature of his conceptualizations of leadership typologies, given--His work persists as a point of departure for most recent studies on the phenomena.[47] Contemporary analysis may disagree with Myrdal's views, and often fundamentally; but the study remains as perhaps the most illuminating of its kind.

Max Weber's conceptual theoretical models of power and authority are additional literary referrants.[48] C. Wright Mills interpretations of Weber, and Mills' independent book, The Power Elite, serve further, in broadening the relevant conceptual field.[49]

In turning to the final theoretical area explored in the study, social change, the reader is presented a complex of literature and professional practice. Note should be made at this point that the 'disjointed' presentation of theoretical and conceptual frameworks used in my analysis of leadership, is essentially for the purpose of clarification re: the dissertation proposal. The reader finds, in the present writing of the dissertation that these various frameworks are interwoven, and serve as continuous elements in reviewing the Haryou mechanism.[50]

The literature and professional practice experience related to Mobilization For Youth, is of particular relevance here. That Dr. Richard Cloward and Dr. Lloyd Ohlin's 'opportunity' theory was instrumental to the original conceptualization of the early Haryou project design.[51] Drs. George Brager and Charles Grosser; Harry Specht and Francis Piven; Alfred J. Kahn and Mitchel Ginsberg; are all among the constellation of Social Work theorists whose contributions in the social change literature are relevant in my study.[52] In most instances these writers participated in the early formulative stages of Haryou, and their insights as colleagues are of immeasureable value in conceptualizing the functional leadership analysis.[53] I am fortunate in knowing many of these authors personally, and in having shared somewhat the experiences and insights about which they have written. Thus, their contributions to the perspective found here goes beyond a purely research one.

To have embarked upon a study of leadership within a black community and notably, Harlem, without a thorough analysis of the literary and research contributions of Dr. E. Franklin Frazier, is inconceivable.[54] Dr. Frazier's consideration of the problem of leadership definition and change is long standing. As early as the 1940's, he is found in the vanguard of social historians articulating the need for research regarding the nature of leadership in Northern ghetto communities. His conceptualization that particular typologies of 'functional' leadership were of greater relevance to such studies, and that the process of leadership transition in Northern communities was the area to be dealt with, is documented in most contemporary leadership literature.[55] Frazier, in 1949 began urging associates in the American Sociological Association to develop more meaningful research into the nature of emerging functional leaders in the black community in contradistinction to the conventional typologies of "Race Leaders"; and in this regard articulates a theme consistent with the present study.[56]

There is, finally a literature seldom referred to in most studies regarding leadership. It is that entire wealth of written accounts of the internal, functional dynamics of the Harlem community. Many of the authors have concerns which fall outside the realm of social science, or empiricism, but as suggested earlier, an account of functional leadership in a ghetto organization as complex as Haryou, is meaningless without establishing an appropriate social historical framework. Thus, in my study, reference is often made to the emotional, subjective writing of men and women who made no claim to rigorous scientific analysis;[57] but rather reflect in their writings the social 'mood' of a community and its people. I find no need to apologize for this. The relevance of the approach is found in the absence of any meaningful alternatives. The dearth of 'objective' literature about Harlem as a self determined socio-cultural community is, perhaps the major shortcoming of the current research effort.

The reader is again reminded that I am here, not primarily concerned with the 'comparative' type of analysis of community and power leadership, conventionally set in a framework of bi-racial or caste considerations. This dissertation is focused on the <u>internal</u> dynamics of a community as they are reflected through the functions of particular types of leaders acting within an organizational context. This consideration may facilitate some generalization beyond the above boundaries. If the analysis adds to knowledge regarding functional leadership in other ghetto communities, as I suspect is the case; then the effort will be professionally rewarding, in terms of additional knowledge, and personally rewarding in terms of having exploded another 'myth' respecting black leadership.

I proceed, then, in exploring the wealth of literature reflected in the writings of: Langston Hughes, Adam Clayton Powell, Sr. and Adam Clayton Powell, Jr., John Henrik Clark, James Baldwin, Paul Zuber, George Brown, John A. Williams, Hope Stevens, Marcus Garvey, Claude Brown, and W.E.B. Dubois. These authors add a particular flavor and insight of importance to the objective analysis undertaken here. I will in some ways be suggesting another subsidiary hypothesis in the study; that Harlem is at base an emotional community, and thus, the expectation that any effective organizational leadership typology could emerge which is non-reflective of this phenomena is unreal.

The theoretical orientation of this study of functional leadership in Haryou-Act is an interdisciplinary one. I am in fundamental agreement with the proposition that an appropriate framework or theory of leadership rests upon a sound theory of organization, but bring to this analysis a concern for linking relevant concepts from theories of power and social change, to one basic assumption:

> that effective identification of leadership styles functional
> for the positive self determination of a Northern ghetto
> community requires the identification and analysis of leader
> functions within legitimate social organizations and instru-
> mentalities.

8

FOOTNOTES TO CHAPTER 1

1. Louise L. Knowles and Kenneth Prewitt; Institutional Racism in
   America. Prentice Hall, Inc. Engelwood Cliffs, N.J. Pages
   12-13. The Authors discuss the historical context in which
   the Ideological roots of Racism resident in concepts of
   manifest destiny and the white man's burden perpetuated the
   myth, that Blacks were generally incapable of leadership
   and Self Government. Gunnar Myrdal, An American Dilemma,
   the Negro Problem and Modern Democracy (Harper and Row,
   N.Y. and Evanston) Chapters 10-15. Chapters and appendix 3.
   Kenneth Clark: Dark Ghetto; Dilemmas of Social Power.
   (Harper and Row, N.Y., Evanston and London), Chapters I-III.

2. Knowles and Prewitt, op. cit., page 174.

3. The Harlem Youth Opportunities Unlimited-Associated Community
   Teams. The term Haryou will be used throughout this study,
   in referring to the Organization.

4. James Q. Wilson, Negro Politics: The Search for Leadership. The
   Free Press, Glencoe, Illinois, p. 79.

5. In this regard I differ with the interpretation of Wilson. He,
   for example, does not include paid staff at any level. However,
   my inclusion of Executives is reflective of the large amounts
   of non-paid, voluntary time required of them and particularly
   during Organizational crisis. Also see Philip Selznick's
   study Leadership in Administration: A Sociological Interpretation (Row, Peterson and Company; Evanston, Ill. and White
   Plains, N.Y.) Chapter I-III re: his discussion of Institutional Leadership types.

6. Philip Selznick, Leadership in Administration, A Sociological
   Interpretation, Ron Peterson and Co., Evanston, Illinois.
   Page 28.

7. William O. Jenkins, "A Review of Leadership Studies with particular reference to Military Problems," Psychological Bulletin
   1947, 44, page 75.

8. M. Elaine Burgess, Leadership in a Southern City, Chapel Hill:
   The University of North Carolina Press, page 4.

9. Gunnar Mydral, An American Dilemma: The Negro Problem and Modern
   Democracy (Revised edition), Harper and Row, Publishers,
   New York and Evanston; appendix 9, page 1133.

9

10. Selznick, op. cit. page 22; see also Mydral op. cit. page 1134-5.
    Burgess op. cit. page 4,526--These authors as well as others
    make this point continually in these analysis. Melvin Seeman
    and Richard Morris. A General Framework for the Study of
    Leadership in, Paul E. Lazarfeld and Morris Rosenberg--
    The Language of Social Research, pages 511-518.

11. Knowles and Prewitt, op. cit. pages 3 and 4. See also The Report
    of the National Advisory Commission on Civil Disorders.
    (Kerner Commission); The Default of National Leadership
    throughout U.S. History with respect to the fulfillment of
    equal rights and opportunities for Black Americans represents
    a major theme throughout the literature on Race Relations:
    For further analysis see also Myrdal op. cit. chapters 1-10
    and appendixes 3, 5, 8, 9, and 13; Stokely Carmichael and
    Charles V. Hamilton, Black Power; The Politics of Liberation
    in America. Vintage Books pages 126 and 127, N.Y. Division
    of Random House; John Romanyshun, Social Welfare; Charity
    to Justice, Random House, N.Y. and Council on Social Work
    Education; pages 129-135 and Robert Perlman and Arnold Gurin:
    Community Organization and Social Planning pages 17-19.

12. The New Yorks Times (Sunday, February 4, 1973) Robert W. Stocks
    Article: The Message; A Basic Change in Social Philosophy.

13. Charles H. King and Arthur L. Ellis et al "Black Youth in Rebellion:"
    in Wilson Library Bulletin--October 1967 page 166-172 also see
    Youth In The Ghetto, The Consequence of Powerlessness, Haryou
    Inc. pages 21-22 and Langston Hughes, "My Early Days in Harlem"
    in John Henrike Clark's Harlem: A Community in Transition,
    Citadel Press. New York, pages 62-63 and Wilson, op. cit.
    pages 88-89.

14. Emory S. Bogardus, Leaders and Leadership, D. Appleton-Century Co.,
    Inc. NY and London, page 274.

15. Many of the questions are included in Morris and Seeman's. Paradigm
    for the Study of Leadership. In Lazarsfeld and Rosenberg op.
    cit. page 513; and see also Robert K. Merton, Social Theory
    and Social Structure (Revised edition), The Free Press, page 50.
    Here, Merton in formulating his paradigm for functional analysis
    in Sociology provides additional referrants for the question
    of relevance to this study.

16. Particularly with respect to the theoretical orientations of
    James Q. Wilson; op. cit., M. Elaine Burgess; Leadership in a
    Southern City, (University of North Carolina Press, Chapel
    Hill, 1962); Everett C. Ladd Jr., Negro Political Leadership
    in the South (Cornell University Press, Ithaca, N.Y.) and
    others.

17. Operational definition of these concepts are found in the appendix
    section: 'Definition of Concepts' at end of dissertation.

18. Richard T. Morris and Melvin Seeman, A General Framework for the
    Study of Leadership in Paul F. Lazarsfeld and Morris Rosenberg's
    The Language of Social Research, page 517.

19. Myrdal, op. cit., page 1133 and Burgess, op. cit., page 123.

20. St. Claire Drake and Horace R. Cayton, Black Metropolis: A Study of Negro Life in a Northern City, Vol, I, Harper and Row Publishers New York and Evanston. page 10-70. James Q. Wilson and Knowles and Prewitt, op. cit., page 1-25.

21. Ralph Ellison, Shadow and Act. A Signet Book, New American Library, N.Y., N.Y., page 301.

22. W.E.B. Dubois, Souls of Black Folk; E. Franklin Frazier, The Negro in the United States; (revised) New York, McMillan Co., 1965. Kenneth Clark, Dark Ghetto, op.cit., page 74. Youth in the Ghetto, Consequences of Powerlessness. (Haryou 1964) Chapter I and II. Knowles and Prewitt, Institutional Racism in American Society, op. cit., pages 10-30. Gunnar Myrdal, An American Dilemma, op. cit., pages 1-50 and others.

23. Morris and Seeman, op. cit., pages 50-70.

24. As noted in earlier section of the proposal many of the questions were generated from an analysis of these Authors Paradigm for the Analysis of Leadership. The work also served as a reference source for analyzing the variety of relationships which might exist between individual, group and organization phenoma relevant to an analysis of Leadership behavior.

25. This is a particularly important point giben current trends in Social policy formulation and Social Work Practice.

26. Philip Selznick, Leadership in Administration A Sociological Interpretation; Row, Peterson and Co., Evanston, Illinois, White Plains, New York.
_____, T.V.A. and the Grass Roots, A Study in the Sociology of Formal Organization, University of California Press, Berkeley and Los Angeles.
_____, The Organizational Weapon: A Study of Bolshevik Strategy and Tactics.

27. Selznick, Leadership in Administration, op. cit. page 16.

28. Ibid. page 17.

29. Ibid. page 23.

30. Selznick. T.V.A. and the Grass Roots, op. cit., page 143. In his analysis of the nuances operative between the three power groups in the forming the authority.

31. Selznick, The Organizational Weapon, op. cit., pages 26-38. These concepts are operationally defined in the section on Definitions (Appendix B) of the Dissertation. It suffices here to mention the importance of these conceptualizations to the formulation of the Haryou Leadership Study.

32. Merton, op. cit. particular note is made to Part I in which he formulates the theory of Functional Analysis. Merton also

discusses manifest and latent functions and presents a
sophisticated procedure for defining concepts of relevance
to my analysis.

33. Talcott Parsons, <u>Essays in Sociological Theory Pure and Applied</u>.
     Glencoe, Illinois: The Free Press, 1949, page 58.
     _____, The Social System, Glencoe, Illinois: Free
     Press, 1951. Malinowski "Anthropology" Encyclopedia Brittani-
     ca, First Supplementary Volume (London and New York, 1926)
     pages 132-133. Emil Durkheim, <u>The Rules of Sociological Method</u>,
     page 110; L'Education Morale (Paris; Felix Alcan, 1925, 9-25
     passim; Durkheim, Anomic suicide in Herman D. Stein and Richard
     A. Cloward's <u>Social Perspectives on Behavior</u>, The Free Press,
     Glencoe, Illinois, pages 506-16.

34. Merton, <u>op. cit</u>., page 225.

35. Harry Bredemier and Richard Stephenson, <u>The Analysis of Social</u>
     <u>Systems</u>, New York, Holt, Rinehart and Winston, 1962. Don
     Martindale, <u>Functionalism in the Social Sciences</u>; Philadelphia,
     American Academy of Political and Social Science, 1965.
     Martin F. Spencer, the Nature and Value of Functionalism in
     Anthropology; Robert T. Holt; <u>A Proposed Structural-Functional</u>
     <u>Framework for Political Science</u>: The Methodology of Compara-
     tive Research Center for comparative studies in Technological
     Development and Social Change and Department of Social Science,
     University of Minnesota. Edited by Halt and John E. Terner,
     New York Free Press, 1970.

36. Youth in the Ghetto: <u>The Consequences of Powerlessness</u>; Harlem
     Youth Opportunities Unlimited Inc. 1964--See particularly
     the Introduction by Clark. Clark, <u>Dark Ghetto</u>, <u>Op. Cit</u>.,
     <u>A Relevant War Against Poverty</u>, <u>A Study of Community Action</u>
     <u>Programs and Observable Social Change</u>. New York, Metropolitan
     Applied Research Center Inc. 1969. Kenneth Clark, Julian Bond
     and Richard G. Hatcher; <u>The Black Man In American Politics</u>:
     <u>Three Views</u>, New York Metropolitan Applied Research Center,
     Inc. 1969.

37. Clark, <u>op. cit</u>., page 197.

38. W.E.B. Dubois, <u>Souls of Black Folks</u>, Chicago, A.C. McClurg, 1904.
     Chapter I.

39. I am concerned here with particular elements of Dr. Clark's leader-
     ship Analysis. It has been my experience that Harlemites are
     most capable of discerning the differences between flamboyant
     "hysterical and cynical" leaders and their rhetoric, as opposed
     to those who have achieved or who show sound judgement. They
     know who is worthy of their trust and/or respect, despite
     ambivalence--the question is; are the types of leaders to
     whom Dr. Clark is oriented functional re: The Internal Com-
     munity Dynamics of Harlem.

40. Hamilton and Carmichael, <u>Black Power</u>, <u>op. cit</u>. Charles V. Hamilton,
     New York Times Magazine Article, October 1, 1972. Charles V.
     Hamilton, Harvard Law Review; <u>The Black Preacher in America</u>,
     Marrow, 1972, New York.

41. Burgess, op. cit. pages 201-216.

42. Floyd Hunter, Community Power Structure; A Study of Decision
    Makers, Chapel Hill, University of North Carolina Press.
    Everett C. Ladd, Negro Political Leadership in the South,
    Cornell University Press, Ithaca, New York.

43. Eugene Litwak and Henry J. Meyer, "A Balance Theory of Coordina-
    tion Between Bureaucratic Organizations and Primary Groups"
    in Administrative Science Quarterly, June 1966, pages 31-58.

44. Wilson, op. cit. See particularly Wilson's analysis in the Intro-
    duction pages 3-13.

45. Ibid. pages 106, 107, 292, 293.

46. Gunnar Myrdal, An American Dilemma: The Negro Problem and Modern
    Democracy, op. cit.

47. I have found that most studies of leadership (since the 1950s);
    quote Myrdal extensively; examples are Burgess, op. cit.,
    pages 4-7; Ladd, op. cit., pages 1-10; Wilson, op. cit.,
    pages 1-4 and others.

48. Max Weber, "Three types of Legitimate Rule". In, Amitai Etzioni,
    Complex Organization: A Sociological Reader, Holt, Rinehart
    and Winston, Inc. New York.

49. H. H. Garth and C. Wright Mills. From Max Weber; Essays in
    Sociology Routledge and Kegan Paul ltd. Broadway House,
    68-74, Carter Lane, London. C. Wright Mills. The Power
    Elite, a Galaxy Book, New York, Oxford University Press, 1959.

50. Borrowing from these varied disciplines effectively serves the
    purpose of integrating into a cohesive conceptual body; ideas,
    propositions and insights fundamental to my study's elements.

51. Youth in the Ghetto, op. cit. Acknowledgements, page XIV.

52. Particular reference is made to these Authors Activities and
    Comments during the period of formulation and implementation
    of the war on poverty; (approximately 1962-1969). See for
    example, George and Purcell's book Community Action Against
    Poverty. Charles Grosser, "Community Organization and the
    Grass Roots" and "Changing Theory and Changing Practice in
    The Practice of Social Intervention: Roles, Goals and Strategies
    A Book of Readings In Social Work Practice, Frank M. Lowenberg
    and Ralph Dolgoff, F.E. Peacock, Publishers, Inc.
    Francis Piven re: "How the Government Caused the Welfare Crisis",
    in Lowenberg and Dolgoff, op. cit., page 411. Alfred J. Kahn
    in Studies in Social Policy and Planning, Russell Sage
    Foundation, NY, 1969 "Trends and Problems in Community Organi-
    zation", in National Conference on Social Welfare, Social Work
    Practice, 1964, New York, Columbia University Press, 1964.
    Mitchel Ginsberg while administrator for the Human Resourses
    Administration.

53. _Youth in the Ghetto_, _op. cit_. It is noteworthy that the Special Relationship which existed between the Columbia University School of Social Work and the Haryou Planners and Leaders though not formally documented; was most instrumental in facilitating early relationship with Federal and Local Funding Sources and the Ford Foundation; perhaps the most substantive relationships, however, were found in the supports and assistance provided by Faculty and Planners at Columbia who were knowledgeable as the result of their functions in establishing the Mobilization for Youth Program on New York City's Lower East Side.

54. Here, as in the case mentioned earlier of Myrdal. Frazier is footnoted in most Leadership Studies related to Black Community. Though many references are in fundmental difference with certain hypothesis: Contributions here are found in _Black Bourgoisie_ (Free Press, Glencoe, Illinois, 1957), _The Negro in the United States_, (Revised) N.Y., McMillan and Co. 1963 and _Race Contacts and The Social Review_, Chapel Hill. University of North Carolina 1953. See also Burgess, _op. cit_., page 3 Ladd, _op. cit_., Introduction; Wilson, _op. cit_., page 72 and others.

55. Burgess, _op. cit_. page 3.

56. Wilson, _op. cit_. pages 205 and 308.

57. Some of which is unpublished: others are reproductions of speeches and lectures. Examples, Arthur L. Smith, _Rhetoric of Black Revolution_, Allyn and Bacon, Inc. Boston, page 154. Marcus Garvey, "The Negroes Greatest Enemy" in Thomas Frazier, _Afro-American History: Primary Resources_. Harcourt, Brace and World, Inc. New York/Chicago/San Francisco/Atlanta. Select writings of the remaining Authors, used for my purposes in the study are found in John Henrike Clarke, _Harlem: A Community in Transition_, Citadel Press, N.Y.; in addition see W.E.B. Dubois, _Black Folk; Then and Now_. _The Philadelphia Negro_, N.Y., Henry Halt and Co., Philadelphia Publications University of Pennsylvania 1899; _The Souls of Black Folks_, Chicago, H.C. McClurg, 1904 and of Mr. Booker T. Washington and others in Smith--_op. cit_., page 221.

CHAPTER 2

The history of the Black community in urban America, is one enriched by the contributions of indigenous functional leadership.[1] Political, religious and educational leadership; artistic, professional and business leadership, race and civic leadership; all, at a time, serve particular civic functions within, and on behalf of, the black urban community.[2]

The forces and circumstances which make this so, are represented by the peculiar circumstances of the black American's social history within his community. An experience enschrouded in racism, exploitation and traumatization, yet one reflective of communal strength, cultural innovation and organizational cohesiveness.[3]

This analysis is about such a community. More particularly, it is about civic leadership in one contemporary ghetto nestled in the heart of the urban north; Harlem in New York City.

We will attempt to trace the process of leadership development, emergence and change in Harlem at a unique period in its history. A period charged with violence and crises, the tensions and, paradoxically, the greatness, of the tumultuous 1960s. These are the years of civil and human rights confrontation, and the "Great Sociaty's" anti-poverty "War".[4] The years of community action demonstration programs and community control strategies. Implicit in my analysis is the proposition that leadership during this period is to some degree a reflection of earlier experiences and styles in Harlem.

In one sense, my story is about a people's organization, The Harlem Youth Opportunities Unlimited, Inc., I approach Haryou from a perspective which related to its conceptual and idealogical "intent";[5] as well as its operational relevance. An approach, which though not intended to represent a total analysis of the organization, is illustrative of its relevance as a legitimate social mechanism for the emergence, function and change of community leadership.

Harlem is located at the northern extremity of Manhattan in New York City.[6] The work "Manhattan" means different things to different people. In some it evokes images of tall buildings and bustling crowds, in others the thought is of high finance and commerce. For others still, Manhattan is the theatre, bohemia, or a cocktail. What is often forgotten, however, is that for some 1,698,281 Americans' Manhattan means home. For them, Manhattan is Yorktown, Chelsea, the Lower East Side, or some other community within this island of 319 square miles. Directly north of Central Park's vast expanse of trees and grass lies one such community -- Central Harlem, the symbolic home of the American urban Negro.

Roughly, the boundaries of Central Harlem may be described as 110th Street on the south; Third Avenue on the east; the Harlem River of the northeast; and the parks bordering St. Nicholas, Morningside, and Manhattan Avenues on the west (see Maps A and B). The community is precisely defined by Health Areas. It embraces Health Areas 8, 10, 12, 13, 15, 16, 19, 24, 85.10.[7] Since Health Areas are groupings of census tracts, the area can be alternately described in terms of thirty-three census tracts. The thirty-three census tracts which comprise Harlem's ten Health Areas are as follows:

Health Areas	Equivalent Census Tracts
8	214,232,234,236.243.1
10	228,230
12	224,226
13	208,212
15	200,220,222
16	196,198,204,206,210
19	190,218
24	186,216
85.10	221.1,227.1,231.1,235.1
85.20	197.1,201.1,207.1,209.1,213.1,217.1

Its history as a black community is relatively recent, as prior to the nineteen twenties few blacks lived within her boundaries. The most important factor underlying the establishment of Harlem as a Black community was substantial increase of the black population in New York City in the years 1890-1914.[8] In 1893, an article appeared in the then shick magazine, The Harlem Monthly Magazine, which captures the sense of community then prevalent,

> It is evident to the most superficial observer that the centre of fashion, wealth, culture and intelligence, must, in the near future be found in the ancient and honorable village of Harlem.[9]

These are the days when Harlem is the upper and upper middle class suburb; New York's first.[10] In 1880, for the first time in its history, the population of Manhattan passed the one million mark (1,164,673). This increase in population coincided with an expansion of business and industrial activity; both made serious inundations on living quarters in formerly staid residential areas of Manhattan. Many New Yorkers, attempting to avoid the bustle of the new metropolis and escape contact with its newest settlers, looked to Harlem as the community of the future. Harlem became "the choicest residential section in the City", according to one former resident.[11]

Practically all of the houses that stand in Harlem today, are the result of the "building boom" during the years 1870-1910. The boom is a direct result of the elevated railroad system, then new to the uptown community. No longer is it difficult to reach the "posh" suburb, heretofore available only after a lengthy buggy ride from the downtown area. New building complexes shot up, almost overnight. Brownstones, and the newest in quality multiple dwelling units are constructed to meet the tastes of the well to do.[12]

Older and wealthier Manhattanites were attracted to the new "residential heaven". In a society whose working class families paid an average of $10-$18 a month rent, the rents for one group of apartments in Harlem in the 1890s started at just under $80 a month, and ranged between $900 to $1700 a year.[13]

The homes of municipal and federal judges, mayors, local politicians, and prominant businessmen were scattered throughout Harlem. Their children could attend Grammar School 68, referred to as the "Silk Stocking School" of the City. Young girls could go to "Mme. De Valencia's Protestant French and English Institute for Young Ladies". Local citizens, after attending a performance at the Harlem Opera House (built in 1889), might dine at the luxurious Pabst Harlem:

> where gentlemen and ladies can enjoy good music and a perfect cuisine amid surroundings which have been rendered as attractive to the eye and senses (as) good tast combined with lavish expenditures, could make them.

Late nineteenth century Harlem was able to support a monthly literary magazine, a weekly magazine of local affairs and a bi-weekly newspaper.[14]

These were the times during which few observers of the Harlem scene would have disagreed with the editor of the Harlem Monthly Review who saw Harlem developing as a

district... distinctly devoted to the mansions of the wealth, the homes of the well to do, and the places of business of the tradespoeple who minister their wants....

"We have no adequate idea of... the greatness that lies in store for Harlem[15] represents another contemporary observer's thoughts on the matter.

The winds of change swirled in Harlem during the first decades of the twentieth century. Forces, initially unrelated to the migration of blacks to this sparkling Harlem community begin to effectively undermine its stability. A wave of land speculation set off by subway construction deeper into the heart of the community, eventuated in overconstruction. Vacant lots, marshes, garbage dumps, any available unimproved property was purchased and turned immediately into flats and tenements. In West Harlem, along Seventh Avenue in the 130s and 140s (the best of Harlem is was called), luxurious apartment houses were built. The entire area was viewed as a place where the rich would find the kind of "high class" accomodations to which they are accustomed. These new dwellings were even equipped with elevators (then first being installed in better houses), maids' quarters and butlers' pantries. In 1899, William Waldorf Astor erected an apartment house on Seventh Avenue which cost $500,000.[16]

In the urge to get rich quickly on Harlem property, few persons realized how artificial market values had become. The inevitable "bust" came in 1904-1905. Speculators sadly realized that too many houses had been constructed at one time, and that the community had been glutted with apartments and "excessive building led to many vacancies".[17]

The individuals and companies that were caught in Harlem's rapidly deflated real estate market were threatened with financial ruin. Rather than face destruction, some landlords and corporations were willing to rent their houses to blacks and collect the traditionally high rents normally charged them. A variety of schemes, ranging from frightening white property owners into selling their homes in the wake of the "black invasion" at grossly deflated prices, and then reselling the property to blacks at phenomenal profit, to the contemporary 'art' of 'block-busting' were embarked upon by shrewd real estate operators. White Harlem fought back, however. Formal opposition to black settlement in Harlem centered in owners' groups. Homeowners protective associations flourished throughout the community. Restrictive covenants were entered into by community property owners (though most were found to be unconstitutional) which promised:

The premises, land, and building of which we...are the owners... shall not be used as a...Negro tenement, leased to colored... tenants, sold to colored... tenants or all (other) persons of African descent.[18]

Some covenants even attempted to put restrictions on the numbers of black janitors, bellboys, laundresses and servants that could be employed in a home. A propoganda 'war' was lodged, as 'White Only' signs began to appear in the windows of Harlem apartments.

Like an enemy negotiating a line of truce, white associations like the Committee of Thirty called meetings with Black Realtors to try drawing a voluntary boundary line that would permanently separate the white and black communities.[19]

17

All these movements fail. The basic cause for the collapse of these organized efforts to exclude blacks from Harlem was the inability to establish a thoroughly united white front. 'Panic selling' and the proverbial 'flight before the black invasions' were essentially the order of the day, despite organized efforts at exclusion. And blacks, offered decent housing and living accomodations for the first time in the City's history "flocked to Harlem and filled houses as fast as they were opened to them".[20]

The creation of black Harlem was only one example of the general development of large, segregated urban communities in many American cities in the years preceeding and following the First World War.[21] That Harlem became the specific center of black population was the result of circumstance, and, in my view, specific Black leadership interests; that some section of the city was destined to become such a neighborhood was the inevitable consequence of the migration of southern blacks to New York City and the commitment of such leaders to achieve better living accomodations. In 1913, George Edmond Haynes, Director of the National Urban League wrote,

There is a growing up in the cities of America a distinct Negro World, isolated from many of the impulses of the common life and little understood by the white world.[22]

Harlem, however, was unique. Its name was a symbol of elegance and distinction, not derogation; its streets and avenues were broad, well paved, clean and tree-lined, not narrow and dirty; its homes were spacious, replete with the best of modern facilities, "finished in highstyle". Harlem was not a slum, but an ideal place in which to live. For the first time in the history of New York City, blacks were able to live in decent homes in a respectable neighborhood. "It is no longer necessary for our people to live in small, dingy, stuffy tenements",[23] editorialized a Black Newspaper in 1906. Harlem was "a community in which Negroes as a whole are....better housed than in any other part of the country" concluded an Urban League report in 1914.[24]

Practically every black institution moved out of its downtown quarters and came to Harlem by 1920: churches, insurance companies, small businesses, real estate firms, fraternal orders, settlement houses, social service agencies, the YMCA and YWCA, branches of the Urban League and the NAACP.[25] That such transition requires the talent, foresight and actions of special kinds of leaders is a matter which I explore below.

The "Fighting Fifteenth", Harlem's Negro National Guard unit, was outfitted in 1916. Harlem's first black assemblyman was elected in 1917. Harlem Hospital hired its first black nurses and a black doctor in 1919. P.S. 89 on Lenox Avenue (three quarters black by 1915) opened a night school, reading rooms and a community center to keep black children off the streets. P.S. 68, the former "Silk Stocking School", became noted for its regular skirmishes between white and black pupils.[26] In 1914, blacks lived in at least 1100 different houses within a twenty-three block area of Harlem. The black population of Harlem was then conservatively estimated at just under 50,000 - the entire black population of Manhattan in 1910 had been 60,534.[27] By 1920, the section of Harlem bordered by 130th Street on the south, 145th Street on the north and west of Madison and Fifth Avenues to Eighth Avenue was predominantly black - and inhabited by some 80,000 people. As the immigrants (Italians and Jews) who lived in surrounding areas moved to better quarters in other boroughs in the 1920s, their homes were filled by blacks. The black section remained and expanded as the other ethnic ghettos disintegrated. By 1930 black Harlem had reached its southern limit, 110th Street - the northern boundary of Central Park. Its population was then approximately 200,000. Harlem became the "Largest colony of colored people, in similar limits, in the world".[28] And so it remains to this day.

A social history, however, includes more than a quotation of the physical and external circumstances of a community or its people. It must also include the major internal dynamics functional respecting community character.[29] The crucial elements in the peculiar ghettoization process in Harlem became relevant historical social factors in this community's identification as the area for the Nations first and largest anti-poverty community action program.[30] Thus, the importance of our historical statement must be found in the social context established by those black New Yorkers who, in assuming leadership, create out of circumstance, a vibrant, exciting and cohesive community. A community in which heretofore unforseen opportunities for black enterprise and institutions emerge.[31]

It is of major importance to recognize, for example, that a certain kind of leadership is required during tumultuous years of migration and change in Harlem. Without the functional leadership of blacks like John M. Royal, George Edmond Haynes, Philip Payton and Pickens; all of whom are civic community activists; there would probably not have been the opportunities which eventually accrue to the new Harlemites.[32] Royals, in particular, demonstrates forsight with respect to the promise that the new area holds for his people. He is, first and foremost, a businessman, a realtor - however owing to the commitment to see, in addition to the potential profits, a new chance for the thousands of blacks, then trapped in the 'Tenderloin';[33] Royale uncompromisingly 'pushes' for 'open' occupancy of the newly available dwellings in Harlem. A forerunner of a type leader which I later define as 'creative elite.' He, for example, ridiculed the proposal of organized white interests such as the Harlem Property Owners' Improvements Corporation (HPOIC) for voluntary lines of segregation as an agreement to "capitalize on prejudice" and "a joke".[34] Other of New York City's most prominent black leaders - The Reverend Dr. Adam Clayton Powell, Sr., Bert Williams, James C. Thomas, Charles W. Anderson - had established residence in Harlem by 1912.

Philip A. Payton, is another business and civic leader during this period.[35] Phil Payton as he was commonly known founded the Afro-American Realty Company, during a fascinating business career. As part of his civic community activity, he served as president of a local Negro defense society, organized to protest police brutality in 1905. He was also a member of Booker T. Washington's National Negro Business League, the leading black businessmen's organization of the time. Payton viewed himself as a "leader of the race",[36] and his public and private statements tended to foster this impression. When, for example, he learned that white landlords in Harlem were organizing to prevent the settlement of blacks there, Payton remarked, "The fight that I am making.. has got to be made soomer or later and I see no better time than now".[37] Four of the apartment houses he rented to blacks were called "The Washington", "The Langston", "The Douglass", and "The Dunbar", in honor of contemporary and past black leaders of National International and local fame. Payton is among the earliest members of a leadership type which I identify as institutional-inspirationalist.

Other Blacks who participated in The Afro-American Realty Company, and who made individual civic leadership contributions to Harlem's transition, were John C. Thomas, first president of the Company; James E. Garner, Wilford H. Smith, Emmett J. Scott, The Reverend Dr. W.H. Brooks, Fred R. Moore and Charles W. Anderson. The Company's life, however is short lived, owing to a series of legal and financial difficulties, and by 1907 it is no longer a relevant force.[38]

After the collapse of the Afro-American Realty enterprise, black churches begin playing a major role in Harlem's development.[39] It is a matter of historical importance, when relating to leadership in the black experience in Harlem, that individual and institutional leaders constantly emerge to meet the kinds of demands of critical importance to the survival of community values and interests.[40] This observation is crucial in understanding the perspective in which Harlem is viewed as the 'Capital' of black America; and is, further of immense relevance to its role as the initial testing ground for the eventual effort related to overcoming poverty by community action strategies. Thus, the role assumed by the black church is viewed, here, somewhat differently than in the traditional manner of its positioning as the 'most stable and wealthy' institution. I want to deal with the churches relevance as a legitimate social mechanism through which leadership of 'functional' relevance to the needs and requirements of black Harlem as an emerging community, is especially important.[41] Thus leaders who emerge through the church are found at each level of my leadership typology though many are early identified as institutional inspirers.

St. Philips Episcopal Church stands out as perhaps the most active in a variety of civic enterprises; particularly in purchasing Harlem real estate.[42] Throughout the nineteenth century, St. Philips was reputed to be the most exclusive Negro Church in New York City. Its members were considered "the better element of colored people",[43] and its services were dignified and refined. This reputation as a fashionable institution made membership in St. Philips a sign of social recognition and many of the more prominent Negroes of the city were its communicants. It was the only black church in Manhattan with a 'pew system' in the nineteenth century - by which members outbid each other for choice seats in the chapel. St. Philips was also recognized as the 'wealthiest Negro Church in the Country", and this reputation has continued until quite recently.[44]

The growth of St. Philips was similar to that of many other important black churches. Founded by a small group of Negroes in the Five Points districts in 1809, it held its first formal services in 1819 in a wooden building, 60' x 50', on what is now Centre Street.[45] In 1856, St. Philips moved to a former Methodist Church on Mulberry Street and in 1889, following the Negro population to the Tenderloin, it came to West Twenty-fifth Street.[46] St. Philips remained in the Tenderloin until 1910, when it moved to a newly constructed church in Harlem.

Because of the opposition of Harlem property owners, the first transactions in the developing Negro section were made in subterfuge. The Reverend Dr. Hutchens C. Bishop, pastor of the Church, and a clear example of an institutional inspirer in my usage, came to New York from Charleston, South Carolina in 1886. He was a tall, thin and almost bald man who easily passed for white.[47] From 1906 through 1910, the Reverend Dr. Bishop bought houses and land in Harlem in his name, including a site for a new church. Some white landlords were glad to sell him their houses and told him they would never sell to Negroes. In 1910, the pastor turned all the property he bought over to the church and prepared to move his congregation to Harlem.

Aside from the church building which St. Philips owned on West Twenty-fifth Street, it also acquired a number of properties on West Thirtieth Street in the 1830s. This property, originally donated to the church as a cemetery, was valued at the time of acquisition at $9,000. As real estate prices rose in mid-Manhattan, the value of St.

Philips holdings skyrocketed. In 1909, the church sold its building on West Twenty-fifth Street for $140,000; the cemetery land was put on the market two years later and bought for $450,000. When the church site in the Tenderloin was sold in 1909, the Reverend Dr. Bishop attempted to purchase a white Protestant Episcopal Church in Harlem. He offered the Church of The Redeemer $50,000 for its property on West One Hundred and Thrity-sixth Street. The neighborhood around the church was obviously changing, its members were moving away, and it would have been to the churches advantage to sell then at a reasonable price; "the coming of so many negroes to the locality has made the property undesireable"48 its pastor said, "most of the members of the congretation having moved away". West One Hundred and Thirty-sixth Street was a Convenant Block, however, and many of the vestry men of the white church felt morally bound (if that is the proper term) to their original agreement. They rejected the offer and St. Philips built its new church a few blocks away. In 1931, the Church of The Redeemer put its property on the market for sale. For one year the vestrymen unseccessfully tried to find a white buyer. In 1914, adhering to the letter not the spirit of the Covenant, the Church of The Redeemer was sold to a white woman who immediately resold it to the African Methodist Episcopal Zion (Mother Zion) Church for $22,000. Within ten years, "Mother Zion" outgrew the premises.49

The new St. Philips, designed by Negro architects, as Madame Walker's mansion had been, was completed in Harlem in 1911. The church was always moderately wealthy, but it never before controlled the vast sums accumulated through the sale of its property in the Tenderloin. Taking advantage of the depressed condition of the real estate market, the decision was made to invest the churches capital in Harlem apartment houses. In 1911, St. Philips bought a row of ten new apartment houses on West One Hundred and Thirty-fifth Street between Seventh and Lenox Avenues for $64,000 - the largest single real estate transaction involving Negroes in the city's history at that time. Before the sale, signs which hung in renting offices of the white realtors who managed these buildings, read: "The agents promise their tenants that these houses will be rented only to white people". Shortly after the transfer of this property to St. Philips, and after its remaining tenants were evicted, a new sign was displayed telling prospective negro tenants, "For Rent, Apply to Nail and Parker".50

I have recounted this experience related to St.Philips Church in detail and at some length for specific reasons. First, the author is, and has been since childhood a member of St. Philips. I was christened at St. Philips by the Reverend Dr. Shelton Hale Bishop, the son and successor of the famed Dr. Hutchens C. Bishop. The experience as a youth of coming to know the Reverend Dr. Bishop, and the ways in which he, in his father's footsteps continued to make major contributions to the lives of Harlem's residents and community institutions serves as additional impetus to the present leadership analysis. For it is from the perspective of observing Dr. Bishop, and members of his family, as well as leaders of the St. Philips vestry that I gain substantive insight into the functional importance of particular institutional leaders. Insight, again, of immeasureable relevance to the leadership typology which I develop of leaders who emerge in the instance of the newer Haryou program.

An additional reason for the above account of St. Philips function as one major church involved in the transition of Harlem, is the manner by which one can observe the actual activities in which her leaders are involved in the change process. One is aware, in this sense, of the kinds

of things leaders 'do' and the ways in which they 'act' in the effort
to enhance specific functions.[51] An account, for example, given by
a senior member of the churches vestry is illuminating. As a newly
immigrated black of Bermudian extraction, in the 1920s Llewelyn
Heyliger recalls,

> When I first came to Harlem, you couldn't walk above 137th
> Street without getting stoned by white people. I had been
> sent to St. Philips Church by a Bishop in Bermuda, and I had
> my papers certifying that I was competent to teach Sunday
> School. Well! You know St. Philips at that time was not
> accustomed to seeing 'dark' Negroes working in the church,
> so they were not really happy about accepting me at first.
> There was this light skinned lady who always used to ask me,
> "how did you ever get to teach Sunday School here". I could
> tell she resented me, cause St. Philips was really known to be
> a church for high class mullatoes, or I think that's what they
> used to call them - yes, that's right. Well I would tell them
> that if they didn't want me there, I would go to St. Martin's
> Church. Finally one Sunday, Reverend Bishop heard about the
> difficulty I was having. He came to me and said, "Lew, I
> want you to know that you are as much a part of this church
> as any other person and I wish you would tell me of any
> further difficulty you have". In addition, he gave a sermon
> the following Sunday about what brotherhood is really about,
> and particularly as it respected black people in this Country.
> Not only didn't I ever have any problem after that, but many
> other people from the community began coming to the church,
> and they were really representative of our people.[52]

This brief recounting of one man's experience provides additional
insight into the leadership function of particular figures during these
early Harlem experiences. One familiar with the internal dynamics of
Harlem at this early period are aware, for example, of the resentments
and rivalries between 'native' New Yorker blacks and the enlarged West
Indian and Southern black communities.[53] The social class, shade of
color syndrome represented a serious issue of dicisiveness and conflict
in Harlem and required the kind of sensitive and astute leader represented
by Dr. Bishop.[54] There are a variety of other examples of leadership of
this kind manifested by other churches in early Harlem. The Reverend
Dr. Adam Clayton Powell, Sr., at the Abssynian Baptist Church, The
Reverend F.A. Cullen, foster father of a gifted poet Countee Cullen, and
others, most of whom are viewed as institutional inspirationalists, made
similar functional contributions to developing Harlem's character. Thus
we gain additional insight into the functional leadership roles reflective of the times, which go behond the normative view of the 'spiritual'
of 'other worldly' leadership relevancies of the black clergy.[55]

Earlier comment was made respecting the arrival in Harlem, of the
variety of black organizations and institutions, which had been part of
the community experiences in the 'Tenderloin' and 'San Juan Hill'
(both former ghetto areas).[56] In addition to those mentioned above, the
United Order of True Reformers; Odd Fellows, Masons, Elks, Pythians
and other fraternal orders, i.e. Kappa Alpha Psi, Omega Psi Phi and
Alpha Kappa Alpha; The Music School Settlement; The Coachmen's Union
League; The African Society of Mutual Relief; The New York Age, (its
monopoly as virtually the only Negro Newspaper was in 1900s was broken
by the publication of two additional weeklies, The New York News, and
the sole contemporary survivor, The Amsterdam News); all arrived in
Harlem at this time.[57]

Harlem at this time.[57]

There are, however, a number of white businesses which remain. Merchants left behind as their former clientelle departed attempted to adjust to new conditions, although a few refused to accept the change. H.C.F. Koch moved into the German section of the community and opened a business on One Hundred and Twenty-fifth Street in 1890. When Negroes came to Harlem, Koch and his children ignored their trade or treated them discourteously: "The Koch family paid scant attention to colored... customers"[58] according to one community person. The family sold out in 1930.

L.M. Blumsteins, a German Jew, opened his store in Harlem in 1896. Blumsteins was as opposed to Negro settlement as Koch, and refused to hire blacks for other than menial positions until 1930.[59] In that year he employed black elevator operators, but still, refused to hire black salesmen, clerks and cashiers. Blacks forced him to change his mind through the pressure of a successful boycott during the great depression.[60] Blumsteins remained in the neighborhood and the department store, founded in 1896, remains one of Harlem's most successful businesses.[61]

It is within the above perspective, that the comment of one black, recently arrived in Harlem, states, "If my race can make Harlem... good Lord, what can't it do?"[62] Harlem had become 'the Mecca of the colored people of New York City'.

There are a variety of other things happening in Harlem at the time, however, of equal and perhaps greater significance to the development of a particular characterology and leadership pattern than the examples reviewed thus far.

James Weldon Johnson, for example, captures the essence of the excitement and emotion which marks Harlem as unique, "gaiety is peculiarly characteristic of Harlem",[63] he remarks.

The people who live there are by nature a pleasure loving people; and though most must take their pleasures in a less expensive manner than in nightly visits to clubs, they still lead gay lives. This emotional pleasure seeking, 'thing'. can be viewed as 'compensatory' for the problems of being black. Aside from things like dancing, picnics for blacks are different than any other kind; the resounding tune of Bongos and special feasts are peculiarly black. Harlemites get a good deal of pleasure from things seemingly very simple; in the evenings of summer and on Sundays 'strolling is a favorite pastime.. Strolling is almost a lost art in New York, at least in the manner in which it is so generally practiced in Harlem. Strolling in Harlem does not merely mean walking along Lenox Avenue or Upper Seventh Avenue, or 135th Street; it means that those streets are placed for socializing.[64]

Churches, fraternal organizations, political clubs and local tenement and block organizations, diverse culture groups within the black community, all interweave within the Harlem community creating a peculiar network of leaders, and a sense of complex participation in, this Manhattans most exciting section.[65] These various organizations, function through cooperative kinds of programs, ranging from annual 'West Indian Day' parades, through to boat excusions up the Hudson. The seasonal activities of 'Debutante Balls', Elks Day, and masonic Dances, affect the total community and the extent of interorganizational activities (including rivalries) serve as integrating mechanisms for diverse population elements. Never before has such an experience in cosmopolitanism and international living been as substantive and important, on the part of the black community as is the Harlem one.[66] The importance of the networks of organizations to the identification and development of a civic leadership typology relevant in my analysis of contemporary Harlem is noteworthy. Anyone who has observed or participated in the tasks inherent in working on a church social or planning committee; or in the organization of one of Harlems major parades can attest to the nature of such participation serving as a testing ground for leadership.[67] The fact of the large numbers of political leaders who have emerged from the black church, gives additional insight into that institution as a particular kind of leadership training ground.[68]

The Harlem of the early Twentieth Century is:
well along the road of development and prosperity. Plenty of work, jobs and money...The community was beginning to feel its growing size and strength...It had entirely rid itself of the sense of apology for its existence; and was beginning to take pride in itself as Harlem, A Negro community.[69]

One black civic organization, The Equity Congress, formed during these years, the first Harlem regiment of State Militia. Charles W. Filmore, an historic precedent for my proto-indigeneous idealist leader, was provisional Colonel. With the coming of Wold War I, blacks through this militia are among the first American Regiment to arms in France. Noble Sissle recounts the regiments attachment to the Eighth Corps of the Fourth French Army, and the Harlem battle groups contribution throughout the entire war. "The stone that the builders rejected",[70] recounts one black soldier embittered by the American Army's discrimination against, and rejection of the early Harlem warriors, "Became the first soldiers of the entire American expeditionary Forces to receive the coveted Croux De Guerre with Star and Palm", Sergeant Henry Johnson of the Fifteenth Regiment New York National Guard (to be exact). This Regiment, now the famed 369th Infantry, arrived back in New York February 12th, 1919 and paraded up 5th Avenue on February 17th.

In 1917, Fifth Avenue had been the scene of a different kind of black people. It was a 'Silent Protest March' organized by Harlem protest leaders irrate over the East St. Louis Riots of July 2nd. Reverend Frank M. Hyden, Reverend F.A. Cullen and James Weldon Johnson were among those present. These men were also among the leaders and local Harlem citizenry, who formed the New York delegation petitioning President Wilson regarding clemency for condemned black soldiers. The soldiers were condemned as the result of racial confrontations involving a military facility at Fort Sam Houston in Texas.[71]

With the end of World War I, and the return of black soldiers, a new radicalism breaks out in Harlem. The new rash of ideology was different from earlier pre-WWI experiences (Harlem has always been the seat of radical black movements in the North), as it manifested for the first time a fierce sense of race consciousness.[72] Heretofore, the Harlem brand of radicalism tended to be more ideological in a political sense (Socialism), than any other. But with the kinds of experiences suffered by black soldiers overseas at the hands of white officials and American Officers, their anger manifested inself in increasingly racial terms.

New Radical Tabloids like The Messenger, Challenge, The Voice, The Crusader, The Emancipator and The Negro World articulated the new art form of an 'old' mood.[73] The names of A. Philip Randolph, Chandler Owen, George Frazier Miller, W.A. Domingo, Edgar Grey, Hubert Harrison, William H. Ferris, William Bridges, Richard B. Moore, Cyril Briggs, William W. Coulson and Anselmo Jackson are familiar signatories on the editorial

24

pages of the above papers and magazines.   W.E.B. DuBois, through the writings in the NAACP's national literary organ "Crisis" is a most substantive contributor to the dialogue.[74]

Harlem's sense of awareness as a community of peculiar substance and attributes grows steadily. Her leaders experience a new exposure to, and reaction from the various local, State and Federal officials, who in their recognition of the potential power resident in so large an aggregation of blacks within the Nation's largest and most affluent City, selectively listen to Harlem's messages.[75] These representatives of the white American power structure are not the only ones who hear Harlem's cries. They are heard and heeded by black people throughout the world, and a new kind of migration begins to occur; one in which black genius participates.[76] Harlem becomes the home of black intelligentsia and art form, of political aspirant and spiritualists; of social reformist and revoluntionary; creative elites, institutional inspirationalists and reacocrats; all forerunners of the leadership types which concern us later, emerge as well. In the midst of it all, a way of life buttressed by the infusion of a particular set of community values, is born. The way of life is essentially the same as any 'average' American community. Average kinds of folks do an average days work (often for less than an 'average' day's pay); raise children; love and hate one another; live and die; but in Harlem with a great intensity. For one finds Harlem to be a peculiarly emotional community. Emotional in the sense that it represents achievement born of historical struggle, fear, idealism, success, failure, frustration and achievement.[77]

The values infused are related to the community's sense of leadership in effecting a particular form of social change. The view of Harlem, as the avante guarde, of black cosmopolitanism in urban America is not to be underestimated. Throughout the black world it is the major topic of discussion; the major theme of dreams.[78]

The social climate is fertile for the emergence of leadership forces which, in a final sense, as we review the functional leadership elements of historical relevance to Harlem's becoming the birthplace of Haryou, are important. What analysis of Harlem's social history is complete, without reference to the revolutionary leadership force of Marcus Garvey, the premier leader par excellance? Or how realistic is any commentary about the functional leadership patterns established in Harlem which does not take into account the political character of the community?

The phenomenon generally described as 'Black Nationalism' was given the clearest and loudest expression by Marcus Mosiah Garvey, who has been described by his biographer, Edmund D. Cronon as a "largely self educated but supremely confident black man".[79] Garvey was born on August 17th, 1887, in Saint Ann's Bay, Saint Ann, Jamaica, West Indies. His experiences in life eventually led him in 1914 to establish, in Jamaica, The Universal Negro Improvement Association and African Communities League (U.N.I.A.). Between 1914 and March 1916, Garvey laboured to unite the Negro masses in Jamaica, and to educate the "black bourgeoisie" to appreciate their responsibility towards the proleterians among their race. His efforts were largely unsuccessful, partly because of the hostility of the mulattoes to the U.N.I.A., and partly because of the apathy of the under-priviledged Negro Masses.[80]

In 1917-1918, Garvey organized the Universal Negro Improvement Association in the United States, with headquarters in Harlem. Together Garvey and his colleague, Hubert Harrison, hammered out the variety of components which comprise the 'movement'. They organized the Liberty League, and built Liberty Hall; Garvey's ecomonic program included the establishment of the auxiliaries of the UNIA i.e.: The African Orthodox Church, The Universal African Legion, a semi-military organization, The Universal Black Cross Nurses, The Universal African Motor Corp, the Juvenile and the Black Flying Eagles and, in 1924, the Negro Political Union.[81]

The leadership qualities which characterize Garvey are precisely the kind needed in Harlem during this period.[82] His bombast and daring; vision and charisma, his appeal to the radical mood of the community, are all timely. In short order, the U.N.I.A. and Garvey find themselves in a fight with most other Negro rights organizations: particularly the NAACP and its profound black creative elite leader, Dr. W.E.B. Dubois.[83] The conflicts are inevitable, as Garvey essentially does what the host of Harlem radicals who precede him failed to do. He established coordinative machinery which link the forces called into action, on a community and national basis, to concrete, planned action programs.[84] Garvey had two major problems, however, in dealing with Harlem. One has to do with the heterogeneous nature of the Harlem black population. We have noted above that the largest West Indian Community in the Nation lived in Harlem. Garvey's movement reached them first and most substantively, as he beamed his earliest messages to those of similar background to his own. As the movement matured, however, Garvey continued making the mistake of disdaining the native American born black, rather than using his newly emerging leadership as a uniting, cohesive force. It is conceivable that had Garvey taken into his confidence, and consulted on issues of planning and strategy with lieutenants of American background, he might have been more successful in avoiding the peculiarly 'American Traps' which ultimately caused his demise.[85]

The final cause of Marcus Garvey's demise is his 'back to Africa' scheme. Most contemporary leadership in Harlem, and around the Nation viewed the plan as a return to the colonization movement and rejected it as 'crazy'.[86] Garvey underestimated the National bond of the average black; who was clear in the commitment that America is not hopelessly racist; and thus as their native land ought to be struggled for, not abandoned.[87] James Weldon Johnson, believed that,

> the tragedy of Garvey, is that to this man came an opportunity such as comes to few men, and he clutched greedily at the glitter and let the substance slip from his fingers.[88]

W.E.B. DuBois was ambivalent about Garvey and ignored him until late 1920. The Crisis editor was profoundly impressed by "this extraordinary leader of men" and acknowledged that Garvey was

> essentially an honest and sincere man with a tremendous vision, great dynamic force, stubborn determination and unselfish desire to serve.[89]

However, he also considered Garvey to be "dictatorial, domineering, inordinately vain and very suspicious...";[90] DuBois had once said of another of his adversaries in race leadership - Booker T. Washington:

> If the best of American Negroes receive by outer pressure a leader whom they had not recognized before, manifestly there is here a certain palpable gain.[91]

"Yet", DuBois continues

> there is also irreparable loss, - a loss of that peculiarly valuable education which a group receives when by search and criticism, it finds and commissions its own leaders.[91]

There is little question but that Garvey represented such leadership to Harlem's thousands.[92] His functional relevance is found in his role as a unifyer of divergent groups and community interests into a singular movement. Garveyism was pomp and circumstance. It was an escape for many thousands away from the humdrum day to day functions of Harlem life into the parading, rhetorical emotionalism of a new movement.[93] Garvey's leadership represented the first clear example of premier leadership to have mobilized from Harlem; and represented a determined effort at self-realization and self-development, despite environmental opinion and pressures outside of the community.

When James Weldon Johnson commented in 1924, that, "The Negro in Harlem has in very large degree emancipated himself from (single party domination) and become an intelligent voter",[94] he was referring to the blacks then traditional allegiance to the Republican party. The unprecedented concentration of blacks in Harlem permitted the entire community to take a more active role in Politics.[95] It was not however, until the 1920s and 1930s, that blacks made significant political advances.[96] Though blacks had been involved in politics as early as the 1890s it was not until their split from the Republicans in 1897 that signigicant political activism becomes a major preoccupation in Harlem.[97] The formation of the United Colored Democracy in January 1898 marked the first instance of a new direction. Edward E. Lee was the first black Democratic leader. His tenure, however, is marked by ridicule and ostracism by the vast majority of blacks, as most remained staunch Republicans.[98]

The Negro Democratic organization existed as a separate and segrated unit outside the pale of the Regular Democratic party machine in New York. The Negro boss theoretically supervised all the Negro wards in the city. His power rose and fell at the disposition of the white Democratic county leader or mayor, not at the will of his constituency.[99] The U.C.D.'s structure prevented the emergence of grass-roots ward leaders and centered Negro Democratic influence in the hands of a single, often autocratic, boss.[100] In retrospect, the tendency is to identify the early Democratic leadership in Harlem as dysfunctional.[101] Bipartisanship did, however, bring some rewards to small numbers of residents, and the very fact of the U.C.D. representing a break from the traditional republicanism, opens new participatory avenues for local leaders to emerge.

The first black politician to take center stage in effecting real power for blacks in Harlem, and throughout New York City is Charles W. Anderson.[102] Anderson's ascendency to political prominence is via the established Republican Party. Originally from Oxford, Ohio, Anderson arrived in New York in 1886. He immediately became active in local Republican politics and was eventually elected president of the Young Men's Colored Republican Club of New York County, a position which accrued to him a patronage position in the Internal Revenue Service. Within a relatively short time, Anderson became "the recognized colored Republican leader of New York".[103] James Weldon Johnson referred to Anderson as "the unfailing observer", who was "much more than an ordianry orator".[104]

Anderson's letters are full of keen insights and predictions about contemporary politics. Throughout his life, he paid the closest attention to detail, an attribute which I later discuss as a relevant leadership skill for certain types of Haryou leaders.[105] As a "cool, calculating player in the game of Politics",[106] Charlie, as he was called, organized and supervised Negro Republican captains in every election district in Manhattan. He was on the closest terms with most Negro religious and business leaders.

In Harlem, if you needed a job, wood in the winter, some contributions for some local charity or boxes of candy for a children's Christmas party, Charlie Anderson was the man to see.[107]

Anderson was a 'doer' in the strictest sense. A close friend of Booker

T. Washington, Anderson is known to have squealched much of the radical Harlem opposition to his champions cause. He kept constant check on the activities of Negro Democrats, the followers of W.E.B. DuBois, and all persons who even remotely threatened Washington's position. To Anderson, the Niagara movement of DuBois, William Monroe Trotter, J. Max Barber and others, articulated demands for racial equality too quickly in a society unwilling to grant it.[108] He hoped for future gains but was willing to settle for something concrete in the present: "We do not belong to a group to whom nothing is desireable but the impossible", he once said. "Some of us are trying to provide opportunities for members of the race."[109] As a 'functional' leader however, Anderson was unprecedented in Harlem. To Charlie Anderson, improving the race most often meant using his influence to find more and better paying jobs for New York's black community.[110] He found positions for blacks as mechanical draftsmen, state examiners, deputy collectors, customs inspectors, messengers, post office employees, immigration inspectors, attorneys to examine election frauds and a host of other positions. Unquestionably Charles Anderson represented the most powerful black politician in Harlem's and New York City's history.[111] And though one can question his concern for the short-run interests of blacks respecting full equality, unity and dignity, Anderson did prove his approach to be an immediate boon for Harlemites, and to New York's black community generally.[112] Reminiscent of Anderson's style of influence and power, is the style and approach of one recent chairman of the Haryou-Act Board of Directors. I comment on the similarities between these functional leaders below.[113]

Perhaps the most significant political advances made by blacks during this period, was the election of Harlemites to legislative offices at the State level. The names of Edward Austin Johnson and Charles H. Roberts (1st district Alderman), and their elections to representative office ushers in an aire of political optimism in the community.[114] "Policital opportunity has knocked on the door of the Harlem Negro",[115] was the general impression held by many. During Johnson's tenure at the New York State Legislature, new civil rights legislation is enacted. He facilitates extension of "equal accomodations" laws which effect N.Y.C., and pressures the legislature to enforce laws already on the books regarding equal access for blacks to all public facilities, businesses, public recreation areas and the like. It is also during Johnson's term, that the first N.Y. State Employment Office is opened in Harlem.

The Democrats in Harlem had to await the 1930s before their ascendency to any meaningful power.[116] The United Colored Democracy, mentioned earlier, had persisted as an independent satellite of the regular party. Its undisputed leader through the early 1930s was Fredinand Q. Morton. Morton was in fact strongly connected with Tammany Hall, and was viewed by some as Harlem's Tamany Boss. I view him as a raceocrat type leader. The fact is that he never ascended to the actual level of 'boss', but for his cooperation with the white bosses running Harlem, he was recognized as the most powerful black functioning within Democratic Party circles.[117] He had absolute control of all patronage which accrued to the Harlem political community and was therefore in a relatively good position. Morton's appointment, by Mayor John F. Hylan in 1921, to the position of Chairman of the Municipal Civil Service Commission, marked "the first appointment in the History of our City of a colored man to head this or any other department"[118] Hylan's successor, James J. Walker, reappointed Morton to this municipal cabinet-rank position. Functionally, Morton served as the cutting edge for the new political bipartisanship emerging in Harlem.[119] No longer could the black community be passed off as a solidly Republican stronghold. Morton also played a significant role in opening Harlem Hospital to black physicians and nurses. The first doctors had been appointed in 1925, and by 1932, more than seventy Negro interns and physicians worked there.[120] This seems a most fortunate circumstance, since I was born in Harlem Hospital a mere matter of three years later (1935)!

There were, then, a variety of politically relevant activities oc-curing in Harlem during the period of the 1920s and early 1930s. Most of the men active in the political arena acted as spokesmen for the Harlem community. Through their initiative, in a political structure now willing to recognize Negro demands.[121] Harlem Negroes received the "solid benefits which accrued" from "an awakening political conscious-ness".[122] The famed 369th Gun Battalion Armory was constructed in the late 1920s, and at the time represented the largest National Guard facili-ty in the country; and though everyone (in the political arena), Repub-licans and Democrats alike claimed the credit for the facilitating legislation; it is clear however, that without the voices of Johnson, Morton, Charles C. Roberts (N.Y. City's first black Republican Alderman), and other civic and political leaders, the Armory might never have been constructed.[123]

But political leadership often inherently involved questions of personal ambition and power that sometimes conflict with, rather than supplement the interests of a community.[124] Competition for power among individual negroes sometimes impeded the progress of the entire group. U.C.D. for example, precluded any struggle for leadership in the Demo-cratic Ward organizations of Harlem; and Morton was viewed as ruling with an iron fist. He is referred to as the 'overlord' of 'Black Tammany', who remained "unaccessible to his constituency",[125] in Harlem.

Change came with the election of Mayor Fiorello H. La Guardia, a Republican. Though La Guardia did reappoint Morton to his commissionor-ship, it was on the condition that he sever his ties with Tammany. Thus, Morton who always viewed politics "as a selfish, desperate game"[126] left the Democratic Party and joined the American Labor Party. Harlem Demo-crats, freed from Mortons control, took over local district organizations from the old white bosses - the Nineteenth Assembly District in 1935; the Twenty-first Assembly District in 1939.

Lest we leave our discussion of Harlem political foundations with the belief that only the Democrats represented problems for the aspiring black leadership, it needs to be clear that blacks within the then tradi-tional Republican Party had their share of problems too. For though Negro Republicans composed the majority of voters of the Nineteenth and Twenty-first ADs through most of the 1920s, and also the majority of county committeemen in each district - whose votes determine district leadership - it took unusual effort to unseat the established white leader-ship, who controlled the party when Harlem was predominantly white.[127] The breakthrough, however, came in 1929 after a battle waged by Negro poli-ticians, Abraham Grenthal, Republican leader of the Nineteenth AD and assemblyman. Grenthal had a long history in Harlem. He had attended public shcools there, including City College and New York Law School. His record as an advocate for his constituency, black or white was a good one; as he fought for low income housing and rent control and introduced bills aimed at bettering conditions in the black wards. The demands for change, then rested not so much on Grenthal's performance in office, as on the fact that Negroes were in the new majority in Harlem and wanted the political leadership their numbers warranted. As power rarely re-linquishes itself 'gracefully', however, Grenthal's unseating required a political struggle. One of the few won by the newly aspiring Harlem leadership.[128]

Two significant outcomes of the struggle were the election of Lieutenant Colonel Charles W. Fillmore, officer in the 369th and auditor in the New York State Tax Bureau to the first district leadership in New York City's history; and a new informal agreement relating to "dual leadership"[129] of the Twenty-first AD. The white section of the district the 'hill' (later to be known as 'Sugar Hill"), continued to be represented by white leadership, Robert S. Conklin; and the black community in Harlem, the 'Valley' became the 'stomping ground', of a Negro Architect and politician, Charles W.B. Mitchell.[130]

Higher political office alluded the Harlem community for some time after these preliminary political victories, owing the peculiarities of the community's geographical boundaries. The Nineteenth and Twenty-first ADs were part of a larger Congressional District - the Twenty-first CD - which included three solidly white and traditionally Democratic assembly districts.[131] The importance of the negro vote, although substantial enough to warrant nominations, was restricted by its very concentration.[132] It was not until Harlem's political boundaries were redrawn in 1944, that New York elected its first black member of the House of Representatives the late, Adam Clayton Powell, Jr.[133]

I have not said much to this point in reviewing the historical roots of Harlem about the emergence of social work leadership. It is an unfortunate fact, in this regard, that such leadership is nonexistent during the community's early development.[134] Less so as Harlem becomes increasingly ghettoized.[135] The absence of social work leadership in the midst of perhaps the most profound socio-political development ever experienced by the black New Yorker, is the more perplexing, given what appeared to be an earlier commitment to help.[136] Despite, however the personal and professional commitments of Mary Ovington, Lillian Wald, Francis Keller, Jacob Riis, Dr. L. Emmet Holt, Mary E. Drier, and the lone black professional social worker among them, George E. Haynes; all of whom made enlightened contributions during the plight of blacks in the 'Tenderloin' and 'San Juan Hill' areas 'avante guarde' of Harlem's aspiring leadership.[137]

Thus despite the fact that the first social work agency primarly designed to deal with the social and human service needs of blacks in New York City, the National Urban League, (formerly the National League on Urban Conditions Among Negroes), is active during this historical period, its recognition as one of the community's relevant leadership structures is unrecognized.[138] The participation of certain of the 'well-to-do' blacks, then viewed as among the community's leaders, (particularly by the predominantly white social welfare power structure); men and women like Dr. William Bulkley, George Haynes, William H. Brooks, Eugene P. Roberts, Fred Moore, R.R. Morton, and Adam Clayton Powell, Sr. appears irrelevant to the emergency of adequate social welfare resources for Harlem.[139]

In its work with the variety of other social services groups, including: The Charity Organization, the Childrens Aid Society, Henry Street Settlement, The New York City Health Department and the Public Education Association, the League merely scratched the surface of the increasingly complex urban problems of Harlemites. Through a network of organizational subcommittees, The League, in cooperation with certain of the above agencies sought involvement in every phase of city life as it affected blacks. Neighborhood improvement, increased employment, decent housing, enhanced educational opportunities and recreational facilities for Harlem's teeming youth; these are among the spectrum of activities in which the League becomes active. In its particular concern for the conditions of juvenile delinquency and the plight of female offenders, the organization is instrumental in effecting separate correctional institutions through organizations like The Utopia Neighborhood Club, the Harlem Utilitarian Neighborhood Club, and the Conference of Organizations for the Assistance of Young Women.[140] It was an Urban Leaguer Eugene Kinkle Jones, who, in 1912 called Mayor William Gaynor's attention to the fact that methods of dealing with black 'wayward' youth was unsatisfactory. Jones maintained that children's court failed to investigate adequately the background of the youthful offender, and early opted for the employment of black probation officers who could achieve, "a closer insight into the family life of colored homes...and as a consequence better results could be obtained".[141]

Finally, it is the Urban League in the early Harlem experience that publicizes the various services furnished by the city and private agencies. In 1916, for example, it published a booklet, What You Need, Where to Find It, How to Use What You Find, thus providing a kind of "ombudsman' for the black New Yorker. Harlemites were provided information as to the locations of hospitals, clinics, milk stations, day and evening schools, playgrounds, recreation centers and libraries.[142] The fact that these efforts only scratched the surface of Harlem's needs is owing to a variety of factors. Paramount among these is the lack of funds to do an adequate job. Additionally, most services were provided paternalistically, that is, there was a failure to develop a meaningful dialogue of participation with those for whom the services are intended; a striking change from the format of other social service institutions with respect to their ethnic constituencies.[143] This latter problem stems from the attitudes of many of those involved in social welfare activites, ranging from racist stereotypes of black 'usurpers', to the segregated nature of agency boards and program operations. Perhaps these agencies viewed the Negro's social and economic problems worthy of separate treatment; still they encouraged the exclusion of the Negro from the wider community. With the exception of the Urban League and The Committee for Improving the Industrial Conditions of Negroes in New York, most charitable organizations and the social workers who staffed them, did little to widen the Negro's vistas, to expand his possibilities, to move him in the direction of first class citizenship.[144] At best, they gave the unemployed poor, jobs at the bottom of the economic ladder, taught people how to keep clean homes in slums, took children off the street for part of the day and returned them to their small crowded apartments at night and to the wider discrimination of the wider community in adulthood.

Essentially then, outside of the Urban League which was comprised of Negroes and whites, white reform and social service groups did little to meet the needs of Harlemites. The Charity Organizaiton, for example, limited its activities to instructing Negroes in better health habits and establishing a kindergarten for Negro children. In general, Negroes were forded to rely on the resources of their own community for any improvement in housing and other conditions. The City Department of Health informed Negroes of the latest health practices; however were indifferent to the plight of their community; irregular and inadequate garbage collection, and default on prosecuting flagrant housing code violations are symptomatic of the contradictions. Blacks therefore only benefited indirectly from the services performed by the city; at least until they began to accrue political inroads in municipal power centers.[145]

Dr. Kenneth Clark, in his review of contemporary social services, adequately summarizes the historical problem of social work in its relationship to Harlem; while at the same time returning to the major consideration of the present leadership analysis; he suggests,

The major social agencies which operate in Harlem depend on

31

sources outside the community for support, and must compete
for limited philanthropic funds. Foundations and philanthro-
pies tend to view the ghetto as a single problem of "civil
rights" or "minority status", and to distinguish less clearly
than they do elsewhere the merits of a particular project.

And further,

to arrange for an agency board dominated by whites instead is
often assumed to solve the problem, but for these whites,
Harlem is necessarily only one of their own many interests.
They agree to serve out a commitment to racial justice, or
because of a personal confidence in an agency's professional
leadership, but they seldom bring power that is transferable
to Negro leadership.[146]

This is the essential nature of the social worker and his service institutions relationship to Harlem, historically, Mary Ovington is perhaps
the singular exception.[147]

The function of black leaders who participate in these early experiences with developing social services in the community is essentially
one of providing access to the community's masses. Legitimatized by
association with emergent black political, real estate, intellectual,
religious and educational leadership, social welfare practitioners sociolo-
gists and emergent psychologists proceed to systematically invade Harlem
in efforts to substantiate theories and doctrines, through research which
in the long run effectively close the ghetto noose around black aspirations.[148]

The functional relevance of the whites who participate is essentially in Myrdal's words, "To lend prestige to some upper and middle class
Negroes creating the illusion that blacks are included in the decision-
making processes which effect their destiny.

It is ultimately as the result of these experiences that increasingly legitimate leadership among Harlem's masses turn their attention and
energies to developing resources in the political arena; with little
more than passing disdain regarding the relevance of the expanding social
welfare institution to their conditions.[150]

American Negro life is, for the Negro who must live it, not only
a burden, (and not always that), but also a discipline just as
any human life which has endured so long is a discipline teaching
its own insights into the human condition, its own strategies of
survival...

For even as his life toughens the Negro, even as it brutalizes
him, sensitizes him, dulls, him, goads him to anger, moves him
to irony, sometimes fracturing and sometimes affirming his
hopes; even as it shapes his attitudes towards family, sex,
love, religion; even as it modulates his humor, tempers his
joy--it conditions him to deal with his life and with himself.
Because it is his life and no mere abstraction in someone's
head. He can change it; must live it as he changes it. He
is no more product of his socio-political predicament. He is
a product of interaction between his racial predicament, his
individual will and the broader American cultural freedom in
which he finds his ambiguous existence.[151]

Ralph Ellison

In the years following the Negro Renaissance period, the Harlem
community became a land of opportunity for new cultists and their leaders.
George Wilson Becton, first of the famous cult leaders to excite the
imagination and stir the enthusiasm of the entire Harlem community, died

32

and left the field open to Father Divine, who expanded the domain of his Kingdom of Peace and found a way to feed Harlem's hungry people at a price they could pay.[152] The insecurity of the depression years had produced widespread discouragement and apathy in Harlem. The mood of the people called for new leaders and new leaders appeared - some were false, and some were true. Joe Louis, perhaps more a symbol than a leader, represented a new kind of hope for Harlem's thousands as he literally writes peotry with his fists. He perhaps more than any single leader during WWII years, lifted the spirit of an entire people giving them an increased sense of pride and self importance.[153] Many aspects of Afro-American life totally removed from the boxing profession were influenced by the the rise of Joe Louis. Dr. Alaine Locke, a professor at Howard University, had recorded what he called "the dramatic flowering of a new race-spirit".[154] in the book The New Negro (1925). Black scholars rewrote those chapters of history which ignored or minimized the part played by their people. "The American Negro must remake his past in order to make his future",[155] said Arthur A. Schomberg, founder of the famous collection of literature that bears his name.

J.A. Rogers, lecturer and traveler and once a member of Marcus Garvey's staff of advisors, became the most widely read pamphleteer in Black America. During the Italian-Ethiopian War, J.A. Rogers and another Harlem resident, Dr. Willis N. Huggins, author of a remarkable book, Introduction to African Civilizations, were assigned to report and explain this war to the people of African descent in the United States.[156] Dr. Huggins went to Geneva and reported on the League of Nations' meetings concerning the War. J.A. Rogers went to the battlefront in Ethiopia. Both Rogers and Huggins saw behind and beyond the headlines and foretold the future reprecussions of Ethiopia's betrayal. Their reports were a highwater mark in Afro-American journalism. In Harlem and in other black communities, the search for the lost African Heritage continued.

The political arena in Harlem at this juncture (early 1940s to 1950s), was essentially, the province of two outstanding politicians; Benjamin J. Davis and the Reverend Adam Clayton Powell, Jr.[157]

The political career of Ben Davis started a long way from Harlem, where Adam Clayton Powell grew up. In 1943, under proportional representation, a progressive and democratic form of election, Benjamin J. Davis, Jr. was elected to the New York City Council to fill the seat vacated by Adam Clayton Powell, Jr., who had been elected to Congress. In the City Council, Davis was a thorn in the side of machine politicians. They were determined to silence him and thereby rid the Council, and if possible, Harlem of this outspoken black politician. Despite Davis' eventual conviction under the Smith Act, and in 1951, his imprisonment where he continued his fight against racism, he remained a popular Harlem political leader.[158]

Adam Clayton Powell, Jr. was born into controversy and his entire political career was marked by it.[159] For more than thirty years, he controlled the political destiny of the Harlem community. From his powerful position as Chairman of the Congressional Committee on Education and Labor, he portrayed perhaps the most colorful and often the most effective politician of his time, black or white. He was a man who always provoked extreme reactions in people. In Washington, reporters and legislators competed in denouncing him. In Harlem and in other communities, he was viewed as the deliverer of the work - spokesman of the black oppressed. As the Congressman from the 18th Congressional District in Harlem, he has been the creator of political mystique and drama.[160] Much of the intrigue and nuance that surround Powell, ultimately, are associated with the program whose launching might never have occurred without his sponsorship in the Congress - Haryou.[161] The Congressman's direct participation in the Haryou program is minimal, but his presumed political 'shadow' serves, functionally, as an enigma to the organizations leadership of the early program effort.

Leadership conflict reminiscent of the DuBois - Washington; Anderson - DuBois, or Garvey - DuBois confrontations; emerge between Powell and Kenneth B. Clark,[162] Haryou's principle designer and early leader. Though this latter antagonism seems more a 'shadow boxing' experience than actual confrontation, it never the less effectively impeded the potential organizational effort in Harlem.

In the years following the Second World War, Harlem's decline accelerates as many of the community's residents are now able to afford better housing, move to Westchester, Long Island, New Jersey and Connecticut suburbs. The community leaders who helped make Harlem the cultural center of Black America have either died or moved away. In the waning years of the 1950s, only noted celebrities like Langston Hughes, Duke Ellington and Lionel Hampton maintain residences in Harlem.[163]

In the midst of the decline, however, Harlem persists as a vibrant exciting community. For those who carve out a day to day existence and view Harlem as home, civic and community social affairs are as important as ever. There are community problems which must be ameliorated and dealt with, there are persistent social problems that effect Harlem, as they have historically; and the absence of a DuBois, a Garvey; and other leaders of notoriety afford no time to lament without addressing them.

Local community leaders, functioning through community churches and block associations; tenants councils, Parents and Teachers Associations, (PTA), youth programs such as the New York City Missions Society's Minisink and Cadet Corps. Programs in Harlem; St. Martins' Cadet Corps., the variety of YMCA-YWCA and New York City Youth Board Council of Social and Athletic Clubs (particularly its Street Club Worker Program); local Harlem W.W.I. and W.W.II. veterans organizations like the Jesse Palmer American Legion Post organization and the 369th A.A.A. Gun Battalion at the now institutionalized Armory faciltiy; all persist as community forms of dealing with ongoing community needs.

Social agencies of both public and private varieties present themselves as supplementary resources for dealing with the individual and collective needs of Harlem and her children. They range from the Lincoln Child Development Center to the Central Harlem Council, a consortium of local and quasi-official social welfare agencies; and public departments of social welfare and health.

The functions of grass roots organizations like the Black Womens' Business and Professionals Association and the variety of Black Men's and Women's Greek letter fraternal and sorority organizations (Omega Psi Phi, Delta Sigma Theta, Alpha Kappa Alpha, Alpha Kappa Psi, Kappa Alpha Kappa and the historical Sigmas), persist as legitimate social mechanisms in Harlem for the activities and emergence of leadership. Lesser known (at the National Black community level), but nevertheless functionally relevant grass roots groups like the Harlem Beavers Club, an association of black men whose interests in hunting and socializing have mushroomed during a twenty year period into community suppers and scholarships for black youth; the Sportsmen, a social and athletic organization for Harlemites, the Ravens Social and Athletic Association, (not only Harlem's only black Semi-professional football team sponsor, but a facilitator of many an athletic scholarship for Harlem youth); are additional though essentially only representative organizations which create in Harlem a network of civic enterprise.

Reflecting on this panorama of organizational activity, the knowledgeable Harlem observer is also impressed with the contributions during the 1950s and early 1960s of the diverse cultural and ethnic community organizations to the raising and resolving of community issues and problems, as well as to the building of new economic enterprise. I am here referring to the host of sub-communities of Haitians, Bermudians, Virgin and West Indian Islanders, who through their New Yorker's associations, have persisted in providing some of Harlems most astute leadership. The current chairmen, of the Haryou-Act community Corporation Board of Directors, is a direct product of such organizations.[164]

Many of those who left Harlem for the 'greener pastures' of suburban living regularly return to her for the activities sponsored by these organizations. What has often appeared as the proverbial 'Sunday Parade' observable as well dressed, affluent black families arrive in the newest automobiles at the doors of St. Philips, St. Martin's, St. James, Abyssinia Baptist, Salem Presbyterian, St. Lukes, and Church of the Master religious institutions, is symptomatic of the returning 'home' to Harlem so crucial to the 'Black New Yorkers' identity, irrespective of where he lives.

It is as these activities recur in the life styles of the black community of Harlem, that potential leadership is identified and trained. The emergence of particular leaders, at particular moments - to meet particular community needs and challenges, is rooted in this on-going process of organizational function. Few 'legitimate' Harlem leaders have arrived upon the community scene, without serving tenure in such organizational experience.

The Courtney Browns, Basil Pattersons, Kenneth Clarks, Adam Clayton Powells, Jesse Grays, Charles Harrisons, Joseph Overtons, Charles Rangels, Harriet Pickens, Eugene Callendars, Andrew Tylers, Percy Suttons, Moran Westons, Edward Dudleys, Helen Testamarks, Herbert Seymours, George Millers and Mark T. Southalls, The George Weavers, Roy Wilkins - all represent direct testimonials to the effective leadership identification functions of the above experiences.

We have in these preliminary remarks concerning the social history of the Harlem community established the foundations for an analysis of functional leadership. Osafsky has suggested that "the dominant patterns of Harlem life were largely set in the 1920s...and have remained remarkably unchanged since then",[165] a comment with which some contemporary Harlemites, who lived in the community at that time, disagree.

The discrepancy resides in the differential perspectives of the external researcher and those who lived the experience. To Eva Robinson, Columbus Austin and other senior Harlem citizens currently participating in Haryou, Harlem has undergone radical change.[166] Harlem's nothing like it once "was", reports Mrs. Robinson,

even though people had lots of problems in the old days, life was different. We had real leaders then, and the community was alive and exciting; always something to do; real organizations actively working in the community.[167]

Mrs. Robinson is reminiscing about a Harlem which alludes even the recent studies of the Harlem community reflected in Youth In the Ghetto and The Harlem Alamanac.[168] A Harlem presistent as an idea which easily alludes those who never lived the experience. It is the 'mind' of Harlem that must be grasped and understood if one is to perform a meaningful analysis of functional leaders. For without such understanding one falls into the 'research pathology' so incapable of illuminating relevant social experience.[169] The indices of social pathology so systematically

35

relied upon by conventional research, do not help in the analysis of community values and syntality.[170] And it is in this arena that the substance of the black experience in Harlem is relevant to the emergence of particular types of leadership.

> The truth about Harlem, is mixed and complex. It is a place of hope and despair. It abounds with churches and bars. Its people reflect determination, courage, apathy and defeat. It is vibrant and it is stagnant. Its children are love, encouraged and ignored. Harlem is a complexity of problems and it is potential. It is in light of its potential that Haryou is conceived and born.[171]

By the 1920s then, there had emerged in New York City a Negro society centered in Harlem. Shut off from white society, it had developed its own churches, fraternal and social organizations, a common culture, and a sense of racial self-consciousness. DuBois had said, much earlier, that

> Here...is a world of itself, closed in from the outer world and almost unknown to it...with its own social distinctions, amusements and ambitions.[172]

The emergence of a peculiarly adaptable and functional leadership, commensurate with this kind of community experience, it appears to me, is an area of inquiry too long ignored, and unenlightened. I now turn to its consideration.

FOOTNOTES TO CHAPTER II

1. E. Franklin Frazier, The Negro in the United States. The MacMillan
    Co., New York, pages 548-63. Gunnar Myrdal, An American
    Dilemma. Harper and Brothers, 1944, New York, pages 709-80.
    James Q. Wilson, Negro Politics The Search for Leadership,
    The Free Press, Glencoe, Illinois, pages 295-315. Louise L.
    Knowles and Kenneth Prewitt, Institutional Racism in America,
    Prentice Hall, Inc., Englewood Cliffs, N.J., pages 12-13.
    Gilbert Osofsky, Harlem: The Making of a Ghetto, New York,
    1890-1930, Harper and Row, New York, pages 5-10. M. Elaine
    Burgess, Negro Leadership in a Southern City. The University
    of North Carolina Press, Chapel Hill, pages 76-107. Floyd
    Hunter, Community Power Structure. University of North Caro-
    lina Press, Chapel Hill, 1953, pages 114-50.

2. Gunnar Myrdal, op.cit., appendix 9, page 1113. St. Clair Drake
    and Horace B. Cayton, Black Metropolis: A Study of Negro
    Life in a Northern City. Harper and Row, New York and
    Evanston, Vol. I, pages 379-98. E. Franklin Frazier, "Race
    Contacts and The Social Structure", American Sociological
    Review, 14, February, 1949, pages 1-11. Ralph Ellison,
    Shadow and Act. Knowles and Prewitt, op. cit. pages 9-10.

3. Kenneth B. Clark, Dark Ghetto: Dilemmas of Social Power. Harper
    and Row, New York, Evanston and London, pages xiii-xxv. John
    Henrike Clark, Harlem: A Community in Transition. The Citadel
    Press, New York, pages 3-10, 62-64. Earl Conrad, The Invention
    of the Negro. Paul S. Erikson, Inc., New York pages 221-226.
    Lerone Bennett, Jr., Confrontation: Black and White. Penquin
    Books, Inc., Baltimore, Maryland, pages 95-168; and Before
    The Mayflower: A History of the Negro in America 1619-1966.
    Johnson Publishing Co., Inc., Chicago, Third Edition, pages
    274-327. Seth M. Scheiner, Negro Mecca: A History of The
    Negro in New York City 1865-1920. University Press, New York
    pages 15-86. James Wledon Johnson, Black Manhattan, Alfred
    A. Knofp, New York, 1930, pages 145-170. Youth in the Ghetto:
    A Study of the Consequences of Powerlessness. Harlem Youth
    Opportunities Unlimited, Inc. New York, Library of Congress
    Catalogue Card Number 64-16399, pages 11-21. Joseph White,
    Toward A Black Psychology: White Theories Ignore Ghetto Life
    Styles. Robert Perlman and Arnold Gurein, Community Organi-
    zation and Social Planning. John Wiley and Sons, Inc., New
    York and The Council on Social Work Education, pages 17-19.

4. Economic Report of the President, Together With the Annual Report
    of the Council of Ecomonic Advisors; Washington, D.C. 1964.
    Michael Harrington, The Other America. MacMillan and Co.,
    New York, 1962, pages 10-33. Norman V. Lourie, "Poverty"

Social Work and Social Problems. Nathan E. Cohen, ed.
New York, National Association of Social Workers, 1964, pages
14-60. Gunnar Myrdal, Challenge to Affluence. Pantheon
Books, New York, pages 20-46. Economic Opportunity Act of
1964 - U.S. Government Printing Office, Washington. 1964.
Harry L. Lurie, ed. Encyclopedia of Social Work. National
Association of Social Workers, New York, 1973 edition,
pages 563-65, and 776. Youth in the Ghetto, Op. cit. pages 1-12.

5. John Henrik Clark, op. cit. Haryou: An Experiment. Kenneth B.
    Clark, pages 210-213. Youth In The Ghetto, op. cit. pages
    353-596. A Proposal For the Planning of A Comprehensive Youth
    Services Program for Central Harlem, Harlem Neighborhood
    Association with Harlem Youth Opportunities Unlimited, Inc.
    Unpublished Report, May 15, 1962 - Public Law pages 87-274
    Section III-V. A Program for Harlem's Youth: A Positive
    Approach to Youth Needs, Harlem Neighborhood Association, Inc.
    December 1961. Unpublished planning report. Charles H. King,
    Arthur L. Ellis, et al, Black Youth In Rebellion. Wilson
    Library Bulletin, October, 1967, pages 166-172. In addition
    to these authors' statements regarding the original intent of
    Haryou, conceptions are also gained from interviews conducted
    among early community planners and Board Members.

6. Youth In The Ghetto, op. cit., pages 95-136. For the purposes of
    my study, the physical boundaries of Central Harlem are as
    presented in the 'Document'. I am aware of somewhat recent
    redefinitions, however, view the above of greater relevance
    here. See for example: Louella Jacqueline Long and Vernon
    Ben Robinson's, How Much Power to the People? A Study of
    the New York Urban Development Corporation's Involvment in
    Black Harlem. Faculty-Student Technical Assistance Project
    Urban Center, Columbia University, New York, 1971.

7. Health Areas are geographical areas originally devised by the Health
    Department for the reporting of health data. Because of their
    utility, many other data, notably juvenile delinquency statistics,
    are also reported by Health Areas. They are larger than census
    tracts, but like census tracts represent relatively homogeneous
    areas.

8. Gilbert Osafsky, op. cit., pages 17-34. Much of the Historical
    section borrows heavily from Osafsky's work on early Harlem.

9. Ibid.

10. Ibid.

11. James Weldon Johnson, Black Manhattan. Alfred A. Knopf, New York,
    1930, pages 3-12.

12. Osafsky, op. cit., pages 17-34. Long and Robinson, op. cit., pages
    1-25. Johnson, op. cit.. pages 145-148.

13. Ibid.

14. Osafsky, op. cit.. pages 20-30.

15. Ibid.

16. Ibid.

17. Ibid.

18. Ibid.

19. Osafsky, op. cit., pages 127-149.

20. Ibid.

21. Ibid.

22. Ibid.

23. John Henrik Clark, op. cit., pages 10 - 30.

24. Ibid.

25. Osafsky, op. cit., pages 150-165.

26. Ibid.

27. Ibid.

28. John Henrik Clark, op. cit., page 25.

29. Gunnar Myrdal, op. cit., pages 10-15.

30. Youth In the Ghetto, op. cit., page 132.

31. Johnson, op. cit., pages 281-284.

32. Ibid. and Osafsky, op. cit. pages 92-149. Also see, Lerone Bennett, op. cit. pages 242-274. Scheiner, Negro Mecca, op. cit. pages 15-38.

33. Ibid.

34. Osafsky, op. cit., pages 92-93.

35. Ibid., see also pages 94-96.

36. Ibid.

37. Ibid.

38. Osafsky, op. cit., pages 113-123.

39. Ibid., also see Myrdal, op. cit. pages

40. Myrdal, op. cit., pages 1133-34. Emory Bogardus, Leaders and Leadership. C. Appleton-Century Co., Inc., New York, London, pages 3-15. Bogardus describes the process of leadership emergence as a response to situational needs as 'conjunctive'. The period described is one during black expansion created a critical need
39

for real estate and housing. It is noteworthy that realtors and real estate professionals have <u>not</u> since the 1930s been prominent in Harlem's leadership - owing to the incredibly prohibitive costs associated with property in New York City.

41.   For a provocative commentary on the Church's role in the develop-
       ment of politics in Harlem, for example see John Henrik Clark,
       <u>op. cit.</u>, <u>Parties and Politics in Harlem</u> by Paul B. Zuber,
       pages 131-135.

42.   Osafsky, <u>op. cit.</u>, pages 115-117.

43.   <u>Ibid.</u>

44.   <u>Ibid.</u>

45.   <u>Ibid.</u>

46.   <u>Ibid.</u>

47.   <u>Ibid.</u>

48.   <u>Ibid.</u>

49.   <u>Ibid.</u>

50.   Osafsky, <u>op. cit.</u>, page 117.

51.   Melvin Seeman and Richard Morris, <u>A General Framework for the Study</u>
       <u>of Leadership</u>, in Paul E. Logarsfeld and Morris Rosenberg;
       <u>The Language of Social Research</u>, pages 511-518. The authors
       present a paradigm of leadership which suggests that certain
       leadership actions are functional in generating certain beliefs
       on the parts of their "followership" or constituency. It is
       in this sense that certain of Harlem's leaders have also been
       functional. See alsy Myrdal, <u>op. cit.</u>, page 1116.

52.   This gentleman, now in his 80s is a leading Vestryman at St. Philips
       Church. He is viewed as one of the Church's top elders. He
       is also the author's uncle.

53.   Osafsky, <u>op. cit.</u>, pages 131-135; also see Johnson, <u>op. cit.</u>,
       pages 251-258.

54.   Shelton Bishop was known throughout Harlem as a leader in effecting
       unity within the community - source- interviews of St. Philip's
       vestrymen and Harlem residents currently on Haryou Board.

55.   John Henrik Clark, <u>op. cit.</u>, page 134. See also Charles V.
       Hamilton, <u>The Black Preacher in America</u>, (Morrow Publishing
       Co., N.Y., 1972)

56.   Scheiner, <u>Negro Mecca</u>, <u>op. cit.</u>, pages 16-19. See also Long and
       Robinson, <u>op. cit.</u>, pages 9-16. Osafsky, <u>op. cit.</u>, page 94.

57.   <u>Ibid.</u>

58. *Ibid.*

59. *Ibid.* See also Hope R. Stevens, "Economic Structure of the Harlem Community", in J.H. Clark, *op. cit.*, pages 105-116.

60. *Ibid.*

61. Blumsteins has only recently become a black enterprise since its purchase from the former owners in 1973.

62. Johnson, *op. cit.*, pages 158-169.

63. *Ibid.*, pages 161-162.

64. *Ibid.*; this is a phenomena that persisted in Harlem well into the 1950s. It begins to decline as an activity with the emergency of narcotics in Harlem.

65. *Ibid.*

66. W.E.B. DuBois, *Souls of Black Folks*.

67. Paul B. Zuber, *Parties and Politics in Harlem*. College and University Press, New Haven, Conn., pages 123-134. Johnson; *op. cit.*, pages 158-169.

68. Myrdal, *ibid*. Stokeley Carmichael and Charles V. Hamilton; *Black Power: The Politics of Liberation in America*. Vintage Books, New York, pages 102,130-131; Kenneth Clark, *op. cit.*, pages 182-186.

69. Johnson, *op. cit.*, pages 145-160.

70. Osafsky, *op. cit.*, pages 136-138.

71. *Ibid.* pages 236-238.

72. Myrdal, *op. cit.*, pages 690-738. Osafsky, *op. cit.*, page 148. Johnson, *ibid*. DuBois, *Souls of Black Folks*, *op. cit.*, pages 48-60.

73. Johnson, *ibid*.

74. Myrdal, *op. cit.*, pages 908-912; 917. Osafsky, *op. cit.*, page 183. Johnson, *op. cit.*, page 260. These leaders have been differentially defined as radicals and militants. In my view, they fit the commutator and creative elite types.

75. Osafsky, *op. cit.*, page 182. Myrdal, *op. cit.*, page 238. Scheiner *op. cit.*, page 86.

76. Johnson, *op. cit.* Langston Hughes, *My Early Days in Harlem* in John Henrik Clark, *Harlem: A Community in Transition*. *op.cit.*, pages 62-64. Also see *op. cit.* pages 26-61.

77. Clark, *Dark Ghetto*, *op. cit.*, pages 63-80. Herbert Krosney, *Beyond Welfare: Poverty in the Supercity*. Holt, Rinehart and Winston,

New York, Chicago, San Francisco. Pages 35-97. Johnson, op. cit., page 168. Joseph White, Toward a Black Psychology op. cit., ibid., Youth in the Ghetto, op. cit., pages 313-352. Myrdal, An American Dilemma. op. cit., page 478.

78. This is certainly true in the historical sense; even today, however, Harlem persists as the reported 'Capital' of Black America; see Long and Robinson, How Much Power to the People, op. cit., pages 1-8; also John Henrik Clark op. cit., pages 14-15.

79. Edward David Cronon, Black Moses: The Story of Marcus Garvey and the Universal Negro Improvement Association. The University of Wisconsin Press, Madison, Wisconsin, 1962. Pages 4-8.

80. Cronen, op. cit., pages 39-72.

81. Ibid.

82. In this sense, Garvey's emergence represents the kind of leader- ship phenomenon identified by Bogardus as "conjuncture". Bogardus, Leaders and Leadership, op. cit., page 274. See also, Mary White Ovington, Portraits in Color. Viking 1927, page 19. Myrdal, op.cit., page 749. This is a phenomena which continues to occur in Harlem.

83. W.E.B. DuBois, Dusk of Dawn, (Harcourt, Brace, N.Y.) Page 277.

84. W.E.B. DuBois, "Marcus Garvey" Crisis XXI 58-60, December 1920 and 112-15 (January 1921).

85. Osafsky, op. cit., page 180. Johnson, op. cit., page 251-9. Cronon, op. cit., page 39-72.

86. Cronon, ibid. DuBois, ibid.

87. DuBois, ibid.

88. Johnson, op. cit., ibid.

89. DuBois, Dusk of Dawn, op. cit., page 260-270.

90. Ibid. These are attributes which persist as characteristics of the Premier and Creative Elite type leaders in Harlem.

91. Ibid.

92. Ibid.

93. Ovington, op. cit., page 20.

94. Johnson, op. cit., page 20.

95. Op. Cit., pages 203-5. See also Osafsky, op. cit., page 159-170.

96. Ibid.

97. Ibid., see also Paul B. Zuber, op. cit., pages 131-135 and
     Clark, Dark Ghetto, op. cit., pages 154-168; Myrdal, op.
     cit., pages 495-496.

98. Ibid.

99. Osafsky, op. cit., ibid.

100. Zuber, op. cit., ibid.

101. Dysfunctional in the sense that such leadership inhibited the
     development of sound political organization, particularly
     given the existence of Tammany Hall and its vulnerability
     to ethnic interests. For additional analysis of this idea
     see; Scheiner, Negro Mecca, op. cit., pages 170-213.

102. Osafsky, op. cit., pages 50, 159, 160. Johnson, op. cit., Scheiner,
     op. cit., page 210.

103. Johnson, ibid.

104. Ibid.

105. Osafsky, ibid.; see also Chapter IX, pages 222-233 of Dissertation.

106. Osagsky, ibid.

107. Ibid.

108. Ibid.; Anderson's critics tended to view him as an 'Uncle Tom'
     a form of leadership comparable to my raceocrat; I, however
     view him as a premier leader.

109. Scheiner, op. cit., ibid. In this regard Anderson was among the
     first to open opportunities for Blacks in State Civil Service.

110. Ibid.

111. Ibid.

112. Ibid.

113. See Chapter VII of Dissertation.

114. Osafsky, op. cit., pages 170-171.

115. Osafsky, op. cit., ibid.

116. Ibid., also see Myrdal, op. cit., pages 507-517.

117. Osafsky, op. cit., and Edward T. Clayton, The Negro Politician:
     His Success and Failure. (Johnson Publishing Company Inc.,
     Chicago) 1964, pages 86-103.

118. Osafsky, ibid.; also see Krosney, op. cit., pages 115-132. The
     Period represents one in which--"New Structures; blacks begin
     inroads into New York City's Civil Service Bureaucracy.

119. Osafsky, _op. cit._, page 171.

120. _Ibid._

121. _Ibid._, also see Myrdal, _op. cit._, _ibid._

122. _Ibid._, and see Johnson, _op. cit._, pages 231-260.

123. _Ibid._

124. Osafsky, _op. cit._, pages 173-175.

125. _Ibid._, see also Paul B. Zuber, _op. cit._, page 133; and Myrdal, _op. cit._, _ibid._

126. Osafsky, _ibid._

127. _Ibid._

128. _Ibid._

129. _Ibid._

130. _Ibid._

131. _Ibid._

132. _Ibid._

133. Scheiner, _op. cit._, page 215.

134. Myrdal, _op. cit._, page 327, 1278-1280. Osafsky, _op. cit._, pages 155-158 and pages 53-67.

135. Clark, _Dark Ghetto_, _op. cit._, pages 173-174. _Youth in the Ghetto_, _op. cit._ page 299. Scheiner, _Negro Mecca_, _op. cit._, pages 27-38 and pages 141-158. I draw from Scheiner's analysis of Social Welfare services agencies in N.Y.C. for this section.

136. Richard Cloward "The War Against Poverty: Are the Poor Left Out," _The Nation_, 201 (August 2, 1965). Richard Cloward, "Private Social Welfare's Disengagement from the Poor". In _Community Action Against Poverty_. Perlman and Gurin, _op. cit._, pages 12-36. See also the Encyclopedia of Social Work, _op. cit._, pages 683-688.

137. Scheiner, _op. cit._, _ibid._

138. _Ibid._ Also see Daniel Thursz "Social Aspects of Poverty", _Public Welfare Forum; The Journal of the American Public Welfare Association_, July 1967, Vol. XXV, No. 3.

139. _Ibid._

140. _Ibid._

141. _Ibid._ Also see DuBois, _op. cit._ page 30.

142. Scheiner, op. cit., ibid.

143. Ibid.

144. Ibid.

145. Ibid.

146. DuBois, op. cit., ibid.

147. Johnson, op. cit., page 140; Osafsky, op. cit., page 58-62. Scheiner, op. cit., page 26-28.

148. Youth in the Ghetto, op. cit.; Kenneth B. Clark; A Relevant War Against Poverty: A Study of Community Action Programs and Observable Social Change, (New York. Metropolitan Applied Research Center, 1968) Pages 1-10; Kenneth B. Clark. Haryou: An Experiment; Portions of a Speech delivered at the Award Luncheon of the Association for the Improvement of Mental Health, Saturday, May 11, 1963; in John Henrik Clark, op. cit., Pages 210-213.

149. Myrdal, op. cit., page 496.

150. Report of the National Advisory Commission on Civil Disorders, (Bantom Books, Toronto, New York (Kerner Commission, London) Pages 457-467. Scheiner, op. cit., ibid.; Kenneth B. Clark, Dark Ghetto, op. cit., page 174.

151. Ellison, op. cit.

152. Osafsky, op. cit., pages 143-145.

153. Johnson, op. cit.

154. Ibid.

155. Jean Blackwell Hutson "The Schomberg Collection" in J.H. Clark, op. cit., page 205.

156. Osafsky, op. cit.

157. Ibid.; see also Scheiner, op. cit., pages 70-72, 94, 100, 156 and 202; Kenneth Clark, op. cit., pages 162-168; Krosney, op. cit. pages 37-95.

158. Ibid.

159. Ibid.

160. Ibid.; see also Wilson, op. cit., pages 229-30 and 44-46.

161. Youth In the Ghetto, op. cit., page XIV also Krosney, op. cit., ibid.

162.   For Bio-sketch, Kenneth Clark and Powell. I use Interview Data
        and The Negro Handbook, (Johnson Publishing Company, Inc.:
        Chicago 1966). Compiled by editors of Ebony. The similarity
        in conflicts and antagonisms are reflective of historical ones
        between Black Idealist-Intellectuals, and politicians. In
        Contemporary Harlem the conflict tends to be manifested between
        politicians and professionals; a matter not reflected in most
        available literature. I have gleened the importance of these
        antagonisms from interviews in Harlem and from piecing together
        specific literary elements.

163.   John Henrik Clark, op. cit., page 43.

164.   See Chapter IX of Dissertation.

165.   Osafsky, op. cit., page 179.

166.   Interviews conducted with these community residents. See Chapter
        IX of Dissertation.

167.   Ibid.

168.   Op. Cit.

169.   Youth in the Ghetto, op. cit., page 47.

170.   Ibid. and see also Raymond B. Cattell "Group Characteristics"
        in Lazarsfeld and Rosenberg, The Languages of Social Re-
        search (Free Press) Page 298.

171.   Johnson, op. cit., ibid.

172.   DuBois, op. cit., page 70.

CHAPTER 3

TYPES OF FUNCTIONAL CIVIC LEADERS:
EMERGING FORM AND SUBSTANCE

We are now ready to consider the peculiar types of leader categories which function within Harlem and the Haryou program. It is
my contention in doing so, that the peculiar nature of the types discussed stem from the unique circumstances of Harlem as a community
and Haryou as an emerging black institution.[1] The reader may sense
the existence of comparable leadership types in other community contexts,
however it is my position that Haryou represents the organizational
'avant guarde' or prototype, later to be imitated in varying degrees,
in other leadership instances.

Before operationalizing my leadership types, it is important to
again comment that I am discussing civic leadership models. Civic
leaders, who, as defined by Wilson, relate to the "raising and settling
of community issues".[2] It is also important to recall, that in my
usage, the term refers to 'functions' performed by leaders, irrespective of their status as paid professionals, volunteer lay people, politicians or bureauocrats and administrators.[3] Thus the point is that
there are community functional leadership contributions made by those
who at various times wear different professional or other leadership
'hats'; at any rate, with respect to their activities in Haryou. As
important, is the realization, that there are those who cannot be viewed
as relevant civic leaders in the Haryou community because they take too
seriously their 'official' classifications (i.e. professionals, politicians etc.); and are not available to commit themselves to the time and
personal sacrafices necessary in Harlem's civic enterprise. These are
the technicians and professionals who are embarrassed by, or defensive
about associations made between their success occupationally and their
racial positions. They reject vehemently any responsibility for civic
leadership not directly associated with their technical or expert skills.
In Myrdal's view these are Blacks who have arranged isolated worlds for
themselves and want to hear as little as possible about their being
'Negroes' or the existence of a Negro problem. Utilizing this perspective,
enables us to legitimately define as a functional civic leader, a Haryou
executive or program director who in addition to his professional roles
in Haryou, commits himself to helping resolve civic community issues by
participation in local community forums over and beyond the requirements
of his professional functions. On the other hand, it is not possible
to view, say, a local politician in the above sense, if his allegiances
and primary concerns conflict with fundamental community needs and
concerns.[4]

The six leadership types are as follows: The creative elites,
the institutional inspirationalists, the raceocrats, the proto-indigenous idealists, the premier leaders and the commutators.[5] The reader
finds in the analysis of the 'types', instances in which individual
leaders move from one type to another. That is, in accordance with
changes in a leader's position within Haryou, it is, from time to time,

found that a concommitant change occurs in that leader's style and function. Additionally, we hypothesize, that part of the culture of leadership in Haryou and Harlem is the phenomenon of 'wearing more than one hat' in any given situation.[6] I will comment on these examples as the analysis proceeds.

The Creative Elites

Creative elite leadership is a type which is creative in the sense discussed by Selznick as "an emobodiment of specific purpose"[7] reflected in the desire to change community conditions, and which leads to the concern for creating new institutions. Beyond this, the creative elite leader is one whose conceptual ability enables him to envision what, in the nature of things, could be with respect to qualitative structural change.

The hyphonated concept - elite, is specifically related to the idea of availability. In C. Wright Mills terminology, elites are above the whim or control of 'ordinary' men, i.e. they are not available or vulnerable in the sense that, for example, grass roots leaders and local political leaders are, to a finite constituency; but tend, rather, to operate outside of the pale of normative community relationships.[8] Elites function in small, near secretive cadres, enschrouding themselves in policy-making and critical decisions which, in their judgement, do not lend themselves to popular consensus or support. Dr. Kenneth Clark, in the book Dark Ghetto, illuminates to some degree the perfect example of elitism.[9] In his discussion of the informal organization known as, The Group, a small leadership cadre of fifteen black leaders. Clark states,

> Members of the Group communicate with one another orally, never
> by written invitation. Its existence has been known to few
> Negroes, fewer whites. For the past four or five years, it has
> met fairly regularly and over brandy and cigars, discussed the
> persistent problems of the Harlem community.[10]

Thus, the Group is a clear example of a kind of leadership which is 'unavailable' to any popular constituency. Ladd also lends conceptual clarity to the idea of availability.[11] In his discussion of specific leadership attributes such as educational achievement, and a style of in-group orientation as criteria for whether leaders are available; he is alluding to a mental and physical involvement in community issues. In my historical statement, above, I discuss men who are viewed as creative elites, utilizing my model. Men for example like W.E. DuBois and Charles Anderson, who are clearly creative in areas of importance to the enhancement of opportunities for the black community in early Harlem. Their contributions, however, are not attended by substantive involvement with the masses of the community, and the decisions they make, the actions they involve themselves in--are in no wise dependent upon any shared perspective from Harlem's black constituency. Anderson, even as a political figure owes his position as much to his allegiences to Booker T. Washington and many of the North's white Republican power figures; as he does to blacks in Harlem.[12] He is functional, nevertheless for Harlem in his service on the Board of Directors of the Urban League; in addition to his function as a political leader who opens opportunities for blacks in the State and municipal civil service bureaucracies. DuBois, on the other hand, as a brilliant intellectual leader, serves the function, through his outspokenness and protestations regarding social injustice, of not only creating new 'institutions', (NAACP), but focussing the attentions of the world on the Urban blacks' problems.

In my use of the creative elite leadership type, I am primarily concerned with contributions made in the early conceptualization and implementation of the Haryou program and idea. The men and women found in the planning, policy-making and critical decisions, persistent in the early Haryou design, share, in my view, certain of those attributes associated with them predecessors. Most are people of vision and ability. They are also leaders, however, who evidence little faith in the relevance and inherent ability of Harlem's masses to deal effectively with the community's problems.[13]

The creative elites, are successful black professionals who, were either born or raised in Harlem. Most have moved beyond the ghetto's walls, establishing residences in surburban Long Island, Westchester or posh West Side and Mid-Manhattan areas.[14] Some few remain in Harlem. Creative elites fit certain criteria respecting age, sex, and educational achievement; and in addition, are mentioned most often by each other and other community leaders as having made early and specific contributions to Haryou. I have identified five creative elite functional leaders of importance here; Kenneth Clark, Eugene Callendar, Arthur Logan, Moran Weston and James Dumpson.[15]

Each of these men share the attributes outlined above. All are, in terms of age, for example, above 40 years old. All are male, (a most relevant point when dealing with Harlem leadership, generally).[16] Educationally, all have ascended to post graduate or professional training, with three holding doctorates in their fields, (a few hold a number of honorary degrees, in addition to formal certifications). Each of these leaders, when discussing Haryou, mention one another as having made major leadership contributions. As a group, they are most often mentioned by lay community people familiar with Haryou effort.[17] Interestingly, however, when mentioned in this latter instance, they are viewed as functional with respect to their porfessional competencies as opposed to general community leadership contributions. An example is presented by the response of one community leader in Haryou to the question as to the major contributions made by Dr. Kenneth Clark. This respondent replied,

> that Dr. Clark is a brilliant educator, and could have been more helpful in helping the children in school if he had remained at Haryou.[18]

Creative elite leaders are participants in a variety of civic and professional organizations in and out of Harlem. They tend to participate in Nationally oriented race organizations, i.e. the NAACP, National Urban League, The United Negro College Fund and in some National Black Fraternal Organizations.[19]

Functionally, creative elites serve the Haryou purpose of, in Alfred J. Kahn's words, "instigating"[20] the Haryou planning and implementation task. They are also functional as stabilizing forces in the determination of goals and organizational structure. Finally, the positions of these leaders in the broader New York and National communities are functional for the early view of Haryou as a serious, substantive program intervention strategy for dealing with the problems of the Harlem community.[21]

The creative elites, then, are leaders of vision and perception. They are professionally trained, middle to upper middle class, relatively successful people. They are highly regarded in the external (non-Harlem) community; and fairly reliant upon these external reputations for acceptance in Harlem. One implication of this finding is that many Harlemites, particularly those within the professional community tend to view achieved status in the external white community as prerequesite to functional relevance as a leader in Harlem. Another implication is that Harlemites still place a premium on leadership which can serve the 'dual functions' suggested by Myrdal, Clark and others. And finally, there is the implication that the elites are correct in their assumption that their power as leaders within Harlem need not be directly sanctioned by the community's masses. This latter factor is a sore spot with many of the elites, as they normally view themselves as the true or responsible representatives of the Harlem community's best interests.[22] There are, presently, in Haryou, leaders who will be identified as fitting these criteria, however, their number is substantially reduced from what it was during the preliminary and beginning Haryou experience. I will discuss these newer leaders in later chapters.

The Institutional Inspirationalist

This leadership type is one reflective of the community values and aspirations of Harlem. The inspirationalist leader is insightful regarding the strengths and weaknesses, as well as the hopes of Harlemites. He is not overly concerned, nor primarily focussed on those social problems, the primary focus of the social researcher; but rather the potential abilities and efforts of the community's people to effect some change in such conditions. Functionally, the inspirationalist leader enhances the collective survival of Harlemites through his participation in formulating organizations and community structures which capitalize upon, and reflect the special culture, history and character of the community's positive aspects.[23] In our historical perspective, leaders like the Bishops; John Royal and Adam Clayton Powell, Sr. are illustrative. Each of these men play some role in the transition of the black community - from the Tenderloin to San Juan Hill; from there, in to Harlem. It is their kind of leadership, once arrived, that sparks the purchasing of large real estate holdings, which, later become the cornerstones of emergent institutions.

The institutional inspirationalist is concerned with the perpetuation of community institutions in Harlem. He finds the social and civic organizational network of community systems relevant in determining and promoting its own leadership.[24] The inspirationalists are radical in their defense of Haryou organizational integrity;[25] and in this regard are found in the vanguard of those individuals who emerge during the critical decisions surrounding Haryou's transition to the Community Corporation for Central Harlem.

In addition to insightfulness regarding community aspirations and values, or 'Harlem's ethos', the inspirationalist leader is also concerned with 'inspiring', within the community the sense of purposiveness and destiny which he feels.[26] This is accomplished through sensitive translation of program objectives and goals, and selective interpretation of organizational policy - often quietly and inconspicuously - though, from time to time, with the 'bombast' and flair associated with Harlem leadership.[27] It is not at all strange to find members of the church community among this leadership type. It is often the case that they are not, however. Even the casual Harlem observer who experiences the phenomenon of the street orator 'doing his thing' on the famed corner of 125th Street and 7th Avenue, can attest to this. Once again, a major criteria for these leaders is tenure in the Community. For those who were not born or raised in Harlem, a minimum criteria is a substantive number of years in pursuing organizational careers within the community. Men like Reverend C. Licorish and Reverend William M. James, who had a profound effect on the life of the well known Harlem author, Claude Brown;[27] Harriet Pickens, Emma Penn and Milton Yale are examples of functional leaders who fit the inspirationalist typology. All of these leaders shared a common perspective, a faith, if you will, regarding Harlem as a community of promise, and

Haryou as a legitimate mechanism for helping in the process. There are a variety of others who fit this leadership category. One man is the owner of a famous Harlem Restaurant; the other, a police captain in one of the community's precincts. Still others are lay community citizens who have ascended to leadership positions in their local block or social organizations as well as in Haryou. A substantial number in this latter group are senior Harlem citizens - in their 60s - a matter of special significance to their relevant status as institutional inspirationalists. They, for example, are in the unique position of comparing Harlem's and Haryou's contemporary leaders, with the major leaders of times long past. Many, for example recall the Harlem "Renaissance"[29] era, and the community issues and problems of the moment. The fact that they persist in participating in Haryou, holding firmly to a vision of a "new Harlem that can be a community of excellence, surpassing the Harlem of old",[30] indicates their inspirational value.

The institutional inspirationalists are functionally relevant in their value as 'alter-egos' for Haryou. They are the main core of leadership responsible for the phenomena which Clark identifies as 'folk sense';[31] and as such, function as stabilizing influences in Haryou's struggle for the achievement of institutional status and relevance. They are masters at the development of community survival strategies, and are persistent in seeking indigenous resources for culture and institution building.[32] A major and fundamental difference between the institutional inspirationalist, and the creative elites resides in their differential views of indigenous Harlem resources and particularly the human ones available as positive strengths for resolving community problems are issues. The inspirationalists are committed to the view that Harlemites are those best equipped to transform their community to meet their needs. Recognizing, however, the requirement for extra-community resources, i.e. money, in order to achieve a variety of objectives, they are nevertheless insistent that such resources be pursued and utilized on terms that do not threaten organizational and community values or integrity.[33]

The Raceocrat Leaders

The raceocrat leader is essentially a black bureaucrat. In modern anti-poverty terms, he or she is a community povertician. I find little precedence to this leadership type in Harlem's earlier history. Primarily because Blacks are only beginning to achieve positions in City and State bureaus and agencies. The closest approximation to the raceocrat discernable in earlier Harlem is the 'uncle tom' or conservative type illuminated by Murdal, Ladd and others. Volunteering for civic community leadership is a device for enhancing personal opportunities such as access to administrative and middle management level positions in civil service, social welfare or City Hall political appointive positions.[34] Haryou, particularly in the early experience, represented the perfect forum for the raceocrat. The program afforded high visibility and a unique opportunity to frequent the insitutional establishments which traditionally have represented power in the City-wide and national communities.[35] Community crisis and conflict represent, to the raceocrat, perfect chances for personal attention. Having mastered polished styles of rhetoric, they opt for recognition as legitimate community representatives, in the hope that as such, they may be "bought-off" by the, in fact, power brokers within municipal and national bureaucratic/administrative systems.[35]

The raceocrat does not share the community values, and institutional concerns of the institutional inspirationalist and view his participation in leadership activities as temporary. Comparable in some ways to the proto-indigenous professional category suggested by Eugene Litwak in his

51

analysis of bureaucratic leaders, the raceocrat in the Haryou experience essentially exploits the existent community pathologies, in the effort to achieve heightened professional/technical status.[37]

There are interesting differences between this type of leader and the creative elites, as well. The fundamental one resides in the fact that the raceocrat has not 'arrived', in the sense that the creative elite has; though he clearly aspires to do so. The raceocrat reference group is the creative elite type, and he tends to view the status positions of the elites as attainable. Once again, however, in contradistinction to his role model, the raceocrat is not as educationally or professionally endowed as the creative elite. He is not privy to the kinds of 'contacts' which are the hallmark of elite leaders, but sensing the importance of such contact, seeks to effect relationships with the elites as facilitators.

In some ways the raceocrat is reminiscent of the conventional 'token' leader of Wilson,[38] or the 'moderate' leadership of Myrdal[39] and Ladd.[40] In Harlem, his genuine purpose tends to be camouflaged by rhetoric as respects the community's major issues and needs, yet though he functions as an organizational representative (i.e. via Haryou); he demonstrates a lack of real concern for such issues. Using his color as a badge of 'expertise' regarding the nature of community life, he vies for inclusion in the 'new leader' or 'young Turks' prespective popular during the mid and late 1960s in civil rights and community action programs.[41] In fact, the raceocrat, though he assumes a posture comparable to one of Harlem or Haryou's 'angry young men'; turns out to be little more than a caricature of the militant. Few really know Harlem or Harlemites, and are disarmed by the community's apparent vulnerability to anyone who would lead. This explains their trauma at finding themselves alienated from the important channels of communication and access which are at the heart of the decision making process in the community.

The raceocrat leader is usually college educated; though he has normally not pursued graduate level training. He is younger than the creative elite leader, (falling within the 20s and early 30s), and is in the beginning years of his occupational career. It is noteworthy that raceocrat leaders often change once they have achieved certain of their status goals. There is the tendency for this leadership type to assume the characteristics of the proto-indigenous idealist though they never fully arrive at the idealism associated with this leader type. One might postulate that the raceocrat ideology is a function of age and inexperience in Harlem and Haryou systems; and that with increased insight born of maturity and recognition of substantive community values and aspirations--there is a normative transformation to a different leadership type. In this sense, the raceocrat is a quite different leader type than the traditional 'Uncle Tom' of earlier theorists. I have identified certain Haryou and/or Harlem actionists as fitting this leadership type. Many of these young men are foreign born and as such evidence a lack of awareness regarding the cultural and organizational values which operate in Harlem.[42] Osafsky illuminates this phenomena in his discussion of the historical culture conflicts which persist even more substantively during Harlem's early development, and Kenneth Clark's comments regarding the Black America's 'folk sense' is illuminating.[43] (See also Chapter II, above.)

The raceocrat leadership type is essentially viewed as dysfunctional with regard to Haryou organizational values and objectives; however, they are found to be positively functional in terms of certain short term goals.[44] In this latter regard, these leaders are masterful at focusing community-wide attention on 'hot' issues, and in facilitating the crystali-

zation and clarification of issue priorities. Litsak, in his analysis
of a balance theory of organizations, discusses a form of public relations or media leadership which is illustrative to some degree of additional functions of the raceocrat.[45]

The Proto-Indigenous Idealist Leader

These are men and women who utilize their differential positions
as public or private administrators, civil service professionals such
as educators, social workers and so on; to the advantage of Harlem and
her citizens.[46] In many ways, they are comparable to the 'race' leadership typologies of a number of theorists; but in the present perspective,
their functional relevance is directly related to the survival of Haryou
as a community program.

As noted earlier, leaders like Charles H. Filmore who launched
the first Harlem regiment of State Militia in New York; Charles W. B.
Mitchell, architect and Harlem politician, and Dr. William Buckley,
Harlem's major leader in public education--these men are essentially
well established in a variety of government positions--yet use themselves so as to be functionally relevant to specific Harlem needs.

Most of the leaders in this category are 'native' Harlem sons and
daughters, and many achieve their positions in various city-wide and
National programs, i.e. O.E.O.; Council Against Poverty; Labor Department Programs; Head Start and other Municipal, State and Federal Agencies, as the result of training and experience gained at Haryou or
some other Harlem agency or organization, i.e. N.Y. Urban League,
HANA, etc. The proto-indigenous idealists normally reside in Harlem;
though many are found at the community's fringe areas.[47] All have
been educated in the New York metropolitan area and are in the approximate 30-40 years of age bracket. A substantial number of these leaders
have spend the major portion of their professional careers in civil
service agencies at the municipal and state level and are represented
in their various areas of competence. I have found a number of administrative and executive secretaries who fit this leadership type, and
have been impressed by their 'influence' in many of the decisions
made by those higher in the organizational charts of their respective
departments.[48]

The proto-indigenous idealist is of particular importance to
Harlem and Haryou. Their astuteness in recognizing that their positions
in many bureaus and agencies are functional for the 'tokenism' concerns
of such enterprises; that they have the jobs because they are 'representative' of, thus proto-typical of, the black community with whom the
bureau or 'bureaucracy' seeks some 'linkages', is a matter to be exploited.[49] The exploitation of their positions is born of a commitment
to make the various institutions for whom they work 'relevant' to the
needs of black constituencies, and in the present instance to Harlem.
In that they take this responsibility seriously, these leaders strive
for perfection in their serveral technical and professional realms, and
are normally above reproach with respect to their competence. This
being the case, they tend to be free in interpreting agency, bureau
and institutional regulations to the advantage of those they seek to
serve.[50]

Leaders of this type are found on the Haryou Board of Directors,
and in many of the 'grass roots' organizations connected with Haryou
programs. In Harlem,[51] allude to the kinds of people who I categorize
above; in their discussion of Project Uplift;

> The supervisors, most of whom were indigenous to the Harlem
> community, had, in general, attained a high degree of formal
> education. Eighty per cent had completed some college training

53

with more than one-fourth (28%) having graduated from college, and about one-third (32%) having attended professional or technical schools....The supervisors employed in the project represented a variety of fields of study;[52]

which, according to the authors, represented education, social science, music, dance, the fine arts, religion, business and physical education. Finally, they conclude, that

In general, then, the picture of the supervisors in the summer project is one of an intelligent well-trained, and dedicated group eager to assist in improving the conditions of Harlem. Their primary concern was with the youth whom they supervised, and the enrollees appeared to feel that, as supervisors, they had performed their functions well.[53]

Many of the people to whom these writers allude, were at the time of their work in the summer program, on vacation, or leave, from regular positions suggested above. A few, interviewed during my analysis, are currently so employed.

Wilson's "New Negro"[54] leadership category, illuminates, to some degree, the attributes of the proto-indigenous leader. He states, for example,

The new Negro will have several attributes. He will respond to the intangible incentives for civic action, and contribute his time and money and energies selflessly or at least without hope of substantial gain. Indeed, he will be willing to perform these duties at some sacrifice to himself and his career. He will be immune to corruption.[55]

And finally, "A new leadership will be created out of civic enterprise, rather than merely co-opted from other areas of achievement".[56] This latter observation speaks directly to the fundamental concerns of my analysis. I take the view that it is only through the emergence of leaders 'created' through the peculiar Harlem community civic organizational enterprise, (as outlined in Chapters II and III above), that we have legitimate functional community leaders. Men and women capable, as the result of their familiarity and internalization of community values and culture, to effect positive institutional and social change; and on Harlem's behalf. This perspective is consistent with the 'idealism' associated with the proto-indigenous idealist. To the creative elites and raceocrat leaders, he is at best, naive in the belief that substantive change in the 'pathological' problems of the ghetto can or will come from an involvement with internal community systems and the people 'trapped' by them. At worst, his idealism serves as 'dysfunctional' for facilitating the recognition of "those Negroes who are worthy of confidence and respect",[57] at least, according to Clark. Finally, even the institutional inspirationalist leaders tend to view the proto-indigenous idealist with some suspicion;

How can they (the idealists), really believe that they can continue to 'bite' the hand that feeds them; by using positions established by white people, for white people; to help black folks in Harlem,[58]

is one representative leaders view.

Irrespective of these conflictual perspectives, the proto-indigenous idealist persists in being functionally relevant to Haryou and other community organizations. They do so by translating, wherever and whenever they can, the policies, services and presumed purposes of public and quasi-public institutions, into specific actions and communications which accrue to Harlem and Haryou's advantage.

The Premier Leaders

The operational definition of 'premier leadership' takes the reader to a somewhat unique conceptualization of an 'old' term;-- professionalism; in addition to being my fifth leadership type.

The literal definition of the term 'premier' comes from the Latin, Premarious - "of the first rank".[59] It is also taken to mean a chief, or principle person or thing. With respect to premier leadership as it is used in this analysis, I will be referring to a qualitative as well as a positional definition. One, however, which does not concern itself with the types of vocations, but rather with the kinds of persons viewed as successful in maintaining themselves, "at the top", or as recognized leaders in a variety of endeavors. I have mentioned earlier, Marcus Garvey's function as a premier leader. He is among the first to emerge in Black Harlem. Other historical examples include "Father Divine" and Daddy Grace.

Utilizing this framework, it is as relevant, in functional terms, to view a street wise 'hustler' of numbers 'banker' as a premier leader in his illegitimate professional career, should he survive, as it is to define a successful Harlem politician who in comparable fashion, though within a legitimate professional arena, is successful in remaining unchallenged in his leadership.[60]

A major factor, I suspect, has to do with who does the defining. In this regard, premier leaders are those defined by Harlemites, as the 'chief' or top 'cats', who are powerful, or who control. An immediate example of premier leadership in Harlem is her former Congressman, now deceased, Reverend Adam Clayton Powell, Jr. Never equalled in his functional relevance to the socio-political community of Harlem, 'big Daddy' Powell reigned as the 'chief' political leader for more than two decades.[61] Other examples of premier leadership are J. Raymond Jones in the political arena, Jessie Gray, in the area of housing rights; Andrew R. Tyler, and in a most contemporary sense, Helen Testamark, Harlem and Haryou's leader in the area of community controlled public education.[62] The premier leadership category is also applicable to youth. Young activists, such as Lloyd Pryor, the early Haryou Associates leader, and Calvin Alston, who at a later stage in Haryou's development essentially replaced Pryor, are examples. I will be expanding my analysis of certain of these premier leaders in subsequent chapters.

At the moment it suffices to note that the premier leaders fall on a continuum; they are not bound by the characteristics associated with the previously discussed leadership types. They are dispersed vocationally in a variety of 'professional pursuits'; some illegitimate. They are young (Pryor, for example was perhaps the most powerful 18 year old Harlem had ever seen);[63] They are middle aged. Premier leaders are drawn from every socio-economic level in Harlem, and range, educationally (formal), from 8th grade drop-outs, to PhD's.

Perhaps the most significant aspect of the premier leader's function, is his relationship to a Harlem constituency. He, more than any of the other leadership types, is a Harlem practitioner. The status accorded him is a reflection of what Harlemites feel, and though a few of the premiers function in areas unrelated to Harlem, (i.e. Powell's national and international reputation, and J. Raymond Jones' city wide responsibilities, they are nevertheless viewed by the community as 'Harlem's own'.[64]

The Commutators

The commutator leader is a community or 'street' administrator. Similar, in some ways to the premier leader, this leadership type is essentially a community technician or 'details' person. In some ways the commutator is a caricature of the premier leader. The term paraprofessional, in contemporary social work terminology; or para-medical in the medical professions approximates my definition of the commutator.[65] James Q. Wilson's analysis of an 'organizer' leadership type approximates my commutator leader.[65] The difference between these early functional concepts resides in the fact that commutators are community leaders in voluntary civic enterprise. As local leaders, they are respected for their technical knowledge and 'contacts' in areas related to housing, education, public assistance, consumerism and legal rights, but they are usually not employed by any social or community action agencies. There is a heavy preponderance of women in this leadership typology, as the amount of time and energy required for gaining the knowledge and reputation essential for prowess in the community are normally only available to those who have large blocks of time to spend in their pursuits.[67] Many commutators are female heads of their households, and have thus found it necessary to become 'involved' in learning to deal with community institutions on behalf of their children and themselves.[68] The absence, in some instances, of men in the household necessitates their assumption of protective or brokerage roles for family survival.[69] In a substantial number of cases, the male heads of the families are just unavailable to assume the kinds of functions associated with commutator leadership on the basis of time, as most work. There are, on the other hand, men who are involved in such leadership. The fact that many are involved in other pursuits ranging from numbers running, to unsuccessful law practices, is essentially irrelevant to their civic community functions.[70]

The commutator, as opposed to the premier leader, associates more clearly with his or her Harlem constituency. More than likely they are neighbors to those they serve, as a prerequisite of acceptance in the role requires constant availability. In addition to availability, the commutator is counted upon as a follow-up person. Matters which require specific action must be pursued to their conclusion, and unless one can be relied upon in this respect, he is not viewed as a commutator leader.

The commutators, are often 'leg men' for premier leaders in whom they believe.[71] The phenomena in Harlem of 'church sisters' or 'soul brothers and sisters', is definable in terms of the functions performed by the commutator leaders in rallying the support of their community constituencies to the cause of some premier leader and his 'program'.[72] Commutators, are often the silent advisors to premier leaders, as well as their intermediaries to the grass roots. Examples of commutator type leaders, are Harlem's 'Pork Chop' Davis, the well known street orator and community 'administrator' of Harlem's street values.[73] Few legitimate Harlem leaders, whether premier, proto-indigenous, or otherwise, would embark upon any community program strategies without, at least, 'consulting' Pork Chop. Even the illusive creative elites are known to 'pick his brain' in the process of making various decision.[74] Haryou's famed executive chauffeur "Mississippi" is another example of a commutator leader. As in the case of the raceocrat leader, it is difficult to identify historical precedents in Harlem during its early development. Only a few such as Lillian "Pig Foot Mary" Harris are documented; and this primarily due to her later emergence as a leading business woman late in her career. The fact that commutators existed in Harlem is assumed; however, the "little man" is not discernable in those written accounts of the community, which have come down to us. Returning to 'Mississippi' as an example, his advice, often, to the executives and Board of Directors' members he had driver, regarding community 'feelings', needs, and reactions to organizational decisions and actions has been critical.[75] Helen Testamark, a woman about whom I say much more in later chapters, is an excellent example of a commutator leader. Through her voluntary participation in the Haryou program she ascends to national prominence; and concommitantly becomes a premier leader in her own right.

Commutators, are in terms of their current visibility inventions of the anti-poverty programs. Their public emergence and status is the result of requirements in Haryou and similar agencies that "maximum feasible participation"[76] of indigenous community representatives accompany all policy and program endeavors. Functionally, however, these leaders have always existed in Harlem. Their roles with respect to Haryou's leadership are essentially interpretive, as they stand as the 'carriers' of community values and mores. There is little question but that without the involvement and loyalty, (though often strained), of representative commutator leaders, in the Haryou enterprise, it would now be but a memory.[77]

The discussion regarding emerging forms of fucntional leadership in Harlem is conceptualized within a framework which views Haryou as one major social mechanism for leadership development, identification and performance. Though I am discussing types of leaders who dominate the community scene for the approximate time frame, 1962-1972, it should be clear to the reader, that the forms and substance of the types are historically relevant.[78] That is, they grow from the peculiar socio-cultural milieu of the Harlem community over an approximate 50 years.

During the course of Haryou's development, particular types of leaders using the above models or categories, are prominent at specific times, and around specific issues.[79] This is a matter which is explored below. Further, one finds a certain tendency towards overlapping leadership styles identified with specific types. Despite such tendencies, I will, in the process of associating major actors on the Haryou scene with various activities and issues of a program and community relevance, attempt to indicate the points at which shifts in leadership types occur. The pressumption, then, that certain individuals may assume different roles or become functional within different leadership types (i.e. creative elite who later becomes an institutional inspirationalist, etc.), is an additional contingency to be dealt with as the analysis proceeds.

FOOTNOTES TO CHAPTER III

1. _Youth In the Ghetto_, A study of the consequences of powerlessness.
   (Harlem Youth Opportunities Unlimited, Inc.) 1964, pages 10-41;
   John Henrik Clark, _Harlem: A Community in Transition_ (The
   Citadel Press, N.Y.) Article by Kenneth Clark, _Haryou: An
   Experiment_, pages 210-213. Alphonso Pinkney and Roger R. Woock,
   Poverty and Politics in Harlem. Report on Project Uplift,
   1965. (College and University Press, New Haven), page 151;
   Herbert Krosney, _Beyond Welfare, Poverty in the Supercity_.
   (Holt, Rinehart and Winston, New York, Chicago, San Francisco),
   pages 35-36 and 94-96; Louella Jacqueline Long, and Vernon
   Ben Robinson, _How Much Power to the People?_ A Study of the
   New York State Urban Development Corporation's Involvement
   in Black Harlem. (Faculty-Student Technical Assistance Project, Urban Center--Columbia University, New York)

2. James Q. Wilson, _Negro Politics: The Search for Leadership_, (The
   Free Press of Glencoe, Illinois), page 255.

3. Though I differ with Wilson as to what categories of leadership
   are functional for civic enterprise, my utilization of the
   term 'function' is synonmuous with his-see Wilson, _op. cit._,
   pages 255-256. Also see Elaine Burgess, _Negro Leadership in
   a Southern City_, (University of North Carolina Press, Chapel
   Hill) pages 81-82; 177; 181-182. Also see Everett Carll Ladd,
   Jr. _Negro Political Leadership in the South_, (Cornell Univer-
   sity Press, New York) pages 137-138; 145-153. Daniel C.
   Thompson, _The Negro Leadership Class_. (Prentice-Hall, Inc.
   Englewood Cliffs, New Jersey) pages 1-4; 31-32; 37; 40-43.
   Philip Selznick, _Leadership in Administration: A Sociologi-
   cal Interpretation_ (Ron Peterson and Company Evanston, Illinois;
   White Plains, New York) pages 22-64. Gunnar Myrdal, _An
   American Dilemma: The Negro Problem and Modern Democracy_
   (Harper and Row, Publichsers, New York and Evanston), page 1133.

4. _Youth in the Ghetto_, _op. cit._, pages 137-161, 313-351. Thompson,
   op. cit., pages 42-44. Also see Clark, _op. cit._, pages 225-226.
   Selznick, _op. cit._, pages 22-24; Myrdal, _op. cit._, page 764-766.

5. In reviewing the leadership literature, I have found the contributions of Eugene Litwak of immense relevance to certain of my
   types; for examples see -- Eugene Litwak and J. Figueira,
   "Technological Innovation and Theoretical Functions of Primary
   Groups and Bureaucratic Structures" (_American Journal of Soci-
   ology_, January 1968.); also Litwak "Extended Kin Relations in
   an Industrial Democratic Society" in Ethal Shanas and Gordon
   F. Streib _Social Structure and the Family_, (Prentice-Hall Inc.,

Englewood Cliffs, New Jersey 1965) pages 295-302; and
Eugene Litwak and Henry J. Meyer, "A Balance Theory of
Coordination Between Bureaucratic Organizations and Community Primary Groups", Administrative Science Quarterly,
11 (June 1966) pages 31-58; see also the contributions to
my typology of Wilson, op. cit., pages 255-280; Burgess
op. cit., pages 176-186; Thompson, op. cit., pages 34-78.
Ladd op. cit., pages 145-232. Myrdal, op. cit., pages
709-780. Selznick, op. cit., pages 22-25; 56-74; 119-149
and 1-4. In addition to borrowing conceptually from these
referents, the typology is a construct growing from my
interviews and analysis with exstent Harlem leaders involved
in Haryou and community organizations of a civic nature.

6. See Wilson, op. cit., pages 255-280.

7. Selznick, op. cit., pages 90-133.

8. C. Wright Mills, The Power Elite (New York, Oxford Press, 1959),
    pages 269-297 and pages 3-4.

9. Kenneth B. Clark, Dark Ghetto, Dilemmas of Social Power (Harper
    and Row), New York, Evanston and London), pages 186-188.

10. Ibid.

11. Ladd, op. cit. pages 122-132.

12. Gilbert Osafsky, Harlem: The Making of a Ghetto: Negro, New
    York. 1890 - 1930 (Harper and Row, New York), page 166.

13. This is a position arrived at as the result of participation
    with many of Haryou's leaders early in the organizations de-
    velopment. The persistent perspective regarding Harlem's
    issues articulated as "Black people in Harlem, just ain't
    ready"-- is a reflection of this attitude. Interview data
    with former and present Harlem leaders is also utilized in
    arriving at this view. Myrdal, also discussed this phenomena
    in The American Dilemma, op. cit., pages 758-764. Also Clark,
    op. cit.

14. This, of course, is a movement which has been accruing in Harlem
    for approximately (2) decades; see for example Pinkney and
    Woock, op. cit., pages 27-28. The authors discuss the decline
    of Harlem population since 1970.

15. Criteria used include these leaders' functions in initiating the
    Haryou Program and Board. Each is an original signer of the
    Haryou Document. See, Youth in the Ghetto, op. cit., XII.

16. See Chapter VI, page 178 of Dissertation.

17. Interviews conducted for analysis.

18. Ibid.

19. Ibid. and see Wilson, op. cit., ibid. and Thompson, op. cit., ibid.,
    also Myrdal, op. cit., ibid. and Burgess, op. cit.

20. Alfred J. Kahn, <u>Theory and Practice of Social Planning</u>. Companion Volume to Studies in Social Policy and Planning (Russell Sage Foundation) New York 1969; pages 60-96. Also in Companion, Volume, see page 157-193.

21. <u>Youth in the Ghetto</u>, <u>op. cit</u>., pages xii-xiv. Krosney, op. cit., page 36-43.

22. Clark, <u>Dark Ghetto</u>. <u>Op. Cit</u>., page 106.

23. Historically, Church based leadership has made the Haryou inspirationalist contributions, this is not to be associated, however with 'spiritualism'; but rather with their 'inspirational functions' re: the establishment of community and race institutions, churches, youth organizations, housing developments, etc. Other inspirationalist leader characteristics are value ladened perspectives on Harlem and its life styles. See for example, Myrdal, <u>op. cit</u>., pages 927-956 and Selznick, <u>op. cit</u>., <u>ibid</u>.

24. Selznick, <u>ibid</u>. <u>Youth in the Ghetto</u>, <u>op. cit</u>., page 461. W.E.B. DuBois, <u>Durkwater, Voices from Within the Veil</u> (New York, Harcourt, Brace and Co., 1921) pages 87-94. Kelly Miller. <u>Out of the House of Bondage</u>, (Arno Press and The New York Times, New York 1969), William Loren Katz, ed. pages 50-60.

25. For a discussion of what is meant by 'organizational integrity' see, Selznick, <u>op. cit</u>., pages 119-133. For issues including Haryou Integrity see, <u>Youth In the Ghetto</u>, <u>op. cit</u>., pages 32-35, pages 37-39. Also see Chapter VI Dissertation, and Wilson, <u>op. cit</u>., page 286.

26. Clark, <u>op. cit</u>., pages 213-215; Krosney, <u>op. cit</u>., pages 50-52.

27. This observation is the direct result of my participation with various Haryou leaders during the study period. There is little question but that bombast, for example as expressed often by Kenneth Clark; is as functional for Harlem leadership as are other styles or actions. See Clark, <u>op. cit</u>. page 164.

28. Claude Brown, <u>Manchild in the Promised Land</u>. (The MacMillan Company, New York; Collier-MacMillan Limited, London), pages 378-385.

29. James Weldon Johnson, <u>Black Manhattan</u>, pages 231-280. And Interviews with senior Harlem residents.

30. Interviews with above contacts.

31. Kenneth Clark, <u>A Relevant War Against Poverty</u>, A study of Community Action Programs and Observable Social Change. (New York Metropolitan Applied Research Center, 1968.)

32. A major location of these community leaders are the various vestry organizations of churches in Harlem. Their familiarity with Harlem community needs and human resources available to participate in various programs is legend.

33. The "purse string" phenomenon is a major consideration of leaders in various Harlem organization; and is manifested in concerns at Haryou regarding the utilization of Federal and City funds for the building of institutional interests-see Richard A. Cloward "The Was on Poverty, Are the Poor Left Out," _The Nation_, August 2, 1965.

34. Interviews with Board and staff members of Haryou are presistent indicators that the Organization is viewed as a stepping stone for leaders who aspire to appointive and administrative positions in municipal and state bureaucracies. The number of organizational participants who hold a variety of such positions, including elective public office tends to substantiate the position.

35. I am talking here, about the new access afforded Harlem leadership to the Mayor's offices of planning budgeting and the City Council; as well as to various Federal and State officials via Executive Orders and the quest for representation from indigenous populations.

36. This had become during the 1960s, a peculiar interpretation of the 'cooptation' syndrome. Given certain leader-aspirants awareness of the predisposition on the parts of controlling forces in the City, to silence outspoken criticism through 'cooptation' and subsequent subservience--there were those who felt that such a devise could be used as a mechanism for access to such power centers--without necessarily giving up specific community concerns. This militant leader might posture himself so as to be coopted--but upon gaining new access to decision making bureaucracies--persist in advocating for community needs.

37. Eugene Litwak and Henry J. Meyer, _op. cit._, pages 53-58.

38. Wilson, _op. cit._, pages 126-134.

39. Myrdal, _op. cit._, pages 1133-1136.

40. Ladd, _op. cit._, pages 76-98.

41. Clark, _Dark Ghetto_, _op. cit._, pages 213-219.

42. See James Weldon Johnson, _Black Manhattan_, _op. cit._, pages 257-258. Osafsky also discusses this phenomenon as 'culture conflict' in _Harlem: The Making of a Ghetto_, _op. cit._, pages 180-184.

43. Kenneth Clark, _A Relevant Was Against Poverty: A Study of Community Action Programs and Observable Social Change_, New York. Metropolitan Applied Research Center, 1968. Page 126.

44. This is in no wise a contradictory assertion; an according to interviews conducted for the study, my leaders are viewed as dysfunctional for certain organizational purposes at one point-around a specific issue; yet functional at some other point. See Myrdal, _op. cit._, page 1133 for additional insights regarding this view.

45. Eugene Litwak and Henry J. Meyer, op. cit., pages 53-58.

46. Ibid. This category, additionally, is generated from Interviews with Haryou and Harlem leaders.

47. Alphonso Pinkney and Roger Woock, Poverty and Politics in Harlem. Report of Project Uplift, (College and University Press, New Haven), pages 48-81; and 123-140. The authors discuss the residential patterns and characterization of the summer staff in such a way as to be relevant to my conceptualization of this leadership type. Also information is based on analysis of interview results.

48. My research indicates that a highly proporation of proto-indigenous leaders are women. They are located along a continuum of technical, administrative and professional positions in various Civil Service and prive Bureaucratic Agencies.

49. My interview data in this regard substantiate and enlarge certain of Litwak's propositions respecting the functions of "primary group" oriented workers in Bureaucracies. See Litwak and Meyer, op. cit., page 58.

50. Ibid.

51. Pinkney and Woock, op. cit., ibid.

52. Ibid.

53. Ibid.

54. Wilson, op. cit., pages 276-280.

55. Ibid. page 278.

56. Ibid., this observation is particularly ciritcal to the relevance of my leadership concerns.

57. Clark, op. cit.

58. Interviews conducted day study.

59. See American College Dictionary.

60. St. Claire Drake and Horace R. Cayton (Harcourt, Brace and Company) New York, pages 524-525. The articles in their discussion of the "Shadies" develop certain of the elements conceptualized in my characterization of the illegitimate premier leader. Harlem's James 'Blue' is an example of 'uptowns' premier numbers banker.

61. See Clark, Dark Ghetto, op. cit., pages 162-168.

62. Interviewing conducted with Harlemites are the primary indicators of these leaders positions. In the case of J. Raymond Jones, his unique emergence as a premier leader is also commented on by Kenneth Clark. See, Dark Ghetto op. cit., pages 159-160.

63. Interviews with members of Haryou's H.Y.U. program; also see Krosney, op. cit., page 37 and page 46-50.

64. Ibid., also see Clark, op. cit., ibid.

65. See Carol H. Meyer, Social Work Practice: A Response to the Urban Crisis. (Collier-MacMillan Limited, London, The Free Press, New York) pages 186-220.

66. Wilson, op. cit., pages 269-276.

67. Ibid. This is a major finding reflected in my interviews in Harlem.

68. Interview with Harlem leader.

69. Ibid.

70. Ibid. and also see Drake and Cayton, op. cit., ibid.

71. See earlier comments above regarding this phenomena.

72. The commutator often uses the church in its 'social' role as a forum for organizing and raising specific community related issues. See James Weldon Johnson's comments on the church as a center for social organization, in Black Manhattan, op. cit., page 86. For further comment also see Clark, op. cit., Myrdal; op. cit. and Charles V. Hamilton, The Black Preacher.

73. Interviews with Harlem residents and Haryou staff.

74. I have observed key Haryou decision makers consult with "pork chop" in the effort to get a "effl" for what the Harlem grass roots community's social climate is at varying points and notably at some moment of community crisis.

75. Field ovservations and interviews.

76. There are a variety of referrents for this idea. Examples can be found in the Economic Opportunity Act of 1965, as amended; also see Daniel C. Moynihan, Maximum Feasible Misunderstanding; and Kenneth B. Clark, A Relevant War Against Poverty, op. cit.

77. Certainly this was true during the public attacks related to Project Uplife (PUL) where community support was crucial. The rioting of the summers of 1964 and 1968 are additional moments of crisis in which such leadership was important.

78. See Commentary in Chapter II and above.

79. This comment is elaborated upon as my analysis proceeds. It is a cue to the reader regarding the importance of specific types of leaders at specific points in Haryou's development. I will expand my view concerning the organizational requirements for certain leadership skills and characteristics during each of the developmental periods conceptualized for the study.

CHAPTER 4

HARYOU: A RESPONSE TO HARLEM COMMUNITY NEEDS

In 1954, the momentum National decision, that "Separate but Equal" doctrines inherent in the 1896 decisions of Plessy vs. Ferguson were unconstitutional, resulting from the outcomes of the Federal Court suit involving five school cases Brown vs. The Topeka Board of Education; and in which racial segregation in public education was legally struck down--ushered in a new wave of enthusiasm and race consciousness in black communities throughout the nation.[1] Harlem, conscious of its identity, views the occasion with reserved optimism.[2] Northern urban communities, generally, tend to associate the new Court Decisions with the problems of the South, as traditionally public education in the North has been 'legally' desegregated. Increased awareness on the part of Harlem's leaders regarding the effects of "De Facto" segregation on the educational and residential opportunities of blacks, however, does spark renewed attention to the issues surrounding 'fair housing' movements. The fair housing movement is essentially a strategy conceived as a component of the newly sparked civil rights movement.[3] Its origins are traceable to the 1940s during that period when public housing and its potential function as a mechanism for breaking down barriers to racially integrated residential communities is at its hiatus.[4] The leadership roles played by organizations like the National Committee Against Discrimination In Housing, The Ethical Culture Society of New York, The New York Urban League and the National Association for the Advancement of Colored People; and spearheaded by men like Algernon D. Black, Paget Alves, Jack Wood and Robert Weaver are important in making inroads in the provision of open housing communities.[5] Restrictive covenants as strategies for maintaining racial exclusion in residential communities, are adjudicated 'unconstitutional' throughout Northern areas, as the direct result of these leaders efforts. Legislative mandates, respecting publicly subsidized 'Urban Renewal' or semi-private construction programs being pursued on a non-racially discriminatory basis, are directly effected by the work of these organizations; and finally, the emergence of the Federal Department of Housing and Urban Development is facilitated by their persistence.[6]

Despite the commitments of these organizations to effectively open opportunity for Northern Blacks, they are unable to gain any real momentum in Harlem. Viewed, primarily as 'middle class' organizations, interested primarily in helping affluent blacks make 'token' inroads to racially exclusive communities, the leaders and their movement are discarded as 'irrelevant' by the bulk of Harlem's blacks.[7] The community mood is one which rejects the idea that one must leave Harlem to achieve; that only by racially integrating can one arrive at the opportunity for experiencing a community of excellence.[8]

The momentum and thrust of the civil rights movement, grows in the years immediately following the Brown decision. The crescendo of events grows as the Montgomery Bus boycott episode in Montgomery, Alabama, adds a new dimension to the American Black community's demands for equality.

64

Dr. Martin Luther King Jr.'s emergence as the leader of the contemporary Southern Christian Leadership Conference (SCLC), in Alabama, is supplemented by the emergence of additional leaders and movements sparked throughout the Nation. The Freedom Rides and Student Sit-Ins; the coordinative protest and confrontation actions of the Student Non-Violent Coordinating Committee (SNCC), under the leadership of John Lewis, James Forman and later Stokely Carmichael; the civil rights and social action demonstrations of The Congress of Racial Equality under the leadership of James Farmer, (CORE had been active since 1942) Floyd McKissick and later, Roy Innis; each lend their talents and commitments to the continuing struggle for human dignity.[9]

The network of Harlem organizations and leaders commit themselves to the struggle through a variety of channels. A Philip Randolph, proverbial Harlem sage and institutional inspirationalist leader of the International Brotherhood of Sleeping Car Porters, seizes the historical moment to gaud organized labor to take a stand on the issue of civil rights in northern communities.[10] This is not a new role for Randolph. In 1925, he is among the activists in the struggle for the rights of Harlemites. He organzied and directed the black communities first 'March on Washington' in 1941 in protest of treatment being afforded blacks in the War economy work force, and thus played a leadership role in moving President Franklin D. Roosevelt to the issuance of the first executive order circumscribing discrimination in government employment.[11] The order eventually led to the Federal Fair Employment Act. Randolph later (1960), organized the Negro American Labor Council, headquartered on 125th Street in Harlem. The NALC, was established as the direct result of leadership conflict within the AF of L-CIO involving Randolph (then vice-president) and George Meany, its president. The leadership of the AF of L-CIO had been under criticism from Randolph and another of Harlem's civil rights leaders, Norman Hill, Associate Director of the A. Philip Randolph Institute. At one point during the AF of L-CIO national convention, Meany, angered at charges levied by Randolph screamed, "Phil, who in the hell made you the guardian of all the Negroes in America?"[12] It was shortly after this episode, and Randolph's censure by the organization's executive committee, that the new NALC was formed. Today the organization has 35 local chapters and in excess of 10,000 members. One of A. Philip Randolph's key lieutenants during these years becomes a major figure in the Haryou program, L. Joseph Overton.

There are innumerable examples of Harlemites 'personal and organizational' involvements in the movement during these years; but the civil rights movement of the 1950s and early 1960s is fundamentally a Southern one. In only two instances, for example, does the new mandate respecting racial exclusion become a matter for the courts in New York City. In 1962, a suit accusing the New York City Board of Education of using 'racial quotas' is lodged in U.S. District Court on behalf of Negro and Puerto Rican children; and earlier, in 1957, New York City became the first Urban community to legislate against racial or religious discrimination in the housing market, with the adoption of the Fair Housing Practices Law (December 5th).[13]

This, then represents part of the social climate in which the conceptulization of Haryou occurs.

Haryou, on the other hand, is an outgrowth of a series of institutional developmental processes and forces which have little to do with the civil rights movement. The program, initially represents an 'idea' "conceived in the general conflict, the normative turmoil, the persistent tensions which comprise the Harlem ghetto';[14] and rooted in the peculiar

social history reviewed above. Haryou is a 'functional' idea born of
the successful experiences of Harlem's leadership during the community's
history. It is functional in the sense that it presents to the Harlem
community, a new opportunity for building upon positive achievements
of the past; a new Harlem Rennaissance. The approximate 40 years experience of Harlem's people, and her leaders, is an indication that,

> Success in removing some barriers feeds the idea of personal
> and community effectiveness and provides the strength and the
> motivation for increased activity.[15]

This is the perspective within which the visionaries of the Haryou idea
initially conceive the program.

But visions are luxuries, shortlived, in the black experience.
And in Harlem, dreams are the stuff of which the next days 'number'
is made; and not the stuff upon which social change is planned. Thus
Haryou becomes a 'creature of controversy' at the moment it begins to
be objectified as an action plan.

Haryou's history begins as the mind-child of the Harlem Neighborhoods Association, (HANA).[16] The drafters of the original Haryou document Youth In The Ghetto: A Study of the Consequences of Powerlessness,
affirm,

> In attempting to acknowledge its gratitude to the Harlem Neigh-
> borhoods Association, (HANA), Haryou is in the awkward position
> of a child seeking to express its feelings toward a parent.[17]

Hana was founded in December, 1958 as the successor to the twenty
year old Central Harlem Council for Community Planning (CHC).[18] CHC
had been the regional arm of the former Welfare and Health Council of
New York and had played an important role in the development of health
and social services in Harlem.[19] Hana was founded to expand the organization to include a larger degree of citizen participation. The 'grass
roots' emphasis was embodied in the inclusion of the word-neighborhoods-
in the name and as the focus of the new association. Hana was incorporated under the membership corporation laws of New York State in April,
1960 and was granted tax exempt status by the United States Treasury in
June, 1961.[20]

The organization's major objective is to strengthen family life
through the provision of improved health and social services. Hana
is oriented to the field of social work (and particularly community organization), for its methods and techniques. Its program is conceived
of as a process in which the people act to meet their own needs. The
major activities of the organization are carried out via citizens committees for health, mental health, recreation, schools and youth. The
program priorities announced by the organization in 1961, are

1. to work with block and neighborhood associations as channels
   of neighborhood development and citizen education
2. to create a Youth Services Council through which agencies
   serving youth, parents groups and churches, can work for
   effective solutions to the needs of youth; and
3. to create a Harlem Council as a public health education
   and social action channel for the citizens and health
   agencies of the community.

It is the second of these priorities which eventuates in the HARYOU
concept. The consultant chairman of the Hana education committee is a
Social Psychologist, at the City College of New York, (now The City University CUNY), and also co-director of the Harlem Northside Center for
Child Development, Dr. Kenneth B. Clark. Dr. Clark, who I earlier identified as a creative elite leader, was born in the Panama Canal Zone, July
24, 1914, and came to Harlem as a youngster. He recounts, that during

his early life in the community, he "first learned about love, about cruelty, about sacrifice, about cowardice, about bombast in Harlem".[21] A critical observer of the Harlem scene for much of his professional life, Dr. Clark has been one of the community's most outspoken leaders. As the social science consultant for the legal and educational division of the NAACP during the early 1950s, his research and testimony during the historic school desegregation cases of the U.S. Supreme Court were instrumental in the eventual Brown decision. Among Dr. Clark's literary contributions, his Dark Ghetto, stands out as perhaps the most critical account of ghetto pathology yet written. A stinging analysis of this power and politics of Harlem during his tenure as Director of the Haryou program, Dark Ghetto, became Clark's final word on what served as a traumatic personal leadership experience.[22] A recipient of the Spingarn Medal, Clark became the first black member of the New York State Board of Regents in 1966. Dr. Clark's reputation as a leader in the field of education, and his respected position in the Harlem professional community were responsible for his assumption of the chairmanship of HANA's education committee and ultimately, HARYOU.

Hana's initial plan is to establish a Harlem Youth Services Council.

The need for this project stems from the community's concern with the future of its young people. The lack of services is well documented in its board outline and much public discussion takes place on what to do. Agencies, churches and civic groups make notable efforts to meet the need.[23]

Through HANA's committee efforts a start is made. The organizations view as to what is needed involved,

a community strategy for youth services which must include strengthening the cooperative efforts of the agencies and strengthening their relationships with the community at large.[24]

It is HANA's perspective, on the need to develop new youth services, that the development of the Haryou program emerges.

Hana's design for youth services is to channel the concern of the community into a concerted effort to 'cut into' the statistics at strategic points. Preventative intervention would be the major guideline.[25]

"Starting at the neighborhood level",[26] Hana proposes the creation of a structure which is to involve the total Harlem community.

Community education and coordination and the development of a stronger social services pattern will aim to create a new community climate--a climate of increased positive expectation for Harlem's youth.[5]

The names of Milton Yale, Harriet I. Pickens, Mrs. Mamie Brunson, Arthur Reed, Mrs. Sieux Taylor, the Honorable Herb Evans, J. Raymond Jones, Marvin Riley, Dr. James Jones, Kenneth Marshal, Clifford Alexander, Cyril Tyson, Charles Ward, Reverend David W. Barry, Reverend Eugene Callendar, Lillian C. Lampkin, Edward S. Lewis, Arthur C. Logan, Emma S. Penn, Father M. Moran Weston, Alice Arrington, Gladys Thorne and Evaline Payne; in addition to those of Dr. Kenneth Clark, Adam Clayton Powell and Livingston Wingate; are all relevant to our considerations here, for functional leadership.[29]

As a social work student in community organization and under the astute observational tutelage of Milton Yale, I was in the position during these early days of Haryou's formation to observe much of the function and decision making involving many of the above leaders.[30] The fascinating process of organizational and leadership cooperation, which as the Haryou project moves closer to realization evolves into competition, crisis and sabotage, serve as relevant analytical references for insight regarding leadership aspirations and objectives.[31]

In the midst of much of the HANA planning outlined above, an incident occurs, which 'triggers' the emergence of HARYOU.

Early in 1961, the New York Times carried a story which announced that the New York City Youth Board and the Community Mental Health Board had entered into a contract with the Jewish Board of Guardians, for an extension of the Youth Board's Street program to include psychiatric services.[32] This program, which would be run and stagged by the Jewish Board of Guardians, was introduced into three communities of the City. Harlem was one of these communities; (as a street club worker for the NYCYB, I recall a similar proposal was to be launched in Brownsville, Brooklyn, where my unit was). Investigation revealed that none of the agencies in Harlem community were consulted or in any way involved in the planning or development of this proposed program. Representatives of the relevant social agencies, civic groups and churches were called together to protest "this form of social welfare colonialism".[33]

Letters of protest were sent to the Mayor, to the Director of the Youth Board, and to the head of the Community Mental Health Board. The community group acting within the framework of HANA, and comprised of the leadership outlined above, sustained its protests and insisted that any meaningful program for Harlem Youth had to involve, both in its planning and in its program stages, those agencies and groups within the community which had responsibility for day to day work with the youth of the community. One later researcher of this aspect of the Haryou process, suggested this point, that Mayor Robert F. Wagner meet with the HANA delegation, and as the direct result of the advocacy of such friends of HANA as J. Raymond Jones, and James R. Dumpson, Commissioner of the Department of Welfare for the City of New York, gained the Mayor's endorsement of the HANA program for Harlem youth. Wagner designated his Deputy City Administrator, Henry Cohen the responsibility for working with the representatives of the Harlem community in developing the machinery for the new approach to the problems of the community's youth.[34]

It is subsequently the result of Cohen's involvement that David Hackett, the executive director of the President's Committee on Juvenile Delinquency, becomes aware of and interested in the Haryou idea. Many of the HANA representatives were suspicious, and somewhat apprehensive about the involvement of a federal representative in the planning consideration. The reason given for this concern relates to the view of Cohen's action as a delaying tactic in the City's interest, but to Harlem's disadvantage. There was another suspicion. Federal governmental involvement in the new idea for a comprehensive program for Harlem's youth also portends the involvement of Harlem's Congressional representative. The Reverend Adam Clayton Powell's name to much of the HANA leadership represents anathema.[35] But 1961, in addition to its relevance as the year during which HARYOU hits the drawing board, is also the year when Powell becomes chairman of the powerful House of Representatives Labor and Education Committee; that committee through which appropriations of Federal expenditures allocated to the President's Committee on J.D. must pass.[36] It is necessary, if one is to understand the perspective of Powell as 'the enemy' to be familiar with the historically significant conflict between the politician and the intellectual in Harlem. Anderson and DuBois alluded to earlier, represent but one example. In tracing Powell's contributions to Harlem as its community representative, first as City Councilman, and finally as congressional representative, the conflict seems contradictory. Powell, for example in addition to the above founded the People's Voice, and was the magazine's editor in chief, and co-publisher, was district Delegate to the Parliamentary World Conference in Geneva in 1961; was decorated Knight of the Golden Cross in Ethiopa; was a member of the World Association of Parilamentarians on World Government, and authored a number of books. Clearly his career is marked by meaningful contributions to Harlem and the World.[37]

Yet in the matter of Haryou, he is projected as 'the corrupter'. A role, which, based on my personal contacts with him during the Haryou crisis seemed inconsistent.[38] Despite the concerns expressed by the HANA professionals the program of planning for Haryou proceeds.

On April 12, 1962, at a meeting of the Board of Directors of the Harlem Neighborhoods Association, Inc., the Reverend Eugene S. Callendar, Chairman of HANA, appointed a committee for the following responsibilities.[39]

1. To recommend to the Board of Directors of HANA an appropriate and effective machinery: (A) for planning a comprehensive youth services program for the Central Harlem Community (B) for submitting a proposal to the appropriate Federal, State and City agencies and private foundations for funds to plan and operate such a program (C) for disbursing such funds and coordinating the over-all program if funds are obtained.
2. The Committee was also charged with the responsibility for planning an appropriate conference to be called by the Mayor of the City of New York in order to involve community leaders in the planning stage of the over-all program.
3. The final responsibility of the Committee was to develop a proposal to be submitted to the Federal Government and private foundations for a grant in support of a planning and pilot program for a comprehensive youth services program involving the various youth services agencies and other appropriate institutions in the Central Harlem community.

The above committee's report recommended the following:

It is hereby recommended, that the Board of Directors of HANA create a new and independent structure consisting of individuals who meet the above standards and whose functions would be to fulfill the responsibilities already stated. This group of individuals would act as a Board of Trustees for the comprehensive youth services program in the Central Harlem community.

It is strongly recommended that such a Board should be representative of HANA, major social agencies, including child care and family agencies, community organization groups, religious groups, labor business, public schools, neighboring colleges and other relevant groups in the community.

At the first meeting of this new Proposal and Machinery Committee, it was agreed unanimously that the members of the Committee with the addition of Reverend Eugene S. Callendar, Chairman of HANA and Reverend W. Barry, Executive Director of the New York City Mission Society would become the incorporators of the new organizational entity. As incorporators they would have the responsibility of selecting an appropriate name for the corporation and selecting the individuals who would comprise the new board.

The name agreed upon for the new Corporation is:
HARLEM YOUTH OPPORTUNITIES UNLIMITED, INC.
The Incorporators and founders of Haryou, Inc. are:

Reverend David W. Barry
Reverend Eugene S. Callendar
Commissioner James R. Dumpson
Mr. J. Raymond Jones
Dr. Edward S. Lewis
Monsignor Gregory Mooney
Mrs. Emma Penn
Reverend M. Moran Weston
Dr. Kenneth B. Clark, Chairman

A formidable and impressive listing, this group was to embark
upon selecting additional Board members utilizing the following criteria:

> That the individuals selected inspire and have the confidence
> of the people of the Central Harlem Community; that they
> have outstanding competence, background training, experience
> in relevant spheres of community activity and planning; and
> that they be individuals who are known and respected for
> soundness and validity of judgement.[40]

> With these acts, Haryou was officially born.
> HANA, however,
> was not content to produce a single child. HANA simultane-
> ously had two offspring, one direct (HARYOU), and one adopted
> (Associated Community Teams). Politics is always a factor
> when one deals with the federal government, and Haryou was no
> exception to the general rule. In this case, Adam Clayton
> Powell was the political fact.[41]

Powell had backed Lyndon Johnson for the Democratic nomination in 1960.
When Kennedy was nominated, Powell gave Kennedy strong support both
because Kennedy was a democrat, and because it was all too apparent
that Harlem would never support Richard Nixon. Because Powell is
chairman of the House Committee on Education and Labor, it is impossible for any important education or labor bills to pass Congress without
support from Powell. For these important reasons, accoring to Krosney,
The Kennedy Administration had an agreement with Powell that any money
to come into Harlem would come through him; and further, that such a
deal should be made is hardly unreasonable in an era when a congressman is chiefly distinguishable by his ability to garner federal patronage.[42] Nor was it unreasonable that the Kennedy administration should
be party to such an agreement. Powell, the most powerful Negro law-
maker in the country, was also one of the ten most powerful Congress-
men in the country. As chairman of the House Committee on Education
and Labor, he could exercise a personal veto on almost any domestic
project which involved these areas, and on many more as well. To alienate such a powerful Congressman for anything but the most vital of
reasons was more than bad politics--it would have been stupidity.[43]

To say, that, "an interesting situation presented itself",[44] is
to underestimate the nuances and pressures that were operative in Central
Harlem during this period. It is true that the President's Committee
wanted to fund Haryou because of Clark's reputation, and that the
dilemma of doing so was inherent in the requirement for such funding
residing in the offices of Powell; that HANA had the intellectual talent
in Kenneth Clark and other professionals, but that Powell had a commitment to ACT.[45] As formulated by the President's Committee with the
approval of both Adam Powell and Kenneth Clark, Haryou would be devoted
to planning on a theoretical level while ACT would be involved in ex-
perimental action programs operative within the Harlem community. And
finally and at some subsequent time, the two organizations would merge

so as to facilitate funding through one major conduit. This presumed 'merger', becomes a critical issue of antagonism and conflict
between Powell's forces and Kenneth Clark.46
    My arrival at HANA occurs at this juncture in Haryou's formu-
lation. It is September 1962, and the actual planning for the newly
spun-off program is in full swing. Though my specific work assignments are related to organizational efforts tied into HANA's Housing
Committee, the intriguing activities surrounding the Haryou program
are inescapable. Milton Yale's perspective on Haryou at the time
is that it is a program which has great 'potential' for helping resolve some of the community's problems, but that it may be doomed to
a take-over by forces outside of its HANA sponsors.47 Milton seemed
committed to keeping me from getting involved in any way with the
Haryou activity. As I continued expressing interest as to what was
really happening with the program, I found that others of the professional HANA staff viewed Haryou as a program "to stay away from".
At one point when talking with another staff worker for HANA's Housing
Committee about my career plans upon completion of graduate training,
including a beginning practice at HARYOU, she flared and responded
"you'd better stay away from that Haryou thing". Continued prodding
as to why, only illicited further warnings about the program's tenuous-
ness and political intrigue.
    This tended to be the general response to questions respecting
Haryou during this period. It was as if the Agency, once having become separately incorporated, had changed in its importance to HANA
and much of the professional community which originally sponsored it.
In discussion, for example, with clergymen, vestrymen and other friends
at St. Philips Church, I received comparable kinds of 'warnings' and
was advised to observe the development of Haryou from a distance before
getting involved.48 In addition to these reactions, there seemed in
the Harlem community to be a sense of suspicion about the new Haryou
project. People were suspicious about the seeming secrecy enshrouding
the Haryou planning stage. Lay people functioning in the variety of
black organizations connected (loosely) to HANA wanted to know
        why is it necessary for them to go off somewhere in the
        mountains, out of the community to plan. Their just spending
        money to party--that's all
and
        hell, its--(HARYOU), really just another political plumb
        for the politicians--not about doing anything for people
        in Harlem.49

    Despite the variety of warnings and suspicions, I found myself
fascinated by the prospects held out for the community by the Haryou
venture. Milton Yale sensing this continuing interest began to
suggest that I talk with individual leaders associated with the
effort. My first opportunity to meet Dr. Clark occurred in a Hana
meeting where Dr. James Jones and Milton Yale were also present. The
purpose of the meeting was to discuss certain aspects of the HARYOU
proposal then being written. I remember Clark's quivering, seemingly
hoarse voice as he talked about the progress of the planning grant. I
also remember how quietly Dr. Jones was during the entire course of the
meeting. It struck me as interesting that he didn't say a word. After
the meeting Milton Yale asked my impression of Clark. My response was
that I had anticipated a more dynamic kind of person, given Dr. Clark's
reputation and contributions in the freedom struggle. He then said,
        you shouldn't judge Ken Clark by his seeming composure, because
        underneath he is seething with anger and emotion about what's

71

happening to Harlem.

It was a comment about the man which I have since referred to in the variety of subsequent meetings and contacts experiences with him.[50]

In conferring with other of the HANA leadership involved with HARYOU, I received varied opinions and insight into their perspectives on the programs relevance. Mrs. Emma Penn, a beautiful woman in her early 60s who has been involved in community affairs for 30 years or more, impressed me as a genuine concerned and brilliant person.[52] She has a quiet, graceful way about her which can disarm the insensitive interviewer, but immediately advised the astute observer that she is experienced in community affairs in Harlem. Mrs. Penn is one of Clark's staunch supporters upon his involvement in HANA and shared with me her feelings of confidence in his ability to make the HARYOU program a success. Her belief, that, "If anyone can get the new program idea across, its Ken Clark",[52] suggests her point of view.

Harriet Pickens, another of the HANA leaders in the early planning stages of HARYOU, was renowned in the Harlem community. She is descended from a family, historically in the avant guarde of black leadership in New York (see Chapter 1); and was, herself, at one time considered one of Harlem's most outspoken radicals.[53] I can recall being very impressed by Miss Pickens' insight and sharpness while dealing with strategies for launching the Haryou program, and some years later, while participating in Haryou directly.[54] I learned much more about this leader's perspective on the Haryou enterprise during talks in the course of driving her to her home after the proverbial late HANA board meetings. On one of these occasions she informed me that she had some concerns about how Clark would hold up under the kinds of community pressures that were imminent upon Haryou's launching. Never questioning Clark's sincerity, or brilliance as a 'thinker', she did feel that "he is out of his element when it comes to dealing with the political and grass roots Harlem scene".[55] Of Milton Yale, she would say "now Milton's a really shrewd professional--his problem is that he's white at the wrong time, in the wrong place".[56] On one occasion, as I was expressing my view of Miss Pickens as truly 'tough minded' to Milton Yale, he responded "Harriet's quiet now compared to what she was like 15 years ago; then she was really militant."[57]

Early contacts with other of HANA's leadership during these days continued to impress upon me the functional and interwoven nature of leadership in Harlem. Other members of the HANA board whose positions in the community facilitate HARYOU's emergence such as Eugene Callendar, J. Raymond Jones, Alice Arrington, Lillian C. Lampkin and Dr. M. Moran Weston are all part of this pattern. Their professional and institutional positions in and out of Harlem make their sponsorship of the new program a matter to be taken seriously by the total community.[58]

Reverend Eugene Callendar, HANA Board Chairman, during this period (Callendar later assumes the chairmanship of Haryou) is a distinguished Minister at Harlem's Church of the Master. My conferences with Reverend Callendar, inclusive of a recent, brief interview, during the present study, are suggestive that his view of Haryou as a social mechanism for the identification and emergence of functional leadership in Harlem is sound. Callendar, in addition to his ministry, is currently Director of New York City's Urban Coalition, and originator commentor of the television program Positively Black. His chairmanship of the HARYOU board occurred at perhaps the most critical stage in the organization's experience, and his insights regarding the major issues requiring civic leadership in the Harlem community at the time are discussed below.

Perhaps the major importance of recapitulating the contributions of

HANA to the development and implementation of HARYOU resides in the finding that many of the HANA leaders, later become key policy makers on the HARYOU Board of Directors. Thus it is clear that the interconnectiveness of leadership elements in Harlem play a major role in the organization's position as a community leadership system. On the other hand, the 'spin-off' of Haryou from HANA marks the effective point at which certain of HANA's leaders divorce themselves from any participation.

In a final sense, the separation of the organizations occurs somewhat traumatically. According to Youth In The Ghetto,

> an objective evaluation of the activities of this agency (HANA) during the past two years would lead to the conclusion that it is not now able to develop and sustain any important social action-oriented community or neighborhood organization program because of its structural and organizational weaknesses, its lack of strong professional leadership, the diffuseness of its lack of planning and follow through, and the inadequacy of its budget and staff. These weaknesses are recognized and attempts at reform are now being initiated by the Board of Directors.[59]

Even so brief a review of the involvement of HANA's executive and policy making Board leadership as provided thus far suggests that the HARYOU findings represent organizational 'sabotage' with respect to HANA. Given the commitment and time spent by HANA's Milton Yale in developing the HARYOU proposal with Doctors Clark and Jones; and the substantive involvement of HANA's leadership in negotiating and planning the eventual launching, it is my judgement that the organization deserved better than the above quotation suggests.[60]

In an interview with the current executive director of HANA, the function of discarding HANA as an irrelevant organization for the purpose of social action and neighborhood organization is clarified. The seeming reneging on the 'deal' that would have given HANA the responsibility for organizaing the Neighborhood Boards program as opposed to Haryou, stripped the organization of both the possibility for new funding as well as renewed relevance in the community.[61] There are those who attribute the undercutting of HANA, to the fact that her executive director was white; a position which loses its substance given the change in leadership shortly after the funding of the program, (James Solar, a black social worker, became HANA's executive director, subsequently); others postulate that had the Neighborhood Boards been structured under HANA, they might have been a political threat to the existent Powell forces in Harlem. This latter consideration is discussed in the next chapter as an element in the ultimate conflict involving Clark, Powell and J. Raymond Jones.

It is in the sense that the drafters of the HARYOU program view existent social services in Harlem as "inadequate", that they project a newer design for effectively meeting the community's human needs.[62] The approach is rooted in the commitment to salvaging Harlem's youth utilizing strategies of social action and institutional change. It is further a commitment to broadening the black professional's base in the newly emerging social welfare industry.[63] The fact, thus, that most of the participants in the Haryou planning enterprise, and later, those who implement the project, are essentially voluntary, civic leaders (as opposed to paid staff or board members), takes on a special significance.

The constant and pervasive emphasis on youth with respect to the HARYOU program triggers a peculiar antagonism within the Harlem community. For one consequence of the focus, unintended or not, is the perspective within sectors of the grass roots adult community that their participation in the new process is irrelevant. It appears to many that they are being passed over as 'unsalvageable". The resentments which result are played out in a variety of ways; ranging from disallowing their children's participation, through to articulated anger directed at the HARYOU effort. I have, during the course of interviews with Haryou board members, found many who resented the fact that,

> kids were making more money than their parents during the early years of Haryou--nobody seemed willing to deal with the problem of unemployed fathers or other adults in the family[64]

and

> that damn Haryou has got the young people disrespecting anybody over 30 years old--as if nothing has ever been done in the community to help--until they came--it's crazy[65]

More sophisticated objections relate to the programs tendency to overlook local community civic leadership when staffing the Haryou operation;

> they brought people in to Haryou for those jobs, who'd never seen Harlem before, supposed elites of some kind; but people who gave the average community person the feeling that they were being looked down on [66]

was the way one community contact expressed the concern.

The current chairman of the Haryou board, when asked why he had only recently (within the last three years), become involved in Haryou--given his 25 years of civic activity; responded that the organization's leadership, intitally seemed predisposed not to include representation from the local political clubs and organizations.[67]

Thus is would seem that the HARYOU theoretical approach which postured the program as salvaging the youth of Harlem from their environing "ghetto pathology" was often interpreted as saving them from the adult population; including their parents in some instances.[68] Now, irrespective of what one's theoretical bias may be respecting, even such matters as whether parents are those best equipped to raise their children; to codify and publicize such a position as the rationale for launching a community based program is a slap in the face to the adults in that community.[69] It was in Harlem.

The manifestations of these resentments reside in such statements as "the program is just a political porkbarrel".[70] Or "they never really intended to do anything for the community--just themselves".[71] And provides a somewhat different view of James Hicks' Amsterdam News editorial during the organization's planning stage:

> I'm fed up with social workers in Harlem because the average social worker in Harlem prostitutes the misery of the community and spends three quarters of his time trying to convert that misery into dollars and cents to put in his own pocket...

> So the folks downtown say in unison to the Harlem "expert": What can we do for these people to prevent this?

> This is what our expert is waiting for.

> I don't have all the answers, gentlemen, he says. But I think I'm on the right track toward a solution to the problem. With about $250,000 I could pull together a research team of emimnent social workers, psychologists, psychiatrist, anthropologists-- the whole bit-- and these young men will come up with the answer for you in the eighteen months.

> "In other words" say the City Fathers, "you need $250,000 to get started, is that right?"

And so the Harlem expert, whom you don't even know, and who doesn't even know you, hops on the "A" train with a quarter of a million dollars of your money and mine to spend studying you.[71]

Harlem felt indicted by a document and an approach which was hailed by the white power structure as "a milestone", in community analysis; and that relegated the community and its institutions to a pathological state.[72] This was not the intent of Haryou's designers. Current analysis of the in fact results however and the perspective held re: many of those at the top echelons of the program's leadership, suggest these to be among the unintended or unanticipated consequences.[73] The major point to be made is that it reflects either a lack of sensitivity as to the history of Harlem's community leadership struggle, and the subsequent failure to build upon existing experience at the grass roots level; or, on the other hand a disregard for existing community systems and leadership. Certain of Krosney's insights regarding Dr. Clark, for example are illuminating with regard to this perspective, as he writes: "Clark consolidated a position as "the Negro representative", on any commission, in any consultant's job in which a psychologist sympathetic to the problems of the Negro community was needed.[74] As much as any man he has benefitted by the "ticket balancing" to which a democratic society must be responsive.[75] There was, however, a price to public prominence, his pursuit of success, and his genuine brilliance and accomplishment. As early as 1960, he had come to be resented in the Negro community. His consultant work, his joint directorship, with his wife, Mamie, of the Northside Center for Child Development, his staff position at City College, garnered him a family income which a friend estimates at well over $50,000. The price of success and an integrated life was a separation from the problems of the lower-class Negroes on which, to a large extend, he built his career. Harlem has lingered as a sore in the back of his mind. Yet years ago he had moved out of New York City to a lovely home in Hastings. Clark had no power base in Harlem or any deep connection with the community.[76]

Clark essentially compounded his weak position as the Director of the Haryou effort by subsequently bringing a cadre of young men, truly brilliant in their own right--granted--but nevertheless as unknown and 'unknowning about the history and leadership nuances of Harlem as himself".[77]

The writer's early experience with the emerging Haryou enterprise provides an additional view. It is early 1962; and one evening while discussing my work at the New York City Youth Board Street Club program with members of my family (at the home of in-laws in Harlem), find myself interested in the remarks of one of my young brother-in-laws teenage friends, regarding a new program in the community called Haryou. He seems very excited about the new project; as according to him, it provides opportunity for youths to work in the community on "surveys and things", and "get paid for it". Presenting, in addition examples in which 'rap sessions' dealing with civil rights and community action programs were also active, I found myself wanting to see what was happening. "After all", I mused, "I'm an involved youth worker, with street gangs, maybe I can find something challenging to do with this HARYOU project." I decided to go to the Harlem "Y", and check things out.

My first (and for some time lasting), impression as I walked into the Harlem YMCA building was that I was not supposed to be there. Now I had been going to this "Y" most of my life. It is an institution where most of my friends and I had participated in clubs, dances, sports activities and other community functions; and suddenly I found myself standing at some receptionists desk receiving the kinds of looks which suggested that I had no business there at all. I was advised that I could see the Director regarding any questions about the program and was pointed in his direction. As I walked through what had formerly been the main vestibule and Men's lounge of the "Y" I had known, I was struck with the numbers of unfamiliar faces at desks placed somewhat randomly. As soon as I saw the director, I knew as much about HARYOU as I wanted or needed to. I had spend the last five to ten minutes wandering amidst a sea of strange faces, only to be confronted with a dude whose facade and appearance suggested that if he knew anything at all about Harlem; it was from the perspective of a member of the "Jack and Jills", an elite upper middle class fair skinned group of young adults who historically shunned associating with Harlem's poor. It may have been an unfair assessment; but its the one I made. I turned and left HARYOU as fast as I could It was not until my residence as a Masters student, placed at HANA, that I again viewed HARYOU with anything less than disdain.

The course of events and experiences which ultimately lead to my becoming an executive at HARYOU and later director of Harlem's Youth Unlimited program are inevitable, given the sense in which I shared this early feeling of alienation from a program, presumably, designed to help my community.

These analytical and experiental comments regarding the conception, planning and early implementation of the Haryou program, are preliminary to establishing the framework in which functional leadership is analyzed. This first phase was one in which it would have been to Haryou's advantage to have had commutator leadership types participating in various staff and volunteer positions. The fact that it was the creative elite who dominated the scene tended to alienate even further, an already suspicious and distrustful indigenous community population. At a time then, when the organizational and community requirements demanded the informal; subjective and warm influences of the grass roots representative; only the aloof objective and intellectual "professional" was discernable. It is now time to comment upon certain assumptions regarding Haryou policy, function and leadership decision as these are responsible for and responsive to, community conflict and crisis.

FOOTNOTES TO CHAPTER IV

1. The Negro Handbook, by editors of Ebony. (Johnson Publishing Company, Inc., 1966), pages 126-127. "The Supreme Court Desegregation Decision of 1954". See also, Youth in the Ghetto, A Study of the Consequences of Powerlessness, (HARYOU) pages 2 and 4. Stokely Carmichael and Charles V. Hamilton, Black Power, The Politics of Liberation in America (Vintage Books, N.Y., Division of Random House), pages 155-157.

2. John Henrik Clark, Harlem A Community in Transition (The Citadel Press), N.Y., pages 3-10; see also Langston Hughes, The Harlem Riot-1964; op. cit., pages 214-220. My observations during the period as a student and community participant; buttressed by interviews conducted for this analysis suggest that Harlemites viewed these decisions as "good for the South but irrelevant for us". Also see Dr. Kenneth B. Clark's Report of the National Advisory Commission on Civil Disorders (Kerner Commission), page 483.

3. Langston Hughes, op. cit., ibid; Report of the National Advisory Commission on Civil Disorders (Kerner Commission) Bantom Books pages 440-441.

4. Charles Abrams, The Housing Problem and the Negro, Daedalus; Journal of the American Academy of Arts and Sciences (Winter 1966) Volume 95, Number 1, pages 64-76; see also Eunice and George Grier, Equality and Beyond: Housing Segregation in the Great Society; op. cit., pages 77-106. See also Charles Abrams, Forbidden Neighbors, (N.Y. 1955), and Eunice and George Grier's, Privately Developed Interracial Housing (Berkeley, California, 1960), Chapter VIII. Additional discussion in Luigi Laurenti, Property Values and Race (Berkeley California, 1960)

5. For elaboration on stragegies for overcoming housing discrimination as component of Civil Rights Movement see; Robert C. Weaver, "Class, Race and Urban Renewal", Land Economics, Vol.XXXVI, No. 3 (August 1960). L.K. Northwood, "The Threat and Potential of Urban Renewal," Journal of Intergroup Relations, Vol. II, No. 2 (Spring 1961), pages 101-114; also see Mel J. Ravity "Effects of Urban Renewal on Community Racial Patterns", Journal of Social Issues, Vol. XIII, No. 4 (1957), pages 38-49. See also Kenneth B. Clark, "The Civil Rights Movement; Momentum and Organization" in Daedalus; op. cit., pages 239-267.

6. The most complete and reliable source of up-to-date information

on the Status of Housing Anti-discrimination laws and
Ordinances throughout the nation is Trends in Housing,
published bi-monthly by the National Committee Against
Discrimination in Housing, 323 Lexington Avenue, New York,
New York. A comprehensive analysis of action at all governmental levels up to the period just before the Federal
Executive Order of 1962 will be found in Margaret Fischer
and Frances Levinson, Federal, State and Local Action Effecting Race and Housing, National Association of International Relations Officials, September 1962. Also see Housing
and Home Finance Agency Monthly Bulletin, Washington, D.C.
I am familiar with this field as the result of my tenure
as Director of the National Center for Fair Housing Organizations, a component program of the National Committee
Against Discrimination in housing during the period February
1966 to October 1967.

7.   Kenneth Clark, A Relevant War Against Poverty: A Study of Community Action Programs and Observable Social Change, N.J.
M.A.R.C. Also Youth In the Ghetto, op. cit. (Haryou) page 97.

8.   Interviews conducted during Course of Study. See also Carmichael
and Hamilton, op. cit., pages 147-177, and Youth in the
Ghetto, ibid.

9.   The reader is referred to the wealth of literature available for
further exploration of the Civil Rights Movement and its
leadership. See for example, Carmichael and Hamilton, Black
Power, op. cit.; Daedalus The Negro American (Speical issue
Fall 1965) Vol. I and II. James Baldwin and Kenneth Clark,
Black America, Accomodation and Confrontation in the Twentieth
Century (D.C. Heath and Company) 1963, Lerone Bennett, Jr.
Before The Mayflower: A History of the Negro in America
1619-1966, Third Edition (Johnson Publishing Company, Inc.,
Chicago). See also Bennett, Confrontation Black and White
(Penquin Books Inc., Baltimore); Report of the National
Advisory Commission on Civil Disorders, op. cit.; Sethard
Fischer (editor) Power and the Black Community: A Reader on
Racial Subordination in the United States; (Random House,
N.Y.) Stokely Carmichael, Stokely Speaks; Black Power and
Pan Africanism, (Random House) Richard P. Young (ed.),
Roots of Rebellion; The Evolution of Black Politics and
Protest since World War II (Harper and Row, NY, Evanston and
London). Joanne Grant (ed.), Black Protest (Fawcett Publi-
cations, Inc., Greenwich, Conn.). Kenneth Clark, Roy Wilkins,
Whitney Young, Jr., James Farmer, Martin Luther King, Jr.,
and James Farmer, "The Management of the Civil Rights
Struggle", in Alan F. Westin (ed.) Freedom Now! The Civil
Rights Struggle in America (N.Y. 1964). Lonis Lomax,
The Negro Revolt (NY, 1963) Howard Zinn, SNCC, The New
Abolitionists (Boston 1964).

10.   This section draws heavily from accounts given of Organized Labor
and Civil Rights found in The Negro Handbook: A Compilation.
Edited by Ebony, pages 205-210.

11.   Ibid.

12.   Ibid.

13.   Op. cit., pages 47-50. See also John Henrik Clark, Harlem A
       Community In Transition, op. cit., pages 214-220.

14.   Youth In the Ghetto, op. cit., page 21; and Clark, Dark Ghetto,
       op. cit. page (preface). Also John Henrik Clark, op. cit.,
       page 210.

15.   Youth in the Ghetto, page 120.

16.   Youth in the Ghetto, op. cit., pages 305-311. See acknowledge-
       ment and Unpublished Documents; A Program for Harlem's Youth:
       A Positive Approach to Youth Needs; proposed by H.A.N.A. The
       Harlem Neighborhoods Association (Dec. 1961); and A Proposal
       For the Planning of A Comprehensive Youth Services Program
       In Central Harlem, (Harlem Youth Opportunities Unlimited
       Inc., in Association with the Harlem Neighborhoods Association
       Inc.) under Public Law 087-274, May 15, 1962.

17.   Youth in the Ghetto, op. cit., Acknowledgement.

18.   H.A.N.A., op. cit., page 1.

19.   Ibid., also Youth in the Ghetto, op. cit., pages 291-311.

20.   Ibid.

21.   Clark, Dark Ghetto. See Introduction, page XV.

22.   Krosney, Beyond Welfare, op. cit., page 62.

23..   H.A.N.A. Proposal, op. cit., pages 4-6.

24.   Ibid.

25.   Ibid.

26.   Ibid.

27.   Ibid.

28.   Ibid.

29.   These individuals plan important roles as members of the Hana,
       and subsequently (in some instances), the Haryou Board of
       Directors.

30.   Milton Yale is during my student tenure at Hana, the Organization's
       Executive Director.

31.   Reference-Field Observation and interviews conducted with current
       Hana leadership.

32.   Youth in the Ghetto, op. cit., pages 22-28.

33. Ibid. page 23; the history of similar paternalistic approaches
     to social services in Harlem is alluded to in Chapter II
     of my dissertation. It grows from a sense of underestimating
     the leadership resources in Harlem, and the community's vul-
     nerability as a 'powerless' enclave.

34. Youth In the Ghetto, op. cit., ibid.

35. See Clark, Dark Ghetto, pages 164-168. Also Korsney, op. cit.,
     page 63.

36. Ibid.

37. Clark, op. cit., pages 164-165; also see The Negro Handbook, op.
     cit., page 411.

38. Interviews with Powell at Abyssinia Baptist Church, Summer 1964.

39. Joint Program and Planning proposal of Haryou and Hana (1962)
     Op. cit. This section draws heavily from various portions
     of the unpublished Board of Directors meetings.

40. Ibid.

41. Krosney, op. cit., page 40.

42. Ibid., page 41.

43. Ibid.

44. Ibid.

45. Ibid.

46. Ibid.

47. This section of references to dialogue with Hana resources
     reflects observations and analysis made during my internship
     as a graduate social work student.

48. As a life-time member of St. Philips I often consulted with these
     clergymen, particularly Father Harrison.

49. Comments recorded at Hana Board Meeting during summer 1963.

50. Most recently, at a speaking engagement in Albany New York
     (Fall 1973), at which time a colleague, accompanying me
     reiterated almost the exact words; I found myself again
     reflecting upon Yale's comment.

51. My experiences in observing Mrs. Penn occured within the above
     Student Internship.

52. Discussion at Mrs. Penn's home, Spring 1963.

53. Per-Conference with Milton Yale (Spring 1963).

54. While at a special Haryou Board Committee meeting, Summer, k968,

55. Comments during dialogue, Spring 1963.

56. Comments during dialogue, Spring 1963.

57. Conference with Milton Yale, Fall 1962.

58. This is an important element in these leaders functional relevance to the emerging Harlem program.

59. Youth in the Ghetto, op. cit., page 308.

60. This comment is also made from my awareness of certain of Hana's leadership's total commitment and involvement in launching the Haryou program. The endless negotiations with the municipality; the constant organizing and placating of competing community organizations and the mind exhausting late night meetings--all are symptoms of Hana's investments.

61. Interview conducted during Fall 1973.

62. Youth In The Ghetto, op. cit., pages 309-311; see also; Clark, Dark Ghetto, op. cit., pages 173-174; and Clark, Haryou: An Experiment, in John Henrik Clark, op. cit., page 211.

63. Ibid.

64. Interview with Haryou Board members during dissertation formulation.

65. Same reference as above. It is interesting in this regard that even among activists in the Haryou Neighborhood Boards-- the essentially adult program component of the project--this view was also reflected. The discrepancy seems to reside in the fact that adult neighborhood board members were volunteers, and thus received no financial inducements to participating. Youths, on the other hand, were paid for making comparable community contributions (i.e. organizing the indigenous population; conducting street campaigns re: Haryou programs and etc.). That the adult 'volunteers' could have used money, no less than the Youths-- is clearly demonstrated in statistics on unemployment and under-employment in Harlem. The priorities seemed skewed in the wrong direction.

66. Interview with newly elected Haryou Board member, Fall 1973.

67. Interview with Haryou Board member, fall 1973.

68. For an interesting perspective on this analytical view see, Joseph White's Toward a Black Psychology; White Theories Ignore Ghetto Life Styles, page 1-7.

69. Ibid.

70. Interviews with community residents.

71. Interviews with community residents.

72. <u>Youth in The Ghetto</u>, <u>op. cit.</u>, page 3.

73. It's impossible for one familiar with the rationales utilized for
   launching Haryou to escape this impression. The writings
   of Dr. Kenneth B. Clark, in particular, reflect a determined
   preoccupation with this theme. See--<u>Youth In The Ghetto</u>,
   page 309. Also see Clark, <u>Dark Ghetto</u>, <u>op. cit.</u>, page
   Introduction and Clark, <u>A Relevant War Against Poverty</u>, <u>op.</u>
   <u>cit.</u>, page Introduction, and finally see Clark, <u>Haryou An</u>
   <u>Experiment</u>, <u>op. cit.</u>, page 183, in J.H. Clark, <u>op. cit.</u>

74. Interviews with current Haryou Board members.

75. Krosney, <u>op. cit.</u>

76. <u>Ibid</u>. Though I tend to agree with Krosney's analysis of Clark's
   power base in Harlem, I disagree with his view that Clark had
   no deep connection with the community; if anything, his connection was of such emotional intensity that it probably served
   as the basis for his apparent irrationality respecting certain
   community issues.

77. Interviews with Harlem residents.

CHAPTER 5

HARYOU-ACT POLITICS AND LEADERSHIP DECISION

In the Spring of 1963, Haryou seems poised for the official launching of its action programs. The approximate 18 month planning and writing phase ends, and the program is tooled up with beginning program staff. An aire of excitement and enthusiasm grips the Harlem community, as expectations rise in anticipation of long awaited change.[1]

The youth of the community, and particularly those involved in the HARYOU Associates (later Harlem Youth Unlimited), are active in setting up storefront coffee shops, and generally creating an atmosphere of promise. These are the days of Lloyd Pryor, Calvin Alston, Frank Willis, Joyce Wilkins, Jim DeBerry, Sharon Jackson, Ronald Wilkerson and many others.[2] As these and others of the Community's youths mobilize for the variety of strategies conceptualized during the planning stage, another drama unfolds. It is a drama which holds profound consequences for the eventual outcome of the above activities: and for HARYOU in general.

Few people are aware of the precise nature of conflict which emerges between Harlem's political leader Adam Clayton Powell and its professional/intellectual leader, Dr. Kenneth B. Clark. One thing becomes increasingly clear, however; the antagonism and hostility were born of more than ideological or programmatic differences. As Krosney has aptly put it, "In discussing Powell, Clark, the psychologist, tends to become Clark, the dogmatist. To deal with Powell in any way is to risk contamination by evil. As Clark explains: "It's like being a little bit pregnant. You are or you aren't. If Powell's in you, even a little bit, he's had you....."[3] Others, more privy to the variety of meetings early in the formulation years of Haryou, between Powell and Clark, also suggest the adamant position of Clark as that bordering on hysteria.[4]

It would appear, thus, that for a professional of Clark's background and knowledge to be so emotionally 'hung-up' on Powell, that some traumatic encounter is at base, responsible. I am aware, for example, that Clark was, during much of the early Haryou experience, viewed by many in and out Harlem as the "carrier" of particular professional values, integrity, and rationality--presumably conflictual with the kind of 'political ractionality" associated with Powell.[5] One active in Harlem at that time could not escape the professional community's anticipation of Powell's downfall within the community, and I recall Milton Yale saying at one point,

> Haryou has the potential for effecting new shifts in the power
> base in Harlem, and Powell's position is not as secure as it
> once was.[6]

The intonation of most professionals seemed anti-Powell. I decided that I would, in some way get to meet the man and determine for myself what his position on HARYOU was. The opportunity presented itself one Sunday afternoon, during the Spring of 1963. Powell was preaching at Abyssinia and I attended. This is the first time I have attended a Powell sermon and the church is so packed, that only standing room remains.[7] I walked

Haryou-Act Organizational

Chart 2
1964

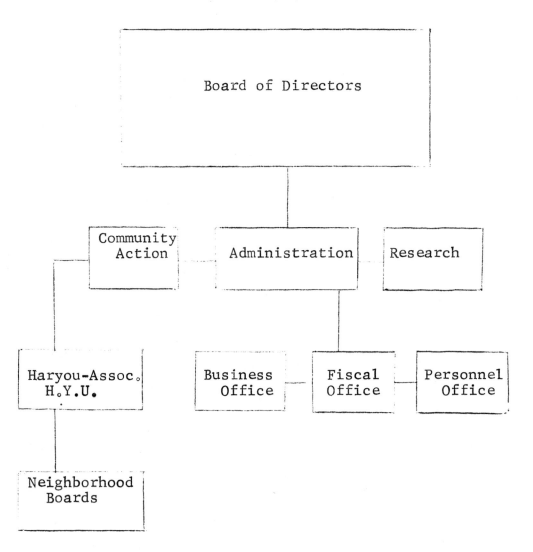

along the side aisle of the church, and standing amidst others of his congregation, I find myself as caught up in his delivery as any of the staunch 'church sisters'. Powell was on this particular Sunday preaching about the ways in which, as God's messenger, he was able constantly to avoid a variety of traps and strategies aimed at his downfall in the Congress. He spoke of powerful enemies in Washington, D.C., and within his own "native Harlem". As he preached, I heard and observed the constant 'amens', and 'wells', that often accompany a warm Baptist experience, but beyond these, I observed how Powell himself was involved in his own words. At the end of the sermon Powell left the podium and began walking up the aisle where I was standing. On his way, he shook hands and spoke briefly to those standing. As he approached me, he smiled and put his hand on my shoulder. Just as he was about to pass, I asked if I might talk with him about Haryou. Without stopping, he turned somewhat and said, "yes. It's a great program. Their doing a find job...come see me in Washington, and we'll talk." I was unable to take the congressman up on the invitation until sometime later. In even so brief an encounter as the above, however, I found in Powell not the hystical, intriguing and villainous person he is reported to be; but a man sufficiently sensitive and available to relate to a strange young man whose eagerness to know, must have reflected in his eyes. Lest the reader assume this to be a small matter, let him ponder the possibilities for addressing Kenneth Clark; the 'unavailable', intellectual.[8]

The analysis is, perhaps enough to suggest that Clark was not the 'haloed' righteous - yet wrongly exploited and betrayed - 'good guy' and Powell, the "devil", pompous and bombastic.[9] It may also suggest that the presumed misunderstanding regarding the merger of Haryou and ACT (Associated Community Teams), was not a misunderstanding at all, but an attempt of Clark to 'betray' earlier agreements with the Congressman.[10] Why for example, would Powell have facilitated the funding of Haryou in the first place, had he not already made some politically satisfactory arrangement with Clark? During interviews with Reverend Callendar and Roy Wingate, it was impressed upon me that there are some things about the conflict that only Clark and Powell knew. There were, for example, some few occasions on which the two men met in private. Whatever the true nature of the conflict, the resultant community strains and nuances eventuate in emotional, often irrational and sporadic program crisis.[11]

The third personality of importance to the Haryou-Act problem is Livingston L. Wingate (Roy Wingate, to friends and the community).[12] Roy Wingate is, both as the result of his directorship of ACT and his former relationship with Adam Powell - usually referred to during these early Haryou days as "Powell's protege".[13] Wingate, in my interviews with him, is outspoken about his earlier (pre-Haryou), relationship with Powell; but repeatedly states that

> Adam liked the idea of Clark's running Haryou, and so did I...
> He (Powell) was not interested in interfering with the program
> and had no direct responsibility in my becoming Executive
> Director...I did that on my own...[14]

By on his own, Wingate refers to his personalized, charismatic assumption of leadership in Harlem. During his tenure at ACT, he has captured the hearts of Harlem's 'little folks', not the least of whom are represented by the newly emerging youth leaders such as Lloyd Pryor, Calvin Alston, and Frank Willis.[15] It is an affair with the people of Harlem that pays off in power dividends for Wingate during crucial times in his poverty career.[16]

There are obvious contrasts between Wingate, the personable, action oriented politico; and Clark, the somber, embittered and distant intellectual.[17] And the differences are among the most important for those who would pursue any leadership in the Harlem community.[18] For leadership in Harlem, if it is to be functional for the achievement of power and influence - must be personable and overtly emotional at appropriate times. The average Harlemite needs to _feel_ as if his leader is available in order to accept him.[19] And Clark, irrespective of his professional and intellectual accomplishments, tended to alienate those he chastised for not 'recognizing' sincere and substantive leaders.[20]

During the final weeks of my student internship at HANA, and in the midst of much of the community excitement related to the announcements of Haryou's launching; I recall the first occasion of my seeing Wingate and Clark together. A press conference had been called at HANA to announce both the promised funding of Haryou and the merger of HARYOU-ACT.[21] The excitement of the moment was shared by everyone involved, Milton Yale, Eugene Callendar, Harriet Pickens, and the variety of HANA Board members and community leaders. In the midst of television cameras and newsmen, poised on the steps of HANA's offices, only Clark appeared grim and uninvolved. Reports had, for a matter of weeks, been circulating in the community that he was stepping down from his leadership position in Haryou, and that Whitney Young, Director of the National Urban League or Roy Wilkins, Secretary of NAACP were being considered as replacements. Milton Yale seemed to sense that neither of these National leaders would respond, though he did view Wilkins as the more astute of the two, respecting Harlem community systems.[22]

As the above group stood, then, ready to go on camera, (I was standing in the background at the time), Wingate and entourage arrived, somewhat bustingly, as he was late. With him were his public relations staff and others. Wingate was quite excited and walked into the group with his hand extended and smiling broadly. As he waded into the group shaking hands and greeting people, he was advised that he could not be photographed well by the T.V. cameras because of the color tie he was wearing. In a kind of frenzied attempt to deal with the emergency, one of the cameramen, pointing to me said, "that's the kind of striped tie you should be wearing...that picks up well". It was all he had to hear. With a big laugh and a very quick move, he had my tie in his hand... and I his. Despite the fact that I never got the tie back, I have been impressed with Wingate ever since.[23]

The press conference was brief, though informative. At one point, the television interviewer, asking how Powell viewed the new HARYOU-ACT enterprise, was calmly informed by Clark, that the Congressman had given his blessings to the program and supported it "unequivacable". There was additional discussion as to how Haryou represented an alternative to the social "dynamite in Harlem's streets" referring to antisocial black youths, who, without some meaningful programs, could explode into rioting and open hostility.[24]

Given the pervasive nuances surrounding Powell and Clark, his comments before the T.V. cameras had to be interpreted as projecting some sense of unity in the community. It is not until sometime later, that Clark openly attempts to indict the congressman for interfering with the program's implementation.[25]

This essentially marks the end of HANA's active participation in the Haryou program. Additionally, of particular importance to my leadership concerns, it also marks the end of the creative elites reign as the major leadership type in the Haryou development process.[26] The emergence of new functional leaders in the organizations experience begins to occur.

Haryou, has essentially arrived at the beginning stages of implementation.

The key leaders involved at this new stage, are Kenneth Clark, Cyril Tyson, Kenneth Marshall, James Jones, Arthur Logan, Roy Wingate, Lloyd Pryor, Dave Barry, Gregory Mooney, Eugene Callendar and others. It is a phase of the Haryou experience marked by beginning efforts at implementing the recently published and Nationally acclaimed study document "Youth In The Ghetto; the Consequences of Powerlessness".[27]

It is a period, the early part of which, is charged with a special sense of accomplishment. The observer of the Harlem scene at this point is impressed with the sophisticated dialogue in which planners, executive staff and youth alike, are involved. Haryou seems to have a well developed cadre of articulate, insightful and brilliant young men and women, who have many of the answers to the ghetto's problems. I recall one of the most impressive experiences during this period being that of observing Jim Jones, Cyril Tyson and Ken Marshall 'doing their thing'. As executive and program technicians, they were unequaled; but beyond their roles as Haryou executives, they assumed a more relevant leadership function as Harlem representatives.[28] Jones, Tyson and Marhsall became the epitome of anti-poverty and community action innovators. They complimented each others style as effectively as if they had been born to work together. To see the trio arrive at a major National or City-wide conference, portfolio's in hand, was to know that a major contribution was about to be made. Normally, their arrival would elicit whispers throughout an audience of the kind that suggests awe and excitement.

Equally as impressive upon occasions, were the HARYOU Associates, headed by Lloyd Pryor.[29] Pryor was a sharp minded and witty ex-'diddy-bopper' from Harlem's streets, who early had been captured by the excitement and possibilities of the Haryou program. Because of his native ability and quickness for 'sizing-up' situations and being strikingly articulate, Pryor had ascended to leadership within Haryou's ranks, practically overnight. Elliot Bovell, a supervisor for the New York City Youth Board (C.S.A.C.), and a personal friend of the writer's, had discovered Pryor, and brought him to the attention of Ken Marshall.[30] Already a leader in the youth community of Harlem, Pryor was functional for Marshall's design for involving cadre's of youths in the Haryou program.[31] What Marshall (and others) did not anticipate, was the speed with which Pryor would become 'acclimated' to the interpersonal and political nuances operative within the program; and effectively use such knowledge to systematically undercut the Haryou planners program intentions.[32] The fact that Pryor did however, is owing to critical errors in judgement on the parts of Marshall, and particularly Clark.[33] It is ultimately the latter's insensitivity to this youth's brilliance and interests, which causes severe problems for the Haryou Board and its leaders.

A major portion of these representatives time is, during this early period (1964), spent in explaining and defining Haryou's structure and function in a variety of public forums. The dialogue, of especially Tyson and Marshall illuminates the relevance of Haryou far as a vehicle for making Harlem a community of excellence; one which ultimately can be self sufficient, utilizing a variety of indigenous community enterprise schemes. The prospectus which Tyson and Marshall present for effective programs aimed at 'culture building' are provocative and insightful regarding the short and long range needs of the Harlem community, and beyond.[35]

Haryou, as the first essentially black community anti-poverty effort in a major city is scrutinized by other black communities throughout the country. Its leadership in this regard is functional for providing a prototype to be emulated by other leaders in Black America. One persistent problem, however, mars the Haryou potential.

With the annexation, (or merger), of ACT to Haryou, the figurehead leaders of the respective organizations, Powell and Clark, heighten to crisis proportions, the issue of power and control. Cyril Tyson, during a recent interview, recounts,

It was a time when Clark was just not available to listen to anyone. I tried to impress upon him and others involved, that we could probably deal so that everybody could get what they wanted out of the effort, without splitting the total thing. What Harlem needed at the time, was a united program effort - hell, we were getting 'crumbs' anyway - for us to fight over them was crazy. But no one would listen.[36]

Other activists involved in Haryou and Act at the time, surmised the "pretentious", struggle to be unreal, on the grounds that,

if you are serious about changing things in Harlem, you have to deal with the community's political structure; and like it or not, that means Adam.[37]

The interesting finding from interviews conducted during the present writing is that view that owing to Kenneth Clark's "illusiveness" respecting what "he really wanted" out of the HARYOU experience, it was impossible to negotiate with him.

These nuances effectively impede the Haryou program's implementation. Ultimately, they usher in conflictual leadership styles which are dysfunctional for Haryou's ever implementing the strategies presented in the Youth In The Ghetto. The fundamental interests in culture and institution building the major considerations of the institutional inspirationalists in my typology seem doomed to failure as leadership elements within the organization and the broader community fight for positions of control. Polarization occurs, as Clark, Tyson, Marshall, Jones, Pryor and Logan; Callendar, Barry, Dumpson and other Haryou actors are postured as struggling to maintain the organization's 'integrity' as an a-political youth and community uplift program. On the other hand, Powell, Wingate, Andrew R. Tyler (then chairman of ACT) and others associated with them are viewed as the corruptors, whose only interests in Haryou are political and personal.[38] It is a time when the institutional inspirationalists and certain creative elite leaders seem to have formed a protective coalition for the purpose of confronting premier leaders around the defense of organizational integrity as defined in the creative elite's terms. The inspirationalists leaders, on the other hand, in their awareness of multi-dimensional nature of leadership--if a genuine process of institutionalization is to occur in Harlem--seems more available to negotiate around issues of differential values and integrity. The problem resides in the relative powerlessness of the inspirationalists during this period for affecting some alliance between the contending elites and premier leaders. These are perspectives created, to some extend, by the public media, who, skillfully utilized by Clark, leap to the opportunity to expose community conflict; and once again attack Harlem's black Congressman.[39] Additionally, they are views perpetuated by leaders in the professional community within and outside of Harlem.[40]

The average Harlem citizen, however, is noncommittal. For one thing, he is somewhat numbed to the rhetoric and infighting which he has come to associate with leadership styles in the community. Bombast, accusation and counter-accusation, crisis and intrigue are elements which are historically familiar. In this regard it is interesting to note the 'functions' served by such seemingly irrelevant and wasteful infighting. The knowledgeable Harlem observer does not cast off these group and organizational behaviorisms and characteristics as dysfunctional; but rather reviews them within the peculiar context of the black American's experience in surviving a generally hostile white environment. In certain ways these activities represent testing mechanisms for aspiring and emerging black leaders, who if they are successful, will presumably have to face comparable conflicts and nuances in larger societal and organizational contexts.

What may often seem then to the purely research or non-participatory observer as unimportant harrassment and piciune 'back-biting' within a black organization, like Haryou--is in fact a 'leadership preparatory' experience. The cliche that "if one survives a leadership experience in Harlem--he or she can survive anywhere" is to be taken seriously. Secondly, the people in the community haven't heard anything from "Adam" directly. Known for his outspokeness about matters that concern him, the people find it of interest that the Congressman has not directly confronted Clark and Company's accusations. Thus the relative importance of "what the newspapers say" is interpreted as "their just out to get Adam again, but he'll survive",[41] as put by one Harlemite interviewed.

It takes approximately one year for this issue of leadership conflict to resolve itself. Through perhaps the clearest example of leadership default observable in contemporary Harlem, Clark, with no more than his persistent style of shadow boxing and rhetoric, resigns as director and board consultant.[42] To the present day no one knows why; and even the most involved Haryou leaders are unable beyond conjecture, to determine what finally caused his leaving, when he did. Krosney has noted that when asked why, Clark's only response is "I had my reasons".[43]

For Marshall, Tyson and Jones, Clark's leaving meant that their vision for Haryou was in serious danger. Their determination not to allow the program to flounder despite his absence, caused a flurry of action to get some part of the show on the road.[44] Their move to hire John C. Johnson, and get the cadet corps program underway is owing to more than the program's high visibility, as suggested by some; it is symptomatic of the non-Harlemites misunderstanding the functional relevance of such programs for the development of community leadership. I view my own experience as a young cadet as perhaps illustrative of the meaning of Harlem's cadetting program.

At thirteen years of age, I became a member of Harlem's St. Martin's Nautical cadet program. I had been a Boy Scout at St. Philips Church, but having lost interest in the scouting approach decided to become involved in cadetting. John C. Johnson was the senior officer in the corps.[48] I remember that awe and excitement experienced on my first night at the 369th's famed Armory in Harlem. The cadet program held for me the opportunity to become part of one of Harlem's elite youth cadres. It was not easy however. Each neophyte cadet had to learn certain traditions. Traditions such as the history of the corp in Harlem, its leaders; Afro-American history, and many of the contributions of black military and community/race leaders. In addition, one had to learn how to function as part of a unit consistent of youths from a variety of class and culture backgrounds. The assumption of personal responsibility for members of the corps and for making oneself as competent in drilling and maneuvering as possible, involved us in working together on and off of the Armory drill floor. Having come from Harlem's 'Sugar Hill', the cadet corps provided the first real opportunity for my coming to know, intimately, youths from central Harlem's 'valley' community. It was a learning experience valued to this day. Thus the elements of leadership identification and development are early found in the experience. Relationships are formed in the cadetting program which persist throughout life. And the military facade is more mimicry than substantive. Comradery and responsibility - not violence - are the ingredients bestowed, and a youth, perhaps without opportunities for such experiences in his general community milieu, can experience them in cadetting.

More profound, however, is the experience, so often repeated in Harlem, of youths who have participated in such programs returning as adults to assume leadership in civic community enterprise.[49] My coming to Haryou as an executive in 1968, and finding John Johnson in the organization's program leadership meant something special with respect to the organizations relevance as a community institution. It also meant something special to John respecting the 'payoffs' possible from his earlier commitment to training youths for leadership.

It is Tyson's sense of awareness respecting Johnson's functional role in Harlem, which leads him to launch the cadetting program among the first implemented during the action phase. Tyson and Marshall encounter some resistance from the Board of Directors, however, on even so relevant a move as this. Krosney documents the Boards concern being one of 'authority' respecting the administrators, "hiring staff and launching the program - unilaterally - and without Board approval".[50] Marshall and Tyson view their actions as essentially sanctioned by the implementation time table of the original Haryou plan; and further, as justified on the basis of the leadership vacuum created by Clark's resignation. In the final analysis, both the action and the conflictual response from the board are viewed as symptoms of the frustration and disappointment precipitated by Clark in the above. Something had to be done, Tyson felt, if Haryou's integrity was going to be maintained. The community and particularly its youth, have been awaiting the promised Haryou intervention strategies for approximately two years. To 'hold off' any longer, and particularly given recent newspaper accounts of community and leadership conflict - could mean disaster for Haryou's impact.[51]

The board of directors, however, does not pursue the matter owing to its involvement with the high priority consideration of finding an executive replacement for Clark. In parting from Haryou, Clark effectively kills Tyson's chances for becoming his successor as he advises the board that "Cyril's brilliant alright, but not quite ready to direct the program, perhaps at some future time...".[52] It is a recommendation, for which, many believe, Tyson has never forgiven Clark. The eventual emergence of Roy Wingate as the principle candidate for the executive director slot is a direct result again of leadership default. In addition to Clark's action, there are other professionals who leave Haryou at perhaps the most crucial moment in its evolution. They do so on the presumption, that if Clark could not maintain himself in the power structure of the new program, then surely it must be currupt and politically contaminated.[53] With Wingates ascendency to the directorship, they are subsequently convinced. There are additional factors which emerge as elements in the transition of leadership at this point. As an organization develops, leadership relevancies and roles change. The types and styles of leadership functional for Haryou at one phase may not be required at another. I have commented on this aspect of leadership phenomena earlier, but again postulate that such did not apply in the changes associated with Haryou's leadership at the time.

Haryou, in 1965, is operational. The Harlem Cadet corps, Neighborhoods Boards, and employment programs; Arts and Culture and Youth activities through the HYU component seem to be moving. In the summer of the year, the organization receives a large summer grant for operating a 'crash program' in Harlem. The project is known as Project Up-lift (PUL).[54] PUL was essentially funded as a measure which was to prevent a repeat of the social frustrations which in the summer of 1964, had erupted in rioting in Harlem. Other black communities had also experienced the 'long hot summer' of '64, and the Federal Government, under the Johnson Administration was determined to avoid their reoccurence.[55] Haryou and the New York Urban League were co-sponsors of operation PUL though Haryou served as the conduit for the funds received for the program's operation.[56] In addition, HANA, and Act were also directly involved. Project Uplift was a crash program which brought together into one entity a highly complex array of organizations and programs. Although it was funded only three days before its eleven week period of performance was to start, the project had to coordinate the activities of scores of organizations; recruit, train and supervise 2,500 (later expanded to 4,000) enrollees; and plan for and implement twelve highly varied program vehicles. Community leaders in Harlem tended to feel that the project was useful, but that it was not directly related to Harlem's basic problems; especially the lack of permanent employment opportunities.[57] They felt that it was insufficient to establish an intensive program lasting less than three months when the problems of the community had developed over decades.

This leadership perspective is shared by key members of the Haryou administration. Jim Jones, for example, recalls his advice to Wingate

I tried to convince Roy, that in addition to the problems inherent in establishing any program utilizing public funds, that to deal with so large an amount as $3,000,000 within an approximate 11 week period; and without sufficient lead time to plan, could cause more problems than it would solve.[58]

Wingate recalling Jones' warning, reflects that,

I knew that Jim was against our accepting the money; but how could I turn down almost $3,000,000 for the people of Harlem?

Wingate reflecting for a moment, as we sat in Harlem's Flash Inn, then adds, "If I knew then, what I know now, I might have acted somewhat differently."[59]

I will not deal substantively with the operation PUL outcomes, but it is significant for the purposes of illuminating relevant leadership issues to deal with the fact that had Haryou not assumed the responsibility for implementing the program; some other agency in the community would have.[60] As the largest and most powerful community agency in Harlem, such an affrontery would have been embarrassing, to say the least. The probability that the New York Urban League could do so, prodded the Haryou leadership to act swiftly and decisively. The League's leadership had been courted by Washington and presumably had already designed a program for doing precisely what the Johnson administration wanted - cooling out Harlem's kids for the summer.[61] The principle leaders involved are, James Solar from HANA, Mrs. Lila Doar, associate executive director of HARYOU, Mr. Frank Stanley, Jr., of the Urban League (later on leave from the Urban League, the PUL project director for HARYOU), Calvin Pressley and David Barry from the Ministerial Interfaith Association, a consortium of religious leaders in Harlem, (and City-side); the Executive Director of the National Urban League, also became involved.[63] Wingate and the Haryou Board of Directors, were, however, primarily responsible for the program.[64]

The planning and program failures of the project PUL effort have been more than reported in a variety of forums; they have essentially been distorted, blown out of proportion and used as indicators of Haryou's inability to function as a responsible community program.[65] Accusations of fiscal mismanagement, never substantiated and designed

Haryou-Act

Organizational Chart
1965-1967

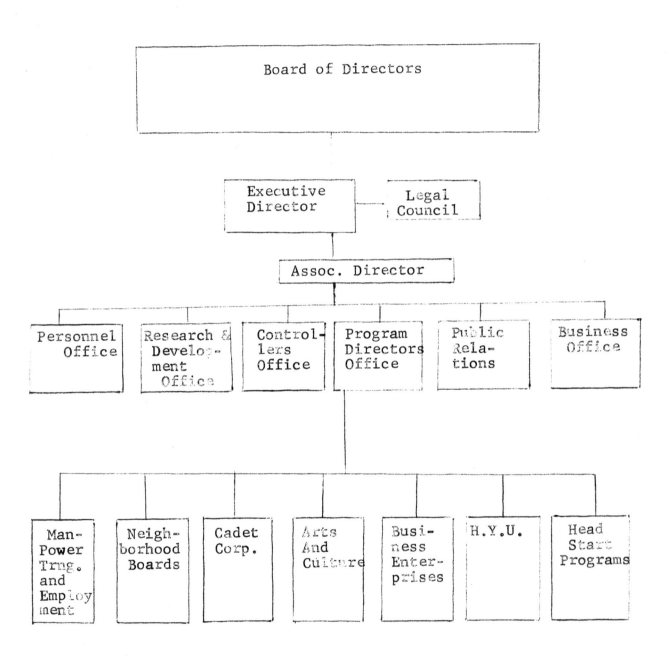

92

to undermine the programs potential, remain even today, as unresolved issues.[66]

There has however, been no attempt at analyzing the miraculous accomplishment of leadership cooperation and program interlock which the effort represented. One Mayoral Task Force evaluation of the program chaired by the then NYC Commissioner of Welfare, James R. Dumpson, notes that,

> The summer project was to be carried out by a number of community organizations... Four community organizations would be delegate (or contract) agencies. They, in turn, would subcontract specific projects to some 89 (itallics mine), other neighborhood groups.[67]

In addition to the effort associated with coordinating leaders from the four major 'contract agencies' (HANA, ACT, HARYOU and NY Urban League), itself a major task; Wingate and the Haryou staff had to deal with 89 autonomous organizations and their grass roots leadership.[68] Interviews conducted with many of these organizational leaders, some of whom are presently serving as Haryou Board Members, further indicate that many become aware of Haryou and its overall program efforts as the result of the summer program experience.

Though many view Haryou's assumption of the responsibility for the PUL program as dysfunctional respecting its institutional roles (i.e. given the recognition that sporadic, short term 'crash' programs could not meet the communities persistent needs, and that long term, substantive efforts were necessary), this analysis does not. Leadership is, in Harlem, fraught with risk. And the attempt to avoid such risk can be more dysfunctional than the consequences which may attend errors in judgement or predictability of outcome.[69] In Dark Ghetto, Kenneth Clark illuminates certain of the risk factors which attend leadership in Harlem as he notes:

> The ghetto is in a manner, self perpetuating, and while it encourages some for attempting change, it rewards others for loyalty to things as they are. Inside the ghetto lie sources of energy that are ordinarily mobilized, overtly or covertly, to prevent change and to perpetuate and exploit the status quo. Outside the ghetto, too, are sources of energy that depend on the ghetto for their own security - all exploitation rests upon real or imagined advantages to the exploiters. Therefore, any social action to transform the ghetto must expect to face apathy and hostility from both Negroes and Whites - for a ghetto can be a cacoon as well as a cage.[70]

In discussing certain of the varieties of black leadership, i.e. James Dumpson, Ralph Bunche, James Robinson and etc.,[71] Clark clarifies additionally, that,

> The ghetto appears to weed out individuals of certain levels of interest and competence, excluding them from effectiveness in the ghetto and thereby contributing to the self perpetuating pathology of the ghetto itself. Such persons may be regarded as deserters, and the ghetto has no role for them to play.[72]

And finally,

> The Negro who dares to move outside of the ghetto, either physically or psychologically, runs the risk of retaliatory hostility, at worst, or of misunderstanding, at best..... Yet escape, whatever the motive, can never be complete as long as racial oppression exists. The Negro, no matter how successful his flight may appear, still remains in conflict, a conflict stemming from his awareness of ambivalence of other Negroes toward him and from his awareness that the larger white society never accepts him completely. He is in conflict

within himself, with whites and with Negroes, confronted by a
sense of guilt, alienation, resentment, and random bitterness
directed as much against Negroes as against whites.[73]

These elements of risk may not be directly applicable to the
Haryou Leaderships' decision to implement operation PUL, but do represent the dysfunctional nature of black leadership which attempts to
avoid the responsibilities inherent in the life styles of America's
Harlems.[74]

Those, then, who assumed the responsibility for the summer program
of 1965, may have acted hastily; but it is unquestionable that they
did act, and on the behalf of Harlem's youth.[75] It is interesting
given Haryou's present function as the Community Corporation of Central
Harlem; one which is essentially coordinative and administrative with
respect to the myriad of Harlem community organizations - that the
assumption of a comparable role during the PUL effort resulted in accusations of fiscal and administrative mismanagement. If there were
instances of malfeasance, they should be shared; as much of the responsibility rests with a panicked Federal Administrative leadership; as
it does with the Harlem implementors.[76]

There is an additional relevance to the functions of Haryou's leaders in pursuing the decision to coordinate the PUL effort. It resides
in the rare occurrence in Harlem of joining partnership between political
and civic leadership. Wilson, for example, in discussing black leadership in the North has stated,

The Politicians and the civic leaders, formerly united, are
drawing further and further apart in Chicago and New York.
The transfer of leadership from the old family elites to the
new business and professional groups is well along toward
realization. The change from personality leadership to
functional leadership, from the era of the "great spokesman",
to the new era of the professionally staffed voluntary association is occuring at varying rates, everywhere.[77]

Additionally, Rossi observes, that the pattern in city politics has
generally been for the political and civic elites to diverge and to
form two relatively independent and often competing sources of civic
influence.[78] The complexity of the problems and issues facing cities
and the increased specialization of interests has stimulated the development of the modern civic association with its board of lay civic
leaders and professional staff. More and more, issues are raised and
agitated, and sentiment is mobilized by these organizations, particularly
by their staffs.[79] Wilson observes, further,

the Negro community has only begun to develop this "agency
approach" to civic issues. In few Northern cities is there
a really vigorous, organized Negro civic life concerned with
race or community issues.[80]

Haryou's leadership contradicts these observations in its assumption of
responsibility during the crucial PUL program; and substantively, step
in the direction of facilitating new linkages between diverse organizational and leadership elements in Harlem.

These kinds of interpretations have never been explored in analyzing the 'fallouts' of the PUL experience. Yet it is clear, given the
present leadership in Haryou, that they were relevant elements.

The actions and decisions of Haryou leaders in 1965 set the
stage for the emergence of new community activists. The community was
embarrassed and traumatized by the attacks which result from their summer project. Despite the myriad evaluations and attempts at exonera-
ting the program and its decision makers; the stigma of failure per-

sisted.[81] Key spokesmen and administrators like Kenneth Marshal and James Jones trickle from the Haryou scene. Marshal leaves on the wings of controversy and conflict, as he is fired by Wingate for open difiance of the new Director's administrative and program decisions.[82] Board members scurry from the now controversial Haryou, with obvious disaffection and dissatisfaction with the organization's direction.[83]

Programs, barely launched, bog down as program and fiscal audits preoccupy administrators and staff alike. City, State and Federal investigators besiege the organization's records; and finally, Wingate is asked to step down as Executive Director until the various charges respecting missing funds and program misjudgements are clarified.[84]

The Haryou enterprise is vulnerable to a new breed of leadership. And, once again, in the 'conjunctive' sense discussed by Bogardus, leadership emerges to meet the circumstance.

The conclusion of this second developmental phase in Haryou's experience marks the end of the institutional inspirationalist leaders focussed effort, as well as the demise of the creative elite as a power force. The time is ripe for the emergence of new types of leadership upon the Haryou scene. Leaders, who, for the most part, share different sets of values, and whose organizational interests and priorities appear substantially different than their predecessors.

FOOTNOTES TO CHAPTER V

1. This marks the onset of the second developmental phase as per the dissertation format.

2. Youth in the Ghetto, see section on "Harlem Youth Unlimited", page 565. See also Appendix 9 of the original document.

3. Herbert Krosney, Beyond Welfare, op. cit., pages 58-65.

4. Interviews with former Haryou Board and Executive Staff members.

5. For an interesting analysis of the concept 'political rationality' see Austin Ramney, Political Science and Public Policy (Markham Publishing Co., Chicago). Article by Aaron Wildavsky, pages 78-82. For a review of the professional values, integrity and rationality see Clark, Dark Ghetto, op. cit., pages 229-231. Also Clark in John Henrik Clark, op. cit., pages 211-212. and Encyclopedia of Social Work "Professional Code of Ethics. Also see Alfred J. Kahn, Theory and Practice of Social Planning, (Russell Sage Foundation, New York 1969) pages 96-129.

6. Conference (Spring 1963).

7. This field experience occured during the Spring of 1963.

8. Particularly during these early Haryou planning and implementation days, Clark seemed so pre-occupied that many of his immediate colleagues felt alienated. Also see Krosney, op. cit., pages 63-64.

9. The Public Media, and particularly the World Telegram and Sunday Daily News were vociferous in their condemnation of Powell. See also Clark, Dark Ghetto, op. cit., pages 168-171 and Krosney, op. cit., pages 63-64.

10. Interviews during Fall (1973). Also see Krosney, ibid.

11. See Krosney's discussion of Clark's refusal to accept director's position in Haryou. Op. cit., page 60.

12. See Negro Handbook and Krosney, op. cit., page 37; also see Alphonso Pickney and Roger R. Woock, Poverty and Politics in Harlem Report on Project Uplift. 1965 (College and University Press). Ibid.

13. Ibid.

14. Interview Fall 1973.

15. During my tenure as Director of the Harlem Youth Unlimited program,
    I came to know these Youth leaders (excepting) Pryor---inti-
    mately. They in fact held Wingate in high regard. See also
    Krosney, op. cit., pages 68-69.

16. Notably during the summer crises of Project 'P.U.L.' (1965); and
    later in Wingate's activities with the Haryou Neighborhoods'
    Boards.

17. See Krosney, op. cit., page 77.

18. Emotionalism and charisma in Harlem are powerful leadership at-
    tributes. Also see Clark, Dark Ghetto, op. cit., pages
    194-196; and Clark, A Relevant War Against Poverty, op. cit.,
    Myrdal also views certain leadership attributes as relevant
    in the Black community generally. In An American Dilemma,
    op. cit., page 1431.

19. Ibid. and see Everett C. Ladd--re: his analysis of 'availability'
    op. cit., page 114.

20. Clark, Dark Ghetto, op. cit., page 197.

21. Field Observation early Spring 1963. I recall that Bill Buetel
    was the Network Commentator covering the Conference.

22. Wilkins' activities in Harlem had a much longer history than
    Young's. See Negro Handbook, etc.

23. It is perhaps noteworthy that Wingate also recalls the occasion,
    and even the inconspicuous students name whose tie he had
    "roughed-off".

24. Reference is made to the period as one during which Black Mili-
    tancy was taking center stage in the national community.
    Clark and others involved in the Anti-Poverty Program often
    related to it as an 'intervening force' an alternative strategy
    for dealing with the energies of Harlem's disenchanted masses.
    If Federal, and other government leaders, it was suggested,
    would avail themselves of the links of leaders involved in the
    Civil Rights and Anti-poverty areas---the potential 'social
    dynamite' in ghetto communities might be 'defused'.

25. See Krosney, op. cit., pages 76-77 and N.Y. Daily News, during
    the period.

26. It is a tenable proposition which suggests that certain of my
    leadership types (i.e. creative elites, commutators, proto-
    indigenous idealists end etc.), are of greater or lesser
    functional relevance to Haryou Organizational needs during
    specific stages. Thus we would expect that the creative
    elite's role and function has essentially been performed with
    the end of the Haryou 'think-tank' phase, and the implemen-
    tation of the action and programming phase. A new leadership
    type will, given this view, emerge to continue the Organiza-
    tions Development. This view is further substantiated by the
    finding that many professional practitioners in the poverty
    program view their roles as 'initiators', 'organizers' and

'advocates' and enter community systems realizing the temporary nature of their involvement. This however does not appear to be the case with Dr. Clark and others identified above. Their participation in Haryou seemed to have been 'aborted' earlier than anticipated and for reasons not anticipated in their assumption of the program's planning and implementation.

27.   The Document, earlier cited, has been hailed as perhaps the most substantive research effort related to a ghetto community ever performed.

28.   This provides an excellent example of my definition of functional leadership; for while it is true that these Haryou executives created a unique and positive image to national citywide communities, interested in the poverty program, they even more substantively created new role models on Harlem's people. One reflective of a new style of technical and creative competence.

29.   In addition to my observations of the Associates at Haryou, I often participated in their presentations at college forums and Youth Group rallies. See also Krosney op. cit., pages 56-58.

30.   Ibid.

31.   Ibid.

32.   Ibid.

33.   Ibid.

34.   One manifestation was Wingates successful election as Haryou Executive Director a power struggle in which the youth vote was critical. See Krosney, op. cit., pages 59-62.

35.   Interviews during course of study. See also Youth in the Ghetto, op. cit., pages 507-598.

36.   Interviews during Fall 1973, see also Krosney, ibid.

37.   Interviews during Fall 1973, ibid.

38.   Ibid.

39.   Krosney, op. cit., pages 62-63; see also N.Y. "World Telegram and Sun" and The New York Daily News. February - March 1966.

40.   Interviews and field observations.

41.   Interviews; also see Amsterdam News; May, 1966. Also see Krosney, op. cit., page 62.

42.   Krosney, op. cit., pages 71-72; also see page 60; and Selznick, op. cit., page 25.

43.   Ibid.

44. _Ibid._ and interviews conducted, Winter 1973.

45. Interview Fall 1973.

46. Interview Fall 1973.

47. Interviews Fall 1973; see also Daily News, September 1965.

48. St. Martins Nautical Cadets. Lt. Colonel Jessie L. Palmer's "Thunderbolts' Drum and Bugle Corps".

49. There are a number of contemporary leaders whose background includes similar experiences; and most fall within my institutional inspirationalist; premier, or proto-indigenous idealist types. A good example is Reverend Calvin O. Pressley; Executive Director of the New York Opportunities Industrialization Centers.

50. Krosney, _op. cit._, page 66; also Interviews conducted during Fall 1973.

51. Interviews Fall 1973.

52. Krosney, _op. cit._, page 61.

53. Krosney, page 71.

54. I draw heavily upon Alphonso Pinkney and Roger R. Woock's analysis in _Poverty and Politics in Harlem: Report on Project Uplift_, 1965 (College and University Press, New Haven)--for documentation in this section.

55. _Ibid._, pages 44-46; see also Krosney, _op. cit._, pages 79-84. See also James Jones, "The Researcher as Policy Scientist" original manuscript.

56. Pinkney and Woock, _op. cit._, _ibid._

57. _Ibid._

58. Interview Fall 1973; see also Krosney, _op. cit._, pages 79-84.

59. Interview, Fall 1973.

60. See Krosney, _op. cit._, pages 78-84 and Pinkney and Wooch, _op. cit._, pages 58-81.

61. _Ibid._

62. _Ibid._

63. _Ibid._

64. _Ibid._

65. In a series of special articles to the New York Amsterdam News beginning June 2, 1966, Roy Wingate publicly responded to the charges related to (P.U.L.) see "The Real Haryou-Act Story"

by Livingston L. Wingate, Executive Director, Haryou-Act Inc. No funds missing, and No Mismanagement. See also, Krosney, op. cit., page 83 and Pinkney and Wooch, op. cit., pages 79-80. and finally see "The Report of the Task Force Appointed to Evaluate Project Up-lift" by James R. Dumpson, Dr. Inabel Lindsay and Reverend Dr. Roy Nichols, December 1965 (unpublished).

66. Ibid. and Interviews Fall 1973.

67. Dumpson Report, op. cit., pages 6-7.

68. Pinkney and Wooch, op. cit., pages 58-81.

69. Wingate in the process of my interviews with him alludes to this possibility when he ponders the question of turning down the money for P.U.L.

70. Clark, Dark Ghetto, op. cit., page 194.

71. Ibid., pages 193-196.

72. Ibid., page 194.

73. Ibid.

74. Ibid.

75. Pinkney and Wooch, op. cit., pages 149-155.

76. Ibid., also see pages 140-143.

77. James Q. Wilson, Negro Politics: The Search for Leadership. (The Free Press of Glencoe, Illinois), page 310; for additional insight regarding, particularly the changing structure of 'civil rights leadership' see Charles V. Hamilton, "Integration on the Move; New Leadership Joins Effort" an article in The Los Angeles Times.

78. Peter Rossi, "The Study of Decision Making in the Local Community," August, 1957 (Mimeographed) Pages 3-4.

79. Ibid.

80. Ibid.

81. See Wingate articles as late as 1967; also see Charles Rangels more recent articles in Amsterdam News. (Chapter IX of dissertation.)

82. Krosney, op. cit., pages 70-71.

83. Interview conducted Fall 1973.

84. Pinkney and Wooch, op. cit., page 84 and Interviews conducted Fall 1973.

CHAPTER 6

THE FIGHT FOR ORGANIZATIONAL INTEGRITY

The leadership of any policy fails when it concentrates on
sheer survival; institutional survival, properly understood
is a matter of maintaining values and distinctive identity.
This is at once one of the most important and least understood functions of leadership. This area.....is a place
where the intuitively knowledgeable leader and the administrative analyst often part company, because the latter has
no tools to deal with. The fallacy of combining agencies
on the basis of <u>logical</u> association of functions is a
characteristic result of the failure to take account of
institutional integrity.[1]

                                        Selznick

The existence of specific community values and distinctive
identity in Harlem is more than an assumption interwoven in my analysis;
it is a fact.[2]   A fact which is inextricably tied to the leadership
typology presented and the relevance of Haryou as one legitimate
social mechanism for its identification. I agree with the sociological
contention, that states;

from the standpoint of social systems, rather than persons,
organizations become infused with value, as they come to
symbolize the community's aspirations; its sense of identity.[3]

In applying this perspective to Haryou, with respect to its conceptualization and implementation, some caution is required. Since we must
look carefully at those leaders responsible for the initial efforts;
and their perceptions of the community, its values and identity.[4] On
the other hand, since according to Selznick, "beginning as a tool, the
organization derives added meaning from the psychological and social
functions it performs".[5] And, "In doing so it (the organization) ital-
lics mine, becomes valued for itself;'[6]our concerns need not interrupt
our considering Haryou's 'infusion with value'.[7]

It may be helpful, at this point, to review certain of these values.
Dr. Kenneth Clark alludes to two of particular relevance to our concerns
for functional leadership: "<u>One basic rule</u> is to present to the hostile
white world a single voice of protest and rebellion. No Negro who is
concerned with his acceptance dares violate this world....Another basic
rule is that no issue can take precedence over the basic issue of race
and, specifically, or racial oppression".[8] These 'rules' are predicated
on community values regarding 'selling out' on the dignity and racial pride
associated with Harlem as a black experience and are also associated with
community values respecting function of 'research' as a method of dis-
torting community culture.[9] Another community value is well documented
by the Haryou document <u>Youth in The Ghetto</u> as it articulates: "that
the youth of Harlem are <u>not expendable</u>",[10] thus positioning the destiny
of the community's youth resources high in the order of value priorities. And finally, there is in Harlem a pervasive value on the critical

importance of culture and institution building. This latter value, though seldom discussed in the literature, is observable in the persistent search for knowledge respecting heritage and Afro-American History; and more profoundly in the determination to survive. There are other values in Harlem, related to the 'work ethic', social justice, civil rights and civil liberties; all relevant to the postures and styles associated with the leadership types being analyzed.[11]

Having defined somewhat, the kinds of community values operative in Harlem, the process by which Haryou as an organization becomes "infused with value"[12] should take on added clarity and significance. The functional relevance of specific leadership types in this process is illuminated by another of Selznick's insights;

> As the individual works out his special problems, seeking his own satisfactions he helps to tie the organization into the community's institutional network. Personal incentives may spark this absorption, and provide the needed energy; but its character and direction will be shaped by values already existent in the community at large.[13]

We can trace a number of circumstances around which Haryou Leadership struggles to maintain perceived organizational integrity.[14] Probably the clearest and earliest example is given by the conflict between Clark and Powell regarding the political vs. a-political contentions effecting the program.[15] Clark, as the embodiment of creative elite leadership is essentially at war with Harlem's prototype premier leader.[16] The conflict is postured as a crisis in which Haryou's integrity as an a-political social services and community action program is threatened by political forces whose interests are essentially inconsistent with such objectives.[17] I have discussed at some length, above, the substance of this conflict and am here, primarily concerned with its consequences regarding assumptions about Haryou organizational and community values. That Dr. Clark lost the 'war', and Haryou, (though there is speculation respecting precisely who lost what), is instructive in this regard.[18] Powell was Harlem's own. He was the embodiment of the communities values and culture. Clark had referred to him as 'part of the pathology' of the community; thereby essentially, categorically relegating the community's fundamental values to the status of pathological.[19] It is not my purpose here to deal with syllogisms for the sake of logical argument; yet it does seem somewhat strange that Clark, concerned as he was with defending Haryou's integrity would attack at the vary foundations of organizational legitimacy. It is probably true that

> leadership sets goals, but in doing so takes account of the conditions that have already determined what the organization can do and to some extend what it must do. Leadership creates and molds an organization embodying - in thought and feeling and habit - the values premises of policy. Leadership reconciles internal strivings and environmental pressures, paying close attention to the way adaptive behavior brings about changes in an organizational character.[20]

Thus the early Haryou leaders were, at a minimum, naive in posturing themselves as the defenders of an organizational integrity which conflicted with fundamental community values and sanctions.[21]

Cyril Tyson, one of Haryou's early administrators, viewed here as representative of the institutional inspirationalist type leader, is adamant in his recognition of the above realities.[22] Symptomatic of this awareness is his persistent efforts at effecting some reconciliation between the protagonists. Tyson's preoccupation with culture and institution building, expressed in his "program interlock",[23] concerns, is a function of his knowledge about the Harlem community's character. This early conflict regarding Haryou organizational integrity is but a prelude to the variety of challenges it subsequently faces. The realization, subsequent to the crisis, that a relevant Haryou would have to incorporate, (beyond mere mention in a planning document), the variety of community elements operative, including those of a political nature, is a major factor in the emergence of new leadership.[24]

The second circumstance responsible for arousing, within the ranks of Haryou's leadership, issues threatening to organizational integrity is related to Project Uplift in the summer of 1965.[25] Again, the concern at this point is the effect of certain leader decisions and functions in facilitating the "persistence of an organization's distinctive values, competence and role".[26] The key leaders involved at this juncture, are Roy Wingate, Executive Director of Haryou, James Jones, Director of Research, Frank Stanley, PUL Director, on leave from the Urban League of Greater New York, Andrew R. Tyler, former Chairman of the Associated Community Teams, Board of Director and now an active officer of Haryou's Board; Eugene Callendar, Chairman of the Haryou Board of Directors. Wingate, during his career at Haryou, shifts from a premier leadership type, to an institutional inspirationalist; an interesting occurrence to be discussed further in the next chapter. Dr. James Jones and Reverend Callendar are viewed as institutional inspirationalists. Tyler is among the creative elites; who interestingly, as in the case of Wingate, undergoes a transitional experience.[27] Stanley is a proto-indigenous idealist.

It is Jones who documents the basic issues related to our concerns for organizational integrity during the "critical decision"[28] respecting Haryou's involvement in PUL:

Research's objections to the program were: (1) no summer program could guarantee the absence of riots; (2) the summer program would divert energies away from developing the basic Haryou programs; (3) Haryou- Act was neither equipped, nor experienced, in effectively spending so much money so fast; (4) the promised funds could be more effectively spent on, and were needed by, the year-round programs; (5) in the long run, the basic programs of Haryou-Act would be much more effective riot preventors than any crash effort; and (6) Haryou-Act would be perverting its mission by accepting short-term funding for alleviating symptoms instead of correcting fundamental social conditions.[29]

It is the essence of 'mission' which concerns us in our analysis of organizational integrity.[30] Further, as Jones subsequently notes,

refusal of the funds could have cost Haryou-Act its grass roots connections, and its newly won position as top social welfare agency in the community. These were risks that the Executive Director and the Board of Haryou-Act were unwilling to take... The great irony in the scandal which subsequently erupted is that the year-round programs of Haryou-Act suffered the reverberations. The ten weeks of the summer program had long since passed when Haryou-Act's personnel were frozen and its funds constricted.[31]

And finally, and once again with particular respect to the major issue of organizational integrity;

a battle had been fought and lost, and research saw its dire predictions come true. The battle was hopeless from the start. The political die had been cast. A multi-million dollar ten-week program was to be consigned to Central Harlem. Haryou-Act had to assume the leadership of this program in order to protect its institutional and political interests.[32]

The fact that Haryou and its leadership were under certain pressures to assume the responsibility for the "Crash" program is clear.[33] The period was charged with demands that community action oriented agencies and programs provide short-run benefits or successes for large numbers of deprived people.[34] In the effort to adapt to such demands, Haryou as a developing social institution, was led into an ill-advised program whose hasty design and formulation evidenced little concern for quality standards or knowledge.[35] Thus Haryou embarked on a course that essentially undermined its special identity and function. It lost its "exclusiveness"[36] or what Selznick had referred to as "that insulation from day-to-day pressures which permit new ideas and skills to mature.[37] Thus, Haryou's leadership had, in terms of directions, articulated in Youth In The Ghetto; obscured its 'vision' and in Dr. Clark's words "legitimized the hustle".[38]

It is only possible to put these circumstances in perspective, to the degree that one associates them with Haryou's announced values and purpose.[39] The question is, whether the organization's leadership was sufficiently aware of, and committed to these ingredients of organizational integrity to adequately defend it. Respondents to interview questions related to the issues surrounding PUL as an organizational crisis speculate that had Dr. Clark been involved in Haryou at the time he would not have sanctioned Haryou's participation; $3,000,000, or not.[40] Clark's comment above substantiates their views. Further, given our view of Clark as a creative elite type leader, we are not surprised that he would rebuff any invasion of the vision as he and his colleagues perceived it. But what of the leaders who made the decision? Why were they vulnerable to the demands and pressures of forces obviously, not concerned about Haryou's integrity?

I have already discussed the relevance of external pressure as a factor. "But in diagnosis, we are mainly concerned with points of special inner weakness",[41] and for present purposes, with the internal leadership structure. The director's background and knowledge, for example--with respect to program implementation represented a serious organizational weakness. He was not a social worker-or administrator-- he was a lawyer with political aspirations. It is conceivable that had he such knowledge-or at a minimum--lieutenants with such training--he might have avoided certain pitfalls. He is correct, however, in his analysis of the total "newness" of the poverty program, and its "guide-lines procedures". Thus his, comment that the

whole O.E.O. thing was an experiment--no one had tried this
thing before and there were no blueprints regarding acceptable procedures for attacking the ghettoes problems;
must be taken into account.[42]

One important factor with respect to all of the leaders identified as key in the decision, excepting Callendar and Jones, is that none were involved in the earliest conceptualization and formulation of Haryou. The director and principle actor, according to one close colleague, "hadn't even read the Haryou document, Youth in the Ghetto";[43] thus, if true, providing us with some insight as to why he was more concerned with "not turning down $3,000,000 for Harlem", than with such 'intangibles' as institutional development and organizational integrity.[44] It is, upon analysis, somewhat characteristic of the premier leader types whether or not the above is true, that they tend to be primarily concerned with immediate, highly visible and tangible 'success' programs. The measurement of success is in terms of a good public relations image, personally and programatically.[45] One can, within this perspective,

judge why the Haryou end-of-summer parade was of such major importance
to some. To one observer,

> that parade showed Harlem in transition. It made Harlem aware
> of itself as a new and significant force. This kind of thing
> is necessary to give people awareness and a real sense of power.[46]

On the other hand, there were those who felt that,

> Harlem needed solid achievement more than it needed symbolism.
> Harlem needed to have its institutions revitalized and new ones
> created so that genuine power and not just the symbols of power
> were the evidence of change.[47]

Though this latter comment tends to ignore the historical place and importance of 'parading' in the Harlem community's experience, it is,
given the stated objection, nevertheless one with which I agree.[48] It
is, as a matter of fact, the recent opinion of a somewhatt more matured
and enlightened interviewer that the parade served as the 'spark' which
ignited the attack on Haryou.

> Ellis, that damned parade scared the hell out of the power structure
> in this city. It represented more black might and power than
> whitey had ever seen come out of Harlem before. We were together
> and the 'man' knew it. If I knew then, what I know now, I might
> have used that power differently...I remember Chuck saying to me..
> "Man this parade could mean real trouble for Haryou"... and he
> was right.[48]

It is true, that immediately after the parade, the scandal broke out.
I will not go into the details and allegations of operation PUL, as
these have been well documented elsewhere.[50] I do, however, believe
that the outcomes were responsible for the director becoming a changed
man; and perhaps more importantly for our purposes, a different type
leader.

The Haryou Board of Director's backing of his involvement in PUL
is an interesting phenomena. There were board members who assumed a
'let's wait and see what happens' attitude as he pushed the organization's involvement; there were others whose receptivity to the idea was
a function of their concern that the Urban League not be given a foot
hold in the community action 'business'.[51] Finally, there were those
who believed that Haryou had a legitimate role to play in facilitating
any special programs that were to be funded by O.E.O. related to Harlem.
There is a second level order of division within the board relevant to
the decision. A large contingent of the formerly autonomous ACT board
of directors held controlling votes in the now merged Haryou enterprise.[52] They were, for the most part, loyal to Wingate, their former
executive director, and were willing to go along with his program recom-
mendations. Those with tenure in the original Haryou effort, on the
other hand, saw the potential for Wingate's victimization, and in the
benign hope that something akin to the "Peter Principle"[53] might operate
to cause his downfall; awaited the predictable crisis. It is interesting
in this regard, that it is Eugene Callendar who, subsequently calls for
Wingate's suspension, pending clarification of the PUL charges.[54]

Few of the board membership, in this latter circle, however, foresaw
the nature or substance of the crisis. There seemed to be a general
lack of awareness regarding the potential danger to the total program
effort. This is the state of affairs in Harlem surrounding the approximate time period of from Winter 1966 to Spring 1967. The early part of
1967, the organization continues its struggle for sheer survival. With
Wingate gone, a complex administrative/policy board of directors' committee assumes the tasks inherent in holding Haryou together. Serving
in Wingate's executive office is Dorothy Orr, interim 'acting' director.
Mrs. Orr, who I discuss somewhat further in the next chapter is respon-

sible for bringing some degree of administrative efficiency to the floundering program components of the organization. I view her as an institutional inspirationalist leader during her activities in Haryou; though, later, as we shall see, she becomes a proto-indigenous idealist.[55] One final aspect of Mrs. Orr's tenure at Haryou (including her resumption of Haryou's leadership subsequent to Charles King's demise), is the manner in which it illustrates the veritable unacceptability of women in certain leadership capacities in Harlem. I will not deal with this matter substantively here, however, though it represents an important area of inquiry for future efforts. Suffice it to say at this point, that the resistances and objections to this brilliant administrator's leadership were resident in a variety of themes; at the community level and in the Haryou organization. These themes range from the requirement that Haryou reflect a positive and strong male leadership image for the purposes of functional 'identity'; to the proposition that the strenuous nature of the executive leadership tasks (late night meetings, highly emotional and from time to time, physical confrontation) preclude a woman's success in the top position. The fact that Mrs. Orr performed these tasks, without 'portfolio' (she never moved beyond 'acting' directorship title), was insufficient to change this perspective.[56]

The third and final issue which threatens organizational integrity, is related to Haryou's becoming the Community Corporation for Central Harlem; a matter which, to some observers, effectively destroys the organization's potential for institutionalization. The analysis of this final threatened the role of certain leaders in organization defense is the major focus of the next chapter.

To summarize my discussion of the fight for organizational integrity, to this point, however, is to remind the reader that I have been concerned with the function of leadership in articulating and protecting basic organizational values and purposes. The experience at Haryou indicates that certain types of leaders; the Creative Elites, the Institutional Inspirationalists and the Proto-indigenous idealists are sensitive to such organizational needs as the maintenance of 'autonomy', the embodiment of purpose and the pursuit of organizational mission and role; they perceive their functions as inextricably tied to achievements in the 'institutionalization' realm.[57] On the other hand, Haryou is organizational host to leadership types such as the raceocrats who, owing to their insensitivity or disregard for such organizational requirements, are available to exploit these institutional requirements. One final point is important. The finding that leaders do change. They do so as the result of organizational requirements and experience; as much as for the purpose of maintaining their leadership status.[58] This is a proposition which, again, I explore in subsequent chapters.

FOOTNOTES TO CHAPTER VI

1. Philip Selznick, <u>Leadership in Administration; A Sociological Interpretation</u>. (Ron, Peterson and Company, Evanston, Illinois) page 63.

2. I am here referring to Harlem 'social values' i.e. as those objects of desire that are capable of sustaining group and/or community identity. This includes any set of goals or standards that can form the basis of shared perspectives and group feeling. See for example Selznick, <u>op. cit.</u> pages 119-121. For additional specification of community values such as "race values"; value respecting 'trust' and community prosperity for a 'present oriented' life style (living for today, for tomorrow may never come); the value placed on "privacy" and "pride in youth" see: <u>Youth in the Ghetto op. cit.</u>, page 17 and pages 31-41; also see Gunnar Myrdal, <u>An American Dilemma</u>, <u>op. cit.</u>, page LXXII; pages 1-25; pages 781-809; pages 681-757 and pages 855-857; Danile C. Thompson, <u>The Negro Leadership Class</u> (Prentice-Hall, Inc., Englewood Cliffs, N.J.) pages 9-11. James Q. Wilson, <u>Negro Politics</u>, <u>op. cit.</u>, pages 169-213. Kenneth B. Clark, <u>Haryou: An Experiment</u> in J.H. Clark <u>op. cit.</u>, page 212 (in this instance note also developing Haryou Organizational Values).

3. Selznick, <u>op. cit.</u>, page 19 and Thompson, <u>op. cit.</u>, page 3.

4. I am here relating to the definitional function of the creative elite leaders in the early formulation of Haryou. As the 'instigators' of the 'planning task', in Alfred Kahn's words it is conceivable that their views of Harlem as fundamentally pathological, may have resulted in their overlooking certain community values, important to organizational institutionalization. See Alfred J. Kahn, <u>Theory and Practice of Social Planning</u>, <u>op. cit.</u>

5. Selznick, <u>op. cit.</u>, page 20.

6. <u>Ibid.</u>

7. <u>Ibid.</u> The point to be made is that varied forms of community pressure demand that Haryou and its organizational leadership assume a posture functional for resolving community concerns.

8. Clark, <u>Dark Ghetto</u>, <u>op. cit.</u>, page 194.

9. Wilson, <u>op. cit.</u>, pages 285-286; see also Clark, <u>Dark Ghetto</u>, <u>op. cit.</u>, pages XIX-XXV; and <u>Youth In The Ghetto</u>, <u>op. cit.</u> pages 20-24.

10. *Ibid*.

11. See Chapter IV of Dissertation for references in these general areas.

12. Selznick, *op. cit*., *ibid*.

13. *Ibid*. Kenneth B. Clark also discusses this phenomena, with respect to certain forms of leadership alienation. See *Dark Ghetto*, *op. cit*., pages 194-195.

14. For illumination of the concept 'organizational integrity' see Selznick *op. cit*., page 119.

15. See Chapter III of Dissertation.

16. See Chapter III of Dissertation

17. See earlier reference to "political rationality" in Ranney, *op. cit*., *ibid*.

18. Interviews with former executives in Haryou and Hana suggest that Clark does not exhibit any such sense of 'loss'.

19. See Clark, *Dark Ghetto*, *op. cit*., pages 163-165.

20. Selznick, *op. cit*., page 63.

21. This is more clearly an example of not recognizing the relevance of divergent values and integrities in Harlem, or at least of ignoring those which did not fit the conceptions of the early Designers. Certain of Alfred Kahn's insights regarding the 'screening' or 'filtering' of 'value preferences' at specific stages in the planning process seem not to have been considered by the Haryou Formulators. See Alfred J. Kahn, *Theory and Practice of Social Planning*, (Russell Sage Foundation, Pages 96-130).

22. Cyril Tyson is currently the Director of Optimum Associates, in New York City; Formerly Director of Administration at Haryou.

23. *Youth in the Ghetto*, *op. cit*., pages 353-504. Krosney, *op. cit*., pages 55-57. Interview held--Fall, 1973.

24. The fact that Tyson was not included in the new Leader Cadre is a function of his status as an institutional Inspirationalist; as well as Clark's Black Bell. His preoccupation with program and institutional concerns left little time (though he seemed predisposed) to deal in the community and organizational politics and intrigues which would have facilitated such emergence.

25. See Dr. James Jones; *op. cit*., pages 17-19 and also in Krosney, *op. cit*., page 83, Pinkney and Woock, *op. cit*., pages 44-57.

26. Selznick, *op. cit*., *ibid*.

27. Interviews conducted Fall, 1973.

28. See Jones, op. cit.,; ibid.; and Pinkney and Woock op. cit., pages 140-155. Also see Krosney, op. cit., page 83.

29. Jones, op. cit., page ibid.; Krosney, op. cit. page ibid.

30. Jones, op. cit., page ibid. Korsney, op. cit., pages 81-91 and Pinkney and Woock, op. cit., ibid. It is conceivable that the Haryou leadership decision to assume the program grew from concerns with organizational interests involving a different constellation of priorities. The existence, according to this perspective, of a continuum of Community and Organizational values would suggest a differential view of relevant mission and integrity. My contention is that given Harlem and her leadership's experience, historically, in dealing with 'stop-gap' or 'bit incremental' types of programs; and further--the precedence found in the problems of mobilization for youth--Haryou leaders should have maintained the 'mission' and priorities established by the Youth in the Ghetto document.

31. Jones, op. cit. pages 19-22.

32. Ibid.; also see Krosney, op. cit., page 81-91.

33. Ibid.

34. See the National Advisory Commission on Civil Disorders (Kerner Commission), op. cit., pages 30-46.

35. Pinkney and Woock, op. cit. page.

36. Krosney, op. cit page 83 and Jones, op. cit., page 18-22.

37. Selznick, op. cit., page 121.

38. Krosney, op. cit., page 83.

39. Youth in the Ghetto, op. cit.; page 9, 30 and 32-41. Clark Haryou: An Experiment, op. cit., in J.H. Clark, Harlem: A Community in Transition.

40. These interviewees further suggested that the rationale for this position relates to posturing Haryou in a better position, in the long run, to demand the kinds of resources it really wanted and needed--within a more relevant planning and implementation framework. Given this approach, agency 'capability' to absorb major funds, with accountability would have been unquestionable.

41. Selznick, op. cit., pages 119-120.

42. New York Amsterdam New Article, June 1966. op. cit.

43. Interview conducted Spring 1973.

44. Interview Fall 1973.

45. Eugene Litwak illuminates the phenomena of the "mass media" type leader in primary groups and organizations; see Eugene Litwak and Meyer _A Balance Theory of Coordination Between Bureaucratic Organization and Community Primary Groups_.

46. Krosney, _op. cit._, page 86 and Interviews conducted Fall, 1973.

47. Krosney, _op. cit._, page 84-86 and Pinkney and Woock, _op. cit._ page 140.

48. The 'Function' of parades in Harlem with respect to cultural development and style has never really been developed. I comment briefly on this activity at a later point in the dissertation; see, however, James Weldon Johnson's _Black Manhattan_, _op. cit._, page 136-140.

49. Interview conducted Fall 1973.

50. See Pinkney and Woock, _op. cit._, pages 44-57 and Krosney, _op. cit._ pages 79-81; also see Wingate's Series of Articles submitted to the _Amsterdam News_, 1966-1967.

51. See Krosney, _op. cit._ page 80.

52. _Ibid_.

53. See Krosney, pages 79-81.

54. Krosney, _ibid_.

55. The change is a function of her changed role. Mrs. Orr is now a top administrator in the New York State Human Rights Commission. I find during the study that comparable changes in leadership involved in the Haryou process, often accompanies changes in their occupational or official organizational positions.

56. Myrdal presents an interesting analysis of the problems confronted by women in assuming leadership generally, see _An American Dilemma_, _op. cit_ page Appendix 5. See also Elaine M. Brugess, _Negro Leadership in a Southern City_, (University of North Carolina Press) page 102.

57. My perspective on institutionalization is akin to Selznick's analysis, see Selznick, _op. cit._, page 16.

58. I arrive at this perspective as the result of findings in my study. The procedure of reviewing the histories of leaders during their activities in Haryou (in addition to field observations as participant observer); and subsequently observing them in their present capacities has facilitated my views.

CHAPTER 7

THE ADMINISTRATIVE COMMITTEE

The Uses of Community Power

In April of 1967, I arrived at Haryou as Special Assistant to the new Haryou-Act Executive Director, Charles H. King. Having come from an approximate one years organizational effort with New York's first Opportunities Industrialization Center (OIC); an experience shared with another of the North's black urban leaders, Reverend Milton Galamison.[1] I felt well equipped to make a contribution to the struggle designed to overcome many of the community's problems. The intervening years since my experience at HANA, had taken me to Mobilization for Youth, the National Committee Against Discrimination In Housing, and OIC. I came to know many powerful and interesting men and women and had traveled throughout the country. Despite these opportunities and adventures, I persisted in my interests in, and concern for, the 'folks' in Harlem: a fact which often irritated my contemporary colleagues.[2] Now, however, a new opportunity presented itself.

My first contacts with Charles King convinced me that here was a man who could effectively revitalize the Haryou program. King, a professional social worker and administrator, had earned a prestigious reputation as the Executive Director of the Wiltwyck School For Boys. A strinkingly sincere and honest man, he seemed somewhat out-of-place at the helm of the controversial Haryou. His insight and commitment to effecting the organization and its staff with the values and purposes for which the program was originally designed, was reminiscent of the earlier institutional inspirationalist leaders, Cyril Tyson, Jim Jones, Milton Yale and others. King has a special kind of dynamism. A contagious sort of open mindedness that affected the entire Haryou staff. I felt confident that as part of the 'new' Haryou team, I was about to share in the revitalization and redirection of the largest black urban anti-poverty program in the country. My idealism was shortlived.

The traumatic organizational experience from which Haryou is still emerging, as outlined in the above chapters, had so effectively dismantled it, that only remnants of the formerly cohesive program elements remained. Wingate has been relieved as Executive Director - permanently; and his former Associate Director, Mrs. Dorothy Orr has been designated 'acting' director. The real controls of the organization, however, are lodged in the new Board of Director's mechanism called "The Administrative Committee'.[3] The Committee is a functional group of Haryou leaders headed by the Chairman of the Board. He is a successful lawyer, highly respected in Harlem both as the result of his professional competence and as the result of his former chairmanship of the Associated Community Teams (ACT), Board of Directors. Currently a Civil Court Judge, the Chairman at the time of his activities in Haryou, held an iron clad 'hold' on all 'critical' decision' making.[4]

The Committee's presumed task is to supervise the day-to-day operations of the Haryou program; while concommitantly conducting an 'in-house' investigation of any instances of agency corruption or mismanagement.[5] Four additional members of the Haryou board were appointed to the com-

Haryou-Act Organizational

Chart
1967-1969

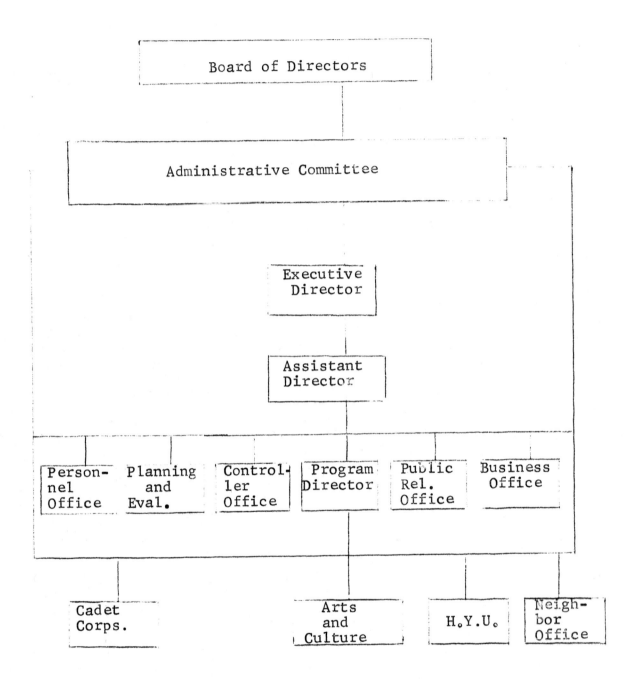

Board of Directors

Administrative Committee

Executive
Director

Assistant
Director

| Person-nel Office | Planning and Eval. | Control-ler Office | Program Director | Public Rel. Office | Business Office |

Cadet Corps.

Arts and Culture

H.Y.U.

Neigh-bor Office

mittee, by the chairman. One is a Labor organizer and head of the Central Harlem Labor Council. He is a lieutenant of the Harlem sage, A. Philip Randolph and was active in the early struggles associated with the labor movement in Harlem and nationally. Two were fairly successful local businessmen and finally, one is a struggling small business entrepeneur.[6] Despite the above association of the Committee's function to that of supervision of Haryou's activities, the immediate effect is the total obliteration of that critical line which separates policy functions from administrative ones.[7] The resultant confusions of program activities, and complete undermining of administrative authority and organizational communications channels was predictable.

This is the Haryou that King inherits. The contemporary program scene is one of administrative and policy chaos. Additionally, the new administrator finds a 'battered' and embattled executive 'cabinet', representative of the once highly qualitative cadre of program directors and administrative officers unique to Haryou.[8] Dorothy Orr, a brilliant administrator in her own right who had brought new executive quality to Wingate's efforts earlier in the Haryou experience, though weary, persists in her commitment to the program. John Young, now deceased, director of Public Relations; James Mitchell, Director of Programs; Julius Cayson, Controller; and Robert Watson, Director of the business office; are representative of this level of leadership. I was early impressed with the potential which these professionals held for building a program of excellence. The fact that it was never realized is a function of the times and realities of the Administrative Committee and its priorities; which as my analysis proceeds, are found to be inconsistent with Haryou program interests. An additional ingredient interwoven in the analysis related to the Committee's actions as manifestations of the distrust which has resided between professionals and politicians from the inception of Haryou.[9] It is noteworthy in this regard, that none of the Committee's members are social service professionals, but its Chairman is an astute politician.

King, in assuming the new Directorship of Haryou, is intuitively aware of these nuances. In the belief, however, that they can be overcome by mobilizing sound programming, he embarks upon the task of getting his staff moving on new program designs.[10] King's resolve to essentially ignore the in-house 'politicing', resides in the chairman's assuring him that he would have no interference from the Committee, or the Board itself.[11] It is a promise unkept, since evidently certain of the Committee members were not party to the deal. Members of the Committee are in the Haryou offices, daily. One in particular is persistent in exploiting his access to agency equipment and transportation resources. King, though he does not confront this Board member directly, is observably distrubed. In trying to deal with the problem indirectly, i.e. through comments to the Chairman, he is able to effect some relief, but at the expense of creating a new 'enemy' in the Committee.

An additional element in the variety of problems faced by the new administration, is the former director. The fact of his resignation (forced), has little to do with his visibility at Board meetings, and at the Haryou program offices.[12] Kings annoyance at the former Director's constant presence at official functions symptomatic of his vying for a new power base in the Haryou organization, is often communicated to his closest associates; 'He represented a real problem to our getting things together and moving again",[13] is a comment reflective of King's strong resentment. The former director, undaunted, however, despite his awareness of King's concerns, persists in 'wheeling and dealing' at the Board

of Directors' meetings, and among the newly emerging Neighborhood Boards'
leaders. Wingate's perspective on the matter is illuminated by him comments during a recent interview:

> I had nothing against King, personally, but he was in my way.
> If it were today, I'd know how to handle the situation. He,
> nor anyone else, would have stayed in my way. My problem was
> ...I was too nice a guy, and nice guys get pushed around.[14]

Wingate's comments during the above interview tended, generally,
to indicate that he had not fully understood the 'power' that he pos-
sessed in his short-lived premier leadership functions.[15] Here was a
man who had evidenced a high degree of charisma among the people of
Harlem (including its youth) at a critical moment in the community's
history; he had represented a mammoth program responsible for facilitating the utilization of millions of dollars, and failed to grasp its
significance.[16] It is my contention that any premier type leader would,
by definition, have done so.[17] Wingate, however, represents a special
instance, in that he might have made a successful return to power had
he not alligned himself with the Haryou Administrative Committee. He
had sensed, and rightly for the moment, that the real decision making
powers rested with the Committee, and thus it represented the mechanism
to be used for his purposes. What he did not realize, was that the actions of the Committee were functional in swelling new resentment of
the existent Haryou leadership. Wingate should have realized this, as
the dissident organizational and community elements resided within the
very constituencies he purported to represent; the neighborhood boards.[18]

King, on the other hadn, was more astute. He knew that a new leadership was emerging, and made himself available to it. He believed in,
and took seriously, (at first), Haryou's possibilities as a potentially
viable community institution. He sought, in various ways such as counselling sincere leader aspirants; interpreting to community people the
institutional intent of Haryou policies; and through publicizing the
positive aspects of the program; through these and other means, to inspire a demoralized staff and community constituency.[19] Functionally,
King was a facilitator of newer and more honest channels of communications between Haryou, its Board of Directors and concerned community
people.[20] In the only written account by King of his perspective on
Haryou, one is again impressed with the rationale for identifying him
as representative of the institutional inspirationalist type leader:

> Haryou is the most controversial of the anti-poverty programs.
> But it also has the greatest potential for significant help to
> the ghetto population. Haryou-Act is controversial and seems
> destined to remain so simply because it represents an ideal
> program; an objective, and aim; the possibility of liberating
> a black ghetto community by making it vitally and powerfully
> aware that, as a community, it has a commonality of interests
> and purpose--that its divergent voices can and must speak a
> single language of desire and ultimate purpose. That in black
> unity, black political and social power can be realized and men;
> black men, can come to have some control over their destinies.[21]

The fact, however, that King stirred once again the imaginations
and sense of 'mission' and purpose, once the prime province of Haryou
was of little importance to the Committee. Two members of the Committee
in particular, tended to view King's concerns as, "naive" and "overly
do-gooder".[22] They did not share his sense of participatory community
programming, and persisted in running the Committee as a kind of 'cloak
and dagger' operation.[23]

114

Why is it so important that the Administrative Committee exercise such control? What is to be gained by a man of the chairman's achievements (he is a successful lawyer and member of the New York City Board of Estimate), by participating in such a process? What were the Committee's real purposes and goals?

I recall the frustrations of Charles King and other Haryou executives in attempting to deal with such questions. King often confided, that "I don't understand what, he (the chairman), really wants out of Haryou; why he just won't let go--but he won't".24 Even at the present writing there are no real answers; only conjecture.25 There are those in the Haryou organization, and the Harlem community at large, who believe that the chairman and his appointed committeemen were so heavily implicated in the issues surrounding Haryou's 'mismanagement of funds' controversy--that they had to extricate themselves (commonly called the 'cover-up' or 'whitewash'), before leaving the Haryou scene. Others are adamant that the committee's purpose was to protect Haryou in its contemporary 'vulnerability' from other community forces, (as well as non-Harlem ones); since the organization represented a "multi-million dollar 'plum'" in crisis and thus available for a 'take-over'. Finally, and probably most tenable, is the position that Haryou represented an effective political platform for certain of the Committee's members who might be inclined towards some public office; a civil court judgeship for example. In this latter instance, effective 'control' of a large black staff and dependent community organizations representing Harlem's masses could be an effective 'vote-getter'.26

An interesting phenomena is observable at Haryou during leadership transitions and change. The peculiar nature of the 'testing' syndrome, is very much a part of the process. New leaders upon arrival at Haryou, are deluged with advisors and well-wishers. Staff members, administrators and a few board of director's members shower the neophyte with flattering remarks, and new ideas, which if followed, presumably will catapault him to immediate success in his new leadership role. The new director is made privy to the variety of organizational 'secrets' representative of informal Haryou 'culture'. and finally he is the object of a facade of 'deference'. His will, for a short time, is respected and implemented. Then the bubble bursts. The leader, if he dares to make an independent decision experiences a complete reversal of attitudes; and it is at this juncture that he must be sufficiently strong to persist in functioning in accordance with what he believes is best for the organization--as opposed to whether he is well liked by all. It is a time when the strengths of the institutional inspirationalist type leader are critical; yet one during which such leadership needs the support of the commutator and proto-indigenous idealists.27

The knowledgeable observer of the Haryou scene, reflecting, recalls that during very few of the organization's leaders have enjoyed a genuine respect during their tenure in office. It seems that only after the leader has left the agency, is there a real assessment of his or her qualities, and a true adjudicating as to his merits. The ongoing, day-to-day analysis of executive leadership activities, on the parts of those involved (staff) is made more on the basis of how much one is able 'not to do', in a work sense, than in terms of what is accomplishable.28 Certainly this is the case during the activities of the Haryou Administrative Committee. Could it have been otherwise? In what sense could genuine respect for executive leadership have emerged given an atmosphere charged with administrative sabotage and 'back biting'. The Committee had effectively created an atmosphere of intrigue and political 'spoils' within Haryou. Favoritism and 'rabbi' seeking were reciprocal relationships of value to be pursued by line staff in the organization as well as some administrators. Personal survival in one's job took precedence over anything else; and if one was to survive, then one had better be on good terms with, or at a minimum—inconspicous to—the Committee's leaders.[29] Functionally, this leadership served as an intimidating fear provoking cadre. King, for example, as he came to know the various members of the Committee, often warned of one member in particular;

> Don't ever underestimate what he will do to get what he wants. Nothing, and I mean—nothing—is impossible for him to try to hold on to the little power he has.[30]

On one separate occasion, while in a Harlem barber shop, I overhead an even more damning remark about the same person King had mentioned. In the broader community, this particular Committee member was viewed as a 'gangster', and 'murderer'.[31]

I must, however, confess that as I came to know the Committeeman to whom the above comments were directed, I found him to be basically honest though in a gruff way; and more importantly, quite likeable.

This essentially is the nature of organizational dynamics which affect Haryou and Harlem leadership during the tenure of the Administrative Committee. The struggle on King's part to cut through this milieu is crucial—though it ultimately eventuates in his resignation, to the emergence of a newer and more community based leadership which ultimately confronts and overturns the Administrative Committee. I discuss this emergence of the commutator leadership phase below.

The King administration in its struggle to maintain some degree of organizational integrity, re-awakened in Haryou and Harlem a greater sense of awareness as to the institutional 'mission' of the organization than had existed since the initial formulation and research.[32]

There are other circumstances which affect the functional relevance of Haryou's leadership during these times. These are times reflective of the issues of community control in local school and government affairs. Desegregation in public education, 'bussing'. and civil rights failures, predicted by many Harlemites, have been realized; and the community demands eminating from northern ghettoes, led by Harlem, is for new priorities. Paramount among these priorities, is that Black communities turn their energies and available resources towards developing self-contained communities of excellence. It is a familiar diologue in Harlem.[33]

Black Muslim and Five Per-Center sects; para-military 'cong' groups and confederated militant organizations, Black Panthers and Elite 'guards'; all are vocal and persistent that the ghetto posture itself anew in a 'death struggle for power'. Haryou leadership and supporting community groups, (neighborhood boards, block associations, etc.), undergo new pressures to assume specific stands on these issues. The organization leadership is intimidated and threatened, (and in specific instances, physically attacked), by representatives of this surging militancy. Uncompromisingly, Haryou is attacked by these community interest groups for their presumed function as representatives of the white man's 'colonialism'.[34] The organization is presented two alternatives; change and assume a relevant community leadership role—or be destroyed. Haryou seems unprepared to do either. The fact that these are legitimate mandates seems irrelevant—given the existence of the Administrative Committee; though it is somewhat painful for many in Haryou who realize it. That special sense of frustration, embarrassment and irrelevance in a most relevant community purpose grips the entire program.[34]

The above should not be taken as an indication that Haryou leadership, including the Administrative Committee leaders, were dysfunctional to Haryou and Harlem during these critical times. It is clear, for example, that had the Committee not been as powerful and uncompromising in their control over the organization and certain community systems; that Haryou would have been torn apart. The Chairman's functional relevance in particular is responsible for maintaining some cohesiveness in the organization under stress. His strengths were repeatedly demonstrated during special kinds of 'crisis'. One example can be used to illustrate the point.

During the course of one of those perpetual 'all night' Haryou Board meetings, (this particular one was attended by some 100 community and board representatives), a loud disturbance is heard at the entrance way. The Board chairman had left directions that no additional people were to be allowed at the meeting as it was already quite overcrowded. I was seated near the rear of the meeting room and observed the Haryou guards struggling to contain a group of people who wanted to enter. Loud swearing and threatening echoed throughout the lobby of the Theresa, and filtering into the board meeting, caused the chairman to ask "what the hell's going on out there". He is advised by one of the guards that there are some 'trouble makers' from one of those radical groups

> trying to 'crash' the meeting. The chairman noticeably annoyed, but convinced (as the result of community people in the back of the room) that if something wasn't done, the meeting would have to be stopped,

said, "well let them in. Let's hear what they have to say".

The guards who had been struggling to keep the group out, were suddenly pushed away from the doorway, and in marched a half-dozen militaristically clad black men, each brandishing the largest machettes I have ever seen. They marched straight to the chairman's table, stuck one of the machettes into it, and threatened that if Haryou didn't get itself together, it would be 'burned' by the new community liberating forces. I later came to know the spokesman as one Charles Kenyatta.

The Chairman sat through this confrontation, unblushed, unexcited, and unintimidated. When Kenyatta had had his say, the Chairman asked "are you through" a few words were passed between the two and then the militants left as they had come. As they left, all kinds of excitement broke out in the room. Some of the community 'sisters' began verbally attacking the men in the audience for allowing the militants to take-over the meeting; other people shouted their feeling that the militants were right and "Haryou had better get itself together". Somewhere near the middle of the packed meeting hall, minor fist fights broke out--but through it all, the Chairman sat--cigar in mouth--uninspired. It is expected that Harlem premier leaders would respond in such fashion. The easily perturbable or flustered person--never emerges as a premier in this highly emotional vibrant community.[36] The point of recounting this episode relates to the knowledgeable Haryou observer's realization that had anyone but the Chairman been presiding so chaotic an experience, the meeting would have ended in shambles.[37] He on the other hand needed only to put one hand in the air, a jesture for which he was renowned, and in a barely audible voice say "Now, Now--let's get on with the business at hand"; and within no time at all, things were settled. Anyone experienced in Haryou during this period can attest to innumerable instances in which he acted accordingly. His function as chairman is paternalistic-- while at the same time placating and uniting.[38]

These latter comments serve to clarify an additional point regarding my perspective on leadership in this analysis. I am primarily concerned about the 'functional' effects of specific leader types within specific action and time references. I am also concerned with a moral-ethical interpretation of such leadership with respect to its relevance or consistency with basic Haryou organizational values and purposes.

Thus it is not of primary concern that I analyze a leader such as the Chairman, interchangeably using one or the other of these criteria in defining him on the one hand as a-moral (with respect to certain organizational values); while subsequently viewing him as positively functional for organizational survival. The reader should keep these distinctions in mind so as not to become even further disoriented when, at a later point, I discuss this leader's transition from a premier type to that of an institutional inspirationalist.

One final example of the effects of the Administive Committee on Haryou and connected community systems relates to the developing crisis with the Neighborhood Boards. The Boards, one of Haryous' major "blue-print' programs, represents a topic which alone could serve as a dissertation.[39] It is a program of singular importance to Haryou's image as 'representative' of Harlem's adult community. The Boards, however, are also viewed as potentially powerful socio-political action groups in their own right.[40] I have mentioned earlier that they represented an early 'bone of contention' between the Harlem Neighborhoods Association, and the early Haryou designers.[41] The perspective then, of the boards as representing potent devices for changing the political power balance in Harlem, persists into the period being discussed above. Thus they also represented a continued threat to the internal Haryou organizational power structure represented in the Committee. It is in the final analysis, leadership which emerges from the Boards that ultimately overturns the Haryou leadership structure.

The Neighborhood Board's program was conceived as a strategy for decentralizing the functions, decision making processes and representativeness of the Haryou organization. According to the framers of Youth in the Ghetto;[42]

> Local Neighborhood Boards, consisting of adults and youth,
> nonprofessionals and professionals, and residents as well
> as those who work in the area and live elsewhere, could form
> the basis for the development of a cohesive neighborhood.

Further, and of particular importance for present purposes, the Document continues, "the basic assumption is that there exist in the local neighborhoods actual and potential leaders, both among the adults and youth", and that

> ...local community leaders, many of whom will be without
> formal education and will lack the usual style and polish
> of social interaction, could be stimulated to develop the
> competence required and become able to utilize the skills
> of professionals in carrying out the mandates of the local
> boards, namely: 1) to develop social action, educational and
> social welfare programs, 2) to conduct systematic community
> research, and 3) to inform local residents about available
> community resources.

Five Neighborhood Boards were developed in Central Harlem, and from their inception threatened the community's power establishment.[42] The earliest instance in which the boards power manifests itself is in the response to Haryou's need for a new leadership.[44]

The initial conceptualization of these community vehicles is, in part, that they serve as mechanisms for the development and emergence of leadership imbued with the organizational values and purposes of importance to Haryou and Harlem. The Boards would then become essentially autonomous 'satellites' of the Haryou program. Their functions within the broader Harlem community once "infused with value",[45] would be to represent and unite diverse community elements around community action issues; inclusive, ultimately of political ones. This latter perspective is responsible for the view of the boards, ultimately as separately incorporated organizations--loosely linked to the quasi-public Haryou.[46]

It is during the tenure of the administrative committee at Haryou, that the above strategy is distorted and postponed.[47] The efforts of the committee at obstructing the process of separation or 'spin-off' of the neighborhood boards, precipitates violent leadership conflict within the organizations involved and the broader community.

An additional element which exacerbates the internal convlict is the newly created, New York City Council Against Poverty.[48] The Council is the policy making mechanism for the Community Action Agency, New York's official conduit for all federal, city and state anti-poverty funds allocated throughout the City's 26 poverty areas. As the coordinative structure for anti-poverty programs, the Council becomes a highly politicized structure. Conceived, initially, as a device for lodging greater control of the formerly autonomous community action programs, in the Mayor's office; the Council quickly becomes the poverticians bureaucracy. Local poverty communities elect representatives to the council for two-three year terms, and expect that their interests for available funding and program resources will have an effective lobby. Actually, the Council is an extension of the federal governments anti-poverty bureaucracy. Functionally, it serves as a "distance creating mechanism" in Litwakian terms, between local community strucures and leadership, and the federal government (represented in this instance by the Office of Economic Opportunity).[49] The informed observer of the anti-poverty program, recalls that this was not the original intent of OEO. Initially the anti-poverty program was envisioned as a politicizing instrument for bringing local urban constituencies into a new alignment with the then Democratic political administration.[50] The 'localizing' of the federal governments presumed concern for the nation's poor, and the generating of the 'Great Society' strategy did not take into account, however, certain consequences for municipal or City power interests.[51] Urban political leaders, in their outspokenness about being 'bypassed' by the federal anti-poverty establishment, demand inclusion. The Council Against Poverty in New York City, is a manifestation of the federal governments placating. It is the White House's 'bone' to New York City's Mayor and his increasingly disenchanted municipal power structure.[52] Effective control, thus, over locally based community action programs, of which Haryou is one, occurs. The Council Against Poverty's elected members, are quasi-public servants. They are unsalaried, but accrue varied degrees of prestige and political 'clout' dependent upon which community they represent and their individual interests or abilities.[53]

In Harlem, the Council is viewed differentially. Those leaders who have vested interests in municipal power circles view it as 'necessary' and realistic. The Haryou board of directors is split on the issue; but its chairman (also of the administrative committee) is pleased. For those primarily interested in Harlem, and Haryou as an aspiring institutions, the Council represented diffusion of the community's newly emergent power base. We now have before us the major factors involved in revolutionizing the Haryou leadership structure.

One community resident is representative of the kind of leadership envisioned by the designers of the Neighborhood Boards program. He is a 'commutator' leader. A man in his fifties, he is a 28 year resident of Harlem. He has been active in civic community activities since first coming to New York City, and is highly respected in the local community. Seymour is the Chairman of Neighborhood Board #5, located at the southern most extremity of Central Harlem on Lenox Avenue. In addition he has served as chairman of the Steven Foster (now Martin

Luther King), Houses Tenants Association; and during the heat of the crisis involving the Boards and Haryou served as chairman of the Central Harlem Council, a consortium of the five boards and other community representatives.[54]

This contact was a functional leaders in Harlem long before the birth of Haryou. His reputation in the community as a 'firebrand' community spokesman, brought him, early, to the attentions of the initial Haryou organizers. In an interview, conducted for this analysis, he recalled how the Haryou organizers sought him out, reminiscing that he was not at all anxious to become involved. He viewed the program as another "political pork barrelling" [55] episode, so familiar to the local Harlem observer, and felt that the community politicians and 'professionals' would only use the Federal moneys to "feather their own caps".[56] Owing, however to the continued prodding of the Haryou community organizers, and some intimation that if he did assume the leadership of developing the Neighborhood Board's program, that there might be a 'piece of the Haryou pie' in it for him, he became involved.

This contact is not alone in this analysis. A staff organizer and prime staff organizer mover of the Boards concept has similar ideas; as do the remaining four Neighborhood Boards chairmen.[57] A former director seems available to help the Boards in their struggle. The fact that the visibility involved in siding with the boards serves his purposes as a platform for returning to power is not construed as in any way dysfunctional to the Board chairman, who observes, for example, "We knew what he wanted, but felt he could still be helpful in helping us gain our independence from Haryou. It wasn't until later", the chairman continues, "that we realized he was an instrument of the Administrative Committee, placed among us to block the spin-off".[58]

The leadership power struggle for control of the Neighborhood Boards comes to a head in 1968. The Administrative Committee, still clinging to its waning power obstructs the spin-off procedure in every way possible. The Boards on the other hand are represented by the 5 chairmen; and key 'friends' in the Haryou staff and Council Against Poverty.[59]

One Board Chairman in his recounting of the struggle recalls instances of intimidation aimed at changing his stand on the issue. Phone threats, bomb scares at his Board office; heated rhetoric and accussations at Haryou Board of Directors' meetings and occasional "pushing and shoving" bouts; all are aimed at those committed to the Board's spinoff.

There is an episode which I recount as illustrative of the intersity of this power struggle. It occurs at Harlem's Salem Methodist Church. Haryou has organized a community-wide meeting, the purpose of which is to clarify certain 'official' Council Against Poverty guidelines regarding Haryou's becoming the new Community Corporation for Central Harlem.

From the very beginning, the atmosphere of the large church meeting area is tense. Present in large numbers are representatives of the Neighborhood Boards, Haryou's full staff, a substantial number of Haryou Board of Directors' members, representatives of the Council Against Poverty, and unaffiliated community people. Conspicuously absent are leaders from the Administrative Committee. The call to order is given, and everyone's attention is focused on the meeting's chairman. Almost immediately, his request for order is interrupted by a man in the rear of the church who petitions to be heard. The Chairman attempts to ignore the man, but he jumps from his seat and escorted by four additional men, walks to the front of the auditorium. In vain, the meeting chairman requests that the intruders take their seats. I am seated in the second row at the front, and surmise that trouble is about to break out. Simultaneously with my insight, one of the four men snatches the microphone at the dais and begins to talk. The Chairman in attempting to

regain the 'mike', is pushed aside. Suddenly a huge Harlemite leaps from
the front row seat, and retrieves the microphone, exchanging at the same
time words to the effect that "If you put your hands on that 'mike' again
I'll crack your head". Evidently not believeing Bobby, the intruder
does precisely what he is warned not to; but never gets a chance to say
another word. He is smashed full in the face, knocking him to the
floor. Then all hell breaks loose. The men who had accompanied each
other to the front of the church attack the Harlemite. Fists are flying
when someone seated directly in front of me leaps up wielding a butch-
er's meat cleaver he had concealed in a gym bag. As he hurls himself
into the fight, screaming breaks out all over the auditorium. Panicked
community people begin jamming the exits in frenzied efforts to get
out. Cries of "Police...Police..." ring throughout the church while
simultaneously, the crunch of fists and bones echo at the dais. I am
frozen to my seat, not knowing what to do, when I spot Charles King, who
had left the scene moments before the frey, struggling to get back into
the jammed auditorium door. Despite the fact that for every step he
took by surging, panic striken people trying to escape, he finally got
in. In a flash, totally, it seemed without regard for his own safety,
King jumped into the middle of the battle - trying to break it up. I
suppose I really had no choice, but in almost the same instant, there
I was - at his side trying to help. In retrospect, I find it hard to
believe, but there we were in the midst of the most violent punching,
cutting and kicking battle I had ever witnessed -- trying to be peace-
makers. It was crazy--we were crazy-- but it worked.

Eventually we had separated enough people to cool things down. As
the screaming and cursing subsided, I noticed, amazingly, that no one
had been seriously injured. One of the men had a slight cut on the
shoulder, evidently from the cleaver; but everyone was able to stand.
Defiantly, the protagonists separated threatening and cursing one another,
and promising a return match 'in the streets'. As they left the auditorium, the police arrived. Within a few moments of their arrival, came
members of the Committee. The fighting was over, but as the Committee
leaders arrived, renewed threats were shouted at them.

Haryou and the streets of Harlem were tense for weeks following the
above confrontation. Members of the Committee were 'sporting' revolvers
in shoulder or hip holsters as they participated in Board of Directors'
meetings and at program locations. Chairmen and others connected with
the Neighborhood Boards travelled in the company of bodyguards. Everyone anticipated more trouble.

My purpose in recounting the above episode is to impress upon those
unfamiliar with the intricacies of leadership conflict and change in
Harlem, (and those who, despite their participation in the process itself,
were unaware of certain nuances), that crisis precipitation and conflict
are functional, not dysfunctional in the change process.[60] The fact
that toughs had been brought to Harlem from Chicago to intimidate and
crush the Neighborhood Board's movement for independence did little
more than strengthen the Board's position in Harlem. The traumatic Salem
experience and its aftermath is responsible for mobilizing a new cadre
of community leaders irate over the exercising of raw power which they
and the Neighborhood Boards laid at the doorstep of the Haryou Administrative Committee.[61]

The new resentment and challenges are articulated by a woman, another
commutator type leader; two additional neighborhood boards activists,
typed here as a proto-indigenous idealists; and other supporters in
addition to the Neighborhood Board chairmen. The manifestation of this
emergent leadership intent is most clearly indicated by their torrid

confrontations with the Administrative Committee prior to the organizations transition to Community Corporation status. These new leaders
demand that 1) in keeping with the guidelines of the Council Against
Poverty, and the intent of the O.E.O. mandate of "maximum feasible participation of indigenous populations" in all community action programs;
that the Haryou Board be revised and expanded to include a cross-
section of the total community (1/3 formula of poor, professional and
elected political representatives),[62] and, 2) that the Administrative
Committee be disbanded.

The mechanism for effecting these changes is a community-wide
election of the new Haryou Board of Directors. I turn to the issues
involved in Haryou's becoming the Community Corporation in the next
chapter.

FOOTNOTES TO CHAPTER VII

1. The Opportunities Industrialization Centers Inc. (O.I.C.) was a unique nationwide program related to developing the technical and manpower training needs of the Blacks and other minorities. The program was conceived and implemented by the Reverend Leon H. Sullivan in Philadelphia, Pa. in 1962. For an insightful history and reivew of the O.I.C. Program see Leon H. Sullivan, Build Brother Build (Macrae Smith Company, Philadelphia).

2. I can recall for example, one colleague who said to me "Why don't you forget about all the social work stuff--you don't have to concern yourself about those people anymore--you don't have a thing to worry about now that you're at this level".

3. This is the designation which the Board gave the Committee-reference-Board of Directors' minutes, Fall, 1967.

4. I use Selznick's definition of 'critical decision' in this analysis. These are organizational or leadership decisions which affect the basic institutional fabric of Haryou. See, Selznick, op. cit., pages 56-58.

5. See Krosney, op. cit., pages 87-88 and the Amsterdam News Article submitted by Livingston L. Wingate, June 1, 1966, "No Funds Missing, No Mismanagement"; also see "Evaluation of Project Uplift" prepared for: Office of Economic Opportunity by International Research Associates, Inc. November, 1965 (unpublished report); and The Mayor Task Force Report (Dumpson Report), op. cit., pages 3-5.

6. Board Minutes-Fall 1967, Spring 1968.

7. In addition to professional and administration literature regarding this phenomena; i.e. Peter Blau and W. Richard Scott, Formal Organizations, A Comparative Approach, (Chandler Publishing Company, San Francisco); Amatai Etzioni, Complex Organizations: A Sociological Reader (Holt, Rinehart and Winston, Inc. New York) see articles by Max Weber, pages 4-14; Philip Selznick 18-31 Robert K. Merton; pages 48-60; Terence K. Hopkins pages 82-98; also see Section 4-Organizational Structures; and Richard H. McCleery, Policy Change in Prison Management, pages 376-399. Additional insight can be gained from Austin Ramney; Political Science and Public Policy, op. cit. pages 3-54; and Philip Selznick; The Organizational Weapon; a Study of Bolshevik Strategy and Tactics; (The Free Press of Glencoe, Illinois); see also Greenleigh Associates Inc. "A Proposal for Administration of Haryou-Act (1969).

8. See Pinkney and Woock's analysis of Haryou's staff in 1965 and 1966; op. cit.; pages 79-81. Also see Krosney, op. cit., pages 36-37; 50-51.

9. Youth In the Ghetto, op. cit. pages 375-384. Clark, Dark Ghetto, op. cit., pages 170-185. Interviews conducted during Fall 1973.

10. This 'programming phenomena' is often utilized as an 'anti-flounder' mechanism during organizational crisis in a number of anti-poverty programs. I recall a comparable activity occuring at Mobilization for Youth during its crisis stage. The persistent efforts on the parts of executives and administrators to keep staff focused on program content despite the variety of organizational nuances and crisis seldom succeeds.

11. This was an agreement with King often articulated during his initial weeks at Haryou.

12. Board of Directors minutes during this period reflect Wingate's substantive involvement in official deliberations, despite the fact that he had no official function with Haryou at the time.

13. Interview conducted Fall 1973.

14. Interview conducted Fall 1973.

15. Krosney, op. cit., page 77.

16. Interviews conducted Spring, 1973.

17. This comment related to my analysis that the premier leader is normally so involved in his own public realtions image that substantive matters re: program, escape him.

18. Interview conducted Fall 1973.

19. See for example Charles H. King and Arthur L. Ellis, et. al; "Black Youth in Rebellion" in the Wilson Library Bulletin, October 1967.

20. Field observation as participant observer; and Interviews conducted Fall 1973.

21. Black Youth in Rebellion, op. cit., pages 1-3.

22. Interviews Fall 1973.

23. Interviews Fall 1973.

24. Field Observation and Conference Spring 1936.

25. I rely quite heavily upon interviews conducted during the study for these conjectures.

26. I say probably most tenable since in fact a number of Haryou's leaders have subsequently become high level public officials; thus

it is not unreasonable to assume some correlation.

27.   It is to King's credit in this regard, that he surrounded himself with representatives of these leadership types, thus avoiding certain of the problems i.e. communications, encountered by other Institutional Inspirationalist predecessors.

28.   Field Observations as participant observer; and Interviews during Fall 1973.

29.   Interviews-Spring 1973.

30.   Conference-**Spring** 1968; Interview Spring 1973.

31.   Field Observation Summer 1969.

32.   Interviews Fall 1973.

33.   See Johnson, Black Manhattan, op. cit., pages 165-170 and Youth in The Ghetto, op. cit., pages 1-10.

34.   These experiences have not been documented in any literature but are the result of my experiences as a participant observer while an executive at Haryou. Corroboration is found in the analysis of interviews conducted for the dissertation however.

35.   Myrdal and others have discussed this conflict; Clark's concept of a pervasive sense of powerlessness as it often affects the community and its institutions at times of crisis, are also relevant. See Myrdal An American Dilemma, op. cit., pages 1133-1138. Clark, Dark Ghetto, op. cit., page 125. The conflict also resides in Haryou's position as a quasi-public agency-funded by Federal and Municipal resources. See Krosney op. cit., pages 91-92. For additional comments regarding this consideration.

36.   Premier leaders, in particular must be conditioned to deal with crisis and bombast. One function of their normally lengthy tenure in a variety of Harlem Community Organizations, including the church--is preparation for such leadership risks. I discussed this phenomena in Chapter V of the disseration.

37.   Upon occasion, the Chairman would relinquish the tasks of running a Board meeting to a lesser Board of Directors' Officer. The stark contrast in meeting decorum and accomplishments are legend in Haryou.

38.   Myrdal has commented on the predisposition of certain types of leaders, the "moderates" in his typology--to be paternalistic and abrasive. See An Amiercan Dilemma, op. cit., page 457.

39.   See Youth in the Ghetto, op. cit., pages 391-340. Documentation of the Neighborhood Board's concept. See also Krosney, op. cit., pages 77-78.

40.   Ibid.

41.   See Chapter IV of dissertation.

42. I draw almost exclusively on this 'Document' for the comments in this section. See Youth in the Ghetto, op. cit., ibid.

43. Krosney, op. cit., pages 78, and Interviews conducted Fall 1973.

44. This comment is based on my analysis of the present leadership structure in Haryou. My findings are elaborated further in Chapter IX of the dissertation.

45. Selznick, Leadership in Administration, op. cit., ibid.

46. The reader is reminded of the legal prescriptions regarding the involvement of publicly funded anti-poverty programs in political activism; see The Economic Opportunity Act as Amended in 1965 and 1967; also see Krosney, op. cit., page 77.

47. We are provided, accordingly, additional insight regarding the community political power concerns of the Administrative Committee in addition to whatever internal organizational considerations determined their interests for organizational control.

48. For a more substantive statement concerning the Council see: the Report of the Mayor's Committee for Developing New York City's Human Resources; (The Mitchel Svirodoff Report), 1966.

49. Eugene Litwak and Meyer, op. cit., page 37.

50. See Krosney, op. cit., page 40-42. I also view the intital intent to be that of broadening the base of Human Service professionals and particularly social workers in a new relationship with the Federal Government. This would explain the Current Chief Executives (Nixon's) persistent attempts to dislodge such professionals and discredit the concept of the Welfare State. Politically, the Social Welfare Industrial Complex had made substantial inroads in terms of coalitions with the Democratically controlled federal bureaucracy.

51. This is clearly demonstrated in the Mobilization for Youth Crisis. See Krosney, op. cit., pages 21-34.

52. Ibid.

53. Interviews Fall 1973.

54. Interveiw Fall 1973.

55. Ibid.

56. Ibid.

57. Interviews conducted Fall 1973.

58. Ibid.

59. Interview conducted Fall 1973.

60. Lewis Coser, in his book, The Functions of Social Conflict. (Free Press, N.Y., Collier-McMillan London) pages 1-80, and Selznick in The Organizatonal Weapon, op. cit., pages 79-160 allude to comparable functions of conflict and crisis.

62. Interviews conducted Fall 1973.

63. New York City Human Resources Administration, Council Against Poverty Guidelines for the Election of Community Corporation Boards of Directors.

CHAPTER 8

THE COMMUNITY CORPORATION STRUGGLE: CONFLICTUAL LEADERSHIP STRATEGIES

The majority of Haryou's present policy leadership are persons who emerged during the evolution of the Community Corporation.[1]

The Community Corporation is an administrative efficiency devise, envisioned as a coordinative mechanism for the funneling of anti-poverty funds to local communities designated as poverty areas. Theoretically, the Corporation is to represent broad ranged community planning, research and development reflective of a community's total resources and needs, and not those which deal with poverty alone.[2] Using the conceptual model of private, industrial and business corporations, there are some similarities discernable in the structuring of these non-profit community entities. Despite the fact that private business enterprise is profit making and the community corporations are not, there are comparable quests for efficiency, and the utilization of 'experts'.[3] In theory, the community corporations relate the development of program priorities and the allocation of scarce monetary resources to deal with them, through a system of 'contracting' and subcontracting with community resources.[4]

Unlike the private corporate model, the community corporation is interested in the development of human resources while persistent in developing strategies for meeting the physical, economic and socio-cultural needs of a finite community. They function as "colleageal"[5] bureaucracies, in Litwakian terms, and are informal, loosely structured social planning mechanisms.

The above represents the conception of the community corporation. In Harlem, the operationalization of the concept is yet to occur. The decision, or rather the community 'elections' which establish Haryou as the community corporation for Central Harlem, occur in 1969. As suggested in the previous chapter, the change represented another issue of leadership conflict. Key figures in the Haryou Administrative Committee take the position that it is only through becoming the community corporation that the program can survive. As the result of his position on New York City's Board of Estimate, The Haryou Board Chairman, for example, is privy to the commitment of the Municipal power structues to effect the corporation in Harlem.[6] The aggressiveness of City Hall, through its coordinative mechanism, the Community Development Agency, (the operational arm of The Council Against Poverty), indicates that he is right in his assessment.[7] It is noteworthy that much of this Municipal aggressiveness occurs simultaneously with the demise of Adam Clayton Powell, Jr's. power in the Congress.[8] The reader recalls that Powell is under suspension in connection with accusations of illegal and illicit conduct. Thus, the political ramifications of Harlem's being without an effective 'spokesman' in the power circles of Congressional and Municipal affairs is an added nuance to Haryou's vulnerability.[9]

One requirement of Community Corporation status, is the disengagement of all direct programming functions.[10] Community corporations are not program operating structures, and for Haryou, this means the 'spinning-off', or disengagement of such components as Harlem Youth Unlimited, (Haryou's historic youth division), its pre-school and 'Head Start' program, Arts and Culture, Cadet Corps and Neighborhood Board's programs.[11] It is in fact, this latter requirement, that is responsible for the pre-Corporation position of the Neighborhood Board's leadership. They, in addition to desiring the independence which the spin-off concept requires; envision the change as the opportunity, long awaited, for revolutionizing the leadership and power structure of the Haryou organization.[12] They are right.

The involved observer of the Haryou Board of Directors and its newly organized "Transition Committee" during these eventful times recalls the process of leadership decision respecting which members of the existing board should 'bow out' - gracefully - prior to being 'unseated' by the new community elections.[13] I can recount a series of such meetings. In some instances the 'voluntary' withdrawals of members from the board represented pitiable instances in which one could observe miniscule vestiges of power being 'snatched' from little people; people to whom Haryou had represented an only chance for participation in policy and important decision making.[14] For the exception of the chairman and his immediate lieutenant, this was the fate of those leaders who served the Board's Administrative Committee.

The decisions as to who should go, or remain, were often made outside of the formal structure of the Board. Frank's, for example, (a famous Harlem restaurant),[15] the location of many important decisions affecting Haryou and Harlem, is privy to discussions by key Haryou power 'barons' as to who on the board ought resign. Some objective criteria are used however; how many Board meetings has he or she attended, or missed, in the last year? How well are certain members known in the general community? How available is this, or, that incumbent on the Board to follow the 'Chairman's' will and decisions? These and other criteria are reviewed by the internal decision making leaders of Haryou. Subsequent, though lengthy, 'official' Board meetings are little more than shams, as, for the most part, the substantive decisions have already been made.[16]

The process of community elections for the corporation board is an interesting one. Haryou is mandated, as the then operating community action agency, by the Council Against Poverty, to effect a plan for community wide voting for new Corporation membership. Council guidelines require that in keeping with the theme of "maximum feasible participation of the poor" in policy decision-making bodies related to anti-poverty programs; as well as in the programs themselves, that one-third (1/3) of the newly structured corporation include 'representatives' of the indigenous poor. Additionally, the new board is to have representation from the professional, elected public official and other community elements.[17]

Haryou leadership in designing the required election procedures, must negotiate with representatives from these various community elements to arrive at 'acceptable' slates of individuals who are to be submitted on the election ballots. The general format is secret ballot. Haryou it is generally agreed, is to be responsible for a slate representing the professional and non-resident portion of the candidates. The neighborhood boards are responsible for presenting a slate of persons from the poor; and both Haryou and the boards are to project candidates from the elected official community.

This approach requires intense bargaining between the boards and Haryou leaders. The culling from preliminary slates of names and individuals not acceptable to one or the other is ongoing; while simultaneously each of the participating parties (Haryou and the Boards), care-

129

Community Corporation

Selection Process*

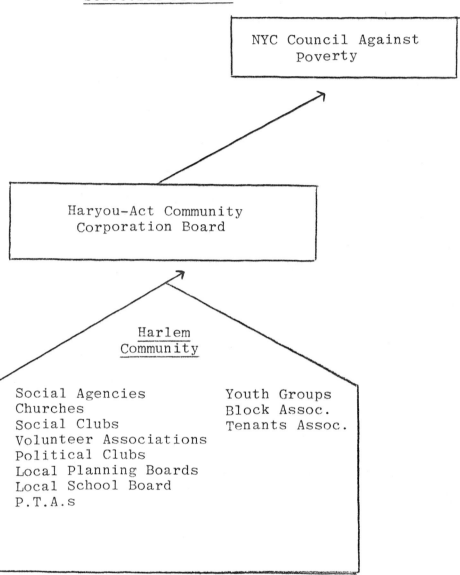

NYC Council Against
Poverty

Haryou-Act Community
Corporation Board

Harlem
Community

Social Agencies   Youth Groups
Churches   Block Assoc.
Social Clubs   Tenants Assoc.
Volunteer Associations
Political Clubs
Local Planning Boards
Local School Board
P.T.A.s

* Corporation Board Members are elected for two and three year terms
  thus allowing for leadership rotation.

130

fully screen their respective candidates.

Finally, the elections are set. Voting booths are set up in local schools, churches and neighborhood centers; and as the result of the effective bargaining and negotiating among the participant parties, an acceptable board of directors for the new Corporation is elected. The internal procedure for the subsequent election of Board officers results in the former Haryou chairman's continuance as corporation chairman, though he must now work with new officers, first and second vice-chairmen, board president, treasurer and secretary, who represent newer constituencies.[18] The new board is on expansion, one of 90 members drawn from all walks of life in Harlem. It is effectively representative of the mandated formula suggested above.

Utilizing my leadership typology, one finds strong commutator representation on the board, particularly as the result of the neighborhood board's influence. There are a number of proto-indigenous iealists, and a few institutional inspirationalists. There are no creative elite leaders on the new board, a finding which I discuss below, however, the raceocrat type leader is a noticeable participant.[19]

There is a third position regarding Haryou's becoming the community corporation for Harlem. This position holds, that such a course corrupts the intent and philosophy of Haryou, as an indigenous community institution, or effectively undermines its potential for ever realizing this goal.[20] In the original Haryou design, the prospectus for decentralizing program decisions and leadership had been built into the Neighborhood Boards idea.[21] True, there are internal leadership struggles and instances of community conflict generated in the process of bringing about this intention; an expected phenomena. To posture Haryou as the Community Corporation, however, is to consummate a relationship with City Hall which takes away the very essence of community decision making. Haryou's becoming the Community Corporation is viewed as creating a new Harlem component fo the City's anti-poverty bureaucracy.[22] The seriousness of these contentions are born out as a new dialogue ensues respecting whether Haryou Corporation staff are to be considered Civil Service employees. In answer to those who view the Corporation route as the only one to take if Haryou is to survive, these latter 'proto-indigenous' idealist leaders respond; far better to forego the immediate short-term benefits of Governmental funding security and certain municipal resources, and seize the opportunity to rally Harlem around salvaging Haryou as an independent program - peculiarly adaptable to Harlem's needs; than to become an additional tentacle of the municipal power structure.[23] These leaders further point to the experience and decision made by Mobilization For Youth as evidence that their's is a viable possibility. The suggestion that MFY, on the other hand had at its disposal a variety of resources, not available to Haryou, is viewed by these leaders as insufficient to warrant 'giving-up' so much that has been struggled for in Harlem.[24]

The issue is clearly one of pragmatism vs. idealism; and as the history of Harlem and Haryou document; the former ensues, as a basic community value.[25]

There are other ramifications of the leadership decision to make Haryou the Community Corporation. The process of program 'spin-off', is an administrative 'nightmare'.[26] Charles King, Dorothy Orr, James N. Mitchell, Robert Watson, John C. Johnson, Alma Lynch, and the writer constituted the executive 'transition' staff at Haryou. The tasks involved in the transition were; 1) design a 'masterplan' for the establishment of program priorities consistent with community needs and preferences, 2) establish priorities for the allocation of Corporation funds, and 3) spin-off the existent Haryou operating programs. This latter process involves help in organizing independent Boards of Directors, or some other policy determining bodies who upon separately incorporating, can assume the leadership responsibilities inherent in program funding and function.[27]   The Youth Development Agency of Central Harlem, for example, represents such an auspice. YDA became the policy Board for Harlem Youth Unlimited, The Cadet Crops, and other youth programs previously operated by Haryou.[28]

The awesome nature of the task is illuminated by the fact that all varieties of political, patronage and program nuances activate around who is going to run, or continue to work in, what programs. Irrespective of the difficulties involved in the transitional stage, the Haryou "Executives" accept the challenge willingly. Many, King included, sense that for the first time in recent memory, legitimate programming and technical competencies, requiring specific and professional type decisions are being required and requested.[29] This represents a stark change from the concerns which normally demanded the staff's attentions.[30] The staff welcomed the opportunity to demonstrate their competence in community planning, and the devising of program priorities.

There are, however, new kinds of pressures with which the staff must deal. The fact of newly emerging leaders in the Corporation Board means new demands for staff alliances re: the sponsorship of this-or-that program priority over some other. New Board members vie for staff time in the formulation of programs related to their priorities, rather than the priorities of the community at large. The Corporation staff responds to these pressures by assuming as professional a stance as is possible without alienating this new community element. King is adamant in requiring staff to structure themselves in roles which are essentially technical, thus, pressumably, avoiding the pitfalls associated with earlier accusations of favoritism and 'rabbi-ing' levied against organizational representatives.[31]

The early Corporation activities represent excellent opportunities for the proto-indigenous idealist type leader, and the institutional inspirationalists, despite their former positions as to what Corporation status portended for organizational integrity and purpose.[32] For in some ways, the new organizational structure represents a new opportunity to 'orient' community representatives to what the corporation might be, if Harlemites are aware of certain potentials. Potentials which relate to their newly united political 'clout' in dealing with City Hall. The community corporation, in this view, is a double edged sword; it can represent a new level of access to municipal resources, in addition to providing the City power structure new inroads into Harlem.

The leadership type of major importance at this juncture in Haryou's development however is the commutator. Helen Testamark is representative of this form of functional leader.[33] Helen has lived in Harlem for approximately 28 years; 25 of which were spent in one block (119th Street). She is a woman of extraordinary character and strength and at age 36 years is among the most powerful of Harlem's grass roots leaders. To walk the streets of Harlem in this woman's presence is to gain a genuine sense of what a community leader is. Helen knows practically everyone living in her community area, and seemingly everyone knows her. To feel that special sense of 'belongingness' or, 'acceptance' so important to one interested in Harlem's community life--is to 'saunter', 'surrey' or 'stroll' her streets or avenues with Helen Testamark.[34]

As an organizer and activist in the area of public education, Helen is unequalled. Her involvement in the community control issues surrounding Harlem's Intermediate School 201 is legend; in and out of Harlem, and she is recognized nationally, as an 'expert' in the variety of Head Start, and community local school board activities contemporary in the late 1960s and early 1970s.[35] Helen's functions as a commutator leader pre-date her connections with Haryou, as she was among the original members of The Harlem Neighborhood's Association (Hana), Board of Direcotrs. I was interested while interviewing Helen, as to why, given her leadership tenure in Harlem, she had never become a staff member of Haryou and only recently a member of the Board of Directors, she responds:

> I was never interested in being on Haryou's staff because the work that needs to be done in the community can't be scheduled from 9 o'clock to 5; it's a twenty-four hour day job - and most of these people left the community at 5 o'clock to go home. I only got on the Baord because we didn't have any real representation with Tyler and those guys--even though they have to count on us for Haryou to survive.[36]

When asked who she felt the key leaders in Haryou were, Helen mentioned Kenneth Clark, Charles Gadsden, Lillian Jordan, Iyantha Maynard, Charles King, Fred Samuels (the current chairman), Mamie Brown, Margaret Gordan, Emma Penn, Andrew Tyler, Dorothy Orr and Roy Wingate.[37] In defining the commutator type leader, above I suggested that a major prerequisite for such leadership is 'availability'. Helen's functional relevance in the community is facilated by the fact that she is a housewife. She is constantly available in the community, day and night to her local constituency. This is also the case with a number of those she identifies as leaders.[38]

Helen's earliest involvement in Haryou is via the Neighborhood Boards, though her organizational skills are earlier demonstrated in the formulation of a local Block Association (128th Street). Her involvement in Neighborhood Board #3, is as a matter of fact, as a representative of this Association. Helen's persistent concern with local educational institutions (the result of personal trauma's associated with her own education and that of her children), catapult her to leadership in Board #3, almost immediately.[39] In reviewing this leader's various community organizational connections we are supplied critical information regarding her functional relevance; for with each new affiliation Helen adds to the number of 'hats' she must wear. As a representative of the 128th Street Block Association, she has specific interests which to some degree are carried-over to her concerns with Neighborhood Board activities. Subsequently, as she becomes a leader in the Haryou Board, and owing to her continued commitments to the Block Association and Board #3, she is in the position to be functionally relevant to both. These functional relevancies are particularly illuminated during Helen's Chairwomanship of the Haryou Community Corporation's Education Committee.[40]

The manner in which Helen emerges as a new leader in Haryou is traceable in the above. Her tenure as a local leader for more than twenty years has accrued to her respect and power. She has developed specific organizational skills related to her commitment to certain community values; particularly those related to quality education for the community's youths.[41]

There is a more important observation to be made here however. It relates to our concern for viewing Haryou as a legitimate community mechanism for the identification and development of community and organizational leadership.[42] Helen, for example, as in the case of Seymour, in responding to my interview guide questions related to the above did not see the organization as reflective of Harlem's leadership.[43] Their view is that the community's legitimate leaders become involved, because of earlier leader 'default' and "feathering their own professional and political hats'".[44] Exploration, however, of these immediate or 'off-the-top-of-the-head' responses illicits that despite certain disenchantments with the 'actions' of Haryou leaders-there is recognition of their 'function' in arousing and mobilizing new leadership elements.[45] There is for example the function which 'open' Haryou community meetings performed for instructing emergent leadership in the techniques and procedures; styles and 'jargons' employed by those who make organizational decisions. Thus an element of 'training' is discernible in these exposures. I take these functions as sufficiently important to persist in the proposition that Haryou is a legitimate social mechanism for the identification, development and training of community and organizational leadership. The Community Corporation shift, then, facilitates the emergence of existent local leadership. A leadership affected with the need for change in Haryou.[46]

There is, finally, with respect to the Haryou Community Corporation's emergent form, a new perspective on youth participation. Haryou, has historically focused on the involvement of youth in the decision making process.[47] With the advent of the Corporation, and the concomitant emergent strength of the Neighborhood Boards, this concern is deemphasized. There has not been a strong youth lobby in Haryou since the days of Wingate, when Lloyd Pryor, Calvin Alston, Frank Willis and others in the leadership of the Harlem Youth Unlimited associates were active.[48] The program, though it continues as one of the newly 'spun-off' components is essentially severed from any meaningful power or leadership in the Corporation. The participation of a youth representative on the new Board of Directors of the revised Haryou is in no way reminiscent of the powerful 'swing vote' position once held.[49] This is not to suggest that the existent youth leadership in the Corporation is without functional relevance, as, below we find the reverse to be true. We gain some insight regarding the functions of youth leadership in Haryou's transition, by tracing the involvements of certain of the young men identified with Harlem Youth Unliminted (HYU). One in particular is certainly representative.

He was born in Harlem, and is one of the original Haryou associates who remains in the leadership spotlight of contemporary Haryou. His earliest participation is linked to Kenneth Marshal, Cyril Tyson, Lloyd Pryor and others. As a youth representative on the Haryou Board, he is familiar with the trials and tribulations of the organization during the eras of Kenneth Clark and Roy Wingate. He recalls, for example, the function of the youth contingent in Wingate's successful bid for the Executive Directorship of the program. "We got Wingate in. We had the swing votes in the Board,"[50] are among his remembrances. He is also quite active as a member of the Haryou Community Corporation board as it is initially set up; though at this point, many of the new Corporation leadership began questioning how long he planned to remain a "youth".[51] It was somewhat amusing to observe this youth's repsonses to being 20 years old and suddently questioned as to his authenticity as a youth representative. Though he was not the only youth representative at the time, he certainly was the most outspoken. As the 'senior' youth member in terms of active tenure in Haryou, he often functioned as the spokesman for Haryou's youth, whether truly representing their perspectives or not.[52]

This young man is also the Youth Mayor of Harlem, during his activities in Haryou, a fact which results as much from his function on the Haryou board, as it does his actual community activities with Harlem's youth population.[53] At the approximate age of 18 and 19 years, he was as sophisticated in the utilization of intrigue and community political systems as elders twice his age. He was fascinated by the leadership process which unfolded before him, and of which he was a part; and

particularly as the process respects the Administrative Committee.[54]
He thoroughly enjoyed the crisis and conflict commensurate with the
evolution of the leadership structure in Haryou, and found himself amused
at the aspirations of emergent leadership.[55]

An interesting aspect of this youth's perspective on Haryou leadership, is the high regard in which he held the Administrative Committee
leaders. In many ways, he emulated those he esteems. He is bombastic
and forceful in dealing with his youth constituency, and whenever he
can, with members of the adult components of the Board of Directors
as well. At one point during Haryou's transition to Community Corporations status, he and a number of his followers are accused by members
of the Neighborhood Boards of harrassment and intimidation regarding the
Board's 'spin-off' objectives. Many leaders of the Boards are convinced
that the youth have been used as 'storm troopers' by adversaries of the
independence movement, and are openly defiant and hostile towards this
youth as a major leader in these activities.[56]

In a sense, he as in the case of those he admires, is basically
honest. He states, or presents his position on an issue 'out front',
"with all the cards on the table",[57] and then embarks on whatever course
of action is necessary to achieve his objectives. In this sense, he
is an uncomplicated person who is easily identifiable as a commutator
type leader. His function as an intermediary between Haryou decision
makers and the youth community of Harlem is well known.[58]

This young man is currently President of Harlem's Local Community
School Board.[59] The astute observer can, upon occasion, find him 'chairing' the characteristic, (to Harlem), luncheon meeting at Harlem's exclusive 'Flash Inn' restaurant (Franks is no longer in existence); where,
seated at the head of a hastily arranged troup of tables--non-chalant
facade and all--he engages in the decision making process. He aspires
to 'premier' leadership stature; a goal which it is conceiveable he
may achieve.

The process of leadership development in Harlem is again illuminated
by the above exmaple. As a young man involved in the Haryou process,
this youth learned much from his mentors. He learned his rhetorical
skills, and the ability to manipulate and coerce, at the feet of Haryou
leaders, and whether one is in total agreement with the style of leadership, there can be no substantive disagreement with its function in
the community.[60]

We now have some picture as to the configuration of leadership and
organizational elements functional in the transition of Haryou from a
community action, programming agency, to that of a community corporation.
There are two remaining aspects of this historic transformation of relevance to our analysis of leadership. One relates to the issue of 'professionalism vs. non-professionalism; the other to the issue of social
service leadership vs. political leadership in Harlem.

It is in the course of an interview with a former Executive of
Haryou, and presently, Assistant Commissioner of the New York State
Human Rights Commission, that I am re-sensitized to the importance of
these issues and particularly the latter one. Having commented earlier
on the dangers inherent in overgeneralizing about the importance of
these concerns in the Haryou experience, it is noteworthy that much of
the distrust and enmity directed against Haryou leaders is often found
to reside in precisely these areas.[61]

Local non-professional community leaders have resented the professional social worker and other human services professionals.[62] Social
engineers have, and to some degree justifiably, been viewed as contri-
buting elements in the community's historic social problems. It is
only recently and as the result of the anti-poverty program efforts in

the community, that this perspective is changed, somewhat. Heretofore, those who represent the above, and particularly their leaders have been identified as being on the wrong side of the 'problem definer' table.[63] Haryou as it becomes the Community Corporation affords new opportunities for black social welfare professionals and community grass-rooters to re-define and redesign their functional relationships to one another. Non-professional leaders for example, find in the corporation staff, professionals who are willing to use their training and skills in a new partnership with their community colleagues. There is a new respect on the parts of both parties for the peculiar contributions each can make and must make if the Haryou Corporation is to survive. The professional's perspective is one which views the new Haryou leaders as the legitimate heirs to the Corporation; and their response to these leaders' requests for assistance and technical guidance in the new planning, research and coordinative tasks implicit in Haryou's new status gives ample evidence of their availability to help. The eager participation of professional staff on the various corporation Board committees (i.e. planning, education, program, personnel, etc.) is unique in the organization's experience.[64]

Community leaders, on the other hand, and probably as the result of their newness in the organization's policy making body, are available to defer technical and 'expert' type decisions to Corporation executives and staff. Even the former Administrative Committee Chairman, successful in maintaining his position as Chairman of the Haryou Corporation Board, seems to have gained some semblance of respect for the professional competence evidenced in the designing of Haryou's new role.[65] One executive recounts,

> He was beginning to see the relevance of the professional
> approach in Haryou. He was, just before his leaving the
> chairmanship, evidencing more confidence in our judgement
> than ever before. Now if we could have arrived at the same
> kind of trust earlier in the Haryou experience, we would
> have a different program today.[66]

The experiences of community leadership in finding the professionals genuinely interested, and competent, are critical in effecting a new community image of the organization and its staff.

There are, however, instances in which some retrogression to the earlier suspicions and distrust emerge. The circumstances of scarce money resources available to the new Corporation is exacerbated by continual 'cut backs' in anticipated allocations to Harlem, from the City.[67] Competing community interests, upon finding 'their' programs are not included in the 'master plans' designed by the Corporation for priority allocations are incensed and accuse the organization staff of favoritism. Once again the important function of the newly involved community leaders is identifiable, as they serve as the primary rebuffers of these accussations.[68]

In those instances where a genuine sense of cooperation does exist (as in the example of the Haryou Corporation education committee, chaired by Helen Testamark), a special kind of accomplishment is experienced. Proposals are made by staff assigned to a particular Board Committee; explanations of technical and funding aspects are discussed openly, and once understood and agreed upon are presented and defended by non-professional committee members to the full Policy Board. Positive experiences of this kind within Haryou program and planning committees serve as additional opportunities for the continued emergence of new leadership.[69]

Georgia McMurray, and Marshal England, for example ascend to new leadership heights, in the Corporation and the community, as the result of their astute participation in the Planning Committee. The committee, responsible for establishing the overall priorities re: funding and program for the Corporation, is viewed as the most controversial within the new organization. McMurray and England are both defined as proto-indigenous idealists, for the purposes of this analysis, and are in the vanguard of the 'new' professional leadership that challenges the former Haryou leadership structure. England becomes President of the Haryou Corporation Board of Directors, as the result of his valuable participation in the committee process, as well as the community.[70]

Lucinda Fox Ward is another example of a community leader, who by virtue of her participation in the above process, as chairwoman of the Haryou Personnel Committee, gains new respect as a community leader.[71] Chairing the personnel committee in Haryou has always been a sensitive task. It assumes added importance at a time when Haryou is undergoing a transition which requires the retrenching of previously funded jobs requiring the trimming of the corporation's operational staff. Miss Ward's impeccable reputation in the Harlem community, the result both of her leadership in Neighborhood Board #1, and her tenure as a community resident (she has lived in Harlem's Dunbar apartments since the 1940s), is functional for accruing legitimacy to an unpopular task.[72] I have often observed Miss Ward in the persistent struggle over decisions respecting the personnel/organizational needs of the new Corporation. She, assisted by her staff assistants, Thomasina Norford and Fran Johnson, (The Director and Assistant Director of Haryou's Personnel Department), have often been deluged with controversy and accussations respecting such decisions, but their well organized and skilled team approach to this highly sensitive task is unchallengeable.

These are but a few examples which indicate the successful cooperation of professional and non-professional leaders in the Haryou Corporation. They are valuable as additional insight regarding the process of leadership development and training.

It is the issue of the relationship between the social services professional and political leadership that is most illusive; yet so critical to our understanding certain of Haryou and Harlem's leaders. One is in this regard tempted to ask; what would Haryou be today had Adam Clayton Powell Jr. and Dr. Kenneth Clark recognized the potential contributions a coalition of resources and skills could have made to the program and the community? Or, had contemporary board chairmen been more available to unite with their executives.

To deal with such questions requires an intensive analysis, not attempted here; but it is clear that much has been lost in Haryou as the result of a naivete respecting this as an area for serious attention. This is especially true for those of us who, representing the Social Work profession, were in positions to diagnose, early, this as a critical area of dysfunction. This is an area in which the political leader, however, is certainly as naive; since even contemporary expressions of new relationships in Haryou and Harlem indicate the politicians approach to be one of providing 'a cloak of protection' for professional activity-rather than a coalition of skills and resources.[73] It is certainly to the Haryou Board Chairman's credit that he is viewed as having 'come around' to recognizing that social service professionals have a contribution to make in Haryou and Harlem; but so long as he viewed his only function to be that of 'protecting' or 'sanctioning' that right, he in fact functioned paternalistically; not colleaguelly. The leadership which Haryou and Harlem so desperately needed, and needs--is represented by the latter.[74]

FOOTNOTES TO CHAPTER VIII

1. Field Observations and Interviews conducted in Fall 1973.

2. See "Council Against Poverty Guidelines", op. cit.,

3. Litwak and Meyer op. cit., pages 31-58. A Balance Theory of Bureaucracy. See also Max Weber, "The Essentials of Bureau-cratic Organizations: An Ideal Type Construction" in Robert K. Merton et al Reader in Bureaucracy. (Glencoe, Illinois, Free Press 1952), pages 18-33; See also Etzioni, op. cit., page 82.

4. The process is one in which an organization like Haryou utilizes the variety of local Harlem businesses and resources as primary contractees--a system of supporting local enterprise, wherever possible for various agency requirements (Guard Ser-vice, Building Maintenance, printing requirements etc.) For further analysis regarding the relevance of this approach see "Council Against Poverty Guidelines", op. cit. Also see Youth in the Ghetto, op. cit., page For additional theoretical perspective see Alfred J. Kahn, Studies in Social Policy and Planning (Russell Sage Foundation, N.Y. 1969) pages 10-67.

5. Litwak and Meyer, op. cit., page 34.

6. Interviews Fall 1973.

7. Haryou during this period is deluged with program site visits, evaluations and Budget reviews; most of which emerge from the C.A.P. and N.Y.C.s Controller's Office.

8. Powell during this period is under suspension from the Congress and secludes himself on the Island of Bimini, in the West Indies.

9. Community residents and Haryou leaders alike, are often out-spoken about the City's increased political inroads in Harlem, during Powell's absence. "If Adam were around they (Downtown City Hall) wouldn't be messing with Haryou this way" expressed the opinion of many in this regard.

10. See C.A.P. Guidelines, op. cit.

11. For a review of these programs see Youth in the Ghetto, op. cit. pages 353-491.

12. Field observations and participant observation during the above period, and Interviews Fall 1973.

13. By "involved observer" I should specify that only a few Board members and executives close to the Chairman; were privy to the meetings and conferences respecting the transition.

14. The process of eliminating Board members was often a manipulative and emotional one. Certain Board members actually broke down in open meetings upon fully realizing they were to be 'phased-out'.

15. At this writing, the famed restaurant is no longer in existence.

16. The full Board (Transition Committee) was seldom consulted during this process.

17. See "Council Against Poverty Guidelines", op. cit., see also Krosney, op. cit., page 89.

18. Particularly neighborhood Board constituencies. The commutator leader is particularly active and important during this selection process.

19. See Chapter III of dissertation for definition of Leadership types.

20. There is the assumption that the Corporation is merely an appendage to the Council Against Poverty; and as such loses its peculiar identity as a Harlem program.

21. Youth in the Ghetto, op. cit., pages 391-400.

22. Interviews Spring 1973; and Board of Directors' minutes Spring 1967.

23. The rationale is comparable to that respecting the earlier Project Uplift. See Chapter V of dissertation.

24. Mobilization for Youth did not become the Community Corporation for the lower East Side poverty area--but elected to remain an independent research and projects development agency.

25. I view Kenneth B. Clark's view of "Folk Sense" as comparable to pragmatism. See Clark, Dark Ghetto, op. cit., page 210-211.

26. See Cyril Tyoson, unpublished paper developed for Optimum, pages 19-21.

27. Haryou Board of Director's Minutes, Summer 1968.

28. Ibid.

29. Interviews conducted Spring 1973.

30. See Chapter VII of dissertation.

31. This 'rabbi' concept is identical to that of "favoritism". At Haryou, staff members were often suspected of having rabbis on the Policy Board of Directors, and thus were given preferred treatment in promotions, salary increases and work assignments.

A given staff member could reciprocate by keeping the Board
member informed about organizational programming issues;
informal communications systems and so on.

32. See Chapter VII of dissertation.

33. Interviews, Fall 1973 and see Chapter III of dissertation.

34. James Weldon Johnson, op. cit., page 38 for definitions of
these terms.

35. Interviews, Fall 1973.

36. Interview conducted Fall 1973.

37. Interview conducted Fall 1973.

38. Todd, op. cit., pages 122-123.

39. Interviews Spring 1973.

40. Interviews, 1973; and see Board of Directors Education Committee
Minutes 1968-1969.

41. I have identified the value placed on Education as a basic one in
Harlem. See Chapter VI of dissertation; also see Myrdal, op.
cit., page 457, Krosney, op. cit., page 79-81 and Youth in the
Ghetto, op. cit. page Introduction.

42. See Chapter I of dissertation.

43. Interviews Fall 1973.

44. Interviews Fall 1973.

45. Interviews Fall 1973; see also Coser; op. cit., pages 38; and
Selznick, The Organizational Weapon, op. cit., page 76.

46. Interviews.

47. See Youth in the Ghetto, op. cit., page Introduction.

48. See Chapter IV of dissertation; also see Krosney, op. cit., page

49. Ibid.

50. Interviews Fall 1973.

51. Interviews Fall 1973.

52. Interviews Fall 1973; participant observation during above
period.

53. Ibid.

54. Though he was not directly involved in the Administrative Committee, he was quite close to one of the Committee members,
and thus was privy to the Committee's interests and plans.

55. Interviews, Fall 1973; and participant observation during Field experience.

56. Ibid.

57. Ibid.

58. Ibid.

59. Interviews, conducted Fall 1973.

60. See Chapter VI of Dissertation.

61. Interviews and see Clark, Dark Ghetto; op. cit., pages 196-198; and Youth in the Ghetto, op. cit., pages 375-387; also see Krosney op. cit., page 81-87.

62. Ibid.

63. Ibid.

64. These comments are the direct result of my participation in Haryou during the period. See, also Pinkney and Woock, op. cit.

65. The reader is reminded that the Chairman was also the leader of the Administrative Committee.

66. Interview, Spring 1973.

67. Haryou-Act Community Corporation Position Paper (unpublished) 1969. This document presented the Corporations petition to the Mayor of New York for some relief regarding cut-backs in Anti-poverty funds to Harlem.

68. Interviews conducted Spring 1973.

69. Helen Testamark's emergence to prominence in Haryou leadership circles is a result of her leadership in the Organization's Education Committee.

70. The emergency of Organizational leadership through the formal Organizational process of committee work is not a phenomena unique to Haryou. Floyd Hunter in the book Community Power Structure a Study of Decision Makers, (The University Press of North Carolina, Chaptel Hill) discusses comparable processes See pages 207-227. See also, Blau and Scott, Formal Organizations op. cit., page 45-47.

71. Miss Ward is currently serving in this capacity in Haryou. (Interviews conducted Fall 1973.)

72. Functional in the sense of instilling trust among her community colleagues.

73. Interview conducted Fall 1973.

74. For additional information regarding the concept of "colleaguel" relationships in varied Organizational settings see Eugene

Litwak "Models of Bureaucracy that Permit Conflict",
American Journal of Sociology, January 1968,

Litwak "Models of Bureaucracy that Permit Conflict",
American Journal of Sociology, January 1968,

CHAPTER 9

THE NEW HARYOU COMMUNITY CORPORATION LEADERSHIP

The preceding chapter was an analysis of the leadership change process during Haryou's transition to the Community Corporation for Central Harlem.

We have traced the vested interests of various leaders within the organization as they anticipate power shifts and new opportunities for access to decision making positions. The leadership types and functions are found to be fluid, in the sense that as Haryou organizational priorities and requirements change, individual leaders often assume different postures.[1] Leadership function often requires the 'wearing of more than one hat' in that Haryou leaders, particularly in the new Corporation, are normally representatives of a number of community organizational interests with varied allegiances and commitments.[2]

Finally, we have taken some preliminary looks at the internal community dynamics which facilitate, and inhibit, emergence and development of new functional leaders.[3] It is now time to analyze what these changes have meant in terms of the present Corporation leadership. First, a reminder. My major focus in on civic leadership, its existence, emergence and function within a particular community and organizational setting. The discussion related to the ideological, or value conflicts between different 'types' of leaders; the comments reflective of chisms between social service professionals and politicians, or professionals and non-professionals are relevant only insofar as they illuminate the functions or outcomes in the arena of civic community enterprise. The reader will, in this regard note, that the analysis of what professional or political leadership is, does not concern us. The concern, rather, is for clarity as to the outcomes of leadership activities in responding to organizational and community needs.

Leaders in Haryou are, presumably, participating for specific organizational purposes; community improvement, increases in the power necessary for the charting of community destiny, institutionalization and the designing of a 'master plan' for meeting Harlem's human resource needs.[4] Most Haryou leaders, however also represent other community organizations; and thus consciously utilize their Haryou leadership positions, for these extra-organizational allegiances.[5] Haryou, given this paradigm of leadership structure, is a microcosm of the broader Harlem community leadership system. This is the current picture. One reflective of a particular 'process' of organizational and leadership change.[6]

The present chairman of the Haryou Community Corporation is Fred Samuels. Samuels is, as in the case of his predecessor, a successful lawyer.[7] The major difference between he and his predecessor, professionally, is that Samuels' success is directly linked to practice in Harlem-the former chairman's is not.[8] Samuels is one of the original organizers of Harlem's Legal services for the poor, The Harlem assertion of Rights (HAR). The HAR is a consortium of volunteer lawyers from Harlem who assist community people in need of legal representation or counselling. They relate to problems ranging from consumer frauds to housing.[9]

Samuels is a 26 year resident of Harlem. Originally from the West Indies, the 47 year old attorney is a leader in the United West Indian Benevolent Association, a consortium of Islander-New Yorkers numbering in the thousands. Samuels is a politician. He holds tenure in the local Harlem political clubs and wards and has emerged as a premier leader at the local level. His name is, increasingly, a commonplace, or household word. Samuels is mentioned by all respondents to my interviews as being among the top four leaders of importance to Haryou and Harlem.[10]

This leader attributes his recent involvement in Haryou to the expressed concerns of certain of his colleagues as well as to a personal sense of commitment. In the latter instance, he views his contributions as important in "repaying many of the little people of Harlem who have helped me become a success";[11] with respect to the former, Samuels recounts that George Miller, Percy Sutton and Mark T. Southall requested that he assume Haryou's leadership. In this regard, Samuels recalls,

> I have always been interested in Haryou, but never became involved because they seemed to avoid any association with local political organizations, and didn't seem to want our participation or assistance. But when George and Percy asked me to become involved--they impressed upon me the need for an honest, non-controversial person, who is well known in the community; I felt a certain obligation to help.[12]

Percy Sutton is the Borough President of Manhattan, and George Miller is a State Assemblyman, as is Mark T. Southall.[13] When I asked Samuels whether his obvious political connections represented problems with his Haryou Board members, he responded,

> They know me better than that, my activities in the organization are not politically motivated, and I am under no pressure nor have I experienced any interference from any of my colleagues in political office. Certainly they are avialable for any advice, and this includes Tyler, but there are no inappropriate requests or pressures.[14]

Ideologically, Samuels is reminiscent of the institutional inspirationalist leader. He is a political leader who is outspoken about the legitimate institutional functions of politics in Harlem.[15] He believes it to be the responsibility of Black elected officials, as well as social services professionals, in his words, "Who exist primarily as the result of the suffereing and problems of Harlem's masses",[16] to make substantive contributions to the community's uplift. "It is not enough", Samuels suggests,

> For middle class Blacks to be returning to Harlem only to be investing in Brown Stone houses. What is required is a commitment to improving people's chances for a better life-helping someone else up the ladder.[17]

And finally, with regard to his institutional insights, Samuels feels,

> Haryou should be the institutional representative for the Harlem community. The public should be able to say 'here is the institution to which you can go for any information respecting Harlem; its people, its organizations - its development.[18]

The new Harlem chairman is also a humanist. He believes that

> We, (successful Blacks) are only as strong as the little folks make us; you must always come back to Harlem; and beyond 'paying you dues' to the brothers and sisters--you must learn to walk with them in the struggle for access to a better life.[19]

Interestingly, the Chairman is a 'law and order' man. He views the major community pathology as one of fear and apathy respecting street crime. He holds the view that better police protection is needed in Harlem, but for purposes of making the community a safer place to live, rather than the traditional rationale of 'keeping the lid on the ghetto'.[20] To the current Board of Directors and staff of Haryou, Samuels is viewed as a "strong", or "well liked", "highly respected", "community man".[21] Though he is often warned by community friends, not to get involved in the program, he is more often implored to assume its leadership by others. Thus far his tenure is a successful one.[22]

As mentioned earlier, the Board which Samuels chairs is comprised substantially of members who made their Haryou leadership debute during the community corporation struggle. Helen Testamark, Lucinda Fox Ward, George Miller, Herbert Seymour (new vice-chairman), Iyantha Maynard, Addie Patterson, Heyward Davenport, Marshal England and others. There are, however substantive additions. I recognized immediately upon attending Haryou Board of Directors' meetings, in the process of this analysis, the large number of elected public officials, Charles Rangel, Harlem's new United States Congressional representive; Hulan Jack, State Assemblyman; Attorney George Miller, State Assemblyman; Mark T. Southall, also State Assemblyman; Sidney Von Luther, State Senator; Percy Sutton, Manhattan Borough President and Councilman; Charles Taylor, City Councilman. Many of these political leaders view their participation in Haryou as functional for "overcoming the Corporations bad image in Harlem and the broader Metropolitan community".[23]

Conspicuously absent in the Corporation's Board leadership is the social or human services professional. There are no social workers; and few educators, no leading doctors or community businessmen. Most Board members interviewed believe that there are two fundamental reasons for this. First,

The professional has gotten all he wants out of Haryou and Harlem for the moment. The community is so 'over-researched', that they find if difficult to gain access.[24]

And secondly,

The professional had been displaced or replaced, in anti-poverty programs at any rate, by indigenous people, who after all function better at the community level.[25]

This latter perspective that the professional's function is no longer relevant in the determination of policy concerning the Haryou enterprise is construed by certain Board and staff members as the legitimate fulfillment of the professional's mandate to 'work himself out of business'.[26] The professed goal of preparing community representatives to assume the responsiblity for running their own 'institutions' is inherent in this position.

What, perhaps needs to be clarified, is precisely what is meant by professional function. It is, in the view taken here, the process by which community and organizational systems are helped to internalize certain professional values.[27] Paramount among such values are those related to the inherent worth and dignity of each individual, and his right to self-determination in charting his destiny. Other values incorporated in the ethics of most human service professions and functional in the development of a community institution like Haryou are associated with legitimate right of people in a democratic society to equal access for the kinds of opportunities which facilitate social and community planning.[28] Included in our meaning of opportunity is access to technical knowledge and skill.

Given this perspective on certain professional functions, I view the 'absence' of black social work professionals in Haryou as a serious leadership vacuum. It is incumbent upon the Black professional to devise ways to create an awareness of the need for his service and its functional relevance to the organization's institutionalization in Harlem. Haryou was in desperate need of professional leadership in its dealings with Columbia University, in its persistent encrouchment on community real-estate; and during its posturing concerning the New York State Capitol building complex in the community.[29] The frustrations experienced by those involved in establishing a Computer Center for manpower development and training needs in Harlem, would clearly have been ameliorated with the advice and assistance of competent professional leadership.[30]

Interviews with professionals who have recently left Haryou indicate the validity of the above assessment. They view current leaders in the Corporation as incompetent in determining the organization's needs, and believe that the anti-professional attitude among many Board members is reflective of their interest to use the Corporation for "personal gain",[31] rather than as an "instrument for dealing with the community's real problems".[32] Certain of these professionals also feel that if the present Corporation were lead by men like Kenneth Clark or Charles King, it would be a more relevant structure. In this instance there is the recognition that these former leaders represent the technical--professional skills and knowledge required for contemporary Haryou and, in a sense, were 'ahead of their time' in their earlier efforts.[33]

> If we only had a Clark, Marshal, Tyson or King in Haryou at
> this point, with the knowledge we have gained about community
> systems and the nature of 'power', something could really be
> done for Harlem,[34]

is the way one professional articulates the above concern.

Finally, the professionals knowlageable of the earlier Haryou feel that 'professionalism;, its values and methods, were never really given a chance to emerge or work in Haryou.[35] The testing of professional skills and approaches as effective change forces in the organization, and the Harlem community, have been 'submerged' by the more visible 'public relations' conflicts of competing leadership representing other-than social welfare concerns.[36]

My analysis of these comments and the observation of professionals making them, indicate that most are reflections of some sense of 'guilt' born of frustration. When asked such questions as, "Why did you leave Haryou?"; responses of the following kind are given: "I felt I had done all I could from within the organization and felt I could make a more positive contribution from a different vantage point", or, "There was no longer any sanction for the professional in Haryou".[37] There are examples in which the former response is legitimized by subsequent actions of certain professionals. Heyward Davenport, is an appropriate example. Davenport represents the singular example in the Haryou experience in which a former staff member emerges to organizational leadership 'through the ranks'.

Heyward has been associated with Haryou since 1965. He began as an employee in the business office. In 1967 he transferred into the program department; where as the result of demonstrated administrative skills he was promoted to an administrative assistantship. By 1969 his ability brought him to the attentions of Dorothy Orr, Associate Executive Director of Haryou; and he joined her staff. Heyward is an interesting example of the fluidity and change potential of leadership in Haryou and Harlem. He came to the organization with an institutional ideology, born of his activities in the civil rights movement in the South (North Carolina). Accordingly, he relates "I wanted to get into something in Harlem at the ground floor and make a contribution in building an institution.[38]

A highly competent 'details man', Heyward made himself indispensable to Haryou administrators and ultimately to the organization's Board leadership. In 1971, he becomes the Haryou Executive Director replacing Dorothy Orr. It is at this point that his functions shift from those of 'facilitator' or 'details man', to the more substantive deicision making functions.[39] Heyward identifies the kinds of tasks he has performed during his tenure as crucial to his eventual emergence as a Haryou leader:

I have always tried to be efficient in handling even the smallest assignments. This approach developed confidence among the Executive and Board leadership. When asked questions about organizational matters, I always used my best judgement and have been right sufficiently often, to have generated trust in its soundness. Increassingly, then, the staff and Board members turned to me for opinions and information-which I make it my business to have readily available.[40]

Heyward is currently an executive Board of Directors' member at Haryou, and was recently appointed to the post of Director of the Department of Administration for New York City's Municipal Planning Department.[41] It is interesting to observe his function in Board of Directors' meetings. He is always called upon to express opinions regarding any major issues; and is listened to when proposing solutions. He often functions as mediator in internal Board conflicts and is sought out as the resource person on matters related to official policy and public administrative guidelines.[42]

Heyward has for much of his tenure in Haryou been referred to by the 'informal' communications system as "Percy's boy"[43] (Percy Sutton is the Manhattan Borough President), and many have attributed his rise in the organization, and most recently City Hall administration, to his friendship with this political leader. Heyward resents these comments, since in his view, "I have made my own way through performance and ability";[44] though he admits, without apology, that Sutton is a close friend. Heyward Davenport, at age 39, was the youngest Executive Director in Haryou's history. He currently weilds as much decision making power in the organization Policy Board of Directors, as any of its senior members.[45]

Davenport, however, is unique. Most professionals who leave Haryou, completely sever any ties or relationships. Thus their response in the above regard are inappropriate, and construed as indicators of some guilt at leaving Haryou in a state of crisis.[46]

The large majority of Haryou's current leadership are lay community volunteers. Most are long time Harlem residents, having lived in the community in excess of twenty years. Their knowledge of Harlem is unquestionable. All have observed the coming and going of the 'professional', 'the Politician', and the 'community organizer' while the community's problems remain.[47] They envision a role, despite these experiences, for each within the corporation; but on somewhat different terms than in the past. These new Haryou leaders put it this way,

Hell, the professionals and all had their chance to do something for the community and things seem to have gotten worse. Now it's our chance. We certainly can do no worse.[48]

One sense this spirit among the lay members of the Haryou Board meetings, as they 'orient' the elected public officials as to what is expected of them in representing Haryou's and the community's interests! It is an interesting experience to observe one of the 'soul sister' Board members dealing with Congressman Charles Rangel, as if he were still a youth playing on one of Harlem's streets. Many of the members, as a matter of fact, remember him in just that way, and make no effort to be overly deferent to his achieved status. Rangel often appears as amused by this 'home' atmosphere as do the Board colleagues. In a special way, it is a warm and, for this observer, a genuine 'community' atmosphere.[49]

The Congressman's participation in the Haryou leadership is, however symptomatic of something else; for he too, is concerned that Haryou become a legitimate community institution.[50]

The Congressman's participation in the Haryou leadership is, however symptomatic of something else; for he too, is concerned that Haryou become a legitimate community institution.[51] He views the Corporation as a potentially powerful 'broker' and wants to purge the organization of any negative images associated with the past.[51] His resignation and subsequent attacks on Haryou during the Spring and Summer of 1972 were the result of finding the program's bookkeeping had not been adequately resolved since the fateful Operation PUL scandal in 1965, resulted in the final clearance of Haryou. He then rejoined the Board and has moved into prominence in re-directing organizational priorities.[52] He fits my premier leadership typology, though in certain respects, he could also be viewed as having institutional inspirationalist tendencies.[53] I have a feeling that given more time in Haryou, the 'sister' may convert him completely.

The new Executive Director of the Haryou Corporation is a Social Worker trained in social work administration at Rutgers University.[54] He comes to Haryou on the heels of directing, the Northwest Queens Community Corporation (formerly known as QUALICAP) for the period of one year. This Corporation, as in the case of Haryou-ACT, is one of the 26 Community Corporations within New York City under the umbrella of the Community Development Agency. The director is not a Harlemite. His knowledge about the community is limited, a fact he readily admits; but he believes that his philosophy as to the institutional mandate of the Haryou Corporation will facilitate the necessary knowledge within a reasonable period of time.[55] He expresses it this way, "I believe that Haryou should serve as the National prototype for all community development programs, and my intent is to make it precisely that kind of program".[56]

The new Executive is reminiscent of one former Haryou Director, Charles King; though I view the former as a proto-indigenous idealist leader rather than an institutional inspirationalist. He, for example generates the same kind of enthusiasm and dynamism as King, but is not as aware seemingly of the organizational and community forces with which he must deal.[57] Having spent nine of the last ten years of his career in various civil service positions within New York City's Department of Social Services, he is accustomed to dealing in bureaucratic systems totally different from Haryou. Despite his brief tenure in the Queens Community Corporation, he does not impress the knowledgeable Haryou and Harlem observer as sufficiently astute in community dynamics to be successful in leading Haryou.[58] The Director at the time of my first interview with him has only been in office for a few weeks, yet even in so short a time, the informal organizational communications structure, (illuminated by interviews with Haryou staff), indicates early discontent with his leadership. The temporary acting Director deluged with additional responsibility for orienting the new Director, is especially suspicious of him competence to "run this show".[59]

The Director is determined not to become enmeshed in the various political and 'power' nuances, which he to some degree has already observed in Haryou. His initial objectives are to build "administrative and managerial efficiency and program soundness 'in the corporation, while concomitantly' finding 'handles', for getting Haryou on the road to being what Harlem really needs".[60] The new leader is impressed with the Corporation Board's Vice-Chairman who he identifies as "a really sharp leader who know what's going on".[61]

The Director's identification with the Board Vice-Chairman is to some degree responsible for the view among 'old-line' Haryou staff members that he will not survive. "He is too naive about the way Haryou operates ...how can he identify himself with the man and expect to remain neutral in Harlem?"[62] Other staff comments are instructive in this analysis,

It is one thing for the Board to search for a 'non-controversial' person for the job. It's quite another thing to hire someone who doesn't know what Harlem is, and how Haryou relates to the community,[63]

and finally in the view of the Corporation's acting Director, "He came out as the best of what we had to interview; certainly he is non-controversial".[64]

In the final analysis, though it is certainly too soon to predict, the new Director's success or failure will depend on his coming to grips with the above perceptions. At the moment, his function seems to be that of diverting the staff's pre-occupation with the Board's activities; while also creating certain concerns over job security on the parts of 'old line' staffers.[65]

Many of the line staff members of the Haryou Community Corporation are functional leaders in their own right. Staffers like Teddy Butler, Columbus Austin and Ed Warner. Teddy Butler clearly fits our commutator type leader, as does Warner. Columbus Austin is an institutional inspirationalist, and one of Central Harlem's most knowledgeable historians.[66] In individual and group interviews conducted with staff representatives, I was advised of staff's apprehensions regarding impending 'purges' of those loyal to the previous administration and its Board leadership.[67] As these informants hasten to give examples of former colleagues already fired or 'retrenched' in lesser positions at lower salaries; a striking observation is made. A number of the secretarial and administrative assistant staff of the former Board of Directors' officers, remain; almost as a separate unit, at the Corporation. The observation is interesting, in that normally, the unspoken 'law' or Haryou culture respecting leadership change is that as the leaders go so too do their closest lieutenants and administrative staffs. The phenomena represents more than a matter of loyalty. It has to do with the 'dysfunction' of such 'carry-over' staff for the new leadership. The expectation is that the new leadership, whether at the policy board level or the Executive, will want to hire its own immediate staff. This circumstance tends to contradict certain fears on the parts of the organization's staff; while on the other hadn substantiating another 'informal' staff perspective;--that former Haryou power 'barons' still hold some control over organizational decisions.[68]

FOOTNOTES TO CHAPTER IX

1. This is a finding seldom dealt with in the general literature
   on leadership. Recent analysis of the effects of the Anti-
   poverty program on the leadership structures within various
   communities does suggest that non-professional persons identified as potential grass roots representatives tended to become over-identified with professional models and in assuming
   the facade alienate themselves from their community constituents. Such finds, however, do not illuminate the process
   of leadership change along the continuum of organizational
   leadership roles. For additional comments, see: Wilson,
   op. cit., pages 255-256.

2. See Wilson, op. cit., page 255.

3. See Chapters IV-VI of the dissertation.

4. See Haryou Organizational By-Laws; also Youth in the Ghetto,
   op. cit., pages I-XII (prefact).

5. Interviews conducted Fall 1973.

6. I have been discussing this process in Chapters IV, V, VI, and VII
   and VIII of the dissertation.

7. Interviews conducted Fall 1973.

8. Interviews conducted Fall 1973; see also Harlem Assertion of
   Rights proposal submitted to Haryou for funding Spring 1969.

9. Interviews Fall 1973.

10. Interviews Fall 1973.

11. Interviews Fall 1973.

12. Interview Fall 1973.

13. Interviews Fall 1973; see also Board of Directors minutes and
    membership lists.

14. Interview, 1973.

15. In this regard I am referring to institutional forms, including
    yet not exclusively political in nature. Samuels, for example
    is also concerned that the church, and networks of local com-
    munity civic and social organizations persist.

16. Interview Fall 1973.

17. *Ibid.*

18. *Ibid.*

19. *Ibid.*

20. *Ibid.*

21. *Ibid.*

22. *Ibid.*

23. *Ibid.* It is interesting to note the difference in orientation regarding the participation of elected officials at Haryou given the earlier perspective (see Chapter IV and V). The defference, I am sure, relates to the fact that my respondents are political fitures. Still there does not appear to be the tenseness and antogonism within the Board of Directors that existed in the earlier Haryou experience. Some answer may be found in the preponderance among the lay board members of Commutator leaders on the one hand; and with respect to the political professionals, premier leaders-on the other. We recall from my earlier discussion that commutators and premier leaders have a special kind of relationship. (See Chapter III of Dissertation.)

24, Interview Fall 1973.

25. Interviews Fall 1973; also see Sumati N. Dubey, "Community Action Programs and Citizen Participation: Issues and Confusions" in Social Work, Journal of the National Association of Social Work, January 1970.

26. *Ibid.* and interviews conducted Fall 1973.

27. Comparable in this regard to Selznick's "value infusion concept". See Selznick, op. cit., page 19.

28. Alfred J. Kahn, Theory and Practice of Social Planning, op. cit. pages 55-56. See also Encyclopedia of Social Work--op. cit. "Code of Ethics".

29. These interpretations of the University's involvement in land development in Harlem, the financing of Office Buildings and etc., grow from the sense of non-involvement on the parts of local indigenous leadership. Interviews during Fall 1973; also see Long and Robinson, op. cit, pages 104-107.

30. Interviews with Haryou leaders; Fall 1973; see also Tyson, Optimum Associates Paper (unpublished).

31 Interviews conducted Fall 1973.

32. *Ibid.*

33. *Ibid.*

34. *Ibid.*

35. Ibid.

36. Ibid.

37. Ibid.

38. Ibid.

39. Interviews conducted Fall 1973.

40. Interview Fall 1973.

41. This change marks his transition from an Institutional Inspira-
        tionalist type leader to a proto-indigenous idealist.

42. In Haryou, it is one thing to talk at Board of Directors' meegings;
        to be listened to, is quite another matter. Only the respected
        receive such attention.

43. Field observation and Interviews, Fall 1973.

44. Interviews, Fall 1973--Participant Observation 1967-1970.

45. Interviews Fall 1973.

46. My inclination is to view their response as an indication of
        leadership default; however such a contention would not be
        documentable.

47. Interviews Fall 1973.

48. Interviews Fall 1973.

49. Field Observation and Interviews, Fall 1973.

50. Interview Fall 1973.

51. Ibid.

52. Ibid.

53. In this regard, Rangel, like Samuels (Chairman of the Board) seems
        to view the role of politics in its institutional relevances
        for Harlem.

54. Interview and Report of Haryou Personnel Committee, Fall 1973.

55. Interviews Fall 1973.

56. Ibid.

57. Interviews and Field Observation, Fall 1973.

58. Interviews, Fall 1973.

59. Interview, Fall 1973.

60. Ibid.

61.   Ibid.

62.   Ibid.

63.   Ibid.

64.   Ibid.

65.   This is a phenomena that occurs at Haryou whenever there are
      major leadership changes. Field Observations and Inter-
      views Fall 1973.

66.   Interviews and Field Observation.

67.   Interviews conducted Fall 1973.

68.   Interviews conducted Fall, 1973. This view suggests that the
      present Board leaders are 'puppets' or figure-heads; while
      former organizational elites continue, behind the scenes,
      to effect all major or critical decisions.

CHAPTER 10

CONCLUSIONS AND IMPLICATIONS

This study has explored the existence of a unique typology of functional leadership in a Northern Urban community. The analysis was conducted within the framework of the community's peculiar social history and milieu. Harlem, the profound black community of New York City, is the setting in which I have attempted further to demonstrate the relevance of particular selective social mechanisms in the selection of black leadership.

There are a number of conclusions drawn from the analysis, which in my judgement increase our knowledge about the phenomenon under investigation. The fact that no comparable studies have been conducted with respect to Harlem leadership during the period under discussion, makes certain of them transitory, but in my view nevertheless relevent.

One conclusion is that in contemporary Harlem, and I suspect in other black communities, one finds a greater awareness and sensitivity on the part of lay community civic activists of the existence of varied forms of leadership and power arrangements than is normally indicated by studies conducted in the leadership area. This suggests, as indicated by Elaine Burgess and others, that the community _is_ the optimum setting for the study of functional leadership, at any rate with respect to black leadership.[1] We in a sense 'explode' then the myth that relevant or 'power' leaders in a community like Harlem can only be successfully identified by reference to noninvolved 'elites' whose professional 'dual' leadership styles are more functional for their positions in the white community than the black. The effective identification of legitimate leaders in the black community requires that the researcher 'go to the people' if his analysis is to be genuine. In this sense it may well be the case ad demonstrated by my experience in conducting the study, that only certain 'proto-indigenous' researchers will be afforded the access to the kinds of community 'data' essential for such inquiry. This is not meant simply to suggest that only Black investigators will be afforded access in black communities for the purpose of similar researches; but more substantively, only blacks with particular constellations of background, interest and understanding in addition to skill. It has become increasingly difficult for any but the most sensitive and well connected research investigator to gain entre to community systems and information.

An additional finding of my study is that the peculiar socio-cultural elements and immediate traditions of Harlem as a black community have profound consequences for the styles and types of leaders identified. Harlem's tenure as a black urban ghetto has ilicited consequences for the patterns and behaviorisms of the leaders who function within her, which in my judgement are without precedence anywhere in American society. This finding goes beyond Myrdal's[2] suggestion that by the very nature of caste as a phenomena in this country, that specific differences would be discerned; to the finding that such differences have become institutionalized.

The conclusion, thus that institutionalization is a process which occurs over time gives some clue respecting the best approaches to understanding the historical, emergent and contemporary forms of leadership which have affected Harlem and other black communities. The tendency of most contemporary leadership studies to overlook this process is at the base of their frustrated efforts for arriving at some 'standard' or singular model of leadership definition and structure. The answer to understanding black leadership in particular contexts is found in the systematic analysis and understanding of the internal systems reflective of cherished cultural and value ladened experiences which determine the roles and importance of individuals in the sphere of socio-political and community power.

One major finding of my study is that Harlem, as a New York City community, experiences the same cosmopolitan and metropolitan types of phenomena associated with the city as a whole. This with particular reference to the tendencies of high residential mobility have a decided effect upon the patterns of leadership which emerge. The 'fluidity potential' of leaders associated with Harlem and Haryou as a social mechanism, is an important aspect of leadership transition; in addition to those of a socio-political nature. Interestingly, however, a peculiar attribute of the community leadership structure appears to be quite similar to elements of stability found in smaller (particularly black communities in the South); urban areas. That is one discern in Harlem, despite the fludity potential, stability connected through family ties and ethno-cultural affiliations over several generations. The lineage of large families, migrated from the South, or established through West Indian and Carribean settlements in Harlem are functional in this regard. And though the spheres of influence of polynucleated structures of specialized leadership cliques, as identified by other leadership theorists, are not found systematically in Harlem, there are leadership resources with long tenure in civic community enterprise.[3] The finding that often, even where former Harlem residents out-migrate they tend to remain within the general metropolitan area (the "Hill', or Bronx, Queens or Brooklyn communities), further indicates some stability, as friends and relatives left in the ghetto remain as important sources of communication and association.

Another finding associated with my leadership analysis concerns the process of leadership change. As we explored the various characteristics and attributes of the six leader types discerned, i.e., the creative elites, proto-indigenous idealists, raceocrats, commutators and premiers, specifying the existent differences and similarities, complimentarities and conflictual styles; certain amounts of overlapping are found. In addition, I found that leaders change in accordance with differential demands placed upon them. They do so by assuming new functions which cause them, often to assume the posture and characteristics of a different type than that with which they were normally associated.

The process of leadership change in Harlem is also a function of changing organizational and community requirements. That is, as indicated by my findings, certian types and styles of leadership are needed during particular organizational and community developmental stages; and once secured, function as part of the institutional process. These leaders move on, however, as these requirements change. Having made specific contributions commensurate with their abilities and skills, they are subsequently replaced by new leaders who possess newly acquired talents. This change process in Harlem was fraught with crisis and intrigue owing to the communities peculiar milieu; an experience which I concluded may well attend leadership change in other black urban communities where scarce opportunities for prestige, status and power are systematically coveted.

My study also indicates an aspect of leadership development and change which is in direct conflict with other leadership theorists. I disagree with those who view black civic leadership in Northern cities as increasingly drawing away from leaders in the political arena. In their view that some degree of transfer of leadership from old elites to new business and professionals groups is occurring, they are partially correct. Further those students of the phenomena who suggest that the change from personality leadership to functional leadership, from the era of the great spokesman to the new era of the professionally staffed volunteer association, is occurring at various rates all over the North, are also partially correct.[4] The missing ingredient, however, and particularly with respect to Harlem, is any systematic analysis of the role and function of grass roots, indigenous representatives and leadership. If it is the case that contemporary leadership shifts are occurring between former civic, professional and political elites, the creative elites and premiers in my analysis, what alternative patterns seem to be emerging? My findings illustrate the emergence of a new form of leadership coalition. A new alignment between the grass roots indigenous poor in Harlem and the new political leaders of the community is occurring.

In our review of the Haryou-Act Community Corporation as one legitimate social mechanism for the analysis of leadership, we found that the major policy makers represented this kind of alliance. I have concluded that this phenomenon is one of the "spill-offs" or consequences of the anti-poverty program which is to some extend generalizable to other poverty communities in the North. It is a consequence of the debate and controversy over the 'maximum feasible participation' theme. This new coalition is presenting specific problems for the traditional forms of middle class professional and civic leadership, as it is for the increasingly defunct 'machine' politician in Harlem, and is responsible for much of the leadership conflict and crisis discussed in the study.

An additional factor of importance is the position in which the black social services professional finds himself. He must function in Harlem and to some extent in Haryou as a marginal man, never fully included or trusted as a contributor to the making of critical community or organizational decisions. This situation is beginning to change however, but as the result of new discretion exercised by the indigenous poor and not the traditional power barons of the community. The professional, suspended in this anomic state has sought through new forms of associations with relevant colleagues, (i.e. ABSW) to achieve some leverage in the leadership system.

Voluntary civic life in Harlem-the church, social organizations, neighborhood associations, and so on, are the legitimate structures designed for the identification, training and launching of black leadership. This is a conclusion which again contradicts the often-times articulated assumption of leadership theorists that civic enterprise in black urban communities is primarily a recreational/social interest, and only secondarily related to the raising and settling of serious community and race issues.

Institutionalization as a process in which organizations and leadership are engaged, are concepts seldom associated with urban black communities. The tendency of most studies related to the role of leadership in the ghetto to focus on those forces designed to disintegrate or disorganize the community, and not those related to culture building and organizational survival are the more conventional social research approaches. I conclude that this is a function of the institutionalized bias built into the assumptions with which social researchers approach the ghetto. A function not to be associated with personal or individual bias on the parts of white social researchers or theorists, (or for that matter, middle class black professionals); but rather with the realities of institutional racism as they affect social science as one subsidiary system in American society.

I have attempted to operationalize the concept of functional leadership as it relates to Harlem, in the belief that E. Franklin Frazier is correct in postulating that contemporary leadership styles and changes in the urban North require more significant classifications than those provided by pure 'race leader' typologies.[5] I have concluded that in fact some innovation in the theoretical paradigms associated with this field are warranted. My study is viewed only as a beginning. As such it seeks to stimulate further research in this most provocative area.

FOOTNOTES TO CHAPTER X

1. Burgess, _op. cit._, pages 23-24.

2. Myrdal, _op. cit._, page 1133.

3. Burgess, _Ibid_.

4. Wilson, _op. cit._, pages 78-83.

5. Frazier, _op. cit._, page 62.

CHAPTER 11

ARE THE GHETTO'S WALLS CRUMBLING?

THE NEW CHALLENGE TO HARLEM LEADERSHIP

The question inevitably arises: Will the Negroes of Harlem be able
to hold it? Will they not be driven still farther northward? Residents of Manhattan, regardless of race, have been driving out when
they lay in the path of business and greatly increased land values.
Harlem lies in the direction that path must take; so there is little
probability that Negroes will always hold it as a residential section.[1]

James Weldon Johnson

If whitey wants to come back to Harlem, he'd better get himself some
'Man Tan' lotion. Man in the Street. We have no adequate idea of
the greatness that lies in store for Harlem.[2]

Osafsky

If the black man can hold on to Harlem as a residential area, it will
be a miracle.[3] Harlem was once the greatest Black community in America;
it can be again.[4] You are a Black wonder Harlem. You survived.[5]

Sylvester Leaks

Haryou is an experiment in community psychiatry. It operates on the
assumption that the personality and emotional problems of the bulk
of youth of the Harlem ghetto must be understood in terms of the
pervasive pathology which characterizes our society and makes the
ghetto possible.[6]

Kenneth B. Clark

   Is Harlem surviving? Even the casual observer walking the community's
streets and avenues notes symptoms of change. A ghetto is first a residential community; and secondly one of predominantly homogenous racio-
economic population, characteristics.[7] In this regard, there is verita-
bly no residential housing left in Harlem, for the exception of a few
modern 'high rise' apartment dwellings. From river to river, crumbling
edifices make the locations where "safe, sound and sanitary" housing
distinguished Harlem as a structurally superior urban location.[8] Sprinkled
amidst these tenements are the 'high risers', small retail businesses,
and public quasi-public office buildings. Even "Strivers Row" and the
once renowned, "Sugar Hill are deteriorating.[9]
   The ghetto criteria of homogeneous population is further, for the
first time since the 1920s undergoinging observable change. This factor
is indicated by the finding that in the approximate decade of 1960 to 1970

the black population in Harlem has declined[10] from 97 percent of the total community population, to approximately 96 percent,[11] this despite the fact that in New York City as a whole, the black population has risen from 1,141,000 in 1960 to 1,847,000 in 1970.[12] Whites, in particular, seem poised at Harlem's extremities for the opportune moment to re-establish themselves as the area's major population.[13] A complete reversal of the rationale utilized in 'fleeing before the Black wave' seems to be operating. Much of this interest is caused by the State's interest in reclaiming parts of this strategically located community; at the gateway of New York City, and the heart of the tri-state urban megalopolis.[14] Little wonder that this strategic intersection of all major transportaion systems to and from the Nation's administrative and financial capitol, is coveted by powerful interest groups. Accelerated investments in Harlem real estate (particularly Brownstone houses, large investments in redevelopment and sponsorship of multiple dwelling unit complexes); strategies related to mass transit proposals, including the monopolization of air space above and surrounding the community; all are symptoms of the above. James Turner, in a recent article; Blacks in the Cities Land and Self-Determination, refers to the above perception as "neo-colonialism".[15] In referring to one serious community issue, mentioned earlier in my analysis,-- the New York State Office Building's construction on 125th Street, Turner relates,

> It is not difficult to imagine what the dynamics of economic
> spin-off from the construction of that building will be and
> the effects it will have on transforming the community and
> the African people there. Even before the building will be
> completed there will be an anticipation of need for a myriad
> of social services for the white people who are to come there
> to work, which will attract a dilluge of white business develop-
> ment. It will not be long before there will be talk of need
> to provide good quality housing and cultural centers in the
> vacinity so that the white office workers will not have to
> travel so far in order to get to work. These forces will
> operate to efffectively move black people out in less than
> a decade and reconstruct this area to fulfill the needs and
> interests of white people who have claimed it as a desirable
> area for themselves.[16]

It is my position here, that these rapid changes are indicative of Harlem's demise as a black community. The ghetto's walls are crumbling.

Having mentioned earlier the vibrant nature of community life, with its peculiarly organized networks of social relationships, institutions and leadership; one laments the predictable disappearance of much that was unique in Harlem. For Harlem youth there are no survivals of the community wide tournaments in 'stick-ball' or 'loddies'; no scooter races; or 'double-dutch rope challenges'. There is a bareness in the community's park and recreation areas, where, often adults established adjuncts to the informal communications channels of the streets through participating in 'checkers' and 'dominoes' tourneys that became the center of a given day's activities. These are particularly adaptable 'City' games; and in Harlem they were integral elements in the culture building process.[17] There are no real parades in Harlem anymore. At least not of the kind that signalled the community's pulse in terms of organizational richness and leadership diversity. The local 'block' with its myraid apartment buildings, simplified by 'unofficial' guardians in the guise of local building superintendents, more commonly call 'supers' in Harlem, has been transformed. The super, often sage and protector to many of the community's children, left in the streets to play, or pivotal in the community's 'stoop' culture, exists no longer.[18] He had either been replaced by the newer civil service public housing projects custodian or engineer, or is without the time or inclination to be so involved.

There are elements of Harlem culture seldom explored, much less built upon. Recent attempts to recreate certain aspects of these various community 'styles' (i.e. NYC Park's Department basketball tournaments, or the Martin Luther King Day Parade on New York's Fifth Avenue), have a sterile, irrelevant flavor.[19] The value of the earlier experiences are in their indigenousness and spontaneity. They were Harlem expressions. The walls of the ghetto, in this sense, were institutional, protective, educational and positive communal experiences.[20] What do the perceived changes portend for leadership in the ghetto--in Harlem? Does the demise of a ghetto signal the end of its leaders functional relevance? Or, do we need to concern ourselves with changed leadership roles and functions?

It is my position that the predicted community changes merely add a new deminsion to the relevance of Harlem leadership. For whether Harlem remains black or not, i.e., should it become a racially integrated community--it must persist as the 'institutional' center of the black urban experience. The Schomburg Collection of black literature, art and history should always be Harlem's; the famed institution, the 369th AAA Gun Battalion Armory must remain in black hands, the Amsterdam News, Harlem and Black America's major chronicle should continue to emminate from the 'apple'; and 125th Street and 7th Avenue, the historic debate corner, with its 'soap box' orators cannot be relinquished. In addition, and perhaps more substantively, basic economic investments and interests must be enlarged and protected. Freedom National Bank and The Carver Federal Savings and Loan Association must persist as resources for Blacks. Referring once again to the new State Capitol Building, Harlem's leadership must demand a representative proportion of the jobs that will be available; and the rotunda or ground floor 'mall' of the building must represent black business enterprises. Any 'new social service or community facilities which emerge as the result of new construction, should have major black entreprenuership as well as clienteles.

This perspective gives some hint regarding leadership dimensions. A new level of leadership 'advocacy' and negotiation for inclusion of specifically and uniquely black vested interests will be required. The Haryou-Act Community Corporation leadership, especially, is in a critical position at its vantage point as organizational spokesman. Haryou leadership is in the unique position, given its experience with official, bureaucratic and governmental systems, to opt for this kind of inclusion through planned community change. There will be a variety of 'cues' available at varying points in the above process. Cues which will serve as signals to sensitive leaders that immediate action and response is needed. But beyond responding, Haryou and Harlem leaders must 'initiate' meaningful planning mechanisms which can establish specific community priorities.[21]

The embarkation upon such planning will require leadership coalition with social and human services' professionals including social workers, planners, public officials, economists, demographers and so on.[22] Republican Senator Edward W. Brooke in a recent statement to the Congressional Black Caucus in Washington, D.C. illuminates the kind of direction which I am suggesting. Brooke suggests, that,

> In the past we (black political leaders) have viewed the notion
> of coalitions too narrowly. We have regarded coalitions as
> permanent. We feared we would lose our identities if we
> coalesced with others, particularly whites. But coalitions need
> not be permanent or erosive. We must form free-floating coalitions

161

across racial lines. And these coalitions must be based on specific and programmatic issues of common interest.[23] Brooke then goes on to specify the issues as those related to economics, i.e. inflation, unemployment health care, housing and etc. Though he is concerned with a National perspective, I nevertheless view his comments as relevant to our concern for a community.

There is however an additional retionale for proposing new forms of leadership coalition, and particularly given my proposition regarding the ghetto's demise. It relates to the perceived decline of the political machine in urban America, an issue of crucial importance to leadership in Harlem. One reason for the decline of the machine is the overall decline of the importance of local political parties. In general, the power center is shifting from the political party to the civil service, the welfare-state bureaucracy. This bureaucracy is constantly expanding and has obtained major political force through coalitions with established unions. Banfield and Wilson point out that city employees constitute one of the most important pressure groups in city politics, yet employee unions are functioning less and less as ajuncts of the party machinery. They are interested, instead, in making the bureaucracy as independent as possible, and they have succeeded both in reducing the amount and nature of patronage available, and in weakening the decision-making power of the political party. As the machine fades, the career bureaucrat becomes the modern-day equivalent of the party boss. As such he may well have more power than the old boss ever had, and this increase in power will be at the expense of the machine and the party.[24] Existent Haryou leadership must be responsive to this reality in the effecting of new coalitions.

The projection of the Haryou Corporation as the social engineering 'firm' for the Harlem community within this change perspective is important. As the coordinative mechanism for newly emergent networks of leadership, Haryou can become to black urban community planning in New York and other Northern communities, what the Metropolitan Applied Research Center Inc. (MARC) is to Metropolitan and City planning on the national level; and what other contemporary New York institutions have become to their divergent, often dispersed interests; the planning research and administrative Center, or prototype.[25] Thus, consistent with the roles currently ascribed to New York as the center of urbanization; the testing ground of megalopolis--is this view of Haryou as the creative, 'innovator' or center of 'inner city' urban planning.

I agree with Dr. Charles Hamilton, who, in a recent newspaper article suggests, that, "The day of the black leadership cluster under one rather small umbrella is over and done with-at least for now".[26] Dr. Hamilton is referring to the National formats of leadership focus in such organizations as the NAACP, CORE and the SCLG. He finds, rather, that "...older organizations are being called upon to share the leadership mantle with relatively new, more locally based leaders and groups".[27] My view is that community mechanisms like Haryou are the logical replacements. Our analysis of functional leadership in Harlem and Haryou substantiates the view, again shared by Harmilton, "the more local the group, the more likely it is to concentrate on those issues and immediate goals which lead toward consolidation of black community resources rather than toward "breaking up the black ghetto".[28] Such groups, continues Hamilton,

> are less interested in such things as scattered site public
> housing and more concerned about replacing the deteriorated
> housing in the black community with low cost structures...One
> crucial point made by local leaders it that policies designed to

disperse black people also operate to dilute the advantages of
the black block vote.[29]
Certainly, these are among the contemporary concerns of black leadership
in most urban ghettoes. In Harlem they are of longer standing than
anywhere in the nation.[30] It is as the result of Harlem and Haryou's
leaderships experience in dealing with these issues, that the inevita-
bility of the ghettoes demise, as a racial enclave is postulated.

Harlem's leadership must concern itself, with the emergent strategies of metropolitanism and megalopolis perceived by some as the major
strategy for overcoming the increasing percentages of blacks in America's
central cities. Piven and Cloward, for example, in their New Republic
article, believe that "Metropolitan government will help to (avert
impending black control of the cities) by usurping many powers of the
city.[31] According to W.H. Ferry, Cloward and Piven also believe that
"blacks may be too immature politically and too habituated to white
dictation to convert even substantial voting majorities into economic
or political power".[33] And would suggest, further that they underestimate the capacities and ambitions of existent leadership in Harlem.

The point is that these must be the legitimate interests of Harlem
and Haryou leadership. Given my proposition as to the realities of
community circumstances and the transformation of the area from a racial
ghetto to an integrated cosmopolitis, it is incumbent upon this leadership to design strategies which maintain certain institutional, power
and decision making handles. Harlem should always have a relevant role,
for example, in determining the voting perogatives of black New Yorkers.
Its power to do so however, must be based on genuine political analysis
and technical insight stimulated by Haryou 'experts' as opposed to certain of the past and current rationales--patronage and so on.[34] Research,
planning and advocacy as proposed in my perspective of the institutional
role of the organization would facilitate this approach.

The observation that functional leaders persist in the organizational and community life of black populations whether they are concen-
trated within ghetto's or not, is demonstrated in the experiences of
communities like Jamaica, Queens; and other 'integrated' Long Island,
and New York suburbs.[35] Certain experiences of the Puerto Rican community in New York are instructive in this regard. The perspective
of an organization like ASPIRA, in dealing with its geographically
dispersed constituency, is suggestive that various 'cultural /institu-
tional' strengths can be maintained.[36] The key to 'successful' leadership function is found in the degree of internalized community, or
ethnic-racial values and purposes, not necessarily, in residential
patterns.[37]

Utilizing my leadership types one can predict that the creative
elites, institutional inspirationalists and the proto-indigenous idealists
will be among those most important for achieving the desired outcomes
in the ghetto's transformation.[38] The premier leaders, raceocrats and
commutators, less so, as they will have lost the required concentration
of blacks essential for their relevance.[39] It is conceivable that some
other leadership type will replace them, but the form and function of
the new leadership is unpredictable. I am struck by the veritable absence, for example, of these latter leadership types in the somewhat
dispersed Puerto Rican community; where the premier leader, in particular, is absent. The efforts, earlier of the Herena Valentine's and
Manual Diaz'; and even the Herman Badillo's for Premier leadership status.
in my terms, have been frustrated.[40] It is true that these men represent
legitimate leadership in the above community, but the heights to which
they might have risen are clearly inhibited by the lack of a highly con-
centrated and outspoken constituency. Badillo, the leader who comes

closest to premiership, finds such status illusive. As former Bronx Borough President, he must represent a heterogeneous population.[41] A comparable situation exists for Percy Sutton. Badillo's black counterpart in the Manhattan Borough Presidency.[42]

The positioning of present Haryou leadership in local block, church and social organizations in Harlem is also viewed as functional given the hypothesis that the ghetto is in transition.[43] The necessity for effective channels of communications will be a high priority; and informed, aware leadership will be essential in facilitating them. Certain forms of consensus, respecting alternate strategies for insuring that the interests and needs of the black community are foremost in the minds of those making critical decisions will require leaders to 'link' their constituencies with one another.[44] These are among the leadership functions to be performed by existent Haryou representatives. I view as perhaps the most important however, those functions which related to designing new coalitions with professional and technical leadership resources; and it is here that social work becomes crucial.[45]

I view the Black social work administrator and planner as a critical resource in the future of the Haryou corporation, and the continued development of relevant leadership. We are sufficient in quantity and technical skill to be effective as partners in the proposed leadership coalitions. In addition, the dispersion of Black social work professionals throughout public and private planning and social service systems could become functional in the planful transformation of Harlem.[46] As participants and allies with existent Haryou leadership, black social workers will be in the position to devote their energies to a specialized area of activity, of importance to their developing technology (i.e. social policy and planning); while concomitantly engaging themselves in organizational policy and decision making. Certain of the new leadership skills particularly those of a technical nature which will be required by indigenous leaders, can be shared by these professionals.

The black social workers training regarding the appropriate use of bureaucracy and 'colleageal' relationships (primarily as the result of experiences in the anti-poverty programs) should facilitate inter-professional alliances of the kind mentioned above.[47] These are pre-requisites for the planning tasks which leadership must assume, given my prospectus for community transition. Mureen Bennis' comment respecting how organizations will change is illuminating in this regard:

> Adaptation, problem solving temporary systems of diverse specialists, linked together by coordinating and task-evaluating executive specialists in an organic flux-this is the organizational form that will gradually replace bureaucracy as we know it.[48]

Though my perspective on Haryou's development as an institution includes certain purposes as the result of 'infused' organizational values. I do find some relevance in Bennis' model. Thus the conceivable function of the social work practitioner or planner will be the continual gleaning for legitimate Haryou and Harlem leadership, of those rationalisties which maintain organizational integrity, even as community systems change.

One is tempted to propose a comparable role for Black social work practitioners throughout the network of Community Corporation programs and communities in Northern Urban areas. That leadership in professional organizations like the National Association of Black Social Workers should envisage these program priorities as opportunities for influencing predictable social change, using positive planning mechanisms, seems plausible.

I am not here proposing that black social workers participate in breaking up urban black communities. Particularly where such communities are approaching models of viability and innovation.[49] In these instances the professionals function would be a maintenance one. What I am proposing is that where a black community, like Harlem, is so strategically located in the path of technological progress--that is in danger of being dispersed by forces beyond its control; Black social workers have a responsibility. It resides in the legitimate function of social work as a 'humanizing' profession and as one committed to social justice; it resides in their position in bureaucratically intense organizations, increasingly more powerful, but beyond these rationales, no one else will care.[50]

The current Haryou leadership has a profound responsibility in this forecast. It must be available to participate in the proposed alliances with a new sense of 'trust'. The petty jealousies and conflicts which have traditionally marked joint experiences with professionals and technicians must now be overcome.[51] There is too much at stake. Functionally, these leaders' several positions as community organizational representatives, civil service employees, public administrators, and elected officials at local, state and federal levels are indispensable input and feedback attributes.[52] The corporation is quite well informed as to the formal and informal priorities circulating through municipal corridors and power circles.[53] These are 'resources' which will be critical in the planning effort.

These comments respecting the perceived roles of functional leaders in Harlem as participating in the transformation of their community are not fundamentally contradictory. My analysis began by focusing on the process of functional civic leadership identification, emergence and change. The tracing of specific leadership 'types' through the peculiar history of Harlem as a Black community is illustrative, "that leadership is specific to the particular situation under investigation; who becomes the leader in a given group (organization or community), engaging in a particular activity and what the leadership characteristics are in a given case are a function of the specific situation".[54] Given this perspective, it is within the legitimate purvue of Harlem and Haryou's leadership to engage in whatever substantive planning, or social policy decisions concern the community; whether related to its transformation and integration, or its perpetuation. I have taken the position that the latter is untenable. Thus the substantive leadership involvement, essential at this point, will relate itself to strategies designed for community transformation and integration.[55]

We are not to be naive, however, in posturing Harlem's organizational and community leadership in the decision making process which will ultimately cause the changes envisaged. Dr. Kenneth Clark is correct in his observation, that,

> If ghettoes are to be transformed, then forces superior to those which resist change must be mobilized to counteract them. The problem of change in the ghetto is essentially, therefore, a problem of power--a confrontation and conflict between the power required for change and the power resistant to change. The proglem of power is crucial and nuclear to any nonsentimental approach to understanding, planning and predicting.[56]

It is conceivable given this perspective, that Harlem leaders will have to carefully research the potential sources of power allies available through the Federal government and those metropolitan bureaucracies they control. The suggestion for example that,

> The double edged sword of national power thus leads to the real question that blacks must face. Any realistic discussion of ghetto problems must focus less on how to change city government (though this is still important), and more on how to influence the national government.

My analysis is consistent with these considerations; since it is in the best interests of the kinds of powerful forces alluded to that Harlem be transformed.[58]

The critical element in my perspective, is the relevance of Harlem and Haryou leadership in advocating for inclusion in the planning process. Any beyond this, in precipitating or initiating certain of the policy concerns which will 'protect' certain institutional and economic vested interests, as the process continues.[59]

The time is at hand for meeting the challenges inherent in Harlem's transformation to a nonsegregated open community system. The leadership skills required are those necessary and prerequisite to success in any single standard competition in a non-segregated context.[60] I have no problem visualizing the emergence, in Harlem of the kinds of collective leadership genius capable of spearheading the process. We will require the skills of the creative elite leader; the institutional inspirationalist, the commutator; and the proto-indigenous idealist-- in the development of critical coalitions with professional and technical leadership.

James Weldon Johnson, once again, provides insight as to the direction comtemporary black leadership in Harlem must take:

It is probably that land through the heart of Harlem will some day so increase in value that Negroes may not be able to hold it--although it is quite as probable that there will be some Negroes able to take full advantage of the increased values-- and will be forced to make a move. But the next move, when it comes, will be unlike the others. It will not be a move made solely at the behest of someone else; it will be more in the nature of a bargain. Nor will it be a move in which the Negro will carry with him only his household goods and utensils; he will move at a financial profit to himself..."[61]

In 1930, Johnson could conclude, "but at the present time such a move is no where in sight".[62] If he were observing contemporary Harlem, 1974, he could not.

FOOTNOTES TO CHAPTER XI

1. James Weldon Johnson, <u>Black Manhattan</u>, op. cit., page 158-159.

2. Gilbert Osafsky, op. cit., page 80.

3. James Weldon Johnson, op. cit., page 135.

4. James Henrik Clark, <u>Harlem a Community in Transition</u>, op. cit., page 262.

5. Sylvester Leaks, op. cit., page 15.

6. Kenneth B. Clark, op. cit., page 210. In J.H. Clark op. cit.

7. Clark, op. cit., pages 11-12.

8. Osafsky, op. cit., page 111. Johnson, op. cit., pages 158-159; also see Pinkney and Wooch, op. cit., pages 29-30. Also See <u>Youth in the Ghetto</u>, op. cit., pages 101-107.

9. Field Observation and Interviews.

10. Pinkney and Woock pages 27-28; the authors in reviewing population characteristics of Central Harlem announced, "As these figures indicate, the proportion of Harlem residents who are black declined (from 98.2 percent to 97.0 percent) between 1950 and 1960; mainly as a result of low-income Puerto Rican Families moving into public housing developments in the area". A later statistic regarding the Black population in Harlem (1965) puts the proportion at 96.3 percent; see Department of City Planning <u>1965 Population for 300 Planning Area</u>, May 1967 as listed by Health Areas in Human Resources Administration, Youth Services Agency <u>Directory of Needs; Selected Social-Economic Characteristics of Youth in New York City</u>, April 1969; thus, an additional decline is discernable.

11. U.S. Department of Labor Bureau of Labor Statistics, Regional Report #29, July 1972; and B.L.S. Regional Report #34, July 1973. <u>New York City in Transition: Population, Jobs, Prices and Pay in a Decade of Change</u>, pages 1-10.

12. One indication of this phenomena is given by the percentage of Whites who have moved to East Harlem at Central Harlem's periphery. They now constitute 22.3 percent of the population in that area. Another indication is found in the Housing Controlled by Columbia University at Harlem's Western extremity (Riverside Drive Apartments). Finally in this regard see James Turner's analysis in "Blacks in Cities: Land and Self-Determina-

tion" in <u>The Black Scholar</u>, April 1970, pages 7-13.

13. See Louella Jacqueline Long and Vernon Ben Robinson, <u>How Much Power to the People, A Study of the New York State Urban Development Corporations Involvement in Black Harlem</u> (Urban Center, Columbia University, NY, 1971.

14. Ibid and see Turner, <u>op. cit.</u>

15. <u>Op. Cit.</u>, page 12.

16. <u>Ibid.</u>

17. Interviews conducted and Field Observations, Fall 1973.

18. <u>Ibid.</u>

19. <u>Ibid.</u>

20. Clark also discusses the protective functions of the Ghetto. He, however, relates to the negative aspects of the phenomena, i.e. in terms of monopolistic and noncompetitive sanctions for exploiting the Community; see Clark, <u>Dark Ghetto, op. cit.</u>

21. See Long and Robinson, <u>op. cit.</u>, pages 117-119.

22. <u>Ibid.</u>

23. <u>Black Enterprise</u>, Vol. 4, No. 6, January 1974, page 18.

24. See Edward C. Banfield and James Q. Wilson, <u>City Politics</u> (New York, Vintage Books, page 213;) see also <u>W.S. Sayre and H. Kaufman, <u>Governing New York City: Politics in the Metropolis</u>, N.Y., W.W. Norton and Co., 1960) pages 73-76 and James Q. Wilson, "The Negro in Politics" in Sethard Fischer (ed.) <u>Power and the Black Community</u>, page 385.

25. This is the view of the institutional inspirationalist. One critical question raised by this perspective, however, has to do with Haryou's being a publicly funded program. Is it possible that an ethnically based institution can be supported by public moneys? According to Richard Cloward's analysis the answer is yes. Cloward points out, for example, that other ethnic or religious oriented organizations receive public funds. On the other hand, Krosney feels that such would be a contradiction in terms and that the onus of responsibility for generating institutions is on Black leadership. The rationale that government may in this regard be financing a revolution that might disrupt its social order presents in Krosney's terms, an obvious dilemma. My position for present purposes is that government does have some responsibility for helping in the financing of certain organizational forms. Institutionalization, however, is a <u>process</u> which requires that major commitments be made by indigenous constituencies. It cannot be dependent upon external resources. Haryou represents a model or test case in my view, which can generate relevant answers regarding the issue. For additional analysis see Krosney, <u>op. cit.</u>, pages 111-114 and Chapter 5 also see Richard Cloward, "The War on Poverty: Are the Poor

Left Out? <u>The Nation</u>, August 2, 1965; see also Long and Robinson, <u>op. cit.</u> pages 97-100.

26. Dr. Charles V. Hamilton, "Integration on the Move: New Leadership Joins Effort", <u>The Los Angeles Times</u>, September 1973.

27. <u>Ibid.</u>

28. <u>Ibid.</u>

29. <u>Ibid.</u>

30. John Henrik Clark, <u>op. cit.</u> pages 198-203. <u>Youth In The Ghetto</u>, <u>op. cit.</u> pages 101-107. Kenneth B. Clark, <u>Dark Ghetto</u>, <u>op. cit.</u> Krosney, <u>op. cit.</u> pages 35-36; 115-116; and pages 149-166.

31. W.H. Ferry, "Farewell to Integration" in Liberator, January 1968, Vol. 8, No. 1. Page 1.

32. <u>Ibid.</u>

33. <u>Ibid.</u>

34. See Krosney, <u>op. cit.</u>, page 116.

35. See Chapter II of dissertation.

36. Interviews conducted Fall 1973.

37. See Chapter VI of dissertation.

38. See Chapter III for definitions.

39. These leaders will have some relevance however; and particularly the commutator--regarding internal communications in Harlem.

40. Interviews Fall 1973; and Field Observations 1966 as Community Organizer, Mobilization for Youth.

41. Interviews, Fall 1973.

42. Interviews, Fall 1973.

43. See Chapter IX of Dissertation, also see Long and Robinson, <u>op. cit.</u> page 99.

44. <u>Ibid.</u> pages 99-100.

45. <u>Ibid.</u> pages 105-107; and <u>Black Enterprise</u> <u>op. cit.</u>, page 18.

46. In this regard I view as important A.B.S.W. involvement in the new planning mechanism The Harlem Urban Development Corporation. See Long and Robinson, <u>op. cit.</u>, page 172.

47. These are requirements which Graduate and Undergraduate Social Work Education must take into account in designing curriculum and in structuring Field experiences. The social work professionals of the 1970s and 80s must be a specialist in dealing with types

of coalitions. He must be equipped to relate effectively with professionals from a variety of disciplines; political, business and industrial, and other Human Service technicians. Such preparation requires an interdisciplinary academic and professional approach to social work practice; the hallmark of the 'generalist' or polyvalent' practitioner. See Kahn, op. cit., Chapter 10.

48.   Mureen Bennis, Planned Change.

49.   I view the Black community of Gary, Indiana as an example of this phenomena.

50.   See James Weldon Johnson, op. cit., pages 158-159; see also Krosney op. cit. pages 199-204 and pages 112-114.

51.   See Chapters VIII and IX of Dissertation.

52.   See Chapter IX of Dissertation; also see Kahn, op.cit. pages 305-327.

53.   Chapter IX of Dissertation.

54.   Selznick, op. cit. page 23.

55.   I am convinced that the indicators discussed above (i.e. new development corporation activities re: Harlem Urban Development Corporation; State Office Building; new Columbia University Housing and Development in East Harlem etc.) point in the direction of Harlem's transformation. But even were my preposition proven wrong, the process of leadership mobilization and coalition would generate positive outcomes for Harlem.

56.   Clark, Dark Ghetto, op. cit., page 212.

57.   See Banfield and Wilson, op. cit., pages 117-119.

58.   See Turner, op. cit., page 3.

59.   Alfred Kahn presents a paradigm of the planning process in which he identifies certain critical phases of relevance to my concerns for leadership involvement. Among them are the definition of the planning task, and Policy formulation. See Kahn, Theory and Practice of Social Planning, op. cit. pages 61-62.

60.   Youth in the Ghetto, op. cit., pages 5-6.

61.   Johnson, op. cit., page 159,

62.   Ibid.

APPENDIX A

METHODOLOGY OF THE STUDY

The study design is that of a qualitative analysis of Haryou leadership over an approximate ten year (10) period.[1] I utilize the case study method in assessing the behavior of selected Board of Directors' members and Executive leadership as they make decisions and implement policies reflecting Haryou positions on various organizational and community issues.[2] Examples of such issues are reflective of the decision, early in the Haryou experience to appendage ACT (The Association Community Teams) to the original Haryou Organization; the decision around Haryou leaderships acceptance of the summer action program "Operation Pull"; and the decision which lead to Haryou ACT becoming the Community Corporation for the Central Harlem Community. Additional issues related to Haryou leadership functions are community issues in housing, education, the Organization of indigenous Neighborhood Boards and the involvement of Harlem Youth in the decision making structure of the Board of directors.

Field observations growing from my involvement in Haryou during the various phases when decisions and leadership actions respecting these issues were resolved are of major relevance to this research. The opportunity to observe first hand the patterns of interaction and influence stimulated my concern for further inquiry.

The present investigation utilized the Focused Interview Method; field study design in which interviewing of those leaders identified by their Board of Executive Participation identified above, is structured.[3] I utilize an interview guide instrument, as it provides the greatest degree of flexibility and allows the gathering of data from semi-structured, open ended questions.[4] The guide is supported by data obtained from a content analysis of relevant documents and records (i.e. Newspapers, Board minutes, Haryou proposal data, and HANA committee reports), contemporary to the particular organizational phase under review. This procedure, in addition to representing perhaps the only realistic one for a qualitative analysis of Haryou and Harlem's leadership phenomena; also facilitates selecting from a repertoire of relevant data.[5] It allows the examination of subtle differences which may exist, as between private feelings and public behavior; observations critical to an analysis of such leadership - since the question of motives is important to my analysis.

Interlocking data also provide a check on certain of my bias' regarding the interpretation of the phenomena under investigation. And, finally, the issue of 'availability' or access to former and present Haryou leaders is critical in selecting the above procedures.

Sources utilized for the identification of leaders to be interviewed range from signers of the original Haryou document, Youth In The Ghetto-- to membership lists of Board of Directors and executive staff during the approximate 10 year period. Seventy interviews were conducted for the study. Responses to a series of interview guide questions were then analyzed and respondents were classified in one of six civic leadership categories, called 'types': 1) creative elite, 2) institutional inspirationalist, 3) proto-indigenous idealist, 4) raceocrat, 5) commutator, and 6) premier. The leaders identified are defined by Harlemites familiar with or active in the Haryou program. A sub-categorization of these major types is borrowed from Bogardus. Thus I am interested in "direct" or "indirect" functions performed by the above; whether their leadership is primarily social or expert, autocratic or democratic regarding community and organizational issues. Finally, are leadership functions administrative or policy-related.

Relevant data regarding leadership characteristics and attributes are collected in the interview process, i.e. respondents race, sex, age, place of birth, educational level, and, in some instances religion. Civic organizational participation, other than Haryou and profession or occupation, length of time active in Harlem and, finally, place of residence during activities in Haryou are additional elements noted. Finally, leadership characteristics extrapolated from the data relate to: sympathy for the objective of Haryou, empathy with Haryou's community constituency, identification with Haryou's organizational values, poise and control of leaders under pressure and astuteness of observation. These are among the relevant leadership elements to be analyzed. The indicators of certain of the above are leaders' behavior in meetings as well as interview questions designed to illicit attitudes and feelings.

In specifying or operationalizing my leadership types, criteria reflective of the above characteristics are used. The process of identifying certain individuals as fitting specific leadership types includes the perceptions of community and Haryou organizational leaders interviewed; and classification categories prestructured as the result of other leadership studies.

In this regard, cross references with existing leadership typologies, i.e., the 'moderate', 'accomodation', and 'protest' leadership categories referred to by Myrdal:[6] the 'militant', 'organizer' and 'radical leadership categories of Wilson,[7] the power and race leaders of Burgess[8] and Ladd,[9] and the 'proto-indigenous' and 'bureaucratic intense' leadership typologies of Litwak;[10] and finally, the conceptualizations of functional leadership articulated by Selznick (i.e., creative, institutional, inspirationalists, etc.) are made. Having the proliferate leadership literature before me, in addition to the invaluable experience of observing first hand the patterns of interaction and influence in which Haryou's leaders operated, facilitated conceptualizing the categories of leadership introduced in my study.

The operationalization of the categories is the result of questions designed to elicit community and/or Haryou organizational activists and leaders (as identified by the criteria of function, recurrent mention and identification with organizational and community issues and life by Harlemites and relevant documents) opinions. These questions are set forth in the enclosed interview instrument utilized in the study.

Leaders are then placed in one of the six categories (i.e., creative elite, commutator, proto-indigenous idealist, raceocrat, institutional inspirationalist and premier), on the basis of respondents perceptions of leader behavior and attributes with respect to relevant civic and Haryou organizational issues. Certain of these criteria are discussed below. The frequency of a given leader's identification as one possessing certain characteristics is important in ultimately being placed in one or another of the leadership types. And thus, those persons identified in the study as falling in a particular category are leaders mentioned most often by Harlemites, (and one another) as demonstrating certain characteristics. In a final sense, leaders are categorized on the basis of their own perceptions of their functions and contributions to Harlem and Haryou.

Topical Outline of Data Collection

As my major approach is that of a functional analysis of leadership behavior in Haryou, I am interested in particular data which illuminates this pehnomena. Thus description of leadership behavior is an essential area of data collection.[1]

1 - <u>What does the leader do?</u> To answer this kind of question, data is
     collected re: (a) time spent in various Haryou activities (i.e.
       planning, evaluation, Board committee work, staff hiring, etc.)
               (b) time spent with various people (i.e. representa-
     tives of funding sources, public relations media, board cliques,
     etc.)
2 - <u>How does the leader do it?</u> (a) Frequency of behavior patterns, (i.e.
     dominance, direct influence, indirect assignments, autocratic
     direction, etc.)
               (b) Responsibility, authority and delega-
     tion of responsibility patterns.
               (c) Leaders ability to predict behavior
     in given circumstances.
               (d) Influence patterns in effecting group
     solidarity in action.

The Method used in securing the data is mentioned above, however, the reader is reminded that an interview guide is the primary research instrument.

Other factors of relevance, for which data is collected have been outlined in the body of the proposal. I will briefly recapitulate them for the purposes of clarity. As mentioned earlier, I will be interested in various Haryou organizational factors. Thus data will be required re: (a) organizational history, (b) present organizational characteristics, (c) informal organizational structure, (d) formal organization structure, (e) relevant communications systems within Haryou, (f) organizational and group ideologies, (g) external/situational factors which affect Haryou, and (h) certain group attitudes and perceptions within Haryou.

These data represent relevant Haryou organizational or groups characteristics which I will suggest are functional with respect to leadership behavior. In this regard, and with respect to the individual characteristics and attributes outlined earlier (i.e. sex, age, etc.), I am interested in specific relationship associated with leadership behavior. Put another way, I am interested in whether certain organizational factors function in a <u>casual</u> relationship with Haryou leadership behavior; or whether many of these organizational factors are the <u>result</u> of leadership behavior. Other possible relationships between the group, individual and behavior variables explored are concomitancy, criterion and conditioner. Are, for example, certain leadership characteristics merely concomitant with behavior i.e. occurences with no discernable functional relevance; are certain forms of leadership behavior appropriate <u>criteria</u> for leadership evaluation; and finally, are certain organizational factors conditioners of relationships between given leadership behavior and other factors.

The following chart graphically demonstrates the variety of relationships suggested.[12]

173

Chart I—A Paradigm for the Study of Leadership

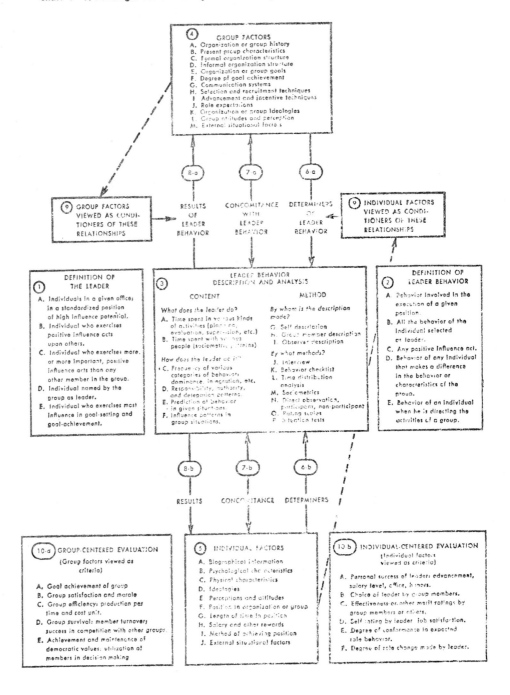

FOOTNOTES TO APPENDIX A

1. This time period (approximately Spring 1962-Winter 1972) is se-
    lected owing to my activity in the anti-poverty program; in-
    clusive of work at Hana, Mobilization for Youth and Haryou
    as an executive. Documentation through the press, recorded
    speeches and written accounts re: public hearings and legis-
    lation are at their height during this period. Finally and
    perhaps, most importantly, these were the years of major
    activities re: the planning, implementation and evaluations
    of Haryou.

2. William J. Goode and Paul K. Hatt, Methods in Social Research;
    McGraw-Hill Book Company, 1952, New York, Toronto and London.
    Particular reference re: The Case Study Method is found on
    pages 313-341. See also, Raymond B. Cattell "Types of Group
    Characteristics in the American Soldier" Lazarfeld, Ibid page
    290; and Daniel M. Goodacre, III "The Use of a Sociometric Test
    as a Predictor of Combat Unit effectiveness", Ibid. page 302.

3. For Relevant Comments re: the utilization of the Field Study
    Method see: Peter M. Blau and Richard Scott: Formal Organi-
    zations; Chandler Publishing Co. San Francisco page 20. Also
    see Goode and Hatt op. cit., pages 92, 119, 296, 313-359.

4. Ibid.

5. See for example Clark's comments re: the methodology used in
    Original Haryou Research in Haryou-Youth in the Ghetto, Op. cit.
    page 47. Also Clark; Dark Ghetto, op. cit. Introduction in
    the Epilogue pages XIII-XXIX.

6. Myrdal, op. cit., pages 436-650.

7. Wilson, op. cit., pages 72-86.

8. Burgess, op. cit., pages 76-187.

9. Ladd, op. cit., pages 43-70.

10. Litwak, op. cit., pages 29-40.

11. The format here is taken from Seeman and Morris, op. cit. See their
    Paradigm for an analysis of Leadership.

12. Ibid.

175

DEFINITION OF CONCEPTS

For the purposes of this study, certain operational definitions of concepts growing out of related literature, theory and practice are presented. As mentioned earlier in the proposal, much of my analysis has benefited from the approach taken by M. Elaine Burgess in her work, <u>Leadership in a Southern City</u>.[1] I am particularly indebted to that study for its conceptual clarifications and in view of the comparable interdisciplinary 'mix' of theoretical approaches used. Thus in presenting the definitions of concepts used in my study of Leadership in Haryou, I have drawn often from comparable ones used in Miss Burgess' works.

<u>Community</u>: A functionally related aggregate of people interacting within a specific geographic locality over time, structurally arranged, and exhibiting some awareness of their identity as a group.

<u>Sub community</u>: A functional sub-system found within a larger community aggregate with organized ways, structures, and patterns of behavior that are distinct from, and yet a part of, and influenced by, the larger whole.

In my study, we will be looking at Harlem as a community, as opposed to the conventional view of her as sub-community. Thus when relating to the Black Community, we will be talking about the above definition of Harlem.[2]

<u>Decision Making</u>:
The effecting of a choice among alternative modes of action made by individuals or groups that involves action toward change or maintenance of organizational or community life or facilities.

<u>Institution</u>: A stable or organized system of behavior developed within a given social context to serve certain needs or social objectives regarded as essential for the survival of a group. The main concern in my study is for the analysis of the <u>process</u> involved in an organization serving institutional needs and the functions of particular leaders in facilitating that process. I agree with the conceptualization of Selznick regarding institutionalization.[3] (See above)

<u>Leader</u>
An individual whose behavior determines the patterning of behavior within a community or its organizations at a given time.

<u>Leadership</u> that process which occurs in a specific social situation and which influences the behavior patterns of others.

<u>Civic Leadership</u>
A voluntary process in which individuals perform functions which influence behavior patterns related to raising and settling of community and organizational issues. As noted in the proposal, my definition of civic leadership represented a departure from that utilized in the conventional literature in that I include paid executive staff within the concept. This though a seeming contradiction, is consistent with my findings through observation of functions performed on a volunteer non paid basis, on the part of Haryou Executive Staff. Thus I differ in this respect from James Q. Wilson in his analysis.[4]

<u>Organization</u>: The process of coordinating activities so that the parts

become interdependent and the system functions as a unit.

Community Organization

As used here, refers to locally based programs or projects which are reflective of community interests and needs.

Position: The individual's place in a given organizational system.

Status: A type of position which is recognized in a given social situation and is spontaneously evolved.

Office: A position which is deliberately created and governed by specific rules.

Power: The ability to induce poeple to take courses of action they might not otherwise have take.

Power Structure: Those leaders and those parts of the community institutional and associational structure which may come into play as a result of various community issues or decision.

Race Leaders

Those leaders who by their stand on certain race issues can be identified in terms of radical, liberal, moderate or accommodating.[5]

Functions: The actions of individual leaders in the organization or community context as dictated by position.

Social Class: Groups of individuals who, through similarity of such criteria as education, occupation, housing and economic background and through similarity of values, attitudes and behavior can be regarded as belonging to a given stratum of a community.

Social Process: The characteristic way interaction occurs, or a series of related events leading to some result.

Social Structure: Relatively fixed, persistent and functionally interrelated units or elements of a social group or social system, such as institutions, social classes, associations, leadership and power groupings, racial groups and other enduring social units.

Social instrumentalities

As defined in the study are organizational structures, indigenous to the community which reflect its values and interests.

Ligitimation: The process by which self determined organizations and institutions are made to reflect the will and needs of their constituents.

Syntality: Defined as organizational character or life style. Syntality is to a group or organization, what personality is to an individual.[6]

Creative elite: a leadership concept defined as one who is creative and brilliant but aloof. As used in the study, this form of leadership is not found to be responsive or responsible to the community constituency it represents.

Proto-indigenous: In my study's terms a person or leader who represents a particular ethnic or racial community as part of his or her function in some external organization or context.

Institutional inspirationalist: A form of leadership which seeks to inspire or promote ethno-community intense organizational and institutional experiences. Culture building and the protection of community and race values are priorities of such leadership.

Commutator: A community or street administrator as defined in my study. A type of leader who serves as an invaluable communications link between indigenous community residents and external/official authorities.

Premier: A leader recognized as a 'top' person in his field. This type of leader as defined in my study is recognized as highly qualitative and unequaled in his or her chosen career.

Raceocrat: A person or leader who uses his racial identity as a devise for access to high level bureaucratic occupations or positions.

FOOTNOTES TO APPENDIX B

1. M. Elaine Burgess, Leadership in A Southern City. (The University of North Carolina Press, Chapel Hill)

2. Louis L. Knowles and Kenneth Prewitt, Institutional Racism in America. (Prentice-Hall, Inc. Spectrum Books, Englewood Cliffs, M.J.) Page 174.

3. Philip Selznick, Leadership in Administration: A Sociological Interpretation. (Ron, Peterson and Company, Evanston, Illinois and White Plains, N.Y.) page 16.

4. James Q. Wilson, Negro Politics: The Search for Leadership, (The Free Press of Glencoe, Illinois) page 255.

5. Ibid.

6. Raymond B. Cottrell, "Types of Group Characteristics" pages 297-299; in The Language of Social Research. Paul F. Lazarsfeld and Morris Rosenberg (editors), (The Free Press, New York-- Collier-MacMillan Limited, London).

APPENDIX C

AVAILABILITY OF RESOURCES

The major resource required for my study is people. I am fortunate in finding those relevant to the Haryou experience under analysis, available to me and positively oriented towards participating in the research process. Many of the sample population are extremely busy with their commitments to tasks unrelated to Haryou; and some give the impression of preferring to forget their earlier associations with the program - but in every instance, I have been impressed with respondents desire to 'have the Haryou story told'.

Entre to Haryou, presently, is facilitated by contacts with the board of directors' chairman and executive staff (acting executive director). Contacts with former Board and executive staff members is facilitated through personal letters, phone calls and inquiries using present Haryou staff and resources.

The variety of documents serving as resources in the study are available through personal files, public records, newspapers, board of directors' minutes, Haryou proposal documents and other studies related to Haryou.

I am fortunate in having the full cooperation of my employer, Skidmore College. The College has made resources available for the typing of the dissertation proposal and final manuscript. Skidmore's flexibility in allowing critical interview time, is or course, essential.

Finally, I am indebted to Dr. James Jones and Dr. Charles Hamilton. They have been available to share precious time with me in the development of the dissertation. Dr. Hamilton is conducting a study of Harlem as a political community, and though my study is not directly related to this broader work, some corroboration regarding the relevant data was possible.

Academic and Experiential Preparation for the Study of Haryou Leadership

My life began in Harlem. I was born in Harlem Hospital, christened in a Harlem Church, paraded her streets as a Boy Scout, fought in them as a gang member; I as is true of Dr. Kenneth Clark; "first learned about love, about cruelty, about sacrifice, about cowardice, about bombast in Harlem".[1] I know Harlem institutions intimately, and prior to assuming professional tasks, was involved in them as a youth. I, for example was a 'cadet' in the youth program which eventually became the major program in Haryou; the Haryou Cadet Corp. Other pre-professional experiences include my role as a Street Club Worker with the New York City Youth Board (SCAC); an innovative anti-delinquency program active in the 1950s and early 1960s.

In 1962, my graduate training in social work became the most prevalent force in crystalizing my interests in Harlem, and specifically in Haryou. As a graduate student concentrating in community organization, my first field work placement is at The Harlem Neighborhoods Association. As noted in the Haryou document Youth in the Ghetto. In attempting to acknowledge its gratitude to the Harlem Neighborhoods Association (HANA), Haryou is in the awkard position of a child seeking to express its feelings toward a parent. I was involved, as a student social worker, in the process of Haryou's evolution from the Education Committee of HANA. The early planning stages and conceptualizations of what Haryou was to be; its relevance as a new community institutional model and opportunity structure represents a major phase in this study and one in which I was substantively involved.

It is through this role as a student for an approximate year, that I came to know the innermost aspirations of the early Haryou leadership, and more importantly, for the purposes of the present study, the various leadership functions they performed.

The next level of experience, of a direct nature, related to Haryou and its leadership occurred during two years of professional practice. For one year, 1968, I served as the special assistant to the Executive Director of Haryou. My office brought me in contact with the major decision makers of Haryou on an intensive basis. During 1969, I became the director of the Harlem Youth Unlimited (HYU) program component of Haryou; an experience which deepened my awareness of the complexities of the Haryou organization and the variety of leadership functions operative.

These are the practical experiences which have equipped me to conduct the present study. When such experiences is buttressed by what, in my judgement, is the best academic and professional preparation conceivable; Community Organization as a MSW candidate, and Social Policy and Planning, as a Doctoral candidate, my qualifications exceed those of most who would attempt such a research effort.

With respect to graduate and post graduate course work, it is difficult to specify or extrapolate discrete contributions to my preparation for the study; for Social Work education, in my experience, has been a continuous, developmental process. It is clear however, that the substantive nature of my two year field placements at HANA and Mobilization for Youth are among the most relevant. Course content in areas of Socio-cultural elements of social structure and social work practice; exposures to content in social theory and social research; community organization and social change theory and practice; course work in administration and social system's theory; and finally in the content areas of group and intergroup relations, political science and community development are among the most relevant during residence as a Masters student.

As a Doctoral resident, I found the course work in administration,

social planning and social policy of immense relevance. The specification within these broad areas, of interests in community organization,
urban education and urban political participation, and theories of
power and decision making are noteworthy.

---

1.   Clark, Kenneth B., Haryou: An Experiment: In - Harlem, A
         Community in Transition, John Henrik Clark, Editor.
         The Citadel Press, New York.

Summary of Pilot Efforts

Most of my preliminary work has related to the availability of key Haryou leaders for the purpose of interviews. A variety of contacts were made by letter, phone and in person to assess the interests of the necessary population. As indicated earlier, the response has been such as to justify the present effort.

Some pretesting of possible interview guide questions was achieved. In informal interviews with present Haryou executives and board members, certain decisions respecting the time parameters of the study were agreed upon. Also, in this regard, conferences held with colleagues regarding research design and appropriate theoretical frameworks for the study were held. I owe to these colleagues at Columbia University School of Social Work, and in the University's Political Science Department a debt of gratitude for facilitating, through prodding and instilling confidence, my embarking upon the research task.

Major Limitations

The major difficulty anticipated in conducting the study, is that related to the deficiencies and pitfalls in mu personal involvement in Haryou, and with its leadership during the period under investigation. I did not view myself as a participant observer in any research sense; I was involved in the social phenomena. Thus at this juncture my concern for an effective bias checking mechanism is a preoccupation. I am confident that the checks built into the collection and analysis of the data will help in this regard; however I am currently discussing the possibility of one or more of my colleagues at Skidmore, serving the function of 'counter checking' my observations, insights and conclusions. At this point, the realization that a potential problem resides in this area, serves as the most effective safeguard.

Finally, in this regard, and with respect to my access to various Haryou leaders, certain aspects of my earlier association with Haryou and Hana are important. My roles and responsibilities as executive assistant and graduate student, respectively, removed me from actual participation in critical decision making. Such removal enhanced my opportunities to view analytically, observational experiences. Owing to my close association with the directors of both organizations, the constant discussion of my impressions and insights benefitted from their experienced, professional knowledge and facilitated a greater degree of objectivity than might otherwise have been the case. Additionally, and of profound importance to my ability to conduct this study, my non-involvement in actual decisions kept me free from the kinds of nuances and associations with issues, which might have blocked subsequent access to important board members and community leadership.

BIBLIOGRAPHY

Abraham, Roger. Deep in The Jungle: Negro Narrative Folklore From
  The Streets of Philadelphia, (Revised Edition), Chicago, Adline
  Publishing Company, 1970.

Abrams, Charles. "The Housing Problem and The Negro", Daedalus, Winter
  1966, Journal of the American Academy of Arts and Sciences.

Allport, Gordon W., The Nature of Prejudice. Boston: Beacon Press, 1954.

Aptheker, Herbert. American Negro Slave Revolts, N.Y. Columbia University Press, 1943.

Baldwin, James, Nobody Knows My Name. New York: Dell Publishing, 1962.

Banfield, Edward C., Political Influence, New York: The Free Press, 1961.

_____, and James Q. Wilson, City Politics, Vintage Books NY, 1966.

Bennett, Lerone, Jr., Before The Mayflower: A History of The Negro in
  America 1610-1964, Penguin Books, Inc., Baltimore, Maryland, 1965.

_____, Confrontation: Black and White.

_____, Black Power USA: The Human Side of Reconstruction,
  Chicago.

Bierstedt, Robert. The Social Order: An Introduction To Sociology,
  McGraw-Hill Book Company, Inc., New York, Toronto, London.

Blau, Peter M., and W. Richard Scott. Formal Organizations: A Comparative Approach, Chandler Publishing Company, San Francisco, 1962.

Burgess, Elaine M. Negro Leadership In A Southern City, University of
  North Carolina Press, Chapel Hill, 1962.

Brazier, Arthur M., Black Self Determination: The Story of The Woodlawn
  Organization, William B. Berdman's Publishing Company, Grand Rapids,
  Michigan, 1969.

Brown, Claude. Manchild in the Promised Land, New York, McMillan Company,
  1965.

Bogardus, Emory S. Leaders and Leadership. D. Appleton-Century Company,
  Inc. New York, London.

Carmichael, Stokely and Charles V. Hamilton. Black Power: The Politics
  of Liberation in America.

Clark, Kenneth B., Dark Ghetto: Dilemmas of Social Power. Harper and
Row Publishers, New York, Evanston, and London.

_____, The Civil Rights Movement: Momentum and Organization
Daedalus, Winter 1965.

_____, A Relevant War Against Poverty: A Study of Community
Action Programs and Observable Social Change, New York. Metropolitan Applied Research Center, 1968.

_____, In American Politics: Three Views in the Black Man
(Clark, K.B., Julian Bond and Richard G. Hatcher) New York Metropolitan Applied Research Center, Inc., 1969.

_____, Haryou: An Experiment: In - Harlem, A Community in
Transition, John Henrik Clark, Editor, The Citadel Press, New York.

Clark John Henrik. Harlem: A Community in Transition, Citadel Press,
N.Y.

Clayton, Edward T., The Negro Politician: His Success and Failure,
Johnson Publishing Company, Inc., Chicago, 1964.

Cloward, Richard A., "The War On Poverty: Are The Poor Left Out?"
The Nation, 201 (August 2, 1965).

_____, and Lloyd E. Ohlin, Delinquency and Opportunity,
Glencoe, Ill: The Free Press, 1960.

_____, and Irwin Epstein, "Private Social Welfare's Disen-
gagement From the Poor". The Case of Family Adjustment Agencies
in Brager and Purcell, Community Action Against Poverty.

_____, and Richard M. Elman. "The Storefront on Stanton
Street: Advocacy in The Ghetto" in Community Action Against
Poverty, op. cit.

_____, and Herman D. Stein, Social Perspectives on Behavior,
Glencoe, Ill., The Free Press.

Coser, Lewis. The Functions of Social Conflict, The Free Press, N.Y.
Collier-McMillan, London.

Conrad, Earl, The Invention of The Negro, New York, Paul S. Eriksson,
Inc.

Cronen, Edward David. Black Moses. The University of Wisconsin Press,
Madison, 1962.

Cruse, Harold. The Crisis of The Negro Intellectual. New York.
William Morrow, 1969.

Drake, St. Clair and Horace R. Clayton. Black Metropolis: A Study
of Negro Life in A Northern City. Volumes I and II, Harper and
Row, Publishers, New York and Evanston, Revised Edition, 1962.

Dahl, Robert A. and Charles Lindblom. "Social Processes for Economizing",
Politics, Economics and Welfare, New York: Harper and Row Torchbook,
paper edition, 1963.
184

Davis, Kinsley, "Mental Hygiene and the Class Structure" in Cloward and Stein, <u>Social Perspective on Behavior</u>.

DuBois, W.E., Burghardt, <u>Black Folk: Then and Now</u>, New York, Henry Holt and Company.

_____, <u>The Philadelphia Negro</u>, Philadelphia Publications of the University of Pennsylvanis, 1899.

_____, <u>The Souls of Black Folk</u>, Chicago, A.C. McClurg, 1904.

Duhl, Leonard, Editor. <u>The Urban Condition</u>, Basic Books, 1964.

Ellis, William W. <u>White Ethics and Black Power</u>, Chicago, Aldine Publishing Co., 1969.

Ellison, Ralph, <u>Shadow and Act</u>, A Signet Book, the New American Library, 1953.

Encyclopedia of Social Work; Harry L. Lurie (ed.) National Association of Social Workers, N.Y. 1970.

Etcioni, Amatai. <u>Complex Organizations: A Sociological Reader</u>, Holt, Rinhart and Winston, Inc., New York.

Fischer, Sethard, <u>Power and the Black Community: A Reader on Racial Subordination</u> in the U.S. Random House, N.Y.

Franklin, John Hope. <u>From Slavery to Freedom: A History of American Negroes</u>, Alfred A. Knopf, New York.

Frazier, E. Franklin. <u>Black Bourgeoisie</u>, The Free Press, Glencoe, Ill.

_____, <u>The Negro in The United States</u> (Revised Edition), New York, McMillan Co., 1963.

_____, "Race Comtracts and the Social Structure" <u>American Sociological Review</u>, Chapel Hill: University of North Carolina Press, 1953.

Frazier, Thomas. <u>Afro-American History: Primary Resources</u>. Harcourt, Brace and World Inc.

Gans, Herbert. <u>People and Plans</u>, New York: Basic Books, 1968.

Gerth, H.H. and C. Wright Mills, From Max Weber: <u>Essays in Sociology</u>, Routledge and Kegan LTD, Broadway House, London.

Gosnell, Harold, F. <u>Negro Politics: The Rise of Negro Politics In Chicago</u>, The University of Chicago Press, Chicago, Ill.

Goode, William J., and Paul K. Hatt. <u>Methods in Social Research</u>. McGraw-Hill Book Company, New York, Toronto, London, 1952.

Hamilton, Charles V. <u>The Black Preacher in America</u>, Morrow, 1972, N.Y.

Harlem Youth Opportunities Unlimited, Inc., <u>Youth in The Ghetto; A Study of the Consequences of Powerlessness, and a Blueprint for Change</u>, N.Y., 1964.

Hunter, David R. The Slums: Challenge and Response. The Free Press, New York. Collier McMillan Limited, London.

Hunter, Floyd. Community Power Structure: A Study of Decision Makers, Chapel Hill, The University of North Carolina Press.

Johnson, James Weldon. Black Manhattan, Alfred A. Knopf, New York, 1930.

Johnson, Charles S. The Negro in American Civilization: A Study of Negro Life and Race Relations in the Light of Social Research, New York, Johnson Reprint Corp., 1930.

Kahn, Alfred J. Studies in Social Policy and Planning, Russell Sage Foundation, New York, 1969.

_____. Theory and Practice of Social Planning: Companion Volume; Russell Sage Foundation.

_____, Planning Community Services for Children in Trouble, New York, Columbia University Press, 1966.

_____, "Trends and Problems in Community Organization", in National Conference on Social Welfare, Social Work Practice, 1962, New York, Columbia University Press, 1964.

Kardiner, Abram and Lionel Ovesey. The Mark of Oppression: A Psycho-social Study of the American Negro, New York, N.Y., W.W. Norton Company, 1951.

King. Martin Luther, Jr., Stride Toward Freedom, New York, Ballantine Books, 1960.

Kogut, Alvin, "The Negro and the Charity Organization Society in the Progessive Era", Social Service Review, March 1970.

Knowles, Louis L. and Kenneth Prewitt. Institutional Racism in America. Prentice-Hall, Inc., Spectrum Books, Englewood Cliffs, N.J.

King, Charles, And Arthur L. Ellis, et. al. Black Youth in Rebellion, Wilson Library, Bulletin, October 1967.

Krosney, Herbert. Beyond Welfare. Holt, Rinehart, and Winston, N.Y., Chicago and San Francisco.

Ladd, Everett Carll, Jr., Negro Political Leadership in the South, Cornell University Press, Ithaca, New York.

Lazarsfeld, Paul F. and Morris Rosenberg, The Language of Social Research: A Reader in the Methodology of Social Research.

Litwak, Eugene and Henry J. Meyer. "A Balance Theory of Coordination Between Bureaucratic Organizations and community Primary Groups" Administrative Science Quarterly II (June 1966).

Litwak, Leon F. North of Slavery: The Negro in the Free States 1790-1860, Chicago, University Press, 1961.

Long, Lollella Jacqueline and Vernon Ben Robinson. How Much Power to the People? A Study of the New York State Urban Development Corporations invovlement in Black Harlem, Urban Center, Columbia University.

Machiavelli, Miccolo. The Prince and The Discourses, The Modern
    Library, New York, Random House, Inc.

Marris, Peter and Martin Rein. Dilemmas of Social Reforem: Poverty
    and Community Action in the United States. New York Athreton Press
    1967.

Merton, Robert K. Contemporary Social Problems.

_____. Social Theory and Social Structure, Revised and Enlarged
    Edition, The Free Press of Glencoe, 1962.

Miller, Kelly. Out of the House of Bondage, Arno Press and The New
    York Times, N.Y., 1969. William Loren Katz (ed.)

Mills, C. Wright. The Power Elite. A Galaxy Book, New York, Oxford
    University Press, 1959.

Myrdal, Gunnar. An American Dilemma, The Negro Problem and Modern
    Democracy, Harper and Row Publishers, New York Evanston.

_____. Challenge to Affluence, New York, Pantheon Books, Div.
    of Random House.

_____. Beyond the Welfare State.

Osofsky, Gilbert. Harlem: The Making of a Ghetto: Negro New York
    1890 - 1930. Harper and Row, N.Y.

Perlman, Robert and Arnold Gurin. Community Organization and Social
    Planning, Published, jointly by John Wiley & Sons, Inc., New
    York, London, Sydney, Toronto, and The Council for Social
    Work Education.

Perloff, Harvey S. Planning and the Urban Community, Carnegie Institute
    of Technology and University of Pittsburgh Press, 1961.

Pinkney, Alphonso and Rober R. Woock. Poverty and Politics in Harlem:
    Report on Project Uplift 1965, College and University Press,
    New Haven.

Quarles, Benjamin. The Negro in the Making of America, New York,
    Collier Books, 1964.

Ranney, Austin. Political Science and Public Policy, Markham
    Publishing Company, Chicago.

Rainwater, Lee. "Neighborhood Action and Lower Class Life Styles",
    in John B. Turner (ed.) Neighborhood Organization for Community
    Action, New York, National Association of Social Workers, 1968.

Romanyshyn, John M. Social Welfare: Charity to Justice, Random House
    N.Y. Council on Social Work Education.

Rose, Peter I (ed.) Americans From Africa, Vol. II - Old Memories
    New Moods, N.Y, Atherton Press.

Rossi, Peter H. and Robert A. Dentler. The Politics of Urban Renewal:
    The Findings, The Free Press of Glencoe.

Rothman, Jack. Promoting Social Justice in the Multigroup Society:
A Casebook for Group Relations Practitioners. Association
Press and the Council on Social Work Education, New York.

Selznick, Philip. Leadership in Administration: A Sociological
Interpretation. Row, Peterson and Company, Evanston, Illinois,
White Plains, N.Y.

_____. The Organizational Weapon: A Study of Bolshevik
Strategy and Tactics, The Free Press of Glencoe.

_____, TVA and The Grass Roots A Study of the Sociology of
Formal Organizations, Univeristy of California Press, Berkeley
and Los Angeles, 1953.

Scheiner, Seth M. Negro Mecca: A History of the Negro in New York
City, 1865-1920, New York University Press, 1965.

Sunquist, James L. Politics and Policy: The Eisenhower, Kennedy and
Johnson Years. The Brookings Institute, Washington D.C.

Suttles Gerald D. The Social Order of the Slums: Ethnicity and
Territory in The Inner City, The University of Chicago Press.

Thompson, Daniel C. The Negro Leadership Class, Prentice-Hall, Inc.,
Englewood Cliffs, N.J., A Spectrum Book.

Wilson, James Q. The Metropolitan Enigma: Inquiries into the Nature
and Dimensions of America's "Urban Crisis", Harvard University
Press, Cambridge, Massachusetts.

_____. Varieties of Police Behavior: The Management of Law
and Order in Eight Communities, Harvard University Press, Cambridge,
Massachusetts.

_____. Negro Politics: The Search for Leadership, The Free
Press of Glencoe, Illinois.

NEWSPAPERS

Tne New York Times - April 1962 - December 1972.

The Amsterdam News, January 1962 - December 1972.

The New York Daily News, April 1962 - December 1972.

The Los Angeles Times.

OTHER TITLES AVAILABLE FROM
CENTURY TWENTY ONE PUBLISHING

Anderson, E. Frederick
The Development of Leadership and Organization Building in the Black Community of Los Angeles From 1900 Through World War II. 1980. Perfect Bound. $12.00. LC# 79-93305. I.S.B.N. 0-86548-000-1.

Bonnett, Aubrey W.
Group Identification Among Negroes: An Examination of the Soul Concept in the United States of America. 1980. Perfect Bound. $9.00. LC# 79-93304. I.S.B.N. 0-86548-001-X.

Butler, John S.
Inequality in the Military: The Black Experience. 1980. Perfect Bound. $10.00. LC# 79-65253. I.S.B.N. 0-86548-002-8.

Cogdell, Roy and Wilson, Sybil
Black Communication in White Society. 1980. Perfect Bound. $13.00. LC# 79-93302. I.S.B.N. 0-86548-004-4.

Collins, Keith E.
Black Los Angeles: The Maturing of the Ghetto, 1940-1950. 1980. Perfect Bound. $11.00. LC# 79-65254. I.S.B.N. 0-86548-005-2.

Dawkins, Marvin P.
Alcohol and the Black Community: Exploratory Studies of Selected Issues. 1980. Perfect Bound. $9.00. LC# 79-93301. I.S.B.N. 0-86548-006-0.

Ellis, Arthur L.
The Black Power Brokers. 1980. Perfect Bound. $12.00. LC# 79-65252. I.S.B.N. 0-86548-009-5.

Fujita, Kuniko
Black Worker's Struggles in Detroit's Auto Industry, 1935-1975. 1980. Perfect Bound. $10.00. LC# 79-93300. I.S.B.N. 0-86548-010-9.

Jones, Marcus E.
Black Migration in the United States with Emphasis on Selected Central Cities. 1980. Perfect Bound. $11.00. LC# 79-93299. I.S.B.N. 0-86548-014-1.